PENGUIN BOOKS

BREAD AND CIRCUSES

Leading historian of the classical world and theoretician of history, Paul Veyne is Professor of Roman History at the Collège de France. Among his other books are *Writing History* (1984), *A History of Private Life, Vol. 1: From Pagan Rome to Byzantium* (1987), *Roman Erotic Elegy* (1988), *René Char en ses poèmes* (1990) and *La société romaine* (1991).

PAUL VEYNE

BREAD AND CIRCUSES

HISTORICAL SOCIOLOGY AND POLITICAL PLURALISM

ABRIDGED
WITH AN INTRODUCTION BY
OSWYN MURRAY
TRANSLATED BY BRIAN PEARCE

PENGUIN BOOKS

PENGUIN BOOKS

Published by the Penguin Group
Penguin Books Ltd, 27 Wrights Lane, London W8 5TZ, England
Penguin Books USA Inc., 375 Hudson Street, New York, New York 10014, USA
Penguin Books Australia Ltd, Ringwood, Victoria, Australia
Penguin Books Canada Ltd, 10 Alcorn Avenue, Toronto, Ontario, Canada M4V 3B2
Penguin Books (NZ) Ltd, 182–190 Wairau Road, Auckland 10, New Zealand

Penguin Books Ltd, Registered Offices: Harmondsworth, Middlesex, England

First published in France, under the title *Le Pain et le cirque*, by Éditions du Seuil 1976
This abridgement in English translation first published by Allen Lane The Penguin Press 1990
Published in Penguin Books 1992
1 3 5 7 9 10 8 6 4 2

Copyright © Éditions du Seuil, 1976
Introduction copyright © Oswyn Murray, 1990
Translation copyright © Brian Pearce, 1990
All rights reserved

Printed in England by Clays Ltd, St Ives plc

Contents

Contents

Introduction

Historians are supposed to write books full of facts, and it is often assumed that their chief function is to tell us new facts or correct old ones about the past. This is a safe and convenient belief, because it means that we can happily leave the writing (and the reading) of those books to professionals, who will sort it all out for us, and save us the trouble of worrying about the past, which is anyway dead and irrelevant to the present. At best historians make good holiday reading, because truth is often stranger and more exciting than fiction, and because history books tend to be longer (whether because historians are more verbose, or because history is more boundless than the imagination), which is always an advantage when there is time to kill.

There are many good and many bad history books of this sort. But historians have often felt that the discovery of facts (even true ones) is only a preliminary to a higher activity, that of understanding the facts. And at this point history becomes dangerous, because it disturbs the dust of the past. It takes what was already perfectly well known, and even quite satisfactorily arranged, and rearranges it into a new pattern, so that the familiar becomes foreign and the past begins to threaten us.

Though it is dangerous to the social order, this activity is also useful, because it is not true that the past is dead. It determines our present lives, not absolutely (we have a certain freedom in at least some societies, some of the time, to make our own mistakes), but certainly more strongly than any power of reason, or any alleged law of politics or sociology or economics. Changing the past therefore means also changing the present, whether by direct example, or by liberating us from our historically determined prejudices so as to enable us to make more rational decisions.

This role of history was well understood in earlier centuries. The Renaissance learned how to free itself from religion through study of the past; in the eighteenth century the history of facts, antiquarian history, was contrasted with the history of explanations, philosophical history, by men like Voltaire, Montesquieu, and the greatest of all English historians, Edward Gibbon. In the nineteenth century, when history became a science, it was immediately recognized as the queen of the social sciences, providing laws for society, reasons for politics, and justifications for legal systems. Scientific history created the nation-states of Europe, and the two world wars which destroyed their power. But that sort of history is now an ageing queen: no one (except politicians) seriously believes that political history has lessons for the present; no one (except lawyers) seriously believes that a legal system should be justified by historical precedent; and no one (except historians) seriously believes that a just society is best built on the past. Nowadays history is an academic discipline, part of the educational system, a device for wasting the time of the young, or a relaxation for consenting adults.

Of course that is not true: the real history, the unsafe philosophical nineteenth-century sort of history, lives on, and the reader should beware. Consider our greatest modern philosophical historian, Michel Foucault. Foucault's histories of madness set out to demonstrate that madness was a social disease, whose nature changed in different periods, but which always reflected the need for society to find outsiders to punish and imprison, in order that the prison of the social order should seem like freedom. These books were read by psychologists in one of the most oppressive European systems of mental care; and as a result it was decided to abolish lunatic asylums, to return the mad into the care of the society which had created them. Approve or disapprove, Foucault had an effect on a country not even his own: the streets of Italy are witness to the liberation of many innocents who owe their freedom to the power of his analysis. The asylums themselves have been given to the universities to keep their ideas in.

Historians (like history) do not always intend their consequences. Take Foucault again: he wrote a *History of Sexuality* to show how society had always sought to problematize sexual activity in order to use natural instincts as an organ of social control: inhibition and repression are weapons in the subordination of the individual to the group. On past experience he might have hoped for a sexual revolution from such a work; but liberating the insane is one thing, liberating the sane quite another. Instead his thesis seems set to be the theory before the times, for we are now experiencing a new wave of sexual puritanism which he could not have predicted and did not live to see, as

viii

governments seek once again to control the sexual mores of their subjects.

So history is dangerous for your health, both too much of it and too little. But ancient history is a long way away (more than 2,000 years ago), and surely safer. Not so; as my scientist son once remarked to me, it is only a hundred generations since Homer: the origins of our civilization are closer to us than we realize. They can also present lessons more clearly, because their systems were simpler, freer from tradition, or merely further away, and therefore less distinct, capable of being seen only in significant outline. The study of the ancient world presents a distinguished tradition of philosophical historians, from Gibbon onwards. In the Romantic period the German historian B. G. Niebuhr, financial adviser to the kings of Denmark and Prussia, studied the peasantry of Rome in order to build an alternative to the revolutionary proletariat of Napoleonic France. Later the liberal politician Theodor Mommsen wrote a *History of Rome* as a precursor to German nationalism, and a *Römisches Staatsrecht* to try to control it through the constitution. In England the banker George Grote wrote a Utilitarian *History of Greece* in order to explain and justify the English radicals. These are, of course, crude simplifications, but they serve to bring out that relationship between past and present which is so necessary and so beneficial to philosophical history, and so deplored by the professional antiquarian.

What makes great historians is not, however, political bias or a time-bound message; it is a quality of the imagination that perceives a grand theme, resonant for the age, and frees discussion of it through placing it in the past: society, not the historian, is responsible for the consequences it may draw. People often deplore in modern historians that fear of the grand theme; but once again the history of the ancient world has not been without its exponents of the art. Rostovtzeff's *Social and Economic Histories* of the Roman and Hellenistic worlds revealed the fascinating complexity of the bourgeois civilization that lay behind the clash of great empires, and perhaps defended the pre-revolutionary values of a Russian exile. Sir Ronald Syme's depiction of the relationship between ideology and oligarchy in the development of a dictatorship, *The Roman Revolution*, was a product of the thirties. Most recently the grand theme has emerged again, in G. E. M. de Sainte-Croix's *The Class Struggle in the Ancient Greek World*, an attempt to reassert the values of orthodox Marxism for 4,000 years of history. It is a waste of time to agree or disagree with such works; they float like icebergs of interpretation, around which lesser books must needs manoeuvre with care if they do not wish to be sunk with all their readers lost.

Paul Veyne belongs to a society where the great historian is a cult figure: it is impossible to understand modern French intellectual attitudes without reference to the influence of a succession of exponents of the historical art, such as Marc Bloch, Fernand Braudel, Georges Duby, Michel Foucault and Tzvetan Todorov. But to mention such names is already to point to the fact that in France the 'sciences of man' are not separated into competing disciplines as they are in England, and therefore the concepts of the grand theme and the unity of history are central to the historian's task. Like others of his generation, Veyne has deliberately sought to bring the history of the ancient world into relationship with this tradition, rescuing it from an older alliance with antiquarian philological and literary studies. A former student at the École Normale Supérieure and the French School at Rome, he was educated in the old style, and his learning and technical expertise remain outstanding. But, Provençal by origin and professor at Aix for many years, he chooses to portray himself deliberately as a provincial, tilting at the Paris establishment. That claim in 1976 won him the paradoxical honour of a place in the inner cabinet of French intellectual life, a professorship at the Collège de France.

His reputation was made by two books of the seventies that complement each other: a book on the theory of history and this present work, which exemplifies that theory in practice. *Comment on écrit l'histoire* (1971) was translated as *Writing History* (1984). In it he sought to demolish all theories of history based on generalizations and social laws, and to claim that history was a common-sense activity devoted to describing the specific, rather than exemplifying the universal; it has no method and no aim other than that of giving an account of anything considered interesting: 'history has neither structure nor method, and it is certain in advance that every theory in this domain is still-born'. History is the account of man's activities in the 'sublunary' world of the particular, which uses generalizations only to illuminate the particular.

Shocking and liberating as such a proclamation appeared in the French world of '-isms', it is more likely to seem shockingly familiar in our citadel of empiric virtue. But even to an English reader there are new aspects to Veyne's defence of common sense, because of its very extremeness. He throws out not only Marxism, Structuralism, liberalism, but also the idea that there are such things as political history, social history, economic history, cultural history. Along with the ideas, all the comfortable unspoken assumptions also disappear: 'sociology has never discovered anything; it has revealed nothing that could not be found in a description'. He is perhaps slightly more tolerant of economics, but even then, 'it is common knowledge that many economic historians do not know much economic theory and that they are none the worse for it. Economic history is much more interested in describing the facts than in explaining them.' Each society has its own structures, its otherness, which we may (if we feel interested) seek to reconstruct, but which we should not falsify by applying our own categories to its differences. The only true history is a history without frontiers and without distinctions: 'the most exemplary historical work of our century is that of Max Weber, which wipes out the frontiers between traditional history, of which it has the realism; sociology, of which it has the ambitions; and comparative history, of which it has the span'. The historian is alone on the sands of time, laboriously picking over the ruins of a buried city of unknown extent and nature. Such an anarchic vision is exhilarating.

In two later papers Veyne sought to explain his position further. His inaugural lecture at the Collège de France, 'L'Inventaire des différences' (1976), portrays the historian's task as that of making an inventory of the differences between social forms; in order to do so, in order to individualize his society, he must use the generalizations of the social sciences or of anthropology: the individuality of the particular requires the descriptive power of the general. And in an essay of 1978, 'Foucault révolutionne l'histoire', he tries to relate his own nihilist theory to that of Foucault; some have interpreted this as a declaration of conversion, but I have a feeling that it is rather an annexation of certain anarchic aspects of Foucault's work to his own views.

What Veyne has succeeded in doing, as no doubt he intended, is to liberate history from preconceptions. His theoretical claims will not convince many, but their practical consequences must be seen in the writing of history itself.

In *Bread and Circuses* Paul Veyne tackles a grand theme such as those I described earlier. In the French original, 800 pages of text and notes explore 1,000 years of history, from the classical Greek city-state of the fifth century B C, through the great expansion of Greek culture in the

Hellenistic world formed by the conquests of Alexander the Great as far as the Punjab in northern India, to the Roman Republic, and the unification of the Mediterranean area under the Roman Empire, until that civilization was in turn transformed by Christianity and barbarian conquests into the origins of modern Europe.

In attempting to follow his theme through its many transformations over a millennium, Veyne was concerned to liberate himself from any theoretical viewpoint that would have obscured the particularity of the phenomenon he was describing. Much of the first 200 pages of the original are taken up with establishing the inadequacy of modern theories to explain the phenomenon of 'euergetism'; at the time of publication these thoughts provoked something of a scandal, but in preparing this English version I have chosen to omit most of them. Essential though these preambles were in the French context of 1976, in a different culture a decade later his arguments seemed in general either accepted or no longer relevant. The main point of these discussions was in any case enshrined in the theoretical works I have already discussed, and concerns the autonomy of historical periods from the general theories that we must use to explain them; those who do not accept history as 'the inventory of differences' will not be persuaded by the theoretical discussions of *Bread and Circuses*.

Indeed, in a curious way I believe that Veyne's obsession with declaring the autonomy of his investigation obscured the fundamental originality of his insight. And in order for the reader to understand the importance of his book it may be necessary to replace his own observations with an alternative reading from the standpoint of ten years on.

Economic history seeks to explain the strengths or weaknesses of civilizations in terms of laws derived from one or other of the great modern theories of economic rationality. Either human society can be explained as an eternal struggle to dominate and exploit the scarce raw materials of wealth, the most important of which in human history has always been labour, man himself, or it must be understood as an attempt to harness scarcity to profit by means of the inventiveness of man and his entrepreneurial skills. Both Marxist and capitalist theories of economic history emphasize the role of scarcity in human affairs, and we shall see in a moment reason to question even this basic assumption. But more importantly, both these theories are in origin social theories belonging to the social sciences, that is, they seek to offer means of understanding and controlling the mechanisms of change: they are designed for societies that believe in change, and for situations where change is possible. The concept of economic history does indeed find itself in a paradox. It uses modern theories for changing the world to explain societies that can no longer be changed because they are dead and gone; moreover in many cases it uses them on societies that, even in their heyday, never had any great desire or any momentum towards change. It is for this reason that most of the disputes about how far economic theories (modern or primitivist) will illuminate the economic life of the ancient world are incapable of solution, because they ignore the difference between the work of the doctor attempting a cure and the forensic scientist carrying out a post-mortem.

The conclusion of most of these debates has been the despairing one that the Greeks and the Romans did not behave as rational economic planners ought to have behaved. This is of course true, for why should they have done so, when even our own societies ignore economic rationality, often for good reason? A second conclusion has usually also been drawn, that the ancient world had not 'discovered the economy'. Again true, or at least they thought it unimportant. The amount of effort great thinkers of the ancient world spent on the fundamental questions of human morality and social and political organization is nowhere matched by any close and well-informed discussion of the principles of economic organization: even the very word 'economy', Greek though it is, denotes the low esteem in which such activity was held, for it means 'household rules' (from *oikos*, 'the house', and *nomos*, 'rule'). Aristotle put the ancient view most clearly, in discussing the various aims that man, a rational animal, could have in life: he could seek knowledge through the 'theoretical life', and so fulfil the demands of his reason; he could seek honour through the 'political life' of community leadership, and so fulfil his social role; or he could seek pleasure through forms of sensual and unharmful self-indulgence, and so fulfil his animal nature. All these aims were autonomous and rational, in that they corresponded to certain necessary aspects of human social psychology. But 'the money-making life is not an end in itself': it is not a separate aim of life; a rational man will indulge in money-making, not for itself, but only in so far as it will buy him pleasure, power or time to think. The millionaire and the miser are specimens of humanity suffering from pathological diseases, cases of arrested development: they do not know the point of life.

Such wise perceptions might lead us to question our own values and assumptions; they will at least serve to suggest that the ancient view of the unimportance of economics was not a mere confusion of thought. The problem remains, when a society is static, uninterested in 'the money-making life', of how we are to describe those areas of its activity that concern the creation and use of wealth, areas that correspond to our sphere of the economy. If we could discover the rules of 'the ancient economy', we might be able to stop complaining on the one hand about the absence of evidence for ancient economic history, and on the other about the primitiveness and irrationality of the ancient economy. For these two complaints are likely to be linked: we do not see the evidence for the ancient economy because we do not allow it to count as economic evidence, unaware that the ancient theory of the economy was different from ours.

It is, I believe, this barrier that Veyne has broken through. In place of the basic laws of modern economics – supply and demand, and the concepts of market exchange and exploitation – he offers us the concept of the gift. Exchange binds together a society unified by its search for the profit principle, exploitation a society dominated by the need to control; the gift demands a new form of economic thought, regulating in a quite different way concepts of scarcity and abundance, power and prestige.

A gift economy is not one based on gift *exchange*: that would be a society half-way to becoming 'rational' in our sense, since people could count the values in this exchange, and establish a market in the gift. The first essential in a gift economy is that return, reciprocity, should be unequal and incommensurable: I give to you because you cannot give to me, being poor; or I give to you so that you may give to me something quite different, incapable of being measured against my gift. To take a typical example from Veyne's book, I give you free oil (or in modern terms, soap) for the public baths, or free dinners, in return for a statue. Such incommensurable forms of exchange are common in all societies (indeed probably more common than ordinary economic exchanges); but what distinguishes a gift economy from an exchange economy is that these activities are at the centre, public and officially recognized by the community.

As Veyne sees, all such theories are capable of reduction to other theories. It is possible to take a gift economy, and interpret it in terms of power relations (the big boss or Mafia type of organization, depoliticizing the political classes through bribery) or class warfare (disguising the exploitation of the proletariat), taxation (the rich pay for public services, because if they do not volunteer they will be compelled) or moral guilt (the eye of the needle gets bigger for the rich man if he practises charity). It is also possible to interpret the gift in terms of social ritual, as the symbolic representation of relations of superiority and dependence. But all these interpretations, though they may be possible ones, are not satisfying, because they do not correspond to the perceptions of those engaged in these activities, and because they do not explain either the specific forms of social response or the ways such forms change in history. These were the arguments that led Veyne to reject modern theories, and to assert the difference, the essential otherness, of ancient economic organization. In order to understand ancient economic history, we must forget economics.

The approach to history that Veyne adopts in this book is not unique; he has had predecessors; and, since he wrote, it has become increasingly clear that his conception of history relates to a general movement of thought among historians of all periods and most national cultures. But in discussing the context of his thought we should always remember that he was one of the first to pioneer a new area of history, and that his study still remains one of the most systematic and complete.

The basic theory behind this attempt to offer a new non-economic theory of economic history was provided by the famous essay, 'The Gift', by the French anthropologist Marcel Mauss: first published in 1925, it laid the foundations for what all later writers have recognized as 'an archaic form of exchange'. But by this Mauss did not mean that the gift was an early form of exchange, which could develop into the economic exchange relationship, or that it was a substitute for exchange in primitive societies. He meant rather that the gift *replaced* exchange in many early societies, operating in the same general area as economic exchange does in more advanced societies, but being fundamentally different in kind, and creating wholly new (economically 'irrational') laws of social interaction. Thus the gift might or might not involve reciprocity; there could be complex rules of interchange, involving return of the gift in the same form, or by other means. The relationship was often one between incommensurable powers: man could give to the gods. There were rules for conspicuous expenditure, leading in some societies to the 'potlatch', or competitive destruction by men of position of their worldly goods in order to affirm their prestige. The gift could serve to establish social relations, in which generosity on the part of the leaders established bonds of obedience for the followers, and in which honour was due to the donor on the basis of his generosity, either to his kin group or to his community in general. The gift could therefore function as the basis for social and political organization, in creating and expressing relationships of power. Although many of the relations might operate in ways analogous to monetary transactions, the value of the gift was determined by its symbolic significance, not in relation to any recognition of its actual worth; the object as gift had a personality unconnected with its economic or scarcity value. The gift could have legal status, as a pledge or sign. Just as there might be an obligation to give, there could also be an obligation to receive: a gift could not be refused, whatever the consequences; there is place in such a world for the unwanted gift or the fatal gift, for the white elephant, the Trojan horse or the poisoned cloak. This theory was not only relevant to history and anthropology: Mauss was concerned to do more than develop 'a science of manners' (*science des mœurs*); he also wished to offer a wholly unfashionable series of ethical conclusions:

The theme of the gift, of freedom and obligation in the gift, of generosity and self-interest in giving, reappears in our own society like the resurrection of a dominant motif long forgotten ... We are returning, as indeed we must do, to the old theme of 'noble expenditure'. It is essential that, as in Anglo-Saxon countries and so many contemporary societies, savage and civilized, the rich should come once more, freely or by obligation, to consider themselves as the treasurers, as it were, of their fellow–citizens. Of the ancient civilizations from which ours has arisen, some had the jubilee, others the liturgy, the choragus, the trierarchy, the syssitia or the obligatory expenses of the aedile or consular official. We should return to customs of this sort.

We may doubt the practicality of such Utopian ideals, we may deplore the social consequences of a system built on such presuppositions, but we cannot deny its contemporary relevance.

More recently, anthropologists and historians have begun to question the fundamental presupposition of economic history, that the material goods of this world are necessarily scarce. All successful societies produce a surplus (that is why they are called successful); it may be that the use of this surplus is what determines the character of the culture. Religious societies build cathedrals with their surplus, secular ones build nuclear power stations or fly to the moon, militaristic ones 'rearm' (one never arms, one only rearms) for a war that will never be fought. The *condottieri* of the Renaissance made their surplus in war, but spent it on paintings and beautiful palaces like that at Urbino – a strange set of priorities to the economically rational man.

Introduction

Modern culture, like Renaissance culture, will be judged by the use it makes of its surplus: 'the money-making life is not an end in itself'.

Early surpluses (like modern ones) were largely agricultural, difficult to store and with a limited shelf-life. Spending them was therefore an urgent problem, one of the chief preoccupations of primitive, as of modern, governmental organizations. One could sacrifice and please the gods, one could have a feast and please the people; best of all, one could combine the two in a religious festival. The rich could provide food and hospitality for idle retainers or (less frequently) the real poor. Most social systems are not, in fact, built on power relations but on the distribution of benefits; one acquires only in order to be able to give away, whether it be the professor with his knowledge or the politician with his jobs for the boys.

A theory of social relations may be built as easily on altruism as on exploitation. The community is (as its name implies) a means of living together, an organization for mutual help, not a system of oppression. Aristotle pointed out that friendship is the basis of association, not self-interest; and societies that forget this destroy themselves in terror. Anthropologists have been particularly aware of the complications introduced into human society by this ineradicable element of altruism, and the pleasures of giving; most recently I would single out the work of the Chicago anthropologist Marshall Sahlins, if only in order to be able to point out that Veyne could not have known his work: the relationship between the two writers is more obscure, and lies in the movement of thought characteristic of an age.

Historians themselves have been more interested in the practicalities of the use of surplus, in the history of food and drink as ritual and as pleasure. The festival, the carnival, was the first centre of interest, because, being infrequent, it is found even in societies that possess only small surpluses, and because it also offers an opportunity for reversing the normal rules and values of society: excessive display, gross consumption, sexual orgies, violent disorder, all these reveal the tensions of normal society in their periodic release. But everyday life ultimately offers more scope for a new history, the history of pleasure. The ritualization of the consumption of food and drink, the social activities of bar and pub, the changes in sexual mores, the values expressed in public entertainment – the history of such phenomena explains the real preoccupations of mankind; and it is politics, not this sort of history, which is trivial and ephemeral.

Thus Veyne's book offers an explanation of a phenomenon that can be seen on the one hand as an alternative theory of economic history; or we may regard it as part of a wider enterprise, to write a new history, an *histoire des mœurs* or history of pleasure. In either case his book does not offer a blueprint for such activity, but rather a practical example, from which we are invited to draw our own conclusions. Not all the problems are solved, but the attentive reader will find that many of them are posed.

It would have been possible for Veyne to have written a description of ancient economic theory, or, as we might call it, the principles of gift-giving. There is plenty of evidence, from the behaviour of the Greek heroes in the Homeric poems, to the works of Aristotle with their emphasis on the 'magnificent' (or gift-giving) man, and the later philosophical treatises on how to give and how to receive, of which the Roman philosopher Seneca's huge treatise *De Beneficiis* may serve as an example. It would also have been possible to discuss how the Christian conception of the gift, though it was similar in its emphasis on non-reciprocity (or rewards in heaven), yet disrupted the pagan system by its different conception of the function and consequences of the gift. It would also have been possible to analyse the language of euergetism in accordance with the belief of generations of text-based historians, that language is reality. Veyne, of course, mentions these aspects: from time to time in his book I catch sight of another book, which a different and perhaps less interesting historian might have written.

Instead Veyne tries to describe in concrete terms the range of phenomena that serves to illustrate such theoretical points: he tries to show that his interpretation *corresponds* to the facts, rather than to fit the facts into an alien framework; he offers 'an inventory of the differences', in which we see the relativity of our own social organization revealed through the coherence of an alternative. We may interpret this in one of two ways. Perhaps he believes (at least partially) in the social order he portrays; or perhaps he offers us a form of carnival, a suspension of the normal laws of history. Does he wish us to regard the society he portrays as merely quaint, a demonstration of the necessity of the modern world? Or does he wish us to believe, like Mauss and Foucault, that history has a lesson for us? That is for the reader to decide.

For the characteristic strength of his book is its attention to the facts and the forms of human conduct in their full complexity. Three social systems are presented to us, with an explicit recognition of their fundamental differences; the ways in which these three systems overlapped and influenced each other in their developments of the 'theory of euergetism', or the economy of the gift, are responsible for the differences between them and for their ineradicable opposition to our own modes of thought.

The first of these societies is the Greek city-state, or *polis*. A political form which originated in equality of wealth and power on a scale small enough to enable all members of the defined community of equals to share in decision-making, it seems at first sight rather infertile ground for the development of an economy of the gift, which normally presupposes inequality of relationships. But the early Greek community had been dominated by an aristocracy of equals, who created their relationships between each other and with their dependants through the gift. So the climate was produced in which inequalities of wealth, unrecognized in the political sphere, could be accepted in the social in return for giving by the rich, not to their retainers but to the community as a whole. The liturgy, or necessary gift established in law, was indeed a form of taxation, devoted largely to unnecessary ends, such as festivals and choruses; in Athens too the armed forces were 'privatized', when the state provided the galley hulks for the navy and the pay of the rowers, while establishing a compulsory contest for the equipment and decoration of the ships by the rich. Thus the practice of euergetism was nationalized into a state taxation system.

But the tensions were always present. The system depended on the willingness of the rich to give without any significant return in political power: surely at least the rich, funding the community, had a right to more say in its running. Hence the prevalence of political systems that the Greeks called oligarchies, meaning by that something still far more democratic than any modern system of government, but one where full voting rights or rights to magistracies were confined to those capable of providing for the survival of the community, whether it was the military class or the wealthy. The result was an inevitable drift towards control of the cities by the notables; and it is this civic economy of the notables as it existed from the fourth century B C to the fourth century A D that Veyne regards as displaying euergetism in its primary form, and to which he devotes his second chapter. In this account therefore the emphasis shifts from the normal one, which regards the Greek city as a political animal of the classical period in the fifth and fourth centuries; now we see the continuity of social life through the so-called Hellenistic period into the Roman Empire and beyond. And we can understand why the civic organization of the *polis* proved the dominant cultural framework for a society that reached from the Mediterranean coast and islands through the irrigated river valleys of Egypt and Mesopotamia and into the barren uplands and the desert fringes of the Asiatic interior – the most successful and most long-lasting form of social organization that man has yet evolved. For an essential part of its success was precisely the continuity of that ethic of 'noble expenditure' that Mauss describes, which united rich and poor in an alternative to the class struggle.

The Roman world was very different, a society of powerful nobles with peasant retainers bound to them in that specifically Roman institution of 'clientship', which has since proved so useful for the understanding of societies as different as those of South America: again an ethic of giving existed, giving by the rich to their retainers in return for unconditional obedience. As the Romans became civilized, that is as they learned how to behave like Greeks, they picked up much of the vocabulary and the customs of euergetism. But the spirit was different: giving to the state was impossible, for the state was composed of myself and my rival nobles: why should I support *their* retainers? All giving was political display, and therefore useful in widening the group of supporters, but also jealously regulated by the senate of notables. The channels that were opened up became sanctified by tradition, as forms of display related to the acquisition of booty from foreign conquest: better a great general should be required to donate a public building than that he should be allowed to keep the wealth of other nations for himself. It was such considerations that created the characteristic ambivalence to public euergetism in the world of the Roman Republic.

When one man took over as ruler of the world, the game had to change. Euergetism in Rome became centralized under his control: public building, bread and circuses were an intrinsic part of his relationship with his people. What functions did they serve? The concentration of traditional activities in the hands of one man transformed their significance, but they remained traditional, time-honoured, and therefore scarcely decipherable as a rational system. He did not need to do these things, they were very expensive, and often counter-productive: the circus was a place for demonstrating the unpopularity of an Emperor as well as his popularity. Buildings provided wages for the poor, some were even useful, like the aqueducts; but mostly they were just reinforced concrete symbols of self-aggrandizement 'given' by the Emperor to 'his' people. More importantly the system no longer served any redistributive purpose; it was merely a way of organizing a gigantic festival of potlatch for the wealth of one of the largest and most efficient empires the world has ever seen. Euergetism had become what it always was in part, a symbolic activity. Perhaps euergetism had reached its logical conclusion, in a system where the emperor owned everything and gave it all away.

Despite its length, Veyne's analysis is not exhaustive; nor could it ever be. He ignores many important aspects of euergetism to concentrate on particular significant types. But the chief criticism of his book must concern its static quality. The three chapters seize three different moments, and scarcely try to explain how these moments came about, or how they relate to one another. Thus we miss a deeper analysis of the origins of euergetism in its relationship to earlier types of liturgical gifts: the Athens of the financier and reformer Lycurgus in the late fourth century BC deserves detailed study, for it displays all the elements of the transition from democracy to euergetism. Similarly Veyne does not fully explore the specifically Roman forms of clientship and the development of a parallel type of euergetism to the Greek, which in turn fused with it. And finally we would like to know what succeeded the Imperial form of euergetism, and how it developed or was replaced in the early Christian and Byzantine periods, finally to succumb to that new form of euergetism that we know as feudalism. That is the problem with an inventory of differences: it offers a static, not a dynamic, view of history. And by so doing it evades the problem of theory in history, for theories are about connections and interrelations between events; and here there are merely events. Veyne, therefore, would not agree with much of my reading of his text, which claims euergetism as one social manifestation of the universal phenomenon of human altruism, harnessed to the specific phenomenon of civic loyalty. But it is the reader's privilege to disagree with his author, and such disagreement is itself a sign of the importance of the book.

It is necessary finally to warn the reader that the text presented here, brilliantly translated by Brian Pearce, is not complete; I am responsible, with the author's agreement, for its present form. I have tried to retain the character of the work, both its immense learning and its originality of insight, while concentrating the theme of a somewhat self-indulgent and discursive author. The main omissions are those areas of least interest to the English reader: in chapter I, the polemic against earlier theorists mentioned above; in chapter III, a long and detailed discussion of the views of Cicero, an author more often read in France than in England; and in chapter IV, a number of detailed discussions of problems in Roman Imperial finance and law.

OSWYN MURRAY

Bibliography

Works by Paul Veyne

Comment on écrit l'histoire (1971); English translation, *Writing History* (1984).
Foucault révolutionne l'histoire (1978).
L'Inventaire des différences (1976).
Les Grecs ont-ils cru à leurs mythes? (1983).
L'Élégie érotique romaine: la poésie et l'occident (1983).
Histoire de la vie privée, vol. I (1985); English translation, *A History of Private Life*, vol. I: *From Pagan Rome to Byzantium* (1987) (edited by Paul Veyne).

Other books discussed

MARCEL MAUSS, *Essai sur le don* (1925); English translation, *The Gift* (1954).

MICHEL FOUCAULT, *Histoire de la folie à l'âge classique* (1961); English translation, *Madness and Civilization: A History of Insanity* (1967).
Naissance de la clinique: une archéologie du regard médical (1963); English translation, *The Birth of the Clinic: An Archaeology of Medical Perception* (1973).
Surveiller et punir: naissance de la prison (1976); English translation, *Discipline and Punish, the Birth of the Prison* (1977).
Histoire de la sexualité, vols. I–III (1977–84); English translations, *The History of Sexuality*, vol. I: *An Introduction* (1978); vol. II: *The Uses of Pleasure* (1987); vol. III: *The Care of the Self* (1990).

MARSHALL SAHLINS, *Stone Age Economic* (1972).
Islands of History (1987).

The Subject of This Book

Panem et circenses: why do gifts to the community and acts of patronage towards the city bulk so large in the life of the ancient world, at least in the Hellenistic and Roman periods, between about 300 BC and AD 300? Every local notable was then required, in accordance with a sort of class morality, to show generosity to the people, and the people expected this of him. The senators of Rome, masters of the world, gave games to the Roman plebs and distributed symbolic gifts among their supporters and their soldiers, openly practising a form of electoral corruption. The Emperor himself guaranteed to the city of Rome both cheap bread and gladiatorial combats, and his subjects eagerly proclaimed him the leading benefactor of his Empire. This giving by an individual to the community is called 'euergetism'. The extent of such gifts was so great that, in a Greek or Roman city like those whose ruins the modern tourist visits in Turkey or Tunisia, most of the public buildings were raised at the expense of local notables. It is as though most town halls, schools and even hydro–electric schemes in France had been gifts from the capitalists of the respective areas – who, moreover, offered the local workers free drinks or film-shows.

Explaining this phenomenon is a delicate matter and, let it be said straight away, has nothing to do with the cliché about 'depoliticization'. Reality is usually more subtle than clichés. Three cases need to be distinguished: first, that of the notables whose wealth or influence placed them at the head of a city; second, that of the senators, members of the Roman oligarchy, the governing or ruling class of the Empire; and third, that of the Emperor himself, who gave Rome bread and provided circuses for it. The true explanation will be different for each case.

In this book I shall deal fully with the Emperor and the Roman oligarchy. As regards the notables, I shall study only those of the Greek cities in the Hellenistic epoch and during the centuries when the Greek world had been reduced to the status of provinces of the Roman

Empire. The reason for this limitation is that I want the book to be read by persons who are not specialists in ancient history. In order not to bore such readers I have therefore left aside for the moment such aspects as municipal life in the Roman Empire, whose treatment would have overburdened the historical narrative with a weight of sociological theory and learned references

This is a work of sociological history: provided, that is, we use the word 'sociology' in the same way as Max Weber did, making it a handy synonym for the human or political sciences. Concerning historical cognition much may be said, the most important point being that there is no such thing as historical method. A historical fact can be explained and consequently described, only by applying to it sociology, political theory, anthropology, economics, and so on. It would be useless to speculate about what might be the historical explanation of an event that could differ from its 'sociological' explanation, its scientific, true explanation. In the same way, there can be no astronomical explanation of astronomical facts: they have to be explained by means of physics.

And yet a book about astronomy is not the same as a book about physics, and a book about history is not quite the same as a book about sociology – although the difference in this case is less than traditional historians are wont to claim. Weber's *Religionssoziologie*, which, despite its title, is a book about history, is not quite the same sort of book as his *Economy and Society*. The fact is that the difference between sociology and history is not material but merely formal. They both seek to explain the same events in the same way, but whereas sociology deals with the generalities (concepts, types, regularities, principles) that serve to explain an event, history is concerned with the event itself, which it explains by means of the generalities that are the concern of sociology. In other words, one and the same event, described and explained in the same way, will be, for a historian, his actual subject, whereas, for a sociologist, it will be merely an example that serves to illustrate some pattern, concept or ideal type (or will have served to discover or construct this).

The difference, as we see, is slight, in the main. From one angle, we have an act of euergetism explained and conceptualized by the ideal types of political science and, from the other, these same ideal types illustrated or discovered by means of an example, namely, an act of euergetism. The flavour is the same, the potential readers are the same, and, above all, the knowledge required of the historian and the sociologist is the same, except for the division of labour implied. Since the 'facts' do not exist (they exist only through and under a concept, otherwise they cannot be conceived), a sociologist needs to know how to constitute them, while a historian has to be able to find his way around in sociology, to estimate its relevance and, where necessary, to create it. History leads to sociological discoveries being made, while sociology solves long-standing historical problems, and also poses fresh ones.

On one point, however, the difference between history and sociology is considerable, and this is what endows history with its specificity. For a sociologist, historical events are only examples (or 'guinea-pigs'). He is not called upon to list all the examples, without exception, that could illustrate one of the generalities that are the true subject of his science. If he constructs the ideal type of 'monarchy by absolute right', he will quote, perhaps, two or three examples (Rome, the *ancien régime*), but not *every* possible example. He does not have to quote Ethiopia as well. For the historian, however, events are not examples, but the actual subject of his science. He cannot leave out any of them, just as a zoologist has to compile the complete inventory of all living species, and an astronomer will not overlook even the least of the galaxies. The historian therefore must talk about Ethiopia, and there have to be historians who specialize in Ethiopian history. They will talk about it in exactly the same terms as a sociologist would, *if* he were to talk about it – but *they* will definitely talk about it.

Accordingly, in this book the reader will sometimes find sociological history (wherein the notions of charisma, expression, professionalization, etc., serve to explain events, or at least to arrange them under a concept), and at other times historical sociology (wherein the notions of charisma, professionalization, etc., are illustrated through examples taken mainly from antiquity). My purpose will have been attained if the reader, when reading, loses sight of this rather pedantic distinction.

CHAPTER I

The Agents and Their Behaviour

Let me begin by explaining what euergetism is and what it is not. It is not redistribution, or ostentation, or depoliticization. Let me list, also, the themes into which I want to try and break it down. Then I will analyse, from among the various public benefactors or *euergetai*, one particular species, namely the municipal notables. The other agents, the Roman senators and the Emperor, will have their turn later.

1. The gift in Roman society: a narrative outline

GIFT BEHAVIOUR

We know how important the giving of gifts was in Roman society. It was as important as in potlatch societies, in those characterized by pious and charitable works, or in those with a redistributive taxation policy and aid to the Third World. Bread and circuses, anniversary gifts, 'presents' to the Emperor and his officials, baksheesh elevated to the plane of an institution (seen through the eyes of a European traveller of the nineteenth or twentieth century, the Roman Empire would look like a triumph of corruption, similar to the Turkish or Chinese empires), banquets to which the whole city was invited, wills mentioning one's old servants, one's friends and the Emperor... It was a confused mass of miscellaneous forms of behaviour (the presents given to officials and the baksheesh were a kind of salary) arising from a wide variety of motives: careerism, paternalism, kingly style, corruption, conspicuous consumption, local patriotism, desire to emulate, concern to uphold one's rank, obedience to public opinion, fear of hostile demonstrations, generosity, belief in ideals.

Every class of the population benefited from gifts. The poor received them as charity, or in the capacity of clients, or in that of free citizens. The slaves received them as a result of philanthropy or paternalism. The peasants, sharecroppers on the estates of the rich, were forgiven their arrears of dues (*reliqua colonorum*) so long as they did not leave their master, this being, for landowners, a way of keeping tenants dependent upon them. Advocates, so long as their occupation was not recognized as a profession and they were forbidden to demand payment, received gifts from their clients as honorariums. The rich circulated their wealth among themselves, giving all the more lavishly because they were giving to the already rich. Corporations also received gifts. From the beginning of the Imperial period, making gifts to the Roman state was a privilege reserved to the Emperor alone. But the cities and municipalities of the Empire received gifts from the state nobility (the senatorial order), the regional nobility (the equestrian order), the notables who made up the municipal nobility (the order of decurions) and the rich freedmen. The notables, to be sure, possessed the privilege of ruling the same cities on which they showered their gifts: but their class interest cannot explain why they also gave no less generously to professional or religious *collegia*, to the private associations of every kind in which the plebs sought human warmth. The provinces of the Empire likewise received gifts, in a particular way. They provided the framework for associations of cities for purposes of worship (the so-called 'provincial assemblies') that came together in order to celebrate public festivals and perform in them that monarchical cult of the Emperor which was obligatory for all. The great notables who presided over these associations ruined themselves in order to make a festival more splendid, or to endow the province with a temple for the Imperial cult, or an amphitheatre.

These gifts had a substantial quantitative importance. They were not mere petty presents or alms, symbolic palliatives or moral gestures. Buildings so characteristic of the Roman spirit as amphitheatres survive today as material indications of the magnitude of the gifts we are discussing: all, or nearly all, were presents from nobles or notables, municipal or provincial. Nor were such gifts made only by patrons whose wealth or whose idealism set them apart, men like Herodes Atticus or others equally rich. Even the poor gave, if only symbolically, for, as in many an 'archaic' society, gifts were in the nature of a rite. For instance, sharecroppers brought solemnly to their master, along with their dues, some products of their farm, to bear witness that they depended upon him and that the land they cultivated did not belong to them. Each of society's orders had the right to make certain gifts. The rich freedmen of the municipalities combined in the *collegia* of *seviri augustales* in order to finance from their resources their town's cult of the Emperor, and sometimes one of them would be given the privilege of offering to all his fellow citizens, the free-born included, a gladiatorial entertainment.

THE GIFT AS VALUE

The free-born rich who made up the various orders of nobility – senators, *equites*, decurions – were naturally required to give more than others. This was not only because they had the means to do so, but because their quality as men who were completely human imposed on them a duty to be responsive to all human ideals. They saw themselves as constituting the type of humanity, which is only a variant of that ideology by which some people think themselves superior in origin to the mass of mankind; and this implied duties of state, in the same way as with a nobility of blood. Whether senator or mere decurion (as we should say, town councillor), a Roman notable felt that if he became a magistrate in Rome or in his city he had to provide the people with splendid spectacles in the arena, the circus or the theatre. He behaved generously to his freedmen and clients. He placed his purse and his influence at the service of his city or even his province (while, for his part, the Emperor exercised the same patronage over Rome itself). He included his friends in his will. He protected arts and letters. Finally, on innumerable occasions he helped the plebeians of his city on an individual basis. This patronage in favour 'of each and every one', as the Latin inscriptions put it, is not well known to us in detail, but the inscriptions allude to it frequently, albeit more vaguely than we should prefer.

The frequency and variety of gifts and, more broadly, of benefactions appears in philosophical writings as something to be taken for granted. When they discuss the virtues of generosity, or *beneficia*, these texts unconsciously depict for us a society in which voluntary relations of giving and benefaction fill the place held in our society by the market and by regulations (where these are protective and charitable). As this book will deal both with Hellenistic euergetism and that of Rome, which succeeded and imitated it, I will take as example a text from the beginning of the Hellenistic epoch, Aristotle's *Nicomachean Ethics*. At the beginning of book IV Aristotle discusses the two virtues related to money, namely the art of giving and of receiving, liberality and that grander form of liberality we call munificence, or magnificence. He discusses this matter at greater length than we should today. We should not, for example, go into such detail on the difference between the man who is truly liberal and those persons who offend by excess; the prodigal on the one hand and, on the other, the person, both miserly and greedy, who is too fond of his money. The prodigal, says Aristotle,

would seem to be in no small degree better than a mean man. For he is easily cured both by age and by poverty, and thus he may move towards the middle state. For he has the characteristics of the liberal man, since he both gives and refrains from taking, though he does neither of these in the right manner and well. Therefore, if he were brought to do so by habituation or in some other way, he would be liberal; for he will then give to the right people, and will not take from the wrong sources.[1]

This scenario is somewhat strange to us. Aristotle talks of presents given or received where our concern would rather be with profits and wages, and we should talk not so much of liberality as of justice, charity or sense of social responsibility. When the philosopher's casuistry comes to consider 'gains', these are, for him, the shameful gains of the thrower of dice and of the usurer; our thoughts would, instead, focus upon the fair wage or the legitimate profit. The Hellenistic world looks like a society of 'friends' and citizens, not one of workers who, whether wage-earners, entrepreneurs or officials, are subject to all-embracing regulations and to the iron law of the market for goods and labour.

Aristotle's portrait of the liberal man is at once still true and yet obsolete. It is an eternal possibility that is not, or is no longer, a feature of our present-day reality. It calls to mind by contrast that other human type, no less true and no less obsolete, the miser (still around in Molière's day), whom moralists have encountered throughout so many centuries on the royal road of the human heart, until the time came when entrepreneurs and managers took over from usurers. The liberal man is the opposite of the miser. He is not tight-fisted. He will not be careless of his fortune, for he needs it in order to be of service to others, but neither will he be greatly inclined to increase it. He does not love money for its own sake, but because, if he has it, he can give it away. He regards close attention to accounts as a sign of meanness. That is how the *Ethics* puts the matter.

Towards the end of this chapter we shall see that, if we look at the facts, the contrast between the liberal man and the person we should call the bourgeois, or the puritan, is more theoretical than real. The contrast is not so much between men as between purposes, which may well coexist within the same man. It remains true, however, that Aristotle's portrait of the liberal or the magnificent man is strikingly correct for Greek and Roman antiquity. Let us consider, four centuries after Aristotle, the senator Pliny the Younger. His *Letters* are, and are meant to be, a handbook for the perfect Roman senator, teaching by example. They are not only autobiographical testimony but are also intended to be didactic, exemplary – which, falsely, makes their author seem highly pleased with himself. Thus Pliny tells us that he has spent 100,000 sesterces to buy a plot of land for his old nurse. On another occasion he gives 300,000 sesterces to one of his friends and dependants, who comes, like himself, from Como. As this friend is already a decurion at Como and possesses the property qualification of 100,000 sesterces required for that office, he will now have at his disposal a fortune that will open for him access to the equestrian order, for which the qualification was fixed at 400,000 sesterces. (Since it is to be feared that figures like this are going to be all too numerous in my book, let me offer the reader this practical advice. When he reads '100,000 sesterces', let him imagine that he is reading Balzac or Dickens, and has come upon the words '50,000 francs' or '2,000 sovereigns'. The Roman world, in its standard of living and way of life, as well as in its economic structure, was much closer to the pre-capitalist, pre-industrial, agrarian and usurer's world described in Dickens, or in Thackeray's *Vanity Fair*, than to the world of the twentieth century. Moreover, a sesterce was, very approximately, equivalent to half a franc in Balzac's time (sixpence sterling of the same period); there may be an error of one to two here, but not of one to ten.) Besides the 300,000 sesterces given to this friend, Pliny writes on behalf of his dependants many letters of recommendation that will give them access to the administrative nobility, those who worked for the Emperor in return for payment. As a landowner he is no less liberal towards his sharecroppers and the merchants who purchase his harvests. He had sold his vintage to these merchants while it was still on the vine, and this vintage turned out to fall short of the estimate, so Pliny refunds part of the price paid. For *noblesse oblige*, and generosity is a lordly virtue. Three centuries after Pliny, when the Roman aristocracy had become Christian, they would found *piae causae*, free their slaves and leave their goods to the poor in the same 'class' spirit. But it is above all towards his home town, Como, that the pagan Pliny shows generosity. He presents his compatriots with a library and subsidizes a school and charitable institutions. During the eleven years covered by his correspondence, he spends nearly two million sesterces on the town. In his will he bequeaths public baths to Como, leaves an annual revenue to its plebs so that they may hold a public banquet, and ensures the payment of allowances to his freedmen. We see the relative importance of liberalities directed to the home town, the city. As Dill writes: 'There has probably seldom been a time when wealth was more generally regarded as a trust, a possession in which the community at large has a share.'[2] This is precisely what we call 'euergetism' and what the subject of this book is. Euergetism means private liberality for public benefit.

2. What is euergetism?

The word euergetism is a neologism – nay, even a new concept – for which we are indebted to André Boulanger and Henri-I. Marrou.[3] It was created from the wording of the honorific decrees of the Hellenistic period by which cities honoured those persons who, through their money or their public activity, 'did good to the city' (*euergetein tēn polin*). The general word for a benefaction was *euergesia*. No word in the languages of antiquity corresponds exactly to euergetism. *Liberalitas* was used not only for liberalities towards the public, the city or a *collegium* but for any and every act of liberality. *Philotimia* is also too wide, and lays stress mainly on the reasons for euergetism, on the virtue that explains it: a noble desire for glory and honours.

THE TWO KINDS OF EUERGETISM

Never mind. Even if the word is lacking, the thing is none the less a wide and well-defined field for study. After all, a word for religion in our sense is also absent from both Latin and Greek. Euergetism means the fact that communities (cities, *collegia*) expected the rich to contribute from their wealth to the public expenses, and that this expectation was not disappointed: the rich contributed indeed, spontaneously or willingly. Their expenditure on behalf of the community was directed above all to entertainments in the circus or the arena, and, more broadly, to public pleasures (banquets) and the construction of public buildings – in short, to pleasures and public works, *voluptates* and *opera publica*. Sometimes *euergesiai* were provided by the notables without their being under any definite obligation to do so (this I shall call 'voluntary euergetism'), and sometimes on the occasion of their election to a public 'honour', a municipal magistracy or function of some kind, in which case I shall write of euergetism *ob honorem*. This was morally, or even legally, obligatory.

The distinction is in fact superficial. At first, voluntary euergetism may have been sometimes (not always or even often) the effect of gentle pressure, of an unfriendly demonstration, of a latent class struggle. Subsequently, and mainly, obligatory euergetism was merely the consequence and codification, in the Roman period, of voluntary euergetism, which made its appearance in the Greek world at the very beginning of the Hellenistic period and was thereafter imitated by the notables of the Roman towns. Alongside this euergetism *ob honorem*, however, voluntary euergetism continued to exist right down to the end of antiquity. Furthermore, many a notable, when elected magistrate, was not always satisfied with giving the community its due, but spontaneously gave it more than that, thereby transforming his *euergesia ob honorem* into a voluntary *euergesia*. It was, of course, to voluntary patronage like this, whether or not exercised on the occasion of accession to an honour, that the most sumptuous edifices owed their construction. In the evolution of euergetism, spontaneous generosity was the primary element and continued to be the principal one. It would therefore be possible to draw two contradictory pictures of euergetism. In one of them we should see notables competing with each other in liberality and inventing unimaginable refinements of munificence. In the other we should see them being pressed by the plebs, or by their peers, fearful of the people, to provide pleasures for the masses. Both pictures are true. It is all a question of circumstances and of individual characters. This duality is just what constitutes the crux of the problem.

THE NOTION OF COLLECTIVE BENEFITS

Nevertheless, the subject is not without unity. Whether Roman senator, Emperor or mere local notable, a *euergetēs* was a man who helped the community out of his own pocket, a patron of public life. What was it, then, that impelled him to give, instead of keeping his money for himself? A number of features make his case even more singular than it seems at first sight. His gifts, or *euergesiai*, were made to the community and not to a few individuals, his dependants or the poor, and that marked him off from the generality of patrons: *euergesiai* were collective benefits. A *euergetēs* obviously had little in common with our conception of an official, yet neither was he a seigneur. If he was the Emperor, he was still not the owner of his Empire, even in words. We should find it suspicious if an official were himself to be meeting the expenses of his office. He serves the public and his office is not his property. He is not required to contribute more than other taxpayers, since he has no right to receive more in return. The man and his office must remain Stoically separate. In more than one civilization, to be sure, it has happened that high officials, governors of provinces, have been left masters of both revenue and expenditure: such a governor, allowed financial independence, was a veritable seigneur. Thus he paid from the revenue of his province, which he hardly distinguished from his private income, the expenses necessitated by the government of the seigniory, to which he devoted his time and resources, and which belonged to him like his own property. But the city, the Republic or the Empire was never the property of the *euergetēs*. Never did a Greek or Roman magistrate enjoy free disposal of the public revenue. And yet, not satisfied with receiving neither salary nor recompense if they were magistrates (all public functions were performed without payment, with rare exceptions, such as the procuratorships, which did not entail euergetism), these patrons contributed from their own resources to public expenses. They took the place of the Treasury in providing collective benefits, or provided such benefits as the Treasury would never itself have provided. It was a curious juxtaposition of the public and private sectors.

Euergetism thus implies that decisions concerning certain collective benefits, which are paid for by patrons, lie outside the scope of the state's sovereignty and are taken by the patrons themselves. Now the collective nature of *euergesiai* entails important consequences. By collective benefits or services we mean those satisfactions which, owing to their external nature, are, like the radio or national defence, at the disposal of all users, without being in principle objects of competition between them. If people have to fight to get a seat on the tiers of an amphitheatre which is too small, that means the *euergetēs* has not done all he should have: the consumption of these benefits by each individual should not entail a diminution of consumption by others. If the public banquet is as it ought to be, there will be enough to eat for everyone. The characteristic feature of collective benefits is that, being provided without discrimination to all who want them, the betterment they bring is the same for everyone, whoever it may be that is making a sacrifice in order to provide them for the community. Since a gladiatorial show will be seen by all, it is best for everyone who wants to be among the spectators to let somebody else pay for it. Everyone is therefore interested in letting other people sacrifice themselves for the public good. In other words, 'the market', by which I mean the activity of isolated economic agents, acting selfishly and freely, cannot provide collective benefits in a satisfactory way. A Pareto optimum cannot even be approximated. In order to achieve it, what is needed is either honest co-operation (for example, the establishment of a roster of duties), or coercion imposed by public authority or public opinion, or else the self-sacrifice of a patron. We shall see as we go on that euergetism was imposed, to some extent, by public opinion and public authority, but also that it originated in the self-sacrifice of certain citizens. I shall explain what their ideals were.

3. Magnificence

THE ETHNOGRAPHICAL QUESTION

History offers examples of cases where gifts to the community have been raised to the level of a system. In our own day, in Mexico and the Andes, the system of *cargos*[4] has revived euergetism. In the villages of these regions the liturgical festivals of the Virgin and the saints are celebrated with exceptional splendour by the poor peasants, and are said to absorb a good third of their activity. In each village the financing of these costly festivals is ensured by a somewhat complex system of institutions. Every year the communities, or rather the village authorities, designate a certain number of individuls who are given honorific titles (*mayordomo* or *capitán*) in return for assuming the financial burden of one of these festivals. These burdens, or *cargos*, are arranged in a hierarchy, and the most honorific of them entail, if not the ruin, at least the lasting impoverishment of the dignitary concerned, who will mortgage his land or lead for several years the life of a migrant worker. The expenses of the *cargos* constitute one reason why peasants leave their villages to go down to the Pacific coast to take jobs in the mines or on public works. Actually, there is one important detail that eludes an outsider like me: is the system a kind of round in which every villager ruins himself in turn for the benefit of the others, so that in the end nobody either gains or loses; or is it the case that an elite of rich peasants, privileged in terms of power or prestige, sacrifice themselves for the rest of the village? We are told, anyway, that if the person nominated to one of these dignities were to refuse to accept the burden that the community laid upon him, he would be 'the target of severe criticism and draw upon himself the reproaches of a pitiless public opinion; it is shameful indeed not to have borne one of these religious burdens at least once in one's life'. Besides this moral sanction, public office would be firmly barred to the recalcitrant person. Nobody may seek to assume the functions of *alcalde* or *fiscal* if he has never been *mayordomo* or *capitán*. 'In these small rural communities, as in ancient Rome, it is by bankrupting oneself that one accedes to power, and the result is that the village headmen are recruited from among the most prosperous of the inhabitants.' For their part, the civil authorities are subject to other liturgical obligations that are less ruinous, such as inviting their colleagues and the religious dignitaries to a banquet during the festival of a particular saint. For the *cargos*, though, the expenses are much heavier. One has to pay for masses to be said, to decorate the church and the saint's own altar, to provide victims for sacrifice (these regions practise a curious mixture of Christianity and paganism) and, above all, to regale the villagers with alcohol and coca. As in the popular celebrations of antiquity, a solemn sacrifice is held in esteem mainly in proportion to the feast that follows it. Such is the principle; in detail, matters are less logical, and some burdens are endowed with a traditional prestige much higher than the moderate expenses they demand. Finally, among the dignitaries there prevails a rivalry that is expressed in striving to outdo each other, to surpass one another in bounty: 'vanity is indeed the weak point in the Indian character'. Pressure of public opinion and vanity: these two phenomena, corresponding like an outside and an inside, would seem to account for Andean euergetism.

But how is the system kept going?

ARISTOTLE: THE CONCEPT OF MAGNIFICENCE

To this question Aristotle gave a famous reply. Euergetism is the manifestation of an 'ethical virtue', of a quality of character, namely magnificence. It can be claimed, in fact, that the analysis of magnificence in the *Nicomachean Ethics* is simply an analysis of what we now call euergetism: 'throughout his study of magnificence Aristotle has all the time in mind the liturgies' and the system of *euergesiai* that was nascent in the decades when the philosopher was teaching.[5] We cannot be surprised at the dated content of his moral doctrine: the description of the qualities of character in books III and IV of the *Ethics* is wholly a 'gallery of portraits, the description of a series of personages who have been turned into types in everyday speech'. A sort of 'method of eidetic variations allows one to determine empirically the content of a semantic nucleus', the point of departure being 'a linguistic usage considered as a mode of manifestation of the things themselves'.[6] Aristotle gives us a history of words, or at least starts from words, particular words, in order to isolate and define, if only conventionally, certain attitudes. Under the name of magnificence, euergetism is explained by the virtue thus designated. The explanation may seem attractive, since it is at the same time historical. The Greeks are explained by a value which is simultaneously Greek and human. Magnificence is presented as an anthropological disposition which is universal (the Greeks were *euergetai* because men in general are *euergetai*) and as a feature of character that conforms to the Hellenic national genius. Here we easily recognize the Greek genius – the Greeks were indeed like that. We can thus respect both the texts and the eternal human being. From the word 'magnificence' we pass to the values. The Greeks accorded considerable esteem to the value of magnificence, which is enough to explain many of the specific features of their civilization. This value was attractive to them all, for it formed part of their national character, so that we see it manifested in widely vary-ing situations and among individuals or groups that were extremely diverse. It will be seen that Aristotle's magnificence is ambiguous: is it a historical value or an anthropological trait? Is it a quality pos-sessed by an elite of individuals or is it a collective tendency? Were the Greeks alone – and *all* the Greeks – inclined towards magnificence?

To begin at the beginning. By 'magnificence', or *megaloprepeia*, common usage designated the motives that moved the liturgists of classical Athens, the ancestors of our *euergetai*. All the examples of this virtue that Aristotle cites show that this was so, together with the definition of the virtue itself, for its exclusive objects, namely collective benefits, distinguish it in the philosopher's eyes from another quality that seems very close, namely liberality.

At the beginning of book IV Aristotle analyses two virtues that are related to the art of spending and receiving properly: liberality and magnificence.[7] How do they differ? Conceptually, the difference is slight. Magnificence does not, 'like liberality, extend to all the actions that are concerned with wealth, but only to those that involve expen-diture, and in these it surpasses liberality in scale'.[8] Thus, magnificence spends more than mere liberality does, and it is only the art of *giving*, whereas liberality consists also in knowing how to receive gifts properly. In fact, as Aristotle's examples show, the difference is not so much philosophical as historical. Magnificence is the variety of liberality which relates to gifts to the community. The magnificent man is a social type: a rich notable.

His acts of magnificence are, in the first place, liturgies (the philosopher mentions trierarchy, *chorēgia* and *architheōria*). He also engages in large private expenditure, notably of the non-recurrent kind − for instance, a wedding. We shall come back to these private ceremonies, weddings or funerals, to which the whole town was invited. The magnificent man also spends generously on 'anything that interests the whole city or the people of position in it, and also the receiving of foreign guests and the sending of them on their way'. His residence, we might say, is a diplomatic and political *salon*, and he himself a public man. The collective nature of his bounty is emphasized: magnificent expenditures are 'of the kind which we call honourable, e.g., those connected with the gods − votive offerings (*anathēmata*), buildings and sacrifices' (at this time all edifices, even secular ones, that individuals offered to their city were verbally consecrated 'to the gods and to the city'). No less magnificent was the bounty that it was a matter of honour to offer for the benefit of the community, 'as when people think they ought to equip a chorus or a trireme or entertain the city'. In short 'the magnificent man spends not on himself but on public objects, and gifts bear some resemblance to votive offerings'. We are to understand that he gives without receiving presents in exchange. He devotes his fortune to higher values, civic or religious, and does not introduce his bounty into the system of exchange of favours that characterizes the more modest virtue of liberality.

The magnificent man is a notable, a rich man who occupies a high position in general esteem.

A poor man cannot be magnificent, since he has not the means with which to spend large sums fittingly; and if he tries he is a fool, since he spends beyond what can be expected of him and what is proper, but it is *right* expenditure that is excellent. But great expenditure is becoming to those who have suitable means to start with, acquired by their own efforts or from ancestors or connections, and to people of high birth or reputation, and so on; for all these things bring with them greatness and prestige.

Sixteen centuries later, St Thomas Aquinas came up against the two difficulties of Aristotle's doctrine: its excessively historical content and the 'class' character of its concept of virtue. The Athenian liturgies were now in the remote past, so the Doctor had to try to give a formal definition of magnificence. He treated it as a variant of magnanimity, that is, of pride (a quality on which the saint heaps hyperbolic eulogies).[9]

The munificent man shows his pride in an edifice, a festival, a work of some kind, for munificence is a pride that is concerned not to act but to make. It does not consist, for example, in acting courageously, but is externalized in a product. Pride suffices to explain the collective character of munificent expenditure: the proud man wants to do something on a grand scale, but everything individual is petty in comparison with divine worship or public affairs. The munificent man does not think of himself: not because he disdains his own property but because there is nothing there that is great.

Euergetism is thus seen as a form of pride that causes collective works to be performed. This pride bears, materially, a class character for which St Thomas tries to console himself in a very Aristotelian way: 'A man who cannot fittingly perform acts of magnanimity can have a magnanimous disposition, which makes him ready to perform a magnanimous act, should it be appropriate to his position in life.' 'Some liberal men are not magnificent in action, for they lack the wherewithal for a magnificent act. But every liberal man has the quality of magnificence either performed or on the verge of performance.'[10] Such are these admirable pages (the doctrine of the virtue of fortitude is one of the finest sections of the *Summa Theologica*). As Gilson writes, the Greek *megaloprepeia* is ready to become, without denying itself, the historical virtue of a Most Christian King or of a Lorenzo the Magnificent. The doctrine of magnificence is an excellent description and, no less, a good definition of euergetism. But is it an explanation that 'fits'?

It is not that the method of the *Nicomachean Ethics* is out of date. Even today, historiography, whether or not it knows this (or wants to know it), naturally tends to isolate and distinguish invariant, transhistorical features in people or things, which every historical context modifies, in a more or less unpredictable way. In euergetism there are one or more invariants, but what are they? Is magnificence among them? No, for this is an ambiguous notion that obliges us to take the analysis further if we want to give it a more definite meaning. Indeed, it is not clear whether magnificence is a universal anthropological trait, or merely a collective historical virtue of the Greeks, or else, among the Greeks as with us, a quality of character possessed by some individuals. Given the first hypothesis, magnificence is an invariant that we can find, either stunted or expanded, in a thousand historical modifications throughout the millennia, with all mankind tending towards magnificence. Given the second interpretation, the Greek doctrine of magnificence is the self-portrait of a civilization: social forces made the Greeks magnificent. In the third case, magnificence is just a virtue which, as such, distinguishes from their fellows those individuals who possess it. If we claim that the social context of antiquity educated everyone to practise this virtue, we shall not be wrong, but then a host of historical and sociological problems arise. How and why were the Greeks educated into that virtue? How and why does the phenomenon called education or socialization take place, causing one group of human beings to be unlike another? One cannot talk vaguely of an entire people as though they were a single virtuous individual: the law of averages forbids us to suppose that the magnificent were numerous through the chance occurrence of individual dispositions. Either magnificence is an invariant, and then we have to discover the sociological and historical explanation of its diffusion; or it is a virtue, collective or individual, and then we have to isolate its invariants.

4. Invariants and modifications

I propose provisionally to reduce euergetism to two or three themes that I shall define, or at least exemplify, in the course of this book. One of them, for which I shall use the conventional term 'patronage', corresponds broadly to voluntary euergetism. This is merely the tendency men have to display themselves, to realize all their potentialities. The second theme, which corresponds rather to euergetism *ob honorem*, is that of the complicated relations men have with the trade of politics. These two themes taken together have given rise to certain explanations of euergetism that I regard as mistaken or confused, but which are well known. One is 'depoliticization', the other is 'conspicuous consumption', and I shall discuss them in a moment. There remains, perhaps, a third theme: desire for immortality, care for what comes after one is dead, for one's 'memory'. Many *euergesiai* were, indeed, offered in men's wills. The following study will tell us whether this theme deserves to retain its specificity, or whether the attitudes of the ancients to death are rather to be reduced to the two preceding themes, however strange this may seem. To quote Aristotle: 'Both evil and good are thought to exist for a dead man, as much as for one who is alive but not aware of them: e.g., honours and dishonours.'[11]

5. Euergetism and Christian charity

One of the advantages of analysis is that it blocks the way to false historical continuities. 'Essay on the Gift', exchange and Structuralism, waste for the sake of prestige, the death portion (*Totenteil*) and 'the accursed share': how can euergetism not remind us vaguely of all that? Does a single mysterious force impel societies to waste or give away their surpluses? Potlatch, *euergesiai*, pious and charitable works – are they all modifications of one species, namely, redistribution? When we look down from an aeroplane on a city of the baroque period and the ruins of a Roman city, separated by sixteen centuries, we are tempted to believe that this is so. In the baroque city we see everywhere the roofs of convents, hospices, charitable establishments. In the Roman ruins, public buildings constructed by *euergetai* seem to cover more ground than dwellings. The observer thinks he is seeing the operation of one and the same function, redistribution, in the two towns across the centuries, to judge by its manifestations, which are on the same scale in both places.

But this is an illusion. Euergetism and pious and charitable works differ in ideology, in beneficiaries and in agents, in the motivations of agents and in their behaviour. Euergetism has no direct connection with religion. The very word 'religion' differs in meaning when applied to pagan ritualism or to an ethical religiosity like Christianity. The relations of the two religions to morality also differ – or rather the word 'morality' does not have the same meaning in the two cases. An analysis of all that would take up many pages. Let me confine myself to a narrative sketch.

POPULAR AND SECTARIAN MORALITY

Charity has a strange history. Here we see three things converging: a virtue that was dear to the Jewish people, loving-kindness, which forbids one to claim everything one has a right to, and makes alms-giving a duty; popular pagan morality, to which this loving-kindness, so natural to all humble people in every clime, was not alien either; and, finally, the solidarity that bound together the members of the Christian sect, like any other. The forms and limits of this convergence will be found to present some surprising agents.

'Thou shalt open thine hand wide unto thy poor brother,' it is written in Deuteronomy. Similarly, in the Egyptian *Book of the Dead*, the deceased takes pride in having given bread to the hungry. Between the book of the Covenant, in Exodus, and the Utopia of Deuteronomy, charity undergoes an increasingly systematic development, which gives us a glimpse of a patriarchal society in which the community of family and neighbours counts for much[12] and the clergy have not remained deaf to the complaints of the just man who is suffering. Almsgiving, which was eventually to become a strict obligation, is the duty of the just man, who does not forget that he himself may in his turn be reduced to beggary, and who has learnt to place himself mentally in his neighbour's shoes. 'Thou shalt not oppress a stranger,' says a remarkable verse in Exodus, 'for ye know the heart of a stranger, seeing we were strangers in the land of Egypt.'[13] One would like to have seen the reaction if a citizen of Athens had been asked to put himself in the place of a resident alien! The son of Sirach is very much aware that there are rich and poor, and he puts himself among the latter: 'When a rich man is fallen, he hath many helpers: he speaketh things not to be spoken, and yet men justify him: the poor man slipped, and yet they rebuked him too; he spake wisely, and could have no place.'[14] There are the rich and there are the poor. Christianity never forgets this great contrast. A citizen of Athens did not think much about it, and the words of the son of Sirach would have sickened him. Pagan literature is full of civic or patrician pride; this harsh climate is the climate of euergetism, which gives edifices and pleasures to the citizens rather than alms to the poor. To be sure, kindness to a slave or a beggar is not unknown in this setting. In the *Odyssey* the suitors discredit themselves when they give a bad welcome to Ulysses dressed as a beggar, and Agamemnon, asking Clytemnestra to treat Cassandra well, observes: 'God from afar looks graciously upon a gentle master; for of free choice no one takes upon him the yoke of slavery.'[15] Who knows, indeed, if the free man may not himself be a slave one day? But patrician pride and a certain spirit of political seriousness more often rejected these feelings of pity: thinking too much about the poor and a possible reversal of conditions is politically demoralizing. A free citizen will not stoop to praise kindness. He will leave that to the lower orders, who are interested in convincing their masters that they should treat them well, and whose only hope lies in prayer. *They* know what poverty is, for they are close to it. The citizen, however, feels solidarity with his fellow citizens, and hardens himself in a haughty attitude. This changed a little only under the Empire, when the citizen had become a faithful subject of his Emperor. Here and there, in epitaphs of the Imperial epoch, we read with surprise that the deceased 'loved the poor' (language that tells us something about popular pagan morality) or that he had pity on everyone.[16] Among the intellectuals too, even those who were aristocrats, the armour of hardness fell away: the Stoicism of the Imperial epoch has notes of philanthropy in it that remind us of popular morality and the spirit of the Gospels.[17]

Gospel morality is both popular and Jewish. Leave aside the often admirable constructions of philosophy and theology erected upon the idea of charity, and keep to the Synoptic Gospels, which give us the already rather platitudinous image of Christ that Christianity was to make official. It has often been said that the Gospel ideal which makes this image so valuable was the least original part of Christ's teaching, being that in which his debt to his own people was greatest, since this ideal was the common property of Judaism in those days. Christ could not fail to adopt it: no popular preacher would have been listened to if he had not done the same.

And why should he not have adopted it? He was himself only a man of the people, one of that crowd who look up from below, marvelling at those who 'in kings' courts' are 'gorgeously apparelled and live delicately' — one of that crowd whose vision does not stretch very far and knows not the great world. 'I am not sent but unto the lost sheep of the house of Israel,' said Jesus himself to the woman of Canaan. If we read the Gospels unencumbered by the interpretation read into them by Christian tradition, we can hardly have any doubt: there is no universalism in Jesus. Could it be that he wanted to be a national prophet of the Jews? Not even that. He never thought either of playing or of not playing that role, for his vision barely transcended the borders of his country: a Samaritan, a Canaanite woman, some soldiers, that was for him the great world. He was neither a universalist nor a conscious nationalist: that dilemma was over his head. Of course he knew and said that all men are descended from Noah, that we are all brothers, all children of God. He knew too how to soften all principles and all exclusions, even national ones. Christian universalism is logically derived from these attitudes, and we must know the tree by its fruits. It remains none the less a fact of history that Jesus did not, himself, follow through that logic, and we must not look for the fruit in the root. Yes, in theory, all men are brothers: but, in practice, Jesus knew, and wished to know, only the sheep of Israel. This is contradictory, but why should it not be? And why should Jesus even have noticed the contradiction? Yet it could not escape him any longer, the day that he encountered the woman of Canaan. And so he was amazed, and hesitated. In the end, his second impulse prevailed. The Canaanite woman had said to him: 'Have mercy on me, O Lord, thou son of David, my daughter is grievously vexed with a devil.' The disciples had urged him to send away this foreigner, and he himself answered her at first saying that she was not one of the lost sheep of Israel. But the woman pleaded so strongly that in the end she obtained a crumb, just as crumbs are thrown to the dogs under the table.[18]

The case of the morality of the Gospels is similar to that of universalism, in that we ought not to ask questions which a man of the people, however great a genius, could not have asked himself. Must charity transform the political order? Is it merely a spiritual refuge? Is it an ethic of conviction, or of responsibility? Jesus did not speculate so far. Only the great ones of this world can ask themselves questions like that – the men who control all things. Jesus does not submit himself deliberately to the established order so as to teach this lesson to everyone; he just renders to Caesar what he owes to Caesar, for how could a man of the people stand up against Caesar, except by resorting to armed revolt? The established order is unshakable, like nature, and the humble cannot but submit to it. What is left for them to do? To help each other, to act as brothers in poverty, to implore those among them who are low-level agents of the powerful not to abuse their little bit of power. Some soldiers and tax-collectors asked him one day what they ought to do. Was he going to tell them to give up their jobs? They were poor people like himself, and such people are not heroes. He advised them to earn their living without showing excessive zeal in their masters' service and without abusing their power. Did he then foresee that the Earthly City would present contingencies to which charity would have to be adjusted? No, for he could not foresee what the Church would one day make him say. All he knew was that everyone has to eat and hold on to his livelihood.

This was an 'irresponsible' ethic, if you wish to put it like that, for the good reason that it was created *by* a man and *for* men who bore no share of responsibility. All they could do was to persuade each other to mitigate, for their mutual advantage, an order and laws of which they were not the authors and which they had never agreed to. This popular ethic was not to develop any abstract principles, but was to be expressed in maxims and typical examples. To love one's neighbour as oneself: this is no longer the nationalistic solidarity of the warlike Israel of old, but the solidarity of the humble. To turn the other cheek, instead of claiming one's right to retaliate against a brother in poverty:

for one ought not to insist on getting one's due absolutely – even when justified, one should concede something to an opponent, and besides, what good would it do for a poor man to plead before those in power? More generally, the humble folk should not consider themselves bound by the rules and prohibitions and all that harsh constraint wherein they find themselves crushed as soon as they are born into the social world, and which the men of power, in order to maintain discipline, uphold in the name of principle, although people matter more than laws and prohibitions. Finally, there is one duty which is incumbent on all Jews and which serves as an emblem of all the rest – almsgiving. He who gives alms mitigates the harsh law of the economic order and puts himself in the place of the poor, feeling solidarity with them.

This was a popular morality of mutual aid and almsgiving, which was also to become a sectarian morality. Before turning into a religion into which one is born, like being born French or Swiss, Christianity was for a long time a sect one chose to join. The practice of mutual aid and the doctrine of love grew in that hothouse atmosphere which engenders intense emotions. Closed in on itself, cut off from the world, the sect had for its only cement the solidarity between its members. Instead of engaging in *euergesiai*, writes Tertullian, we give to our poor, our orphans, our old people. 'But it is mainly the deeds of a love so noble that lead many to put a brand upon us. See, they say, how they love one another.'[19] For this exclusive freemasonry disquieted society, being felt as a threat.

Apol.
39.7

The sectarian solidarity of the Christians goes back to Jesus himself, as witnessed by St John's Gospel, which shows us a picture of him so intimate, so violent and so unconventional that many who are fond of the Synoptic Vulgate regard this other testimony as 'late' and 'suspect', though it cries out its authenticity. Once again, Jesus has gone to Jerusalem, hoping to succeed there with his message, but he has a premonition that this journey will be his last. 'Little children,' he says to his disciples, 'yet a little while I am with you ... A new commandment I give unto you, That ye love one another; as I have loved you, that ye also love one another. By this shall all men know that ye are my disciples, if ye have love one to another.'[20] This time, the commandment is not addressed to all men but to the disciples alone. They are to stay together, to keep solidarity after their master has gone: they are to form a sect so as to perpetuate his teaching. Mutual aid will be one of the effects of this solidarity, as was traditional in the Jewish sects: one of the Essene scrolls from the Dead Sea, the *Damascus*

Document, prescribes the levying of a tax for the purpose of forming a common chest from which the poor and the old can be succoured.[21] From the second century at least, the Christian Church was to be no longer satisfied with urging the faithful to show beneficence privately but would institutionalize it, setting up a 'chest' (*arca*) for aid to widows, orphans, the poor, the old, the sick and those in prison, under the control of the hierarchy.[22]

ETHICS AS PROFESSED AND AS PRACTISED

When the inhabitants of the Empire had been converted *en masse*, or at least had changed their labels, and the sect had become a Church, these charitable practices continued to flourish because they found in popular pagan ethics a field ready for sowing. Christianity thus led to an 'upsurge' of popular morality within Roman aristocratic morality (the two moralities had become differentiated since Rome began to be Hellenized). One is reminded of Rousseau's success in making the practices and prohibitions of bourgeois morality fashionable among the nobility of his time. The Roman aristocracy accepted the new morality on the plane of principles to be avowed and respected, and put as much of it into practice as they could; we shall soon see what this amounted to. As a rigorist sect, Christianity did what such sects often do: they impose on their members a morality that does not differ from the morality of their time, for they cannot imagine any other, but they impose it with great vigour, and also make obligatory certain articles of this morality that current usage has not treated as absolute duties. Or else they adopt the popular morality of their time, which is stricter on many points than that of the nobles (popular pagan morality, like Christianity, did not make light of clean living or of suicide). Moreover, Christianity, being a religion of the Book, had no hesitation in imposing new or alien practices such as almsgiving, for no better reason than that these were prescribed by the Scriptures.

With what success did the Christians impose these practices? Did their rigorism and evangelical spirit transform, if not the social structure and the major institutions, at least everyday relationships and the national spirit? This is a question hard to answer, for realities as intangible as these cannot be tracked down in the sources. Accordingly, I shall be brief, and offer no firm conclusions. There are cases in history of an ethic of kindness spreading among certain social groups or even entire peoples, and modifying the human relationships of everyday life.

The effects of Buddhism are noticeable in more than one nation of Central Asia, and it is said that, over several centuries, Lamaism has transformed the Mongols. Where our Western world is concerned, it is not easy to say what we owe to Christianity. Did paganism already include the duty to show consideration, equity, mildness, mutual aid, and everything we could call the spirit of the Gospels; or does the West owe its everyday physiognomy to Christianity? In fact, we should begin by making distinctions. The style of unequal relationships between master and subordinate or between judge and accused, which may be authoritarian, legalistic or paternal, can be very different from relationships between equals, whether these be brutal, competitive, distant or amiable. Attitudes towards those who do not form part of society – children, animals, beggars, invalids, lunatics, handicapped persons – often constitute a separate domain. Institutional or ritual atrocities, public executions or human sacrifices, are generally treated as a separate sphere, as are military atrocities. Similarly, seemliness and elementary courtesy have little to do with ethical rigorism or laxity.

Charity was an alien morality that became acculturated in Rome: the morality of a sect that had become a Church, a popular morality imposed on everyone in the name of religious principle. Its success was very uneven. We must distinguish carefully between the ethic that a society practises (whether it does this consciously or whether this ethic is merely implicit in people's behaviour) and the ethic that this society professes. These two ethics usually have little in common. Different social groups may practise the same morality in the name of opposing faiths: Julian the Apostate differed from the Christians only in his principles. The professed morality is never discredited, because it is not translated into deeds. People hardly notice that its principles are not put into practice: what is important is that these principles should not be challenged. This was what happened with charity. In some respects it became part of morality as practised: it continued some long-established forms of behaviour, or it served certain interests or, on the contrary, it occupied without opposition a sphere that was considered unimportant. In other respects it remained an ethic that was professed, which it would be indecent to repudiate, and which people sincerely believed that they practised in all circumstances.

Charity, or, more generally, pious behaviour, engendered three new practices. The Roman aristocracy had certain styles of formal behaviour and social responsibility. It was euergetistic and caused civil edifices to be built: henceforth it would build churches. The concern of individuals for their fate in the next world multiplied pious liberalities in the form of legacies to the Church, in numbers so great that we get the impression that people were obsessed with their salvation. Finally and most important, charitable practices occupied without hindrance, in between political or social concerns, what I shall call the margin of charity, and there achieved results that have to be taken quite seriously.

LIBERALITIES AND LEGACIES TO THE CHURCH

In the fourth century the aristocrats of Rome and the notables of the municipalities continued to be *euergetai*. 'They vie with one another in exhausting their patrimony in order to embellish their city,' wrote the pagan Symmachus.[23] Municipal life changed so little, indeed, that the Fathers of the Greek Church are among our richest sources for the history of euergetism.[24] The Christian notables did not lag behind those who had remained pagan, for the same obligations, formal or moral, were binding on both sets – with some differences, however. A Christian *euergetēs* could not be expected to build a temple. In the fourth century secular building work was rarely undertaken in Roman Africa: at most, edifices falling into ruin would be repaired, because the Emperor and the governor wanted this done. What had happened? Had there been an economic crisis or a decline in the spirit of munificence? To believe this would mean overlooking the fact that in the same period Roman Africa was being covered with a garment of Christian basilicas. Euergetism had new objects in view. At other times, euergetism changed its intention. St Ambrose called on the rich to distribute bread to the poor by charitable intention,[25] and St Augustine contrasted pagan euergetism, which distributed pleasures, with charity, which looks after the true interests of the poor.[26] Almsgiving thus succeeded euergetism. St Cyprian compares almsgiving to a public spectacle presented by a *euergetēs*, but with God and the angels as spectators.[27] The money spent on games would be better given to the poor, writes St Augustine.[28] Moral rigorism plays a part as important as charity in this condemnation of public entertainments.

The Christian notables were charitable and built churches. The bishops, even before the Peace of the Church and the triumph of the new religion, inherited the social responsibilities of the notables, along with those specific to their own charge: when he became a bishop, St Cyprian ruined himself in the performance of his office, opening his door to everyone who sought his advice and giving support to the humble against the insolence of the powerful.[29] These welcome attitudes on the part of the notables conformed to the hopes placed in them by the people, who expected no less. From the new ethical religion the masses looked to receive the same satisfactions they had found in paganism: festivals and feasts. It is well known that, towards the end of antiquity, there was a vogue for funeral banquets in memory of the martyrs. Sometimes things went further still. In the *Life of Porphyry of Gaza* we see a bishop who, to honour the consecration of his church, 'spares no expense' (the formula always used in connection with the munificence of a *euergetēs*) and provides a banquet for the entire population – priests, monks and lay folk – in a celebration that lasts throughout Holy Week.[30] The pagan *euergetai* had similarly given banquets for the inauguration of secular edifices, and the public eulogy awarded to them by the city did not fail to list the categories of the population who had been invited and to specify the number of days the merrymaking had lasted.

The Christian notables ruined themselves in pious and charitable works because they were notables. Their power gave them responsibility for all spheres of social life, and also obliged them to make a certain show. Their wealth imposed a duty to realize in their persons the human ideal that was highest in the eyes of their contemporaries, since this very wealth endowed them with the means to do so. If they did not actualize that potentiality they would remain unworthy of themselves and suffer contempt in their own eyes.

But they also ruined themselves in this way because they were Christians. A pagan would have sought to realize in his person an ideal different from that of the pious and charitable soul. Another new practice, that of pious liberalities and legacies to the Church, owed almost everything to the content of religious beliefs, almost nothing to the social ostentation or Pharisaism of the rich man – even though the latter was indeed ready to believe that his soul was not so cheap as that of one of the poor.

The legacies left by the pagans of former times and the pious liberalities of the Christian period had in common only the immensity of their effects. Considerable quantities of goods were both offered to the cities and consecrated to the Church, but the respective motivations were almost opposite. The *euergetai* gave what they gave in order to acquire social standing, or out of patriotism and a sense of civic responsibility – in any case, from interest in the things of this world. Bequests to the Church, however, were intended to redeem the sins of the testator at the expense of the interests of his heirs: they were made for the sake of the other world.

I believe that this was the case. And I believe that, even more powerful than fear of what comes after death, love of the Church was the chief motivation of these legacies. But let me first strengthen myself in this belief by letting the devil's advocate speak. The history of religion is a difficult art, in which one must neither be too Voltairean nor surrender to the unquestioning faith of the ignorant. Is it then really enough, the devil's advocate might ask, that a religion should swear that there is a future life, for hordes of people to believe this and put their belief into practice? On other points religions seem powerless to change the old Adam. And besides, belief takes several different forms. Nobody has seen the Beyond with his own eyes. Its existence is of a different ontological order from the world in which we live, so that one cannot believe in it in the same way as one believes in the existence of cities that witnesses have seen with their own eyes in lands which, though distant, are yet real. Let us admit, too, with Gabriel Le Bras, that Christendom never existed – that beneath the surface of orthodoxy there were always unbelievers hidden, more numerous than one thinks, even in the Middle Ages.[31] Let us go further: people believe only what they have no interest in *not* believing. There are orthodoxies that enjoy unanimous adhesion, but which exist in a separate world of the spirit, a world of statements, regarded as noble or sacred, which do not conflict with other statements or clash with the interests of other worlds. In such cases, anyone who might choose to challenge these beliefs would provoke a general outcry. His questioning of them could be ascribed only to a gratuitous hatred of the good and the sacred, a sort of perversity. If this is so, how are we to explain why so many testators have sacrificed so much wealth to fear of the Beyond, and neglected, on that account, the ontologically very solid interests of the real world? The explanation is quite simple. Many of these pious liberalities are made in men's wills. They come into force when the testator is no longer there to enjoy his property. He therefore has nothing to lose by securing, through a stroke of the pen, a guarantee against the vague possibility of an after-life: this is easier than having to reform one's life day after day. At a stroke, he is redeemed of his sins, with an absolute guarantee and without self-deprivation. Do we not have examples of testators who waited until what they thought was going to be their last hour before leaving a legacy to the Church, and then, on recovering their health, proceeded to revoke their wills?[32]

The devil's advocate is right in principle (the forms of belief are many indeed) but wrong in the case in point. People are not uninterested in what will happen after their deaths. They are capable of dying voluntarily for a cause of which they will not see the victory. They may compromise the future of their souls because they are *not* willing to neglect the interests of their heirs and the future of their house. If they give to the Church, they do it in spite of these future interests, and not out of ultimate indifference. Do they redeem themselves from all their sins at a single stroke, instead of reforming their lives, as they doubtless would if they shared the unquestioning faith of the ignorant? That merely shows that they esteem present benefits more highly than future ones: one could say the same of hardened drinkers and smokers, but that does not mean that the latter do not believe in the reality of cirrhosis or lung cancer. Do they prefer to leave their goods to the Church when they die rather than present them while they are still alive? But who is not even a little calculating? What rich man never contemplates a little low cunning, what logician does not reckon on God's disinterestedness?[33] It remains true that, for everyone, the idea of the after-life is always a little unreal and that, even with the strongest of believers (think of Bernanos), it is still overshadowed by fear of death. So that it is not so much fear of what comes after death as love of the Church that motivates pious liberalities, whether or not these are embodied in men's wills.

Redemption of sins and assurance of the life to come are hardly more than the occasion that is seized by the believer and for which ready-made institutions are available to him. We ought not to imagine him to be an unbeliever who is suddenly confronted with the prospect of hell and wonders if he really believes and how he is going to place his bet. Nor ought we to imagine him to be someone ready to set aside all his interests for the sake of his soul's salvation; he is more likely to try to find some compromise that safeguards them. But in between men's major interests there is still a wide margin of everyday life, and within this margin religion can infiltrate everywhere, weaving itself into all aspects of behaviour, shaping gestures and inflections, linking itself with many joys, being present on a wide front. And it can cause the Church to be loved. Men often left something to a servant they had been fond of, or to an old nurse of theirs. They also left something to the Church they had loved and respected – and, into the bargain, such a legacy was an insurance policy for the after-life.

ALMSGIVING AS COMPROMISE

Almsgiving was that, too: insurance for the next life, but, above all, an effect of pity for the disinherited, that pity which is so natural a sentiment when felt, but which societies can endure for thousands of years without feeling, and which, in any case, they feel only when major interests allow this to happen.

Histories of public assistance through the ages have been written in which charity is shown as continuing euergetism and as taking over its function. This is, needless to say, a false continuity. In an excellent book,[34] Bolkestein has convincingly shown the contrast between civic assistance in pagan antiquity and Christian charity to the poor. The very word 'poor', he wrote, is peculiar to the vocabulary of the Jews and the Christians: paganism does not have this concept. In Greece or in Rome what we should call assistance, redistribution or euergetism was directed, or was thought of as being directed, to the people as such, to all the citizens, and to them alone; the slaves were excluded on principle, apart from exceptional cases of generosity. Agrarian laws, *euergesiai*, distributions of cheap bread, were civic measures: it was the Roman people who had the right to free bread and it was for the citizens that colonies were founded.

Ought we to take this vocabulary literally? Ought we not, on the contrary, to consider whether the pagans were perhaps just as charitable as anyone else, though they lacked the relevant language? After all, though the conceptualization of that epoch dissolved the social category of the poor in the civic universalism of the law, it was none the less true that only *poor* citizens benefited from the agrarian laws or emigrated to the new colonies. When a pagan established a fund for the education of citizens (of *poor* citizens, obviously), Roman lawyers did not know under what heading to classify this foundation: eventually, they decided to treat it as intended to honour the city, and thus as euergetic in character.[35]

Which gives us the truth: the history of words or the critique of ideology? Neither, for language is sometimes true and sometimes false. The fact is that paganism helped some of the poor without naming them. It helped others on the grounds that they were destitute. (Sometimes a *euergetēs* allowed slaves to share in his bounty, emphasizing when he did so that this resulted from unusual benevolence on his part.)[36] But there were also many poor whom paganism did not help at all. On the whole, paganism showed itself much less charitable in deeds than Christianity was to be, even if it *was* charitable to a small extent. That is understandable. The attitude of charity, though greatly developed by certain religions, was not invented by them. In paganism it coexisted with another theme, that of the civic patrimony.

Agrarian laws and colonies: as Claude Vatin has pointed out to me, these institutions were based on the idea that a citizen who had no patrimony could not be a real citizen. The Gracchi wanted to distribute land among the poor citizens of Rome, not so much in order to relieve poverty as to ensure a sound foundation for society. Every community has its poor. Under paganism they were the citizens who lacked a patrimony. For the Christians the poor man was anyone who needed alms. Paganism was aware of the poor man only in his most commonplace shape, that of the beggar encountered in the street. 'The wise man,' writes Seneca, 'will give a coin to a beggar without dropping it in a contemptuous manner, as do those who wish to be charitable only for the sake of appearances.'[37] The coin given to a beggar was thus a feature of everyday reality, but this reality did not include welfare institutions, which the Christians invented. The philanthropic actions in which a Demosthenes or a Cicero took pride[38] consisted of ransoming a captured citizen or providing a dowry for a citizen's orphaned daughter. Philanthropy was noble only if it relieved elevated misfortunes. Almsgiving was an everyday action but not a duty of the state or an act of high morality, and philosophers barely mention it.

All this changed with the coming of Christianity, in which alms-giving resulted from the new ethical religiosity. Now that it had become a highly significant form of behaviour, charity was worthy to rank as a state duty of the upper class, for whom it took the place of munificence. By its material importance, its spiritual implications and the institutions it engendered, charity became the new historical virtue.

Almsgiving was the central imperative of the new religious morality, its *Kerngebot*, as Max Weber calls it.[39] Of all the commandments to show kindness, almsgiving is the one that a person can most commonly take the initiative in fulfilling; the others are concerned, rather, to prescribe how a person should behave in particular situations. It is also a pledge of disinterestedness and the simplest proof that a believer can offer of the sincerity of his faith. It is all the more in the nature of a symbolic act in that the believer can bring his deeds into line with his words at small cost, and multiply proofs of his sincerity, by giving little at a time, but giving often. Our rich men, writes St Justin, give what they choose and when they choose.[40] Of all meritorious acts, this is the cheapest psychologically: it enables a person to redeem at one stroke a whole lifetime of sins. Almsgiving conforms to God's will and constitutes merit in his eyes, and so it is soon looked upon as a gift made to God himself, as an exchange and a ransom. The Epistle to the Hebrews says that doing good is equivalent to a 'sacrifice',[41] and St Cyprian sees in it the only means open to a man for redeeming his sins after being baptized[42] (the sacrament of penance had, of course, not yet been introduced in his time).

Pious and charitable works finally effected a compromise between asceticism and worldly life. Was one to renounce the things of this world? Now that the entire population of the Empire was Christian, Christianity was no longer solely 'the religion of the poor and the slaves'. That has often been said, perhaps too often. Let me say that, above all, Christianity had become a religion into which a person was born, and was no longer a sect. Was one to flee from the world? That could be required only of volunteers. What was to become of those who were born both rich and Christian, if, for them, the entrance to heaven was no bigger than the eye of a needle? As early as the third century a realistic and moderate thinker, Clement of Alexandria, declared that what mattered was not riches but the way riches were used. In a treatise entitled 'How Can a Rich Man be Saved?' he called upon the rich to assume a Stoic attitude to their riches. External things that do not depend on us are neither good nor bad: they become one or the other by the use we make of them. God, he writes in another place,[43] has allowed us to use all things, but has set a limit to such use, namely need. What is sinful is to have an unlimited desire for riches for their own sake, and not merely to meet one's need. Almsgiving and the spirit behind it are the best pledge of a sound attitude towards the goods of this world. And so, from the fourth century, a dual morality was established:[44] perfect Christians fled from the world and the flesh, while other Christians, the greater number, remained in the world, and these latter were to save their souls through almsgiving and leaving property to the Church.

Almsgiving is not merely a compromise with the ascetic ideal, in a religion that conceives of no half-way house between poverty and damnation; it is also a consequence of that ideal. In the New Testament almsgiving had at least two origins: namely popular morality, of which I have already spoken, and an ascetic ideal, which needs further discussion. Now, if we take a hard line, we have to say that asceticism has nothing to do with philanthropy. The person who gives his goods to the poor in order to flee from the world is less concerned to help his neighbour than to rid himself of obstacles to his own salvation. There will therefore be an easy transition from asceticism to a 'class morality' in which almsgiving is a merit for the rich man, who shows himself obedient to God's commandment, but not a right for the poor. God has called on the rich to give, but has not willed that the poor be poor no longer. Furthermore, it remains understood that the rich man gives *if* he wants to and *what* he wants to.

HISTORICAL EFFECTS OF CHARITY

The triumph of the Christian religion enabled a strong minority to make an entire society sensitive to poverty. This minority would never have succeeded in doing that if it had preached charity for the love of charity. Almsgiving was merely the corollary of a faith to which the majority had been converted. Alms were to be given in obedience to God's commandment. In this way the popular morality of the Jews became acculturated in Rome, after having conquered its own 'margin of charity' and turned almsgiving into an obligatory institution (as England was later to do, with its Poor Laws). The consequences of this triumph were very marked. Paganism had abandoned without much remorse the starving, the old and the sick. Old people's homes, orphanages, hospitals and so on are institutions that appear only with the Christian epoch, the very names for them being neologisms in Latin and Greek.[45]

True, the pagans deposited many of their sick slaves in certain temples, but they did this mainly in order to get rid of them in a decent manner, by entrusting their fate to the gods. Paganism was so completely unaware of charitable institutions that when Julian the Apostate sought to combat Christianity (which he called atheism) with its own weapons, he found he had to start from scratch. 'Why do we not observe,' he writes, 'that it is their benevolence to strangers, their care for the graves of the dead and the pretended holiness of their lives that have done most to increase atheism?' (It was Christianity, indeed, that provided that every person must be buried with some ceremony, whatever his social status. Among the pagans, the corpses of slaves and destitute persons were thrown on the refuse-dump.) And Julian goes on: 'For when it came about that the poor were neglected and overlooked by the priests, then I think the impious Galilaeans observed this fact and devoted themselves to philanthropy. And they have gained ascendancy in the worst of their deeds through the credit they win for such practices.'[46] For a purist like Julian, 'philanthropy' was better Greek than 'charity' – a word of sectarian jargon.

If we think of the mass of destitute people to be found generally in pre-industrial societies (in France and England in the seventeenth century between 5 and 10 per cent of the population were in receipt of relief),[47] pagan society must have presented a dreadful sight, similar to what Father Huc beheld in the Chinese empire a century ago.

In the great towns the multitude of paupers is terrific ... The Chinese who are in easy circumstances do not object to bestow a few sapecks in alms, but they know nothing of the feeling of charity that induces anyone to interest themselves in the poor ... They give a handful of rice, or a piece of money, to the sick and unfortunate, merely to rid themselves of their presence ... The Chinese, so ready and skilful at organizing every kind of society ... have never yet formed any benevolent society for the solace of the sick and the unfortunate, with the single exception of a society to provide coffins gratis for the dead who have no relatives to undertake their funerals.[48]

The Romans were no less skilful than the Chinese at organizing confraternities of every sort, and the rules of many of these associations are known to us: the subscriptions to be paid by members and the allotment of the funds collected in this way are carefully defined. We note that none of these associations ever allotted anything for assistance to members who had become poor or sick.[49] Charity and euergetism have only this in common, namely, the responsible and ostentatious attitude of the ruling class – in other words, the circumstance that the society of antiquity was an unequal society. It would therefore not be very illuminating if we were to subsume almsgiving and *euergesiai* under the one concept of 'redistribution', along with gifts, potlatch and social security.

6. The Hellenistic and Roman city

Euergetism would be incomprehensible outside the city of antiquity. The *euergetai*, who were notables, were the natural leaders of the city's population, and this explains why the primary theme of their euergetism is voluntary patronage. Moreover, these notables lived in towns that were cities: their town was a political corporation, with a territory. As political rulers, the notables were required to apply themselves to the second theme I have indicated, that is, political euergetism, or euergetism *ob honorem*.

As a town, the city was the principal setting for voluntary euergetism. As a city, it was the primary cause of political euergetism. There were other settings, certainly, in which patronage was exercised: the province, with its provincial assemblies and festivals of the Imperial cult, or private associations, with religious or professional objects. But to study them would require a special monograph, and I shall confine myself to euergetism in cities.

Throughout the whole period covered by this book, the framework of social life was not the nation but the city, whether this was independent, a 'city-state', like the cities of classical Greece and a certain number of Hellenistic cities, or whether it was a mere autonomous community within one of the Hellenistic kingdoms or a province of the Roman Empire. Our *euergetai* were benefactors of a particular city, usually the one of which they were citizens. The states of those days were either very small, being the cities themselves, or very big – kingdoms or the Empire – in which case their fabric was largely composed of cells consisting of autonomous cities, such as Athens in the Roman Empire, or Pompeii. That was so, at least, in the civilized regions; but, as other regions came within the pale of civilization and were Hellenized, they too organized themselves into cities. The 'city' system thus spread over most of the eastern Mediterranean and the Near East in the Hellenistic epoch, and later, in the Roman epoch, throughout almost all the Latin West, from the Rhine and the Danube to the Sahara. This presents us with a curious problem, that of the absolute dimensions of human groups in history. Between the city of yesterday and the nation of today there is an enormous difference of scale, with the city's population measured in thousands but the nation's in millions. In each epoch, rivalry and example doubtless contribute to make general a certain standard size.

THE PRE-INDUSTRIAL TOWN

The city is at once an urban fact, a political or administrative unit and the framework of social life. It stands for urbanization, local autonomy (we can even say autarchy, if not sovereignty) and municipal spirit. But firstly, why were there towns, and why did people live in them? Spatial economy and the geography of central locations provide the answer to the first question, and history to the second. Economics does *not* provide the answer, whatever may have been said. The urban phenomenon and the roughly regular scattering of towns over the earth's surface, at the centre of regions which are their geographical territory, are accounted for by the different functions that a town performs for its territory and by its need to receive subsistence there-from.[50] The technical and economic constraints on transport, the short radius within which a town can supply services, and the limited availability of information divide the earth's surface into regions that are so many Thünen's circles.[51] Each region has its central location, the town. Of course, the individuals whose functions extend to the region as a whole – notables, priests, craftsmen, shopkeepers – could live scattered all over the territory. But (and this is the essence of the urban fact) they tend to form groups, to live together, because this proximity enables them to optimize their interrelations, and ensures external savings. Everyone benefits from the urban setting and its advantages. The craftsmen live near the notables who are their principal customers; the notables like to live among their own kind, for their glory and pleasure; and the countryfolk, when they visit the town, make a round of the shops.

The town is thus a rational solution, but history alone will tell whether or not a particular society will listen to reason. Not all ruling classes choose to live in groups. There is the classic contrast between the rural nobility of old-time France and the urban nobility of medieval and modern Italy.[52] Conversely, peasants may prefer the town to the village. Even today, in southern Italy, some towns are actually huge villages, from which long files of carts set out each morning for plots of land that are sometimes far distant. The grouped habitat is a historical fact, something 'arbitrary', in Mauss's sense of the word.

A town's functions are not necessarily economic. The pre-industrial town corresponded to a tradition of living in groups. It was the central location of the ruling or possessing class, but it had little productive activity and was rarely a commercial centre. Not every town could aspire to be a base for trade like Genoa or Venice. Its function was social rather than economic. It was rich in everything that facilitated life in common, as regards politics, religion and leisure. The town was where the public buildings stood, both secular ones and places of worship.[53]

Historiography of the ancient world has much to learn from the debate among medievalists about the origin of medieval towns, in which the views of Sombart and Pirenne stand opposed. As is known, for Pirenne the towns of the Middle Ages 'were the work of the merchants: they existed only for them';[54] the town, he claims, was born of the market and signalized the beginnings of commercial capitalism. This opinion – which, unless I am mistaken, has acquired classic status in France – was criticized by Sombart on the grounds that it takes no account of the relevant orders of magnitude. Trade was a source of income inadequate to support an entire urban population. Sombart, in his brisk and sometimes haughty way, wrote, 'The non-specialist (and most of those who have written about the origin of towns are not specialists in economics) does not clearly realize that the stream of commodities which enters and leaves a town would not support a single sparrow.'[55] What the town gains from this flow of goods is no more than the merchants' own profit, which, even when high, would not suffice to maintain a whole town. The medieval town, Sombart concludes, was not the offspring of trade. It did not promote trade until *after* it had been formed, and then did this in order to satisfy the needs of its inhabitants. The latter were above all persons who drew rent from land, or were political leaders (kings, and lay or ecclesiastical lords) who controlled the revenue derived from the countryside round about, or the taxes received from the region. It was they who caused the craftsmen who served them to settle in the towns, and likewise the shopkeepers who served the craftsmen. The king of England alone maintained between ten and thirty times as many people as did trading centres such as the Hanseatic towns of Lübeck and Reval.

Orders of magnitude are no less dominant in antiquity than in the Middle Ages. Standing at the centre of a circle some tens of kilometres in diameter, an ancient city had several thousand inhabitants – some-times several tens of thousands. These inhabitants were, primarily, the notables of the region, who traditionally had their homes in the town and spent there the income from their lands. Around them assembled the craftsmen for whom they provided employment, and also their numerous households, usually made up of slaves, who may have constituted the majority of the city's inhabitants. Nobles, their servants, and the craftsmen who worked for them: this was Cantillon's portrait of a town.[56] Pompeii consisted of buildings of three kinds: public buildings, private residences, which occupied most of the town, and shops. A few very large towns were political capitals or centres of trade, drawing profits, either commercial or fiscal, from places far beyond the limits of their 'circle'. Yet it is hard to believe that maritime trade or caravans from Central Asia sufficed to maintain such accumu-lations of people as Antioch or Alexandria. These cities must have lived, mainly, off the revenues of their own locality. Their famous commercial activity is like fishing in present-day Brittany. That is, it is the conspicuous and characteristic part of their economy; but, if we look at the figures, we see that it does not support a large number of people. Finally, around the notables and their slaves there sometimes swarmed a lumpenproletariat of landless peasants, who came to the town because means of surviving without a patrimony were more plentiful there than in the country.

THE CITY

Such was a town of the pre-industrial period. However, by no means every pre-industrial town was a city. For the possessing and socially dominant class, if indeed it lived in the town, was not necessarily a ruling class of lords or notables. The town, product not of trade but of the countryside's surplus, assembles those who draw income from the land: it will not be a city unless these *rentiers* form a political class. They may not do this. Ancient China resembled the Roman Empire in many respects (structure of the central authority, foreign policy of aggressive isolationism, economy of interregional exchanges) but was unlike it in that its towns were not cities. In some well-known passages Max Weber[57] contrasts the autonomous cities of the ancient West with the cities of China and India. In China, he writes, the town has no autonomy; it is where the mandarins live, those organs of the central authority. It is the villages that enjoy autonomy, and are without mandarins.

In contrast to this, in the ancient West the village counted for little. Our documents give us far fewer names of villages than of cities. How could the village matter much when there was no parish priest there, nor any lord in his castle? A mere group of houses, it performed no administrative role, unless it was on the way to becoming a city, and endowed with embryonic autonomous institutions. The significant divisions of the rural world were not the villages but the great estates.[58] We have a very poor idea of how that world was peopled. Where were there villages? Was dispersed settlement the more frequent case? When the Emperors, in order to provide support for veteran legionaries in their retirement, settled them on plots of land, they did not scatter these men around in villages. They founded a city, a colony for them, or else installed them in an old city which received the honourable title of 'colony' as compensation for the lands it gave up. These soldiers who had become peasants were not villagers but city-dwellers. The great landowners filled the magistracies of the city, and exercised their powers over the whole area of the city without distinction: in this respect the essential feature of the Roman municipal system was the union of country and town.[59] Town or city? Given what might be identical economic foundations, the choice made by different societies was political. Would they or would they not opt for local autonomy? If they did, political power fell into the hands of the notables of the region.

Whether independent or merely autonomous in relation to the central authority, the city was the ultimate framework of social life, even when the Empire had become the ultimate framework of political life, because it was the place where decisions were taken on all matters of everyday importance, and the reference point for social distinctions. Comparisons were drawn between one city and another. It was in their city that the *euergetai* shone by their munificence, it was their city that they wanted to render more brilliant than its neighbours, by erecting finer monuments 'in competition with another city' ('*ad aemulationem alterius civitatis*'), as the *Digest* has it.[60] Socially, psychologically, and at least administratively, the city was self-sufficient. It was autarchic in Aristotle's sense of the word. When a Roman or a Greek, a subject of the Emperor of Rome, spoke of his *patria*, this word always meant his city, never the Empire. There was no Roman bourgeoisie, but only a Pompeian, an Athenian or an Ephesian bourgeoisie. The craftsmen who belonged to professional associations were not members of an international or of a trade union. The only associations that existed were local ones, and a man belonged to the *collegium* of the carpenters of Lyons or of the bakers of Sétif.[61]

Everything for which men ruined themselves, over which they fought or of which they boasted was bounded by the city. The cities could multiply like living cells, or they could be subordinated to a higher entity – kingdom or Empire – but they could not be merged: or, at least, to do this was as difficult as to merge several individuals or several nations. The *patria* was a visible thing, for it was possible to assemble it physically in a public place (in classical Greece it even happened that whole cities literally transferred themselves from one spot to another). In those days it was in a town that 'everybody knew everybody else' just as today we say this of a village.[62]

Some passages in *Democracy in America* where de Tocqueville eulogizes 'self-government' give such a good idea of what an ancient city could have been like that they are worth quoting:

The township [*commune*] is the only association which is so perfectly natural that wherever a number of men are collected, it seems to constitute itself ... If man makes monarchies and establishes republics, the first association of mankind seems constituted by the hand of God.

The federal government confers power and honour on the men who conduct it; but these individuals can never be very numerous. The high station of the Presidency can only be reached at an advanced period of life; and the other federal functionaries are generally men who have been favoured by fortune, or distinguished in some other career. Such cannot be the permanent aim of the ambitious. But the township serves as a centre for the desire of public esteem, the want of exciting interests and the taste for authority and popularity, in the midst of the ordinary relations of life.

The American attaches himself to his home [i.e., home town, *cité*] as the mountaineer clings to his hills, because the characteristic features of his country are there more distinctly marked than elewhere.[63]

SOVEREIGNTY OR AUTARCHY

The city is autarchic, and for this reason it hardly matters whether it be independent or only an autonomous commune, whether it engages in high politics or only in municipal affairs. The city is sufficient unto itself, complete, and this is more important when we come to define it than the question of whether it is its own sole ruler. For the notables of the Greek cities, obedience to the Roman Emperor did not mean submission to a foreign power, because this was not submission to another city. In the first century AD the Greek publicist Dio of Prusa was at once fiercely nationalistic and an unconditional supporter of Imperial authority. He passionately desired that the Hellenic race should preserve its original character and recover its pride, but, in relation to Roman sovereignty, his political loyalism as a rich notable was beyond doubt, and that is understandable.

The idea of autarchy without sovereignty may seem strange to us, because we are accustomed to define the state in terms of sovereignty. Our touchy nationalism is not satisfied with mere autonomy. But what if reality was less monolithic and the state not an 'essence'? In his study of the political thought of Aristotle, Hermann Rehm[64] has shown that, for this philosopher, dependence, lack of sovereignty, did not contradict autarchy, which was the sole true criterion of a state. The ideal of Aristotle's state does, to be sure, remain independence; but this desire springs from its autarchy. For an individuality that is sufficient unto itself it is better to be free than dependent, but dependence does not prevent individuality from being complete. Even when merely autonomous, the city nevertheless has a complete existence and is not an abstraction. No other community is more complete. (The Emperor is hardly more than a specialist in foreign policy.) Sub-groups, associations of one kind or another, possess only fragments of existence.

Depending on whether we are stressing foreign policy, the 'high politics' that presuppose national sovereignty, or, on the contrary, autarchy, we shall say either that the Hellenistic period saw the deca-dence of the city or that it was marked by the city's triumphant diffusion – representing the triumph of the urban phenomenon, with the Hellenized East covering itself with cities in the Hellenistic period and the West becoming urbanized under the Empire. Whether new or old, the cities did not count for much when the Hellenistic kingdoms put their own weight into the balance. On the international chessboard the cities, apart from a few exceptions, retained some importance only if they organized themselves into confederations. The era of the sovereign city was over. But as an autarchic entity the city triumphed in the Hellenistic period, and even more under the Empire, when the Mediterranean world, henceforth urbanized, lived under a regime of local autonomy.[65] When C. B. Welles expressed, for the first time, the idea that, in a sense, the great period of the city began after Alexander's conquests, some said that this was a paradox. It is none the less true that the social and mental framework of life was not the kingdom or the Empire but one's home town. For half a millennium the way of life of tens of millions of people could be summed up as follows: resigned submission to the remote authorities who governed the kingdom or the Empire, but keen interest in the affairs of the city. After all, the Imperial authority, though an alien sovereignty, was neither more nor less alien to the inhabitants of the cities than are our own rulers, even if they be our compatriots, to us, the ruled, at the present day.

In the narrow circle of the town, where everyone lived face to face, individuals were gripped by a group dynamic that has its equivalent today in the enterprise or office where people work. As Louis Robert has taught us, it must not be said that the Hellenistic epoch was the era of individualism or of universalism, and that its people felt lost within kingdoms that were too big. We ought, rather, to marvel at the way their cultural and religious life completely transcended a municipal framework that was in other respects so restrictive, a fact that is doubtless adequately explained by the possession of a common language.

However, even if sovereignty is not essential, even if high politics are not everything, those who engage in high politics are very ready to believe that they are, and their sentiments are moulded accordingly. Therefore, depending on whether the scene for euergetism was an autarchic city or a sovereign and hegemonic state like Rome, this activity differed very greatly. The springs of high politics are not those of homely civic affairs. A Roman senator and a municipal magistrate both gave bread and circuses, but for very different reasons. I shall confine the title of oligarch to the members of ruling groups engaged in high politics: the title appropriate to the elites of the autonomous cities is that of notable.[66]

7. The regime of the notables

Weber's political 'ideal type' of the notable is an illuminating concept for the whole of the period here considered, if we extend it to the social domain.

POLITICAL POWER OF THE NOTABLES

Politically, notables are persons who, thanks to their economic situation, are in a position to manage, as a secondary activity, the affairs of some community without being paid a wage, or for a wage that is purely symbolic. The leadership of the group has been entrusted to them because, for whatever reason, they enjoy general esteem. A notable lives for politics but not by politics. Consequently he needs to have an income from another source, either as landowner or slave-owner or by engaging in one of the professions, that is, in a socially respected activity. He carries out his public functions voluntarily and even at his own expense. 'Such a person is partly himself in possession of the means of administration or provides them out of his own private resources.'[67]

The Hellenistic and Roman cities, whether independent or auton-omous, were governed by notables, by a class or order of rich and prestigious individuals who saw politics as a state duty rather than as a profession or vocation. What surprises the modern observer about this system is that the possessing class is itself the governing class, because, in our day, the capitalists are not the same people as the members of parliament: with us, politics is a profession. The notable is an amateur who devotes his leisure to an unpaid activity, and thereby differs from both the professional politician and the civil servant. Yet he is not a privileged person, a nobleman, in this sense, that no formal rule, written or unwritten, reserves the activity in question to him alone, excluding commoners. Many communities headed by notables are officially democratic.

In short, a regime of notables has as its formal condition free access to politics for all citizens, and as its material condition, the wealth of some citizens, who alone engage in politics. When this is the case, two other possibilities exist. Either the distribution of income is such that access to political activity is open only to a small minority of rich men, and then we have the regime of notables: or else income is distributed more equally, so that it is possible for there to be many politicians, and political activity is undertaken only by those persons, and those alone, who find it interesting, and then we have government by professional politicians. In other words, when everybody has the right to take part in politics, this right is exercised either by those who are able to do it or by those who like to do it.

The regime of notables is particularly well adapted to the city system, for it is effective above all in small communities, in local administration or in tiny states. It presupposes that the tasks of government are not too demanding. The functions involved must not be time-consuming, otherwise a group of specialists will emerge, and the other notables will object to that: putting it quite simply, these functions must not be such as to discourage amateurs. Finally, the competence of the magistrates must be limited by that of the assembly of notables, who claim to be the actual rulers and will not let themselves be tyrannized by any of their peers. In the Roman cities the four magistrates who were at the head of local affairs were appointed for one year from among the members of the municipal Council, which usually comprised about a hundred notables, and all important decisions had to take the form of a decree by the Council.[68]

A regime like this can function only if continuity of policy is not required and if the tasks involved are not too technical. The notables are amateurs who run the city because they have the leisure to do this and because their social superiority brings them general respect. They thus have two activities (neither of which is considered to be work or a profession), namely, their economic activity, which enables them to live as rich men, and their political activity, which is looked upon as their true dignity. Their state duty is to devote their care and their fortune to the government of the city, to the *bios politikos*. They must engage in politics (*politeuesthai*). This does not mean choosing a party, but occupying themselves with public affairs instead of doing nothing. When they become the exclusive masters of the cities, the notables pass gradually from being a class to being an order, either formal or informal. As a result of constantly seeing the government of the city in their hands, public opinion eventually accepts that it is right for this to be so and that these matters are no one else's concern. This political privilege becomes part of the class interest of the notables. When a class, a group or an individual possesses social superiority, they interest themselves fervently in all aspects of this superiority and every means of maintaining it. This includes, of course, means and possible aspects of an *economic* nature, though not exclusively or primarily: for why should that be so?

Once they are the exclusive masters of the cities, the notables, like all privileged groups, turn their social superiority into a duty and a doctrine. They feel a lively patriotism for the town that belongs to them, they exalt the duty they owe to their colleagues, they bring pressure to bear on each other to fulfil their state duties, they try to restrict their privilege to as small a number of participants as possible, and they consider themselves indispensable for the defence of society's values. Local autonomy is the bastion of their social superiority.

SOCIAL AUTHORITY AND PATRONAGE

This must also be said: the notables are in power by virtue of their prestige, which results from their wealth, and that same wealth which gives them the political authority described by Weber confers upon them power in all other spheres. A man who owns a thousand acres is materially and morally the master of a whole district: everyday life also knows the phenomenon of authority and the distinction between rulers and ruled. The political power of the notables is only one aspect of their social authority in general. This authority accounts for their voluntary euergetism.

The voluntary patronage of notables (using the word in the social sense, this time) is an almost universal fact. In the last century Europe still knew municipal administrations entrusted to an elite of landowners. Here is the enthusiasm with which Taine (the post-Commune Taine) describes the public life of the English countryside. The country people, he says, need a leader.

Without popular election, or selection from government, [they] find him ready made and recognized in the large landed proprietor, a man whose family has been long in the county, influential through his connections, dependants, tenantry, interested above all else by his great estates in the affairs of the neighbourhood, expert in directing these affairs which his family have managed for three generations, most fitted by education to give good advice, and by his influence to lead the common enterprise to a good result.[69]

Taine adds to his description of the English county families a point that would be applicable to the Greek notables, who were men of culture, and to the Roman notables, who often knew Greek: 'In contrast to other aristocracies, they are well educated, liberal.' They have often travelled, they know foreign languages, are familiar with literature, can speak in public. And they are euergetists. 'One has built a bridge at his own expense, another a chapel or a school ... in fact, they provide for the ignorant and poor, at their own expense, justice, administration, civilization.' Thus, Taine concludes, 'below the legal constitution is the social, and human action is forced into a solid mould prepared for it'.

All right, but whence comes this 'mould'? How does it happen that, especially in pre-industrial societies, political and social power lies in the hands of those who own the land? 'Those who in former times founded our institutions,' wrote the Emperor Justinian, 'judged it necessary to group together in each city the notables [*nobiles viros*] and form from them a council to administer the common interest in an orderly manner.'[70] In the Roman Empire the great landowners formed the order of public officials and, consequently, the judicial order as well. The state apparatus expresses the relation of forces among the groups in society: but what are the processes by which it expresses this relation?

The power of the possessing classes is derived from their 'material' advantages: that we understand (economic means are materials that are scarce and almost everywhere indispensable), but the reasons for this derivation are many. Wealth enables a man to dispose of more time: the notables are men of leisure, for their peasants (slaves or, much more commonly, sharecroppers) work for them. They possess competence (Taine stresses this) and, above all, they possess the confidence to command. Their chief advantage is that they learnt when young that they had the *right* to command: Gaetano Mosca ascribed the survival of political aristocracies to the fact that it is easier to instil into children a trait of character like the sense of command than to transmit intellectual qualities to them. Furthermore, the notables have learnt about public affairs not through teaching but, like craftsmen, through family apprenticeship. Nevertheless, they would not be the only persons capable of ruling. In a Roman city the municipal slaves (experienced officials who must have been the only persons familiar with the paperwork) or the stewards of the big landlords were certainly possessed of that capacity. But the notables, because they were rich, wanted to have the government to themselves, in so far as they saw it as a dignity, and they had the means to keep it for themselves. An ancient city was so constituted that the sharecroppers and, in the town, the household servants and craftsmen, who all depended on the orders (in one sense or other of that word) of the notables, made up the majority of the population. Each notable had power only over those who were actually dependent on him, but the notables as a group possessed power greater than the sum of their individual powers, because everyone knew that they were ready to band together.

The responsibility for patronage entrusted to the notables lasts as long as the people do not organize themselves, in the American manner, and so long as the central authority, splendid and remote, appeals to men's imaginations more than it interferes in everyday life. In other contexts the initiatives are taken by priests or by political activists, or else the government alone has the right to do this without offending egalitarian sentiments.

8. *Work and leisure*

'Leisure' is not synonymous with idleness or even with genteel beggary, but rather with riches. 'Disdain to work' does not mean 'neglect your economic interests', but 'be independent, thanks to your fortune'. Six or seven different notions need to be distinguished here. Each notable possessed, objectively, an activity that made him rich and which perhaps kept him as busy as any worker, but which was not regarded as work, for the essence of a notable was that he was a man of leisure, independent and fully human. According to a stereotype, this activity could only be agriculture. The notable might also choose to fulfil himself in a profession: he could teach rhetoric, or be a philosopher, a poet, a doctor or an athlete. As a rule he followed a career in politics, which was his only *dignity*, and in this career he acquired titles that were socially recognized and were the only ones to be inscribed in his epitaph. I shall leave out of account those individuals who withdrew from this social setting in order to devote themselves to a mission, temporary or otherwise, in the Emperor's service. The essence of a notable was that he was a man of leisure, with an economic activity, a political dignity and perhaps a cultural profession. He is to be contrasted with the merchant, who, in those days, had as his 'essence' his economic activity, which was not a socially recognized profession but merely a specialized occupation. The only person who was fully a man and a citizen was the one whose essence was leisure. 'What, then,' writes Plato, 'should life be like with men whose necessities have been moderately provided for, their trades and crafts put into other hands, their lands let out to villeins who render from the produce such rent as is sufficient for sober livers . . .?' This was the semi-Utopia of the *Laws*.[71] The realistic moralists saw things no differently. If we are asked to say what happiness is, writes Aristotle, certain ways of life are not even to be considered, namely, those that are taken up in order to meet the necessities of existence. Slaves, peasants, craftsmen and shopkeepers cannot be happy – only those persons who have the means to organize their lives as they wish. We observe that the latter choose between three modes of existence: the life of enjoyment, wherein one ascribes no ideal purpose to existence; the political life; and the life of the philosopher, in which one becomes a man of culture.[72] Only men of leisure are truly citizens: 'Our definition of the excellence of a citizen will not apply to every citizen, nor to every free man as such but only to those who are freed from necessary services. The necessary people are either slaves who minister to the wants of individuals, or mechanics and labourers who are the servants of the community . . . No man can practise excellence who is living the life of a mechanic or labourer,' and so he cannot be a citizen under a government 'in which honours are given according to excellence and merit'.[73]

It was still thought decent to express such ideas down to the beginning of the industrial age, and this is exactly how Kant and Hegel spoke.[74] Because leisure means economic independence, antiquity's praise of agriculture meant praise of landownership.[75] There could be no great family without a great fortune. Being a notable presupposed a minimum of wealth, at least, and the status of notable could not long survive the loss of that wealth. However, as high positions were cumulative and the grades of prestige had no great gaps between them, wealth was merely the means of ensuring social superiority. It was not, in itself, the sign of one's success in a professional hierarchy. It enabled a man to belong to a class of notables who did not look like a plutocracy because they possessed other excellences as well. He who belonged to this class did not work, for 'work' meant working with one's hands like a serf, or working for others, like a steward.[76] Not that the notable was not a busy man; but, when he supervised the management of his patrimony, or carried on whatever activity it was that ensured his independence, he did this without anxiety for the morrow. We do not *work* if we are not dependent economically on things or on other people. The notable's activity was not a profession, since economic activity was not recognized as such, nor was it a specialized occupation, because it was not part of the notable's essence. He was not defined by it: he was Socrates or Crito, not a shipowner or an owner of olive-groves.[77]

Besides his activity, the notable possessed a dignity, namely, politics. He was, for life, a Roman senator or a municipal councillor, and three or four times in his lifetime he fulfilled for one year some magistracy or priestly function, acquiring thereby titles that would be engraved in his epitaph. We can speak of a 'dignity' when some activity involves not merely social recognition, like the professions, but also public institutions. Such a dignity *can* be exercised full time (though it will not, even so, be called a profession, since its aspect as a public responsibility eclipses the notion of individual choice, but is more often exercised by an amateur. In our day, when we read 'former Minister' in an announcement of someone's death, we can assume that the deceased had been a professional politician. In antiquity, however, the words 'former archon' meant that the deceased, a large-scale merchant, had been an archon for one year: he attended the municipal council as one might go to one's club, but his mind was mainly occupied by his business.

There was no ladder of social esteem other than politics, with the exception of those cultural activities called the professions: 'Platonic philosopher', 'teacher of rhetoric', or private priest of a favoured deity. The man of leisure may well pursue activities both economic and political and yet still have time to spare that he will employ, perhaps, in one of the professions recognized by society, instead of remaining satisfied with enjoyment of his honourable independence. This profession will be chosen freely, without any economic constraint. It matters little if this profession is also an economic activity by means of which the notable ensures his independence, or if, on the contrary, it earns him nothing and he has to find resources elsewhere. What is important is that the profession be so highly esteemed that people may not presume that need alone has impelled him to adopt it: and also that this profession shall enable him to live independently, with a substantial income.

'LIFE-STYLE', GRADING, STEREOTYPE

The notable will, consequently, be careful not to choose as his profession a speciality that does not enjoy social esteem. Until the nineteenth century an economic occupation was either an 'inessential' activity or a mere speciality that did not enable a businessman to raise himself, on his own social scale, to the same level as the gentry. To be sure, even when a notable engaged in trade he was not looked upon as a trader, because in his case trade was no more than an inessential detail: he was not engaging in trade as a profession. It was not a question of life-style or the quality ascribed to different activities, but of the grading of the individuals themselves.[78]

Ancient epitaphs give us a deceptive idea of men's actual activities but a correct idea of the way things were seen by the communities concerned. They rarely mention occupations, even in the case of men of the people, but merely list political titles, which are enough to show that the deceased was a notable. One and the same economic activity will either be classed as a speciality or treated as inessential, depending on whether the man who engaged in it was or was not included among the notables. With us, an ironmaster is only an ironmaster, whereas a duke who happens to be an ironmaster continues to be, essentially, a duke, for the ladder of roles in economic activity does not reach so high as that of the nobility. In Hellenistic and Roman society, the man in the street would not have said of a notable, 'He is a shipowner,' but 'He is one of the leading men in our city,' perhaps adding later, 'He fits out ships.' The Medici were seen as nobles who lived by banking rather than as bankers, and that was not because of their life-style, as Max Weber says, for in that case they could have been taken to be merely bankers who 'lived nobly'. It was a pure matter of grading, based on the way the community looked at things. We shall see later that economic development has turned modern society topsy-turvy more by multiplying the scales of social grading on which individuals stand than by changing their economic mentality from within. For a notable of antiquity not to be seen as a farmer, which he was, there was no need for him to have a noble life-style or to pretend to look down with aristocratic contempt upon agricultural activity, which his society respected. He would only have been considered incompetent in business matters, which was no compliment from anyone. In order not to be seen as a farmer, it was enough for him to be a notable. In contrast, a mere freedman who was a farmer would be defined by his trade, as a farmer.

But suppose one day a rich farmer joins the municipal council and becomes a notable. In that plutocratic society it was not beyond the bounds of possibility. In those days, moreover, when the social barrier consisted not of nobility of blood but of people's ideas about what was essential, one was careful not to be too contemptuous of economic activity that brought in a lot of money. 'Trade,' writes Cicero, 'if it is on a small scale, is to be considered vulgar; but if wholesale and on a large scale ... it is not to be greatly disparaged.'[79] 'But,' he hastily adds, 'of all the occupations by which gain is secured, none is better than agriculture ... none more becoming to a free man.' Yes, indeed, since in this economy which consisted almost entirely of the primary sector, most free men, or, let us say, notables, owed their independence to landed property. Essentially, every notable would thus be presumed to live on income derived from land: that went without saying.

But what if the notable does *not* derive his income from the land? What if he gets his resources from commerce or from some industrial activity? Our documents will tell us little about that, for another reason. The classification of individuals becomes a matter of stereotypes. Since a man is a notable, he can engage in trade only incidentally, and that is something that cannot discredit the essence of the notables as such, nor even this particular person, who, whatever he may do, cannot cease to be what he is.

Modern observers have sometimes concluded from this circumstance that notables had no other fortunes but what they derived from the land. According to Libanius, writes Paul Petit in his excellent book, the notables of Antioch were exclusively landowners.[80] But ought we to accept the silences of Libanius, who is a snob, keen on his own caste and on upholding the respectability of his peers? Other sources, literary and epigraphic, are less discreet. The agriculture of antiquity was far from being mere subsistence farming. Certain areas specialized in production for export, if we are to judge by the scale on which they produced. It goes without saying that landowners themselves sold to specialist merchants the produce of their estates, or the surplus of that produce (one of Senator Pliny's letters shows him engaged in this activity). Moreover, certain economic activities such as mining and quarrying, or pottery-making, were regarded as activities associated with agriculture, because they used raw materials extracted from the estate, and also used the unoccupied labour-time of the agricultural workers.[81] But, above all, doing and being are not the same thing. A man can engage in business while being no less a genuine farmer. Income derived from land was invested in secondary or tertiary enterprises and the notable did not have to look far for capital. Add the profits from occasional trade (*Gelegenheitshandel*): landowners used their income from the land in a variety of ways.[82] Even so, there were notables who specialized in trade and engaged in it as their habitual and continuous occupation. Proclus of Naucratis, a very rich man, an Athenian by adoption and a person of culture, increased his already enormous fortune by importing goods from Egypt. 'He used to receive direct from Egypt regular supplies of incense, ivory, myrrh, papyrus, books, and all such merchandise, and would sell them to those who traded in such things.' [83]

Finally, every single city of the ancient world was unlike any other, and there were even towns, Aquileia and Palmyra,[84] which were commercial centres, wherein the upper class were specialists in trade, just like the patricians of Venice or Genoa at a later period. Let us leave aside those persons who were merchants by occupation and called themselves such, and who became notables of their cities, as we learn from certain inscriptions.[85] Between the notables and the secondary and tertiary sectors the bulkhead was not watertight. It allowed passage in both directions for activities and persons, if not for principles.

For principles survived, in words at least. Of Proclus of Naucratis we learn, also, that 'on no occasion did he show himself avaricious or illiberal or a lover of gain; for he did not seek after profits or usury but was content with his actual principal.' As we see, Proclus preserved his honour as a notable. Pliny, too: he insists that he is accommodating and far from stingy when he deals with the merchants who buy his crops.[86] Let us not conclude too soon that a lordly outlook inhibited the capitalist reflex, for these testimonies are too edifying to be instructive. The contrasting type of the great lord who is very polite, except when money is involved, belongs also to every epoch, and is doubtless close to reality. Let us conclude merely that the notables used terms that reconciled their actual behaviour with their stereotypes as lords. Monsieur Jourdain gave many goods to his friends, in return for money.

CONTEMPT FOR TRADE

To the above must be added another stereotype: contempt for trade and merchants. The notables would have shared this contempt all the more because the merchants were their only rivals in wealth. This was an already age-old contempt that was to endure until economic development brought the secondary and tertiary sectors to the forefront and even made them the principal source of wealth.[87] The universal disparagement of commercial activity is a curious phenomenon that already fascinated Plato:

Internal retail trade, when one considers its essential function, is not a mischievous thing but much the reverse. Can a man be other than a benefactor if he effects the even and proportionate diffusion of anything in its own nature so disproportionately and unevenly diffused as commodities of all sorts? This, we should remind ourselves, is the function achieved by a currency, and this, we should recognize, the function assigned to the trader. What, then, can be the reason why the calling is of no good credit or repute?[88]

There is no shortage of replies. Agriculture lives off nature, whereas trade lives off other people. An agricultural enterprise is not essentially speculative (it may be carried on merely for subsistence, or may sell only its surplus), whereas trade is speculative in essence. A merchant is not somebody who sells goods of which he has an excess. Men cultivate the soil to live, whereas trade, that exploitation of man by man, aims at making money, which signifies substituting the means for the end: 'The life of money-making is one undertaken under compulsion, and wealth is evidently not the good we are seeking; for it is merely useful and for the sake of something else.'[89]

In order to make money, the merchant falsifies the value of things. He sells space, an incorporeal entity that does not belong to him. Time, too, belongs to no one, and that is why it is dishonest to lend money at interest. Commerce is no less dishonest. Furthermore, the merchant, thanks to his position as intermediary, inflates the prices of goods as he passes them on. This is his profit. People are convinced that the intermediary is responsible for the dearness from which he gains. We know that matters are less simple, for the marginalists have taught us that scarcity and the market are the only sources of the value of goods. Except where there is monopoly or a cartel, an intermediary profits from the level at which prices stand at the final stage, and does not himself increase them on the way thither; for value does not increase between the producer and the consumer but, on the contrary, follows back along the stages of distribution and manufacture. People produce and sell only the things which will find a buyer, at the price which will find a buyer. When it comes down to the level of the intermediary, the value of goods is already less, for what buyer would pay dear for goods that he himself has to travel to find? This difference in value provides the merchant's profit: he gains from dearth and shortages without being responsible for them. But the naïve mind does not see matters like that. In its view, the merchant does not just slip into the gap that separates intermediate values, but himself creates this gap. For the naïve mind thinks that value arises from below. It believes in labour-value. It would agree that if one were to manufacture knick-knacks lacking in any utility whatsoever, but 'with lots of work in them', then these would possess a lot of value. Labour-value alone is the basis for the *justum pretium*. The merchant, however, is said to falsify the just price, for he inflates it without incorporating any additional labour in the object concerned. Of course the merchant is not inactive, but the very trouble that he takes is suspect. He travels, he is an unstable person, and his efforts do not change the object he sells, wherein is embodied solely the fatigue of the honest craftsman – who, himself, does not make a fortune.[90]

Besides, the dishonest conduct of merchants does not even provide them with that independence which is alone deserving of respect. They depend on their clientele and have to struggle constantly with competitors who threaten to strangle them. Though exploiters of others, they are also their slaves. All their thoughts are concentrated on survival, just like those of animals. In agriculture, however, infra-marginal enterprises do not go bankrupt: the owner simply lives by consuming his own produce. A farmer does not have to maintain a position of strength in the market. All he need do is to organize production physically and wait to see what nature will be so good as to give him. The value of a commodity depends on the market, that is, on other people, whereas the physical value of the fruits of the earth is directly appreciable by the person who lives on them. The farmer is always master of his fate, but the merchant resembles the gambler or the drinker. Drawn on by competition, he is compelled to make more and more money, for he cannot leave the gaming-table without suffering final ruin. In the end, he is himself the slave of his occupation.

These condemnations, which go back three thousand years, have never stopped merchants from trading, or even notables from engaging in trade. They have not 'restricted the exchange economy', any more than other condemnations have prevented governments from governing or administrations from abusing their power. Nor did antiquity's well-known contempt for work discourage the poor from working in order to live. As we have seen, the word 'work' covers many different things, some of which are shams while others permit of many compromises with useful reality. Contempt for manual work and respect for property are features of every age. The fact remains that every society grades activities in its own way, that the relation of these gradings to reality is dubious, and that the very principle of grading is not always the same. Today we are contemptuous of work, but without ascribing significance to leisure, so that our respect for wealth must imply some other principle than the ancient ideal of independence.

9. Economic analysis of sumptuary expenditure

Euergetism, or, more generally, sumptuary expenditure, 'waste', would not have been possible without economic growth. The Hellenistic epoch and the Principate were the most prosperous period of antiquity, as the ruins of ancient towns, with their monuments, suffice to prove. During the half-millennium between the death of Alexander the Great and the Imperial crisis of the third century and the spread of Christianity, the Mediterranean world enjoyed a standard of living that it was not to know again for many hundreds of years. This growth made possible sumptuousness and *euergesiai*: how did it come about? Conversely, did sumptuary expenditure favour this growth or hinder it?

To answer these two questions one would need to distinguish between centuries and regions. It would be necessary, also, for the economic history of the ancient world to have been written. So, what can one do except treat the two problems *ex hypothesi*? I am not going to improvise a version of the economic history of 500 years, but merely to recall the various paths that were available for pre-industrial growth in general, and the influence that sumptuary expenditure can have upon growth. For lack of knowing how the Roman economy in fact grew, I shall show how it *could* have grown. It is simple courtesy to warn readers who have the slightest knowledge of economics that they will learn nothing from the pages that follow.

WASTE AND FOCALIZATION

'The fundamental problem in the history of the Roman Empire,' writes Gilbert-Charles Picard,[91] 'was the meagre opportunity for creative investment, which obliged it to live from day to day, spending its profits without care for the future.' It is true that, in this respect, 'the situation of the Empire did not differ fundamentally from that of all human societies before the eighteenth century'; like the Romans, they 'petrified their surplus in decorative monuments that, from the economic standpoint, appear to us as constituting a magnificent but sterile epiphenomenon'. Were opportunities for investment so lacking as these penetrating lines allege? Let us not think of industrial investments, for until the eighteenth century agriculture continued to be the driving force of growth. Now, ancient agriculture did not lack opportunities for investment. The Roman world was still covered with forests and grassland (some of which later became desert), and it did nothing to develop them. In any case, these possibilities, if they existed, were not grasped. The Romans preferred to waste their surplus in the form of the monumental epiphenomenon described by Picard.

Are these value-judgements? Certainly 'waste' can mean many different things: not using a source of wealth, using it in a way that is less productive than another way, consuming it instead of investing it, using it for purposes that we do not consider justified ... But what purpose would be justified? Nobody has ever been able to define national income unambiguously. If a community ascribes great importance to religious practices, or regards cows as sacred creatures, have we the right to say that cathedrals or a huge number of unproductive cattle constitute waste?[92] Fortunately, we do not need to face this difficulty. We shall not speculate as to whether the pyramids were indeed seen by the Egyptians as indispensable, but will merely note that a pyramid was not a means of producing anything else. even another pyramid, and yet it possessed utility in the view of those who built it or of their Pharaoh. This is enough for the economist, who is not required to be the judge of ultimate utilities.

By waste, then, we mean that the rich classes consumed their surplus to a much greater extent than they invested it. We can, therefore, speak of an epiphenomenon. As a result of big differences in income, a large part of the surplus was concentrated in the hands of the possessing class, and this class used it for splendours that were out of proportion to the level of prosperity attained by society as a whole. In short: very unequal incomes, and more consumption than investment.

This ought not to surprise us. Even today, the poorest countries are the ones where the possessing class lives most sumptuously: differences in income are relatively greater in the Third World than in the United States or in Europe. This concentration of income in an economy with a low level of productivity does not result in a cumulative movement of growth, but in extreme inequality in consumption by the different classes of society. While the majority of the population barely rises above subsistence level, the rich devote their substantial incomes to luxury consumption and ostentatious expenditure. Only a small part is allotted to productive expenditure. The underdeveloped countries that invest do this not with private savings but with public credits or through self-financing by enterprises.[93]

Inequality results in a focalization effect, a deceptive epiphenomenon. When even a small fraction of the total income of an entire society is concentrated on a particular objective, whether this be decorative monuments or nuclear weapons, the results seem gigantic on the individual scale, even if the society in question is a poor peasant society. This gigantism is misleading. It is much less costly to build what archaeologists and tourists call a high culture, rich in monuments, than to feed a population more or less adequately. Everything depends on the possessing class, which controls the surplus and decides what is to be done with it. The mere splendour of the monuments arouses suspicion. Even the buildings intended for everyday purposes have an imperishable look that points to their irrationality. Everything has been built to last for ever, which means that everything is too solid for its purpose. The least important aqueduct becomes a prestige enterprise which reveals that a class of notables is making a vainglorious use of its resources. Euergetism is based on unequal distribution of the surplus and unequal power in deciding how the surplus is to be used.

Focalization was easier for the societies of antiquity than for us, because we are obliged to reinvest, so as to allow for the depreciation of an enormous capital of reproducible assets: dwellings, infrastructures, factories and stocks of goods. The wealth of the ancient civilizations seems not disproportionate to our own, if we judge by their luxury and their cultural achievements, because they consumed nearly everything, whereas we both consume *and* reinvest. Allowance for depreciation was, moreover, among the least concerns of ancient societies that were too poor to provide for the future. A few good harvests succeeded one another unexpectedly, or a *euergetēs* suddenly displayed generosity: it was thereupon decided to build a theatre or an aqueduct; then the money ran out, and the building never reached completion. If it was completed, the means to maintain it were not always available. If we could go back in time and visit the Roman Empire, we should doubtless observe that the monuments with which it was decorated were poorly maintained and badly weathered, and that their walls were crumbling.

OPTIMIZE OR SATISFY

The active members of a society have, a priori, a choice between two attitudes: either to promote growth or to mark time, that is, either to optimize or to satisfy.

Let us visualize some economic agents and their needs. In order to obtain what they want, they follow a certain procedure, a certain 'path', and their quest entails a certain cost, at least psychologically. As soon as their gains arising from the path adopted exceed this cost, they may declare themselves satisfied: they will not necessarily seek the optimum path. By following their routine path they find that they can obtain resources, and when their needs are satisfied they may stop and go no further, without trying to maximize their gains. This is how the agents may act, if they are rich. They will have no desire to make their gains grow. And if they are poor, they will be unable to do so, for even though their routine path hardly secures them enough to live on, finding a better one would necessitate investments that are beyond their means.

History has seen rich societies and poor ones, and it is conceivable that their varying fates have depended on a very simple choice, between trying to grow and not worrying about growth – a question of yes or no. In the case of our society the choice has been affirmative, so that growth seems to us only a matter of less or more, and we are constantly comparing rates of investment, saving, growth. We invest less or we invest more, but we always invest; certain social categories, certain entities, make a profession of this activity, and institutions have been established for the purpose. Other societies, however, do not even think of growing: they follow a routine and remain satisfied with what they have. They are racked by want – but the point is that want does not impel them to adopt the luxury attitude called optimization.

Social reasons may cause a community to remain content with a path that is merely satisfying. Economic enterprise is a source of wealth that demands too much knowledge and that is too indirect, and it is less amusing than the profits to be derived from war and politics or from mere saving. 'If a man will keep but of even hand,' writes Bacon, 'his ordinary expenses ought to be but to the half of his receipts, and if he think to wax rich, but to the third part.'[94] Everywhere there have been noble families that lived in a state of sordid miserliness: they saved in order to round off their estates, and the bare walls of their country houses were their only pomp. Their stinginess enriched them permanently, at the expense of their peasants and relatively to the other nobles, but without increasing the national product. This was a path that was satisfactory for them. It was enough for them to get ahead of their rivals and ensure for themselves the margin of security that they considered adequate. Not every possessing class has had the spirit of enterprise, the capitalist outlook, of the notables of antiquity.

In ancient societies, when investment was undertaken by the possessing classes and not by professionals backed by institutions, growth had only a psychological foundation. It depended on what went on in the notables' heads. For example, a politically uneasy situation could have the same economic consequences as, in our society, result from fear of a recession. Notable and entrepreneur were the same man, and the fears of the former influenced the conduct of the latter. This accounts for some strange developments. The war with the barbarians on the frontier did not bring decisive victory, but went on and on. The various armies, discontented with the progress of the campaign, blamed the Imperial authority and staged frequent *pronunciamentos*. This political agitation in no way threatened economic life. The barbarians were far away and the state itself was remote. In the countryside the peasants continued to harvest the crops, just as they do nowadays during wartime summers. But the notables felt alarmed. Like someone who, in our time, decides against building himself a villa if the international situation looks grim, they stopped reclaiming land, stopped making improvements, stopped planting and abandoned their building projects. The clothing of the land with monuments suffered several years, or even decades, of interruption. Was this an economic crisis? No, it was a moral crisis, and *euergesiai* will be the first activities to be affected if the notables start hoarding their money through fear of the political future.

INCIDENCE OF EUERGETISM

Notables and entrepreneurs were, then, the same persons: but so were notables and *euergetai*. Did their *euergesiai* encroach on their investments? The answer depends on a certain number of hypotheses.

1. If the *euergetēs* has the impression that all the money he makes is being wrested from him by the people, who demand bread and circuses, he will be discouraged from increasing the yield of his property, because euergetism will seem to him like a tax on production.

2. If, on the contrary, the *euergetēs* has the impression that he himself is taking the initiative in *euergesiai* that will enable him to improve his status or enhance his social superiority, he will try to increase his income, since wealth is the condition for being a notable. Euergetism will have the effect of inducing greater production.

3. However, this effect will not operate if the *euergetēs* considers the bounty for which he alone holds the initiative as a form of display enabling him to keep up his existing rank among his peers, rather than as a means of raising him to a rank higher than that of his rivals. This is because, in order to keep up his rank, it is enough to devote to expenditure on display merely the surplus he happens to possess: thereby, the degree of display will be automatically proportionate to the wealth of which it is meant to be the sign. Which is not at all the same as trying to acquire more surplus than one possesses already, so as to get the better of rivals by showing, through one's bounty, that one is more deserving than they are of a rank one has not yet attained.

4. Instead of inducing greater production, euergetism will, on the contrary, entail a reduction in saving and investment if *euergesiai* are seen as a sort of tax, distinct from expenditure on consumption and additional to this. If, however, instead of being obligatory, *euergesiai* are inspired by the same motivation as voluntary expenditure, they will form part of habitual consumption, the other components of which will be reduced so as to make room for them, without saving having to be reduced so as to keep up the standard of living. In short, *euergesiai* will be charged to consumption and not to saving.

5. The least grave case, for the community at least, would be for *euergesiai* to be felt as obligations which come upon the notables unpredictably (they try to get out of them but do not know if they will succeed) and on dates that are no less unpredictable, in the same way as illnesses or disasters. In this case they will not be provided for either at the expense of consumption or at the expense of saving: when

the misfortune happens, the notable will cope with it by selling a piece of land.

Depending on the time, the place and the individual, euergetism must have had one of these effects rather than another: the documents are, naturally, silent on such matters. Let us hope that my analysis *ex hypothesi* may make up to some degree for this disappointing silence, by supplying ideas in lieu of knowledge.

My aim will have been realized if I have managed to define the conditions that make possible the following paradox. Euergetism, a form of waste, seems to contradict the prosperity that it presupposes. Hellenistic and Roman society is no less paradoxical to our modern eyes. It presents the spectacle of prosperity without a bourgeoisie and without professional economic agents: the problem, once much discussed, of capitalism in antiquity really amounts to that. In the ancient world we find brought together features that seem contradictory: a standard of living that may have reached the level of our seventeenth century, and even, at certain times and in certain regions, that of the eighteenth; euergetic behaviour whose scale and prima-facie archaism remind us momentarily of the primitive mentality and tempt us to talk of potlatch; a class of notables who ensure this prosperity, a situation which would be unthinkable if they were not animated by a spirit of economic enterprise. And yet this same class, euergetist through sense of duty and through taste, declines to define itself by economic activities and affects to despise them – so that, when Rostovtzeff calls this class a bourgeoisie, the word rings false.

Notes

1. *Nicomachean Ethics*, IV, 1, 30 (1121a20).
2. S. Dill, *Roman Society from Nero to Marcus Aurelius* (Meridian Books, 1957), p. 231.
3. A. Boulanger, *Aelius Aristide et la sophistique dans la province d'Asie* (De Boccard, 1923), p. 25; H.-I. Marrou, *Histoire de l'éducation dans l'Antiquité* (second edn, Seuil, 1950), index of *notabilia* and p. 405. In modern Greek the word *euergetēs* is currently used to mean a public benefactor or patron, and the word *évergétisme*, in the sense of patronage, was introduced into French from modern Greek by Boulanger, who was a member of the French School in Athens. Around 1900 the term *euergetēs* was applied to the rich Greek merchants established in Egypt or Anatolia who founded schools or public buildings in their motherland. (In the

English translation of Marrou's book, *A History of Education in Antiquity*, 1956, p. 305, *évergétisme* is translated as 'private munificence'.)

4. A. Métraux, *Religion et Magie indiennes* (Gallimard, 1966), pp. 240, 267; F. Cancian, *Economics and Prestige in a Maya Community* (Stanford University Press, 1965).

5. J. Tricot, note to his translation of the *Nicomachean Ethics* (*Éthique à Nicomaque*, Vrin, 1967, p. 133). The ideal of munificence is thus not at all the same thing as the old aristocratic ideal, despite W. Jaeger, *Paideia*, vol. I, p. 29.

6. J. Aubenque, *La Prudence chez Aristote* (PUF, 1963), p. 37.

7. *Nicomachean Ethics*, IV, 4–6 (1220a20ff.); cf. 1107b15.

8. Ibid., 1122a30.

9. *Summa Theologica*, Secunda secundae, qu. 134, cf. 129:

These properties as found in the magnanimous man call not for blame but for abundant praise [*superexcedenter laudabiles*] ... it is said that he employs irony [*ironia*]; not that he controverts the truth by falsely belittling himself or by denying some of his great qualities. He merely refrains from displaying the whole of his greatness, especially to the huge crowd of lesser men. For as Aristotle further says in that same passage, the role of the magnanimous man is to be lofty towards men of high rank and wealth, but courteous to those of moderate station. The fourth trait is that he cannot associate with others intimately, except with his friends.

This whole passage, which interprets Aristotle as indulgently as possible, would seem to be actually a self-portrait. We know that, in Thomism, the virtue of humility holds a much humbler place than in the Augustinian tradition. On 'magnanimity' I have looked through U. Knoche, *Magnitudo animi*, Philologus, Supplementband XXVII, 5, 1935, and R.-A. Gauthier, *Magnanimité: l'idéal de grandeur* (Bibliothèque thomiste, XXVIII, Vrin, 1951).

10. Ibid., Secunda secundae, qu. 129, art. 3 and art. 134, 2; cf. art. 6.

11. *Nicomachean Ethics*, I, 10, 3–5 (1100a15); I, 11 (1101a20); I, 7, 6 (1097b10); IX, 9, 3 (1169b15).

12. M. Weber, *Ancient Judaism* (Free Press, New York, 1952), pp. 46–9, 255–62, 370–71.

13. Exodus 22: 21 and 23: 9.

14. Ecclesiasticus 13: 22; cf. 8: 2 and 13: 18, 21.

15. Aeschylus, *Agamemnon*, 951–3.

16. Dessau, *Inscriptiones Latinae Selectae*, no. 7602; Buecheler, *Carmina Epigraphica*, no. 74; *Inscriptions latines de l'Algérie*, vol. II (Pflaum), 820. See the comments of H. Bolkestein, *Wohltätigkeit und Armenpflege*, p. 473, and M. MacGuire, 'Epigraphical evidences for social charity in the Roman West', in *American Journal of Philology*, 1946, pp. 126–50. This accent, so much unlike civic sternness, is to be found elsewhere also.

We know how the kindness found in the Old Testament resembles that of Egypt, where, around 2000 B C, a nobleman says of himself, in his epitaph: 'I was a father to the orphan and took care of widows.' See, e.g., E. Suys, *Vie de Petosiris, prêtre de Thot à Hermoupolis-la-Grande* (Fondation égyptologique Reine Élisabeth, Brussels, 1927), pp. 127, 134, 144.

17. Besides Epictetus, see Musonius, 19, on luxury, p. 108 (Hense).

18. On the episode of the woman of Canaan I have followed A. Harnack, *Mission und Ausbreitung*, vol. I, pp. 39–48; A. D. Nock, *Essays on Religion and the Ancient World*, vol. I (1972), p. 69, note 72 speaks of 'the universalism *implicit* in the *behaviour* of Jesus' (Veyne's emphases).

19. Tertullian, *Apologetica*, 39, 7; *Epistle to Diognetus*, I; Minucius Felix, 9, 2, cf. 31, 8.

20. John 13: 34–5 and 15: 12, 17; cf. I John 2: 7; I Peter 2: 17: 'Honour all men. Love the brotherhood. Honour the king.' On St John's Gospel, besides the appendix to Renan's *Life of Jesus*, I have read the works of Loisy, Bultmann, H. Odeberg, O. Cullmann, C. H. Dodd and J. Blinzler. There is a hermeneutic circle between the historicity that that one is prepared to grant to St John's Gospel and one's idea of Jesus.

21. A. Dupont-Sommer, *Les Écrits esséniens découverts près de la mer Morte* (third edn, Payot, 1968), p. 75; cf. J. Daniélou, *Philon d'Alexandrie* (Fayard, 1958), p. 19.

22. A. Harnack, *Mission und Ausbreitung*, vol. I, pp. 178–83. Two typical texts are the letter of Dionysius of Corinth to Pope Soter, in Eusebius, *Ecclesiastical History*, IV, 23, 10, and Aristides, *Apologia*, XV, 6–7.

23. Symmachus, *Epistolae*, I, 3: 'Deos magna pars veneratur; privatam pecuniam pro civitatis ornatu certatim fatigant.'

24. L. Robert, *Hellenica*, XI–XII, p. 569ff. On euergetism, both pagan and Christian, in fourth-century Africa, see P.-A. Février in *Bulletin d'archéologie algérienne*, I (1962–5), p. 212.

25. St Ambrose, *De Officiis Ministrorum*, III, 36–44; cf. J.-R. Palanque, *Saint Ambroise et l'Empire*, p. 340, note 80.

26. St Augustine, *De Civitate Dei*, II, 20; cf. V, 15. These passages are particularly striking.

27. St Cyprian, *De Opere et Eleemosynis*, 21–2.

28. W. Weismann, *Kirche und Schauspiele: Die Schauspiele im Urteil der lateinischen Kirchenväter*, p. 164.

29. *Cypriani Opera*, vol. III, Hartel (ed.), Vienna *Corpus*, *Vita*, p. xciv: 'contemptis dispendiis rei familiaris'. On the building of churches by bishops, see the epitaph of the notable M. Julius Eugenius, Bishop of Laodicea Cambusta in the second half of the third century, quoted by A. Harnack, *Mission und Ausbreitung*, vol. II, pp. 616, 774 (the best text is that published by W. M. Calder in *Klio*, 1910, p. 233). Be it noted in

this connection that the *tituli* of Rome were private foundations: see A. Harnack, vol. II, p. 855.

30. Commented on by L. Robert, *Hellenica*, XI–XII, p. 13, note; see also *Hellenica*, X, p. 200.

31. G. Le Bras, *Études de sociologie religieuse*, vol. II (PUF, 1955), p. 564.

32. Ibid., p. 573.

33. Ibid., p. 574. On legacies to the Church, besides these two rich pages of Le Bras, see J. Gaudemet, *L'Église dans l'Empire romain* (Sirey, 1958), pp. 294–8, cf. 167–8; and E. F. Bruck, *Kirchenväter und soziales Erbrecht* (Springer-Verlag, 1956).

34. H. Bolkestein, *Wohltätigkeit und Armenpflege in vorchristlichen Altertum* (Utrecht, 1939). See how the Christian Emperors transformed the traditional Imperial liberalities into works of charity: H. Kloft, *Liberalitas Principis* (1970), pp. 171–5 (on Constantine); D. van Berchem, *Les Distributions de blé et d'argent à la plèbe romaine*, p. 103 (the *panis gradilis* of the Byzantine Empire was a work of charity).

35. *Digest*, XXX, 122, pr.

36. E.g., Dessau, *Inscriptiones Latinae*, no. 6271: 'sine distinctione libertatis'; cf. L. Robert, *Études anatoliennes*, p. 388, note 2.

37. Seneca, *De Clementia*, 8; cf. Pohlenz, *La Stoa*, vol. II (Italian trans.), p. 82; other passages are quoted by H. Pétré, *Caritas, étude sur le vocabulaire latin de la charité chrétienne* (Louvain, 1948), p. 223.

38. Society being an exchange of 'benefits', the poor lie outside the circuit, because they can provide none: see J. Kabiersch, *Untersuchungen zum Begriff der Philanthropia bei Kaiser Julian* (Harassowitz, 1960), p. 31.

39. M. Weber, *Religionssoziologie*, vol. I, p. 495. The whole passage contrasts civic sternness with popular charity.

40. St Justin, *First Apologia*, 67; Tertullian, *Apologetica*, 39: 'Nemo compellitur, sed sponte confert.' It was important for the apologists to emphasize this voluntariness. Alms must not resemble the subscriptions that had to be paid by the members of a *collegium*, for every *collegium* needed approval by the Imperial authority.

41. Hebrews 13: 16, quoted by A. Harnack, *Lehrbuch der Dogmengeschichte*, vol. I, pp. 227, 231, 465.

42. *De Opere et Eleemosynis*, 1, quoted by A. Harnack.

43. Clement of Alexandria, *Tutor*, II, 12, 5.

44. E. F. Bruck, *Kirchenväter und soziales Erbrecht*, p. 69.

45. 'Xenodochium, orphanotrophium, ptochotrophium, gerontocomium, brephtotrophium': on this point we need only read article I, 2 of the *Codex Justiniani* dealing with the Churches and their privileges. On the importance of these innovations in the history of civilization, see J. Daniélou and H.-I. Marrou, in *Nouvelle Histoire de l'Église*, vol. I (Seuil, 1963), p. 369.

46. Julian, *Works*, vol. III (Loeb Classical Library, 1973), p. 69, and vol. II (1913), p. 337.

47. In the England of 1688, according to the well-known statistics of Gregory King, ancestor of all who engage in national accounting, over a million poor people, out of a total population of five million, were occasionally in receipt of poor relief. In seventeenth-century Beauvais, in good years, the Bureau des Pauvres relieved 6 per cent of the inhabitants of the town (charity took no cognizance of the countryside); see P. Goubert, *Cent mille provinciaux au XVIIe siècle*, p. 339.

48. *Souvenirs d'un voyage dans la Chine*, vol. II, A. de Tizac (ed.), p. 228 (Eng. trans., *The Chinese Empire*, vol. II, 1855, pp. 325–6).

49. Waltzing, *Étude historique sur les corporations romaines*, vol. I, p. 32; G. Boissier, *Le Religion romaine d'Auguste aux Antonins*, vol. II, p. 334.

50. On the geography of the town and of central locations, see the outstanding article by Paul Caval, 'La théorie des villes', in *Revue géographique de l'Est*, VIII (1968), pp. 3–56, and C. Ponsard, *Histoire des théories économiques spatiales* (A. Colin, 1958).

51. *Der isolierte Staat*, by J. H. von Thünen, was reprinted in 1966 by the Wissenschaftliche Buchgesellschaft. Numerous publications and reprints on the spatial theory are appearing at present and I have glanced at some of them.

52. On the urban nobility, see W. Sombart, *Der moderne Kapitalismus*, vol. I, part 1, p. 151.

53. G. Sjoberg, *The Pre-industrial City: Past and Present* (Free Press Paperbacks, New York, 1965).

54. H. Pirenne, 'L'origine des constitutions urbaines', in *Revue historique*, vol. LVII, p. 70. Sombart's work is rarely mentioned in historical writings published in French.

55. W. Sombart, *Der moderne Kapitalismus*, vol. I, part 1, particularly pp. 131, 142, 156, 160, 168, 173, 175, 230; cf., for example, J. Weulersse, *Paysans de Syrie et du Proche-Orient* (Gallimard, 1946), p. 88.

56. *Essai sur la nature du commerce en général*, part 1, chapter 5.

57. M. Weber, *Religionssoziologie*, vol. I, pp. 291–5, 330–35, 380–85. Weber's view is confirmed by a sinologist, E. Balazs, *La Bureaucratie céleste* (Gallimard, 1968), p. 210.

58. F. de Coulanges, *L'Alleu et le Domaine rural*, pp. 38–42.

59. Id., *La Gaule romaine*, p. 238.

60. *Digest*, L, 10, 3.

61. Mommsen, *Römisches Staatsrecht*, vol. II, p. 887.

62. What is best for a city is that all citizens know each other and that the group be close-knit: Plato, *Laws*, 738e: Aristotle, *Politics*, IV, 4 (1326a25) and III, 3 (1276a25); cf. J. Moreau, 'Les théories démographiques dans l'Antiquité grecque' in *Population*, 1949, especially p. 604; see also

Isocrates, *Antidosis*, 172. The idea was no less widespread in the Italian republics of the Middle Ages.

63. *Democracy in America*, vol. I, trans. H. Reeve (1855), pp. 72, 83–4, 85.

64. H. Rehm, *Geschichte der Staatsrechtswissenschaft* (Wiss. Buchgesellschaft, reprinted 1970), p. 91; G. Jellinek, *Allgemeine Staatslehre*, p. 436.

65. On this immense subject I will refer only to D. Nörr, *Imperium und Polis in der hohen Prinzipatszeit* (C. H. Beck, 1966); and, for the Roman municipal towns, to Marquardt, *Römisches Staatsverwaltung*, vol. I, pp. 52–3 and 88; Mommsen, *Staatsrecht*, vol. III, part I, p. 811, note 2. C. B. Welles's study appeared in the *Studi in onore di Calderini e Paribeni*.

66. In conclusion, it should be observed that two types of self-government can be conceived. In one case, local administration is a duty, performed by officials. In the other, it is a right possessed by the governed. In practice, 'participation' becomes, in the latter case, the privilege of the notables.

67. M. Weber, *Economy and Society*, vol. I (Eng. trans., Berkeley, 1978), p. 291. This passage is remarkably rich in ideas.

68. On relations between the Council and the annual magistrates, Mommsen, *Juristische Schriften*, vol. I, pp. 226 and 254; Marquardt, *Staatsverwaltung*, vol. I, p. 193. See, for example, in the *Corpus Inscriptionum Latinarum*, II, 5221, and X, 4842, line 37ff. (Augustus's edict for the aqueduct at Venafrum).

69. *Histoire de la littérature anglaise*, vol. IV, p. 422. (Eng. trans., *History of English Literature*, vol. IV (1890), pp. 98, 99.)

70. *Novellae*, IV, 17.

71. Plato, *Laws*, 806de; cf. 881c, 832d, 846d. It is indeed necessary to distinguish between masters and slaves (777b). The advantage of this Utopian constitution is that 'it provides more ample leisure than any other' (832d).

72. *Eudemian Ethics*, I, 4, 2 (1215a25). See R.-A. Gauthier and J. Y. Jolif, *L'Éthique à Nicomaque*, vol. II, *Commentaire*, part I, p. 34, with other references.

73. Aristotle, *Politics*, III, 5, 5 (1278a20). In Ecclesiasticus, the same thing is said by the son of Sirach (38: 24–34), but, in his case, in a tone of sadness. The words of Plato, in *The Republic*, 590c, are even more contemptuous, for in him there is an element of the aristocrat and even of the snob (*Theaetetus*, 175e–176a). But how could that element not be there, as well, in Plato? 'The most complete monad that ever existed' was certainly Plato rather than Goethe.

74. N. Machiavelli, *Discorsi*, I, 54; G. Lebrun, *Kant et la Fin de la métaphysique* (A. Colin), p. 394; G. Hegel, *Philosophy of Right*, trans. T. M. Knox (Oxford, 1942), vol. III, 2, sections 199–208, pp. 129–34. Dionysius of

Halicarnassus ascribes the same ideas to Romulus (*Roman Antiquities*, 2, 28).

75. O. Neurath, in his study of Cicero on labour, in *Jahrbücher für National-ökonomie*, XXXII, 1906, p. 600. Nobility presupposes wealth and cannot long survive it. Julian, in *The Heroic Deeds of the Emperor Constantius, or On Kingship*, notes that there is a view that 'even a man who is born of noble ancestors, but himself sinks down in the opposite scale of life, could not justly claim kinship with those ancestors'. Julian is indignant at this prevailing absurdity. It should not be necessary to say that nobility is neither the reflection nor the mask of wealth: the relation between these two entities is less simple than such dualism (even if it be called 'dialectical'). When we are dealing with an aristocracy, wealth counts above all because of the display it makes possible: wealth is a means and a sign rather than a qualifying excellence. Consequently, a nobleman may prefer genteel beggary to derogation. However, genteel beggary is only a temporary expedient. After a generation or two, a ruined noble family disappears among the mass of commoners, for lack of economic means prevents it from keeping up the characteristic way of life of the nobility and expressing its noble status through display (and any superiority that does not express itself becomes of suspect authenticity). Finally it prevents such a family from exemplifying, among other forms of excellence, *wealth* – and people expect of a highly placed person that he exemplify all possible forms of excellence, among which wealth is included.

76. On work for others: Aristotle, *Metaphysics*, A, 2 (982b25); *Politics*, VIII, 2 (1337b15); *Rhetoric*, I, 9, 27. Passages dealing with work in Greece and Rome have been brought together by G. Kühn, *De Opificum Romanorum Condicione*, pp. 5–14.

77. The best illustration of this ideal of independence is the theory of chrematistics in Aristotle, *Politics*, I, 8–11, which is ideological rather than philosophical: the writer rationalizes the prejudices of his time. Economic activity should be restricted to the satisfaction of one's needs, which are not infinite, at least for 'living well' and not for 'living only' (1256b30 and 1257b25 and 40). But what is the limit to needs and where does chrematistics begin? A big farmer certainly lives beyond his needs, since he lives more opulently than the mass of the population, who get by on less. Yet Aristotle does not accuse him of chrematistics and keeps well away from inquiring what is the just size of a patrimony. As against this, he describes as chrematistic all poorly paid and servile activities, such as those of the merchant and the manual worker (1258b20–25).

78. On 'life-style', see M. Weber, *The City*, trans. Martindale (Free Press, New York, 1958), p. 155.

79. Cicero, *De Officiis*, I, 42, 151. The passage is commented on by Mommsen, *Römische Geschichte*, vol. III, p. 520; by Pöhlmann, *Soziale Frage*, vol. II, p. 359; and by H. Bolkestein, *Wohltätigkeit*, p. 322. Cicero is recording not a philosophical doctrine but the opinion current in Rome. (This is the meaning of the phrase 'hoc fere accepimus', which corresponds to the Hellenistic *paralambanein*: cf. W. Spoerri, *Späthellenistische Berichte*, p. 34, note 1, and p. 163, note 15.

80. P. Petit, *Libanius et la vie municipale à Antioche* (Geuthner, 1955), pp. 33, 330, discussed by J. H. W. G. Liebeschuetz, *Antioch: City and Imperial Administration in the Later Roman Empire* (Oxford, 1972), p. 38. Libanius carefully avoids saying that his peers were traders and industrialists, admitting this only in one place, where he has greater reason to speak than to remain silent. His secretary, Thalassius, who was an arms manufacturer (and a large-scale one, Libanius adds, comparing him nobly with Demosthenes' father: *Orationes*. XLII, 21, quoted by Petit, pp. 31, 37), was in danger of being conscripted into the Senate of Antioch, and tried to escape by fleeing upward, applying to enter the Senate of Constantinople. That body rejected him, however, on the grounds that he was engaged in industry, an attitude that grieves Libanius. Historians of the Later Empire mention the case of a duumvir of Aptungi, Caecilianus, who owned a mill where linen yarn was made (Optatus of Milevi, App. 2, in the *Corpus Script. Eccl. Latin.*, vol. 26). In the few works about Julian or about Antioch that I have consulted, I have found no allusion to a phrase in the *Misopogon*, 20 (350ab), which says that 'the councillors of Antioch enjoyed a twofold income, as landowners and as traders'. Julian boasts of stopping them from continuing to enjoy this twofold income. This might be understood to mean that he subjected them to the *collatio lustralis*, but I think what happened was that Julian forbade the curiales to keep shop (compare a law of later date, *Codex Justiniani*, IV, 63, 3). The Emperor wished to compel them to conform to their own ideology. Finally, I will quote a law of Julian's, *Codex Theodosii*, XII, 1, 50 and XIII, 1, 4: 'nisi forte decurionem aliquid mercari constiterit'.

81. *Digest*, XXXIII, 7, 25, 1: 'A certain man had potteries on his estate and employed the potters as workers on the land during the greater part of the year.' On mines, quarries and pottery workshops as annexes to a rural estate, see *Digest*, VIII, 3, 6 pr. and 1: 'If a man has pottery workshops wherein vessels are made for containing the products of the estate when these are sent out, such as, quite often, *amphorae* for the wine dispatched from the estate . . .'; also *Digest*, XVIII, 1, 77; XXIII, 5, 18 pr.; VII, 1, 9, 2–3; XXIII, 3, 32, XXIV, 3, 7, 13–14; XXIV, 3, 8 pr.

82. *Palatine Anthology*, XIV, 72: 'Oracle given to Rufinus, who asked how

to make his ship's captain swear an oath.' This Rufinus has been identified by L. Robert as a man of consular rank, a *euergetēs* of Ephesus in the second century (*Comptes rendus de l'Académie des inscriptions*, 1968, p. 599: 'We learn that Rufinus, a very rich man, had, in particular, a business in maritime trade'). In the collection of amusing stories entitled *Philogelôs* (Thierfelder, ed., *Philogelôs, Der Lachfreund*, Tusculum-Bücherei), which Robert has dated to the third century AD, the hero of these tales, a notable who is a man of culture, absent-minded and absurd, lends money to a ship's captain (no. 50); I cannot resist the temptation to quote no. 57: 'The Absent-Minded One has a child by a slave: his father advises him to kill the child' – this being followed by a witty remark. Cf. Diogenes Laertius, VI, 99 and VII, 13.

83. Philostratus, *Lives of the Sophists*, II, 21.
84. P. Collart, 'Quelques aspects de la vie économique à Palmyre à la lumière de découvertes récentes', in *Mélanges d'histoire économique et sociale*, vol. I (A. Babel, Geneva, 1963), pp. 37–46.
85. Dittenberger, *Sylloge Inscriptionum Graecarum* (third edn), no. 838; *Corpus Inscriptionum Latinarum*, vol. VI, no. 33887 (an *omnibus honoribus et muneribus functus* of Misenum, who is a *negotiator*); vol. XIV, no. 4142 (Dessau, no. 6140): 'decurio adlectus ... mercator frumentarius'. Cf. also *Corpus*, vol. V, no. 785 (Dessau, no. 7592).
86. Pliny the Younger, *Letters*, VIII, 2.
87. An impressive testimony is provided by chapter 6 of Benjamin Constant's *Principes de politique* (*Œuvres choisies*, Bibl. de la Pléiade, pp. 1115–18). On the eve of the Industrial Revolution we see Constant, in this treatise which is a remarkably lucid work, setting out in good faith the most sophistical arguments to justify restricting political rights to landowners and refusing them to 'industrialists' (this word being used to mean merchants as well as factory-owners). Few passages, among the writings of reasonable men, illustrate so well the power exercised over us by stereotypes and belief in 'eternal verities'.
88. *Laws*, 918b. But, in another place, Plato says that in the maritime cities men become greedy and cowardly: *Laws*, 704b–707b: cf. 842d.
89. Aristotle, *Nicomachean Ethics*, 1095b15.
90. On the concept of the *justum pretium* (which, even in the *Digest*, is ethical and not juridical), see E. Albertario, *Studi di diritto romano* (Milan, 1936), vol. III, p. 403, and P. de Franciscis in *Studi Paoli*, p. 211. On the role played by space and time in the pricing of goods, see P. Oertmann, *Die Volkswirtschaftslehre des Corpus Juris Civilis* (Scientia Verlag, reprinted 1971), p. 110. The concept of the just price would be meaningless unless prices, instead of fluctuating in accordance with the state of the market where goods end up, were indeed, as the naïve view of things supposes, to be determined at the start by the costs and the labour incorporated

in them. According to A. Sauvy, *Histoire économique de la France entre les deux guerres*, vol. II (Fayard, 1967): 'The ultimate price results from the commodity's market-value, and this dictates the preceding prices. The order in which operations of manufacture succeed each other seems, wrongly, to govern the formation of prices. This is a classic example of a social "optical illusion".' Cf. J. A. Schumpeter, *The Theory of Economic Development*, pp. 142, 204, 207. The labour theory of value is normative, not descriptive. One cannot say, without falling into absurdity, that a market price is 'unjust'; but one can legitimately say that it is unjust for prices to be decided by the market.

91. *La Civilisation de l'Afrique romaine* (Peon, 1959), pp. 98–9.

92. S. Kuznets, *Modern Economic Growth: Rate, Structure and Spread* (Yale University Press, 1966), p. 21.

93. D.-C. Lambert, *Les Économies du Tiers Monde* (A. Colin, 1974), p. 297.

94. Francis Bacon, *Essays*: 'Of Expence'.

CHAPTER II

Greek Euergetism

We have seen that euergetism was very different from the gift as primary form of exchange. It does not enable a person to obtain goods and services through an informal exchange. It belongs to a different species, political gifts, which are bound up in a certain way (which this chapter will explain) with relations of authority (and it is not to be forgotten that these are also relations of prestige). A political gift is a symbolic gift.

We have seen also that euergetism could be connected with three themes of which it constitutes a historical modification. In the first place, patronage, which Thorstein Veblen satirically equated with ostentation, but which is, rather, the effect of a tendency possessed by individuals or groups to actualize their potentialities, together with a tendency to express their superiorities, even if only for their own satisfaction, without any audience being present. The second theme is what I have called euergetism *ob honorem*. Every magistrate and dignitary had to make a *euergesia* to his city, by virtue of his office. Was this done as payment for the public function he had assumed? Was it done to console the people for the loss of their political rights, because the plebs of the cities had surrendered the role of government to the notables, and all the *euergetai* to be discussed in this chapter were notables? Or is the explanation less commonplace? The third theme, which I have put forward only provisionally (and that provisionality will be disposed of during the present chapter), is preoccupation with the after-life. Many *euergesiai* were, in fact, foundations provided for in men's wills, and it is momentarily tempting to identify them with legacies left to the Christian Church.

The present chapter will analyse Greek euergetism in the Hellenistic period and subsequently, in the period when Greece and the Greek East were subject to Roman hegemony and formed part of the Empire – an epoch extending roughly from 350 BC to AD 400. The scene is set in the Greek city, either independent or autonomous, and the principals are the notables of these cities. In order to define better what euergetism was I shall first show what it was not, and, to this end, shall begin by considering classical Athens, where euergetism was unknown. If we look at the subsequent evolution in its material aspect, the genesis of euergetism can be set out under three headings. There was transition from oligarchy or direct democracy to a regime of notables. Euergetism appeared as a supplement to an archaic system of public finance – the liturgy. Finally, from a society divided into classes there was transition to a society in which – formally, informally or symbolically (thanks to a system of 'honours to *euergetai*') – the notables constituted an order, which public opinion recognized as possessing the right to govern and the duty to perform patronage, this situation being ratified by public law during the period of Roman domination.

1. Before euergetism: classical Athens

In Athens in the days of its political and cultural glory, approximately between 500 and 350 BC, though the future system of euergetism did not exist, it was already heralded. We note, first, the existence of gifts to the community, such as those which are familiar to us in most 'primitive' societies: generosity on the part of rich men, collective feasting. We see, especially, in the city's political and fiscal organization, some features which could open the way to euergetism. And, finally, one institution, the liturgy, foreshadows oligarchy: it consecrates the division of the democratic city into poor and rich, and testifies to a euergetic mentality among the rich. Helped by the depoliticization of the mass of citizens, the transition to an oligarchy of euergetistic notables would take place almost automatically. It is a pity that my exposition is restricted to the example of Athens. No Greek city was exactly the same as another, and Athens was only one city among others; but it is the only one that is well enough known.

A passage in Xenophon's *Oeconomicus*[1] supplies us with a more or less complete inventory of the varieties of gift to the community that existed in the Greek world in the classical epoch. The wealth you possess cannot be enough, says Socrates to young Critobulus: 'Because, in the first place, I notice that you are bound to offer many large sacrifices; else, I fancy, you would get into trouble with gods and men alike.[2] Secondly, it is your duty to entertain many strangers, on a generous scale too.[3] Thirdly, you have to give dinners and play the benefactor to the citizens,[4] or you lose your following.' Here we have a primary species of gift which, owing to its commonplace character, we discover in almost any 'primitive' civilization: hospitality, banquets which the members of a certain group offer, each in turn, to their fellow citizens, generosity and protection on the part of the 'big men' towards the poor. A second species of gift is, however, much more characteristic, namely, the liturgies. 'Moreover,' Socrates goes on, 'I observe that already the state is exacting heavy contributions from you; you must needs keep horses, pay for choruses and gymnastic competitions, and accept presidencies,[5] and if war breaks out, I know they will require you to maintain a ship and pay taxes that will nearly crush you.' Horse-breeding,[6] choruses, gymnasiarchy, trierarchy, not to mention the extraordinary *eisphora*, these were all so many obligations laid upon the rich to contribute, in person and from their own purses, to the public festivals of Athens or to national defence. These liturgies had to be fulfilled less as a tax than as an honour. What was needed for this system to operate was a certain attitude, that of a notable more inclined towards spending, for whatever purpose, than towards making money. 'Whenever you seem to fall short of what is expected of you, the Athenians will certainly punish you as though they had caught you robbing them. Besides all this, I notice that you imagine yourself to be a rich man, you are indifferent to money, and yet go courting minions, as though the cost were nothing to you.' 'Primitive' acts of generosity – *largesses* – and democratic liturgies: such was the fate of the rich Athenian.

ARCHAIC *LARGESSES*

Such acts of generosity were ageless. They had always existed in the Greek world and were to go on existing. Their object was not the city but a narrower and nearer group of human beings, the tribe or the deme. In those old subdivisions of the city, social realities, rich and poor, natural leaders and men of the people, were more important than institutions. It had been necessary to cease sharing among the demes the urban magistracies whose holders were chosen by lot, because the demesmen sold them.[7] In the tribes, the custom survived for periodical feasts which were provided by the rich, turn and turn about, and this was to become a veritable liturgy, the *hestiasis*.[8] But the old name of this function is revealing. It was called *phylarchia*,[9] the person who invited people to the feast having been named chief of the tribe. In many parts of the world we come upon enthronement feasts such as these, and often the actual role of the chief is merely to provide food[10] at this own expense; in fact, he is nominated for that purpose alone. There is nothing more widespread, with or without a chief, than these peasant merrymakings: one could mention Flemish festivals to which each farmer in turn invited the whole village, because in the village everyone knows everyone else, or dinners to which a priest invited, once a year, all the peasants of his parish.

Three reasons, at least, explain the frequency of these tontines, in which all the members of a group (or, at least, all the rich ones) do what is needful, one after another, and the same reasons underlie many of the cases of euergetism which I shall describe in the rest of this book. First, the small size of the group means that the better-off find it hard to resist the demands of the poorer members who try to extract from them some of their superfluity. The word 'demands' is, moreover, not very appropriate here, since, through either shame or prudence, the rich forestall such demands, so as to avoid an embarrassing encounter with the poor. This same small size of the group means that the tontine system, by which successive victims are designated, is easier to establish than a system of taxes, under which everyone's quota has to be collected at the same time. Administratively, a tax is more complicated than a liturgy and, psychologically, a rich man pays up more willingly if he sees where his money is to go, and if it is to result in some 'work' – a building or a feast – that will be his, and associated with his name. Finally, in a small group, even in a city (but not in a large nation), the behaviour of every citizen is visible to and foreseeable by his fellow citizens.[11] Everyone feels that his contribution influences the attitude of the rest. Dodging the trierarchy or the tribal feast means setting a bad example and ruining the social order (which, in modern nations, one does not consider one is ruining when defrauding the Inland Revenue), whereas, by assuming the responsibility, one is obliging others to do the same for oneself at some future date. This transparency renders voluntary co-operation, and the negotiation that results in it, easier than in larger groups.

The embarrassment involved in a confrontation explains another phenomenon that must have been more important than is apparent from our texts, by whose authors it was doubtless taken for granted, namely, gratuitous loans between equals. Theophrastus's Pretentious Man, we learn,[12] 'contributed more than five talents, in a time of famine, to the relief of citizens who were in need'. No doubt he had put his name down for the sum in question on a list of voluntary subscriptions (*epidosis*), of which we know many from the beginning of the Hellenistic period onward. This was an organized form of mutual aid. But the Pretentious Man had also laid out ten talents in loans to friends (*eranos*), because 'he can't say no'. 'Why should we want to be rich,' writes a comic poet, 'if not to be able to help our friends and sow the good seed of gratitude?'[13]

We should like to know more about this. We do at least know that there were friendly societies for loans, called *eranoi*, which were tontines of a kind: their members pooled their resources so as to accept, turn and turn about, the duty of offering interest-free loans. An institution like this, the exact equivalent of which exists in many a poor country, is undoubtedly symptomatic. Athens must have been one of those societies where everyone needs at some time to borrow money, where everyone is morally bound to lend, and where everyone owes something to everyone else. This establishes a sort of equality and suggests to everyone concerned that he should be as long-suffering towards a debtor as he would like a creditor to be towards him. Nobody pays back what he has borrowed, at least unless asked, and, if he does pay, only after being asked several times. This is justice. It is presumed that the person who shows himself the harsher in demanding or refusing is the one who has the greater need for the money, and it accords with indulgence and equity that the poorer person should prevail in such a situation. If that was indeed how things were in Athens, a conclusion relevant to our subject emerges, namely, that, in that society, the economic agents did not pursue their activity to the bitter end; they did not insist on getting everything to which they had a right.

There is one form of ageless *largesse*, about which it is even more regrettable that we know so little, namely, the generosity of the men of power who maintained numerous clients. In Aristotle's *Constitution of Athens*, we read these significant lines: 'Pericles was ... the first to institute pay for service in the law-courts, as a bid for popular favour to counterbalance the wealth of Cimon. The latter, having private possessions on a regal scale, not only performed the regular public services magnificently, but also maintained a large number of his fellow demesmen. Any member of the deme of Lacia could go every day to Cimon's house and there receive a reasonable provision; while his estate was guarded by no fences, so that anyone who liked might help himself to the fruit from it. Pericles' private property was quite unequal to this magnificence,' and he acted on advice to 'make gifts to the people from their own property; and accordingly he instituted pay for the members of the juries'.[14]

74

The aristocrat Cimon behaved as a worthy representative of his caste.[15] Maintaining one's own people and also offering splendid hospitality to foreigners[16] – that was the old morality of the nobles. Athenian democracy took shape outside these networks of clientage and, as our quotation shows, in opposition to them. We may suppose, despite the silence of the documents, that the networks never ceased to exist and that the later euergetism was often a disguise for them, in civic costume.

A disguise, I say, for, on a crucial point, euergetism is diametrically opposed to these archaic liberalities offered to foreigners, to friends, to clients or to anybody at all. *Euergesiai* were, on the contrary, offered to the city as a whole and only to the city. They were civic. The *euergetēs* does not maintain a group of clients, but pays homage to the city, that is, to his fellow citizens as a body. We shall see that the *euergetēs* is a magistrate who provides from his purse proofs of his disinterestedness, or else he is a notable who regards public functions as honours, or a member of an order for whom ruling the city is a right and a duty. In all three cases the *euergetēs'* responsibility is to the city as such. If his *euergesia* was aimed merely at *some* of the citizens, that would constitute corruption, or even the purchasing of a clientele. This was to be seen clearly in Rome. According to the public law of the Roman Republic, it amounted to electoral corruption if a candidate who made *euergesiai* during his campaign for election invited to the feast only a *section* of the citizenry, if he sent out individual invitations (*viritim*); whereas, if he invited everybody to his banquet or to the entertainment he provided, that was not corruption. This was why the city, be it Rome or Athens, felt no shame in accepting the gifts made to it; such gifts created no personal bond between the least of the citizens and the *euergetēs*. As nobody doubted that the citizens as a body were superior to any single citizen, even the richest of all, *euergesiai* were regarded not as gifts from on high but as acts of homage offered up to the city. To the end of antiquity, euergetism was to retain a civic, even deferential style, and to proceed from below upward. Since the manner of giving meant more than the gift itself, a *euergetēs* had to avoid all arrogance and boasting: first and foremost, he was a citizen.

LITURGIES AND LIBERTIES

At first sight, there was nothing more civic, either, than the liturgies, those obligations laid upon the rich to contribute, with their persons and property, to public festivals or the defence of the city. Nothing less euergetistic, one could also say. The liturgies were obligatory and the liturgists were not patrons: we should regard them, rather, as taxpayers who were taxed more heavily than other citizens for the good reason that they were richer. The trouble is that the Greeks had no conception of taxes or taxpayers. In the Greek cities where, as modern writers sometimes claim, the citizens were wholly devoted to the city, a permanent direct tax would have been considered an intolerable act of tyranny. Nobody contributed to the common expenses, except the rich with their liturgies. Theirs was therefore the outlook of patrons and *euergetai* rather than of taxpayers. Let us consider the matter in its fundamental aspect. A liturgy was primarily a civic task which, since it could not be seen as a tax, was considered as an honour exclusive to an elite – something hardly civic. Why was it not felt to be a tax, if it could be felt as a task? Because Athenian democracy could allot tasks to some which it did not allot to others. It was a direct democracy, free of legal formality, so that the public authority was not an entity: such an authority existed, but it was not named. And the liturgy did not become a tax because the authority would not have been able to allow itself to institute permanent taxes: liberties existed in ancient Greece, but they were not named, nor were these liberties the same as ours.

The Greeks did not distinguish in every respect between the city and the totality of its citizens, nor did they set forth systematically the rights and duties of the citizen, any more than it occurs to anyone to define the duties of every member of a closely knit family. What could be simpler than that an Athenian should dedicate himself to Athens, and do more in that line than others? Only in the Hellenistic epoch would it be said of a citizen that he was the *euergetēs* of his own city. Previously, the title of *euergetēs*, of public benefactor, had been awarded only to foreigners. Themistocles was the *euergetēs* of Corcyra,[17] and we know that this title was awarded by decree at the same time as the office of *proxenos*.

The origin and evolution of the liturgy are accounted for by this lack of legal precision. Liturgies are, strictly speaking, tasks the performance of which has been entrusted to certain citizens who are capable of performing them, but there is no concern to systematize and establish the principle of a contribution to be made by all the citizens to the life of the community, in proportion to their abilities. There is not even any concern to allot the tasks more or less equitably; it is simpler to make the rich pay. Each year, the Athenian people allotted hundreds of liturgies to the well-to-do citizens. How was the burden to be shared equally? By what common scale could one measure the contribution of a trierarch who fitted out and commanded a ship because he knew how to do this, and that of a *chorēgos* who staged a theatrical or musical entertainment? In a closely knit group each member does what he can, and there are neither rights nor duties. A liturgy is a task in exactly the same sense as a magistracy. Is playing the role of commander a right or a duty? Neither the one nor the other; it is a public service.[18]

Now whereas liturgies became taxes instead of tasks, the Athenian people, who found it normal for the citizens to devote their time and their lives to the city, did *not* find it normal for them to devote their money to it. They could not have put themselves in a more self-contradictory position. But an insurmountable moral barrier prevented them from accepting the principle of a permanent direct tax levied on the citizens. Taxation could be no more than a makeshift solution, a momentary expedient in case of a grave crisis – that is, if it were not a tribute signalizing the subjection of one people to another, a mark of slavery. The city, like every citizen, had to live by its own income, obtained from indirect taxes, plus tribute paid by subjects, the tax levied on residents who were not citizens, and the produce of its estates. The absence of direct taxation, strange to our eyes, had historical reasons, and I shall come back to it. But this absence should suffice to warn us against the notion, still too commonly believed, that the citizen owed everything to his city. Let us say, instead, that the limits of his devotion and of intrusion by the community upon the individual sphere were not fixed in advance and for ever, any more than they are among us today. The notion of 'liberties' is a principle whose content is purely historical. Let us also say that this principle existed in Greece without being conceptualized.

SOCIOLOGY OF THE LITURGIES: PLATO

But since the city of Athens did not accept the principle of taxation, how did it arrive at that direct tax, albeit not so called, which the liturgy actually was? It slipped into this without any set principle. The rich were too ready to pay for the people not to yield to the temptation to let them pay.

The liturgical system appealed, in fact, to some of the moral springs which are also those of euergetism: desire to display one's wealth, to express one's personality, to put oneself forward so as to stand

77

out from the people (especially when the rich man was aiming at a career as a political orator), desire to leave one's name on a 'work', the spirit of competition. As only the rich had liturgical obligations, a liturgy was not a tax but a mission. Since it was a contribution made in kind, and the liturgist's money was not going to mingle in the public coffers with the contributions made by other citizens – on the contrary, the whole city would see with its own eyes the feast or the ship of which the liturgist was personally the creator – a liturgy was an act of patronage. This meant that, altogether, the liturgical system bore an equivocal character upon which euergetism would play: it was sometimes imposed, sometimes voluntary, for there is nothing easier or more difficult than doing what *noblesse oblige*. Sometimes the rich Athenians tried to avoid performing a liturgy, resorting to the procedure of *antidosis*, but sometimes also these ruinous honours were accepted voluntarily. One year, when no *chorēgos* had been nominated and the day of the festival drew near with lively disputes still going on in the Assembly about the unfillable appointment, Demosthenes 'came forward and volunteered to act as chorus-master'.[19]

There were even virtuosi of the liturgy. A client of the advocate Lysias was able to boast to his judges that in nine years he had spent more than 72,000 drachmas on tragic choruses, male choruses, dancers at the Panathenaea, cyclic choruses, trierarchies, gymnasiarchies, comic choruses, extraordinary war-contributions, and so on.[20] For many liturgies were, as we have seen, contests in which the prize was competed for at great expense. The Greeks' taste for competition, the 'agonistic attitude',[21] found full expression here. 'Spending so as to be honoured, competing – that old Greek sentiment – in expenditure and in honours',[22] that was the motive of the liturgies as it was of euergetism.

Books VIII and IX of *The Republic* are a work of sociology, if by that word we mean, conventionally, political philosophy which relates a political regime to the social material to which it gives form. Plato here established reciprocal relations of resemblance and causality between types of regime and types of human being.[23] The infinite diversity of existing societies can be reduced to four ideal types. These are: (1) aristocracy, or rather timocracy; (2) plutocracy, or rather 'oligarchy' (for the Greeks, oligarchy meant a regime wherein the rich, as such, monopolize power); (3) democracy; and (4) tyranny. Therefore four basic types of human being must be distinguished. To oligarchy corresponds the oligarchic person who has no interest in the community and lives only for money. To timocracy corresponds the authoritarian personality who is avid to compete, in order to win and be honoured. At first sight, this sociology sets one thinking of book III of *L'Esprit des lois*: but it is in fact very different, and even more sociological. Montesquieu wonders what particular psychological trait is needed if a given regime is to function. For example, in the absence of coercion from above, a democracy can function only if each citizen individually loves the public good. In an aristocracy, on the contrary, the people have no need of this civic virtue, because the rulers keep them under control – but these rulers need to possess a different sort of virtue if they are to control themselves. Plato, however, thinks not in terms of function but of causality, with each regime turning out to produce an entire human personality in its own image. For Montesquieu the functional virtue may be lacking in a given society, in which case the regime will not function, and that is that. But for Plato, a regime cannot fail to engender a man in its own image – who, in his turn, will reproduce the regime. Regimes result from the character of the citizens who inhabit states and, reciprocally, the citizens are formed in their youth in the image of the state. The child is impregnated with what he hears said by his father, his mother, the servants and other people. But while each regime thus produces an entire personality and does not appeal merely to one particular virtue, on the other hand it does not itself create all the features of this personality. It merely shapes the potentialities of the human soul: socialization teaches the child to 'practise what is admired and neglect what is despised' in the regime under which he lives.[24] For example, in a plutocracy, the love of riches which is natural to everyone is reinforced in the child by what he hears around him, and it shapes his whole personality. His other potentialities are still there, but are more or less repressed. It goes without saying that this 'more or less' will give rise to mixed types and all the diversity of real human characters.

To come back to patronage or competition: what regimes favour these tendencies in people? Timocracy alone. 'Thanks to the predominance of the spirited part of our nature, it has one most conspicuous feature: ambition and the passion to excel (*philonikia, philotimia*)'; for timocracy, as we see, gives ascendancy to that psychological potentiality called ardour, *thymos*. On the other hand, nothing is meaner than oligarchy. The plutocrat is a man who represses his desires as best he can because 'he trembles for the safety of his whole fortune'. He 'will not be single-minded, but torn in two by internal conflict'. As the *Laws* teaches us, 'the passion for wealth ... leaves a man not a moment of leisure to attend to anything beyond his personal fortunes. So long as a citizen's whole soul is wrapped up in these, he cannot give a thought to anything but the day's takings.' All pursuits which do not tend to that result 'are laughed to scorn'. Consequently, the oligarch's stinginess 'weakens him as a competitor for any personal success or honourable distinction. He is unwilling to spend his money in a struggle for that sort of renown, being afraid to stir up his expensive desires by calling upon them to second his ambition.'[25] Oligarchy is too much afraid of ruining itself to be magnificent. Because in this regime money is the criterion of all distinctions (the oligarchic constitution is based on property qualification), children born under it learn that what is important is to accumulate rather than to shine. As for democracy, it does not even dream of emulating. It is a regime that ensures the supremacy of a potentiality different from ardour or avarice, namely, desire or rather the crowd of desires. This anarchic regime renders men's souls anarchic: since no moral order exists any more, the individual no longer controls himself, and everyone spends in order to gratify his appetites.

The agonistic attitude is thus characteristic solely of warlike aristocracies, 'timocracies', because it requires that men have a heart that is ardent (*thymos*); and this is not a mercantile virtue. Such was the traditional view, which is Plato's inspiration here. According to him, socialization operates at the level of society as a whole, of the regime, and not at that of the subgroups in which everyone is born and lives his life. Though more sociological than Montesquieu when he links the entire personality with the regime, he is less so when he explains this personality by the regime rather than by the social 'conditioning' of individuals. What results, among other things, is that, unknown to Plato, his timocratic man is really the portrait of a mere subgroup, the ruling caste of a timocracy; the education and personality of the subgroup of the ruled was certainly different.

THE OLIGARCHS

Besides the democrats, however, there was in Athens a party whose attitude with regard to liturgies was very different and, from another point of view which will be of cardinal importance for the rest of this exposition, very revealing. These were the oligarchs, or, as they called themselves, the good men, the nobles, the rich, in contrast to the bad men, the poor, the people. We should not have in mind here the oligarchical personality described by Plato, greedy for riches. Nor should we believe that these men were the heirs of the old nobility of Athens, the victims of democracy. They did not unite in order to defend the material interests of their class; the object of their efforts was a different satisfaction, power, which they sought for its own sake and which was the principal issue in the social struggles of that time. They found it hateful or ruinous that everybody in Athens took a hand in government. They aimed either to secure a share of power proportionate to their wealth and influence, that is, to monopolize the government of the city, or to take that government away from the populace (who certainly had shown themselves incapable of giving proper direction to policy) in order to entrust it to a class, their own, which had the ability to perform that role. The principle of their struggle was an idea characteristic of pre-industrial societies, namely that wealth confers the right to wield power, that power should belong to the rich (a claim which seems to us excessive, so that we imagine, at first, that the oligarchs were merely defending their material class interest). And as, in Athens, the rich did not hold power, the oligarchs thought themselves victims of a standing injustice and oppressed by a clique. Since the democrats constantly violated justice where they were concerned, the social contract had been broken and they no longer owed anything to the city: 'We should give up dallying with office and suffering ourselves to be insulted or exalted by such persons, when either we or these fellows must govern the city.'[26]

Their attitude towards the liturgies was therefore ambiguous. On the one hand, these were yet another tyranny; on the other, the oligarchs noted sarcastically that the populace could not do without their talents and their wealth. How shaming it is 'when some lean and ill-kempt fellow sits next to him in the Assembly', says the Oligarch whose portrait is drawn by Theophrastus. And he goes on: 'When shall we cease to be victims of these state-services and trierarchies?' We ought not to think here of the avarice of Plato's oligarch. This one merely considers that, since beggars unjustly refuse him power, he is not going to ruin himself for them. We shall see, however, that when the oligarchy of notables came to power, they ruined themselves in *euergesiai*. Meanwhile, liturgies not being a tax, since there were no taxes, they could only be a tribute or an honour, depending on whether the liturgist himself was oppressed or in a position of honour. An oligarch would feel honoured to be a liturgist if he and his peers were honoured as an elite. For governing was an honour that belonged to an elite. Here we have already the conception of government as the right of a class, which would be the principle of euergetism.

On other occasions the oligarchs considered that, by making them liturgists, the democracy acknowledged their superiority. Of course, 'the demagogues wrong the notables [*gnōrimoi*]'; either they make a division of their property or diminish their incomes by the imposition of public services,'27 but, by so doing, they recognize that the notables are indispensable. Under the title *On the Government of Athens* there has come down to us, mingled with the works of Xenophon, a pamphlet by an unknown oligarch who lived in the period of the Peloponnesian War and was a man of undoubted talent (he develops, in particular, an interesting theory of hegemony through sea-power). This writer is sarcastic about liturgies.

The people have ceased to tolerate those who practise gymnastic exercises and cultivate music, thinking that such pursuits do not become them, and knowing that the lower class are not competent to study such arts. In the furnishing of choruses, as well as in the government of the gymnasia, and the equipment of triremes, they are aware not only that the rich furnish the expense for the choruses, while the lower class of people enjoy the pleasure of them, but that the rich also supply triremes and preside over the gymnasia, while the poor have the benefit of both; the plebeians are accordingly ready to take money for singing, and running, and dancing and serving in the galleys, that they themselves may have some advantage, and that the rich may become poorer.

And he notes that, while indifferent to posts that are merely burdensome, 'whatever posts are held for pay ... these the people try to gain'.28

The liturgical system prefigured the regime of the notables. It divided the city into two groups, the liturgists and the rest. It was viable only because the liturgists had the outlook of notables or patrons rather than of modest taxpayers. The liturgists were a group who were able to do what the majority of the Athenians were incapable of doing. Owing to their wealth and their education, they alone could practise that virtue of the *euergetēs* which the *Nicomachean Ethics* calls magnificence. It was natural for the rich notables to want to wield power, since they were capable of it. And we shall see that, for their part, the people, through their political absenteeism, let power slip into the hands of the notables. In this way there was established in

Athens, or in many other Greek cities there continued to exist, the regime that was to be dominant in the Hellenistic and Roman epoch – the epoch of euergetism – namely government by the notables. A return from democracy to oligarchy was possible because, even in the democracies, this society was not universalist.

2. The oligarchy of the notables

How did the regime of the notables come to be established? 'A democracy may change into an oligarchy,' writes Aristotle, 'if the wealthy class are stronger than the people, and the one are euergetic, and the other indifferent,'[29] and Max Weber writes: 'Every type of immediate democracy has a tendency to shift to a form of government by notables.'[30]

Athens, where such a government succeeded a democracy, is a somewhat special case, as it is possible that most of the Greek cities had always been oligarchic. But this matters little. The reasons that explain why the notables gradually took power in Athens explain equally well why they held power as a matter of course in the cities where power had not at first belonged to the people. We have just seen why this was: every direct democracy is burdensome, and also, inequalities being cumulative, the rich class tended naturally to be the ruling class.

THE NOTABLES

The old warrior caste, the aristocracy of horsemen, had faded away, and the possessing class which economic inequality now placed at the head of society bore a less distinctive physiognomy, so that historians of the Hellenistic epoch are disposed to call it a bourgeoisie. Everywhere, the conduct of politics was in the hands of this relatively narrow stratum, a ruling and possessing class of right-thinking and moderate persons, as Maurice Holleaux calls them.[31] This bourgeoisie of the cities regarded it as normal to wield power itself and not to be the object of political decisions taken by others who were less clever or socially less highly placed than they were. Did this bourgeoisie *seek* power? What happened was, rather, that power fell naturally into its hands. Power goes to the abilities, material and moral, which are usually a privilege of wealth; that is precisely what is meant by a government of notables. The epoch of the militant oligarchy which tried to seize power by force had been left behind. Institutions counted for nothing in this matter, nor did any ruthlessness of the rich, allegedly blocking access to power. Institutions differed from one Hellenistic city to another, the various cities being either more democratic or less, but their constitutions were not drawn into any kind of general evolutionary process (the Roman conquest itself did not mark any break in this respect).[32] The most that can be said is that, more or less everywhere, the Council or the Executive (*synarchiai*) gradually grew stronger at the expense of the Assembly. But the outward appearance of the institutions remained democratic (oligarchy was an idea that conflicted with the spirit of the age), even if the functioning of these institutions was less so. Politics continued, as Louis Robert has shown, to be the business of the orators, just as in the days of Demosthenes, and was consequently a career open to merit. Consider the city of Mylasa, in Caria, in the first century B C. It possessed among its citizens more than one famous orator who was both professor of rhetoric and politician. One of these, Euthydemus, 'having inherited from his ancestors great wealth and high repute, and having added to these his own cleverness, was not only a great man in his native land, but was also thought worthy of the foremost honour in Asia'. The story of another orator, Hybreas, was quite different. He had to begin by acquiring some money through his own efforts:

As he himself used to tell the story in his school and as confirmed by his fellow citizens, his father left him a mule-driver and a wood-carrying mule. And, being supported by these, he became a pupil of Diotrephes of Antiocheia for a short time, and then came back and 'surrendered himself to the office of market-clerk'. But when he had been 'tossed about' in this office and had made but little money, he began to apply himself to the affairs of state and to follow closely the speakers of the forum. He quickly grew in power, and was already an object of amazement in the lifetime of Euthydemus, but in particular after his death, having become master of the city.[33]

Without money, a man had neither the leisure nor the social rank appropriate to a political career. Euergetism itself, which meant that one could not become a magistrate without paying, raised the money barrier still higher. As Louis Robert writes: 'The regime of the Greek city continues, with those modifications in political practice increasingly entailed by the system of *euergesia*, of benefactors who assume offices and magistracies and accumulate honours.'[34] In short, a political career remained open to merit; blood, property qualification, the arrogance of the rich constituted no barrier; but leisure, culture and *euergesiai* were needed to such an extent that this 'merit' was accessible only to those who had either inherited or acquired some affluence. In this way democracy fell into the hands of the notables. Nobody fought them for it: the issue at stake in the class struggles was no longer the sharing of power, the conflict between democrats and oligarchs, but the cancellation of debts and the redistribution of landownership.

The regime of the notables was the normal outcome of a direct democracy, in the absence of a tyranny or of an aristocratic caste exercising traditional authority. Since social inequality entailed inequality in talent, leisure and prestige, the result was never in doubt. The diversity of regimes, says Aristotle, is due to the diversity of the social material to which they give shape.[35] In a direct democracy, social inequality has effects much more far-reaching than in a representative democracy, in which the participation of the body of the citizens takes only a few minutes of their time every four or five years. It was not simply that the plebs of the Greek cities let the notables rule alone; in a direct democracy, even political participation is burdensome, without bringing to the individual any satisfaction markedly greater than that enjoyed by an elector in our society.

3. The origins of euergetism

Euergetism is a union of three 'themes' – patronage; the more or less symbolic *largesses* that politicians confer out of their own pockets, by virtue of their office (*ob honorem*); and funerary liberalities and foundations. I shall describe the beginnings of these practices in the Greek world during the fourth century and especially after 350, for it is in the latter half of that century that we see euergetism nascent. Actually we have no evidence for funerary foundations before the end of the century,[36] and I shall come back later to this point. Euergetism is manifested in the form of pious donations or foundations, choregic monuments in which a liturgist becomes a patron in order to express and perpetuate his glory in a building, public subscriptions (*epidoseis*) and public promises of *largesses*, called pollicitations, and the generosity shown by magistrates who meet the expenses of their offices out of their own pockets, or offer liberalities in honour of the function they have assumed.

BIRTH OF PATRONAGE

1. Gifts to the gods are ageless. Since the city had its own gods and cults, just as individuals had theirs, men shared in public expenditure when they contributed personally to the costs of the city's cult, whether this was done from piety or as a kind of patronage. When the illustrious family of the Alcmeonids, who had undertaken to build the temple at Delphi, made it more magnificent than the plan required,[37] how can we determine here the relative weight of devotion and of aristocratic pride? How are we to distinguish piety from patriotism when we note, in the accounts for the Parthenon and the statue of Athena,[38] that several Athenians saw fit to add their modest contributions to the mass of public funds thanks to which the people of Athens raised the buildings that stand on their Acropolis and thereby honoured their goddess? All these motives explain why – doubtless earlier than our sources tell us – public personages who assumed a religious function were expected, from piety or in the name of piety, to add something from their own resources to the public credits made available to them. Consider, for example, the procession of the Greater Dionysia. It was financed by voluntary contributors, by liturgists, and organized by curators.[39] In theory, a commissioner was not the same as a contributor: nevertheless, these commissioners 'formerly met all the expenses incurred for the procession; nowadays, the people hand over to them (*didōsin*) a hundred minas to pay for organizing it'. The festival certainly cost them much more than that. In the name of piety these commissioners acted as true liturgists, and did so in connection with their official function – that is, they were *euergetai ob honorem*.

2. Piety and the games were thus the school of patronage. Like the Italians of the pre-Renaissance period who left us their names with the Bardi or the Scrovegni chapel, the Greeks learnt that a building for religious or sporting purposes made its donor a public personage and immortalized his name. At the end of the archaic period dynasts or tyrants glorified their names by the splendid offerings they presented to the temple at Delphi. The Hellenistic kings were to present to the free cities, as well as to those that were their subjects, buildings both sacred and secular, in order to win over these free cities to support of their policies, and, even more, so as to shine on the international stage. On the stage of their own city the Athenian notables learnt to do likewise: several choregic monuments, erected in the second half of the fourth century, illustrate for us the transition from the ex-voto to the building, from the *anathēma* to the *ergon*.[40]

It was customary for the victors in the games to dedicate to the gods the prizes they had won. In Athens the successful liturgists were given a tripod which they consecrated to Dionysus or to Apollo, in the Pythium or the Street of the Tripods. 'As witnesses to the liturgies of your ancestors,' said the advocate Isaeus to the Athenian judges, 'you have the *anathēmata* that they consecrated as memorials to their excellence: tripods in the precincts of Dionysus for their victories in the *chorēgiai*, *anathēmata* in the Pythium.'[41] The tripod was set up in the open air on a pedestal bearing the name of the victor or of his tribe. This pedestal, originally just a support, later became the essential element, and expanded to the size of a monument. Thus the tower of Lysicrates, who was victor in 334, is a rotunda a dozen metres high. The choregic monuments of Nicias and Thrasyllus, who were both victors in 320, are, respectively, a small temple of which only the foundations survive, and a portico which serves as façade to the natural grotto above the theatre of Dionysus. The consecration of the tripod was, for the victor, no longer anything but a pretext to give lustre to his name by beautifying the city and doing on a small scale what the people, in Pericles' time, had done on a large scale on the Acropolis.

The year 320 also saw the appearance of what was perhaps the first building to bear the name of a *euergetēs*, to wit, the bridge on the river Cephisus between Athens and Eleusis. Indeed, there is in the *Greek Anthology* a little poem which runs like this: 'Hie ye, hie ye, initiated, to the temple of Demeter, fearing not the winter floods. So safe a bridge for you hath Xenocles, the son of Xeinis, thrown across this broad river.'[42] The epigram is more indicative than poetic. It would even be without interest if it had not actually been engraved on the bridge, to tell travellers (and, in particular, those who were on their way to initiation into the Eleusinian mysteries) of the benefactor to whom they owed this bridge. This must be a genuine 'epigram' (that is, an inscription) rather than a mere poetic fiction like most of the 'epigrams' that make up the *Anthology*. The bridge actually existed, and Xenocles also, and a decree was found at Eleusis by which he was honoured for having had it built, together with several other epigraphic documents which enable us to glimpse the personality of this *euergetēs*. Hellenistic Athens was ruled by a few rich families who formed an oligarchy of notables.[43] Xenocles was, in particular, a gymnasiarch and an agonothete (these being two expensive liturgies). It was as an *epimelētēs* of the Eleusinian mysteries that he displayed his pride and his taste for honour, and, as the decree mentioned goes on, 'wishing that the images of the gods and the sacred objects might safely and properly make the journey' from Athens to Eleusis and that 'the crowd of Greek pilgrims who come to Eleusis and to its sanctuary, together with the inhabitants of the suburb of Athens and the peasants, should run no risk, he is causing a bridge of marble to be built, advancing the funds from his own pocket'.[44] He never asked to be reimbursed, and this was why his name was carved on the bridge. It will thus be seen that, in the Hellenistic epoch, rich men, magistrates or liturgists stood in for the city, out of patriotism, in order to build public edifices, religious or secular, in return for having their names inscribed thereon.

POLITICAL *LARGESSES*

3. For patriotism was the third motive of the *euergetai*. They gave from piety, they gave so as to be honoured, and they might also give because they were interested in a cause. Patriotic gifts went back a very long way, in Athens and elsewhere. Participation in collective enterprises was appreciated more or less immediately and the mechanisms of the state were simple enough for this conduct, quite natural in itself, to encounter no obstacle. The size of the state was sufficiently small for personal gifts not to be disproportionate to the collective enterprises and for the donor not to feel that he was adding a mere drop to an ocean. The money-changer Pasion gave his city a thousand shields manufactured in his workshops.[45] Others gave money towards some military expedition.[46] Gellias, a rich burgher of Agrigentum, billeted 500 cavalrymen.[47] If a man did not make gifts to his city, at least he agreed not to make any profit when he had dealings with it: Andocides sold the Athenian state at cost price timber with which to make oars,[48] while bankers and notables lent money to their cities interest-free.[49]

This patriotic attitude found an outlet, on the eve of the Hellenistic epoch, in a new institution, the public subscriptions or *epidoseis*,[50] which were semi-voluntary and served as channels for collective and organized patronage. It can be claimed that in the fourth century, when Athens no longer had any 'allies' to pay her tribute, the city was able to carry on high politics, to wage war, and to build, only through extraordinary and obligatory contributions and voluntary subscriptions. The only large-scale construction works of the fourth century – the improvements to the port of Zea, the stone theatre and the Panathenaic stadium – were carried out, in part at least, thanks to subscriptions 'for the fortification of the port' and 'for the building of the stadium'.[51] Every *epidosis* had a specific purpose: an expedition to Euboea,[52] a famine,[53] a war. 'Let those citizens and inhabitants of the city record their names who wish to subscribe for the salvation of the city and the defence of the country.'[54] *Epidoseis* were voluntary, in the sense that they were imposed solely by the conscience of each individual and by public opinion. 'Voluntary gifts were first introduced at Athens for the expedition to Euboea. Meidias was not one of those volunteers ... There was a second call subsequently for Olynthus. Meidias was not one of those volunteers either ...'[55] 'Dicaeogenes subscribed only 300 drachmas, less than Cleonymus of Crete!'[56] 'Why, you incorrigible knave, even at the time when every man who ever spoke from the tribune gave freely to the national defence ... you never came forward and put your name down for a farthing.'[57] This bad citizen was none other than Aeschines: Demosthenes' reproach shows that, to a greater degree perhaps than all other citizens, politicians were morally bound to subscribe and that the politician was not merely an orator but also a rich man, a *euergetēs*. We can at least say that the view taken was that a politician ought to prove by patriotic gifts the sincerity of his convictions.

4. Furthermore, the *epidoseis* show us, in its nascent phase, one of the great institutions of Hellenistic euergetism, namely promises of *euergesiai*, or pollicitations (*epangeliai, hyposcheseis*).

In the Hellenistic epoch, many *euergesiai* were preceded by an announcement or solemn promise to perform them, given in the Assembly or the Council, and usually confirmed by a letter which the city carefully preserved in its archives as written proof of a promise the implementation of which sometimes took a long time. These declarations of intent became a rather theatrical kind of rite, carried out even when the *euergesia* was to take place immediately. Under the name of *pollicitatio*, this institution was later adopted by Roman euergetism. From the beginning of the fourth century[58] the *epidoseis* already present this dual character of promise and performance. There was more than one reason for this duality. First, some promises to subscribe were made conditionally: in 330, while Alexander was conquering Central Asia, Greece was tempted to take advantage of the opportunity to free itself from the Macedonian yoke: an *epidosis* was opened in Athens, the subscribers to which undertook to lay out their money 'in case of need'.[59] But the chief reason for pollicitations was that *epidoseis* were proposed in the form of bills presented at a plenary meeting of the Assembly, so that the effect of surprise, and that of the crowd of people present, might put the rich on the spot.[60] There was always some extempore orator ready to harangue any rich man who tried to get out unobserved.[61] When one was under the eyes of the whole people, how could one refuse, if not to give money there and then (for naturally the man would not have the sum on him, and perhaps would have to dig out some treasure or sell some land in order to obtain it), at least to promise to pay it? This 'Assembly' strategy also had a great future before it. The number of *euergesiai* that were to be extracted by such 'crowd effects' is beyond counting. But it is understandable, too, that more than one pollicitator, when on his own again, wished only to forget his promise. The people were then reduced to setting up in the agora a placard of dishonour reading: 'Here are the names of the men who voluntarily promised to give money to the people for the salvation of the city and who have not done this.'[62]

LARGESSES OB HONOREM

5. Finally there was another practice destined for a long future – that of the magistrates or curators who met from their own resources all or part of the expenses of their functions. This is attested to by Demosthenes, because it gave rise to the point of law at issue in the famous case of the Crown. Demosthenes' work shows us also how the transition took place from the man of leisure, a liturgist or political orator, to the notable, politician and *euergetēs ob honorem*.

We certainly observe, in the speeches of Demosthenes, the old Athenian ideal: a politician is an orator, a good citizen is a liturgist. 'If anyone were to ask me to say what good *I* had really done to the city ... I could tell how often I had been trierarch and *chorēgos*, how I had contributed funds, ransomed prisoners, and done other like acts of generosity ...' However, he adds, the greatest good he has done for the people is that he has given them only good counsel and has not been a demagogue.[63] The political orator thus conceived is a man of culture and leisure, moved by desire to be honoured, by *philotimia*, who looks upon public honours as his true reward. Let us recall the famous passage:

In my boyhood, Aeschines, I had the advantage of attending respectable schools: and my means were sufficient for one who was not to be driven by poverty into disreputable occupations. When I had come of age, my circumstances were in accordance with my upbringing. I was in a position to provide a chorus, to pay for a war-galley, and to be assessed for property tax. I renounced no honourable ambition either in public or in private life: and rendered good service both to the commonwealth and to my own good friends. When I decided to take part in public affairs, the political services I chose were such that I was repeatedly decorated both by my own country and by many other Greek cities . . .[64]

To the good conscience of the notable corresponds the euergetism *ob honorem* of the politician: we learn, through the case of the Crown, that Demosthenes, when appointed inspector of the fortifications, received ten talents from the public treasury, these being put into his own hand (as was the financial practice of the time) and that, for the work on the fortifications, he spent 100 minas more than that, which he drew from his own resources and did not charge to the state.[65] This behaviour was no isolated case, but tended to become the rule. Demosthenes mentions other curators and even magistrates, *stratēgoi*, who had been as generous as he. 'Nausicles . . . has been repeatedly decorated by you for the money he spent out of his own pocket when serving as military commander.'[66] Demosthenes sacrificed his 100 minas following a pollicitation. He speaks of 'the donations that I promised and gave at my own expense'.[67] Had he promised, when the decree appointing him inspector was put forward in the Assembly, to take upon himself the possible excess charges (without saying anything about their amount) and not to ask for a decree granting him extra-ordinary credits? Or did he undertake to pay out, in any event, an extra amount of 100 minas, mentioning that figure? In either case we see here one of the other reasons why *euergesiai* would more and more frequently be preceded by public promises to make them. The future magistrate or curator announced officially, when he was elected or appointed, or shortly afterwards, what *euergesiai* he would undertake during his term of office. Pollicitations were thus in the nature of election programmes or promises.

Political life tended, from the time of Demosthenes, to be the prerogative of the notables. A well-known passage in *De Corona* reveals that in the minds of everyone the Assembly, in which all citizens were equal, was in fact a hierarchy determined by wealth and liturgies. The scene is set at the fateful moment when Athens learns of the taking of Elateia. The panic-stricken people have rushed to the Assembly, but who will have the courage to take power in such dramatic circumstances? Nobody went up to the tribune; and yet, says Demosthenes, if a merely patriotic citizen had been needed, each and every Athenian might have been the man of the moment.

Now, had it been the duty of every man who desired the salvation of Athens to come forward, all of you, aye, every Athenian citizen, would have risen in your places and made your way to the tribune, for that salvation, I am well assured, was the desire of every heart. If that duty had fallen upon the wealthy, the Three Hundred (the biggest taxpayers) would have risen; if upon those who were alike wealthy and patriotic, the men who thereafter gave those generous donations [*epidoseis*] . . .[68]

But what had been needed was a man who was patriotic, rich *and* clear-sighted – and that meant Demosthenes and no one else. We see here sketched out the portrait of a new social type, the *euergetēs* of the early Hellenistic epoch who served his city by virtue of both his gifts as a political orator and his fortune. The mass of ordinary citizens would then fall, *de facto*, under an obligation to the notables. And in the course of the third century the title of *euergetēs*, with the corresponding verb, 'to do good' to the city, was to be applied, even in the style of the·decrees, to fellow citizens and no longer only to foreigners and *proxenoi*. One of the first Athenians to be accorded this title in Athens, for his generous participation in an *epidosis*, was a certain Xenocles – none other than the grandson and namesake of the Xenocles whom we have seen inscribing his name on a bridge he had caused to be built not far from Eleusis.[69]

   6. And the fourth century saw the appearance of another variety of liberalities *ob honorem*, namely, the *largesses* of magistrates on the occasion of their entry into office, or in gratitude for their nomination to honours. There is a page in Aristotle's *Politics*, book VI, which tells us of this. The facts it sets out have already a strongly Hellenistic flavour (it is generally agreed that book VI was composed during Aristotle's second stay in Athens, after 335). The philosopher presents the symbolic *largesses* of the magistrates as a practice which, though normal, is not observed universally: 'not yet', we are tempted to add. The passage is worth quoting in its entirety. In oligarchies,

The magistracies of highest rank, which ought to be in the hands of the governing body, should have expensive duties attached to them, and then the people will not desire them and will take no offence at the privileges of their rulers when they see that they pay a heavy fine for their dignity. It is fitting also that the magistrates on entering office should offer magnificent sacrifices or erect some public edifice, and then the people who participate in the entertainments, and see the city decorated with votive offerings and buildings, will not desire an alteration in the government, and the notables will have memorials of their munificence.[70]

Here, then, is one reason (of secondary importance, no doubt) for the *largesses ob honorem*: they allowed the notables to exercise their instincts as patrons and to perpetuate the memory of their personal merits. The chief reason is recalled implicitly in the rest of the passage: 'This, however, is anything but the fashion of our modern oligarchs, who are as covetous of gain as they are of honour; oligarchies like theirs may well be described as petty democracies.'

The oligarchs were too preoccupied with money: that was the dominant feature of their personalities, and it clashed with the oligarchical system, the logic of which required that the ruling group should compensate by means of *largesses* for their monopoly of power. Only in a democracy would such compensation have been pointless. We shall see later the sense in which it can be said that a *largesse* compensates for a frustration. Let us conclude for the moment that liberalities *ob honorem* are a special feature characteristic of oligarchies and that they serve as symbolic compensations, without talking about patronage.

These liberalities are of two kinds. First, public offices having become burdensome, 'liturgies' are associated with the exercise of magistracies. We must not think, in this connection, of liturgies of the Athenian type, which were in no way linked with the exercise of public functions: here, the word 'liturgy' bears the meaning it would often bear in the Hellenistic epoch, where it signified *largesses* and services to the public generally – where, in fact, it was almost a synonym of *euergesia*. The 'liturgy' of a magistrate consists, for instance, in meeting the expenses of his office out of his own pocket. Secondly, public offices having become honours, the magistrate thanks the city which honours him by offering it a banquet, the usual follow-up to a sacrifice, or else he commemorates the honour done to him by consecrating some precious object in a sanctuary, or by paying for the construction of a public building of some kind. These were old-established practices in Greece, which the oligarchies perpetuated, while modifying their nature and significance. The official year began regularly with public sacrifices celebrated by the City Council and the magistrates newly taking up office. These sacrifices made on entry into public office, or *eisitēria*, were naturally followed by banquets at which the flesh of the sacrificial offerings was eaten. In that civilization where poverty was widespread, few people ever ate meat except on these solemn occasions, and so the public sacrifices aroused among the poor a degree of interest in which piety was not the only element, as the Old Oligarch known to us as 'Pseudo-Xenophon' confirms: 'The people, knowing that it is imposs-ible for every poor man to make offerings and feasts . . . have discovered by what means these privileges may be secured to them. The state accordingly sacrifices many victims at the public expense, while it is the people that feast on them, and distribute them among themselves by lot.' Leaving office was also an occasion for banquets in some cities. Outgoing magistrates alone participated in these, unless they happened to bring along some courtesans. In the logic of the oligarchical system as Aristotle describes it, the public sacrifices celebrated at the beginning of the official year became a pretext for feasting all the citizens, and the new magistrates doubtless bought the sacrificial victims themselves, as a 'liturgy'.[71]

Offerings to the gods and building of public edifices by the magis-trates were another old tradition. In more than one city, when officials left office, they would consecrate in a sanctuary some object of no great value – a cup, or a statuette – to thank the gods and also, no doubt, to testify that they had presented their accounts and the city had approved their management of its affairs. Later, a priest would consecrate to the gods a statue of himself (in accordance with a well-known Greek custom) on the expiry of his year of priesthood. To conform to Aristotle's prescriptions it was enough for magistrates to consecrate more sumptuous offerings, which would embellish the city no less than they would please the gods. The magistrates might even consecrate to the gods buildings of a secular character, useful to men: all that was needed was for the dedicatory inscription on the monument to state that it was offered 'to the gods and to the city', as we see from many examples provided by epigraphy.[72]

EUERGETISM NOT REDISTRIBUTION

Our survey of the facts is concluded. The reader has seen how euer-getism began and how varied were its motives. He has been able to observe that euergetism was not a response to any cause or requirement of high politics: it was not a tax under another name; nor did it serve to ensure the social equilibrium, domination by the oligarchs or the rich. It was not a case of social redistribution. It was external to the social problems and conflicts of the Hellenistic epoch. To be sure, in some instances, *euergesiai* effected something that a city's inadequate revenues prevented it from effecting, or provided material satisfactions to the poor. But they did not serve only or always for such purposes. *Euergesiai* had a great variety of objects: the *euergetēs* offered his city a statue or a banquet, or undertook to meet the expenses of his office. Some of these objects were 'social' in character, while others could or should have been covered by the city itself, out of its own fiscal resources. Thus euergetism did sometimes fulfil a fiscal or redistributive function, but it did this only partially and secondarily, just as it sometimes fulfilled a religious function. More often, however, it peopled the cities with useless statues or gave from some persons' excess income to persons who lacked the necessities of life. For the *euergetai* wished, first and foremost, to please themselves. They had motives for giving which were not those of a taxpayer or of a big businessman who is 'demonstrating his social conscience'.

Euergetism was external to the social problem in its motives, its workings and its effects. In the Hellenistic epoch social conflicts were as noisy as, in the classical epoch, had been the struggle for power between democrats and oligarchs. The issues at stake were cancellation of debts and redistribution of landed property, not to mention the difficulties caused by economic ups and downs – in other words, famines (when corn was in short supply, or rather was too dear, there were riots in the cities).[73] *Euergesiai* could remedy these ills to a slight extent only: a long queue of citizens might subscribe to an *epidosis* to buy grain for the poor citizens, or a rich benefactor might sell at a low price the corn from his storehouses. But a social problem is not solved by means of more or less symbolic gestures like these. It needs remedies on a very much larger scale, the scale of the community. Consequently, when 'demagogues' took power in a city, it was into the public funds that they delved in order to solve the social problem, or else they confiscated the lands of the rich. This was done by one Molpagoras, at Cius, on the Propontis. He was 'a capable speaker and politician, but in character a demagogue, greedy of power. This man, by flattering the populace, by inciting the rabble against men of means, by finally killing some of the latter and banishing others whose property he confiscated and distributed among the people, soon attained by these means to supreme power ...'[74]

Euergetism appears only in the margins of the picture that we can draw of the social problem. If the euergetistic spirit and social 'demagogy' were sometimes connected, the connection was hardly ideological. In the eyes of the conservatives, the supporters of authority and firmness, social policy and *euergesiai* had this in common, that they were equally contrary to sound tradition. We see this in a passage in Polybius which is so instructive in other ways, too, that it deserves to be quoted in full. The scene is Boeotia, about the beginning of the second century. Demagogy prevails. It is not possible for justice to be administered; the cities grant *largesses* at the expense of the Treasury; and rich men who die without issue endow foundations whose beneficiaries are to hold banquets in their memory.

Public affairs in Boeotia had fallen into such a state of disorder that for nearly twenty-five years justice, both civil and criminal, had ceased to be administered there, the magistrates by issuing orders, some of them for the dispatch of garrisons and others for general campaigns, always contriving to abolish legal proceedings. Certain *stratēgoi* even provided pay out of the public funds for the indigent, the populace thus learning to court and invest with power those men who would help them to escape the legal consequences of their crimes and debts and even in addition to get something out of the public funds as a favour from the magistrates ... Incident upon all this was another most unfortunate mania. For childless men, when they died, did not leave their property to their nearest heirs, as had formerly been the custom there, but disposed of it for purposes of junketing and banqueting and made it the common property of their friends. Even many who had families distributed the greater part of their fortune among their clubs, so that there were many Boeotians who had each month more dinners than there were days in the calendar.[75]

The endowments left by these testators for their own commemoration are lumped together by Polybius with the social policy of redistribution because both were the actions of a social class which was letting go and showing indulgence both to itself and to its proletariat. To an old, poor society, ruled by an authoritarian and rigid oligarchy, had succeeded a richer society in which the principle of authority was mitigated, class struggle wrested social concessions, and easy-going use of wealth made possible both luxury, which was conspicuous consumption, and euergetism, which was conspicuous giving. Demagogy could then dissipate the public funds in sacrifices at which the whole population came to dine and in allowances paid to those citizens who saw fit to take part in the assemblies – alms in disguise[76] (a practice long established in Athens, as will be seen). The interruption in the administration of justice was due also to the social conflict. The point was to prevent the courts from sentencing insolvent debtors.

More generally, confidence in class justice had disappeared. A few pages later Polybius tells us that, in that same Boeotia, as a result of Rome's victory over Antiochus the Great, 'the hopes of all those who had revolutionary aims were cut short, and there was a radical change of character in the various states. The course of justice had been at a standstill there for nearly twenty-five years, and now it was common matter of talk in the different cities that a final end must be put to all the disputes between the citizens. The matter, however, continued to be keenly disputed, as the indigent were much more numerous than those in affluent circumstances . . .'[77] Preventing the magistrates from imprisoning insolvent debtors was a typical demagogic measure.[78] Nor was the interruption in the course of justice a phenomenon peculiar to Boeotia. Everywhere, 'when social crises broke out, the courts were suspected of partiality and reduced to paralysis.'[79] Hence one of the most curious practices of the Hellenistic epoch, the calling-in of judges from other cities: as nobody had confidence any longer in fellow members of that narrow group which comprised their city, people preferred to appeal to the impartiality of the foreign judges that another city might agree to send them.[80]

REDISTRIBUTION

The class struggle, obstructing the work of the courts and wresting payments for the poor, took money from wherever it lay – usually from public funds, but sometimes from the coffers of the rich, who subscribed to an *epidosis*, either willingly or under threat of class guerrilla warfare, hostile demonstrations: 'The Athenians were once asking contributions [*epidoseis*] for a public sacrifice, and the rest were contributing, but Phocion (a politician well-to-do but with old-fashioned ideas) said: "Ask from someone richer than me." And once, when his audience would not cease from shouting and crying him down, he told them: "You may croak with all your might, but you shall not get a taste of me."'[81] We shall see that, in Roman euergetism, the charivari became the people's way of replying to the recalcitrance of rich men.

Allowances paid out of public funds and *epidoseis* out of private wealth: of these, the first were traditional in democratic cities, and Athens was no exception. It had long been understood that, in critical situations (the Persian invasion, the Peloponnesian War),[82] the city should distribute corn, meat and money to indigent citizens. It was accepted, too, that in case of need, if not always, the city's surplus revenue might be divided among its citizens. To take a single example, the theoric fund:[83] when there were theatrical performances and public festivals, the surplus of Athens' resources was shared out in this way. Without going into the details, which are uncertain anyway, let us simply note that, in principle at least, the theoric fund was not public assistance, charity or social justice. By virtue of a rule that remained unchangeable throughout antiquity, these distributions were not restricted to the poor but were made to all the citizens, whether poor or not, and to citizens alone. A man who was rich and had no children received the same amount – if he cared to collect it – as a poor man with a family, while foreign residents and (of course) slaves got nothing. In antiquity public assistance went not to the social category of the poor but, without differentiation, to the citizens as a whole.[84] And the rich did not always disdain to collect their share.[85] In actual fact, it *was* public assistance, because the poor, being more numerous than the rich, were the principal beneficiaries. In the minds of contemporaries, too, it was that. When Demosthenes talks about the theoric fund, he speaks constantly of 'citizens who are in need' and 'poor citizens'.[86] The theoric fund resulted in a huge redistribution of income among the citizens. The rich paid for the poor, in the sense that the city's surplus went into the theoric fund, instead of serving to relieve the rich taxpayers and liturgists.[87] It was the pact that 'cemented'[88] democracy.

The rich were fully conscious of this and proclaimed, in their fury, that they had become the real poor. Xenophon excelled in expounding this sort of idea.[89] He searched desperately for fresh sources of revenue for Athens, so that the city could thereafter relieve the poor without impoverishing the rich[90] and so that the tax burden might be lifted from the latter. The democrats replied that the city was one big family,[91] and proposed to the Athenian democracy a compromise between rich and poor. The former would tolerate the existence of the theoric fund, while the latter would agree that part of the surplus intended for these distributions should be used instead to reduce the tax obligations of the rich.[92] That was the social problem of the time. In such a democracy as Rhodes 'the demagogues not only provided pay for the multitude, but prevented them from making good to the trierarchs the sums which had been expended by them,' says Aristotle in the *Politics*.[93] In this way a redistribution of income was carried out 'imperceptibly'.[94] When allowances or a theoric were paid to the people, the sums needed could be obtained only by means of a property tax.[95] Thereafter, a democracy that wished to be moderate and lasting would agree to a pact on these lines: the rich would contribute to the payment of public assistance and, in exchange, would be freed from liturgies which were more ruinous than useful.[96]

Free bread is one of the best-known institutions of the Hellenistic cities. No better example could be imagined for examining the problem of euergetism. 'The Rhodians,' writes Strabo, 'are concerned for the people in general, although their rule is not democratic; still, they wish to take care of their multitude of poor people. Accordingly, the people are supplied with provisions and the needy are supported by the well-to-do, by a certain ancestral custom ...' 'There are certain liturgies that supply provisions, so that at the same time the city does not run short of useful men, and in particular for the manning of the fleets.' Thus, in Rhodes, the liturgies were divided between the maintenance of the poor and the city's needs: in particular, the needs of the navy. A well-known inscription tells us in some detail how the supply of free bread was organized at Samos.[97] During the second century, a subscription was opened to which more than a hundred rich Samians contributed sums of between 100 and 1,000 drachmas without hope of reimbursement. From the fund formed in this way interest-bearing loans were granted, this being the most usual way in which money was made to increase in antiquity. The interest received was used to buy the corn which was distributed free to the citizens each month, until stocks ran out. In other cities cheap or free bread was not guaranteed by a permanent fund, but when famine struck, a city would open a subscription list or appeal to the generosity of a *euergetēs*. One year at Priene, 'the supply of corn falling short', a citizen named Moschion, 'seeing that the situation was urgent, and cherishing a devotion for the people which forbade him to wait to be asked, presented himself spontaneously before the Assembly and, in his own name and that of his brother', distributed corn at four drachmas the measure (an extremely low price at that time).[98] He performed what was called a *paraprasis*, a cut-price sale for charity. Another year this Moschion, along with his brother, 'gave the city corn without hope of reimbursement, as public documents testify' (the drafter of this honorific decree put that in lest the person being honoured should decide to try and recover the price of his corn). A third year when, once more, 'the supply of corn fell short, Moschion, desiring to follow the example he himself had set, and seeing the urgency of the situation, undertook to procure the corn that was lacking and, furthermore, made a promise' (a pollicitation, to use the technical term) to sell it to the citizens over a period of several months at a price below the market rate so that the entire people might be saved, 'women and children included'. Perhaps this *euergetēs* bought corn from merchants at famine prices, in order to resell it at a low price: but perhaps, also, he had hoarded it in his own granaries (this was a current practice)[99] and distributed it at a low price in order to save himself from becoming the target of a riot.

EUERGETISM NOT A TAX

Euergetism was not a quasi-tax. Euergetism and taxation were not interlinked. Neither by its motives, nor by the destination of the resources it procured, nor by the volume of these resources was euergetism equivalent to direct taxation. It did not take the place of inadequate public revenues. On the contrary, the richer the city, the larger its revenue and, at the same time, the greater the number of large-scale *euergetai*. The yield from *euergesiai* is not to be compared with what would have been brought in by a tax levied on either an assessment or a quota basis. The yield was uncertain and variable: it sometimes remedied difficulties due to economic conditions, it provided unexpected savings (when a magistrate undertook to defray the expenses of his office), or it supplied the city with a surplus which was more or less useless. Euergetism bore no proportion to a city's needs: it yielded the amount of money which, for reasons of their own, the *euergetai* allowed to be taken from them and which they assigned to whatever purpose they chose. A special case is that of the religious festivals for which, officially, a priest met the cost, either partly or wholly (as was to happen, under the Empire, with the Imperial cult); euergetism served to mount these festivals. But where serious matters were concerned, notably war, means of raising finance were adopted that were more compulsory than acts of patronage. The Egypt of the Ptolemies obtained ships in its external possessions by imposing upon the subject cities a liturgy, the trierarchy.[100] In 146, when Achaea, which had for so long been the pillar of Roman hegemony, at last revolted against its foreign rulers, the 'demagogues' in power resorted, in order to finance the struggle, to the tried and tested methods: an extraordinary tax (*eisphora*) and a promise (*epangelia*) to subscribe to an *epidosis*.[101] On the other hand, the festivals and games which became so frequent in the Hellenistic epoch were maintained by benefactors.

In Boeotia the agonistic movement which developed at the end of the third century kept going only through the generosity of local patrons and foreign kings. A great athletic tournament like the Mouseia at Thespiae, which was Panhellenic and where crowns were awarded, survived on *largesses*.[102]

It is very hard to estimate the share represented by *euergesiai* in the revenues of a city, but it seems certain that the amount of these public revenues differed greatly from one city to another. Among the cities there were both rich and poor, and those that were poor existed only through patronage. Euergetism brought them from time to time a public building, a statue or a banquet; enabled them to resume the holding of some games which had been interrupted for many years, to keep the public baths heated or to repair (*episkeuazein*) buildings which were in sore need of attention. But the revenues of the rich cities could be considerable. There, the *euergetai* added still more to their public luxury of festivals and buildings, and multiplied little monuments, symbols of the public honours they had held. While the Greeks' aversion to direct taxation seems odd to us, it did not mean that the cities were deprived of resources. Their chief source of revenue was, as with us today, indirect taxes.[103] Some cities had the luck to possess extensive estates or mines, or to draw tribute from their continental possessions. If these various resources ever proved insufficient, all repugnance was overcome, and resort was had to an ordinary direct tax. Taking this action seems to have been much less exceptional than might be supposed.[104] In Athens the *eisphora* was a tax which, though in principle extraordinary, tended to become ordinary: sometimes, during wars, it came to be levied for many years in succession. However, the *eisphora* remained outside the normal budget. It was always assigned to a particular purpose and justified by special circumstances – war, or the building of an arsenal. Paying it was a matter of merit as well as duty. In the pleading of Attic orators, defendants made much of their *eisphorai*, just as of their liturgies, and the two terms went together. The same could be said of the *epidosis*.[105]

4. Hellenistic euergetism: a general survey

There was no finer virtue than to be open-handed, or, as they said in those days, to have a great soul[106] – provided that the recipient himself or itself was also great: not a slave, a poor wretch, some unknown passer-by, but a god, a foreign people or a city. Nevertheless, the exercise of this virtue cannot be understood, as regards its motives and its choice of objects, unless we visualize the political situation or the social role of the donors. Otherwise, we should be supposing that the men of that time were not like us, and that disinterestedness was less exceptional then than now.

THE GIFTS OF KINGS

Kings have souls as great as or greater than those of notables, but for different reasons. Giving is the kingly gesture *par excellence*, with the king's courtiers and soldiers as primary beneficiaries.[107] As for the gifts that the Hellenistic kings made to cities and foreign peoples, a whole chapter would not suffice to list them: monuments sacred and secular, minted coins, cargoes of corn . . .[108] I will say merely that there were three main reasons for these *largesses*: keeping up useful political relations, making gratuitous display of the monarchy's splendour, and giving symbolic form to a relationship of dependence. We read in book IV of Polybius that Attalus of Pergamum had 'undertaken for the Aetolians the expense of construction' of the ramparts of their strong fortress of Elaos, and we see why when we find, in book IX, Attalus and the Aetolians allied against Philip V of Macedon.[109] More simply still, a king provides a friendly state with money or corn in order to sustain military operations and pay mercenaries.[110] Two dramatic turns of events, the liberation of Sicyon by Aratus and the departure of the Macedonian garrison from Athens, were made possible by foreign money: Aratus and Cleomenes of Sparta were financed for a time by the Ptolemies.[111] But the gifts of kings and peoples were also often disinterested. The international community, too, had its euergetism. Thebes, destroyed by Alexander the Great, was rebuilt thanks to a genuine *epidosis* in which all Greece took part.[112] It would be wrong to talk of propaganda, which seems to imply calculation. The need to display oneself, to express one's splendour, is as natural to social groups as to individuals. If Hiero II 'conferred great benefits on the Greeks and studied to win their high opinion',[113] this was not because, in his distant Sicily, he expected great services from them, but so that his remoteness should not cause him to be forgotten. Certain cities which were neutralist or very independent, such as Athens or Rhodes, served as 'shop-windows' for international ostentation, but this applied even more to the major sanctuaries, where the kings set up the trophies of their victories and the statues of their servants or allies.[114] Finally, a foreigner's gifts might be symbols of dependence. The people which accepts them does not sell itself for that price, but its acceptance of them signifies a promise of obedience which it is induced to give for one reason or another. Thus, the Achaeans were unwilling to accept gifts from certain kings. Either, they said, we shall sacrifice our interests to the interests of those kings, or else we shall seem ungrateful if we oppose the wishes of our paymasters.[115] To refuse a gift meant declining a friendship that could be domineering. Phocion refused the gifts of Alexander, who angrily informed him that he did not regard as true 'friends' those who were unwilling to accept any-thing from him. In fact, Phocion did not wish to be Alexander's unconditional friend,[116] and accepting a gift and not obeying all the giver's commands would be equivalent to not keeping one's word. As a symbol, the gift may follow the opposite path, proceeding from below up towards a protector. Prusias of Bithynia was cut to the quick by the failure of Byzantium to erect the statues it had promised him and to send a sacred embassy to the religious festival of the Bithynian monarchy.[117] He wanted to wield over Byzantium a sort of negative protectorate, a 'Finlandization' according to which the city would not ally itself with the enemies of Bithynia or impose a tax on navigation through the Straits. Byzantium's discourtesy was significant on the plane of high politics. In short, the *largesses* of one state to another were sometimes gratuitous display or international euergetism, and sometimes symbols of dependence or protection. How are we to tell the difference? Tact was needed if no ambiguity was to be in the air when one accepted a gift, and the Rhodians possessed that tact to a high degree. When their island had suffered grave damage from an earthquake, they sought the help of all the peoples; but their ambassa-dors did this with such nobility and dignity that everyone appreciated, by their attitude, that Rhodes intended to receive help without com-mitting itself in any way.[118]

THE NOTABLES AND CONSTRAINT TO GIVE

Let us return to our notables and their cities. Like the kings, they gave *largesse* sometimes for the sake of gratuitous display (voluntary euergetism or patronage) and sometimes symbolically (this was the case, and we shall see why, of their *euergesiai ob honorem*). But their magnificence had a very special character, which is a good reason for coining the word 'euergetism', with its ending in 'ism'. It was both spontaneous and forced, voluntary and constrained. Every *euergesia* is to be explained both by the generosity of the *euergetēs*, who has his own motives, and by the constraint imposed upon him by the expectations of others, public opinion, the 'role' in which the *euergetēs* is caught. This dual character makes euergetism something almost unique: if there were only constraint, *euergesiai* would be in the nature of taxes or liturgies, while if there were only spontaneity, there would be no difference between a *euergetēs* of antiquity and an American patron of the arts today, who gives if he chooses to, without such patronage constituting a moral obligation.

In euergetism are present both the pleasure of giving and the moral duty of giving: the city expects its rich citizens to be generous. How are spontaneity and constraint to be reconciled? By the circumstance that the constraint is informal: it involves no regulation, no definite sanction, but only reproach and possible acts of retaliation. Euergetism consists, for a city, in profiting by the generous disposition that a certain class possesses spontaneously, and turning this into a duty, but one that is purely moral and informal, so as not to destroy the rich men's wish to give, which would mean killing the goose that lays the golden eggs. If euergetism was easier to establish than a system of taxation, as we have seen, this was because the notables were inclined towards ostentatious giving. Resistance broke at the weakest link in the chain, the notables being readier to engage in *largesse* than were the citizens as a whole to pay taxes. If the disposition to give had not existed, there would not have been any euergetism. If an informal constraint had not been added to that disposition, there would have been isolated acts of patronage, such as occur in all societies, but not a permanent system, an abundant and perennial source of benefits to the community.

PATRONAGE OF THE NOTABLES

Spontaneous generosity multiplied by constraint – euergetism, whether gratuitous ostentation or *ob honorem* symbolic payment, always had two sides. It was civic, in that it benefited the city or the citizens as a whole, and it was the act of a class, the notables, who gave because they felt they were superior to the mass of the people. That second aspect was essential: euergetism was the expression of a political ascendancy – the city was split in two, between those who received and those who gave. Every superiority tends to express itself, not because of some sort of machiavellian calculation but through a kind of natural expansiveness. An essential and necessary condition for euergetism is

the establishment of a regime of notables, for nobody indulges in ostentation unless he feels superior to the rest. In the Athenian democracy
this superiority was an individual matter. Alcibiades expressed his
personal excellence (or the dignity of a group on its way out, namely
the old aristocracy to which he belonged) when he performed the
chorēgia so splendidly that he made his fellow citizens envious, or
when he ran seven chariots at Olympia on his own account.[119] In the
Hellenistic cities euergetism expressed the superiority of the class of
notables in its entirety: *notabilité oblige*. The specific historical feature
of this epoch was that their social superiority obliged them to express
themselves not through conspicuous consumption but through conspicuous patronage: they had to spend as individuals for the benefit
of collective purposes. And these purposes were themselves civic in
character. *Euergesiai* were gifts to the city and not, for example, for
the benefit of the poor, or of arts and letters. This amounts to saying
that the class which displayed its superiority in this way behaved as a
political class: the notables were defined by their participation in the
government of their city. Examination of some documents, honorific
decrees celebrating the *largesses* of a *euergetēs*, will afford us proof of
this. Let us look at the notables at work.

Seen through these decrees, the Hellenistic *euergetēs* appears as an
all-round political man who does good to his city by means of his
counsel, his high connections and his wealth. A decree of Miletus
discovered fifteen years ago has enabled us to become acquainted with
one of these politicians, the rich Irenias, leader of the pro-Pergamene
party and inevitable intermediary between his city and King Eumenes
of Pergamum.[120] His father had already set him an example of munificence (being a form of class behaviour, euergetism is necessarily also a
family tradition). He himself succeeded in persuading King Eumenes
to show generosity, and as the decree tells us: 'Irenias constantly exerts
himself with zeal in the interests of our city, always bringing greater
glory and renown to our homeland. Having obtained an audience
with King Eumenes, he persuaded the king, whose ear he has, to donate
to our city [6,000 tonnes] of corn towards the construction of a
gymnasium, together with the wood needed for the work. The people
having awarded to the king the honours merited by these gifts, and
having charged Irenias to convey this news to the king,' Irenias proved
able to persuade the king not only to increase his promised liberality
but also to pay the cost of the honours Miletus had awarded him. Such
'bouncing back' of magnificence was much in the political style of the

time. For his own part, Irenias was liberal towards his city and each of his fellow citizens. He lent money free of interest and even without recovering the principal, he undertook many liturgies or *epidoseis*, and he helped sustain the public finances 'during this difficult period'.

A *euergetēs* comes to the rescue of the public treasury and also both feeds and entertains the population. In the agora of Priene the whole length of the wall of the northern portico was covered with honorific decrees. These form a select group which has remained free from the hazards to which the conservation of documents is sometimes subject. One of the decrees concerns that same Moschion whom we have already seen on three occasions, giving corn to his compatriots or selling it to them at a low price. He could boast of many other benefactions: 'he looked on his personal fortune as belonging to all his fellow citizens',[121] he lived a life of piety towards the gods, his conduct to his parents, those around him and his fellow citizens was beyond reproach, he was just, he was eager for the renown of his homeland[122] – in short, a man worthy of the reputation his ancestors had enjoyed. On at least four occasions, when the public finances were in difficulty, he advanced or donated money to the city. Besides his distribution of corn, he distributed 1,000 drachmas in honour of his mother.[123] He contributed towards the building of a gymnasium; when the city found itself unable, for lack of funds, to complete this work (because the kings who had promised the city money for the purpose had either changed their minds or lost their thrones), Moschion saved the situation once again. The sanctuary of Alexander the Great needed repairing: Moschion advanced the necessary money. While he never performed governmental functions (he never became *stratēgos*), he did take on expensive responsibilities. He was three times nominated to lead a sacred embassy and, on those occasions, offered public sacrifice at his own expense, as well as returning to the city the funds allotted for his mission. Finally he assumed the priesthood of Olympian Zeus, which was the highest honour, for at Priene the years were dated by the name of the bearer of this 'crown-wearing' office. On that occasion Moschion offered a serving of sweet wine[124] to all the inhabitants of Priene, foreigners and slaves included, to celebrate his entry into office and the beginning of the year. Subsequently he gave a banquet to the citizens every month, following his monthly sacrifice to Zeus.[125]

We see, then, that *euergetai* came to the aid of the public finances in the times of distress which are frequently mentioned in inscriptions.[126] They gave the people entertainments of a traditional kind. They took upon themselves all or part of the public expenditure connected with their functions. Finally, they left to the city some building to serve as a monument to their political activity. Another decree, from the city of Sestos, on the Hellespont, will complete the picture.[127] From his youth the *euergetēs* Menas had considered that nothing was nobler than to make oneself useful to one's homeland, and to this end he spared no expense. For example, he thought nothing of the dangers and the loss of money involved in an embassy. All of that seemed secondary to the renown that his patriotic conduct would bring. What was important, in his eyes, was to win the gratitude of the people, for himself and his descendants, and so he participated in embassies. Later he became priest in charge of the cult of King Attalus, and contributed largely to the expenses of this function. His generosity extended, indeed, not only to the citizens but also to all the residents in the city and the foreigners passing through, which meant that the city had a good name abroad. He was also gymnasiarch and built baths for the ephebi. Altogether, in all his magistracies and liturgies, he was true to himself and to what the people expected of him. To crown it all, when the city awarded a bronze statue to Menas, he, knowing how short of money the city was, undertook to meet the cost of his own statue.[128]

These examples[129] will be enough to give the reader a notion of the usual nature of these *euergesiai*. The phraseology used is itself significant in its stereotyped character. The epigraphic, or rather scribal, style consists of stock formulae which are repeated more or less verbatim from one decree to another. This fine Hellenistic prose, clear, scholarly and without bombast (the baroque style of the decrees of the Imperial epoch would be very different),[130] contains many expressions which become conventional, like our standard expressions of politeness. The aim of the decrees is honorific and didactic. The wording has been carefully weighed, for each *euergetēs*, with consideration of what was said in earlier inscriptions, so as to proportion exactly the degree of honour he deserves. The ready-made phrases define a conception of euergetism, establish a norm. The solemnity and application with which the decrees were drawn up show that the *euergesiai* were matters of state importance, and the local event of the year.

Composed under the supervision of the Council, that is, of the notables, the decrees reveal the conception this class held of itself and of the state duties it imposed on itself. At this point a difficulty arising from our documentation has to be admitted. The style of the Greek decrees is much more civic than oligarchic, and that was to be true of

the Roman documents as well. The city does not humble itself before
the *euergetēs*. The eulogy it awards proceeds from above downwards,
and the citizen, even when meritorious, is considered only a part of
the city. Even in the Imperial epoch the decrees, both Greek and
Latin, contain bombast rather than platitudes. But does this civic
condescension not, perhaps, conceal social realities that come close to
clientage? Let us look at the great decree of Olbia in honour of its
benefactor Protogenes.[131] The city of Olbia, on the Black Sea, not far
from the mouth of the Bug, lived precariously under the threat of the
barbarians and their King Saitapharnes, to whom it paid tribute.[132]
From the decree we learn that the city survived only thanks to the
largesses of the citizen Protogenes, who himself paid the tribute to the
king, obtained cheap corn when the movements of the barbarians
hindered normal supplies, and restored the ramparts when a Celtic
incursion loomed. The people habitually appealed to his generosity,
examples of which would fill several pages. As we read the decree we
realize that Protogenes is richer than the city, that he is its absolute
master, just as Cosimo de' Medici's wealth made him master of Florence; that he maintains the city out of his own pocket, just as a feudal
lord would with his manor. Yet nothing in the wording of the
decree reveals that dependence. If we were to judge by the style alone
(ignoring the content), we should see the community honouring a
benefactor who has merely behaved as a good citizen.

PATRIOTISM?

It is customary, nowadays as in ancient times, to explain this patronage
in a different way – by patriotism, by the feeling of solidarity, as strong
among the Hellenes of those times as today. This explanation is half-
true. 'Patriotism' is, up to a point, a vaguer synonym for everything
already described; beyond that point, it is a polite interpretation or an
ideological cloak.

The Hellenistic decrees do, to be sure, ascribe *euergesiai* to two
virtues – to emulation or competition (*philotimia*) among good citizens
who want to distinguish themselves and be honoured for having
rendered some signal service to the city; and to their patriotism, their
good attitude to the common interest. And, of course, a notable who
regards the city as belonging to him and his peers cannot but be well
disposed towards it. But we know that this idea of patriotism covers
attitudes that differ very markedly. On the one hand we have the
attitude of the member of the ruling group who identifies himself with

a great cause, that of his city, and merges his personal pride with the lively nationalism of the Greek cities. On the other, we have the feeling of 'us' that may possess all the citizens, humble and powerful alike, of a community which is unanimous at a moment of crisis or of triumph. And then, again, there is the benevolence of a 'father of his people' towards obedient children for whom he feels responsible. Widely differing craft sail under the flag of patriotsism. Itself a form without content, patriotism includes as many varieties as an individual can have different relations with and interests in a community. Consequently, if we ascribe to the notables, as a matter of course, the feeling of solidarity, the patriotism of 'us', we are taking advantage of the flag's ambivalence to commit a psychological error.

Officially, Greek patriotism was that of a good citizen, an equal among equals, who differed from the rest only in his greater degree of devotion to the public weal. The decrees and the speeches of Attic orators reiterate this idea. The ideal of this patriotism of 'us' is, in short, that moment of unanimity and emulation, the departure of the Athenian expedition against Syracuse, when, Thucydides tells us, 'there was a passion for the enterprise which affected everyone alike' and 'competition among the Athenians themselves, each with regard to his own particular piece of responsibility'. On that day the humblest citizen could feel that he was a *euergetēs*.

Let us take care, though, not to make men out to be greater liars than they are. The ideology of 'us' included also an element of genuine local colour; it was not so much machiavellian as nostalgic. True, by glossing over the social gap, it preserved the city's pride before a rich benefactor. But it also reflected the sentiment that the potential for unanimity was always there in those precariously situated groups, the cities. International politics was sufficiently troubled for every citizen to have had the opportunity to enjoy that feeling of 'us' once in his lifetime, and evocation of that unanimity could not but warm the heart of the *euergetēs*.

For the *euergetēs* is a patriot in his own way, which is that of a notable. Being responsible for his city, he is highly sensitive to national pride. But it is not that patriotism that makes him a *euergetēs*. As a nationalist he wants his city to enjoy greatness, or at least independence (or autonomy if nothing better can be had) – but, for all that, he is not going to provide banquets for his fellow citizens. In intensity, this nationalism is equal to the patriotism of 'us' and to the paternalism of the 'fathers of the people', but it differs in its effects and in the part played in it by the mass of the citizens. The patriotic pride of Hellenistic Athens produced all its effects on the international scene. The old city tried to play the great kingdoms off one against another, and sought, for preference, to find allies who were powerful but distant. Out of nostalgia for its former greatness (its *polypragmosynē*, as Thucydides would say), Athens refused to join the league of cities, its peers and neighbours, among which it would have retained its independence but lost the possibility of setting its personal mark on events. Athens had invented for itself a role on the scale of its potential: it was a centre of culture and, much as others award Nobel Prizes, it distributed around the world pompous decrees which irritated Polybius – so many certificates of good behaviour or Philhellenism. One sees there a certain notion of patriotism.

But when notables offer to their fellow citizens a banquet or a building, a different sort of patriotism is at work. The feeling of 'us' does, certainly, explain the voluntary subscriptions, the *epidoseis* to which thousands of citizens sometimes contributed, to save their homeland or to construct a rampart which would protect them all: but individual *euergesiai* are something different. The *euergetēs* is a 'big man' who would speak of 'my people' rather than of 'us': the mass of the citizens are his family and he loves them no less than he controls them. Let us admit, however, that here, too, there is genuine local colour in the language of the decrees. Magnificence is the historic virtue of the Greek notables, who showed more benevolence towards the mass of their fellow citizens than other notables did. But the fact remains that they were benevolent *as notables*. In order to have the feeling of duty towards everybody, one has to have a lofty idea of oneself and one's mission. Altruism and the tendency to actualize one's role are not separable here, because what the role in question entails is, precisely, altruism: *notabilité oblige*. And, of course, for all that it differs from the patriotism of 'us', this relation between an individual and his community is none the less a variety of patriotism. There are so many!

FUNERARY EUERGETISM

There is a marked contrast with the charitable works of the Christian world, with its huge quantity of legacies to the Church and pious foundations. It is this contrast that should provide the occasion, now that we have discussed civic patronage and before we consider *euergesiai ob honorem*, to analyse a pagan institution which has certain superficial relations with the pious foundations of Christianity, and also other relations with euergetism, namely testamentary foundations, which were very important. We have seen, above, that in Boeotia too many persons for Polybius's liking left some of their goods to drinking clubs which held banquets in memory of them. Was this posthumous patronage, whether civic or not? Was concern about the after-life the main thing? In this extremely delicate matter we must be careful to draw many distinctions.[133]

Let us begin by drawing the ground plan. First, a *euergetēs* might make gifts during his lifetime, and might also bequeath in his will some *largesse* to his city (legacies to a city, whatever their motive, are known to go back a long way).[134] The legacy might be left to a definite person who would do with it as he thought fit; but a testator might also leave a sum to an indefinite person (a group of men and their heirs in perpetuity, or an association) and specify a particular and permanent destination for the sum bequeathed, in which case what we have is a permanent foundation. A *euergetēs* might, of course, set up a foundation during his lifetime, if he found it expedient to use this legal instrument. It is no less evident that not all foundations were in the nature of *euergesiai*: many had a religious purpose and these were the oldest-established. Many others were not set up for the benefit of a city but for that of an association. Euergetistic foundations began to proliferate at the start of the Hellenistic epoch. When a couple of *euergetai* set up a fund the income from which was to be used to establish a musical contest in honour of Dionysus, and entrusted this fund to the city of Corcyra, this pious work was to bring joy to men no less than to the god.[135] From the third century, a century no less warlike than any other, patriotic citizens dedicated to their city, by bequest or in their lifetimes, a capital sum, the income from which was to be used to maintain the ramparts.[136] The same period saw the appearance of foundations of a more 'social' nature. Funds were established or bequeathed so that the club of the junior citizens (*neoi*) might have the oil necessary for cleanliness, according to the ideas of the time, or so that, after their gymnastic exercises, the *neoi* might have a hot bath.[137] But the best-known foundations (though these were no more typical than the others) were the ones established for the upkeep or improvement of schools.[138] For example, a benefactor of Teos left in his will, in fulfilment of a pollicitation, a capital sum which was to provide for the education of boys and girls of free birth and to be 'the finest monument to his love of renown'. The annual income from this investment would pay the salaries of teachers of writing, music and gymnastics. The legal device of the foundation left plenty of room for inventiveness and enabled patrons to make available public services for which no institutional framework existed. The inscriptions tell us what the motives of these benefactors were: patriotism, love of renown and the desire to leave behind a great memorial.[139] One Milesian, creator of another educational foundation which he established in his lifetime by pollicitation, 'decided to do good to the people and leave the best possible lasting memorial of his love of renown'.[140] Under the Empire the title of 'eternal gymnasiarch' or 'eternal agonothete' was to be the reward of liturgists who, in the exercise of their function, established a foundation to guarantee or to improve the performance of their liturgy for all time to come. For example, if a certain Leonidas established, as agonothete, a local games which he would endow with prizes for the victors (*themis*), he was to receive officially the title of eternal agonothete, and the games itself would bear his name, as the 'Leonidian *themis*',[141] and likewise the fund.[142] Thus, a *euergetēs* who wanted to guarantee a certain public service in perpetuity and promote for the future the values he held dear (for the field of our interests is not limited by the length of our lives) succeeded also in perpetuating his own memory, for the city would be grateful for his benefaction and would express its gratitude by perpetual honours. Euergetism would make the *euergetēs* immortal.

Second, however, by a contrary movement, concern about the after-life led, from the beginning of the Hellenistic epoch, to a desire to immortalize one's memory and to funerary *euergesiai*. A mortal wants to ensure some care for his soul in the beyond. In classical Greece his descendants had the duty of rendering to him the cult which is due to the dead, offering sacrifices or libations every year upon his tomb. The fate of the dead depended, in fact, not on their conduct in this world but on the care of them taken by the living.[143] Furthermore, objects were placed with the corpse to accompany him in his life beyond the tomb. The quantity and quality of this funerary furniture varied a great deal, less in accordance with the wealth of the deceased than with periods and regions.[144] To these almost universal customs was added, from the 300s at the latest, a new practice which became widespread among the upper class, namely funerary foundations. A capital sum was set aside, the income from which enabled a sacrifice to be offered annually in the dead man's honour. A dead man could receive sacrifices, because he was heroized or associated with gods – something that was not at all shocking in the Hellenistic period, when the contrast between mortals and immortals became less sharp because the new piety sensed divinity everywhere. Added to the sacrifices was a reception[145] or a banquet[146] for the members of the society to which the fund had been entrusted for the purpose of rendering to the deceased the cult founded by him. This society might have been constituted for the foundation itself, and have consisted of the dead man's family and his future descendants, or else a group of friends chosen by the founder,[147] so that the funerary foundations thus continued the family cult of the dead. But the deceased might also entrust the fund to an already existing group. In the case of the richest men, this would be the city itself, and for others merely a part of the city such as the Council, or the old men's club (*gerousia*).[148] That, at least, was to be the custom in the Imperial epoch. The foundation might also be entrusted to a trade association.[149] A group of shopkeepers or craftsmen might honour the memory of the departed and receive from the founder a sum that would produce income sufficient for them to hold banquets in his memory. If the founder was very rich, he would entrust the management and the profits of his foundation to the city as a whole, and all the citizens would take part in the annual banquet. That became the practice in the Hellenistic epoch. It the second century B C a certain Critolaus established a fund for the benefit of the city of Aegiale,[150] which, to thank him, heroized by decree the son he had lost. The income from this fund made it possible to celebrate his memory every year with all that composed a cult in Greece: a procession, games, a banquet and a sacrifice (we are not told to whom this was offered). Was this a cult of the gods or of the dead? Was it religion or euergetism? For the people of the Hellenistic epoch these two ambiguities did not exist. Another sacrifice, which took place at the opening of the games, was offered to the heroized son before his statue (*agalma*). The banquet was enjoyed by all the citizens, the resident foreigners, other foreigners, the Romans living in the city (this was at the beginning of the later Hellenistic period) and even the women. The prescriptions for the banquet were much more detailed than those for the sacrifice: the regulation specified the dishes to be served and how much was to be spent on them.

Critolaus of Aegiale ensured for his son a perpetual cult in which a great number of people participated. Euergetism here served as means, as subsidy, for a funerary cult. It could also serve to honour the memory of a dead man, even without a cult. Towards the end of the third century the philosopher Lyco, successor of Aristotle and Theophrastus at the head of the Peripatetic sect, allocated in his will, 'for the use of the young men, the oil from the olive-trees belonging to me in Aegina, for the due commemoration – so long as they use it – of myself . . .'[151] What was essential was no longer the cult of the dead, since the foundation aimed only to obtain agents who would perform these rites. What mattered was the memory that the beneficiaries would retain of the dead man and his generosity. In the Imperial epoch many foundations were established to guarantee the provision every year, for a city, its Council or some association, of a banquet and a distribution of money to take place at the founder's tomb or in front of his statue, on the occasion of his birthday.[152] We have already seen cases of patrons whose memories were perpetuated by their establishment of a foundation. Here we see people establishing a foundation for the sole purpose of perpetuating their memory. The two forms of behaviour merged together, and when the fund was entrusted to a city, they merged with euergetism.

ATTITUDES TO DEATH

The origin of funerary foundations and the change of outlook to which they testify become easier to understand if we start from the oldest known foundation established in honour of the gods. Its founder was Nicias, an Athenian politician well known for his piety, and it dated from the Peloponnesian War. While on a mission to Delos, Nicias 'consecrated to [Apollo's] service a tract of land which he bought at the price of 10,000 drachmas, the revenues from which the Delians were to expend in sacrificial banquets, at which many blessings should be invoked upon Nicias from the gods'.[153] This was the starting-point of the funerary foundations. A person no less illustrious, Xenophon, one day consecrated a tract of land to Artemis. The sacrifice was followed by a banquet at Scillus, with 'all the citizens and the men and women of the neighbourhood taking part'.[154]

Nicias belonged to an age when people still believed in the gods as real persons, just as substantial as human beings. Also he had confidence in the efficacy of religious rites – he doubtless felt the traditional cult of the dead to be adequate. And he 'knew himself' in the sense that he was aware of being a mere mortal. He did not claim to be on the same level as the gods, even after death, and was content to ask for prayers to the immortals to grant him their favour in this life. All this changed in the Hellenistic epoch. The dead and the gods were both held to belong to a higher category, the divine, and this was why pious foundations could become funerary as well, and the deceased could be heroized. Did this indicate an advance in scepticism and individualism? The concept of individualism, which we owe to Burckhardt, is not a very exact one, and so we find *some* sort of individualism in every epoch – during the Renaissance, but also in the Middle Ages. We find it in the Hellenistic epoch, but also in the age of wrathful Achilles. An advance in scepticism? This cannot be accepted, either. The transition from the old Greek religion to a more 'modern' type of religiosity did not mean a loss of religious feeling, even if a tinge of scepticism did creep in; after all, the new religiosity made possible the birth of Christianity. This new religiosity no longer trusted in the automatic efficacy of rites, but required that certain sentiments be experienced; the remembering of a dead person by the living, ensured by a foundation, satisfied it better than mere ritualistic gestures. Also, it was less mythological than the old beliefs. A god was no longer an imaginary person like the fictitious beings children believe in, but a force, a protecting power, a semi-abstraction, both more rational and more exalting, for how could the feeling that the divine is present everywhere, in a man or an idea or a god, not be accompanied by fervour? When this almost poetic fervour is joined with lack of trust in rituals, which are no longer any more than the outward sign of the feelings that the worshipper puts behind his gestures, the distinction between worship on the one hand and veneration or homage on the other tends to fade. The dead, the gods, great ideas, mysterious forces, great men, all will be on the same level and will be equally capable of receiving sacrifices and worship, because worship is only the outward expression of fervour. Divine society is overturned, ranks are confused, and the old protocol, which used to mark distinctions between ranks, is now employed somewhat at random, because the worshippers think little of these empty forms and value only the feeling which is expressed by their means. In the beginning the gods were asked to extend their protection to the mortal who established the foundation. When that mortal died, was he not divine, too? So he was heroized and worshipped along with the gods.

But the gods and the dead both need people. If they are no longer substances, if they no longer exist by themselves like mythological beings, they need to be thought about in order that they may exist. The dead want to live in the piety of those who survive them, and ritualistic automatism is no longer enough for them: they must live in people's memories. This was the primary reason for the foundations.

There was another, too, more prosaic, namely, the desire for luxury. We must not forget that a foundation was costly, and guaranteed a sumptuous cult of the dead person. The creator of a foundation could just as well have had a rich tomb built for his corpse, but he preferred to live in the memory of a certain group of people. Besides which, the euergetistic spirit encouraged preference for conspicuous giving rather than conspicuous consumption, patronage rather than egoistic luxury.

Desire to be remembered; conspicuous giving. The reader may be surprised to find a funerary practice being explained by something other than religion alone. Is not our first impulse to relate all of a people's funerary customs to their beliefs about the after-life? However, as Philippe Ariès has said, it would be mistaken to suppose that religion is coextensive with culture. Some attitudes to the after-life vary in accordance with beliefs, but only some. Belief in personal immortality did not stop the Christians wishing also to survive in their descendants. Nor did it rule out another 'vanity', namely, splendid funerals. As well as being a metaphysical event, death was also a social occasion. Under France's *ancien régime*, what happened in the bedroom where a rich farmer awaited his approaching death and took the sacraments was something different from the public aspect of the occasion, his ostentatious funeral. Nevertheless, for all that funerals might be ostentatious, they did not eliminate religious feeling. These were two thematically distinct parts of a total event, of a confused whole within which we have to make the distinctions that will alone enable us to take account of the '*eschatologische Inkonsequenzen*'. Unless we do that, we are in danger, for example, of diagnosing de-Christianization because of a conspicuous luxury which is merely one of several funerary themes (and one in which religion does not figure). If we suppose that religion is present everywhere, we shall end by supposing that it has been banished from everywhere.

To conclude on the subject of funerary foundations. At the beginning of this book I provisionally reduced euergetism to three 'themes': ostentation or patronage, concern about the after-life, and political responsibilities. We have just seen that, in paganism, the second theme is reducible to the first. 'Attitude to death' is a spurious historical subject in which we can distinguish several different concepts that are obviously mixed up together in reality. For example, funeral ceremonies are related to the socialization of death, but also to the metaphysical aspect of death, since they are also a ritualization, usually religious in character, of the transition to the after-life. Now, unlike the pious and charitable foundations of Christianity, which largely derived from religion, the pagan foundations owed little to the meta-physical aspect of death. A pagan did not leave a lot of money in his will because of the fact of death and in order to save his soul. It would be more correct to say that he indulged in such *largesse* in spite of death, projecting into an indefinite future, without thinking of the limits of his own life on earth, the same interests and the same sensibility to public opinion that caused the notables to be *euergetai* in their lifetimes.

EUERGETISM *OB HONOREM*

The third theme, that of political responsibility or euergetism *ob honorem*, to which I now turn, is another matter, and cannot be reduced to ostentation. Euergetism *ob honorem* is a by-product of the essence of politics, and is part of the problem of whether governing can be a trade by which one earns one's living.

Governing can be a duty, a right or a profession. Less easily can it be a trade, for one would not entrust the task of government to persons motivated solely by desire for gain. But governing can certainly be a duty, a task which a democratic group entrusts to one of its members or that the sovereign entrusts to one of his subjects. In this case it is unlikely that euergetism *ob honorem* will make an appearance, since people do not usually pay or leave gratuities in order to perform a task. Governing can be a profession, too, an activity which an indi-vidual chooses freely because he finds it interesting in itself, with the community taking advantage of this disinterested vocation. The professional clearly does not receive a salary in order to perform the activity which he had wanted to perform anyway (at most, he receives an allowance), and it is even expected of him that he should show his disinterestedness by behaving generously or by not claiming what is due to him. Finally, governing can be a right, an absolute right like private property. A dynasty, or an order of nobles or notables, may look on itself as the owner of power, and this right may be acknow-ledged by the governed. This situation is far from rare, and was that of the Hellenistic notables. The governed found it quite proper to be governed by rich and cultivated men of leisure. With the regime of the notables, politics, originally a liberal profession chosen by certain individuals who possessed the means to follow their vocation, became the absolute right of an order.

Euergetism *ob honorem* is a by-product of politics considered as an absolute right – because it can be just as difficult for governing to be a right as to be a trade. Even the people most deferential towards their masters wish to believe that the shepherd is doing his duty to his flock, and every authority must legitimize itself, in words at least. Between the right to reign and the occupational duties of a king there is a gap in which secondary affects bloom and have to be reduced to symbols. Euergetism *ob honorem* plays this symbolic role. It is not payment for the right to perform public functions, but is a sort of gratuity. If governing is an absolute right, power becomes the property, the privilege and the honour of the class or order which wields this power. It is normal for a proprietor to meet the costs of his enterprise, for a privilege to be worth compensation, and for an honour to oblige its holder to offer *largesse*. This is the true content of the muddled idea that *euergesiai* console the people for the loss of their political rights, that they cause (or compensate for) depoliticization, and are the price of public honours.

POLITICS AS PROFESSION AND ENTERPRISE

Demosthenes held the exercise of power to be a liberal profession which he practised because he was personally rich and cultivated, and therefore honourable. If, however, it is understood, once for all, that politics is the business of the notables, their state duty, and power has been finally handed over to them without any prospect of return, the notables as a group become the owners of the government. The city is now their enterprise. They will therefore defray, when necessary, the expenses of their function, just as a businessman finances his own business. The *euergetēs* no longer gives pledges of his disinterestedness: he pays what has to be paid in order that the machine which belongs to him and for which he is responsible may operate.

From individual vocation to state duty and from pledge to expenses of office: the evolution is imperceptible but more or less inevitable. Euergetism exists, nascently at least, in most regimes of notables – in the Morvan of Le Play's time and in the English counties of Taine's. At the outset, public offices are not accompanied by any salary, but neither does the notable pay anything. The public treasury covers the expenses of office, and the notable may even receive some indemnity for the time he can no longer devote to his own affairs. In short, he neither gains nor loses. He will start to lose without even thinking about it. If, when he has become a magistrate, he finds he cannot rely on a well-organized financial department, it will be simpler for him to pay something out of his own pocket in order to cope with the many unexpected petty difficulties that constantly arise. *Noblesse oblige.* Correspondingly, we cannot expect that such a man will distinguish scrupulously between his own finances and those of the state: he may dip into the public coffers just as he dips into his own. Demosthenes paid out of his own pocket for part of the cost of the ramparts of Athens, and also put his hand into the treasure-chests of Harpalus as if they belonged to him. We need only read the orations of Demosthenes and Aeschines in the case of the Crown[155] to see that, once a functionary had behaved as a *euergetēs* while in office, the city no longer troubled to check his accounts. Euergetism goes easily with peculation and corruption. In 169 Archon, *stratēgos* of the Achaean Confederation, did not dare support a decree in honour of the Attalids, lest he seem to be doing it so as to obtain a gratuity from Eumenes, 'having spent a considerable sum of money during his term of office'.[156] Others were certainly less scrupulous. It remains true that the people were spontaneously obedient and trusting in their attitude to the notables, who thereafter could regard the city as an undertaking subject to their control. This change in the social and political outlook was apparent quite early in the case of some favoured individuals, who became presidents or protectors of their cities. We have spoken of Protogenes of Olbia. A similar story is that of Polydamas, the man who, around 375, was the master of Pharsalus, whose acropolis and finances were in his hands

This man was not only held in very high repute throughout all Thessaly, but in his own city was regarded as so honourable a man that, when the Pharsalians fell into factional strife, they put their acropolis in his hands and entrusted to him the duty of receiving the revenues, and of expending, both for religious purposes and for the administration in general, all the sums which were prescribed in their laws. And he did, in fact, use these funds to guard the acropolis and keep it safe for them, and likewise to administer their other affairs, rendering them an account yearly. And whenever there was a deficit, he made it up from his own private purse and whenever there was a surplus of revenue he paid himself back. Besides, he was hospitable and magnificent, after the Thessalian manner.[157]

We deduce that, when necessary, Polydamas would advance money without thought of return, so that he might continue to exercise an authority which had grown dear to him. The regime of the notables, once it is accepted by public opinion and legitimized, is the collective property of an elite who undertake whatever financial sacrifices are required for the good functioning of the city which has become their private enterprise. We see, too, that the notables do not hold power in return for their *euergesiai*: they do not pay to govern but because they govern, and they govern because power has fallen into their hands for the reasons analysed earlier.

POLITICS AS HONORIFIC PRIVILEGE

The primary condition for euergetism was, therefore, this major fact of Hellenistic history: the establishment in the cities of a regime of notables who looked upon public office as their responsibility and, as prisoners of their own system, gave pledges or paid the price for this. For euergetism to develop thoroughly, however, for public office to be considered also as an honour and a privilege, which would oblige its holders to pay still more, a second condition was needed, and that was another major fact of the period, namely the decadence of the cities on the international plane. This meant that public functions in the cities now usually entailed responsibilities at the municipal level only, and became, in the main, just costly marks of social distinction. Besides which, quite apart from the question of decadence on the international plane, most of these functions were of reduced importance, and equivalent to the county administrations in Taine's England. With this difference: in England the notables of the county were appointed by the monarch (except for the coroner, who was elected), whereas the Greek dignitaries were designated by the city itself. They owed their positions to the city which honoured them and were not entrusted with a task handed down from above.

However, if we were to suppose that the dignities of the Greek cities were equivalent to ministries, or to imagine a grave political situation in which the city faced a life-or-death choice, the snobbery of the municipal dignities would no longer be conceivable, nor the euergetism which was, to a large extent, the consequence thereof. One does not become a minister in return for a statue or an enthronement banquet, for the seriousness of the function takes precedence over its decorative aspect. If the Parthians, Pompey, Brutus or Octavius threaten and the fate of the city hangs in the balance, then politics becomes once more a serious matter, attended to by the orators. The time of Demosthenes and his like returns. One does not ask for a gratuity from a saviour. In troubled times, the *euergetēs* helps the city with his advice and his influence no less than with his money (like Theophanes of Mytilene, who obtained the protection of Pompey for his city and persuaded him to restore its autonomy).[158] But all times are not troubled, nor all functions important. The more politics sinks into mediocrity, the more the *euergetēs* becomes a man who does good to the city essentially by opening his purse. The relation between euergetism and the municipal scale of functions becomes clear if we compare the Roman Senate with the dignitaries of the Greek cities. In the municipal towns of the Roman Empire there was, of course, euergetism very similar to that of the Greeks. In Rome itself, though, there was nothing of the *euergetēs* about a senator. The senators did indeed give gifts, but very differently: for example, there was electoral 'corruption'. However, senators, consuls and praetors, heads of a gigantic city, masters of the Italian race, sent out to rule vast territories and wielding an informal hegemony over two other races, the Carthaginians and the Greeks, and over the three parts of the world, cared nothing for honorific dignities and *euergesiai*; they possessed real power and were in command.

Let this be clear. Even if the cities no longer weighed very much in the international scales, or had become no more than autonomous communes, the city remained psychologically the principal framework of life, and that was why euergetism was so important. For the bulk of the population what mattered most was not foreign policy and independence, but the totality of everyday life, autarchy, for which mere autonomy sufficed, and within which *euergesiai* produced their effects, material or moral. For the notables, public functions were what created social superiority: they were not nobles by blood but *politeuomenoi* who marked themselves off from commoners by their participation in local politics. The strongest of their interests as a class (or rather as an order) were thus bound up with the system of the city.

Now the public dignities were, mostly or most often, merely municipal in scale. They were dignities for which any dilettante would do. The profession of politics no longer presupposed talent and a personal vocation. Public functions were the natural consequence of a position of social superiority. They gave distinction to notables who would have been interchangeable among themselves, and that was why they were honours. A function becomes an honour when it is reserved for an elite and when it has no very serious implications. Public functions were tasks – often of a modest nature, no doubt – and not honours, so long as the Greek democracies entrusted them indiscriminately to any of their citizens. One could easily add other conditions to these two. First, the dignity must not be regarded as recognizing personal merit, like membership of the Académie Française. Nor must it be the birthright of a nobility of blood, which has only to take the trouble to be born in order to find this in its cradle as an absolute right. Finally, the authority which confers the honour must not be higher than the new dignitary and his peers: the notables of the English counties about whom Taine writes were *euergetai*, but they were not *euergetai ob honorem*. They were patrons, local benefactors, by virtue of conspicuous social superiority, but they did not have to give a gratuity in return for their appointment. They would not have written what the Greek notables wrote: 'I obtained the position of first magistrate in return for a distribution of money,' or even (an exception that proves the rule, and of which the person concerned boasts as an exceptional honour done to him) 'I was made *stratēgos* for nothing,' that is, the city did me the honour of appointing me free of charge. The conditions for fully developed euergetism are thus many, which is why the phenomenon is rare, even unique, in history.

EUERGETISM AS SYMBOLIC COUNTER-AFFECT

When a function is a somewhat empty dignity, conferred by their peers upon interchangeable persons of privilege who have no personal right to it, it entails payment. This is the origin of euergetism *ob honorem*. It entails payment, in the sense that it engenders psychological side-effects which have to be compensated for symbolically. The function is a privilege and an honour, and so it calls for the giving of a gratuity. The notables are, of course, spontaneously generous, quite apart from any public function. But now something new appears: for public functions, the giving of a gratuity is obligatory. Originally, in Demosthenes' day, euergetism was, if not the price of the profession of politics, at least its consequence; now, euergetism becomes, if not the price, at least the condition of public honours.

THE HONOURS AWARDED TO THE *EUERGETĒS*

Functions and *euergesiai*: these two terms go together and characterize the notables. Few were the notables who failed to express their membership of the upper class by conspicuous patronage, voluntary euergetism. Every notable who exercised public functions, magistracies or liturgies was, on that account, a *euergetēs ob honorem*. To belong to the elite it was not enough to be rich. Public life was what marked the upper class, rather than wealth or birth. A rich man who stayed out of politics would have lived only a diminished life and maintained his rank poorly. This political ideal became inevitable from the moment when the administrative system, even in the kingdoms and empires, became one of local autonomy. Since local government was there for the taking, the upper class would lose prestige if it left this to others and failed to claim a political importance proportionate to its social importance. And we know that the people entrusted authority to the notables – that is, they gave it up for good. Now, since there was no authority without *euergesiai*, the city was divided into two camps – the camp of those who gave and the camp of those who received. From the epitaphs of a Greek city under the Empire we get the impression that the population is divided into two classes, the notables and the rest (or into three classes if we add those who pursue a career in the Emperor's service). The epitaphs of notables are the most numerous (the rest of the population lacking either the money or the self-esteem needed to perpetuate their own memory), and what do they mention? Not the activities of the deceased or his individual characteristics, whatever these may have been, but one thing only: his public functions and his *euergesiai*. Social superiority depended on them, and an epitaph mentions them just as, in other epochs, it would mention titles of nobility.

Functions and *euergesiai*: a third term needs to be added, namely, the public honours of the *euergetēs*, and these we shall now consider, after which the circle will be closed. In exchange for their benefactions, the *euergetai* had conferred on them by decree all manner of distinctions: public eulogies, crowns, statues and so on. The quantity of extant documentation represented by these honours awarded by cities to their *euergetai* and the importance they possessed in the outlook of the time are so considerable that they must certainly be more than they seem. They are evidently a cog in the system, but which cog? They are not confined to the rewarding of deserving individuals and the promotion of a certain rivalry, like the honorific distinctions of our democracies or of classical Greece. They ratify a person's membership of the order of notables and express the superiority of that order. They erect a symbolical class barrier, on the pretext of honouring a *euergetēs*. For their quantity, their flashiness and their role as an ideological barrier we can compare them to the obsession with symbols of nobility under the *ancien régime*, its armorial bearings, gable-ends, weathercocks and privileges. The rich vain man of whom St John Chrysostom speaks and who ruins himself in *euergesiai* so as to be solemnly acclaimed is the equivalent of a squire or an *hidalgo* infatuated with his titles – except that in *his* case it was not enough merely to take the trouble to be born.

THE HYPERTROPHY OF HONOURS

Euergetai in the restricted sense in which we conventionally use the word, those who helped the city with their purses, were the principal recipients of honours. A Greek city under the Empire would honour with a statue (or 'consecrate a statue of') three sorts of person: the reigning Emperor, governors of the province (*hēgoumenoi*), and public benefactors[159] – in other words the notables, or certain notables. Not every notable, to be sure, received public honours. It was not enough, in order to be so distinguished, to have 'filled all the magistracies and all the liturgies' of one's city, according to the stock phrase that under the Empire could be read, in Greek or Latin, in many a notable's epitaph, from Asia to Roman Africa. One had to have done more than that, and, in fact, many did more, in proportion to their personal fortunes and to the importance of their city. It was good form for a notable to perform an act of patronage once in his lifetime, building a public edifice or giving a banquet to the population. He would be honoured for that, because custom did not strictly oblige him to do it. He would also be honoured if, when appointed to a public function, or having volunteered to assume it, he took advantage of this occasion to perform his act of patronage, by paying, *ob honorem*, a gratuity that was larger, or more ingeniously conceived, than prescribed by custom. Voluntary patronage or payment of more than the obligatory gratuity: these were the actions which entitled one to crowns and statues, and it was more and more exclusively on grounds of this sort that the cities decreed them. Honours were not prostituted or devalued, they remained a distinction and an incentive: but many notables deserved them, and only notables cared to deserve them. Consequently, it is of little importance to know (if we could know) what precise proportion of the notables performed acts of patronage. Euergetism was regarded as typical of the upper class, just as in other periods charitable duties were, and that is what matters. We are only too well aware that our thinking about social life is dominated by types and essences, from which we get national, racial or social prejudices.[160] This is wrong of us, no doubt, but none the less it entails very real consequences. If 'the' notable is a *euergetēs* and the recipient of honours, it follows that this must or should be true of every notable, and that honours reward those who deserve them for a generosity which is typical of their class. *Euergesiai* and honours become the stuff of an ideology, a belief which results in a type of behaviour. By decreeing statues or crowns, the city, that is, the body of notables, on the pretext of honouring one of its members, reminds the rest that *largesse* is a state duty, to be performed for the better reputation of the whole body. When they acclaim a *euergetēs*, the people encourage and even constrain the other notables to follow his example. When they honour patrons, the notables make known to the people merits which are those of their order as a whole, and proclaim that this order is essentially honourable. Honours show to everyone just what the established order is.

Since both camps have an interest in this system of bowing and scraping, there is plenty of scope for ingenious developments in it. The raising of a statue becomes the pretext for polite exchanges and renewed *euergesiai*. There are a thousand possible nuances to the wording of the decree which awards the statue. The city may decide, in so many words, that the statue is to be set up 'in the busiest part of the town', or may even allow the *euergetēs* himself to choose where it is to stand: he may set it up 'wherever he likes'.[161] All the same, a statue is expensive. The right sort of *euergetēs* will relieve the public finances by taking upon himself the cost of his own statue. Or resting content with the honour constituted by the piece of parchment which the law awards him, he will restrict himself to having the text of the decree engraved on marble, excusing the people from actually erecting the statue.[162] If the statue is erected, the day of its inauguration will be marked by a public festival, paid for once again by the *euergetēs*.[163] New honours are invented, which lend colour to the life of the time, or illuminate its social reality. When he arrives in the town, the public benefactor may be officially received by the entire local population, who hail him, so that the occasion resembles the solemn entry of a monarch.[164] The people invent fresh ways of acclaiming their benefactors or those from whom they want to extract benefits:[165] 'Foster-father!', meaning that the person greeted has nourished the population (or ought to nourish it); 'Ocean!', meaning that he is, or ought to be, an inexhaustible ocean of benefits (others would say 'River!'). These popular cries may be reproduced in the honorific decrees, which will assign to the *euergetēs* the official title of foster-father, founder (or refounder), patriot, beautifier of the city, first person of the city, or even father, mother, son or daughter thereof (depending on the age and sex of the *euergetēs*). The adoption of these terms shows how the affective vocabulary of the family rubs off on to the civic vocabulary in and after the later Hellenistic period.[166]

The qualification of notable, as has been mentioned, was not hereditary in law. The idea was rather to contrive to fill the Council with men who were rich and capable of performing the liturgies, even if they were of humble origin and engaged in trade. However, through inheritance, notable status did usually become *de facto* hereditary, and later antiquity was to invent the title of *patroboulos*,[167] meaning a man whose father had been a member of the Council before him. It was not out of the ordinary for a father to pay from his own pocket for the *euergesiai* of his still adolescent son, thereby opening for him the door to a career. From the early Hellenistic epoch onward, numerous honorific decrees tell us that a *euergetēs* has followed in his father's footsteps and shown the city the same benevolence. In this way there began to appear the type of honorific decree known as 'consolatory'.[168] If a family of notables lost a child, the decree lavished expressions of condolence on them, for the loss of an offspring who had already given the city cause to place great hopes in him.

In the Roman epoch the institutions of the cities were increasingly built around the question of money, or, rather, of euergetism. Democracy disappeared, as has been said, not because the notables despoiled the people of it, but because the problem was no longer to choose the man who would govern the city, and who, notables or people, would choose him, but, rather, to find even one man who could be persuaded to sacrifice himself to this ruinous task. It did happen, nevertheless, that the *vox populi* was still sought – to secure acclamation by the entire people of a decree in honour of a public benefactor. By the late Hellenistic epoch, in the second century B C, it was mainly at the end of honorific decrees that were recorded the number of popular votes cast in favour of the honours awarded.[169] Soon there was no more voting except by acclamation, and the civic assembly became merely a popular audience whose presence increased the glamour of the ceremony. A decree of one of the cities of Euboea, in the third century A D, provides a very vivid example of this. It was the time when the Greek lands were under threat of invasion by the Goths. On one occasion the Heruli succeeded in penetrating as far as Athens and Sparta. To defend themselves the cities had to rely first and foremost on their own resources. At Chalcis in Euboea the city's priest for life had the sanctuary of its goddess surrounded by a rampart, and added thereto some buildings intended for embellishment and piety. In exchange for this he asked to be given the title of 'eternal priest' and to be allowed to pass on his priestly function to his descendants, like a title of nobility. This request was granted, and, to enhance and confirm this concession, the Council and the people each voted for it separately, in the following manner. One of the leading councillors, Pamphilos, presented the proposal to make the priesthood hereditary in the *euergetēs*' family. 'The other councillors cried: "Up with Pamphilos's proposal! Let it be so!"' The secretary then put the proposal to the vote, suggesting that unanimity would be desirable: '"All those in favour of this honour passing also to the honorand's descendants, according to the will of you all and in conformity with the proposal our colleague Pamphilos, raise your hands." The councillors cried: "Adopted!"' The next scene took place before the people. The chief magistrate said to them: '" You would do well to reward those who have deserved it, and let the honours granted pass to their children instead of remaining with them alone. Only thus can we induce others to do great things for us. The Council has already been quick to vote in favour of the proposal. If you too are for it, raise your hands. And the people cried: "Adopted!" Long live these priests!"' [170]

But it might be that, of all these honours, the one that was closest to the heart of the *euergetēs* was not so much the honour itself as the engraving of the decree which awarded it and which posterity would be able to read. When, nowadays, we walk among the ruins of an ancient city, or in the modern town which occupies its site, we see, still in place or else reused in modern walls, some pedestals, steles, epitaphs or architraves on which we can read engraved the names of *euergetai* of ancient times, and we are struck by the recurrence of the same names. At Perge, in the south of Asia Minor, we see everywhere the name of the Plancii, and at Saepinum, in the Abruzzi, that of the Neratii. The effect must have been even greater upon the passer-by in antiquity. Our documentation is not misleading: inscriptions held a place in the mind of that time as important as they hold in our collections of documents. A great family owed it to itself to have its name inscribed all over the city, and if a decree in its honour was set up in a public place or on the family tomb, it was certain to be read. Indeed, for the people of antiquity an inscription possessed a dignity equal to that of a book. Inscription (*epigraphē*) and book were two modes of publication of like value. What were engraved were not 'documents', if by that word we mean the equivalent of our posters or our bureaucratic paperwork, but monuments intended to be read by posterity.[171] And there was no shortage of readers. When a Greek or a Roman wanted to read a little, he could either go to a library or walk around a sanctuary or a public square, or along a road whose shoulders served as a cemetery, where he could read the votive offerings, the decrees, the pedestals of statues or the epitaphs.[172] How was a great lord like Petronius able to get to know the way of life of lesser people, which he describes with clear-sighted condescension? The *Satyricon* gives us the answer: by frequenting low company, yes, but also by reading these people's inscriptions, just as we read them today.

It was thus no less honorific to enable people to read that a benefactor had been crowned than it was to crown him. There could be two ways of honouring someone – by awarding him a crown or a statue, and by simply saying to him: 'I honour you.' Among the honorific decrees, some, for example, award a statue with an honorific inscription on its pedestal, while others provide, in addition, for a copy of the decree to be transcribed on a stele and set up in a public place. It is this copy that we read today. It might also happen that the person honoured had the decree engraved himself. What epigraphists call, for short, the Greek (or Roman) 'decrees' are thus in reality copies, more or less abridged (the original, written on perishable material, being kept in the city archives). It was not a matter of course for a decree to be engraved, and we need always to consider why it *was* engraved, for the answer is always significant. Nine times out of ten, the decree is honorific and the engraving of it constitutes an extra honour. If it was engraved as a result of an official decision, the decree will be seen on a stele set up, for example, in the agora, the gymnasium or a sanctuary. If the person concerned had it engraved by his private decision, the decree will be seen, for example, on his tomb. The official engraving is a 'witness' (*martyria, testimonium*) to the merits of the *euergetēs* and to public gratitude.[173] In the later Hellenistic period there was even a type of decree in which the honouring consisted merely of the statement 'I honour you' and a list of the person's merits, without any particular marks of honour being awarded: these certificates were called testimonial decrees.[174] When a city honoured an international athlete or some foreign judges, it sent to the home city of the athlete or the judges the text of the honours awarded, so as thereby to acknowledge their merits and make them known. Cities were not the only authorities to award certificates. The governor of a province, or even the Emperor himself, might testify by means of a letter to the merits of a man he thought well of. Under the Empire great *euergetai* like Opramoas, of whom I shall have more to say, were to cover their monuments with entire epigraphic portfolios consisting of all the honorific decrees and letters they had been awarded during their lives as patrons. A tomb offering so much reading matter would indeed be worth a funerary foundation.

By honouring one of their number or honouring themselves, the notables who issued these decrees honoured their order as such. The Athenian democracy considered that the public proclamation of the award of crowns was an instrument of education: 'For the whole vast audience is stimulated to the service of the commonwealth.'[175]

Did these occasions have educational value? Let us say, rather, that it was a case of moral constraint, brought to bear by the order of notables upon the individuals composing that order. The honorific decrees always end with what epigraphists call the exhortatory formula: the city, says the text, has honoured its *euergetai* in this way in order to show that it is not ungrateful and that it knows how to pay homage to good citizens, in order that these citizens may find many imitators, in order to exhort everyone to do as they did and to bring them to even greater devotion in the future.[176] In appearance, what could be more civic than this style? The city does not humbly thank a powerful benefactor but acts as though superior to every citizen, even if he be a notable and a *euergetēs*. The city expects that every citizen will do his best and it honours the good citizens just as it punishes the bad; it keeps the upper hand, unquestionably – in the sense that the notables who rule over it exert pressure on one another, in the interest of their order as a whole. To find a more deferential style we have to read the decrees by which the cities honour not one of their citizens but the Imperial authorities. So long as a notable is the one involved, even though he be the richest of all, the other notables treat him as their peer, and civic appearances are thus respected.

THE REAL REASON FOR THE PROLIFERATION OF HONOURS

At the end of this long survey, let us not fail to see the wood for the trees. Were the honours what made a notable honourable, or was it the dignity of a notable that constituted the real worth of the honours? Taken one by one, the various honours seem to have played the role of honorific distinctions anywhere: in classical Greece, in Rome, or even among ourselves today. If, however, we consider the mass effect, this analogy fails and an original historical fact appears. The proliferation of honours could not serve to designate the meritorious citizens, but distinguished an order as such, like titles of nobility. Even today, the star worn by an ambassador is not there to distinguish the individual so that we may honour him; it is there to pay tribute to the dignity of the diplomatic corps and it is this corps that supplies the value of the honour.

We need only read the inscriptions of a Greek city under the Empire to see that functions, *euergesiai* and honours overlapped each other and marked off two camps among the citizens – those who had them and those who did not. If these too numerous honours had not distinguished a class which was honourable in itself, they would soon have lost their value through inflation and become no more than courtesy titles or formulas of politeness. Too many people held them; but all these people belonged to a respected order which, by awarding these distinctions to itself, merely expressed before everyone its acknowledged superiority. Conversely, the honours became so numerous and so nuanced because they had become a class distinction.

So this distinction existed, in spite of appearances of universalism, and this is why the honours awarded to *euergetai* are not a mere epigraphic curiosity but one of the major political facts of the Hellenistic and Roman epoch. Marks of honour which were in theory civic, conferred in order to reward individuals, made possible the surreptitious introduction of a distinction of prestige which set the order of notables apart from the mass of citizens. The notables' privilege of being at the head of the city, although accepted by public opinion, remained *de facto* and was not usually sanctioned by public law. It did not contradict the equality of the citizens before the law (membership of the order of decurions became hereditary *de facto* but never *de jure*). Moreover, civic egalitarianism forbade one to boast of this *de facto* superiority in the way in which, in other periods, persons were to boast of the better birth which raised them above the common herd. The honours awarded to *euergetai* made it possible to circumvent the difficulty, to create an inequality of prestige and to satisfy the need human groups feel to express their superiority, even if only through symbols. The irrational and symbolic nature of this superiority (an order and marks of honour) admittedly signifies a departure from the habitual rationalism of ancient politics; it is not in antiquity that we are used to seeing so much importance attached to the arbitrary and the palpable, to privileges and their symbols. Notability was a sort of non-hereditary nobility, and the honours awarded to *euergetai* were titles of nobility which had to be re-earned in every generation. The scion of a family of notables knew that he would fail somewhat in his dignity if he did not cause himself to be awarded one of the public honours appropriate to his peers, and he did what was necessary to that end: performed an action of voluntary patronage, or gave a gratuity *ob honorem* that was bigger than customary.

5. The system in detail

Most of the facts which I shall now describe in some detail belong to the Imperial epoch, which is unquestionably the golden age of euergetism. The economic apogee of the Greek East was attained under the early Empire.

Three kinds of *euergesiai* can be distinguished. First, popular demand obtained fom the rich the *largesses* which every plebeian could easily agree to accept — banquets, entertainments, pleasures of all kinds. Secondly, the rulers of the cities were led, in order to operate the machinery of government, to take public expenditure upon themselves, whether this expenditure was destined to procure pleasures for the people or to serve more utilitarian purposes. It followed that every public function tended to become a liturgy: the rulers paid in order to rule. Soon, the function was no more than a pretext for making the rulers pay: the rulers ruled in order to pay. Finally the situation was reached where the rich ruled the city and these same rich were willing patrons. In order to be politicians or public figures they looked upon their whole life as a liturgy and sacrificed part of their fortune so as to leave a memorial of their role. The consequence was that, soon, it became no less impossible to distinguish voluntary euergetism from euergetism *ob honorem* than it was to distinguish magistracies from liturgies. Ruling and giving were one and the same.

FROM THE EXPENSES OF OFFICE TO THE PRICE OF HONOUR

The point of departure for this development was the fact that, from the early Hellenistic period, the magistrates performed the duties of their offices at their own expense, *ex idiōn dapanēmatōn*, according to the formula which appears in innumerable inscriptions.[177]

A liberality of the same sort was the practice followed by many ambassadors of willingly renouncing their travel allowances,[178] and by many voluntary officials (for example, the Council's secretaries) of refraining from collecting their salaries.[179] To understand the way these *euergesiai* worked we need to know what the budgetary system of the

Greek cities was.[180] Each magistrate received a defined sum with which to carry out his functions, just like a minister in France today. (The difference is that the authorization of expenses, or of a maximum figure for expenses, is now voted annually, whereas among the Greeks it was fixed by a law which remained in force, apart from modifications introduced by decree.) For example, the funds which a gymnasiarch was authorized to spend, and which were called *gymnasiarchika chrē-mata*,[181] might amount in a given city to 15,000 *denarii* (about 1,200 sovereigns of Dickens's time).[182] The amount having thus been fixed, it was tempting for the magistrate to leave it untouched: the maximum expenditure having been laid down, it was tempting to exceed it at his own charge.[183] Here we see a gymnasiarch who 'distributed oil to his most worthy home city, at his own charge, without drawing on the funds provided by the Treasury and which amounted to 15,000 *denarii*'. The father of this gymnasiarch had, in his time, been granted the same authorization for expenditure and had shown the same generosity. He had 'given back to the city the money it had paid out, as was customary, to the gymnasiarch, namely 15,000 *denarii*'.[184] It should be added that when a public task was entrusted to a curator, the latter often had to advance the money for his expenses and then be reimbursed by the city, if his accounts were approved by it – and if he insisted.

The inscriptions I have quoted date from the Empire. In that period the performance of public functions 'at one's own expense' was tending to be made the rule and was in any case the ideal.[185] This was the culmination of a process whose beginning in Demosthenes' time I have described. Very soon the cities had become used to expecting the rich to advance the money for some public expenditure, this advance to be reimbursed to them when the city was able to do so, or else deducted from their tax obligations.[186] The cities were often short of money. This was due, to some slight extent, to their poor budgetary technique. The absence of a unified budget and the multiplication of special budgets meant that the cities had no overall view of their revenues and led them to live from one day to the next. The assignment of a particular receipt to a particular expenditure meant that a city found itself in difficulty when the expected receipt failed to materialize. Finally, the extraordinary budget was a huge stumbling-block. When an unexpected necessity arose, the Treasury was empty, and then the only recourse was to appeal to the rich, who were also the magistrates.[187] Even more important, though, than lack of organization or of receipts, was excessive expenditure: the cities regarded it as normal to live at the expense of their magistrates.

Since it was understood that a good magistrate paid the charges of his office or, as people said, of his 'honour', it could happen that the city might ask him to devote to a more urgent need, or to a greater public pleasure, the sum which he had in any case invested in his magistracy. Did the city need to send an ambassador to Rome? The *stratēgos* would make the journey at his own expense, for the honour of his function.[188] Did the city need, or desire, some building? A sebastophant[189] 'presents to the city the money constituting the funds of the sebastophancy, for the construction of a building, instead of using it for the purchase of oil, as all his predecessors had done'.[190] It was in this roundabout way that the idea gradually took root that every magistrate ought to give the city something – this something no longer being connected with his office, but amounting to a sort of gratuity. Every year, the cities decided what gifts they would arrange to be given by the persons they honoured with a public office. To different offices corresponded different *euergesiai*. The only rule was that no office was to be held free of charge. Men no longer carried out a duty, even at their own expense; instead, they bought an honour, or found themselves forced by the city to buy it.[191]

This change was accompanied by a quantitative evolution. The city required the successors of a magistrate to continue his *euergesiai*, while the successors, for their part, tried to do no less than their predecessors, or even to do more. The decrees often tell us that a *euergetēs* behaved generously because he did not want to be outdone by anyone in this respect, because he wanted to emulate his ancestors, or because he wanted to raise liberality to its highest pitch.[192] Sometimes they say even more. A certain gymnasiarch undertook, 'at his own cost, considerable provision and expense, desiring to contribute no less than his predecessors'.[193] The agonistic style in which inscriptions speak of record-breakers in athletic contests is also used of *euergetai*.[194] Of both it is said that they were 'the first and the very first', either to pay for the heating of a portico or to win some brilliant victory at Olympia. The taste for giving and the taste for outbidding converged to produce showers of *largesse*, according to this regular pattern: the *euergetēs* assumed an honour in return for a promise of liberality he had made; he did more than he had promised, and consequently received from the city the honour of a statue; he took upon himself the cost of erecting the statue and gave a public banquet to celebrate its dedication.[195] This pattern was to be reproduced quite unchanged in Roman euergetism, in which, indeed, almost all the features of Greek euergetism were to reappear.

Two facts emerge from all this: it is impossible from that time onwards to distinguish between magistracies and liturgies, and pointless to distinguish between voluntary euergetism and euergetism *ob honorem*.

From then on, every public function implied a *euergesia*, performed or promised. The *stratēgoi* helped the city when it was in financial difficulties. The priests and the crown-wearers offered banquets to the people. The agonothetes set up at their own expense statues to victorious athletes.[196] The gymnasiarchs distributed the oil needed for the baths to the users of the gymnasium or to all who went to the baths – unless, instead, given the splendour of their office, they erected a public building. The *agoranomoi* sold corn cheap to the people, decorated the market or repaired the public buildings. Even the archons or the *dēmiourgoi* did not enjoy their offices for nothing, any more than the *stratēgoi*; the inscriptions praise them for having performed their duties not just 'scrupulously' (*hosiōs*), 'irreproachably' or 'with kindness', but also 'generously', 'with munificence' (*philotimōs*), 'brilliantly', all adverbs which make us think of the gleam of gold. At the very least, they performed their duties at their own expense. Finally, under Roman influence, entry into the Council itself, the title of councillor, came to be regarded as an honour, and consequently had to be paid for. With these conditions it is no longer possible to distinguish between magistracies and liturgies.[197]

What had become of the system of classical Athens, where magistracies were free and liturgies were payments imposed on rich private individuals? Henceforth, magistracies entailed money payments (this applied even to magistracies of command, like the *stratēgia*, the archonship and the *prytaneia*), while the old liturgies always included an element of direct activity: an agonothete organized the athletic contest which he partly financed, and a gymnasiarch directed the education of the adolescent citizens. Consequently, magistracies and liturgies became indistinguishable. Historians are uncertain whether a gymnasiarch of the Hellenistic period should be described as a magistrate or a liturgist, nor did the Greeks themselves know.[198] They sometimes called him a magistrate, but, contrariwise, authentic magistracies were often called liturgies.[199] The two words tend to become synonyms, since the ruling class is the same as the possessing class. The

Hellenistic liturgies, the office of gymnasiarch and agonothete, became stages in every political career, alongside the old magistracies. The same men, the notables, filled both sets of positions.

This was the real nature of the evolution that took place. It is sometimes claimed that the liturgies disappeared at the beginning of the Hellenistic period, when Demetrius of Phaleron abolished them in Athens. That is not the case. In the Hellenistic and Roman epochs liturgies existed, in Athens and everywhere else.[200] Demetrius abolished the trierarchy – unless that liturgy disappeared of its own accord, along with the political power of Athens – and he reorganized the theatrical contests, financing them out of public funds and arranging for them to be organized by a commissioner, the agonothete: but the latter made it a point of honour to add something from his own pocket to the public credits.[201] Thus, when hardly in its grave, liturgy revived. In fact, in the Hellenistic epoch all official personages, magistrates or commissioners, were liturgists.

Then began the great turnaround in which the fate of the ancient city was at stake. Public functions were no longer regarded as much more than a pretext to make the rich pay. It became more important to attract patrons willing to take on these jobs than to appoint persons possessing some administrative talent. The consequence was a deterioration in public life.[202] Priesthoods and crowns, lamented a Roman governor, were 'sold as though at auction, and sold to anyone at all: they no longer choose the persons most worthy to wear the crowns of these functions properly, but are concerned only to sell these crowns as dear as possible'.[203]

This selling of public functions entered so thoroughly into the way of life that the inscriptions mention it in formulas so condensed that they are sometimes hard to interpret. Such-and-such a notable, they tell us, was eponymous archon 'upon distribution', or on the contrary he decorated a building 'for nothing', that is, through a voluntary *euergesia* performed when he was not occupying a public function.[204] The public functions were regarded from the standpoint of their cost. Those persons were praised who were magnificent enough to assume these functions in a period when the expenses entailed were higher than usual, because of a stay in the city by the Emperor, or the passage of troops, or the presence of the governor, his entourage and the pleaders during the assizes.[205] Some offices were so ruinous that they ceased to be performed by one person for a whole year: they were divided into half-yearly or monthly offices.[206] The financial aspect of things henceforth dominated public law, to the extent that sometimes magistracies were assumed by gods, women, children, dead persons and sovereigns. For lack of candidates, the city sometimes persuaded the priests of a temple to meet the cost of *euergesiai* out of the god's treasury, and this god was then appointed magistrate. Children became magistrates when their father paid what was required, so as to prepare a brilliant political career for them. The parents of a young man who had died caused him to be appointed to a public function so that his name might be inscribed for ever in the city's annals.[207] Finally, the Hellenistic kings and the Roman Emperors sometimes assumed the supreme magistracy of a city, heaping their favour upon it on this occasion.[208] Nevertheless, it was not always possible to find a patron and the magistracies were sometimes left unoccupied. One had then to resign oneself to a year of 'anarchy'.[209]

New honours were created so that they might be sold. The Greeks dated the years by the names of particular magistrates, and it was highly honorific to assume such an eponymous magistracy. In the Hellenistic period this eponymy was usually conferred on the priest of some great local god, who wore his god's crown as symbol of his eponymy (hence the title of 'crown-wearer', *stephanēphoros*). In return, he had to offer banquets to the people, or to show himself magnificent in some other way. Crown-wearing was thus a liturgy imposed upon the vanity of the rich.[210]

'INDUCING' TO PAY

Public functions became commodities which were sold by a process of haggling[211] in which the buyers were not always very anxious to buy and it was often necessary to bring gentle pressure to bear in order to 'induce' them to pay. 'Induce', *protrepein*, that is indeed the right word.[212] Euergetism was not a right the city had in relation to the rich, but a moral duty the rich had in relation to the city. The city could not force the rich to pay, but the rich could not flatly refuse to do their duty: they needed to find pretexts. The rest followed automatically. It did not matter if the pretexts were false, if the city knew it, and if the rich man knew the city knew it. What mattered was to navigate between two shoals: neither refusing brusquely, nor lying shamelessly. The opponent's strategy would therefore be to drive the rich man into a position where he had either to lie shamelessly or accept the liturgy. Every sort of haggling was allowed. The rich man had to refrain from putting up an absolute defence of his right not to be a magistrate, because such dry legalism would have been discourteous to his fellow citizens. He had to sacrifice part of his right, meet his opponent half-way, so as to keep everyone happy and make it easier to reach agreement. Nobody could argue against public opinion. Even if one had right wholly on one's side, one owed it to a neighbour to sacrifice to him a part of that right.

A chance bringing-together of documents provides me with a specimen of this art of exhortation, composed entirely of adroit hints. When a magistrate or a liturgist had to be appointed, the choice, in the Imperial epoch, was limited to members of the municipal Council, and it was this same Council that took the decision. Now this Council was also responsible for the tax which the property-owners of the city paid to the state. In other words, all the councillors had a very precise idea of the fortune possessed by each of them. Besides which, these cities were often no more than big villages, where everybody knew everybody else. The Council knew very well who were the richest men, who ought to be the first to sacrifice themselves, but decency forbade telling them so to their faces. Instead, one alluded to the prosperity being enjoyed by the Empire, under the rule of the good Emperor now on the throne. This reference to the general prosperity was a delicate allusion to the particular prosperity of the person addressed. Was it a matter of getting a rich man to distribute oil for the baths? The happiness everyone was enjoying under Trajan would be recalled. Was it necessary to name an *exēgētēs*? Pointed allusion would be made to the prosperity of the current reign. The rich man could, of course, offer a reply that would not involve lying too shamelessly: 'Despite my seeming fortune, I am poor, and if you oblige me to give *largesses*, I shall risk sinking to the level of a tramp.'[213] In contrast to these unwilling *euergetai*, those who came forward as candidates 'voluntarily' and 'spontaneously' had praise heaped upon them.[214] And, for their part, these model candidates did not fail to boast of their spontaneity in the epitaphs in which they surveyed their political careers, or in the inscriptions engraved on the pedestals of the statues given them as honours by the city, which dictated or authorized their wording.

When a rich man had at last allowed himself to be persuaded to assume a public function, the game was not yet over, for the *euergesiai* obtained from him existed, to start with, only in the form of promises, pollicitations. The victim had no ready money, or the promised *largesse* would take the form of a banquet to be held some time in the future, or perhaps what had been promised was a building, which could not be constructed in a day. Most *euergesiai ob honorem* appear as pollicitations haggled for and obtained by the city on the actual day of nomination. Consequently some dignitaries, such as the priests of Zeus Panamaros, were described, in a significantly laconic expression, as 'priests upon pollicitation'.[215] It remained to be seen if the pollicitator would keep his promise and not put off its performance indefinitely. As a sanction could hardly be applied *de facto*, and none was provided for in law,[216] no period was laid down within which promises had to be fulfilled. The only guarantee the city had was the official declaration that the *euergetēs* made, embodying his pollicitation to the city, which went into the city's archives. At Priene a pollicitator 'gave his promise, on the nomination day, and in writing'. Elsewhere the creator of a foundation 'made it known by this present letter, so that his promise might not be unwitnessed or without written proof'.[217] Nevertheless, it happened all too often that a father's pollicitation came to be honoured only by his son or his heirs.[218] It was some achievement if the *euergetēs* performed his promise during the actual year of his public function.[219] Particular fervour went into the celebration of a benefactor who performed what he had promised, there and then,[220] that is, one whose *euergesia* ceased to be just a pollicitation.

'Inducing' a rich man to pay, and getting him to pay on the spot, those were the two problems. We can see them set forth in a document which leaves nothing unclear. The scene is at Hermupolis, in Egypt, in AD 192. In the presence of the *stratēgos*, who was the head of the whole nome, the local population gathered in an assembly (for the towns of Egypt had no councils at that time) and prepared to appoint a *cosmētēs* to take charge of the gymnasium and the ephebi.[221] 'The townspeople who were there cried: "Crown Achilles as *cosmētēs*! Do as your father did, that munificent and venerable old man!" But Achilles said: "To satisfy the demands of my home town I accept the dignity of crown-wearing *exēgētēs* at the price of an annual contribution of two talents, and on condition that I be released from responsibility for the leased-out public land." '[222] In order to understand the preference he expressed, one needs to know that it was more distinguished to be *exēgētēs* than to be *cosmētēs* and less expensive, too, so that there was no shortage of candidates for the office of *exēgētēs*. But Achilles' manoeuvre was doomed to fail. 'Then Olympiodorus spoke: "The Fortune of our master the Emperor enables us all to assume magistracies and develop the wealth of our city. How could this not be when

Larcius Memor is a prefect of Egypt who delights his subjects? Well, then, since Achilles wants to be crowned *exēgētēs* let him be crowned, but on condition that he pays the dues of entry into office here and now.[223] Otherwise, he will, by his refusal, have appointed himself *cosmētēs*, which fate he sees as a threat!"' The counter-manoeuvre is plain: rejection of a mere pollicitation and insistence on payment on the spot. Achilles could only reply: 'I accepted the office of *exēgētēs* for two talents, but I cannot accept the office of *cosmētēs*.' A confused discussion followed. One of those present complained that Achilles had struck him. Others tried to cite an Imperial edict. At last a former *cosmētēs* took it upon himself to crown Achilles as *cosmētēs*, on his own responsibility. He would be the one who paid if Achilles should refuse. Doubtless he possessed the means to force Achilles to pay. We understand the bad temper displayed by those present: if Achilles had not taken on the office of *cosmētēs* one of *them* would have had to do it.

We see how pressure was brought to bear on the notables in order to extract liberalities from them. It was the notables who, among themselves, each tried to put the burden on somebody else, or to prevent him from rejecting it. The same embarrassed confrontation now took place among the notables which had been so painful when it occurred between the grandees and the people. This embarrassment took many forms, depending on the occasion: shame at not sacrificing oneself when one's peers were sacrificing themselves; shame at forcing an equal to sacrifice himself in one's place; desire to obtain the respect of one's peers (for the satisfaction of being respected, the desire to be recognized, counted for as much as the satisfactions of power, money or social superiority); the duty to be modest, not to set oneself above one's peers, not to lie shamelessly to them, not to repudiate what they regarded as true and good, not to isolate oneself; the complaisance that impelled one to do spontaneously whatever they might ask, and unwillingness to wound the feelings of others even when one did not share those feelings; finally, the precise fear of vague sanctions and the vague fear of precise sanctions which the future might have in store.

THE 'LEGITIMATE SUM'

But since the wrangling was so vigorous, would it not have been more convenient to bring in a rule, to make the arrangement more systematic; that is, on the one hand to establish a roster of duties, and on the other to fix the rates for *euergesiai ob honorem* (as the Romans

were to do)? To all appearances that is just what happened. Gratuities
ob honorem were fixed at a figure decided once for all. These obligatory,
fixed-rate *euergesiai* corresponded to what the Romans, in their own
system of *euergesiai*, called the 'honorary sum' which every newly
appointed dignitary paid to the city, to thank it for the honour
conferred on him, or the 'legitimate sum', because the law laid down
the obligation to pay it and determined the amount (which it was not
forbidden to exceed, of course, if one had the true spirit of a patron).

There were thus, to all appearances, two types of payment *ob
honorem*, both in the Greek world and in the Roman West. There was
the legitimate sum, of which the documents hardly speak, and the
voluntary additions to that sum, which alone called for public honours
to be rendered to the new dignitary, so that only these exceptional
extra payments are known to us, whereas the rule itself is barely
recorded. Yet it seems that this rule did exist and that it became
widespread from the first century AD, partly through the action of the
Roman authorities, wishful to codify the custom for reasons of good
administration. In Latin this determination of the rate for the gratuity
was called *taxatio*, 'fixing', and in Greek it was *timēma*, 'estimation'.[224]
What was it that was thus fixed or estimated at a definite price laid
down once for all? The gratuities *ob honorem*, which had until then
been left at the discretion of each new dignitary, when they had not
been a matter for haggling over by the Council and the interested
party. Two things now happened. Once the gratuity had been fixed,
it lay outside the realm of euergetism. In their epitaphs, the notables
do not deign even to mention that they paid it, just as, in the Roman
West, the legitimate sum is hardly ever mentioned, except when it is
exceeded. Moreover, in conformity with the logic of euergetism, a
gratuity would not be required from magistrates and priests alone.
The obligation would be extended to ordinary councillors, and in
order to become a member of the city Council, that is, in order to
qualify as a notable, one would have to pay the legitimate sum. Finally,
hardly had euergetism been expelled through the door than it came
back through the window. Once fixed, the honorary sum was often
exceeded by generous notables, so true is it that spontaneity and
constraint always coexisted happily in the hearts of *euergetai*. The
legitimate sum came to signify little more than a legal minimum.

How was this minimum determined? Did it represent, as has been
supposed, the amount of the public expenses connected with the
various functions, which, as we know, the dignitaries often took

upon themselves? I do not think so. Paying the expenses of a function was only a stage, and a stage now left behind in the development of euergetism. A new principle was born. Every honorific privilege called for the payment of a gratuity. The legitimate sum was therefore not proportioned to the expenses of the function, but to the glory attached thereto. In a decree of Istros a mere priestess of Cybele is praised for having made *largesses* greater than had been expected of her and which were equivalent to the generous gifts made 'in respect of great honours'.[225] Being also regarded as an honour, the position of councillor was made subject to the payment of a legitimate sum, even though this position entailed no public expenses at all. One paid for the honour of being a notable.

Unfortunately the documents, which are usually honorific in nature, rarely deign to mention these payments. When they do mention the payment of a sum to the city, this is *not* the legitimate sum. For the same function, the sum mentioned is different as between one dignitary and another, and it is not usually a round figure, as it would certainly have been if the amount had been fixed once for all by legislation.[226] In practice, for magistracies, the amount of the legitimate sum is known to us only where small towns are concerned. This was a *euergesia* only in the eyes of villagers. In the valley of the Cayster, in Lydia, in the third century AD, it cost a thousand sesterces to become first magistrate of a village.[227]

What is abundantly clear is that the Roman authorities favoured the fixing of rates for the gratuities *ob honorem*. There is a papyrus which enables us to imagine, by analogy, their motives and procedures.[228] Towards the end of Trajan's reign, the archons of Hermupolis, following an order from the prefect of Egypt, told the *epistratēgos* what economies they would be able to effect in the expenses of the gymnasiarchy. Thanks to the reduction of these expenses, says the document, future gymnasiarchs will bear the burden of their office with more enthusiasm – in other words, the town will have less trouble in finding candidates (a hope often expressed around that time). As a result, the prefect formally fixed the new level of expenses for the future. The motives here are clear. This high official had no pre-conceived theory in favour of uniformity throughout the Empire or against local autonomy. Quite pragmatically, he wanted the finances of the towns for which he was responsible to be in order, and he fulfilled that aim by introducing a regulation and fixing a rate.

In addition the authorities preferred payment in coin, which the city could dispose of as it chose, to a *euergesia* in kind, which might prove to be a gift of no great use. In the eyes of the Emperor's representatives, the legitimate sum looked increasingly like one of the city's ordinary revenues, and they did all they could to ensure that this spring flowed as abundantly as possible. Hence the legitimate sum introduced for entry into the Council. The dignity of councillor was much sought after and when new councillors were being elected or nominated the struggles between clubs, *hetaireiai*, were sometimes sharp;[229] could the man lucky enough to be chosen not show his gratitude in some active way? One new councillor offers the city a building, 'in exchange for [membership of] the Council'.[230] During the second century, at the latest, payment of the legitimate sum was obligatory in all cities. Wishing to reward a navigator who had served him well, the Emperor Hadrian had him made a councillor of Ephesus, the metropolis of Asia, and recommended him in these terms to the local authorities: 'I leave it to you to co-opt him yourselves. If there is nothing against this, and if he seems to you worthy of the honour, I will myself pay, for his nomination, the sum that has to be paid by Council members.'[231] It was then an exceptional honour to be a 'councillor free of charge'.[232]

Euergetism had developed around public functions – magistracies, liturgies or priesthoods. When it was extended to the dignity of councillor, this confirmed that political activity was no longer anything but a mark of social distinction. One paid to enter the Council as one might pay to enter a certain *collegium*, that of the notables.[233] The legitimate sums of the councillors having become an ordinary resource, the authorities tried to ensure that they were paid by as large a number of persons as possible. In Bithynia, under the Pompeian law, the members of the Council were nominated by censors, and paid nothing. Under Trajan, certain cities having received permission to create extra councillorships, the fortunate persons privileged to assume these had to pay to enter into office, and their legitimate sums served, for example, to build public baths. However, the proconsul 'ordained (though his edict extended to some few cities only) that those who were elected by the censors should also pay into the treasury a certain sum'.[234] The privilege resulted in an abuse which the administration tended to turn into a rule. Eventually the rule became general. Antoninus Pius, when founding a city in Macedonia, laid down in its charter the number of councillors and the sum they would have to pay.[235] The councillors were the milch-cow of the cities, not only through their entrance-payments but also because, for the rest of their lives, they were destined to be the future magistrates and liturgists. Giving a city the right to add to its number of councillors meant giving it fresh resources. The prosperity of a city was measured by that of its councillors and, before founding a new town, Emperors made sure that there were enough rich men in the region to compose a Council that would enable the new city to survive.[236]

But the legitimate sum was merely a legal minimum. It did not put an end to the history of euergetism, which, since it had its own motivation, exceeded that minimum, or else continued to exist alongside the legitimate sum in the form of voluntary patronage. For quite a few dignitaries, of course, the fixed rate, or even a contractual price, was a way of limiting their expenditure. In a decree of Iasos a certain Caninius Synallasson makes a pollicitation to be *stephanēphoros* and 'pays 5,000 *denarii* for all the expenses of the office'.[237] This echoes what must have been a lively discussion in the Council. It ended in a compromise at 5,000 *denarii*, but Caninius made it quite clear that he would not pay a farthing more, even if the expenditure exceeded the estimates. This was not a legitimate sum fixed once for all but simply a contractual price, and doubtless the next year saw another discussion about money with the new *stephanēphoros*. The words 'for all the expenses' do not mean that the honorary sum was a fixing of the expenses of a public function, but merely that Caninius specified that he did not intend to be a milch-cow for his fellow citizens for a whole year. But other dignitaries were more magnificent than he was. They paid more than the minimum, and are naturally the ones we know most about. For example, 'over and above the expenses of the priesthood', a pair of priests of Zeus Panamaros 'have had the floors of the temple of Hera covered with mosaics, and have promised to have the wall of a portico decorated with inlaid work'.[238]

PUBLIC ENTERTAINMENTS

More generally, voluntary patronage continued as before, and even reached its apogee in the second century when the legitimate sum became general. That century was indeed the golden age of the Greek East. Forms of patronage were as various as the individual inclinations of the different *euergetai*. However, certain types of *largesse* were much more widespread than others, namely entertainments and buildings. Lucian draws the portrait of a dreamer who is building castles in Spain and imagines what he would do with his money if he were rich. He would acquire real estate as extensive as Attica, he would have rich men as his clients and make them wait in his anteroom, he would be served by 2,000 slaves. 'I should set apart something for the public service too: a monthly distribution of [100 drachmas] a head to citizens and half that to foreigners; and the most beautiful theatres and baths you can imagine . . .'[239] Distributions of money or banquets on the one hand, buildings, sacred or secular, on the other, were the favourite themes of patronage in the later Hellenistic epoch and the Roman era. To these should be added the most ambitious of *euergesiai*, the supreme *philotimia* – the great festivals of the Imperial cult, celebrated throughout the province, in which a dignitary who was also a priest, the asiarch or high priest of the Emperors,[240] provided, in honour of the sovereigns, the most ruinous of all forms of entertainment, a gladiatorial combat. The survival of spontaneous patronage explains why a statutory duty roster was not established along with the honorary sum: the less generous could always hope to leave the burden to be borne by the more generous.

The patrons erected public buildings to express their grandeur. They gave entertainments to the people because the people asked for them and because they could also express their grandeur by presiding over these occasions. Thus they provided banquets for their fellow citizens, procured for them, free or at a low price, the oil needed for the baths,[241] or simply distributed money at so many *denarii* per head. These *largesses* had several origins. Piety had always required that a priest or a commissioner should exhibit feelings appropriate to his mission and not be miserly towards the gods. For example, he paid for the sacrificial victim.[242] Other forms of *largesse* had their roots in folklore and are accounted for by the face-to-face relationships of a well-defined community (just as nowadays when we announce 'Drinks are on me', or issue a general invitation). The new dignitaries, when presenting themselves to the public for the first time, invited everybody to enjoy themselves at their expense.[243] The notables invited to their family festivals all whom they considered 'their people', which meant the whole city.[244] In Bithynia it was the custom to invite the town Council and a large number of citizens and distribute money to them on four occasions – on assuming the *toga virilis*, on getting married, on assuming a magistracy and on inaugurating a public building.[245] From the late Hellenistic period, honorific decrees are full of indulgent descriptions of public banquets.[246] Sometimes the citizens alone were invited, sometimes the foreigners resident in or passing through the city, sometimes even the slaves, at least under the Empire. Sometimes the citizens' wives were also invited, or at least a meal was provided for them separately.

The simplest illustration is provided by a graphic document, a decree of Acraiphia, in the poverty-stricken Boeotia of the beginning of the Christian era. The rich notable Epaminondas, 'having assumed, in his turn, the supreme magistracy, was tireless in displaying his magnificence. When he sacrificed a bull to the Emperors, he offered in connection therewith a banquet and celebration for the city lasting a whole day, so that, in the cities round about, as well as here, people wondered at the boundlessness and endlessness of his spending.' The festival and games of the Ptoia

having been broken off for thirty years past, Epaminondas, on being appointed to preside over the games, accepted the responsibility with much eagerness and made it a matter of honour to re-establish these ancient games, so becoming the new founder of the Great Ptoia Caesarea. As soon as he had assumed this function, he set himself to carry out the orders of the god's oracle, offering five sumptuous annual dinners to the magistrates and councillors during the four years he was in office, and he never put off till later a sacrifice or any other expenditure. In the eighth year, during the games, he distributed food and drink to all the citizens, to the resident foreigners and to those who held property in the country, for the approaching festival, giving [ten litres] of corn and [a quarter of a litre] of wine to everyone. Furthermore, he piously celebrated the great traditional processions and the traditional dances of the *syrtes*,[247] and after sacrificing a bull to the gods and the Emperors, he never ceased to distribute food and to give lunches, servings of sweet wine, and dinners. Again, between the 20th and 30th of the month his wife provided lunches every day, by category, for the citizens' sons, the adult slaves, the citizens' wives, the girls, and the adult female slaves. Nor did Epaminondas neglect the pilgrims who camped in the city and who enhanced the glory of the festival by their presence. He had them invited to lunch by a special proclamation read by the town crier, something nobody had previously done. He wanted there to be no one who did not share in his philanthropy. When plays were being performed in the theatre, he offered a light meal there to all the spectators and to those who had come from neighbouring cities, and he threw sweets to the spectators,[248] so that, even in the cities round about, people talked much about the money he spent. During the celebration of the games, after the dinner offered to the entire people, he spent the same amount a second time: he distributed a sum of eleven *denarii* per dining-couch,[249] and, with the rest of the money, a jar of old wine and six *denarii* for a cooked dish. Having accomplished all that, he walked down from the sanctuary towards the town, and all the citizens crowded forward to meet him and give full expression of their zeal and their gratitude. After which, far from belying his magnificence, he sacrificed, in the town, a bull to Zeus the Preserver and at once regaled the people who came to thank him.[250]

Hunger, piety, a taste for display and solemnity, the pleasure of social-izing under a pretext, concentration into a short period of the small surplus available, so as to get the maximum enjoyment therefrom by consuming it all at once – all this explains the explosive rhythm of collective life in poor societies and the considerable place occupied in them by banquets. Feasting is a regular institution in such societies, figuring in all sorts of combined activities, and religion is sometimes the principal motive and sometimes just the pretext for it.[251]

Another pleasure results from the fact that banquets are accompanied by a certain amount of display. The *euergetai* placed dining-couches at the disposal of the guests, so that on that day the poor dined lying down, like the rich who possessed whole suites of furniture. Finally, in a well-defined community, there is some pleasure and interest simply in being together. People do not live shut up in bourgeois privacy, and the entire community is both actor and spectator. Thus poor children, who have no toys, find amusement among themselves, using each other as toys. However, in order to enjoy without embarrassment the pleasure of being together, it is necessary to have a pretext which allows people to keep countenance and avoid the necessity of confessing this pleasure to each other. The banquet permits them to withhold that dampening admission. (The same complication of affectivity explains the very widespread diffusion of the marriage-bed and of institutions of sociability like public baths and cafés.)

In the Hellenistic and Roman epochs, true religiosity increasingly turned away from the communal religion and sought refuge in the sects. The Greeks were well aware that their public sacrifices were mainly pretexts for providing banquets. The priests or commissioners who offered them, say the decrees, both honoured the gods and heaped benefits upon men; they showed both piety and patriotism.[252] As for the *euergetēs*, he had the satisfaction of being applauded. One day the philosopher Peregrinus came before the Assembly of the people at Paros 'with the announcement that the property left him by his father of blessed memory is entirely at their disposal! Being a needy folk, with a keen eye to charity, they received the information with ready applause: "Here is true philosophy, true patriotism . . .!" '[253]

Largesse became the essential feature of many public dignities. One example will suffice, that of the gymnasiarchy, the history of which can perhaps be summed up as follows. Originally, the gymnasiarch was responsible for running the gymnasium and supervising there the instruction and education of the ephebi. The young men's parents expected him to enforce strict discipline and teach proper behaviour to his charges. We can still read several decrees which, in a high style, eulogize gymnasiarchs who performed that task well.[254] A gymnasium was merely a sports ground fitted with some equipment for training and physical exercises or care of the body – in particular, a bath.[255] One of the gymnasiarch's duties was to see that the swimming-pool of the ephebi was kept warm and to provide them with the oil they needed for the bath. Now in the Hellenistic period the fashion for bathing became more widespread, while dignitaries of every sort were to an increasing extent paying the expenses of their dignities.[256] A day would come, therefore, when 'to be gymnasiarch' no longer meant 'to be in charge of the gymnasium', but rather 'to guarantee from his own resources the heating of the public baths and the supply of oil, not just to the ephebi, but to the whole population', old men included, if the gymnasiarch was generous.[257] Under the Empire the word *gymnasion* would not always mean 'gymnasium', but also 'public bath',[258] and *gymnasia* (the word entered into Latin with this meaning) would mean 'distributions of oil'.[259] Gymnasiarchs would assume their dignity for periods of ten days, i.e. they agreed to pay for ten days' heating of the bath and supply of oil. The function was so ruinously expensive, when assumed on a yearly basis, and the Greek population were so fond of their baths, that in Egypt the gymnasiarchs were regarded as the greatest dignitaries in a city.[260] (There is an amusing testimony to this: in one of Aesop's fables, the crocodile, an Egyptian creature, boasts of belonging to a family of gymnasiarchs.)[261]

PUBLIC BUILDINGS

For one was a *euergetēs* by dint of belonging to one's family, since the status of notable was passed on to descendants through inheritance, tending to become almost a *de facto* hereditary nobility. Under the Empire, decrees regularly praise a benefactor's ancestors and say that he has inherited their worth, or that he follows their example.[262] Since there are dynasties of *euergetai*, euergetism ought not to be expressed merely in ephemeral *largesses*, but should have more lasting monuments. To all the personal reasons that led patrons to establish or re-establish games, institute a permanent foundation or erect a public building,[263] another reason was added – to put down dynastic roots in the city. The games, the building and the foundation (and even the income of the foundation) would bear the name of the *euergetēs* and make it known to posterity; his descendants would complete, repair or enlarge the works of their ancestor (*erga progonika*) and add their own works.[264] Just as the lord's castle would for centuries dominate the village and the countryside, and just as the town houses of the principal families in Florence and Rome, Dijon and Aix, are dynastic monuments no less than the Bardi or Medici chapels, so every family of notables had to have its public building, either in the city or in some great sanctuary of the city, at Miletus or at Didyma, at Stratonicaea or at Panamara.

A family of notables had to set a mark on the face of the city which was proportionate to its rank in local society. Throughout the city, monuments had to bear its name (it is hard to believe what importance was attached in those days to the right to inscribe one's name in the dedication of a building – a right evidently reserved to the builder – or the amount of litigation and dispute over precedence to which it gave rise).[265] In one very large town, Ephesus, the name of the great *euergetēs* Vedius could be read on the temple of Hadrian which he had promised to build, and also on a huge 'gymnasium' and an odeum.[266] One of his relatives, Damianos, a famous man of letters, built the 'eastern gymnasium' (which has been excavated and where his statue and that of his wife were found)[267] and several other edifices, both secular and sacred.[268] Ephesus was so used to having its public buildings erected by rich individuals that when, by way of exception, the city itself built such an edifice – the theatre – using public funds, it mentioned in the dedication that the theatre had been built by the city 'out of its own resources'.[269] The old Greek ideal of the founder of a city, the *oikistēs*, was still alive; 'embellishing the town', being a *cosmopolis*, was almost the same as founding or refounding it, and merited the award of the title *ktistēs*, 'founder'.[270]

Embellishing the city was the notables' duty and their exclusive right. Public opinion would certainly have seen it as effrontery if a plebeian had sought to include his name in dedications.[271] The grandeur of the notables was expressed by public buildings. These constructions corresponded to a need to symbolize the notables' own grandeur: they were not addressed to a plebeian audience. They reflected a class psychology without serving class interests. They could not serve to make the notables popular with the people (who would have preferred entertainments) and they ruined the patron's family.

ROLE, SELECTION AND 'PERFECTION'

It was thus necessary to spend a great deal if one was to maintain one's rank as a notable, and necessary also to save enough to leave to one's descendants the means to do as much in their turn. A sure sense of equilibrium between well-managed saving and opportune *largesse* was required:[272] 'No one could say of my grandfather,' writes Dio of Prusa, 'either that he disgraced the city or that he spent nothing on it out of his own means. For he spent on public benefactions all that he had from his father and his grandfather, so that he had nothing left at all, and then he acquired a second fortune by his learning and from Imperial favour.'[273] This family history can be translated as meaning that his grandfather's *euergesiai* made a hole in his patrimony, but he recovered some of his losses through the *largesse* of Emperors and his own activity as a teacher of rhetoric.

From the second century A D there existed, in the Greek world as in the Latin West, some patrons whose liberalities were so immense that they cannot be accounted for by this policy of equilibrium between spending and saving, nor by an individual taste for patronage, and these virtuosi of euergetism undoubtedly constitute a special group.[274] Rather than Herodes Atticus[275] I will take as my example Opramoas of Rhodiapolis.[276] The name of the former was already proverbial in antiquity as that of a millionaire patron, as famous for his quarrels with his Athenian compatriots as for his *largesse* to all the Greeks and for his royal airs. The latter is known to modern epigraphists as the champion *euergetēs*. The tomb of this Opramoas, who lived in the first half of the second century, was found in a little city of the Lycian Confederation. The walls of the building are covered with inscriptions (occupying twenty folio pages of modern print) which celebrate the *largesses* and the honours of this ultra-rich patron – letters from the Emperor and the governors which testify to his merits, and honorific decrees of the Confederation. Opramoas had all these details carved on his tomb as proof of the vocation of *euergetēs* that he had followed all his life. The total of his benefactions is amazing: more than a million and a half sesterces (nearly £1 million), even when many figures are missing through gaps in the inscription. Though Opramoas had children, his vocation took priority.

To explain the case of such a virtuoso we need to start, I think, with a revealing phrase uttered by Marcus Aurelius. 'When I was young,' wrote the philosopher-king, 'I was never tempted to pose as an ascetic or as a *euergetēs*.' [277] From this we learn that around the second century AD there were ideals of 'perfection' (in the sense in which that word would be used in Christian theology), and that one of these perfections was euergetism. A great personage became a *euergetēs* and sacrificed his patrimony to that vocation. He might equally well have become a convert to Pythagoreanism or Neoplatonism and led an ascetic life. Similarly, later on a Christian might take orders or become a tertiary of St Francis. An eighteenth-century duke might become a freemason and imitate the virtues of Tamino in *The Magic Flute*. A perfection is not the same as a profession, such as philosopher, teacher of rhetoric, etc., which is a specialization, whereas a perfection is an example to everyone – the realization of what every man ought to become. Every believer is called to sainthood,[278] and every man worthy of the name ought either to be a *euergetēs* or an ascetic. A perfection is thus a religious or moral ideal, since ethico-religious values are the only ones that are considered obligatory upon all (whereas nobody is obliged to become keen on literature). Nevertheless, it is observed that, in practice, only a handful of virtuosi have the vocation to devote their lives to a perfection. Opramoas was one of those few.

An adept of euergetism, Opramoas was thus the *euergetēs par excellence*. Other notables were no more than lay votaries who now and again performed a voluntary *euergesia*, or were even careerists, when assuming a public function obliged them to perform some *euergesia ob honorem*. The circle is closed. At the beginning of the Hellenistic epoch a patron could be satisfied with a single act of *largesse* and a magistrate became an object of popular comment if he added something to the public funds out of his own pocket. But now everyone was a *euergetēs*, and to distinguish oneself it was necessary to become a *euergetēs* by vocation.

However, the field of municipal life was occupied by a profession, politics. Were euergetism and politics good bed-fellows? They were united by compulsion. *Euergesiai* had become the condition for any political career. Now political activity has its own logic, since in the end there is a task to be performed, namely to govern. It is not certain that good government is always compatible with a policy of *largesse*, nor that munificence or a taste for popularity are virtues that can serve as reliable criteria in the selection of good politicians. Dio of Prusa[279] and Plutarch were acutely aware of this problem. Plutarch was all the more aware of it because he had an interest in the matter. This Platonist, a supporter, like Polybius, of a policy of authority and moral order (we must not be misled by his seeming good nature) was opposed on principle to *euergesiai*. But Plutarch was also aware that it was hardly possible in his time to govern without doing good to the people. This philosopher therefore sought the elements of a compromise, while at the same time developing, in his *Life of Pericles*, a consoling myth. We shall see in the next chapter that Cicero, on the basis of the same principles, arrived at the same happy mean.

Plutarch is all too well aware that, in the cities, most ambitious men win the hearts of the people by giving them banquets and *largesse*,[280] distributions, gladiatorial combats and spectacles of every kind.[281] Yet the political career ought to be open to notables of no great fortune: they ought to be able to please the people with nothing but their sincerity and honesty.[282] In that event, public life would be like Plato's banquet: there would be room for the *euergetēs*, but it would be Socrates, who pays nothing, that the public would listen to.[283] This ideal was realized only rarely, and euergetism resulted in a distortion in political recruitment. As Max Weber says, when we set about estimating any social system, we need to study it from this angle, among others: of what type of man does it facilitate the recruitment to political leadership?[284]

Let the politician, even if he be talented, give *largesse* then, since he must, but let him at least preserve his honour by finding elevated pretexts for his *euergesiai* and by not compromising on certain principles. He needs to realize that the crowd must be led like horses or children, its minor faults being treated with indulgence, so that one may resist and contain it when it deviates too far from the proper path. He must know how to slacken the reins at the right moment and give the people, with good grace, sacrifices, games, theatrical shows[285] and even distributions of money, if a religious festival or the cult of a god provides the pretext. Pericles himself followed such a course.[286] Gifts 'should be given on some occasion which offers a good and excellent pretext, one which is connected with the worship of a god and leads the people to piety; for at the same time there springs up in the minds of the masses a strong disposition to believe that the deity is great and majestic, when they see the men whom they themselves honour and regard as great so liberally and zealously vying with each other in honouring the divinity'.[287] But he will not compromise on the principle that *euergesiai* are not a right possessed by the people and so will refuse to distribute public money.[288]

6. *Envy, legitimation, social superiority*

There has been another interpretation of euergetism, which has enjoyed much success among modern writers. According to this, far from being a trick aimed at getting round the people's ill-nature, *euergesiai* are satisfactions granted to the indefeasible rights of individuals or groups. They redistribute social advantages between the ruling class and the ruled and in this way ensure the equilibrium of the community. The people receive collective benefits which compensate for the unequal sharing of wealth and power. The theory of depoliticization is a satirical and machiavellian variant of this doctrine of balancing redistribution.

The two doctrines have in common the assumption that euergetism was an element in the political and social machinery and fulfilled a function therein – to relax tension, or to redistribute. We shall see that this is not so, that euergetism did not guarantee possession of power to the notables or the tranquil possession of their property to the property-owners. The regime of the notables and the power of the rich were completely independent of euergetism, which is merely a curious special feature, even a sort of 'fad'. The regime of the notables would have functioned just as well without it, and the notables had no interest in doing good to the people, for the idea of social equilibrium is only a deceptive metaphor, and that of class interest is much too rigid.

CLASS INTEREST OR SOCIAL SUPERIORITY?

We thus have an order, formal or informal, of rich notables who fiercely defended their exclusiveness and were ready to pay the price for it. Shall we say that it was out of 'class interest' that this order paid and governed? Will the expected appearance of this expression be for us like the coming of one of the beasts in the Apocalypse, to open the last seal (assuming that there is a last one any more than a first) of historical analysis? Yes, if we take the notion of class interest in a vague sense, meaning by it that classes defend whatever happens to interest them. No, if what is assumed is that the notables governed and paid merely in order to defend the material relations of production. In the first case, talk about class interest means committing oneself to nothing, while still calling oneself a Marxist: it will be for us to determine what it is that interested the notables. In the second case, we protest that men do not essentially strive to defend the relations of production, but rather their social superiority, if they possess this, and whatever it is that endows them with such superiority. The notables were not magistrates and *euergetai* in order to defend their landed property, but because the status of notable separated them from the people. Once more, the functionalist interpretation is false; euergetism did not serve to maintain the relations of production any more than to give balance to political society.

The notables had no need to govern the cities in order to defend these relations. If the city had been the state, one might claim that it was the instrument of the dominant class. But it was hardly more than an autonomous commune. It was the place where one acquired and displayed social superiority, but not the place where one defended the 'material' privileges that were the principal condition, if not the essence, of that superiority. We speculate in vain about what material interest could lie in being liturgist and municipal magistrate in order to defend a social order which was upheld by the Emperor with his legions and the governor with his tribunal. With us, today, do the relations of production depend on mayors and municipal councillors? Dio of Prusa, threatened with lynching for starving the people, threatened the people in return that he would appeal to the Roman governor.[289] The peace of the cities was troubled by food riots and strikes about which the notables could do nothing, for there was no police force in those days. The cities were also disturbed by charivaris intended to evoke *euergesiai*, and also by the pride of the most powerful notables, and by clan conflicts comparable to the famous quarrel of the Capulets and the Montagues – not to mention conflicts between cities over frontier questions or precedence at the provincial Assembly.[290] All these troubles, strikes included, were dealt with or repressed by the Roman authorities; the notables, like the people, had no choice but to submit. In short, as the city was not the state, the interests of the notables as *euergetai* and as property-owners were not at all the same. The only 'material' interest that the rich could have in governing the cities was more concerned with maladministration than with the relations of production. They undoubtedly pillaged the town's finances, shared among themselves the public contracts and tax-farms,[291] and placed on the backs of the poor the main burden of the Imperial taxation.[292] On the other hand, *euergesiai* and liturgies cost them dear, and, as Paul Petit writes, weighed heavier than the Emperor's taxes.[293] Yet it was those taxes which most aroused their discontent – because, unlike *euergesiai*, paying them conferred no social superiority.

The autonomy of the cities, which was not enough to make them a social battlefield (the machinery of state would have fulfilled that function), *was* enough to clothe municipal politics with a prestige that the rich did not want to abandon to others and which increased their social superiority. The notables therefore clung fiercely to two things: their wealth and their position at the head of the city. But they did not cling to the latter in order to defend the former. Their interests were many, as we have seen. Why should class interest consist of one thing only? Politics constituted one half of their class interest, if by that expression we mean what a certain class is interested in, what it is ready to defend fiercely, and what it justifies by the most ingenious ideological tricks. That is indeed the confused and violent phenomenon we commonly call class interest. I prefer to speak of social superiority, so as to eliminate the too directly and narrowly economic connotation of the other expression. Politics was in that epoch a mode of this theme of superiority. This superiority is not, like interest in Marx's sense, a sort of instinct of preservation of the relations of production. It means everything in which the historical context causes a certain class, in a certain society, to interest itself.

Nobody denies that this superiority is most often acquired through *economic* superiority (with some rare exceptions, such as, sometimes, cultural, religious and other excellences). For in the first place economic superiority is itself the most commonly appreciated excellence (and so the notables held on to their wealth). And then it is with superiority and excellence like most other things in this world: they call for the use of 'material' means, of scarce goods (in order to be a notable and govern the city, one had to possess resources). If these truisms are all that is required to be a Marxist, who is not one? Wealth is almost always the condition for superiority, but does not itself constitute that superiority. If we were to suppose that distinction to be meaningless, we should find ourselves believing that wealth is always sought after for its own sake and that everything else is sought after as a means to wealth; and we should deprive ourselves of the possibility of understanding that in different ages people have sought, by means of one and the same economic superiority, different types of advantage: the status of notable, economic achievement, nobility, religious excellence, politics and so on. The heuristic value of Marxism has been exhausted long since and it no longer serves to do more than disguise the vagueness of an analysis. I will not even accept that the political superiority of the notables was a symbolic satisfaction, for it is hard to see what it could be symbolizing. Power is a satisfaction no more and no less than 'material' advantage or religious authority, and symbolizes nothing but itself.

It so happens that men, in the great majority of cases, are sensible of a certain number of excellences – wealth, power or prestige; that possession of the excellences that a society puts in the forefront confers superiority; and that those who possess this superiority cling to it fiercely. Not everyone possesses superiority. Most of us have only modest status, mediocre advantages, which do not separate us from the crowd: we defend our humble interests, our daily bread, but not a superiority. It happens, furthermore, that those who possess this superiority have a curious tendency to express it, to display conspicuous consumption or ostentatious patronage, in order to manifest their superiority. And they are ready to do anything to safeguard this superiority. For example, if it consists, for them, of being at the head of their city, and if, through the many springs of human nature, holding a public sinecure calls for the payment of a symbolic gratuity, they will not refuse to pay that gratuity.

THE HISTORICAL PACT

Thus the givers made it a duty and a pleasure to give, and the people adapted themselves to the regime of the notables by regarding their benefactions as something to which they were entitled. It would take too long to show how the Imperial authorities themselves, in the interests of public order, did not hesitate on occasion to remind the notables of their duty and to impose on them a legal obligation to be *euergetai*. We can now conclude by revealing the element of truth in the accepted idea by which euergetism ensured political and social equilibrium: it ended in the establishment of an implicit contract between the notables and the plebs, but this contract was historical, 'arbitrary' in Mauss's sense of the word, conventional or ideological, according to taste. In other words, between everyday political reactions and the essence of politics, we have to accept the existence of an intermediate level which I shall call the historical contract. This contract is not derived from the essence of politics. We saw in chapter I that euergetism did not serve to ensure political equilibrium and we have just seen that the social equilibrium was no less non-determined. But the contract is not to be reduced, either, to everyday reactions. On the contrary, it explains them and limits them – it is their presupposition. For example, the plebs does not revolt against the principle of social inequality, but it will launch a hostile demonstration if the rich break the historic contract which obliges them to be generous to the public. 'Envy' is a function of this implicit pact. We should not be surprised at the existence of this intermediate level in every society. The ideal list of the tasks of the state or the bases of foreign policy are no less non-determined and historical. We see that there is both truth and falsehood in the idea that euergetism ensured a half-millennium of equilibrium and peace. It ensured this in the sense that, since it was one of the chief clauses in the contract, there would have been trouble if the notables had tried to infringe it. On the other hand, it is not at all certain that a different society, essentially comparable to or even almost identical with Greek society, would have accepted the same contract and remained peaceful at that price; for this inessential contract was the result of the specific peculiarities of Greek society or just of its individual past. The Greek plebs eventually adjusted itself to the fate that its history had created for it, and the small advantages that this offered. A people which had not had the same history would have been either more restive or more accommodating.

Historical contracts, which tend to be classified indiscriminately as ideology, are usually preconceptual, or at least their arbitrary character is not apparent. In France, certainly, the 'ideological' nature of the contract represented by the Third Republic (nationalism, equality before the law, government by the new social strata, public education ensuring social mobility on the basis of 'merit') was never misunderstood, because this contract was challenged by oppositions on the Right and on the extreme Left. But in the United States, till quite recently, the very general acceptance of the dogmas of government by consent and free competition has concealed the purely local character of this contract, which has passed for the essence of democracy. It was the same with the euergetistic contract, so that even to-day modern observers readily believe that bread and circuses ensured social peace, though all that they actually did was not to disturb it.

Notes

1. Xenophon, *Oeconomicus*, 2, 5–6.
2. The sacrifice was also a gift to mortals. We shall see later that, as every sacrifice was followed by a banquet at which the flesh of the victims

was eaten, giving to the gods meant also giving to men. This piety is hard to distinguish from the virtue of *largesse*.

3. Similarly, for Aristotle, the virtue of magnificence (*megaloprepeia*) leads to splendid performance of 'the receiving of foreign guests and the sending of them on their way', an allusion to the role of the *proxenos* (*Nicomachean Ethics*, IV, 2, 1123a3).

4. Allusion to the *hestiasis*, when a liturgist gave a banquet to his tribe; cf. *Nicomachean Ethics*, IV, 5, 1122b20.

5. A note by Chantraine points out that *prostateia* here means 'high office' in general, as in Xenophon's *Memorabilia*, III, 6.

6. On hippotrophy, a little-known liturgy, see A. Boeckh, *Staatshaushaltung der Athener*, Fraenkel (ed.) (1886), vol. I, p. 318, note d; vol. II, note 755; vol. I, p. 585, note d.

7. Aristotle, *Constitution of Athens*, 62, 1.

8. Boeckh, vol. I, p. 554; vol. II, notes 756 and 779; A. M. Andreades, *A History of Greek Public Finance*, vol. I (Harvard University Press, 1933), p. 292.

9. This is in fact the meaning of the word as used in the *Economics* of the Pseudo-Aristotle, II, 2, 4; see Boeckh, vol. I, pp. 534 and 585; vol. II, note 810. See also B. A. van Groningen, *Aristote, le second livre de l'Économique* (Sijthoff, 1933), p. 73. See also Theophrastus, *Characters*, 10, 11 for *hestiasis* of the members of the deme; 30, 16 for that of the members of a phratry.

10. See, e.g., L. Molet, 'La cérémonie d'intronisation à Madagascar et ses implications économiques', in *Cahiers internationaux de sociologie*, XXIV (1958), pp. 80–87.

11. M. Olson, *The Logic of Collective Action: public goods and the theory of groups* (Harvard University Press).

12. Theophrastus, *Characters*, 23, 5–6.

13. Antiphanes, in Kock's *Comicorum Atticorum Fragmenta*, vol. II, p. 111, no. 228. The 'cadger' must be distinguished from the parasite: on the latter, see K. Beloch, *Griechische Geschichte* second edn, vol. IV, 1, p. 411.

14. Aristotle, *Constitution of Athens*, 27, 3; Plutarch, *Life of Cimon*, 10, depends on Aristotle, whom he quotes with acknowledgement.

15. Cf. L. Gernet, 'Les nobles dans la Grèce antique', in *Annales d'histoire économique et sociale*, 1938, p. 39.

16. Other famous feasts were those of the Spartan Lichas, who kept open table for the foreigners who came to Sparta to attend the gymnopaedia (Xenophon, *Memorabilia*, I, 2, 61; *Hellenica*, III, 2, 11; cf. Thucydides, V, 51).

17. Thucydides, I, 136, 1. See E. Skard, *Zwei religiös-politische Begriffe: Euergetes, Concordia* (Oslo, 1931); this study does not deal with the Hellenistic period. In the mouths of demagogues or ambitious men,

'doing good to the city' was, however, a common formula: thus Cleon in Aristophanes, *Knights*, 741 and 1153.

18. For the true meaning of the word 'liturgy' see how it is used by Aristotle, *Politics*, 1272a19, where it means 'service to the state', which in the given case is backed by the public funds. It should be added that the liturgist received money from the state (Demosthenes, *First Philippic*, 36). We may suppose that liturgies originated because the rich were morally required to add something from their own pockets to the public credits; and in particular, trierarchs sometimes paid the wages of their crewmen (Thucydides, VI, 31, 3; Isocrates, XVIII, *Against Callimachus*, 60).

19. Demosthenes, XXI, *Against Meidias*, 13 and 156. 'Voluntarily', ἐθελοντής, is a word that was to enter the vocabulary of euergetism. On the psychology of the liturgies there are good passages in P. Guiraud, *La Propriété foncière en Grèce* (1893), p. 531, and *Études économiques sur l'Antiquité*, 1905, p. 112, and also in Wilamowitz (Kromayer–Heisenberg), *Staat und Gesellschaft der Griechen und Römer* (1910), p. 114.

20. Lysias, XVI, 1–5.

21. On this taste for glory, there are some fine pages in Burckhardt's classic work on Greek civilization, vol. II, p. 353, and vol. IV, p. 32. See also H. W. Pleket, 'Griekse Ethiek en de "competitive society"', in *Lampas*, 1971, no. 4.

22. L. Robert, *Les Gladiateurs en Orient grec*, p. 257.

23. Plato, *The Republic*, 544c–576b.

24. Ibid., 551a.

25. Id., *Laws*, 831c; *The Republic*, 555a.

26. Theophrastus, *Characters*, 26, 6.

27. Aristotle, *Politics*, V, 5 (1305a5). There was no lack of complaints about crushing burdens laid on the rich: Isocrates, *On the Peace*, 128. Similarly, the Oligarch described by Theophrastus declares (XXVI, 6) that liturgies and trierarchies are ruining decent people.

28. Pseudo-Xenophon, *On the Government of Athens*, 1, 13 and 3.

29. Aristotle, *Politics*, V, 12 (1316b10).

30. *Economy and Society*, vol. I, p. 291. On the connection between non-payment of functionaries and oligarchy, see also Tocqueville, *Démocratie en Amérique*, in *Œuvres complètes*, vol. I (Gallimard, 1961), p. 211.

31. *Rome, la Grèce et les monarchies hellénistiques au IIIe siècle*, p. 221: cf. *Études d'épigraphie et d'histoire grecques*, L. Robert (ed.), vol. V, pp. 376, 384–5, 398. See also J. Deininger, *Der politische Widerstand gegen Rom in Griechenland* (De Gruyter, 1971), p. 17.

32. A well-known statement by Pausanias affirms that, everywhere, Rome put an end to democracies and established regimes based on property

qualification (VII, 16, 9). However, J. Touloumakos, *Der Einfluss Roms auf die Staatsform der Stadtstaaten des Festlandes und der Inseln in ersten und zweiten Jhdt v. Chr.* (Göttingen University dissertation, 1967), pp. 11 and 150–54, has shown that the reality was much more varied and the evolution more continuous. For the reinforcement of the executive, see Touloumakos p. 151, and I. Lévy, 'Études sur la vie municipale de l'Asie Mineure', in *Revue des études grecques*, XII (1899), especially p. 266.

33. Strabo, XIV, 24, p. 659c, a passage kindly brought to my notice by L. Robert. Hybreas was in no sense a man of the people. He belonged to a family with a tradition of education, culture and, of course, good manners, but which was either not well–off, or else ruined. It would not have occurred to a mere peasant to study rhetoric, any more than a nineteenth–century French peasant would have thought for a moment of preparing to enter a *grande école*. Hybreas established, or re-established, his fortune by one of those 'occasional enterprises' (*Gelegenheitshandel*) which were characteristic of the upper class, as we have seen in chapter I. For mule–back transport enterprises, see chapter III, note 111. I am not clear what he did in the *agoranomian* (the premises of the *agoranomoi*). Perhaps he acted as advocate in petty cases before the court of the *agoranomoi*, or held a job (*hyperēsia*), paid or farmed, in the service of the *agoranomoi*. Hybreas may have farmed the market-tax, or have been a registrar or an auctioneer. In any case, *agoranomion* definitely cannot mean 'the dignity of *agoranomos*', since the passage tells us that Hybreas entered public functions only later. An 'occasional enterprise', access to culture, enrichment through minor offices, public or judicial: we have here the story of a talented 'petty-bourgeois' from the world of Furetière or Balzac. The mule continued until the nineteenth century to be the principal means of land transport.

34. L. Robert in *Annuaire du Collège de France*, 1971, p. 541, also in *Opuscula Minora Selecta*, vol. II (Hakkert, 1969), p. 841: 'More and more, the evolution of society removed the business of the cities from the sovereign action of the people's assembly and the democracy and put it into the hands of a more or less hereditary minority of notables who financed from their fortunes many of the essential services of the state, receiving in return honours that were increasingly numerous and brilliant.' On the Athenian aristocracy, for instance, see P. MacKendrick, *The Athenian Aristocracy, 399 to 31 BC* (Harvard University Press, 1969). There is no good general treatment of the constitution of the Hellenistic cities. See the brief studies by Wilamowitz in *Staat und Gesellschaft der Griechen und Römer* (1910), pp. 172–9; by A. H. M. Jones, *The Greek City from Alexander to Justinian* (Oxford, 1940 and 1966); and especially by C. Préaux, 'Les villes hellénistiques', in *Recueils de la Société Jean-Bodin*, VI: *La Ville*, vol. I (1953). On the 'bourgeois'

nature of the notables, see also M. Rostovtzeff, *The Social and Economic History of the Hellenistic World*, p. 897. On the Roman period, see the excellent studies by I. Lévy and J. Touloumakos (note 32). I have also read H. Swoboda, *Die griechischen Volksbeschlüsse* (Hakkert, reprinted 1971). See also below, note 158.

35. *Politics*, IV, 3 (1289b25).

36. For the date, E. F. Bruck, *Totenteil und Seelgerät im griechischen Recht*, second edn, (C. H. Beck, 1970), p. 167, note 1.

37. Herodotus, V, 62.

38. *Inscriptiones Graecae*, editio minor, vol. I, no. 348, lines 65–6, and no. 354, line 8. Cf. E. Cavaignac, *Études sur l'histoire financière d'Athènes au Ve siècle* (1908), pp. xlix and lxvii.

39. By *epimelētai*. On all this see Aristotle, *Constitution of Athens*, 56, 4, and Demosthenes, XXI, *Against Meidias*, 15–18.

40. Contests were also one of the origins of the *largesses* by *euergetai*. Thus the poet Ion of Chios, victor in a tragedy contest in Athens, offered wine to the Athenians after his victory (Athenaeus, I, 3, quoted by L. Robert in *Arkhaiologikē Ephemeris*, 1969, p. 38, note 4).

41. Isaeus, V, 41. With this should be compared a very similar passage in the *Gorgias*, 472ab (in which the mention of the Pythium is a correction by Boeckh, vol. II, p. 515).

42. *Palatine Anthology*, IX, 147. The principal epigraphic documents concerning Xenocles are in Dittenberger's *Sylloge*, no. 334, line 8; no. 962, line 299; no. 1089, cf. note 3. For the epigram, see A. S. F. Gow and D. L. Page, *The Greek Anthology*, part 1: *Hellenistic Epigrams*, vol. II (Cambridge, 1967), pp. 29–30. In the manuscripts it is attributed to Antagoras of Rhodes. Xenocles must have asked this well-known poet to compose a verse inscription for his bridge. I shall not go into the details of the chronological difficulties and textual corrections (the Rhodian origin of the poet has caused an assertion to appear in the manuscripts that Xenocles came from Lindos). The epigraphical references are assembled in *Inscriptiones Graecae*, II–III (2), no. 2840. For a new document, see J. and L. Robert, 'Bulletin épigraphique', in *Revue des études grecques*, 1961, no. 264.

43. Athens is the 'Tory democracy' spoken of by W. S. Ferguson, *Hellenistic Athens* (1911), p. 287. Cf. P. MacKendrick, *The Athenian Aristocracy, 399 to 31 BC* (Harvard University Press, 1969). In the Hellenistic epoch 'democracy' was counterposed not to 'oligarchy' but to the pejorative term 'monarch'. Saying that Athens was democratic meant that it was not subject to a king, whether Athenian or foreign, but was an independent non-monarchical city. I shall return to this meaning of the word in a study, now in course of publication, of Roman imperialism.

44. Dittenberger, *Sylloge*, no. 1048. The use of the present tense shows that the bridge was being built when the decree was voted.

45. Demosthenes, XLV, *Against Stephanus*, 1, 85. Other liberalities, such as the one in XXXIV, *Against Phormio*, 38, were more in the nature of *epidoseis*.

46. Lysias, XIX, *On the Property of Aristophanes*, 43.

47. Diodorus Siculus, XIII, 83, 2, quoting Timaeus. The event was earlier than the capture of Agrigentum by Hamilcar in 406, in which Gellias played a role (Diodorus, XIII, 90, 2). Here arises a curious problem of investigation of sources. It was by means of Diodorus's account that Jacoby reconstituted the account given by Timaeus (*Fragm. griech. Hist.*, 3. Teil, Band B, p. 605, no. 566). But there is another author who, without mentioning his source, talks about Gellias in the greatest detail, namely Valerius Maximus, IV, 8, 2, who lists the *euergesiai* of Gellias. Now this passage in Valerius Maximus cannot be fantasy. The description given of Gellias's *euergesiai* has an undeniable tone of Hellenistic (if not Hellenic) authenticity. A detail like 'everything that Gellias possessed was like a patrimony common to all' has many parallels in Hellenistic decrees in favour of *euergetai*, at Priene especially. In fact this passage in Valerius Maximus seems to be the Latin translation of a Hellenistic decree, enough so to serve as a good exercise for a seminar on Greek epigraphy. Consequently, three things are clear. Valerius Maximus's source, like that of Diodorus, is Timaeus; Valerius Maximus gives us what Timaeus wrote much better than Diodorus does; and Timaeus had imagined and ascribed to Gellias *euergesiai* which are anachronistic for the fifth century, but invented on the basis of honorific decrees of the early Hellenistic epoch.

48. Andocides, II, 11.

49. Numerous examples, e.g. at Amorgos as early as 357 (*Sylloge*, no. 193). Cf. Boeckh, vol. I, p. 688.

50. A. Kuenzi, *Epidosis, Sammlung freiwilliger Beiträge zur Zeit des Not in Athen* (dissertation, Berne, 1923): this does not deal with the Hellenistic epoch.

51. *Inscriptiones Graecae*, II–III (2), nos. 835 and 351 (*Sylloge*, no. 288). The text says: 'for the building of the Panathenaic stadium and theatre'. We may suppose either that the wording was muddled, and we should read 'of the Panathenaic stadium, and of the theatre', or else that *theatron* means here not the theatre of Dionysus but the tiers of the stadium. For an *epidosis* for the building of the theatre in the Piraeus, see *Inscriptiones Graecae*, II–III (2), no. 2334.

52. Demosthenes, XXI, *Against Meidias*, 161.

53. Among other examples, see *Sylloge*, no. 304, or *Inscriptiones Graecae*, II–III (2), no. 1628, line 384.

54. Cf. *Sylloge*, no. 491, line 15.

55. Demosthenes, XXI, *Against Meidias*, 161.

56. Isaeus, V, 37.

57. Demosthenes, XVIII, *De Corona*, 312 (329).

58. The *epidosis* with unfulfilled pollicitation referred to by Isaeus, V, 37–8, occurred in 393.

59. *Sylloge*, no. 288, line 14. In the end, war did not break out until several years later, after the conqueror's death.

60. Plutarch, *Life of Alcibiades*, 10; Demosthenes, XXI, *Against Meidias*, 161. From the decree in *Sylloge*, no. 491, line 15, it emerges that citizens who, being absent from the Assembly, had not been able to give their subscription to the Council, could also pay the money to the *stratēgoi*. It was customary to fix a lower limit for pollicitations, but sometimes an upper limit was fixed so as not to discourage small subscribers, when a large number of small contributions were being counted on rather than a single generous donation. There were examples of this in Athens; let us cite one from Tanagra, for an *epidosis* destined for the building of a temple of Demeter (Dareste–Haussoulier–Reinach, *Recueil des inscriptions juridiques grecques*, vol. II (Bretschneider, reprinted 1965), p. 354; *Sylloge*, no. 1185): 'It will be permissible for any woman who so wishes to pledge and to pay within twenty days, to the commissioners, a sum not exceeding five drachmas per head.'

61. Isaeus, V, 37: 'At the time of the taking of Lechaion [in 393], in response to the appeal [κληθείς] of another citizen, my opponent subscribed, before the Assembly, a sum of 300 drachmas.'

62. Isaeus, V, 38: 'voluntarily', ἐθελονταί. See, on this word, my note 19. I do not think that – in our documents at least – the procedure called προβολή was invoked against recalcitrant pollicitators, a procedure by which it was possible to prosecute persons who did not keep promises they had given to the people. Cf. J. H. Lipsius, *Das attische Recht und Rechtsverfahren* (Olms, reprinted 1966), p. 213.

63. Demosthenes, VIII, *On the Chersonese*, 70.

64. Demosthenes, XVIII, *De Corona*, 257.

65. The papers of the case include *De Corona*, 110–19, and Aeschines' *Against Ctesiphon*, 17–31.

66. *De Corona*, 114; Nausicles was *stratēgos* in 334–3.

67. *De Corona*, 112. Throughout this passage the payments made by Demosthenes out of his own pocket and added to the public credits made available to him are referred to by the verb ἐπιδιδόναι, used in a vague sense ('to give to the community'), which is just as common as its precise meaning of 'subscribe': see, e.g., Lysias, XXX, 26.

68. *De Corona*, 171.

69. *Sylloge*, no. 491, line 56. He was the grandson, or great-grandson, of

Xenocles. On *euergesia* as a purely honorific distinction, implying no real advantage, see H. Francotte, *Mélanges de droit public grec* (Bretschneider, reprinted 1964), pp. 194–7. In literary works the word '*euergetēs*' had long been used of a fellow citizen: besides the passage in Aristophanes mentioned above, see Xenophon, *Poroi*, 3, 11, where we find a proposal to open a subscription to improve the maritime trade of Athens, the subscribers' names to be 'enrolled for transmission to posterity' on the list of *euergetai* of Athens (an expression that reminds us of the 'perpetual *euergetai*' of the later Hellenistic epoch: an 'eternal gymnasiarch' would be one who had established a permanent foundation for the gymnasiarchy, thereby giving an imperishable example of magnificence).

70. *Politics*, VI, 7 (1321a30).

71. I shall come back to the officials who defray the expenses of their office and to the enthronement banquets. As regards the *eisitēria*, a distinction must be drawn, because it seems that this word has three very different meanings, only the first of which concerns us. (1) Public sacrifice at the beginning of the civil year (Demosthenes, XIX, *On the Embassy*, 190: XXI, *Against Meidias*, 114; cf. G. Busolt, *Griechische Staatskunde*, vol. I, p. 518 and note 1; P. Stengel, *Griech. Kultusaltertümer*, third edn (1920), p. 249; L. Deubner, *Attische Feste*, p. 175). It does not appear that, in Athens, the *eisitēria* occasioned great public feasts, but other sacrifices did provide food for the people (Pseudo-Xenophon, *On the Government of Athens*, 2, 9). (2) Festival celebrating the anniversary of the installation of a divinity in its sanctuary, when a statue of the cult was set up: thus, at Magnesia-on-the-Maeander (O. Kern, *Die Inschriften von Magnesia*, no. 100 = Dittenberger, *Sylloge*, no. 695, line a25; M. Nilsson, *Griechische Feste*, p. 248; *Geschichte der griech. Religion*, vol. II, pp. 87, 388, 392; cf. P. Herrmann, 'Antiochos der Grosse und Teos', in *Anadolu (Anatolia)*, IX (1965), p. 66 and note 33). (3) Dues for entry into a public function or an association (see below, note 223). For the banquets of magistrates leaving office, see Xenophon, *Hellenica*, V, 4, 4 (on this passage see the following note). See also note 243.

72. Dedications of *phialai* or statuettes or statues when a priesthood or a public function was given up were well known in the Greek world. See W. Rouse, *Greek Votive Offerings* (1902), p. 260; M. Holleaux, *Études d'épigraphie et d'histoire grecques*, vol. II, p. 182; A. Wilhelm, 'Neue Beiträge V', (*Akad. der Wiss. in Wien, Sitzungsberichte* CCXIV, 4, 1932), pp. 9–10; F. Sokolowski, *Lois sacrées de l'Asie Mineure* (De Boccard, 1955), p. 155; L. Robert, *Hellenica*, XI–XII, pp. 268–9; Bernard and Salviat, in *Bulletin de correspondance hellénique*, 1962, p. 589. See also below, note 173, on a decree of Sestos, and note 265. The following examples can be mentioned: Plato, *Critias*, 120b; *Inscriptiones*

Graecae, editio minor, I, no. 1215; II–III, nos. 2891–931; Hiller von Gärtringen, *Inschriften von Priene*, no. 113, line 92. At Paros in the second century B C (*Inscriptiones Graecae*, XII, 5, 129, line 44) a former *agoranomos*, having performed his task well, was given the right to install a marble statue in the *agoranomion* (Salviat, in *Bulletin de correspondance hellénique*, 1958, p. 328, note 4). The custom existed in Rome. In the Narbonne tablet (Dessau, no. 6964), the outgoing *flamen* was authorized to set up a statue of himself in the sacred enclosure, and evidence has been found of a similar privilege granted to the provincial priest of Africa (D. Fishwick, in *Hermes*, 1964, p. 342ff.; for Hispania Tarraconensis, however, see P. Veyne, in *Les Empereurs romains d'Espagne* (Colloques du CNRS, 1965), p. 121. For the Greek custom whereby a priest consecrated a statue of himself in the sanctuary, cf. *Latomus*, XXI (1962), p. 86, note 3. F. Salviat has related the feasts given by certain outgoing magistrates in honour of Aphrodite (Xenophon, *Hellenica*, V, 4, 4, quoted in previous note) to the dedications to Aphrodite by *gynaikonomoi* leaving office (*Bulletin de correspondance hellénique*, 1966, p. 460). In Rome the *jus imaginis ad posteritatem prodendae* of the magistrates is well known (Pliny, *Natural History*, XXXIV, 14, 30; Cicero, *In Verrem*, II, 5; Mommsen, *Staatsrecht*, index, see under 'Bildnisrecht'; also vol. II, p. 437, note 4). At Pompeii the ministers of Fortuna Augusta were obliged by law to consecrate a statue of Fortuna (*Corpus Inscriptionum Latinarum*, X, 825–7). The same could be said of the *magistri Campani*, of the *magistri* of Minturnae, and of numberless statues, human and divine, erected *ex officio* in Italy and throughout the Empire by priests and magistrates: from the Republican period examples are plentiful and deserve systematic study. Sometimes the series is exceptionally full: at Syros (*Inscriptiones Graecae*, XII, 5, no. 659ff.), the *stephanēphoroi* for the year offered the people a sacrifice and a banquet with a *largitio*, and also put up a dedication to the Emperor, for his health – 'since when', the dedications conclude, 'there has been a good harvest, a good year and a healthy year'. Many examples could be given of these *largesses* and dedications on the occasion of entry into or departure from office. In the Tarentum tablet (Dessau, no. 6086, line 37), the magistrates can, at their discretion, use the money from fines either for their games or 'for their monument' (*seive ad monumentum suom in publico consumere volet*).

73. Polybius, XXI, 6, 2 (Phocaea, 190 B C).
74. Ibid., XV, 21; see also IV, 17; VII, 10; XIII, 1.
75. Ibid., XX, 6–7, cf. 4–5. I think that *dietithento* in this passage means a legacy in the form of a permanent foundation, and that Polybius is alluding to the fashion for foundations in memory of the deceased; on

this point I follow E. F. Bruck, *Totenteil und Seelgerät im griech. Recht*, p. 276 and note 1.

76. M. Feyel, *Polybe et l'histoire de Béotie au IIIe siècle avant notre ère* (De Boccard, 1942), pp. 280–83: cf., e.g., Polybius, XXIV, 7, 4.

77. Polybius, XXII, 4, 1. The distinction between 'collaborators' and 'Resistance' in Greece did not at all coincide with the distinction between the notables and the people. The anti-Roman parties were headed by notables. See, on all this and on the affairs of Boeotia, the excellent work by J. Deininger mentioned in note 31.

78. Cf. Polybius, XXXVIII, 11, 10.

79. L. Robert in *Annuaire du Collège de France*, 1971, p. 514; Feyel, pp. 274–9.

80. L. Robert, 'Les juges étrangers dans les cités grecques', in *Xenion: Festschrift für P. J. Zepos*, vol. I (C. Katsikalis Verlag, 1973), p. 775.

81. Plutarch, *Life of Phocion*, 9; *Precepts of Statecraft*, 31 (*Moralia*, 882d); *Sayings of Kings and Commanders* (*Moralia*, 188a); *On False Shame*, 10 (*Moralia*, 533a).

82. In 480, when Attica was evacuated before the victory at Salamis, each emigrant received eight drachmas. I will not go into the details, which are too well known.

83. A. M. Andreades, *Storia delle finanze greche*, pp. 306–10. Bibliography in A. R. Hands, *Charities and Social Aid in Greece and Rome* (Thames and Hudson, 1968), p. 165, notes 116 and 117. After Demetrius of Phaleron our documents make no further mention of the theoric fund; it may have been abolished.

84. The resident foreigners had no right to the theoric fund, which was distributed on the basis of the registers of citizenship (Boeckh, *Staatshaushaltung*, vol. I, p. 279). Generally speaking, the resident foreigners received no *misthos* from the state (Xenophon, or Pseudo-Xenophon, *Poroi*, 2, 1). The idea that public assistance in antiquity was conditioned by citizenship and took no cognizance of the category 'the poor' is central to H. Bolkestein's excellent study of the subject.

85. Pseudo-Demosthenes, X, *Fourth Philippic*, 38.

86. Demosthenes, XVIII, *De Corona*, 107 (262) or 311 (329).

87. It should be remembered that the liturgists received funds from the state; but these funds were quite inadequate, and, in any case, the liturgists felt bound to spend more than they received, out of a spirit of competition. Also, the rich paid a heavy *eisphora*.

88. According to a famous remark by the orator Demades, quoted by Plutarch, *Quaestiones Platonicae*, 10, 4 (*Moralia*, p. 1011b): 'the glue of the democracy'.

89. Xenophon, *Symposium*, 4, 30–33.

90. Xenophon (or Pseudo-Xenophon), *Poroi*, 6, 1.

91. This is the picture drawn in the *Fourth Philippic*, 40–41. The orator is embarrassed by the paternalistic connotation of the 'family' analogy, so he says, awkwardly, that the 'father' of this family is the whole body of citizens.

92. *Fourth Philippic*, 35ff.

93. Aristotle, *Politics*, V, 5 (1304b25); cf. 1305a5.

94. Ibid., V, 8 (1309a15).

95. An *eisphora*. I have paraphrased *Politics*, VI, 5 (1320a15). The word *eisphora* always means a tax that is *extraordinary* – in theory, at least.

96. *Politics*, VI, 5 (1320b1). For useless liturgies, see V, 8 (1309a15). In fact Aristotle touches here upon another problem, namely the proliferation of liturgies which served to provide festivals for the people. In this age of collective leisure occupations, the people's pleasures were collective, and these festivals were somewhat like the social security payments or the paid holidays of our time. The oligarchs and moralists attacked them as demagogic waste. In the fifth century Athens had supported its citizens to a large extent on the tribute paid by its 'allies' (cf. Aristophanes, *Wasps*, 655). When this source of income dried up in the fourth century, the rich had to pay for the feeding and the leisure of the poor. For the financial reorganization of Athens by Demetrius, see E. Bayer, *Demetrios Phalereus der Athener*, pp. 46–7 and 70–71, who shows that the transformation of the regime of liturgies by Demetrius had nothing particularly 'Peripatetic' about it. Aristotle and Demetrius simply reflected the conditions and difficulties of their time, and expressed them in the style of the moderate oligarchy. Also, Demetrius celebrated the public festivals in sumptuous style (Plutarch, *Precepts of Statecraft*, 24, p. 818d). On the real spirit of Demetrius's austerity measures, see Bayer, p. 47, note 1, on Cicero, *De Officiis*, II, 60.

97. Strabo, XIV, 2, 5, p. 653, on Rhodes; Wiegand and Wilamowitz, 'Ein Gesetz von Samos über die Beschaffung von Brotkorn aus öffentlichen Mitteln', in *Sitzungsberichte der Akad. Berlin*, 1904, pp. 917–31 (not collected in Wilamowitz's *Kleine Schriften*). The text is reproduced in full in J. Pouilloux, *Choix d'inscriptions grecques* (Les Belles Lettres, 1960), no. 34, and, in part, in Dittenberger, *Sylloge Inscriptionum Graecarum*, third edn, no. 976. The institution was permanent, as the funds remained untouched and the interest alone was used for the purchase of corn. See also G. Busolt, *Griechische Staatskunde*, p. 434.

98. Hiller von Gärtringen, *Inschriften von Priene* (1906, reprinted by De Gruyter, 1968), no. 108, lines 42, 57 and 68. See, more generally, H. Francotte, 'Le pain à bon marché et le pain gratuit dans les cités grecques', in *Mélanges Nicole* (1905), pp. 143–54 (reproduced in Francotte's *Mélanges de droit public grec* (1910), p. 291; A. Wilhelm, 'Sitometria', in *Mélanges Glotz*, vol. II, pp. 899–908; for the supply of

corn in normal years, see L. Robert, *Bulletin de correspondance hellénique*, LII (1928), pp. 426–32 (reproduced in his *Opuscula Minora Selecta*, vol. I, p. 108).

99. In pre-industrial economies, landowners store corn in their granaries either to speculate (waiting for a price-rise) or merely to ensure their own survival. These stocks of corn are stored in their town houses, not in the countryside. I examine elsewhere the passages in the *Digest* that deal with the hoarding of corn. I will also quote Proverbs 11: 26: 'He that withholdeth corn,' (so as to sell it during a famine) 'the people shall curse him: but blessing shall be upon the head of him that selleth it.' For *paraprasis*, see L. Robert, *Études anatoliennes*, pp. 346, 347 and note 3, 547; J. and L. Robert, *La Carie*, vol. II, p. 322; J. Triantaphyllopoulos, in *Acts of the Fifth International Congress of Greek and Latin Epigraphy* (Oxford, 1971), p. 65. Cf. an inscription from Roman Africa (*Corpus*, VIII, 26121): 'exigente annona, frumenta quantacumq[ue] habuit populo, multo minore pretio quam tunc erat, benignissime praestitit.'

100. C. Préaux, *L'Économie royale des Lagides*, pp. 41 and 294, following a papyrus of Zeno (Edgar and Hunt, *Select Papyri, Public Documents*, no. 410).

101. Polybius, XXXVIII, 15, 6 and 11.

102. M. Feyel, *Polybe et l'histoire de Béotie*, pp. 256–62.

103. The essential study is that by G. Busolt, *Griechische Staatskunde*, vol. I, especially p. 612.

104. On real direct taxation, see especially Busolt, pp. 609–11, who shows that there was nothing extraordinary about this: see also H. Francotte, *Les Finances des cités grecques*, p. 49; A. Wilhelm, in *Akad. der Wiss. in Wien, phil.-hist. Klasse, Sitzungsberichte*, CCXXIV, 4 (1947): 'Zu den Inschriften aus dem Heiligtum des Gottes Sinuri', p. 17; B.A. van Groningen, *Aristote, Second livre de l'Économique*, p. 143; H.W. Pleket in *Bulletin of the American Society of Papyrology*, 1972, p. 46.

105. R. Thomsen, *Eisphora, a study of direct taxation in ancient Athens* (1964).

106. In later spoken Greek, *megalopsychia*, 'greatness of soul', 'magnanimity', eventually came to mean liberality, and even an *act* of liberality. The same thing happened to the Latin *magnanimitas*. This explains a phrase in the *Satyricon*, 45, 5, where it is said of a *euergetes* '*magnum animum habet*', which does not mean 'he has big ideas', but 'he is open-handed'. For *megalopsychia*, to the references already mentioned one could add Ptolemy, *Tetrabiblos*, IV, 3, 177: the stars of Jupiter and Venus predispose ἐπὶ χάρισι καὶ δωρεαῖς καὶ τιμαῖς καὶ μεγαλοψυχίαις. The meaning of the word was established during discussions about a famous mosaic in Antioch: see G. Downey, 'The pagan virtue of *megalopsychia*', in *Proceedings of the American Philological Association*, LXXVI (1945),

pp. 279–86 (who sees *megalopsychia* as signifying 'courage') and E. Weigand in *Byzantinische Zeitschrift*, XXXV (1935), p. 428 (who saw in it the generosity of the *euergetēs*); subsequently, D. Levi, *Antioch Mosaic Pavements*, vol. I, p. 339, and P. Petit, *Libanius et la Vie municipale à Antioche* (1955), p. 142, note 5, and p. 282, notes 5 and 10. For Latin *magnanimitas* and *magnitudo animi*, see J. Aymard, 'La *mégalopsychia* de Yakto et la *magnanimitas* de Marc Aurèle', in *Revue des études anciennes*, LV (1953), pp. 301–6, concerning a passage in the *Historia Augusta*; Aymard gives other references (Symmachus, *Codex Justiniani*). I will mention one that is especially interesting: *Sallust's Second Letter to Caesar*, 5, 5, a reference given by R. A. Gauthier, *Magnanimitas, l'idéal de grandeur dans la philosophie païenne et dans la théologie chrétienne*, Bibliothèque thomiste, XXVIII (Vrin, 1951), p. 167, note 4, and p. 170, note 4. On *magnitudo animi* in Tacitus, see R. Syme, *Tacitus*, p. 417, note 2. Many more references could be given (the *Thesaurus Linguae Latinae* being of no help here): thus, the inscription *Corpus*, VIII, 27382, where *majore animo* is equivalent to *ampliata pecunia* or *ampliata liberalitate*; Pliny, *Natural History*, VII, 26; Caesar *magnanimitatis perhibuit exemplum* by his entertainments and distributions; Pliny the Younger, *Letters*, IV, 13, 9, where the *euergetēs* tries to instil into his peers the same feelings of liberality that inspire him, should probably be translated: 'be more generous in response to my generosity' (*majorem animum ex meo* [*animo*] *sumite*).

107. E.g. Theocritus, *Eulogy of Ptolemy*, 106: far from clinging to his riches, Ptolemy has distributed them among the gods, the princes, the cities and his courtiers.

108. Study of the *largesses* of the Hellenistic kings would require a volume to itself. See the references assembled by C. Préaux, 'Les villes hellénistiques', in *Recueils de la Société Jean-Bodin*, VI: *La Ville*, vol. I (1953), p. 119, note 1, and p. 122, note 1. I will refer only to Polybius, V, 88–90 (gifts by the kings and princes to Rhodes after the earthquake) and to Livy, XLI, 20 (following Polybius: the magnificences of Antiochus Epiphanes). What Livy writes is interesting: 'Nevertheless, in two great and important respects his soul was truly royal – in his benefactions to cities and in the honours paid to the gods' – a significant testimony to the connection between religious offerings and euergetistic gifts. Moreover, gifts to temples were hard to distinguish from gifts to cities, since the cities controlled the treasuries of the temples: giving to Athene meant giving to Athens. A statue or a sacred building was both an offering to a god and an ornament for the town. Festivals, games and sacrifices were at once homage to the gods and also nourishment and distraction for the people. The dedications of public buildings clearly reveal the dual significance. For example, the hall of the Council

at Miletus, built by two courtiers of Antiochus Epiphanes (Roehm, *Milet*, I, 2, *Das Rathaus*, inscriptions 1 and 2, and p. 95), was consecrated 'to Apollo, to Hestia the Counsellor, and to the People [of Miletus]' – it was both a sacred offering to the gods and a present to the city. On the custom of consecrating many buildings, sacred and secular alike (and even sundials), to the god of the city, to the city itself (or to its people) and also, later, to the Emperor, cf. P. Veyne in *Latomus*, 1962, pp. 66 and 82; G. F. Maier, *Griech. Mauerbauinschriften*, vol. II (Quelle und Meyer, 1961), p. 26.

109. Polybius, IV, 65, 6–7 and IX, 30, 7; E. V. Hansen, *The Attalids of Pergamon*, second edn (Cornell University, 1971), pp. 46 and 292; R. B. MacShane, *The Foreign Policy of the Attalids of Pergamon* (University of Illinois, 1964), pp. 101 and 109.

110. É. Will, *Histoire politique du monde hellénistique*, vol. I (Annales de l'Est, 1966), p. 162, note 1.

111. See, *inter alia*, Will, vol. I, pp. 289, 290, 329, 363. Traces of these gifts have been sought in the circulation of money: T. Hackens, in *Antidorum W. Peremans* (Studia Hellenistica, XVI), especially pp. 82–90.

112. M. Holleaux, *Études*, vol. I, pp. 1–40.

113. Polybius, VII, 8, 6.

114. For Rhodes, see note 108: for Athens, H. H. Thompson, 'Athens and the Hellenistic princes', in *Proceedings of the American Philosophical Society*, XCVII (1953), pp. 254–61; for the major sanctuaries, Will, vol. I, pp. 14 and note 1, 206–7, 218, 292, 364; vol. II, p. 242.

115. Polybius, XXII, 8, 7; cf. XX, 12, 5–7.

116. Plutarch, *Life of Phocion*, 18.

117. Polybius, IV, 49 (cf. XXVII, 18, 1).

118. Ibid., V, 88, 4 and 90, 5.

119. Thucydides, VI, 16, 2–5.

120. P. Herrmann, 'Neue Urkunden zur Geschichte von Milet', in *Istanbuler Mitteilungen*, XV (1965), pp. 71–117; for the decree *Didyma* no. 142 (quoted by Herrmann, p. 77), see L. Robert in *Gnomon*, XXXI (1959), p. 663, now in *Opuscula Minora Selecta*, vol. III, p. 1628: Irenias 'induced' the king to give his corn ($\pi\rho\sigma\tau\rho\epsilon\psi\acute{\alpha}\mu\epsilon\nu\sigma\varsigma$). On this word, see my note 212; I shall return to the point later. For the king who takes upon himself the cost of the honours awarded to him, see note 162 (and, for the Roman period, a decree of Pagai: cf. P. Veyne in *Latomus*, 1962, p. 65, note 1). The 160,000 *medimnoi* are 6,000 or 7,000 tonnes of corn; as the editor explains, quoting Polybius, XXXI, 31, 1, this corn was destined to be sold, and the money obtained from the sale would be lent out at interest by the city: the gymnasium would be built by means of this interest and the city would still possess the capital produced by the sale of the corn. A king, says the Pseudo-Aristotle's

Economics, must consider 'whether one should pay what is expended in coin or in commodities which have an equivalent value'. For another good example of the great *euergetēs* who helped his country through his connections, see decree no. 4 in Dittenberger, *Orientis Graeci Inscriptiones Selectae*. For *euergetai* who helped their country through their connections not with the Hellenistic kings, but with the Romans, see L. Robert, in *L'Antiquité classique*, XXXV (1966), p. 420, and in *Comptes rendus de l'Académie des inscriptions*, 1969, p. 43; for the services rendered to the cities by financiers, see L. Robert in *Revue des études grecques*, LXX (1957), p. 374, now in *Opuscula Minora Selecta*, vol. III, p. 1491.

121. F. Hiller von Gärtringen, *Inschriften von Priene* (1906, reprinted by De Gruyter 1968), no. 108, line 91.

122. Note this use of the word πατρίς which, in the inscriptions, belongs rather to the later Hellenistic age; cf. B. Laum, *Stiftungen in der griechischen und römischen Antike* (1914, reprinted by Scientia Verlag 1964), pp. 44 and 162. This phraseology, as I have heard Louis Robert explain at the École des Hautes Études, applies to the city the language of family relations: a very commonly used formula is 'my very dear home town', like 'my very dear wife', which we read in epitaphs. A *euergetēs* will say, for example: 'I give and present such-and-such a piece of real estate to my very dear home town' or else τῇ κυρίᾳ πατρίδι, 'to her ladyship my home town' (in inscriptions in Lycia). The most impressive example of ἡ γλυκυτάτη πατρίς is in the Acts of the Alexandrians: the gymnasiarch Appianus, condemned to death, hears his companions say to him that it will be his glory to die for his very dear home town (H. A. Musurillo, *The Acts of the Pagan Martyrs* (Oxford, 1954), p. 66). Similarly, the language of the *agapē* is applied to the city (Dio of Prusa, *Orationes*, XLIV, 6); see A. D. Nock, 'A Vision of Mandulis Aion', in *Harvard Theological Review*, 1934, p. 67 (*Essays*, vol. I, p. 368). This 'family' language was copied by the Romans: 'Why, shameless man, do you not measure out something from that great heap [of gold] for your dear country [*cara patria*]?' says Horace to a rich miser (*Satires*, II, 2, 105).

123. Line 66, restored by Wilamowitz.

124. A γλυκισμός. On the meaning of this word, see, most recently, L. Robert, in *Studi Clasice*, X (1968), p. 84, and *Arkhaiologiké Ephemeris*, 1969, p. 35, note 4. The Romans were to copy this usage: their *euergetai* would distribute *mulsum*. The day when the *stephanēphoros* took up office was also the first day of the year; the γλυκισμός offered by Moschion thus recalls the *largesses* which, Aristotle tells us, the magistrates offered on the occasion of their taking up office. At the same time it was equivalent to *eisitēria*, sacrifices offered for the New Year.

125. Which implies that he bought, evidently out of his own pocket, a substantial number of victims. Cf. decree no. 113, at Priene itself, line 61, which should be restored as [πάνδ] ημον εὐωχία[ν]; cf. L. Robert in *Hermes*, 1930, p. 115, now in *Opuscula Minora Selecta*, vol. I, p. 663.

126. *Inschriften von Priene*, no. 108, lines 43, 48, 70; *Sylloge*, no. 570, line 12; no. 569, line 5; *Supplementum Epigraphicum Graecum*, vol. I, no. 336 (J. Pouilloux, *Choix*, no. 3), line 437; Dittenberger, *Orientis Graeci Inscriptiones Selectae*, no. 339, lines 24 and 54.

127. Dittenberger, *Orientis Graeci Inscriptiones Selectae*, no. 339; cf. A.-J. Festugière, *La Révélation d'Hermès Trismégiste*, vol. II, *Le Dieu cosmique*, p. 305, note 2. I had the good fortune to hear L. Robert explain this decree at the École des Hautes Études.

128. It happened often that an honoured person relieved the city of the cost of his honours, and this practice was passed on to Rome, where innumerable honorific pedestals were to bear the formula *honore contentus impensam remisit*; see B. Laum, *Stiftungen*, vol. II, p. 35, note 5; W. Liebenam, *Städteverwaltung in römischen Kaiserreiche* (Bretschneider, reprinted 1967), p. 128, note 1. See notes 120 and 162.

129. I could also have quoted the decree of Istros for Aristagoras (*Sylloge*, no. 708), that of Mantinea for a pair of *euergetai*, husband and wife (no. 783), and that of Samos for Bulagoras (J. Pouilloux, *Choix*, no. 2).

130. On the style of the inscriptions, see E. Norden, *Die antike Kunstprosa*, pp. 140 and 443; L. Robert, in *Revue des études anciennes*, LXII (1960), p. 325, now in *Opuscula Minora Selecta*, vol. II, p. 841.

131. *Sylloge*, no. 495: see E. H. Minns, *Scythians and Greeks* (Biblo and Tannen, reprinted 1965), vol. II, p. 462ff.

132. It can be seen from the decree that this tribute consisted of more or less sumptuous presents. When the king desired these presents, or had need of them, he visited the city, and the city offered them to him on that occasion. If the king considered the presents inadequate, he threatened to take offence, and to give the order to depart from the city – unpleasantness which portended formidable reprisals.

133. At this point let me express my deep gratitude to Philippe Ariès. This great historian did me the honour of discussing his current work on attitudes to death in the Christian world.

134. Thucydides, II, 13, 1. On foundations in Greece, see E. F. Bruck, *Totenteil und Seelgerät in griech. Recht*; B. Laum, *Stiftungen in der griech. und römischen Antike* (Scientia Verlag, reprinted 1964); M. Nilsson, *Geschichte der griech. Religion*, second edn, vol. II, pp. 113–19; H. Bolkestein, *Wohltätigkeit und Armenpflege im vorchristlichen Altertum* (1939), pp. 232–5.

135. Laum, *Stiftungen*, vol. II, p. 3, note 1; cf. vol. I, no. 90, and p. 24, note

1. It could happen that a foundation in honour of a god was entrusted to a city, which received and administered the funds (Laum, vol. I, p. 156). On the other hand, when a *euergetēs* established a fund to supply sacrifices, he thereby ensured a feast for the city's inhabitants (Laum, vol. II, no. 21; cf. Nilsson, p. 114).

136. Laum, vol. II, no. 46.

137. Ibid., vol. I, pp. 89 and 105; vol. II, nos. 68 and 62; Marrou, *Histoire de l'éducation dans l'Antiquité*, pp. 178 and 500. I have not been able to see Ziebarth's *Aus dem griech. Schulwesen* (1914).

138. Laum, vol. I, p. 105; vol. II, no. 90; Marrou, ibid., p. 161.

139. Laum, vol. I, pp. 40–45.

140. Ibid., vol. II, no. 129.

141. Ibid., vol. I, p. 47, and vol. II, no. 151. In 182 a certain Alcesippus founded, in honour of Apollo and of the city of Delphi, a sacrifice which came to be called the Alcesippeia (Laum, vol. II, no. 27). For foundations intended to cover the cost of a liturgy or a priesthood, see Laum, vol. I, p. 97, and vol. II, no. 162, for example: in order to ensure the performance of the gymnasiarchy for ever, a gymnasiarch established a fund to meet the costs of that office; but if a future gymnasiarch should wish to meet these costs himself, the unexpended income from the fund was to revert to the city, which would use it to purchase cornfields. A person who in this way rendered a certain function permanent, 'eternal', gave thereby a no less eternal example of generosity and became an 'eternal' gymnasiarch. See Heberdey and Wilhelm, *Reisen in Kilikien*, p. 153; Laum, vol. I, pp. 46 and 97; L. Robert in *Revue des études anciennes*, LXII (1960), p. 294, and in *Revue de philologie*, XLI (1967), pp. 42–3.

142. Laum, vol. I, p. 133 and note 3.

143. Bruck, *Totenteil*, p. 166; E. Rohde, *Psyche, the Cult of Souls and Belief in Immortality among the Greeks* (Eng. tr., 1925), pp. 162–74.

144. Bruck, pp. 119–45.

145. Reception or *dexiōsis*: Laum, vol. I, p. 70, and vol. II, no. 45, the text of which is better read in Dittenberger, *Sylloge*, no. 1106, with note 23.

146. Banquet or *hestiasis*: Laum, vol. I, p. 72, and vol. II, no. 50.

147. The three oldest foundations (Posidonius at Halicarnassus, Diomedon at Cos, and Epicteta at Thera) are family foundations (Laum, vol. II, nos. 117, 45 and 43).

148. Laum, vol. I, pp. 160–61 and 248–9.

149. Ibid., vol. I, pp. 160 and 249.

150. Ibid., vol. I, p. 72, and vol. II, no. 50; for the blurring of distinction between the cult of the dead and the cult of the gods, see Nilsson, vol. II, pp. 116–17.

151. Diogenes Laertius, V, 71 (Laum, vol. II, no. 16); cf. Bruck, p. 159, note 8. For the 'cultural' immortality of the philosophers and for the cult of the Muses, I refer the reader once for all to P. Boyancé, *Le Culte des muses chez les philosophes grecs* (De Boccard, 1937).

152. Laum, vol. I, pp. 74, 98, 103.

153. Plutarch, *Life of Nicias*, 3, 7.

154. Xenophon, *Anabasis*, V, 3, 9; cf. Laum, vol. II, nos. 12 and 3.

155. Aeschines (who seems to be in the right on this, from the standpoint of us rationalists) has to make desperate efforts to get the Athenian people to understand that a functionary's promise to add something to the public funds from his own pocket does not justify the loss of the city's right to check his accounts (*Against Ctesiphon*, 17–23). Besides which, says Aeschines, one ought first to establish whether this *euergetēs* has really spent a larger sum than he received. And even if the functionary had declined any public money, presentation of accounts would still be justified, in order that he might state in writing that he neither received nor spent anything from the public funds (*Against Ctesiphon*, 22).

156. Polybius, XXVIII, 7, 7.

157. Xenophon, *Hellenica*, VI, 1 and 2; G. Busolt, *Griechische Staatskunde*, vol. I, p. 360; cf. the power of Protogenes at Olbia (Busolt, p. 484, note 1).

158. In the Hellenistic era and even in the Roman era, the policy of the cities continued to be shaped by orators, as in Demosthenes' day (Dio of Prusa was a sort of Panhellenic councillor). 'It was political speaking and adjuration that mattered,' writes L. Robert in *Laodicée du Lycos, le Nymphée* (Université Laval Recherches archéologiques, De Boccard, 1969), p. 306. See also L. Robert, *Monnaies grecques* (Droz, 1967), p. 25; 'Les juges étrangers dans la cité grecque', in *Festschrift für P. J. Zepos*, vol. I, p. 778; 'Théophane de Mytilène à Constantinople', in *Comptes rendus de l'Académie des inscriptions*, 1969, p. 42: 'The Greek city did not die at Chaeronea.'

159. Friedländer, *Sittengeschichte Roms*, vol. III, pp. 65–9 (Eng. tr. *Roman Life and Manners*, vol. II (1908), pp. 260–63).

160. On this thinking in terms of types or essences, see G. Jellinek, *Allgemeine Staatslehre*, third edn (1922), p. 36; Husserl, *Expérience et Jugement* (tr. Souche, PUF, 1970), p. 233.

161. 'In the busiest part': e.g. Dittenberger, *Sylloge*, no. 711, L, 42; 'wherever he likes': e.g. A. Wilhelm, 'Neue Beiträge, IV' in *Akad. der Wiss. in Wien, Sitzungsberichte*, CLXXIX, 6 (1915), p. 44, and in *Jahreshefte des österr. arch. Instituts*, X (1907), p. 17. In the great decree of the *koinon* of Asia in honour of Menogenes which was discovered at Sardis, Menogenes is given the right to erect a portrait of himself in whichever

city of Asia he chooses. It was an additional honour to leave the choice of location in this way to the person being honoured (Pliny, *Letters*, X, 8, 2). In Pliny the Elder, *Natural History*, XXXIV, 11, 25 we read that the Vestal Gaia Taracia (heroine of a legend which duplicates that of Acca Larentia) had a statue decreed to her – 'the same, too, to be placed wherever she might think fit' (*ut poneretur ubi vellet*). This wording suffices to indicate that it is the invention of a Hellenistic historian. As Roman public honours, from the last century of the Republic onward, are a very faithful copy of Hellenistic honours, there is often mention in the Roman texts of statues set up *celebri loco* or *ubi vellet*: thus, Cicero, *In Pisonem*, XXXVIII, 93; Pliny the Elder, *Natural History*, XXXIV, 2; Pliny, *Letters*, VIII, 6, 14; Apuleius, *Florida*, XVI, 36 (a text of great interest for the mechanism of public honours, which deserves a full epigraphic commentary).

162. This feature is familiar to Latin epigraphists, who also know the wording *honore contentus impensam remisit*. However, like most features of Latin epigraphy, it is of Hellenistic origin. I quoted above (notes 120 and 128) the case of Irenias and King Eumenes. I will add here a decree of Pagae (Wilhelm, in *Jahreshefte des österr. arch. Instituts*, X (1907), p. 17), a decree of Pergamum (Hepding, in *Mitteilungen des deutschen archäol. Instituts, Athen. Abteil.*, XXXII (1907), pp. 264 and 271), the decree of Sestos in honour of Menas (Dittenberger, *Orientis Graeci Inscriptiones*, no. 339, line 42). The person concerned could either take upon himself the cost of his statue, or exempt the city from erecting the statue and also refrain from erecting it himself, resting content with the decree that awarded it to him and bore witness to his merits (compare, in Pliny, *Letters*, VII, 29, 2, the conduct of the freedman Pallas: the Senate awarded him 15 million sesterces, but he declined to accept this money, being satisfied with the honour of the *senatus consultum* which awarded it). See Dio of Prusa, XXXI, *Discourse to the People of Rhodes*, 114–15. A city could either itself award a statue and provide credits for this purpose, or simply authorize someone by decree to erect the statue himself. In both cases the person honoured could rest content with the honour of the decree, that is, could exempt the city from erecting the statue, without doing this himself, or could take over from the city the expense of the statue, or could refrain from erecting himself the statue he was authorized to erect. When a city awarded a statue and decided to pay for this itself, it could give the money to the person concerned, who would then be able either to use this money to erect the statue, or to keep it, or to use it for a different purpose. When the Emperor Vespasian heard that a certain city had just awarded him a statue of considerable cost, he held out his open palm to the city's ambassadors and said: 'The pedestal is waiting'

(Suetonius, *Vespasian*, 23). It sometimes happened that a notable took upon himself the expense of a statue awarded to someone else (L. Robert, *Hellenica*, IV, p. 141, note 2), and also that the person honoured used the money to erect a statue not of himself but of a god (hence an epigram in the *Anthology*, XVI, appendix by Planudes, 267; cf. Dio Cassius, LIV, 35: Augustus used the money from a collection not to erect statues to himself, but instead to erect statues of Concord and Peace). A very different case is that of statues erected by subscription: e.g. at Rhodes, the statue of a gymnasiarch was erected by more than 500 persons (*Inscriptiones Graecae*, XII, 1, no. 46). In the Roman sphere the best example is doubtless the pedestal of Sulpicius Felix, at Sala, set up by his *amici* (J. Carcopino, *Le Maroc antique*, p. 200).

163. See again the decree of Pagae mentioned in notes 161 and 162 (Wilhelm, *Jahreshefte des österr. arch. Instituts*, X (1907), pp. 28–9).

164. *Euergetai* might be hailed in the theatre, or at their entry into the town, by the whole population (St John Chrysostom, *On Vain Glory and the Education of Children*, Malingrey (ed.) (*Sources chrétiennes*, no. 188), pp. 75–83, vividly describes such an occasion; see also note 165); we shall see the population hailing a notable so as to induce him to make *largesse* (note 250). In Apuleius, *Metamorphoses*, X, 19, a procession greets a notable as he enters the town. Pliny writes that the people of a city of which he is patron 'celebrate my arrival among them' (*adventus meos celebrat*) (*Letters*, IV, 1, 4). An inscription at Marathon describes a solemn entry by Herodes Atticus (Svenson in *Bulletin de correspondance hellénique*, 1926, p. 527). This occasioned a decree 'of reception' (a splendid example: *Sylloge*, no. 798, lines 15 to end).

165. See note 221. Compare Dessau, *Inscriptiones Latinae Selectae*, no. 5062: a notable of Minturnae undertook the charge of a gladiatorial combat 'which the people had asked of him during the celebration of his procession', *postul[ante] populo q[uando] process[us] editio celebrata est* (this was the *processus* of new municipal magistrates or *duumviri*, comparable to that of new consuls, on which see H. Stern, *Le Calendrier de 354*, p. 158).

166. On the language of family feeling as applied to the city, see my note 122. For the titles given to the *euergetai*, especially 'foster-father', see L. Robert, *Hellenica*, XI–XII, pp. 569–76. The name '*euergetēs*' was itself an officially awarded title (see, e.g., the list of the *euergetai* of Pergamum compiled by C. Habicht in *Istanbuler Mitteilungen*, IX–X (1959–60), p. 118, note 2). For the title 'son of the town', see now L. Robert in *Laodicée du Lycos, le Nymphée*, p. 317, note 4 (*filius publicus* is Apuleius's translation, in *Metamorphoses*, IV, 26). Also found are titles such as 'mother of the metropolis', or, at Sparta, 'Hestia of the city'. For 'foster-father', see L. Robert, *Monnaies grecques* (Droz, 1967), p.

66. 'Foster-father and founder' is found in the colony of Parlais (L. Robert, *Hellenica*, VII, p. 78); a founder, under the Empire, was a *euergetēs* who had won for the city the protection or the mercy of the Emperor (J. and L. Robert, *La Carie*, vol. II, p. 163) or had had public buildings erected (*Hellenica*, XI–XII, p. 575): in the colony of Sinope we find the Latin translation of this title, *conditori patriae* (*L'Année épigraphique*, 1916, p. 339, no. 120). A 'founder' is someone who has 'embellished his city', a *kosmopolis* (L. Robert, *Études anatoliennes*, p. 349), and this has an equivalent in Tripolitania, where *euergetai* bear the title *ornator patriae*. (These inscriptions are in both Latin and neo-Punic, the Latin title being accompanied by its neo-Punic translation: see J. M. Reynolds and J. B. Ward Perkins, *The Inscriptions of Roman Tripolitania*, index, p. 264. It will be seen that, despite what has been alleged, the title *ornator patriae* is not of Punic origin, but Greek: the neo-Punic version is a translation from the Latin, which is itself a translation from the Greek.) For the exclamation 'Ocean!' (or 'Nile!'), see J. and L. Robert, 'Bulletin épigraphique', in *Revue des études grecques*, 1958, p. 207, no. 105. In the *Key to Dreams* by Artemidorus of Daldis, he who dreams of a river will be a *euergetēs* (p. 147, 2–7 (Pack)) and also head of his city. Another honorific title is 'chief man of the city' or 'chief man of the island' (in Malta, in *Inscriptiones Graecae*, XIV, 601, with a reference to Acts 28: 7), together with 'chief man of the province', or (in Asia) 'chief man of the Greeks' (Dittenberger, *Orientis Graeci Inscriptiones*, no. 528; L. Robert, in *Annuaire des Hautes Études*, 1964–5, p. 180; cf. P. Veyne in *Bulletin de correspondance hellénique*, 1966, p. 150, note 2). In this connection, it seems to me that the patronate of cities in the Roman world needs fresh study. The patronate was not a function imposing precise activities, but a title, *patronus*, which was awarded to benefactors as a gesture of thanks: it is a word (and not a thing), comparable to 'son of the town' or 'founder'. The title *patronus* could be awarded for a great variety of merits, and study of these merits is not study of 'the patronate of cities' but of the benefits which could be brought to Roman cities; just as, in our day, studying decorations or the Legion of Honour is not the same as studying the very diverse reasons why a person may be decorated – which would mean studying much of the functioning of French society.

167. L. Robert, 'Sur une liste de Courètes à Ephèse', in *Arkhaiologiké Ephemeris*, 1967, p. 131. A *patroboulos* is a son of a member of the Council, successor-designate of his father, and as such associated from adolescence with the work of the Council. Cf. J. Declareuil, *Quelques problèmes d'histoire des institutions municipales* (1911), p. 188.

168. On the consolatory decrees, see E. Norden, *Die antike Kunstprosa*, vol. I, p. 448; L. Robert, *Hellenica*, III, p. 15; also in his *Laodicée du Lycos,*

le *Nymphée*, p. 324, and in *L'Antiquité classique*, XXXVII (1968), p. 407, note 6. I have not read O. Gottwald, 'Zu den griech. Trost-beschlüssen', in *Commentationes Vindobonenses*, 3 (1938), pp. 5–19. This topos, the theory of which was expounded by Menander the Rhetorician, is summarized by Pliny, *Letters*, II, 7, 5: it serves to keep fresh the memory of the deceased, to comfort his relatives, and to offer a good example; it is a variant of the decree of honorific testimony, as we see from Cicero's *Fourteenth Philippic*, 11, 31. Examples include, in Greek, the decree *Sylloge* no. 889, and in Latin a decree of Sicca, *Corpus*, VIII, 15880. For public funerals, see a decree of Capua, *Corpus*, X, 3903, and numerous Greek examples (Athens, Epidaurus, Amorgos, Aphrodisias, Olbia, Odessus etc.; cf. J. and L. Robert, *La Carie*, vol. II, p. 176, on a hybrid type of inscription, at once funerary and honorific.

169.   For example, in two honorific decrees of Magnesia-on-the-Maeander (O. Kern, *Inschriften von Magnesia*, no. 92 a and b and no. 94). On mention of the number of votes cast, at the end of a decree, see Wilhelm, 'Neue Beiträge, VI' in *Akad. der Wiss. in Wien, Sitzungs-berichte*, CLXXXIII, 3 (1921), p. 5; L. Robert, in *Revue des études anciennes*, 1963, p. 304, and in *Annuaire du Collège de France*, 1963–4, p. 365.

170.   *Sylloge*, no. 898. In the Latin part of the Empire things were done in the same way as in this Greek document. For honorific decrees, and for these alone, the people were associated with the Council and voting was by acclamation – a fact which Latin epigraphy, always sparing of explanations (and anxious to avoid the expense of engraving long texts), expresses in the simple words *decreto Ordinis et populi* (or sometimes *Ordo censuit consentiente populo*, Dessau, no. 6530; *succlamante populo*, no. 6113). On the voting of honorific decrees by popular acclamation, see I. Lévy, 'Études sur la vie municipale de l'Asie Min-eure', in *Revue des études grecques*, VIII (1895), pp. 208, 212, 214. This provides an opportunity to point out that the famous formula S P Q R, 'the Senate and the Roman people' (or, rather, 'the Roman Senate and people', as the adjective qualifies both nouns, since Sallust writes *populus senatusque Romanus*) does not mean anything very different. It appears in epigraphy about the time of the beginning of the Empire, not earlier; that is, at a time when the people had recently been deprived of any political role at all, except in so far as the representatives of the urban tribes played in Rome the role of cheer-leaders. The formula S P Q R signified that, thenceforth, the Senate would be the people's sole representative and its decrees would be regarded as expressing the popular will: cf. Mommsen, *Staatsrecht*, vol. III, p. 1258, note 4.

171.   L. Robert, 'Épigraphie', in *Encyclopédie de la Pléiade: L'histoire et ses méthodes*, pp. 8–10 of the offprint; L. Wenger, *Die Quellen des römischen*

Rechts (1953), p. 61, note 1. Let me take this opportunity to mention once more all that I owe to the teaching of Louis Robert at the École des Hautes Études.

172. Read them aloud in a low voice, is what is implied, not read silently. In antiquity nobody read silently, or rather the ability to do this was considered a feat of which only superior minds were capable. Hence the point of the formula we see on so many ancient tombs: 'Traveller, stop and read.' Reading aloud, in a low voice, gave new life to the epitaph, and it was aloud that the reader spoke the farewell which the epitaph asked of him. The reader also spoke the name of the deceased and thereby made him live again; cf. A. D. Nock, *Essays on Religion and the Ancient World*, vol. I, p. 359; C. Jullian, *Histoire de la Gaule*, vol. VI, p. 253, note 6; E. Norden, *Die antike Kunstprosa*, vol. II, p. 451; H.-I. Marrou, *Histoire de l'éducation dans l'Antiquité*, pp. 124, 215, 270. Hence Dio of Prusa, XVIII, 6, advises the reading of certain writers 'not casually by reading them to yourself but by having them read to you by others . . . For the effect is enhanced when one is relieved of the preoccupation of reading.'

173. The use of *martyria* in connection with an epigraphic text is found in Demosthenes, *Against Leptines*, 149: decrees engraved in sanctuaries are so many 'witnesses' to the people's favour. An honorific decree does two things: it witnesses to a man's merits (*martyria*) and it awards him an honour (*timē*). The testimonial is in itself a first degree of reward and of honour; it is even the only honour one can receive from the highest authorities, the Emperor and the provincial governor, who award no others and confine themselves to issuing certificates, so to speak, in letter form: the inscriptions on the tomb of Opramoas, which I shall discuss later, and, in the Latin West, the Thorigny Marble are examples. There is a second variety of quasi-honour: having the testimonial engraved, instead of letting it lie in the city's archives. Any person awarded an honour could, of course, if he chose, commission an engraving of the decree which honoured him and whose text the city would certainly have conveyed to him. He could, for example, have it engraved on his tomb. But the quasi-honour consisted in the city itself deciding to have the decree engraved, in some public place (whereas of course no private person, even the recipient of an honour, had the right to have a text engraved in a public place). The city could also have the text engraved on a bronze tablet, to be presented to the person concerned (*Sylloge*, no. 889, line 36). This was called *epigraphē*, a word used for any inscription honouring someone, which could be a decree which the city had had engraved, or the right granted by the city to a *euergetēs* to include his name in the monumental inscription on a public building constructed at his expense, cf. note 265; or the

right granted by the city to a deserving magistrate or liturgist to mention his name on the *anathēmata*, *phialai* or statue which he was authorized, after presenting his accounts, to consecrate to the gods in order to thank them for his fortunate and honest administration, cf. note 72. For example, in the decree of Sestos, *Sylloge*, no. 339, lines 40 and 94, with note 20, the *euergetēs* Menas is allowed to engrave his name on the *imagines clipeatae* which he will consecrate to the gods when he leaves office. An example, taken at random, of the quasi-honour of permission to engrave is the decree *Sylloge*, no. 721, wherein the Cretan city of Cnossos awards honours and privileges to a foreigner, a writer from Tarsus who was the author of a book in praise of Cnossos. The city also resolves to have the text of the decree engraved in the sanctuary of the chief god of Cnossos, Apollo Delphidius, and to request the Athenians of Delos to set it up in their sanctuary as well. In addition, the city sends a copy of the decree to Tarsus, so that the writer's compatriots may know of his glory. Naturally the Romans imitated all these usages. For example, the Roman Senate could decide to inscribe on bronze an honorific *senatus consultum* (Pliny, *Letters*, VIII, 6, 13–14). The Senate evidently knew all these Hellenistic usages through the Greek decrees, copies of which had been sent to it, or through having seen the provincials practising them. Cicero is aware that in the province of Sicily the cities honour a *euergetēs* by sending him a copy on bronze of the decree honouring him (Cicero, *In Verrem*, IV, 65, 145) or by posting a copy of the decree on the wall of the Council hall (Cicero, *In Verrem*,. II, 46, 112). These were all ways of bearing witness to the merits of the person being honoured: Latin *testimonium* is the standard translation of *martyria* in Cicero, and the word designates a decree or a *senatus consultum* in someone's honour. Besides *martyria* and *epigraphē*, another word worth studying would be *hypomnēma*.

174. On testimonial decrees, see L. Robert, *Opuscula Minora Selecta*, vol. I, p. 617; *Hellenica*, III, p. 123 and XIII, p. 207; and in *L'Antiquité classique*, XXXVII (1968), p. 409. For Opramoas, see below, note 276.

175. Demosthenes, *De Corona*, 120 (267); Aeschines, *Against Ctesiphon*, 246.

176. On the exhortatory clause, see L. Robert, *Annuaire de l'École des Hautes Études*, 1968–9, p. 165. The Romans did not fail to copy this clause in their *senatus consulta* (e.g. Pliny, *Letters*, VIII, 6, 13) and municipal decrees.

177. These inscriptions are honorific decrees, or rather copies of decrees; pedestals of statues erected to dignitaries by virtue of an honorific decree (in the Roman period such pedestals became more numerous than copies of decrees); epitaphs of notables boasting of their *euergesiai* (especially in the Roman period); dedications of buildings or works

of art presented to the city as a *euergesia*. The formulas vary: ἐκ τῶν ἰδίων, ἐξ οἰκείων ἀναλωμάτων or δαπανημάτων, or even οἴκοθεν (*Inscriptiones Graecae*, editio minor, II–III, nos. 3592, 3687, 3669, and references; A. Wilhelm, *Beiträge*, pp. 101–2; L. Robert, in *Revue des études anciennes*, LXII (1960), p. 321, now in *Opuscula Minora Selecta*, vol. II, p. 321. There is an excellent example of the word in Lydus Magister, where he contrasts the consulship, which obliges its holder to make *largesse*, and the prefecture of the city, which is free of charge: *De Magistratibus*, 2, 8, p. 173, Bekker); or αὐτόθεν (*Inscriptiones Graecae*, V, 1, no. 536). See, in general, A. Wilhelm, *Attische Urkunden*, 5. Teil, p. 115. The same phenomenon is observed in private associations, whose dignitaries perform their functions at their own expense; see F. Poland, *Griech. Vereinswesen* (1909), p. 496.

178. There are innumerable examples of this. When an ambassador declines in this way to take his allowances (ἐφόδιον, or less often μεθόδιον), his embassy is performed προῖκα or δωρεάν, free of charge. This is the *legatio gratuita* of Roman euergetism. For an early Greek example of such an embassy, see the decree of Samos for Boulagoras (Pouilloux, *Choix*, no. 3) and that of Araxa for Orthagoras (no. 4).

179. Wilhelm, *Attische Urkunden*, 5. Teil, p. 116. In the Peraea Rhodiorum there was an 'unpaid governor', *hāgemōn amisthos* (*Sammlung der griech. Dialektinschriften*, no. 4275).

180. There is a general survey by H. Francotte, *Les Finances des cités grecques* (Bretschneider, reprinted 1964), pp. 129–56. He points out the differences from the modern budgetary system. The Greek budgetary law ('finance act') was not annual; there was no principle of unity of the budget, and the budget was made up of several separate mini-budgets; and there was no principle of unity of the funds (non-linking of particular expenditure to particular income). In this connection I have studied L. Trotabas, *Les Finances publiques* (Dalloz), and Leroy-Beaulieu, *Traité de la science des finances* (1879). On extraordinary expenditure, see E. Szanto, *Ausgewählte Abhandlungen*, p. 112. On τὸ γυμνασιαρχικόν, A. Wilhelm, *Neue Beiträge*, V, p. 44; on the διοίκησις and advances of funds, *Neue Beiträge*, VI, p. 69; on the ἐξαιρούμενον, *Attische Urkunden*, V, pp. 110–14.

181. L. Robert, in *Arkhaiologiké Ephemeris*, 1969, p. 28; *Monumenta Asiae Minoris*, vol. VI, p. 87, no. 180.

182. This sum thus perhaps represents £12,000, if we assume that the relation between prices and utilities was the same in antiquity as today, and that the dimensions of a Greek 'budget' were comparable to our enormous budgets (even the municipal ones).

183. προσαναλίσκειν or προσδαπανᾶν. Thus, *Sylloge*, no. 691, line 5. Before 130 BC, a gymnasiarch, 'in order to distribute oil, contributed money

from his purse in addition to the sum which had been given to him'
(πρὸς τὸ μερισθέν). For μερίζειν, see Francotte, *Finances*, p. 236.

184. L. Robert, in *Laodicée du Lycos, le Nymphée*, p. 314.

185. For example, at Attaleia in Lydia, the inscription *Athenische Mit-
     teilungen*, XXIV (1899), p. 221, no. 55: a man 'loving his country,
     and a *euergetēs*,' has executed 'splendidly and honourably, at his own
     expense', the offices of *stratēgos, hipparchos, nomophylax, agoranomos* and
     sitonēs.

186. See a very explicit passage in Aeneas the Tactician, XIII, 1–4. For
     interest-free loans, see, e.g., *Orientis Graeci Inscriptiones*, no. 46, and C.
     Michel, *Recueil d'inscriptions grecques*, no. 456. In the early Hellenistic
     epoch it was interest-free loans that made possible the erection at
     Halicarnassus of a portico and a gymnasium. More generally, see
     E. Szanto, *Ausgewählte Abhandlungen* (1906), pp. 11–73: *Anleihen
     griechischer Staaten*.

187. Thus, about 274, at Erythraea, the *stratēgoi* found ἐκ τῶν ἰδίων the
     sums needed to pay the mercenaries who had just occupied the town
     (*Sylloge*, no. 410).

188. L. Robert, in *Laodicée du Lycos*, p. 359.

189. On the sebastophants, who concerned themselves with the Imperial
     cult (the word was formed on analogy with 'hierophant'), see L.
     Robert in *Revue des études anciennes*, 1960, p. 321, now in *Opuscula
     Minora Selecta*, vol. II, p. 837; H. W. Pleket, 'An aspect of the Emperor
     cult: imperial mysteries', in *Harvard Theological Review*, LVIII (1965),
     p. 338.

190. L. Robert in *Laodicée du Lycos*, p. 314, note 10. Similarly, in Athens
     under the Empire it was not unusual for the *agōnothetai*, instead of
     organizing and financing the festivals that included games, which was
     their official task, to repair the roads or equip a ship (D. J. Geagan,
     The Athenian Constitution after Sulla (Princeton, 1967), p. 133). The
     same transfer of liberalities took place in Roman euergetism. See my
     chapter IV, notes 333–9.

191. To this was added another development. The magistrates were fond
     of offering a building, or part of a building, so that it might serve as
     a monument of their term of office. For example, the *agoranomoi* would
     present some object that could be used to equip or decorate the
     market: a bench, tables, a portico, shops, measures of volume, statues of
     divinities such as Justice or Plenty (L. Robert, in *Laodicée du Lycos*, p.
     259). The purpose of these offerings was above all to carry the magis-
     trate's name. The desire to inscribe one's name thus led to a great
     increase in buildings and statues. It was the same in Roman Africa,
     where erecting statues became a sort of mania.

192. To raise liberality to its highest pitch, μηδεμίαν ὑπερβολήν καταλιπεῖν

or ἀπολιπεῖν: see Dunant and Pouilloux, *Thasos*, vol. II, p. 105, note 1. In Philostratus, *Lives of the Sophists*, the formula is used for the generosities of Herodes Atticus (p. 552, beginning) and of a *prostatēs* of the Pythian games (II, 27, p. 616).

193. L. Robert, *Monnaies antiques en Troade* (Droz, 1966), p. 26. 'Contribute' here translates χορηγεῖν (A. Wilhelm, *Neue Beiträge*, V, p. 46; L. Robert, *Hellenica*, XI–XII, p. 123, note 2).

194. L. Robert, in *Laodicée du Lycos*, p. 268.

195. Among many examples there is the decree of Pagae in honour of Soteles, commented on by A. Wilhelm in *Jahreshefte des österr. arch. Instituts*, X (1907), pp. 28–9.

196. L. Robert in *Revue de philologie*, XLI (1967), p. 43.

197. See, e.g., the table of the magistracies and liturgies of Athens under the Empire, and the corresponding payments, in D. J. Geagan, *The Athenian Constitution after Sulla*, p. 128.

198. The inscriptions call the gymnasiarchy sometimes a liturgy and some-times a magistracy; see J. Oehler's long article on 'Gymnasiarchos' in Pauly and Wissowa's *Encyclopaedia*, cols. 1975–6 and 1981. It is also called *philotimia* (1985), i.e. munificence. For the transformation of magistracies into liturgies, see, e.g., U. Wilcken, *Einführung in die Papyruskunde*, vol. I, pp. 342 and 350; I. Lévy, 'Études sur la vie municipale en Asie Mineure', in *Revue des études grecques*, 1899, p. 256; E. P. Wegener, 'The Boule and the nomination to the Arkhai in the Metropoleis of Roman Egypt', in *Mnemosyne*, 1948, pp. 15–42 and 296–326: 'Already in the second century the ἀρχαί were no longer *honores* in the sense that the elite of the *metropoleis* offered themselves out of their own free will; the difference between ἀρχαί and λειτουργίαι is vanishing.'

199. Philostratus, *Lives of the Sophists*, II, 20, writes of the liturgies 'which the Athenians rank highest', the eponymous archonship and the generalship of the hoplites. These were the two highest magistracies. Similarly II, 1: Herodes Atticus performs the liturgy of eponymous archon. I shall return to this question when examining the distinction between *honores*, *munera* and *munera sordida* in Rome.

200. On the transformation of the liturgies by Demetrius, or at the time of Demetrius, see W. S. Ferguson, *Hellenistic Athens* (1911), pp. 55, 99, 290, 473; E. Bayer, *Demetrios Phalereus der Athener* (1942), pp. 47 and 70–71; P. Roussel in *Histoire grecque* in the Glotz collection, vol. IV, part 1, p. 327. Hellenistic Athens had another liturgy, concerned with the currency: liturgists provided the 'stephanophoric' ('new-style') coinage, as has been convincingly established by Margaret Thompson, *The New Style Silver Coinage of Athens* (The American Numismatic Society, New York, 1961).

201. For the office of *agōnothetēs* the document is the inscription *Sylloge*, no. 1809. The *agōnothetēs* undertook to pay the cost of the *chorēgiai*, says Beloch, *Griechische Geschichte*, vol. IV, part 1, p. 148, note 3. For example, Euryclides, who was all-powerful in Athens during the wars of Demetrius II, spent seven talents for his appointment as *agōnothetēs* (*Sylloge*, no. 497). But already in classical Athens it was expected of the commissioners for festivals that they should contribute, out of piety, to the splendour of a festival (Boeckh, *Staatshaushaltung*, vol. I, p. 273). Thus in Athens, of the two major old liturgies, one, the *chorēgia*, was revived in the Hellenistic form of the *agōnothesia*, while the other, the *triērarchia*, obscurely disappeared; and an evolution in the way of life gave great importance to an old liturgy which had been of secondary status, the *gymnasiarchia* (see below). For the personal generosities of an *agōnothetēs* I will quote an inscription from Lebadea, where, in the second century BC, the *agonōthetēs* of a federal games established in honour of Zeus declares: 'I have returned to the cities the whole of the contribution they had to pay for the games; I have paid personally all the expenses for the sacrifices and for the games; I have not charged for the money paid to the staff and to the under-secretary, or for the preparation of the stele, or for the transcription of the victors' names, or for the engraving of the accounts, decrees and other texts; the money I have received I have passed on to my successor as *agōnothetēs*, after deducting what was needed to make a *phialē* which I have consecrated to Zeus' (*Nouveau Choix d'inscriptions grecques par l'Institut Fernand-Courby* (Les Belles Lettres, 1971), no. 22).

202. A second and even more serious reason for the deterioration of public life was that the notables were also demoralized by the collective responsibility resting upon them with respect to Imperial taxation. Public functions were no longer anything but a pretext for *euergesiai* and taxes, and this, morally even more than financially, deprived the city system of its meaning. On euergetism as a factor in the breakdown of public life, it is enough to refer to the comments of a wandering orator of the Second Sophistic whose vigorous language derives from the tradition of political harangues and cynical diatribes (Dio of Prusa, XXXIV, *Second Tarsic Discourse*, 28–32).

203. F. K. Dörner, *Der Erlass des Statthalters von Asia Paullus Fabius Persicus* (Griefswald University dissertation, 1935), p. 8, text IV, line 14. The sale of priesthoods which took place in the Hellenistic age was quite another matter. Priesthoods of the Emperor were glorious and ruinous functions, whereas priesthoods of the gods were a source of profit for their holders, since the worshippers left part of the sacrificed victim for the priest, as a sort of tax. On the sale of priesthoods, see M. Nilsson, *Geschichte der griech. Religion*, second edn, vol. II, pp. 77 and

99. For the sale of freedom of the city, see L. Robert, in *Revue de philologie*, 1967, p. 29. There were, in Greece as in Rome, *euergesiai* performed as the price of freedom of the city: see L. Robert, in *Bulletin de correspondance hellénique*, 1936, p. 196, now in *Opuscula Minora Selecta*, vol. II, p. 903.

204. 'On distribution', ἐπ' ἐπιδόσει χρημάτων (in the late Hellenistic and Imperial periods ἐπίδοσις commonly means a distribution, a *divisio nummorum*). For this use of the conditional dative, see an inscription in Athens, *Inscriptiones Graecae*, editio minor, II–III, no. 3546. The same person was herald of the Council and of the people ἐπὶ δηναρίοις δυσί, at the price of a distribution of two *denarii* per head. See A. Wilhelm, 'Inschrift aus Pagai', in *Jahreshefte des österr. arch. Instituts*, X (1907), p. 29; 'Zu neuen Inschriften aus Pergamon', in *Sitzungsberichte preuss. Akad. Berlin*, 1933, p. 854; L. Robert, in *Anatolian Studies Buckler*, p. 237, now in *Opuscula Minora Selecta*, vol. I, p. 621; in *Revue de philologie*, 1959, p. 204; and in *Études anatoliennes*, 1937, p. 340, note 8. The dative is also used without a preposition: γυμνασίαρχος ἐλαίου θέσει. A *euergesia* is performed 'for nothing', ἀντ' οὐδενός, without any dignity being received in return: L. Robert in *Bulletin de correspondance hellénique*, LX (1936), p. 197, now in *Opuscula Minora Selecta*, vol. II, p. 904 (Wilhelm, *Jahreshefte*, 1907, p. 25, read 'in the absence of any other candidate for the function' in another inscription). Other formulas: the *euergesia* was performed '*ex officio*', ὑπὲρ ἀγορανομίας (L. Robert, *Hellenica*, I, p. 49; in *Revue de philologie*, 1958, p. 41; in *Revue des études grecques*, 1957, p. 363, note 1, and in *Gnomon*, 1959, p. 662; now in *Opuscula Minora Selecta*, vol. III, pp. 1480 and 1627); 'by reason of the office', ἀγωνοθεσίας ἕνεκεν (J. Vanseveren, 'Inscriptions d'Amorgos et de Chios', in *Revue de philologie*, 1937, p. 335); 'in exchange for the office', ἀντί τῆς ἀρχῆς (L. Robert in *Bulletin de correspondance hellénique*, 1936, p. 196, now in *Opuscula Minora Selecta*, vol. II, p. 903; in *Laodicée du Lycos*, p. 264, note 3, and p. 359, note 2; *Études anatoliennes*, p. 414, note 7); the genitive alone has the same value: γυμνασίου, 'in respect of the gymnasiarchy' (L. Robert, *Études anatoliennes*, p. 414, note 7; *Hellenica*, XI–XII, p. 479, note 5). Or else it would simply be stated that the *euergetēs* performed his benefaction during his year of office (I. Lévy, 'L'honorarium municipal à Palmyre', in *Revue archéologique*, 1900, vol. I, p. 128). The adverbs which express the fact that a function has been performed 'with munificence' are πολυτελῶς, μεγαλοψυχῶς, φιλοδόξως, φιλοτίμως, λαμπρῶς, etc.

205. For an *epidēmia* of the Emperor, see *Orientis Graeci Inscriptiones*, nos. 516–17; Keil and Premerstein, *Zweite Reise in Lydien* (*Denkschriften Wiener Akad.*, LIV (1911)), no. 116; cf. L. Robert in *Revue de philologie*, LX (1934), p. 278, now in *Opuscula Minora Selecta*, vol. II, p. 1177

(whence C. B. Welles in *Gerasa, City of the Decapolis*, p. 425, note 144). There is another good example at Ephesus: *Jahreshefte der österreich. Akad.*, XLIV (1959), Beiblatt, p. 258, no. 3. For the passage of troops and the *conventus juridicus*, see L. Robert in *Laodicée du Lycos*, p. 314. In the third century BC it was specified that a notable of Athens was *stratēgos* in the year of the Great Eleusinian Mysteries, which brought a huge gathering of foreigners, and that on this occasion he offered fine sacrifices (*Sylloge*, no. 457).

206. L. Robert, in *Laodicée du Lycos*, p. 262, and D. J. Geagan, *The Athenian Constitution after Sulla*, p. 129. In Egypt a rather special function, the gymnasiarchy, which no longer meant more than ensuring that the public baths were kept heated and oil supplied, was eventually performed on a daily basis, with the gymnasiarchs each taking a certain day of the month as their responsibility (G. Méautis, *Hermoupolis-la-Grande* (dissertation, Neuchâtel, 1918), p. 103). At Chalcis, when financial circumstances were difficult, gymnasiarchs were appointed on a monthly basis: Wilhelm, 'Neue Beiträge', IV (1915), p. 52.

207. It was so important to have one's name recorded in the annals or on the official monuments that in the 'law' of Ilion against tyranny (*Orientis Graeci Inscriptiones*, no. 218, line 120) it was laid down that, among the measures of purgation which should follow a tyranny, the names of the tyrant's adherents should be deleted from the public monuments, and that the town should sell the site where these names had been inscribed, the purchaser being allowed to replace them with whatever name he chose. See also note 265.

208. Magistracies of women: O. Braunstein, *Die politische Wirksamkeit der griechischen Frau* (Leipzig University dissertation, 1911), did not always appreciate that female magistracies were in every case explicable by money considerations (e.g., for the women gymnasiarchs in Egypt, see G. Méautis, *Hermoupolis-la-Grande*, pp. 100–103). I offer an example from Priene, just before or just after the beginning of our era: a certain lady 'was the first woman' (in Priene) 'to be *stephanēphoros*' and presented to the city a fountain-basin and water-pipes (*Inschriften von Priene*, no. 208). Again, at Pogla a father bequeathed money to his daughter so that she could distribute it publicly, and in return for these distributions the daughter was appointed demiurge (V. Bérard in *Bulletin de correspondance hellénique*, XVI (1892), p. 425). For child magistrates see L. Robert, *Hellenica*, XI–XII, p. 560, note 6. For dead men (the term 'heroes' meant nothing more) who were made magistrates, see L. Robert, *Hellenica*, XIII, p. 207 (the dead man had set up a foundation to cover the costs of the office of *stephanēphoros*); in *L'Antiquité classique*, XXXV (1966), p. 389, note 4; and in *Comptes rendus de l'Académie des inscriptions*, 1968, p. 581, note 4. For gods made

eponymous magistrates, see J. and L. Robert, *La Carie*, vol. II, p. 210, note 1; in Sparta, under the Empire, Lycurgus became eponym when the opportunity presented itself (*Inscriptiones Graecae*, vol. V, 1, no. 45). For the Hellenistic kings who were eponymous magistrates of a city, see L. Robert, *Études épigraphiques et philologiques*, pp. 143–50.

209. P. Graindor, *Athènes de Tibère à Trajan* (Cairo, 1931), p. 73: 'Formerly these years without archons were due to external troubles,' but under the Empire 'they had economic causes: no candidate offered himself for election' (for the archons were no longer chosen by lot), because nobody was ready 'to assume the heavy expenses of entry into office, as required by tradition'. When the cities were unable to find gym‐nasiarchs or *agōnothetai*, they sometimes replaced them by com‐missioners who donated their time to the city while the costs of the gymnasium and the games were met from public funds.

210. Wilamowitz (Kromayer–Heisenberg), *Staat und Gesellschaft der Grie‐chen und Römer*, p. 182. An example is the decree for Aristagoras (*Sylloge*, no. 708), in which we see how, through euergetism, this citizen of Istros assumed 'the crown of the god' several times and on those occasions made *largesses*: the text would be worth quoting in full. The proliferation of expensive functions led, from the late Hellenistic period, to double eponymies: L. Robert, in *Revue des études anciennes*, 1960, p. 344, now in *Opuscula Minora Selecta*, vol. II, p. 860.

211. And not at a fixed price, under the name of 'legitimate sum' or 'honorary sum'.

212. For the word *protrepein*, see L. Robert in *Anatolian Studies Buckler*, p. 237, now in *Opuscula Minora Selecta*, vol. I, p. 621. 'The exhortation must have been extremely pressing, and was doubtless not very pleasant for the persons concerned.' In an inscription in the sanctuary of Zeus Panamaros it is said that a statue was erected by the two curators, 'induced to do this by the town' – which means, I suppose, that they did not offer themselves spontaneously for the curatorship. The Council, which had final authority for the text of the inscription, did not want the reader to believe that the curators had shown exceptional generosity (Le Bas and Waddington, *Inscriptions grecques et latines*, no. 743; cf. A. Wilhelm, 'Neue Beiträge, VI' (1921), p. 74). In *Oxyrhynchus Papyri*, XII, no. 1416, line 5, which lists the subjects discussed by the Council, we see that it considered 'inducing one of those nominated as magistrates to assume the office of *agōnothetēs*'. The list of the victims had already been drawn up, but it had not yet been decided with what sauce each should be eaten. Cf. A. K. Bowman, *The Town Councils of Roman Egypt* (Hakkert, 1971), pp. 103, 106, 110. At Lindos (Soko‐lowski, *Lois sacrées des cités grecques, Supplément*, no. 90, p. 157) the *epistatai* of the cult were instructed to induce the sacrificers to perform

their functions free of charge. Finally I will point out the use of the verb *protrepein* in connection with the honours rendered to *euergetai*: honorific statues served to 'induce' euergetism in persons who saw that the city honoured *euergetai* in this way (Latyschev, *Inscriptiones Ponti Euxini*, vol. I, no. 22). The word *protrepein* is used by Demosthenes, *De Corona*, 120, in relation to the 'exhortatory clause' of the honorific decrees.

213. Funds for the distribution of oil: *Inschriften von Magnesia*, no. 116, lines 6–8. One could not refuse to be *exēgētēs* in so prosperous a reign: *Rylands Papyrus*, II, 77, line 35. See also the *Oxyrhynchus Papyri*, XII, no. 1413. 'I am poor, I am in danger of becoming a vagrant': Apollinarion's petition, *Oxyrhynchus Papyri*, VI, 899. The reason why this theme lent itself to allusions which were perfidious but polite is that it was traditional. The Emperors and high officials never failed to acclaim the prosperity of the Empire in the current reign. See, e.g., the edict of Ti. Julius Alexander (*Orientis Graeci Inscriptiones*, no. 669, line 4), the *senatus consultum* of Herculaneum (*Corpus Inscriptionum Latinarum*, X, 1401), or the edict of Nerva mentioned by Pliny the Younger (*Letters*, X, 58).

214. R. von Jhering, *Das Zweck im Recht*, vol. I (Olms, reprinted 1970), p. 141. The *euergetēs* could also, with the town's permission, boast of his spontaneity in the dedication engraved on the building erected at his expense. For the functions assumed by a 'volunteer' (see note 19) or αὐθαίρετος (L. Robert in *Bulletin de correspondance hellénique*, LIX (1935), p. 447, note 2, now in *Opuscula Minora Selecta*, vol. I, p. 288), there are innumerable examples. They were referred to, when the occasion arose, by such ready-made expressions as 'spontaneous gymnasiarch' (*Orientis Graeci Inscriptiones*, no. 583). Also worth mentioning is *Oxyrhynchus Papyri*, III, no. 473, line 3: 'voluntary gymnasiarch'.

215. See the inscriptions published by G. Cousin in *Bulletin de correspondance hellénique*, 1904; L. Robert, *Études anatoliennes*, p. 549.

216. We shall see later that Roman law attempted to apply a public sanction to pollicitations.

217. *Inschriften von Priene*, no. 113, line 37; L. Robert, *Études anatoliennes*, p. 378, who makes this comment: 'We see that the negotiations between [the pollicitator] and his home town were arduous; for once, we glimpse the realities and the haggling which are concealed by so many honorific inscriptions.' On Greek pollicitations in general, see B. Laum, *Stiftungen*, pp. 118–20 and 224.

218. The written document had served to extract performance of the promise, with or without intervention by the Roman governor of the province. See, e.g., *Inscriptiones Graecae*, IV, no. 593; O. Kern, *Inschriften von Magnesia*, no. 92; L. Robert, 'Inscription d'Adalia', in

Revue de philologie, LV (1929), p. 122 and note 4, now in *Opuscula Minora Selecta*, vol. II, p. 1088. Of King Antiochus Epiphanes, Livy writes (XLI, 20): 'many other things he promised in other places, but by reason of the very short duration of his reign he did not finish them.'

219. L. Robert, *Études anatoliennes*, p. 549.

220. For promises given immediate effect, see A. Wilhelm in *Jahreshefte des österr. arch. Instituts*, X (1907), p. 28; B. Laum, *Stiftungen*, p. 119; J. Robert, 'Inscriptions de Carie', in *Revue de philologie*, LXVI (1940), p. 243. Protogenes, we read in the great decree of Olbia I have summarized above, brought and paid out immediately all the money he had promised for the purchase of corn. For pollicitations made and implemented not just immediately, but unexpectedly, see L. Robert, *Études anatoliennes*, p. 343.

221. *Rylands Papyrus*, II, 77 (reproduced in Hunt and Edgar, *Select Papyri*, vol. II, no. 241); cf. G. Méautis, *Hermoupolis-la-Grande*, pp. 117–25; A. K. Bowman, *The Town Councils of Roman Egypt*, pp. 16, 43, 122.

222. Two talents was equivalent, perhaps, to 1,000 sovereigns of Dickens's time. Responsibility for the public lands (Imperial or municipal?) must indeed have been ruinous, since the person who assumed it was certainly liable from his own pocket for rents that remained unpaid. Preference for the office of *exēgētēs* can be accounted for in a different way. Achilles was prepared to pay a great deal for a function which represented the end of his career, and after which he could not decently be asked to assume another one. In fact, it was understood at this time that a notable could be called upon to assume all the dignities, one after another ('omnibus honoribus et muneribus fungi', say the Latin epigraphs, in a formula whose literal translation also occurs frequently in Greek epigraphy). Compare Dessau, no. 6821 ('ob honorem aedilitatis intermissae') and no. 6570 ('aedilitate intermissa duumvir'). The *Digest* mentions the case of notables who promised a *euergesia* in order to be relieved of assuming a public honour, which amounted to jumping over one of the stages in a career (L, 4, 16 pr., and L, 12, 12, 1).

223. The right of entry, *eisitērion* (on two other meanings of the word, see note 71). The word is used in the sense of 'entrance fee' in private associations (H. Hepding in *Athenische Mitteilungen*, XXXIII (1907), p. 301; F. Poland, *Geschichte des griech. Vereinswesens*, p. 547). For the meaning of the word in our papyrus, see S. Le Roy Wallace, *Taxation in Egypt from Augustus to Diocletian* (Princeton, 1938), p. 278: 'Apparently a fee paid for a sacrifice by an *exēgētēs* upon entering office'; A. K. Bowman, *The Town Councils of Roman Egypt*, pp. 26, 41, 171.

224. On the honorary sum in Greece, see A. Wilhelm, 'Zu einer Stiftungs-urkunde aus Iasos', in his 'Neue Beiträge, IV' (1915), especially pp. 43

and 49–52 (the reader may find it useful to know that the summary of this study by Wilhelm given by D. Magie in a note on the honorary sum, *Roman Rule in Asia Minor*, vol. I, p. 650, and vol. II, p. 1519, note 52, is very inaccurate); I. Lévy, 'La vie municipale de l'Asie Mineure', in *Revue des études grecques*, XII (1899), especially pp. 259–62; by the same author, 'L'honorarium municipal à Palmyre', in *Revue archéologique*, 1900, vol. I, p. 128, and the entry 'Honorarium' (in the Greek cities) in the *Dictionnaire des antiquités* of Daremberg, Saglio and Pottier (all these studies are quoted by L. Robert in *Bulletin de correspondance hellénique*, LX (1936), p. 196). See also T. R. S. Broughton, 'Roman Asia Minor', in Tenney Frank, *An Economic Survey of Ancient Rome*, vol. IV, pp. 802–3; A. H. M. Jones, *The Greek City from Alexander to Justinian* (Oxford, 1940), p. 247. For *timēma*, see a Lydian inscription quoted by Wilhelm, p. 49. This meaning of *timēma* is confirmed also in a papyrus published by N. Lewis, 'Leitourgia papyri: documents on compulsory public service in Egypt under Roman rule', in *Transactions of the American Philosophical Society*, LIII, 9 (1963), p. 19, note 8, where the editor interprets the word as meaning 'the expenses of the office of *exēgētēs*'. (A petition was sent to the prefect of Egypt on behalf of an under-age orphan, a rich heir, whom the prefect had obliged to become *exēgētēs*; in this connection the editor compiles a list of examples of children appointed to municipal functions in Egypt.) It will be observed that in the *Digest* (L, 4, 16 pr.: 'aestimationem honoris aut muneris in pecunia') the word *aestimatio*, a translation of Greek *timēma*, is used for an honorary sum. For *taxatio*, see Wilhelm, p. 50; the word appears in several African inscriptions which have most recently been discussed by A. Beschaouch, *Mustitana: recueil de nouvelles inscriptions de Mustis* (Klincksieck, 1968), pp. 38–42. In the glossaries, *taxatio* is glossed as *nominatio, designatio* (G. Goetz, '*Thesaurus Glossarum Emendatarum*', under 'Taxatio', in *Corpus Glossariorum Latinorum*, vol. VII).

225. Decree quoted by J. and L. Robert, 'Bulletin épigraphique', in *Revue des études grecques*, LXXV (1962), no. 239.

226. At Sebastopolis, in Caria, a notable, before becoming *argyrotamias* for 4,000 *denarii*, was three times *apodocheus* for 11,200 *denarii* – a figure not divisible by three (J. and L. Robert, *La Carie*, vol. II, p. 317, no. 168). At Telmessos a notable gave, 'for the gymnasium', 56,058 drachmas: this cannot have been a sum fixed in advance, but the total of actual expenses (*Tituli Asiae Minoris*, vol. II, 1, no. 15; for the 'drachmas of small change' mentioned in this document and which were worth one-sixth of the normal drachma and *denarius*, compare *Sylloge*, no. 1109, note 48; *Orientis Graeci Inscriptiones*, no. 484, note 14; *Inscriptiones Graecae*, vol. II–III, editio minor, no. 2776, entire

commentary; cf. also J. Day, *An Economic History of Athens under Roman Domination*, p. 221). On the other hand, when, for one and the same function, the same round figure is recorded in two neighbouring cities, we may presume that it represents an honorary sum, one of the cities having imitated the other in determining the amount. Thus the honorary sum for the *dēmiourgos* was the same, namely 1,000 *denarii*, in two cities of Cilicia – Olba (*Monumenta Asiae Minoris Antiqua*, vol. III, no. 103) and Cestros (according to J. and L. Robert, 'Bulletin épigraphique', in *Revue des études grecques*, LXXVIII (1965), no. 428).

227. One of these small towns in the valley of the Cayster was Apateira, which was attached to Ephesus. In 206–7 the *logistai* nominated 'for the price of a single liberality' were 'induced to pay in addition' 250 *denarii* for repairing the bath (Keil and Premerstein, *Bericht über eine dritte Reise in Lydien*, p. 86, note 116; cf. L. Robert, in *Anatolian Studies Buckler*, p. 237, note 6. The date 206–7, and not 170, is that of the Pharsalan era, used in this region along with those of Sulla and Actium; cf. P. Herrmann, *Neue Inschriften zur histor. Landeskunde von Lydien*, p. 9; 'in addition' is here *exōthen*; cf. L. Robert, *Hellenica*, XIII, p. 205). About the same time, another *logistēs* paid the same sum of 250 *denarii*, which was allocated to pay for the *aurum tironicum* (Keil and Premerstein, p. 87; for the *aurum tironicum*, see Rostovtzeff in *Journal of Roman Studies*, 1918, p. 26; J. and L. Robert in *Revue des études grecques*, LXIII (1960), p. 170, no. 230, in connection with the *Inscriptiones Graecae in Bulgaria* by Mihailov, vol. II, no. 517). There is a third inscription by a *logistēs* at Apateira, but the figure for the *summa honoraria* is not legible (references in L. Robert, *Hellenica*, XI–XII, p. 18, notes 4 and 5). In the same valley, the small town of Hypaipa was headed by comarchs. See Keil and Premerstein, pp. 66 and 78–9; Fontrier in the *Mouseion kai Bibliothēkē* of Smyrna, 1885–6, p. 88 (in the Bibliothèque Nationale, Paris). The comarchs paid an honorary sum to their town, 'traditionally' and 'in accordance with the decree of the community': five inscriptions show us the honorary sum increasing in the course of the third century, by leaps of 250 *denarii* at a time, which reflect both inflation and the arbitrary fixing of a round-figure rate. In 213–14 the sum stood at 250 *denarii* (Fontrier: date according to the Pharsalan era; for *gentilicius* the *euergetēs* had M. Aurelius (in 213–14 the *Constitutio Antoniniana* was already having its onomastic effects); previously the *euergetēs* had paid 50 *denarii* for repairing the baths; on *tacheion*, 'previously', in this inscription and in the inscription of 272–3, see L. Robert, *Hellenica*, XI–XII, p. 18). In 225–6 the sum had risen to 500 *denarii* (Keil and Premerstein, p. 78, no. 109); at an unknown date it had reached 750 *denarii* (p. 79, no. 110); in 272–3 it was 1,000 *denarii* (p. 79), and at the same level at an unknown later

date (Fontrier). Cf. also H. V. Pleket, 'Nine Greek inscriptions of the Cayster valley, a republication', in *Talanta*, II (1970), p. 80.

228. *Amherst Papyrus*, II, no. 70, in U. Wilcken and L. Mitteis, *Grundzüge und Chrestomathie der Papyruskunde*, vol. I, 2, p. 175, no. 149.

229. Dio of Prusa, *Orationes*, XLV, 8.

230. Inscription at Laodicea (Latakia), now in Toulon Museum: L. Robert in *Bulletin de correspondance hellénique*, LX (1936), p. 192.

231. Dittenberger, *Sylloge*, no. 838.

232. A 'councillor free of charge' is mentioned in a bilingual inscription in Galatia in 145 (*Corpus Inscriptionum Latinarum*, III, 282, line 49). This must show Roman influence (*decuriones gratuiti* are not rare in Latin inscriptions). I know of no other examples.

233. On the *summa honoraria* of the *bouleutai*, see L. Robert, in *Bulletin de correspondance hellénique*, LX (1936), p. 197, note 6. On subscriptions and entrance fees in associations, see F. Poland, *Vereinswesen*, p. 492 (the best example is the statute of the *hymnōdoi* of Pergamum, in M. Fränkel, *Inschriften von Pergamon*, vol. II, no. 374, e.g. face D, line 13, on page 262, reproduced in L. Ziehen and I. von Prott, *Leges Graecorum Sacrae e Titulis Collectae*, vol. I, no. 27. Another document, unfortunately obscure, on the honorary sum of the *bouleutēs* is *Oxyrhynchus Papyri*, XII, no. 1413. During the debates in the Council of Oxyrhynchus in 270–75 mention was made of a tax called *steptika*, paid by *bouleutai* and *exēgētai*. This tax, unknown elsewhere, seems to have been an honorary sum (A. H. M. Jones, *The Greek City from Alexander to Justinian*, p. 247, note 70; A. C. Johnson, 'Roman Egypt', in *An Economic Survey*, vol. II, p. 576; S. Le Roy Wallace, *Taxation in Egypt from Augustus to Diocletian* (Princeton, 1938), p. 281); but we do not know whether it was a question of nominating *bouleutai* to be *exēgētai*, the honorary sum being that of an *exēgētēs* (thus P. Jouguet, 'Les boulai égyptiennes à la fin du IIIe siècle', in *Revue égyptologique*, I (1919), especially p. 67) or whether it was a question of nominating new *bouleutai* for whom the Senate would pay the honorary sum (E. P. Wegener, 'The Boulè and the nomination to the archai in the metropoleis of Roman Egypt', in *Mnemosyne*, I (1948), especially p. 21).

234. Pliny the Younger, *Letters*, X, 112, 2. In Bithynia, under the Pompeian law, councillors did not pay the honorary sum, and were nominated in the Roman manner by the censors or *timētai* (on whom see L. Robert in *Bulletin de correspondance hellénique*, LII (1928), p. 411; F. K. Dörner, *Bericht über eine Reise in Bithynien* (*Denkschriften Akad. Wien*, LXXV, 1 (1952)), p. 13, no. 5; and 'Vorbericht über eine Reise in Bithynien', in *Anzeiger der Akad. Wien*, 1963, p. 137; L. Vidman, 'Étude sur la correspondance de Pline avec Trajan' in *Rozpravy Československé Akademie Ved.*, 1960, fasc. 14, pp. 66–9; A. N. Sherwin-White, *The*

Letters of Pliny, a historical and social commentary (Oxford, 1966), p. 669). However, Pliny's letters later tell us that the cities were authorized, for the purpose of raising revenue, to appoint an extra number of councillors. These supernumeraries were elected, not nominated by the censors, and they paid an honorary sum. Some public buildings were erected by the cities out of the revenue from this source; and Pliny, a provincial governor, considered it his duty to check that the honorary sums were actually paid, for the sake of the cities' finances (Pliny, *Letters*, X, 39). In this case, too, the new *bouleutai* were the cities' milch-cows. On this point, it will be noted that these supernumerary *bouleutai* were also mentioned in the Bithynian discourses of Dio of Prusa — which brings up the question of the actual date of these discourses. Dio obtained for Prusa the right to have, apparently, up to a hundred *bouleutai* paying an honorary sum (H. von Arnim, *Leben und Werke des Dio von Prusa*, pp. 327 and 334–9: cf. Dio, *Orationes*, XLV, 7, and XL, 14; also XLVIII, 11). These men were elected, not nominated by the censors (Dio, *Orationes*, XLV, 7–10), so the discourses in question must have antedated the governor mentioned by Pliny, who merely extended to the ordinary *bouleutai*, appointed by the censors, the obligation to pay an honorary sum which had originally been imposed on the supernumeraries alone. This governor was named Anicius Maximus: unfortunately the date of his governorship is, so far as I am aware, as yet unknown. On the Pompeian law in Bithynia, see especially G. Vitucci, 'Gli ordinamenti costitutivi di Pompeo in terra d'Asia', in *Rendiconti dell'Accademia nazionale dei Lincei*, 1947, vol. II, p. 248. The Pompeian law was still in force in the third century (Dio Cassius, XXXVII, 20, 2); the *Digest* (L, 2, 3, 2 and 50, 2, 11) and also the *Codex Theodosii* (XII, 1, 5, with Godefroy's note) mention it, as does Gaius, *Institutes*, I, 193.

235. Inscription of Sveti Vrač, in the Strymon valley: D. Detschew, 'Ein neuer Brief des Kaisers Antoninus Pius', in *Jahreshefte des österr. arch. Instituts*, XLI (1954), p. 110; cf. J. and L. Robert, 'Bulletin épigraphique', in *Revue des études grecques*, 1956, no. 159; J. H. Oliver, 'A new letter of Antoninus Pius', in *American Journal of Philology*, LXXIX (1958), p. 53: 'Let your Council be one of 80 councillors,' wrote the sovereign, 'and let each contribute 500 Attic drachmas, in order that there may come to you prestige from the importance of your Council and an income from the sums which they will contribute.' On the identification of the city, which is undoubtedly Parthicopolis, see L. Robert, *Hellenica*, XI–XII, p. 253, and F. Papazoglou, in *Bulletin de correspondance hellénique*, 1963, pp. 535–44.

236. This is proved by a number of Imperial letters concerning the foundation or refoundation of cities, in which the sovereign provides that

the number of decurions shall be large enough for the city to have adequate resources. E.g. the letter concerning Tymandus (Dessau, no. 6090; *Monumenta Asiae Minoris Antiqua*, vol. IV, no. 236, lines 14 and 35), Constantine's letter concerning Orcistus (Dessau, no. 6091, line 11), and Antoninus's letter about Parthicopolis (previous note); see also a decree of Trieste (Dessau, no. 6680, section 2, line 8). Julian, *Misopogon*, 40, p. 367d; Pliny, *Letters*, X, 39, 5.

237. Mentioned by Wilhelm, 'Neue Beiträge, IV', p. 43, following T. Reinach, in *Revue des études grecques*, 1893, p. 159. For the proper name Synallasson, cf. L. Robert in *Revue des études grecques*, 1957, p. 362, note 2.

238. G. Cousin, in *Bulletin de correspondance hellénique*, XXVIII (1904), p. 45. For the inlay-work, see L. Robert, *Nouvelles Inscriptions de Sardes*, p. 50.

239. Lucian, *The Ship: or the Wishes*, 24; one drachma was worth about 1s. 6d. of Dickens's time.

240. On the provincial assemblies, see J. Deininger, *Die Provinziallandtage der römischen Kaiserzeit* (C. H. Beck, 1966). On the entertainments, see L. Robert, *Les Gladiateurs dans l'Orient grec*. On the identity of the high priest and the asiarch, see some references in *Bulletin de correspondance hellénique*, 1966, p. 151, note 3, and especially Deininger, pp. 41–50.

241. On the distributions of oil, see J. and L. Robert, *La Carie*, vol. II, p. 320; L. Robert, *Hellenica*, VI, p. 127. Bath-oil and banquets go together when public rejoicings are listed: see, e.g., Giessen Papyrus 3, concerning a public festival to celebrate the 'good news' of Hadrian's accession to the throne (O. Weinreich, *Ausgewählte Schriften*, vol. I (Grüner, 1969), p. 282. On the *euangelia* of good news, victories or accessions, and on the public rejoicings, see a vivid passage in L. Robert, *Laodicée du Lycos, le Nymphée*, p. 274: 'The people were ready to vote for the institution of a festival day, as this would be a signal for the rich citizens to increase the rejoicing through their generosity.'

242. This *euergesia* was not infrequent, on the part of a great variety of dignitaries; see Dittenberger, *Orientis Graeci Inscriptiones*, no. 764, note 61; L. Robert, *Hellenica*, XI–XII, p. 120: in the procession to the place of sacrifice, 'each man walks with the victim that he is personally offering in his capacity as magistrate'; cf. M. Holleaux, *Études*, vol. II, p. 101. As evidence, I reproduce the following translation of a decree of Amorgos dating from the third century BC (*Inscriptiones Graecae*, XII, 7, no. 241): 'Whereas Epinomides, son of Theogenes, having fulfilled the highest dignity for the festival of the Ithonia, showed all the zeal desirable in order that the goddess might have the finest possible sacrifice and procession, and concerned himself well and generously with those persons who came to take part in the festival

[cf. A. Wilhelm, *Griechische Königsbriefe* (*Klio*, Beiheft 48 (1943)), pp. 37 and 61]; and after giving to the *collegium* of the *dēmiourgoi*, for construction work in the sanctuary, the interest due to him on the taxes [*pelanoi*] paid to the goddess, and which hitherto went to finance the sacrifices; and after paying out of his own pocket for the sacrificial cow and all the other expenses, he levied no contribution from the persons attending the festival, who numbered no fewer than 500 ... considering that nothing was greater or finer than to maintain observance of the devotion due to the people and the piety due to the gods', etc.

243. Soteles of Pagae, in the decree already several times referred to (republication and commentary by Wilhelm in the *Jahreshefte des österr. arch. Instituts*, 1907), offers rejoicings for his first public appearance as dignitary. At the sanctuary of Zeus Panamaros a four-day festival marked the entry into office of the priest of Zeus (J. Robert, in *Revue de Philologie*, 1940, p. 239). See also note 71 above.

244. Diodorus Siculus, XIII, 84: H. von Gärtringen, *Inschriften von Priene*, no. 109, lines 162–8: Pliny, *Letters*, X, 116.

245. Pliny, *Letters*, X, 116. The mention of the *toga virilis*, which has surprised commentators, is due to the fact that a substantial minority of the Bithynian notables possessed Roman citizenship.

246. L. Robert, *Décrets d'Acraiphia*, now in *Opuscula*, vol. I, p. 279; *Hellenica*, XI–XII, p. 569; *Hellenica*, XIII, p. 244. For a late example, in AD 251, see Dittenberger, *Sylloge*, no. 851. It is revealing that the Greek word *philothytēs* (literally, 'he who sacrifices gladly') does not mean a devout person, but a hospitable one. For a comparison with Roman customs regarding consumption of meat and sacrifices, see the illuminating remarks of E. Fraenkel, *Elementi plautini in Plauto* (La Nuova Italia, 1960), pp. 124, 239, 408–13. L. Robert, *Hellenica*, XIII, p. 224: 'The essential part of the sacrifice is the banquet that follows it.' Thus bread was carried in the sacrificial processions (Athenaeus, 111 B); only the inedible parts of the animal were left for the gods (Tertullian, *Ad Nationes*, I, 10, 35).

247. Both the thing and the word are unknown in any other connection.

248. Throwing sweets or coins to the crowd of spectators, or ῥίμματα: this word, deciphered on the stone by M. Feyel, has been interpreted by L. Robert in *Arkhaiologikē Ephemeris*, 1969, pp. 34–9. In Aristophanes' time sweets were already being thrown to the spectators: the fashion of the Roman *missilia* is of Greek origin.

249. About a sovereign of Dickens's time, for three persons. It was a further magnificence to install dining-couches for the public banquets. This allowed the poor to eat lying on rich men's furniture.

250. *Inscriptiones Graecae*, VII, no. 2712 (lines 22–7: see M. Holleaux in

Bulletin de correspondance hellénique, 1935, p. 446, cf. p. 443, line 48; A. Wilhelm, in 'Neue Beiträge, III', p. 45). For the historical context, see L. Robert in *Bulletin de correspondance hellénique*, 1935, p. 447, now in *Opuscula*, vol. I, p. 288: 'We see how narrow was the circle of rich *euergetai* who could serve as milch-cows for the republic. The same men had to assume all at once all the essential magistracies ... The situation was one of general poverty, from which emerged a few rare fortunes whose possessors were alone able to bear the expenses of the city's administration.' Cf. U. Kahrstedt, *Das wirtschaftliche Gesicht Griechenlands in der Kaiserzeit* (Dissertationes Bernenses, VII (1954)), p. 82. Nero was to attempt, in a very praiseworthy and reasonable move, to relieve poverty-stricken Greece by exempting it from state taxation. On some difficult words in the text, like διάδομα, see L. Robert, *Hellenica*, XI–XII, p. 472; for θεωρία, see *Études anatoliennes*, p. 318; for εἰς φιλόπατρις, H. Seyrig, *Antiquités syriennes*, vol. I, p. 119; cf. L. Robert, *Hellenica*, XIII, p. 215.

251. It should be obvious that a religion does not exist in itself but in the souls of its believers, that what exists in men's souls is inevitably individual, and that the attitude of no two individuals is the same. Also that religions that rely essentially on ritual are religions of festivals and popular merrymakings, and must not be looked at with puritanical eyes (Nilsson, *Geschichte der griech. Religion*, vol. I, p. 827). Further, that there is no conflict between giving pleasure to the people and giving honour to the gods, since piety consists in enjoying oneself at the festival, from which the gods derived the same sort of pleasure as the people – by whom, indeed, they had literally been invited. Piety thus means passing an agreeable day in the company of these guests.

252. Paganism, writes a historian of religions, 'brought together in a single feeling all the emotions which transcended the monotony of everyday life' (B. Groethuysen, *Origines de l'esprit bourgeois en France*, p. 23). A ritualistic religion is the opposite of a religion that is empty of feelings. It combines feelings of different kinds and does not break down, through either rationalism or fervour, the plurality of satisfactions. Let me quote, as proof of this synthesis, the decree translated in note 242, the decrees *Sylloge*, no. 783, line 40, and no. 900, line 13 ('he performed his priestly duty, throughout the year, with piety towards the gods and munificence towards men'), and the decree of Ptoion, *Inscriptiones Graecae*, VII, no. 4148 ('he procured, continually and splendidly, the sacrifices due to the gods and the feasts due to the citizens'). To the banquets could be added distributions of money: at Syros the *archon stephanēphoros* and his wife offered a sacrifice with a public feast and distribution of coins (*Inscriptiones Graecae*, XII, 5, nos. 659–68).

253. Lucian, *The Death of Peregrinus*, 15, with L. Robert's remarks in *Hellenica*, XIII, p. 215, note 4. Peregrinus presented himself before the Assembly to *announce solemnly* his pollicitation. This was the customary procedure, in order to commit oneself. I shall come back to this point in chapter IV.

254. The key word in these decrees is *eutaxia*, 'discipline'.

255. H.-I. Marrou, *Histoire de l'éducation dans l'Antiquité*, p. 180. See also Marrou's excellent passage on the financing of the gymnasia by *euergetai* (pp. 160–64). I presume that the evolution was as follows. On the one hand, the gymnasia included baths for the pupils, for which the gymnasiarch often provided the necessary oil; on the other, the gymnasia were not closed to the public, as in our schools and colleges, but played the role of a 'second *agora*', as L. Robert puts it. Besides which, the population came to the gymnasium to watch the games of the ephebi, to the sacrifices and banquets held in that connection, and to the crowning of the victors. The bath of the gymnasium eventually became the public bath of the city. Finally, other baths, bearing the name *gymnasion*, were built, unconnected with any gymnasium, for use by the city's population, and the liturgist who made the distributions of oil (*gymnasia*) could also bear the name of gymnasiarch.

256. A gymnasiarch honoured by the cleruchs of Salamis 'spent money from his purse in addition to the credits made available to him for the oil' (*Inscriptiones Graecae*, editio minor, II–III, no. 1227, line 8). τό ἀνάλωμα πεπλήρωκα, writes another (*Oxyrhynchus Papyri*, XII, no. 1418, line 21).

257. The inscriptions of the Imperial epoch give enough precise information on these points to provide material for a whole book. See L. Robert, *Hellenica*, VI, pp. 128–30; J. Robert, in *Revue de philologie*, 1940, p. 241; L. Robert, ibid., 1943, p. 115 ('the public bath is regarded as a prime necessity'); J. and L. Robert, *La Carie*, vol. II, p. 320.

258. Cf. P. Veyne in *Latomus*, 1967, p. 744.

259. The fact had already been noted by I. Lévy, *Revue des études grecques*, XIV (1901), p. 371. The Latin word *gymnasium*, 'distribution of oil', figures in an inscription at Ain Nechma published by S. Lancel in *Libyca*, VI (1958), p. 143 (*L'Année épigraphique*, 1960, no. 214). The bath, the *hammam*, was as traditional in those countries in antiquity as it is today. I have been shown a translation of an article published in 1974 in the Turkish periodical *Yuruyus*, in which one reads that, in order to put a stop to the flight from the countryside, the leader of the Party of National Salvation proposes to have a *hammam* built in every village. The difficulty is the lack of water, and also of fuel (owing to deforestation, dried cow dung is used for fuel, as in Central Asia and China), as well as of finance. Should the village *hammams* be built by the state, but their management entrusted to the private sector? Each

one of these three points: water-supply, heating with wood (for there were more forests in antiquity than today) and the source of funding, can be illustrated from the Greek inscriptions.

260. B. A. van Groningen, *Le Gymnasiarque des métropoles de l'Égypte romaine* (Groningen,.1924); J. G. Milne, in *Journal of Roman Studies*, XVI (1926), p. 132, and 'Pap. Oxy. 1416 and the history of the gymnasiarchy', in *Actes du cinquième Congrès international de papyrologie*, 1937, p. 505. The old-established activities of the *gymnasium* continued, and at Oxyrhynchus the ephebi were still engaged in them in 323, under the direction of *cosmētai*.

261. *Fabulae Aesopicae*, no. 37, Halm, quoted by van Groningen.

262. Decree of Olbia (Latyschev, vol. I, no. 42): 'Callisthenes, descended from illustrious forebears who were known to and esteemed by the Emperors and who founded the city [they must have made use of their links with the sovereigns to render an exceptional service to their town: on these 'founders', see L. Robert, in *L'Antiquité classique*, 1966, p. 420] and did much good to it in difficult circumstances; descended from such forebears and having inherited their fortune and also their excellence ...' Decree of Istros (*Sylloge*, no. 708): 'Aristagoras, son of a worthy father and with as forebears *euergetai* who were priests of all the various gods, wishing to imitate them and follow in their footsteps ...' Decree of Mantinea (*Sylloge*, no. 783): 'Euphrosynus, our fellow citizen, who has continued the devotion to the homeland shown by his forebears ...' Finally, the decree of a city in Lycia (*Tituli Asiae Minoris*, vol. III, no. 838): Ctesicles, 'our fellow citizen, who belongs to the first rank in our city for his birth and dignity, distinguished also among the [Lycian] nation, from a brilliant and distinguished family of the first rank in our city, descended from brilliant and distinguished ancestors who did much good to the city', is himself 'a further ornament to the qualities and renown of his ancestors, and surpasses them'.

263. I imitate Menander the Rhetorician (*Rhetores Graeci*, vol. III, p. 413 (Spengel)): if you are praising someone who is too young and who is rich, you can always predict 'that he will be munificent to the cities, will establish games, will ornament great sanctuaries ($\pi\alpha\nu\eta\gamma\acute{\upsilon}\rho\epsilon\iota\varsigma$) with monuments, and so on'.

264. On $\check{\epsilon}\rho\gamma\text{ον}$ in the sense of *opus*, building or part thereof, see L. Robert, *Hellenica*, IV, p. 12, note 1. For $\check{\epsilon}\rho\gamma\text{οις}$ $\grave{\iota}\delta\acute{\iota}\text{οις}$ $\tau\epsilon$ $\kappa\alpha\grave{\iota}$ $\pi\rho\text{ογονικοῖς}$, see J. and L. Robert, 'Bulletin épigraphique', in *Revue des études grecques*, 1958, no. 476 (cf. *Hellenica*, XI–XII, p. 478, note 6). The Latin counterpart of $\check{\epsilon}\rho\gamma\alpha$ $\pi\rho\text{ογονικά}$ can be read at Thugga (*Corpus Inscriptionum Latinarum*, VIII, 26602: 'avita opera'; cf. VIII, 26616, and Cagnat-Merlin, *Inscriptions latines d'Afrique*, no. 538: 'avita et

paterna o[pera]'. I shall examine at length, in another book, these semantic superimpositions between Imperial Greek and Latin. It can be said that, in the Roman Empire, there was an 'Imperial language' in two versions, Greek and Latin. For the ideology of ancestral monuments, see Cicero, *In Verrem*, II, 4: 'It is an old tradition with us for everyone to look after the monuments of his ancestors just as he looks after his own, and not even to let them be decorated in the name of anyone else.'

265. For the right to inscribe one's name on a monument, see, e.g., Dittenberger, *Sylloge*, nos. 277 (Alexander the Great) and 756; Plutarch, *Life of Pericles*, 14 (explained by *Orientis Graeci Inscriptiones*, no. 339, note 20; cf., in the present chapter, note 173). This casuistry was passed on to Rome, finding its definitive formulation in the *Digest*, L, 10, 3, 2: 'It is forbidden to inscribe on a public building a name other than that of the Emperor or of the person who had the building erected at his own expense'; cf. L, 10, 2 pr.; L, 8, 6 (4) (end).

266. Vedius Antoninus alone would deserve a whole memoir; cf. F. Miltner, *Ephesos* (Vienna, 1958), pp. 42, 60, 68, 74. Ephesus had awarded him the honorific title of 'founder', κτίστης.

267. J. Keil, in *Jahreshefte des österr. arch. Inst.*, XXVII (1932), Beiblatt, p. 25, and XXVIII (1933), Beiblatt, p. 6.

268. See the list of them and the portrait of Damianus drawn by Philostratus, *Lives of the Sophists*, II, 23, p. 605, with details concerning his eloquence and his landed property.

269. *Orientis Graeci Inscriptiones*, no. 510, note 8: ἐκ τῶν ἰδίων. The explanation is that, by Hellenistic times, ἴδιος had come to indicate possession: the expression means 'the town, out of its own funds', and not 'out of private funds'.

270. On κοσμόπολις and κοσμεῖν, see L. Robert, *Études anatoliennes*, p. 349, note 1. They spoke also of αὐξάνειν a city (which was done, for example, by a Roman governor who granted it a favour). On this verb see A. Wilhelm in *Mélanges Glotz*, vol. II, p. 902. For the efflorescence of monuments in the Greek East during the Imperial epoch, see the lists of buildings compiled by T. R. S. Broughton ('buildings, gifts and foundations, wealthy families') in Tenney Frank, *An Economic Survey*, vol. III, pp. 715–34 and 746–97; cf. also D. Magie, *Roman Rule in Asia Minor*, vol. I, p. 582. On the important role of the gymnasiarchs in this building activity, see L. Robert, *Études anatoliennes*, p. 77.

271. Of Demetrius of Phaleron, Diogenes Laertius says that he 'enriched the city with revenues and buildings, though he was not of noble birth' (V, 75). Needless to say, when patronage became a class duty, those who did not belong to the class in question no longer had the moral

right to engage in patronage. In Rome, Martial waxes ironical about the people of the lower orders who take it into their heads to mount gladiatorial performances (III, 16 and 59; cf. Juvenal, III, 36).

272. A. Aymard in Aymard and Auboyer, *Rome et son empire* (PUF, 1954), p. 344.

273. Dio of Prusa, *Orationes*, XLVI, 3–6; cf. von Arnim, *Dio*, p. 122.

274. In the Latin West the example to mention would be Gamala of Ostia, whom we place in the second century AD. The astrologers knew this type of professional: Firmicus Maternus, *Mathesis*, III, 4, 1.

275. On Herodes Atticus, see P. Graindor, *Un milliardaire antique: Hérode Atticus et sa famille* (Cairo, 1930); J. Day, *An Economic History of Athens under Roman Domination* (Anno Press, reprinted 1973), index.

276. *Tituli Asiae Minoris*, vol. II, fasc. 3, no. 905.

277. Marcus Aurelius, *Meditations*, I, 7, 2.

278. All Christians without exception must strive towards holiness, wrote Pius XI in an encyclical of 26 January 1923, on St Francis de Sales.

279. See note 202.

280. Literally 'hestiaseis and chorēgiai' (*Precepts of Statecraft*, 31 (*Moralia*, 822)).

281. *Precepts of Statecraft*, 5 and 29 (*Moralia*, 802d and 821f).

282. Ibid., 31 (822f).

283. Ibid., 31 (823de).

284. M. Weber, *Essais sur la théorie de la science*, trans. Freund, p. 443.

285. *Precepts of Statecraft*, 24 (*Moralia*, 818b).

286. Ibid., 24 (818cd).

287. Ibid., 30 (822b).

288. Ibid., 24 (818c). Cicero uses the same language.

289. Dio of Prusa, *Orationes*, XLVI, 14; cf. also Plutarch, *Precepts of Statecraft*, 32 (*Moralia*, 824a to end). For an example of bloody repression of municipal disturbances, see Suetonius, *Tiberius*, 37. On the police, see O. Hirschfeld, *Kleine Schriften*, p. 576: *Die Sicherheitspolizei in röm. Kaiserreich*.

290. For quarrels over borders or precedence, see R. MacMullen, *Enemies of the Roman Order* (Harvard, 1966), pp. 163–91 and 336–50. For strikes and their repression, see an inscription at Ephesus published among those from Magnesia-on-the-Maeander (Kern, *Inschriften von Magnesia*, no. 114) and commented on by Buckler in *Anatolian Studies Ramsay*, p. 30. For conflicts between cliques, see Plutarch, *Precepts of Statecraft*, 32 (*Moralia*, 824f–825d) and 19 (815d). For local potentates the *loci classici* are those of Tacitus, *Annals*, XV, 20 (cf. Syme, *Tacitus*, pp. 467 and 556) and those quoted by J. H. Oliver, 'The ruling power: the Roman *oratio* of Aelius Aristides', in *Transactions of the American Philosophical Society*, XLIII (1953), pp. 929 and 954.

291. Plutarch, *Precepts of Statecraft*, 13 (809a).

292. In Cicero's time, in Sicily, 'all the wealthiest men had their assessments reduced, while the poorest had theirs increased' (*In Verrem*, II, 2). A law of 313 says: 'The *tabularii* of the cities, in collusion with the powerful, shift the burden of taxes on to the lesser people' (*Codex Justiniani*, X I, 58 (57), 1). Cf. Godefroy's commentary on Law X I I I, 10, 1, of the *Codex Theodosii*. In vain did the law decree that the *defensores civitatis*, whose task it was 'to defend the plebs against the injustices of the powerful', should not be recruited from the decurions (*Codex Theodosii*, I, 29, 1 and 3). On the *superindicta*, see E. Stein, *Histoire du Bas-Empire*, J.-R. Palanque (ed.), vol. I, pp. 76 and 346.

293. *Libanius et la Vie municipale à Antioche*, p. 163.

CHAPTER III

The Republican Oligarchy in Rome

The word 'oligarchy' is ambiguous. The notables of the Hellenistic cities, and also those of the Roman municipal towns which I shall discuss in the next chapter, formed a sort of privileged order in relation to the mass of the citizens. But the great oligarchs of Rome, the senators who were the masters of Rome, Italy and the world, were not such an order, privileged by wealth, influence and prestige, from among whom the governing personnel were recruited turn and turn about. There was indeed such an order in Rome – the *equites*.[1] The senators were, themselves, recruits. They did not constitute a ruling order, coextensive, if you like, with a social class, but a ruling group consisting of a few hundred individuals, a body of specialists which, by the end of the Republican period, had become practically hereditary (those newcomers who managed to join it could be counted on the fingers of one hand). The Senate was not defined by its social position, as was the case with the notables (social position, though necessary, was not sufficient), but by its function. It was composed of the council of annually elected magistrates currently in office, together with all former magistrates; and, in practice, future magistrates were all recruited from among the senators or their sons. The Senate was the government of Rome (Polybius says that when a Greek thought of the Roman state, he saw it as being ruled by the Senate). More precisely, it was a body which supervised the annually elected magistrates by reminding them, through the obligation under which they lay to seek its advice, that they were not free to ignore the views and wishes of their colleagues, past and to come. The Senate embodied the solidarity of a governing caste, and even the complicity of that caste. As Montesquieu says, the easier it is for an aristocratic government to curb the people, the more difficult is it for such a government to curb itself.

All this entailed far-reaching consequences with regard to euergetism. As the Senate was defined by its function, not by its social position (a Roman would have thought it too obvious, and at the same time improper, to say that the senators were rich men), the senators were prouder of their function than of their wealth. Did a senator wish to be the *euergetēs* of Rome? He would check himself, and think again: he would be a *euergetēs* not in his capacity as senator but merely as a rich man. Therefore, the euergetism of senators has only name and content in common with that of notables. Its motives were quite different. When senators wished to be magnificent they were magnificent privately, for the benefit of individuals, their clients, who were bound to them by a personal tie.

It will be appreciated that the senators of Rome, those consuls and praetors who, in accordance with the protocol of the time, ranked with a Hellenistic king,[2] had an outlook different from that of municipal notables. They were not caught up in the dynamic of a narrow group, and felt no embarrassment in dialogue with their compatriots, or rather with the plebeians. The city of Rome was only their capital or their electoral constituency, not the sole object of their political activity. They were statesmen who ruled an empire. There was no question of the plebs besieging the homes of these oligarchs in order to force games or bread out of them. The Roman plebs themselves, patriotic and imperialistic, saw the senators primarily as statesmen, and, whatever may have been said, did not elect them mainly on account of the splendour of the games they had provided. They did indeed provide games for the plebs of Rome, and paid for them. To judge by appearances, then, they were *euergetai* of that city. But if we judge by reality, they gave the people games for reasons of high policy or out of electoral considerations, and did this with a degree of condescension that would have been outrageous in the Athenian democracy. There was no guerrilla warfare between classes here, but there certainly was a class struggle which extracted from these great conservative lords bread for which the state had to pay.

The euergetism of this republican oligarchy was inspired by several motives quite different from those analysed in the previous chapter. When the oligarchs were magistrates they gave the people games so that they might be loved, and in order to facilitate the exercise of their authority (we shall examine this delicate matter in detail). Furthermore, they cultivated an electoral clientele in Rome and Roman Italy, by offering it pleasures on a great variety of pretexts. They also had buildings erected. When they had commanded an army and triumphed over the enemy, they commemorated their glory by erecting some public (and in principle religious) edifice. That would be more or less the whole story, were there not also two rather special features to be mentioned: state-provided bread, which was wrested from the government of the oligarchy, if not from individual oligarchs, and state patronage. Towards the end of the Republican period, when the advent of Imperial monarchy was already imminent, great lords came to look upon public responsibilities as their personal enterprises and consequently met, out of their own pockets, expenses entailed by these responsibilities. One of them, luckier than the rest, became the first Emperor, under the name of Augustus, and was to become indeed the patron of the state. The city of Rome never had *euergetai* in the true sense, comparable to the notables of Greece or of Roman Italy: the Republican oligarchy, followed by the Emperor, made many *euergesiai* in Rome's favour, but did this for reasons of state, or through state channels.

There is thus an almost complete contrast between Rome, Imperial city and capital of the world, and the Greek cities studied earlier. The contrast can be outlined as follows.

1. We have seen that euergetism begins when the exercise of power is looked upon as a profession, and is mainly the property of politicians, who resemble managers. Rome might certainly have known, therefore, a beginning of euergetism. The Roman senators were deeply convinced of their absolute right to rule Rome and the world, and even of their exclusive right to do that, and so they would have been quite ready to dip into their private coffers for the purpose. However, this did not happen, for an accidental reason. Thanks to the Eldorado of the Spanish mines and to the plundering of conquered peoples, the Roman Republic was glutted with money, and the senators were much more concerned to dip deeply into the public funds for their private profit, as will be seen, than to supplement those funds privately. It should be added that, in Rome, public life was much more oligarchic than civic in the true sense of the word. Between a senator and a plebeian the gap was infinitely wider than between a Greek notable and a man of the people. We can therefore hardly imagine a senator feeling the need to engage in *largesse* in order to reassure the people as to his professional disinterestedness.

2. Euergetism attains its full development when public functions are no longer anything more than honorific privileges and when

politics has ceased to be a serious matter. But nothing was more serious than the politics of Rome, with its world-wide scope. A senator possessed real power, and did not have to cultivate his social superiority. At the level of high politics there could be no question of gratuities *ob honorem*.

3. For the same reason, Rome did not foster the awarding of honours to *euergetai,* as happened in Greece. A senator had nothing more to prove, no 'life peerage' to acquire. It is hard to imagine him caring to receive a statue from the plebs in return for providing them with games. If he aspired to some distinction he would want to owe it to his merits in the sphere of high politics: to have a triumph or to be elected consul.

4. Finally, a senator would become a *euergetēs* only in order to give expression to his political glory (so that a *triumphator* gave *largesse* to the plebs) or else to symbolize relations in the sphere of high politics. 'Electoral corruption' was to be the typical form of these symbolic gifts which served to mark relations of clientage.

1. *The government of the oligarchy*

For the history of euergetism the domination of the oligarchy presents three interesting aspects.

1. The rich possess the moral right to rule, and are the only persons to possess it. Even more than a *de facto* situation, this is a reality accepted by popular opinion. Let us think of this oligarchy as a group of landowners and warriors, not much different from the nobles of archaic Greece or ancient Germany, a *Herrenvolk*: we shall then have a better idea of them than if we were to think of Cincinnatus.[3] There is no salary for servants of the state, and only men enjoying an income from the land can become magistrates and senators. The concentration of power is extreme: it has been said, without exaggeration, that in the second century BC twenty families decided Rome's policies.[4] While the electoral system favoured the 'middle class' (in the English sense of that expression), this middle class did not elect representatives from its own midst, but voted for oligarchs. In Athens in the age of democracy there was no class possessing the right to rule, but in Rome there was such a class. We never see, in Rome, any equivalent to the middle class who ruled Athens momentarily, and whose members came to the forefront through the eloquence they displayed before the popular assembly – Cleon the rich tanner, Lysicles the sheep-merchant,

Hyperbolus the manufacturer of lamps. The Senate and the magistrates were recruited, *de facto* if not *de jure*, exclusively from the ranks of the upper class, known as the order of *equites*. This oligarchy of rich men, these *optimates*, possessed *de facto* the privilege of governing, the rest of the citizens being content to vote. Even the leaders of what modern historians call the popular party were recruited from among the *optimates*. They were oligarchs who were ambitious, intelligent or generous (all three varieties existed) rather than 'demagogues' in the Greek sense of the word. Actually, the Romans never spoke of a popular party opposed to that of the oligarchy: the name of *populares* was given not to members of this alleged party but to statesmen, senators of course, who appealed to the popular assembly against the Senate.[5]

THE OLIGARCHS' POINT OF HONOUR

2. The oligarchs' assumption of public functions, far from being a public mission, was, in the full sense of the expression, a personal point of honour as demanding and quixotic as was honour in the Middle Ages. We should not see these oligarchs as men of duty, great servants of the Republic; through insistence on a political point of honour, they put Rome to fire and sword and brought the Republic to the brink of the abyss.

The point of honour in question was to occupy the highest magistracies, so that one's family might include the largest possible number of consuls and praetors: for, as in the *mestnichestvo* of tsarist Russia, distinctions of rank within the Roman oligarchy were based on the offices which had been held by one's ancestors. More generally, the point of honour for each oligarch was his *dignitas*, that is, his rank, his prestige in the political sphere. *Dignitas* was not 'dignity', a bourgeois virtue, but glory (*decus*),[6] an aristocratic ideal. A Roman oligarch was as greatly concerned for his political *dignitas* as the Cid for the honour of his house. But medieval honour consisted in not having failed to fulfil certain minimum requirements (first and foremost, to be brave) which every nobleman was presumed to satisfy until there was proof to the contrary: one had one's honour, or one lost it. Roman *dignitas*, on the other hand, was acquired, preserved and enhanced as a senator's political importance grew. Take Cicero, for example.[7] Throughout his life he thought about his *dignitas* as a medieval lord thought about his honour. In the course of a career which, until then, had been remarkably skilful and successful, he suffered exile. He was in despair, his *dignitas* was lost. He was recalled from exile: his *dignitas* had been restored to him. We understand, therefore, that these oligarchs did not perform their functions as modest servants of the state. It was accepted that a man who became a magistrate should glory in his office and defend his prerogative just as a king defends his crown. This zeal to defend one's *dignitas* was excused and absolved by public opinion, which could not really blame Caesar for talking on equal terms with the state, the Republic, and unleashing his civil war because the Senate encroached on his *dignitas*. Had he not made it known that he would give priority to his honour over everything else, even life itself?[8] Any more than one can reproach the Cid for killing his king's best general: honour demanded it. This cult of political *dignitas* is comprehensible. The Roman magistracies were very few in number: in the second century there were, each year, only thirty magistrates, of whom twelve at most were available to take command of the armies and govern the provinces, while the rest were kept busy in Rome. Athens, one-twentieth the size of Rome, had scores of public offices. Moreover, these thirty annually elected magistrates did not form a government; each had his own domain, his 'province', where he was more or less master, so that the magistrates constituted a plurality of sovereigns.[9]

3. Finally, in the matter of public finance, the Romans had as much sense of the state as the Greeks had, and more: was not the public Treasury the treasury of the ruling oligarchy?

THE OLIGARCHS AND THE PUBLIC TREASURY

Once the Republic had established a Treasury, two principles took root, which the Greeks also had discovered: the Republic must live off its own revenues and not levy taxes except in special circumstances;[10] and every public function must be paid for out of the Treasury. The land tax was levied irregularly down to 167 BC.[11] After that date, Rome, enriched by its plundering of the Hellenistic states, levied no more taxes from its Italian citizens, but lived instead from its domains and the tribute paid by its subjects. Italy was not subjected to the land tax again until four centuries later, at the end of the first period of the Empire, under Diocletian. All public expenditure was met by the Treasury. When a magistrate or a commissioner had to incur some expense for the Republic, the Treasury advanced him the money required. This sum remained the property of the Roman people: the magistrate's coffers were not separate from the state's, for a state quaestor had charge of them and any unexpended amounts were returned to the Treasury.[12]

However, Rome was an oligarchical state. Two consequences followed from this: hostility to 'largesses' made at the Treasury's expense, and absence of the liturgical spirit. The oligarchy considered that the *aerarium* no more belonged to the citizens than it did to their magistrates, but was at the disposal of an entity, the Republic, which was under the tutelage of the senatorial oligarchy. A guardian had no right to engage in liberalities at the expense of his ward's patrimony,[13] and likewise the magistrates and the Senate could not spend public money on what the oligarchy would have regarded as demagogic liberalities.[14] This was to be one of the points of friction between *optimates* and *populares*: the problem of the public corn. The most solid foundation of the Senate's power was the rule that no magistrate might spend public money without the Senate's permission. This oligarchy made its point of honour, as we know, the assumption of magistracies, *honores*, as they were called. It did not see its *dignitas* as demanding that it should ruin itself in expensive liturgies. Accordingly the *munera* were not to enjoy the brilliant expansion of the Athenian liturgies, but, on the contrary, would be regarded as somewhat sordid obligations. The *munera*, as forced contributions or taxes, were imposed by the magistrates; it was the *honores*, awarded by the people's votes, that distinguished one man from another.

In the third century BC there were already three sensitive areas in which the principle that the state's money did not belong to the magistrate, or his own money to the state, was giving rise to various difficulties. What was to be done with the money from fines imposed by the magistrates? What should a general do to whom the Senate had permitted free disposal of part of his booty? And when a magistrate had received a sum from the Treasury in order to provide games for the people, might he not add thereto something out of his own pocket? We can appreciate that these three questions were embarrassing. The proceeds of fines burnt the fingers of the magistrate who had imposed them. He would have to dedicate them to the gods – that is, to buildings or entertainments – if he did not want to be suspected of condemning an innocent person in order to enrich the Treasury; I shall examine this matter in more detail in the next chapter. As for booty and the cost of the games, these were the oldest starting-points for euergetism. Booty, too, burnt the fingers of the *triumphator*, and he would dedicate it to the gods instead of keeping it for himself. And the public games were so important to the Romans and played such a part in their political psychology that, as we shall see, the magistrates were soon, in this sphere, transformed into *euergetai*.

2. Why the magistrates provided games

WHO WAS TO PAY FOR THE GAMES?

Every year the Roman Republic celebrated officially, in honour of certain divinities, religious festivals which took place on fixed dates and were called the public games. They consisted mainly of chariot races in the Circus and theatrical performances. These games were organized and presided over by some of the magistrates of the year; namely, for historical reasons, the aediles and the praetors. The two consuls were not subject to any obligation of this sort. For the performance of their duty the aediles and praetors received from the Treasury a fixed sum,[15] but this was quite inadequate. To ensure the splendour of the festival and to win popularity for themselves, the magistrates who 'produced' the games – that is the Latin expression – had to meet most of the cost from their own resources. From the second century B C the games became a ruinous obligation – to which, nevertheless, the magistrates submitted cheerfully or even with enthusiasm. What we have to do is to explain the enthusiasm of these *euergetai*, to explain why the Romans found it normal to see their magistrates producing the games, presiding over them in person, giving with their own hands the starting signal for the chariot-races, and ruining themselves for the sake of these very popular festivals, whereas it would seem to us absurd for one of our ministers to be subjected to this glorious obligation. The reasons are many, and the religious character of the games is only the most superficial of them. Nor should we invoke 'depoliticization': the public games did not serve to resolve the agrarian crisis of the second century or the problem of state-provided bread. Conversely, if the Roman plebs had obtained free bread, that bread would not have been for them any substitute for the Circus. Nor should we compare the producing of the games by the Roman magistrates to the *largesses ob honorem* of the officials in the Hellenistic cities. Those *largesses*, which took very varied forms, were the price of the honour that the officials had received from their fellow citizens, and were not among the duties of their office. But producing games *was* one of the two functions of the aediles. These ministers of public works were at the same time ministers of sport or of religious affairs.

There was no question of their providing the people with pleasures other than these solemn games, and no Roman ever considered that producing games was the price of a magistracy. The euergetism of the Roman magistrates is a unique phenomenon, to be explained by a convergence of several special features, many of which are peculiar to Rome.

Let us first recall how Rome's public finances evolved. The Romans had a very clear idea about public money. The sums placed at magistrates' disposal by the Senate remained the state's property; but this principle, if we are to believe Mommsen, was subject to one or two exceptions – the money for the games, and also booty.[16] The money for the games, it is said, became the property of the magistrate who received it, was not administered by the quaestor, and did not have to be accounted for. The magistrate was merely required by the community to spend, from his now increased personal fortune, an amount corresponding to the sum he had received. If he spent less he would be charged with embezzlement. What is the aim of this theory which, however logical, lacks foundation in any text? To justify (to modern minds especially) the fact that, for their games, the magistrates spent a sum greater than they had received from the Treasury. If the state's money became their private property and they did not have to render accounts, they would have been doing as they wished with their money and it would no longer seem strange for a public man to have dipped into his own pocket to meet the cost of exercising his functions. Needless to say, Mommsen's theory is only a fiction, corresponding to legalistic preoccupations that were alien to the Romans. The latter were not troubled by any scruples about letting their magistrates pay for their pleasures. It remains to be discovered why the generosity of the oligarchs was expressed principally in the form of games, and how, historically, they came to be spending more than they received from the Treasury.

The details of this evolution are easy to reconstruct if we accept (contrary to Mommsen's theory) that, with the credits intended for the games, it was the same as with other public credits: the magistrate who had the power to dispose of them was not their owner, and it was the Treasury's quaestors who themselves administered these sums. What do we actually know about the credits for the games? I hope the reader will forgive me for the somewhat pedantic details which we now have to investigate. The sources tell us first that, for the Circus games, the procurement of racehorses was farmed out by the Treasury, so that under that head the Treasury itself chose and paid its suppliers.[17] And what about the theatrical games? There is an old word, *lucar*, which we find five or six times in the Latin texts that have come down to us and which means, it is generally believed, the credits which the Treasury placed at the disposal of the magistrates responsible for providing the public games. The texts tell us, for example, that a *euergetēs* of Ostia excused his city from payment of the *lucar* allotted to him for his games,[18] or that, following a scandal (an actor had demanded a very large payment for performing in the public games), the Roman Senate fixed a maximum figure for the *lucar*.[19] When we look more closely at the sources, however, we see that *lucar* actually means the payments made to the actors or buffoons who took part in the theatrical games. Thus the Treasury does not pay a sum to the magistrates, under the name of *lucar*, but itself makes the payments, or *lucar*, due to the performer or to the impresario.[20] We can conclude then that, at the beginning of this evolution, the magistrate was content to preside over and organize the games which were within his field of concern, while the actors and suppliers were paid by the Treasury. It was the Senate's responsibility, as was normal, to authorize the Treasury to undertake this expenditure. Texts inform us that for each game the expenditure in question was fixed, once for all, at 200,000 sesterces[21] — sometimes at 333,333 sesterces, as a consequence of a superstition whose Greek origin has been demonstrated.[22] The magistrate had nothing to pay.

Not for long, however. Soon he was to pay a great deal, so as to make the festival grander, and the state and the citizens would expect this of him; for the public games were religious ceremonies, i.e. festivals, at which men enjoyed themselves no less than the gods. What were the games, indeed? They were entertainments which the city offered to the gods because it was certain that the gods would enjoy them just as mortals did.[23] In the same way, the city invited the gods to banquets and offered sacrifices to them; believers consecrated precious objects to them, or sacrificed to them a day (a 'holy-day') and what they would have earned by working on that day. Since the gods took the same pleasure as men in the games, they too could only wish that the festival should last as long as possible; merrymaking and piety were inseparable. It remained to find some decent pretext for prolonging the festival without burdening the Treasury. Two were found.

FESTIVITY OR 'RELIGION'?

First, 'instauration'. When a religious ceremony had not been performed in accordance with the rules, even if unwittingly, what was to be done to expiate this failure? The person responsible must do the whole thing over again at his own expense. 'Instauration' of the games meant repeating the day or days of the festival when things did not go as they should have done, or even repeating the entire games, i.e. prolonging or doubling their duration, or extending it even further. In a ritualistic religion the most trivial slip was sufficient for a pretext: 'that year,' writes Livy, 'the Roman Games in their entirety were repeated three times, the Plebeian Games five times.'[24] The annalistic tradition carefully preserved the memory of these cases, which were excellent events for the plebs to recall and were greatly to the honour of the magistrate's euergetism; for it was obviously he who paid for the instauration, since he was responsible for the conduct of the games and he alone could decide whether or not everything had to be begun again.

The second decent pretext for making the magistrate rather than the Treasury pay was to take up a collection. This was how it was done. Livy tells us that in 212, when the Apollinarian Games were initiated, the oracle which prescribed their institution also gave this order: the Treasury must pay for the sacrifice at the end of the games, and the spectators must subscribe to pay for the entertainments. A *senatus consultum* laid it down that, for the sacrifice, the praetor who produced the games would have his expenses paid up to 12,000 *asses*, while the praetor, for his part, called on the people to subscribe according to each person's means.[25] Public funds and a collection – the recipe must have been inspired by the Greeks. At Amorgos in the third century BC the festival of the Itonia was financed partly by the city and partly by the contributions of pilgrims. It should be added that a *euergetēs* did not fail to 'decline the contributions of those who came to attend the festival, and who numbered no less than five hundred'.[26] This was exactly what everyone expected the Roman praetor to do: for as time passed there was no further question of this sort of collection, or rather we shall see that, if the custom was not absolutely abandoned, it was now the spectators themselves who, to honour a magistrate, took the initiative in reviving it on special occasions. At the end of the Republican period the Apollinarian Games were financed by the Treasury, which paid 380,000 sesterces, and by the praetors themselves.

Moreover, ever since 212 the praetor must have had to find some of the money, for he was certainly expected to spend more than the 12,000 *asses* for which the Treasury was obliged to reimburse him; he knew that the results of the collection would be added to that sum, but nothing guaranteed that this would prove sufficient to save him from being out of pocket.

Piety, merrymaking, solemnity – this was a balancing of functions which was always unstable and required much tact to keep in being. If the religious rites were manipulated too much for the benefit of the last two functions, if the games were 'instaurated' excessively to give pleasure to people rather than to satisfy piety, the confusion of functions would become impossible. Men would thenceforth go to the entertainment to distract themselves and as though to some secular ceremony, with the religious origin of the games nothing more than a survival or a pretext. The functions became separated; piety became purer, while losing most of the intertwined roots which attached it firmly to the soil of society. During the last two centuries of the Republic, and even more under the Empire, the games lost their religious dimension in the minds of their organizers and of all their spectators.

EUERGETISM

The secularization of the Roman games put an end to their multi-functional character. Henceforth they were merely an occasion of entertaining and ceremonial revelry. Since they gave so much pleasure to people, why should the magistrate who produced them not make himself popular, if he was open-handed? How could he fail to be elected when he offered himself for some other magistracy higher up the *cursus honorum*? And how could he fail to be defeated, if he had shown meanness? The public at the games was a public of electors. The Senate could with impunity refrain from increasing the public credits destined for the games: it knew that the magistrates would dip into their own pockets. The story of the Roman Games at the end of the Republican period is the story of how they grew ever more expensive and ever more sumptuous. It became sometimes necessary and often sufficient, in order to be elected to a magistracy, to have provided the plebs with magnificent games when one was an aedile. Euergetism became an instrument in a political career. From the beginning of the second century BC a person who had not held the aedileship, which involved responsibility for producing the costliest games, stood little chance of being elected praetor or consul. Euergetism thus contributed to determining a *cursus honorum* in which the aedileship, with its splendid games, and then the praetorship, which also had its games, were necessary stages before the consulate.[27] Every politician therefore sought 'to surpass all his predecessors in the magnificence of his exhibition'[28] – for they had acquired the outlook and the language of *euergetai*. The games were no longer regarded as a public ceremony but as a gift from their producer, a *munus*.[29] In principle it was the college of the aediles as a whole, or that of the praetors, who organized the various games. The public credits were assigned to the college and not to individual magistrates.[30] But each magistrate could, of course, add to these funds whatever sum he liked, and show himself more generous than his colleague. The public knew what each had paid, and was well aware of which had been the more generous: for the games that the aediles Scaurus and Hypsaeus gave together, posterity retained only the name of Scaurus.[31] The annals carefully preserved the memory of those aedileships which had been particularly sumptuous (those of Scaurus and Lucullus were remembered by all).[32] The coins of the last century of the Republic sometimes celebrate the memory of some aedile of the past, or of legend, who was 'the first' to produce the games of the Floralia or Cerealia, or that of some praetor who was 'the first' to produce the Sullan Games, in the year of their initiation.[33] For great euergetistic importance attached to being the first to practise a particular *euergesia*: both Greeks and Romans highly prized this sort of priority.[34] The magistrates ruined themselves for these splendours. Milo could boast that he had spent three inheritances on them.[35] One of the rules of friendship, in the senatorial class, was to open one's purse for a friend when he became an aedile.[36] In fairness one must add that producers of games were happy to extort money from the subject and 'allied' peoples,[37] that the yield of a special tax levied on Asia was assigned to finance the aediles' games,[38] and that when they became provincial governors aediles and praetors could recoup their losses to a very large extent by plundering the people under their administration and by eating up in 'entertainment allowances' a substantial slice of the public revenue.[39]

We should therefore not explain the senators' taste for making themselves prominent by mere human vanity. In that authoritarian oligarchy, a taste for popularity meant a taste for command. We know what satisfaction a real leader feels when, mixing with his men, he senses that they love and are ready to obey him, and he relishes the sensation of his power. Moreover, his taste was selective. The oligarchs sought the applause of Rome for the entertainments they provided, but they were not concerned, in the provinces they governed, to win the applause of their subjects by their justice and disinterestedness. However, the Roman people were not merely a passive object of political activity. They had a role to play in legislation: assembled in *comitia tributa* they acted as the instrument of the tribunes of the plebs, who relied on them to vote for their laws. As regards elections, these were in the hands of the 'middle class', the equestrian order, which controlled the *comitia centuriata*; but the equestrian order also attended the public games, where it demonstrated its opinion by giving or withholding the signal for applause.[40] The public games were not distractions for the proletariat: the division between plebeian amusements and those favoured by the elite had not yet taken place, and the entire population was interested in the spectacles provided.[41]

3. Symbolic gifts

Largesse has this in common with politeness, that both serve a protector as means of giving his protégé the feeling that a relationship of equality exists between them, so that the protégé accepts more willingly the protection given by his master. It would be unjust to conclude from this that *largesse* served to buy men's consciences. Both ancients and moderns are sometimes guilty of this unjust conclusion.

WHAT GIFTS SYMBOLIZED

Business is not transacted to the accompaniment of symbolic gifts unless the two parties are independent of each other. An elected person cannot decently give a present to his electors unless he considers himself to be something more than their shadow. Have we not seen, earlier, that the Roman magistrates did not consider themselves the mandatories of their electors? When two parties deal with each other only on condition that a symbolic gift changes hands, each of them considers that it possesses autonomy, or that its interests are not identical with those of the other party. It would be wrong to assume that *largesses* to the electors signified, in Rome, homage to the sovereign people. The reverse, rather, was the case: the candidate would not have made *largesse* unless it was understood that his authority was a sort of private property in his possession and that he was not the servant of his fellow citizens. The power he held was his personal interest rather than a mission he was fulfilling on behalf of his electors. He sought an enhancement of his honour (*dignitas*), a glorious title. For power was a benefit one received from the Roman people, whose votes were so many services rendered to the candidate.[42] The two parties were mutually independent. The candidate might not be elected, for the people owed him nothing; but if he was elected, the people would have no claim upon him. Since they were independent of each other, the election resembled a negotiation, and that was precisely why it was accompanied by symbolic gifts on the part of the person seeking election. These gifts established the principle that respect should prevail around the negotiating table, so as to emphasize more clearly that the matter in hand would not be settled merely on the basis of power relations. Thus, the candidates negotiated amiably with their electors, instead of stoically awaiting the verdict of the sovereign people.

What applied to the electorate applied also to the people as a whole. Symbolic *largesses* conferred on the relations between oligarchy and plebs a style of amiable condescension. We still need to grasp why the politicians, from ordinary candidates up to a Caesar or an Octavius, seemed to regard the plebs as so important. What political power did the plebs actually wield? It is hard to answer this fundamental question. Are the means and ends of politics to be reduced to power relations and material interests, to a quest for security and prosperity and ways of rationally ensuring both of these?

It was of course important for the oligarchs to make themselves popular, so that in the *comitia tributa* the tribunes of the plebs would not be able to manoeuvre the lower orders against them, and so that a compliant tribune would be able more easily to pass some law in their favour. In the last century of the Republic the magistrates who dominated political life through their wealth, prestige and political clientage – a Pompey or a Caesar – dreamt only of obtaining special commands in the Empire. The provinces, which concerned the senatorial oligarchy, with its narrowly Roman outlook, less than did the contests in the Forum, served instead as the magnates' arena and jumping-off point. It is significant that the laws which granted to Pompey (*Lex Gabinia*, *Lex Manilia*, *Rogatio Messia*) and to the 'first triumvirate' (*Lex Vatinia*, *Lex Trebonia*) extraordinary powers in the Empire were all voted at *comitia* of the plebs, on the initiative of the tribunes. It was therefore important to win the hearts of the plebs.

We need to distinguish between two cases. Either the donor and the beneficiary are already linked in some way (patron and client, general and soldier), or they are as yet not linked in any way, though the possibility of such a bond is already hinted at in their hearts or in the power relations between them. In the second case the gift merely proposes, or seals, the creation of the bond. Thus Octavius made a political agreement with the veterans to whom his father had granted land, and who had the same reason to desire the victory of the Caesarean party as had, in France, the purchasers of *biens nationaux* to desire the success of the Revolution. In the first case the gifts are not the price of the bond. A client does not sell himself for life to a patron for thirty pieces of silver. The gifts merely symbolize the fact that the patron's authority is not unconditional and that both parties must gain from it. 'When elections take place the candidate presents his followers with gifts in kind or in money, but what would be corruption in an advanced society is here only the legitimate result of the relations of personal solidarity that unite the leader and his followers. The leader is not buying their votes: they were already his.' These lines were not written about elections in ancient Rome but about elections in Brazil in 1958, as they took place in the provinces dominated by the *cacicat* of the latifundists.[43] Petty gifts maintained the relation of clientage, which often consisted in an exchange of services very widely separated in time. In order that the obligation to return the service received might be kept up, there had to be a bond of affection between protector and protégé, and this affection was symbolized by petty gifts which seemed to create the bond but in fact merely served to maintain friendship and the memory of a service which still awaited its reward. It is only when I pay cash for a service done to me, and I have no intention of remaining any longer in a business relationship with my partner, that I can consider that I owe him nothing more and that he is not my benefactor but merely a vendor. If a gracious gesture, even one that costs little, seems to create for me the duty not to be ungrateful, and to lay me under considerable obligation ('he did not give me much but he did it so nicely that I can't decently refuse him anything now, without being ungrateful'), this is an illusion. I have forgotten that my benefactor and I are already linked in a lasting bond that should bring me more substantial satisfactions – otherwise, I should find that my alleged benefactor takes me for a fool. To this pre-existent bond the symbolic gift indeed adds a supplement of real authority, but the value thereof remains proportional to the gift. The boss who treats his staff well may from time to time ask his secretary to stay behind for half an hour after the office has closed, and 'do it as a favour to him'.

THE *DONATIVUM*

In none of these cases is there room for a symbolic gift unless the two parties have independent interests and neither owes the other statutory obedience. Such was the state of affairs between Roman soldiers and their generals from the end of the third century BC. The following story is well known. When he was sent as quaestor attached to Scipio during that general's campaign in Africa, Cato the Elder noticed that Scipio was showing his usual extravagance and distributing the state's money carelessly among his troops. This angered Cato and he reproached the general with demoralizing his men and undermining discipline.[44] Yet Scipio was not buying his soldiers; he was simply showing awareness of the fact that they felt they were more their general's followers than defenders of the Republic, something which Cato did not, or did not want to, understand. The armies of the civil wars thus tore the state apart by fighting each other for their respective generals. The personal bond between the soldiers and their chief came to acquire features not very consistent with that passive obedience which may be thought essential where military discipline is concerned. The generals granted *donativa* to their troops and allowed them to sack cities.[45] On one occasion some troops refused to march, so their general went personally to plead with his men, going from tent to tent, taking the soldiers by the hand and weeping.[46] This general's mistake had been that 'he was not disposed to court the favour of the common soldier, and thought that everything that was done to please one's command only dishonoured and undermined one's authority'.[47] As for the *donativa* (distributions of money among the soldiers), these were originally military rewards; but from the time of the Scipios they lost that character by reason of their frequency, and became *largesses* from the leader to his men.

Elections, clientage, politics, the army: symbolic gifts are found everywhere in Roman civilization. It was not that in this case the gift was a primitive form of exchange. On the contrary, the gifts reveal that exchange, or rather the market, was much less important then than nowadays (the labour market in particular). Nor were laws and regulations very important: personalized relations prevailed. For example, we find patrons who had as clients an architect or a shoemaker who devoted most of their efforts to their master's service: 'in exchange', the master fed them every day the gods sent. Perhaps the master gained by this, or perhaps, on the contrary, he maintained his architect in idleness. At all events, the food supplied would be payment for the architect's labour, but the master was not buying this labour at the price it would have commanded on the market. It established between him and his client a bond of personal affection, to justify the continuation of their relationship, and small mutual gifts would from time to time symbolize this bond and seem to maintain it.[48]

THE DUAL FUNCTIONING OF ROMAN SOCIETY

From the beginning of the second century BC Roman society was based on two parallel systems: public institutions and interpersonal relations. On the one hand there was the Republic, the magistracies, the legions; on the other, the new-style clientage, exchange of services, *largesses*. The last-mentioned, if interpreted according to the second system, were only symbols. But interpreted according to the first system they pointed to a corruption of morals, being the price at which consciences were bought. Always, or almost always, when *largesses* are mentioned, ancient authors say, either calmly or with indignation, that he who made them bought the favour of the plebs. This was a somewhat unjust interpretation, as we know, but not a hanging offence: casuists and sociologists had not yet been born. Two types of men were sworn enemies of the new style of human relations and of the gifts that symbolized them: those who regretted that the old obedience existed *no more* and those who regretted that the sense of legality was *not yet* present. Among the first I will mention Lucullus (he it was who feared to dishonour his authority by complaisance towards his soldiers) and, much later, the Emperor Galba, a man behind the times who, failing to understand the sociology of the *donativum*, was unwilling to distribute it among his soldiers because he claimed to give them orders, not to buy their obedience: he treated this as a matter of principle.

Among those who regretted that the sense of legality did not yet exist (or who affected to believe that it existed already and behaved accordingly), the most interesting is the Stoic Cato of Utica. To parody Weber, it could be said that Stoicism was the Puritanism of antiquity, which, applied to political life rather than to economic activity, advanced its rationalization. Sallust, the leading political thinker of his time, who carried a taste for impartiality to the point of being fair to Cicero, of whom he had a poor opinion, held that Cato was, with Caesar, one of the two greatest politicians of the age. When the other oligarchs talked of serving the state and sacrificing themselves for the general interest, in their mouths these were empty phrases. One day, when Crassus was asked if he would seek election as consul and he did not want to answer, he declared nobly 'that if it was for the interest of the city he would be a candidate for the office, but otherwise he would desist'.[49] Cato, however, took seriously the idea that magistracies were missions. When he failed to win the consulship he remained ice-cold and showed not the slightest resentment. The people owed him nothing; if they did not want him, he must bow to their decision; if they had chosen him, they would thereby have entrusted him with a mission rather than done him a favour.[50] Moreover, that mission ought to be acquired on grounds of merit alone.[51] Cato refused to corrupt the electorate, did nothing to win the people's support, and never succeeded in becoming consul.[52] He himself declined to accept presents from kings, which he saw as attempts to corrupt him[53] rather than as symbolic gestures which had become customary in the diplomatic relations of his time.[54] Politics was, in his eyes, a serious activity which called for application and method. From his youth he had studied public affairs and he was one of the least amateurish statesmen of his time.[55] In his view politics was work. He spent whole days working on his documents[56] and regularly attended the sessions of the Senate,[57] whereas many others stayed away. He had a legalistic, even bureaucratic turn of mind.[58] A stern watchdog over public finance,[59] he also deserves a place in the history of book-keeping and red tape: he knew how important it is to keep proper accounts.[60] If Puritanism be regarded as the spiritual father of capitalism, Stoicism can figure as the ancestor of the bureaucratic state. As a way of life, Stoicism provided the sense of methodical effort and justified it by glorifying it. Cato of Utica was perhaps the only politician of his age for whom the description 'servant of the state' would not be anachronistic. Because he refused to play the game of clientage in politics, Cicero, while respecting him, held that he was actually not very intelligent and even rather limited.

4. Electoral 'corruption'

In Rome itself we can distinguish two systems of gifts. Within the oligarchy, where personal relations and political positions were intertwined to the point of ambiguity, services or 'benefits' were exchanged between equals in accordance with their real value, which was very substantial. But between this oligarchy and the plebs, who were reduced to obeying and had only their faces to save, *largesses* were merely symbolic – which amounts to saying that the faces in question were correctly estimated at their poor worth. It remains to consider a third system, that which applied in the relations between candidates for magistracies and the people who were their electors. In this sphere, it is said, electoral corruption prevailed. Let us see if things were as simple as that.

ORIGINS IN FOLKLORE

Public banquets in which all citizens participated were a civic custom that was widespread in the Greek world.[61] It was much less widespread in Rome, where the senatorial oligarchy reserved for itself the right to banquet at the state's expense (*jus epulandi publice*). If a feast was offered to the population as a whole, the oligarchs had reserved tables to which the plebs were not admitted.[62] The feasts of the Senate and of certain priestly *collegia* were famous for their gastronomic refinement,[63] but the plebs had no place there. At public sacrifices the meat of the victims was not distributed among the crowd of persons present, but probably set aside for the senators.[64] On the other hand, some great personages did, in their private capacity, willingly provide dinners for plebeians – a form of behaviour more lordly than civic. When Octavius shaved for the first time (four years had passed since he came into his fortune and he was now the master of the Roman West), 'he held a magnificent entertainment himself, besides granting all the other citizens a festival at public expense'.[65]

But most often it was funerals that provided the opportunity or pretext for feasting. For the great families of the oligarchy, funerals, when portraits of their ancestors were displayed, were a sort of dynastic ceremony. Through the years, the life of the plebs in Rome was punctuated by free banquets in memory of the illustrious departed. These were events of some interest to the market, too, for in the years when a feast was given the price of thrushes would rise.[66] Collective memory piously retained the dates of particular feasts: the one offered in 59 by Arrius in his father's memory (and also, doubtless, with a view to his own candidature for the consulship) became proverbial.[67] A technical vocabulary came into being: *epulum* was a banquet, *visceratio* a distribution of meat, *crustum* and *mulsum* were sweets. Officially these enjoyments were funerals, but this troubled no one, and it was out of place to come to the feast dressed in mourning garments.[68] For banquets, dining-couches were set up in the Forum and the people lay on them, while the senators had tables reserved for them in the Capitol.[69] The earliest *visceratio* recorded in the annals goes back to

328, when one Flavius distributed a dole of meat to persons who walked in his mother's funeral procession: 'the dole was ... the cause of his receiving an office; and at the next election he was chosen tribune of the plebs in his absence, in preference to some who canvassed.'[70] Sweets were given to the people during the funeral of Scipio Africanus, the conqueror of Hannibal: a friend of the family, who owed much to the dead man, 'at the Porta Capena served wine and honey to those who had attended the funeral'.[71] Besides the pleasures of the palate, funerals brought still more intense enjoyments, namely gladiatorial combats — for in origin these were a funerary rite. In 174 a certain Flamininus gave the people, in memory of his father, a banquet, a dole of meat, theatrical performances in the guise of funerary games, and a gladiatorial show (*munus*) in which seventy-four combatants took part.[72]

Thereafter, the process of evolution became bifurcated towards a kind of euergetism and towards electoral corruption. It was not uncommon for the deceased to have made arrangements in his will for his own funeral and himself to have ordered his heir to provide pleasures for the people on that occasion, so as to perpetuate the memory of his name and to enhance the ceremony. Soon, pleasures other than those that were customary came to be provided for the plebs. Seneca was later to satirize persons who, out of desire for immortality, sought to arrange what was to happen after they died, and ordered that gladiatorial combats and the dedication of a public building should accompany their cremation.[73] The dictator Sulla ordered his heir to give a feast and a gladiatorial show to the people in his name, together with free entry to the baths and the oil needed for cleansing the body.[74] In this way a testamentary euergetism developed, associated with foundations in memory of dead men and with the funeral ceremony as no more than a pretext. Sulla's son carried out his father's long-awaited liberalities nearly twenty years after the dictator's death.[75] From this to bequeathing money was but a step: Balbus was to leave 100 sesterces to each citizen of Rome.[76] This is worth knowing if we are to understand the origins of legacies to cities, as dealt with in Roman law.[77]

But the best example of a funeral practice that became a *euergesia* is provided by the gladiators, that institution, unique in world history, which is one of the most original creations of the Italic genius.[78]

Achilles celebrated the funeral of Patroclus with games. Paintings in Etruscan tombs depict funeral games. In Rome the citizens did not take part in the spectacles, which were left to professionals, persons both admired and despised.[79] This was the case with the private games held by great families to commemorate the death of one of their members. From the third century these games consisted mainly or solely of gladiatorial combats,[80] the introduction of which to Rome can be attributed to one of the oligarchical cliques which dominated the Republic at that time, the clique of Junius Brutus and Aemilius Lepidus.[81] Under the pretext or in the name of funeral games, gladiators were thus at first associated with funerals, and until the end of the Republic it was the funerals of great men which, almost without exception, served as an excuse for their combats. All the people were admitted to watch these combats, which were advertised by public proclamation,[82] their organizer having the right to be formally preceded by the lictors.[83]

So the people became the true beneficiary of these spectacles, rather than the memory of the deceased. 'Giving gladiators' became the best way to make oneself popular; from 'funeral games' the gladiators thus became a 'gift' presented to the people, a *munus*.[84] This was how the word acquired the meaning of 'a gladiatorial spectacle'. In this way there came into being the contrasting pair which dominated the organization of entertainments under the Republic and during the early period of the Empire, both in Rome and in the municipal towns: on the one hand 'the games', the public games, in the theatre or the Circus, which were organized by the state and presided over by a magistrate, and which came round every year, in conformity with the religious calendar; on the other 'the gladiators', a secular and private spectacle given irregularly,[85] when a *euergetēs* happened to take the initiative in his own name. When it became a *euergesia* pure and simple, the *munus* was not even disguised any more by the pretext of a funeral.[86] Other pretexts were equally valid for presenting this 'gift' to the people: in Pompeii combats were held in honour of the Imperial house or for the dedication of some public building.

How did the transition take place from these funeral *largesses* to electoral corruption? In two ways. Intending candidates postponed the celebration of their *munus* until the year of their candidature, and invited to share in their *largesses*, as was the custom, the entire plebs or at least all the members of their constituency, their 'tribe'. In this manner Caesar enhanced the brilliance of his aedileship, the foundation of a fine career, by adding to his public games a *munus* in memory of his father, who had died twenty years earlier.[87] In vain did the laws against canvassing, which multiplied in the first century and which their very authors were sometimes the first to violate,[88] attempt to forbid candidates to give a *munus* in the year when they put their names forward, and to invite the whole population to attend.[89] But how, in decency, could a son be forbidden to honour his father's memory, even if there had been some delay?[90] Candidates' memories consequently turned towards the dear departed with special force during election periods, and they invited to the celebration the entire plebs or at least all members of their own tribe. In vain did the law declare that canvassing had occurred when a candidate, following the ancient funerary custom, invited everybody to his feast, to his gladiators, or when he reserved the best seats at the public games for the electors of his tribe, instead of issuing invitations by name.[91] It goes without saying that, no less than the public games, the *munus* and the *largesses* of all kinds which candidates provided for their electors were so expensive that only the very rich could compete. Even in the time of the Scipios a good funerary *munus* cost the equivalent of hundreds of thousands of pounds.[92] At the election of 54 something scandalous occurred: two candidates announced that they were ready to distribute to the few dozen electors of the *centuria praerogativa* (whose vote was usually decisive) a sum which today would amount to tens of thousands of pounds if these electors would declare in their favour.[93]

ELECTORAL SOCIOLOGY

But what actual influence did entertainments and *largesses* have on the outcome of elections? This question needs to be countered by another: what actual influence did election results have on policy? Could the Roman electors take their ballot papers seriously? The *largesses* played a role in the electors' choice, but it would be a caricature of the truth to claim that this role was decisive: the elections involved many other interests – personal, regional, even sentimental[94] – but rarely (if ever) interests of high politics. What was really at stake in elections was not anything of importance to the electors, who usually saw in them only a charade from which they might at best expect to make a little profit, but something that mattered to the oligarchs, who competed in them for honours, in this society in which political dignity was not one career among others but the only career worthy of an oligarch.[95]

Was it decisive to have made *largesse* when one was an aedile and fatal not to have done so?

Sulla now thought that the reputation which he had won in war was sufficient to justify political activities, and therefore at once exchanged military service for public life, offered himself as a candidate for the city praetorship, and was defeated. The responsibility for his defeat, however, he lays upon the populace. They ... expected that if he should be made aedile before his praetorship, he would treat them to splendid hunting scenes and combats of Libyan wild beasts, and therefore appointed others to the praetorship, in order to force him into the aedileship.[96]

On the other hand, a certain Flavius was elected tribune of the plebs for having distributed meat, and a *triumphator* became censor for having distributed oil.[97] Murena lacked an advantage in seeking the praetorship which did not matter when seeking the consulship, namely the reputation of a provider of splendid games.[98]

The electors' interests were manifold and the means available to candidates for making themselves popular were consequently numerous. Each chose his method in accordance with his capacities; had not there been a few cases when the public subscribed to reimburse a particularly respected magistrate for the cost of his games?[99] 'From their other praetors,' said Cassius to Brutus when introducing his plan of conspiracy to him, 'they demand gifts and spectacles and gladiatorial combats; but from thee, as a debt thou owest to thy lineage, the abolition of tyranny.'[100] In 53 Curio lost his father and became preoccupied with giving the plebs a funerary *munus*. Cicero, who had taken this young man under his wing, wanted to dissuade him from doing this: Curio had received advantages enough from nature and fortune to reach the greatest heights in his career without need of gladiators, and had services quite different from a *munus* to render to the state and to his friends.[101] This was a reminder to the young man that the electors were far from being the only persons to decide who should be elected, and that the protection of a Cicero, the intrigues and influence of the oligarchs, the manipulation of voting procedures by the president of the *comitia*, were just as useful to an ambitious man as a dubious popularity. It amounted to telling him that if he earned the esteem of the senatorial order, that order and Cicero himself would be there to help him.

Entertainments were only one electoral argument among others; the relations of every kind which clientage, in the widest sense of the word, created between candidates and electors counted for just as much. 'I have never seen candidates more evenly matched,' wrote Cicero to a correspondent before the consular elections of 54. 'Scaurus has been called into court by Triarius: without any great sympathy for him being aroused, if you want to know. However, his aedileship recalls no unpleasant memories, and their remembrance of his father has some weight with the country voters.' This Scaurus was the one who, when aedile, had given games of unforgettable splendour.[102] As an ardent defender of oligarchical privileges, his father had won the hearts of the Italian notables and landowners. Cicero goes on: 'The other two plebeian candidates are about equal, as Domitius is strong in friends and his very popular gladiatorial exhibition will count for him too, while Memmius is popular with Caesar's soldiers and relies on the support of Pompey's Gaul.'

The pomp surrounding the candidate counted for as much as and more than his *largesses*, nor should we discount his personal prestige, if he had any. Cicero was elected to his four magistracies by a very big majority.[103] This prestige, or *existimatio*, depended on many things: birth, the deeds of one's ancestors, personal merit, comportment, liberality, number of supporters. The electors voted for the candidate for whom their protectors or their friends had requested their votes as a personal service. Respectful of the natural authorities, they chose the man whom eminent members of the Senate took the trouble to recommend. Ever deferential to a great lord, they gave their votes to the figure who trailed an impressive retinue of supporters and clients behind him everywhere, to do him honour: these processions were the picturesque element in the Roman elections.[104] In their turn, however, pomp and clientage had, like *largesses*, only relative importance, given the absence of any serious political issue at stake. For these elections were barely serious: they could not bring about an alteration in policy; the electors merely made their choice between candidates who were politically interchangeable and belonged to the same ruling class.

Politics entered only rarely into the elections. Not that this society was immune to social or political antagonisms or that the struggles in the Forum were confined to rivalry between cliques, but the electoral arena was not the setting for the major antagonisms. These were fought out on the legislative plane: the political action of the *populares* consisted in getting revolutionary laws voted.[105] In serious cases the possessing class always won the day, and in normal times the electors made their choice between lords and did not vote for a policy.[106] Many plebeians were certainly favourable to the *populares*, but no 'popular' party ever existed, except potentially. It was not a mass party, the candidates did not campaign under its banner, and there was no continuity in 'popular' policy. There was not a 'popular' candidate up for election every year. The action of the *populares* was nothing more than political guerrilla warfare; the *optimates* kept control of the country.

It was important for the *dignitas* of every oligarch to get elected, but it mattered little, politically, to the electors which oligarch was successful in an election; hence the demoralization of the electorate and the triumph of corruption. Quite non-political considerations (nobility, services rendered, games, clientage) usually determined the way votes were cast.[107] Sometimes *largesses* in the crudest form were enough to ensure that one candidate was preferred to another. The easiest way to win the electors' support was still to distribute money among them on the actual day of the election. For this purpose the candidates employed professionals, the *divisores*, who paid out the appropriate sums to the appropriate persons; this was one of the minor trades of ancient Rome.[108] However, let us not caricature the reality; the electors who, under the Roman electoral system, decided the way the vote would go were not poor wretches whose ballot papers could be bought for the price of a dinner or a pair of shoes, but rich landowners. True, they sold themselves, though indeed at a higher price than that; but perhaps they did not *always* sell themselves, and they chose their buyers. A courtesan is not a prostitute. Let us consult some texts. Cato of Utica was a candidate for the praetorship. Against him the consuls 'brought forward henchmen and friends of their own as candidates for the praetorship, themselves offering money for votes, and themselves standing by when the votes were cast. But even to these measures the virtue and fame of Cato were superior, since shame made most of the people think it a terrible thing to sell Cato by their votes, when the city might well buy him into the praetorship; and therefore the first tribe called upon voted for him.' Cato's election seemed assured, and in order to block it Pompey was reduced to manipulating the state religion. He 'lyingly declared that he heard thunder, and most shamefully dissolved the assembly'.[109] Not everyone who wanted to buy votes was able to do so. When Cicero was a candidate for the aedileship, Verres wanted to spoil his chances and instructed the *divisores* to promise the moon to whoever would vote for other candidates. In vain: all the constituencies, the 'tribes', refused to sell themselves, except the Romilia, to which Verres belonged, and whose electors, with the usual deference of the tribes towards their eminent members, would have voted as Verres wished in any case, for was it not unusual and dishonouring for a candidate to fail to receive the votes of his own tribe? This sort of mishap became almost proverbial. The votes of the Romilia were assured to Verres in advance, and that was why this tribe had accepted his money, regarding it as merely a traditional gratuity, since it was customary, and approved by the law, for a candidate to give money to his own tribe.[110]

What was forbidden by law, however, was to offer money to other tribes. That amounted purely and simply to buying consciences, and constituted the offence of canvassing. It was towards the end of the Republic, around the 50s, that canvassing began to be practised on a scale unheard of until then: as has been mentioned, in 54 the *centuria praerogativa* was offered some £500,000. This shameless act, which was an exception rather than the rule or even an extreme case, has to be understood as the folly of a moment, comparable to the South Sea Bubble in England around 1720, or the fever of speculation in the United States in 1927–9 – except that in Rome men speculated in the Forum rather than on the Stock Exchange, and in votes rather than shares. But the taste for speculation was the same. Favoured in our society by the separation between ownership and the profession of entrepreneur, it was favoured in Rome by a taste for money and cleverness in making money, together with refusal to consider enterprise as a genuine profession. Men wanted to be rich while remaining idle; therefore they had to speculate, so as to have an economic activity which, though perhaps absorbing, was diffuse, and they had to profit from possible opportunities rather than be continuously engaged in doing a job. Economic life in the upper class was thus varied, improvised and discontinuous. Senators, *equites*, rich men of every sort were always on the look-out for opportunities not to be missed and speculative coups to attempt. All was grist to their mill: regional famines, loans to a city or a king, auctions (very fashionable at that time), state tax-farms – not to mention pursuit of legacies, buying up the property of exiles, and simple brigandage. What we should regard as normal forms of business (maritime trade, transport by mule-pack, pottery-making) were considered varieties of speculation. A person who speculates can at least *think* that he is not working. Everyone specialized in one or more distinct kinds of speculation, and within the same upper class the variety of activities as between one individual and another was wide and picturesque. Some manufactured amphorae, others sold books, and Crassus bought cheap, from the distressed owners, the land under houses which had burned down.[111] In this lively and sharp climate the sale of votes became for a moment just one speculation among others, and a collective folly.

Finally, if we are to understand the psychology of this handful of rich electors and voters who controlled the *comitia*, it is necessary to take account of another attitude of theirs, a disinterested one this time. When they ensured success for the candidate who had given the best games, did they do this in their own name, because these games had pleased them? Rather than being straightforward electors, did they not see themselves as forming a jury responsible for representing the opinion of the plebs, whose votes hardly mattered? Did they say, 'I liked Scaurus's games, I'll vote for him,' or 'Scaurus succeeded in making himself popular, the plebs liked his games: he's the one who deserves to win'? After all, we have seen that the oligarchs made *largesse* not so much in order to win over electors for a practical purpose as out of a desire to make themselves popular. Why should not the electors, who belonged to the same social class as the candidates, have seen things in the same way, and considered, like them, that popularity with the plebs was an advantage?

The distributions of money to the tribes tended eventually to become an automatic and inconsequential gift, like the '*épices*' which litigants used to give to their judges: this hardly answered the candidates' purpose. Laws against canvassing were passed again and again in the last century of the Republic. Despite the social order dominated by clientage, the legalistic façade was upheld. Characteristically, however, these laws were directed against the candidate who sought to corrupt, and never against the electors who let themselves be corrupted: the legislator understood them too well. Another significant fact was that these laws against canvassing gave the greatest pleasure to the candidates themselves.[112] Did they not result in putting an end to a process of mutual outbidding that was ruinous for all the candidates (outbidding is the curse of euergetism) and to unfair competition? If the Republic had not been replaced by the Imperial monarchy, which eventually abolished the elections, we can guess how the matter would have culminated – in the fixing of a price-list. A decision by Augustus points towards this: while introducing many penalties to suppress canvassing, the Emperor consoled the members of his own constituency, who were nostalgic for the *largesses* of the candidates in the good old days, by having distributed to them, on election day, a payment fixed at the rate of 1,000 sesterces per elector.[113]

EUERGETISM THROUGHOUT ITALY

Distributions of money were only one argument amongst other *largesses* and amongst all the bonds of clientage. A feature of the electoral system made it much more important for candidates to form these bonds throughout Italy rather than in Rome itself. To be sure, the actual voting took place only in Rome: votes could not be cast elsewhere and there was no postal voting.[114] Election campaigns were also carried on in Rome alone, so that the first concern of a candidate was to rent a house not too far from the Forum.[115] The city-state had grown too big. As against this, the Italian electors' votes counted for more than those of the inhabitants of Rome. Electors voted by corporation, not as individuals; each of the thirty-five constituencies or 'tribes' had one vote, and only four of them were Roman ('urban'), the remaining thirty-one being Italian ('rural'). The Italian electors had to travel to Rome. This they did if they were rich, and if the candidate was able to persuade them to do it for his sake.

In order to win the election it was often enough to take part, so that the main concern of the candidates was not to win over the 'don't knows' but to assemble supporters, 'clients', who would go and vote.[116] One of the duties of friendship was to cast one's vote when a friend was a candidate: for that purpose Atticus travelled from Athens to Rome.[117] There was no quorum for each tribe, but all the tribes had to be represented. If it so happened that not a single representative of a certain tribe turned up, the magistrate presiding over the vote dispatched five electors from another tribe to vote on behalf of the missing one.[118] The unwanted presence of certain electors could upset the results. Thus the elections of 63 were decided to some extent by the arrival in Rome of a crowd of veterans who came to take part in Lucullus's triumph.[119] During the Gallic War Caesar took care to grant leave to his soldiers so that they could go to Rome and vote for their general's political allies.[120]

The presence of Italian notables was more usual, and ensured that the elections were dominated by the middle class. The electoral *comitia* coincided with the public games, which brought many Italians to Rome.[121] Although the rich definitely dominated the *comitia centuriata*, they could control the *comitia tributa* only if the notables came to Rome to counterbalance the votes of the Roman plebs.[122] When they were there, the senatorial oligarchy took the opportunity to get laws adopted by the *comitia* which conformed to the wishes of the *optimates*.[123] The honours and laws of Rome were thus largely subject to control by a handful of Italian notables, a few rich families from Atina, Lanuvium or Arpinum. These notables consequently became ardent defenders of the system of voting by corporation, which guaranteed their supremacy, and in relation to which historians often refer to the 'pocket boroughs' and 'rotten boroughs' of eighteenth-century England. They opposed all proposals to introduce individual balloting, 'a random system of voting'.[124] An ambitious man therefore needed, in order to attain honours, to cultivate the goodwill of the Italian towns and of the municipal notables who ruled the roost there. Consequently the oligarchs of Rome formed or maintained close ties with what we should call 'the provinces', and a senatorial euergetism developed in Italy. Memories were long in the provinces: a service rendered was not forgotten and a clientage was durable. Cicero recommended to Brutus his fellow townsmen of Arpinum: 'You will find that you have added some men of excellent character to the list of your intimate friends, and that by your kindness you have laid under obligation a most grateful municipality.'[125]

Municipal gratitude was indeed not without its uses. Murena was elected consul partly through the votes of his own tribe, the Maecia, which consisted mainly of inhabitants of Lanuvium, his home town, only about twenty kilometres from Rome.[126] We can be sure that those people had covered that distance on the day of the election. The other cities of the Maecia – Naples, Brindisi and Paestum[127] – were much further off, so that Murena could neglect them without incurring the risk that they might come in to vote against him. His opponent Sulpicius had as his fief the Aniensis tribe.[128] But on Murena's side were Umbria and the tribes of Umbria: 'He held a levy in Umbria. The political situation enabled him to display a generosity which won him the support of the many tribes which are composed of the towns of Umbria.'[129] In order to have a tribe's votes it was, in practice, enough if one's clientage embraced one of the towns of that tribe,[130] provided that this town was not at the far end of Italy.

Not resting content, however, with becoming the benefactor of certain Italian cities, every Roman senator went further: he became, or if he actually originated from some small town he remained, an Italian. The figures speak for themselves: of more than 200 senators whose tribe is known to us with greater or less certainty, Lily Ross Taylor has listed ten at the most who were members of one of the four tribes of Rome, all the others belonging to rural tribes.[131] Caesar, the only Latin writer who was born in Rome itself, nevertheless belonged to a rural tribe, the Fabia. Senators never lost contact with their home towns. They went back there from time to time and kept up good relations with the notables, meaning 'those persons who carry weight with some of their tribesmen by reason of their home town, district or college'.[132] They did not disdain to assume local magistracies in their home towns. When Clodius and Milo, followed by their 'heavies' (as in Stendhal's Italy, a great lord never travelled without an escort of *buli*), met by chance in the open country, and one killed the other, Milo was returning from Lanuvium, which was his home town and of which he was *dictator* that year, while Clodius was on his way back from addressing the municipal councillors of Aricia – these being two towns close to Rome.[133] After becoming all-powerful in a city, senators could use their influence in aid of an ally of the moment and get their fellow citizens to vote for him. One year, Plautius and Plancius 'gave' a friend their respective tribes in this way: the Aniensis tribe in the case of Plautius, with the town of Trebula Suffenas, and the Teretina tribe in that of Plancius, with the town of Atina where he was the great man, as we shall see.[134]

Cicero's speech *Pro Plancio* illuminates this electoral sociology so vividly that we need only paraphrase a few lines from it.[135] One year the rivals before the *comitia tributa* were a certain Lateranensis, from an old noble family,[136] and Plancius, a 'new man' (his father, the chief notable of Atina, was a mere *eques*). The noble candidate belonged to the Papiria tribe, which included, in particular, a small town at the gates of Rome called Tusculum, while the son of the *eques* reigned over Atina and thereby over the Teretina tribe. Unfortunately for the nobleman, Tusculum 'numbers among the inhabitants more families of consular rank ... than all the other corporations put together', and these blasé people did not put themselves out when the time of the *comitia* came round. Atina, on the contrary, was enthusiastic for the candidature of its great notable. The *equites* of the town went to vote for him, the plebs themselves turned up *en masse*, and in the other places of the same tribe, round Atina, it was the same, for the power of Plancius's family extended throughout the region. So Plancius was elected. There you see, Cicero concludes with humour (a quality he did not lack), what advantages we enjoy who come from modest little towns. 'Need I refer to my own case or to that of my brother?' he adds. 'Our distinctions have been acclaimed by our very fields and hills ... Whenever you come across a man of Arpinum, you will have to listen, willy-nilly, to some fragment of gossip, possibly even about me, but certainly about Gaius Marius.'[137]

In the country areas and the municipal towns personal and informal ties could be established between a great man, or even a mere notable, and his peasants or the plebs of his town. Things were not the same in Rome, where the agglomeration of human beings was too large and where, moreover, personal relations were crushed beneath the weight of the central institutions of a vast empire: instead of notables and men of the people, Rome had only senators and electors. Consequently, in Rome the oligarchs did not behave as *euergetai*, or rather their euergetism had a special colouring.

5. Euergetism political, not social

We do not find in Rome the abundance and diversity of *euergesiai* that we found in the Greek cities (and which we should find, almost exactly the same, in the municipal towns of Italy). In particular, voluntary euergetism did not exist in Rome. As for euergetism *ob honorem*, its motives were political ambition rather than social zeal. And it was performed only by the politicians, the few hundred senators, not by the equestrian order, the middle class, or the rich in general. One small fact can be dignified as symbolic: Pompeii had had an amphitheatre for a century and a half while Rome was still without one,[138] and this for the good reason that in Pompeii the amphitheatre was built by *euergetai*, whereas in Rome there were no real *euergetai*. The *triumphatores*, who alone followed the custom of erecting public buildings, put up only religious monuments.

Sallust says somewhere that liberality was an ancestral virtue among the Romans. Polybius, on the contrary, wondered at the magnificence of Scipio, as being a quality he is astonished to find in Rome, 'for there no one ever thinks of giving any of his private property to anyone if he can help it'.[139] It would be a waste of time to try to solve these apparent contradictions and study the evolution of 'liberality' in Rome. In Polybius's day the Romans were not magnificent in the way the Hellenistic *euergetai* and kings had been. In Cicero's time the same lord who had starved debtors to death when they refused to pay him could also keep his word when once he had promised his protection to a client, and open his purse freely to his political friends.[140] The oligarchs could also perform *euergesiai* like those of the Greek or Italian notables, but the motives of their euergetism were different, and guerrilla war between classes did not enter into it. Instead, what mattered was the point of honour – that is, the quest for honours. They provided games, made *largesse* when they were aediles, distributed money among their electors, and sometimes contributed from their fortunes to support the more or less personal policy they pursued when they became proconsuls or praetors. The same point of honour also required them to manifest their splendour. Nevertheless, this mistrustful oligarchy did not allow its members to commemorate their glory in monumental forms in Rome itself, except in one specific case, namely the triumph. A day came, at the end of the Republic, when *largesses*, private financing of policy and triumphal monuments announced that monocracy was close at hand; Augustus was to reign over a state which he would run as patron, thanks to his gigantic fortune.

THE 'BUDGET'

If there was not much euergetism in Rome, this was partly due to the fact that the Republic was not short of revenue. In 62 the plebs were restless because corn was dear. Cato of Utica persuaded the Senate to distribute corn to the people, at the Treasury's expense, of course – the orator did not propose to his colleagues that he would meet the cost, the aediles did not rise to make a pollicitation, and nobody tried to induce a *euergetēs* to sacrifice himself, as would have happened in a Greek or Italian city.

In 62, as a result of his conquests in the Greek East, Pompey added to the public revenue, which at that time amounted to 200 million sesterces, another 300 million, and also paid into the Treasury booty worth nearly 500 million.[141] These were considerable resources. The structure of the budget was altered. The army, which cost no more than about 50 million sesterces, no longer absorbed the major share of the revenue. The tasks of the Roman state and the items of expenditure in its budget had not grown, but its resources had increased through fiscal exploitation of the conquered peoples. Rome had revenue greatly in excess of its expenditure on the army and on distributions of grain. What did it do with the surplus? P. A. Brunt suspects, and may be right, that the provincial governors pocketed the money, in the guise of 'expenses'.[142] Cicero frequently laments that the Treasury is empty, adding that the *largesses* to the plebs made by demagogues are the reason. In short, the Republic did not have enough money for everything.

As any special credit advanced to the magistrates had to be the subject of a formal act by the Senate,[143] as the Senate had a horror of *largesses*, and as the magistrates were often dilettanti and their ordinary credits inadequate for serious expenditure (a famine, a road or a building to be built or repaired), business was held up, corn was often lacking, and the Republic bequeathed to Augustus a city where the public buildings were falling to pieces and the roads were pitted with pot-holes.[144] Not only were the censors doing no more building, or hardly any, in Italy,[145] but they were undertaking nothing in Rome – neither theatre nor amphitheatre. The regular institutions were no longer capable of ensuring the functioning of public life. At the same time, this oligarchy, whose sense of organization has often been contrasted with the amiable aestheticism of the Greeks, was no longer able, entangled as it was in its internal rivalries and its passion for power, to carry out the simplest administrative reform, for every abuse and every prejudice was presented as the outward form of some hidden wisdom and involved too many vested interests.[146] It was a sign of the times that the simplest initiative was no longer taken by the competent magistrates.[147] Extraordinary commissioners were needed, armed with credits which also had to be extraordinary: a commissioner for corn,[148] or a commissioner for repairing an aqueduct.[149] If, as a coin testifies, the public Villa could be restored, that was due to a *triumphator* who wished to devote his share of the booty to this useful but unprestigious work.[150] The Empire alone was to bring a little order into this domain.

In comparable circumstances, in the Greek or Italian cities, magistrates, curators or patrons hastened to open their purses, or were 'induced' to do so by their peers. In Rome itself the senators began to open theirs only in the last half-century of the Republic and (sinister omen) the first to do so was Caesar, who is said to have repaired at his own expense the Appian Way, of which he was curator.[151] The only edifice built or rebuilt by a *euergetēs* who was not a *triumphator*, as far as I know, was the Basilica Aemilia, which Aemilius Paullus rebuilt because the name of an ancestor of his was associated with this monument, and because Caesar, out of political calculation, gave him the necessary money from his Gallic booty.[152] We shall see later that the real begetter of this undertaking was Caesar, and that it portended the age of personal power and patronage of the state that would soon begin.

THE *TRIUMPHATORES*

Buildings were less useful for a political career than games or distributions of money. The *triumphatores* were almost the only ones who built, because they did not need to encroach on their patrimony for this purpose, but used their booty. Decency decreed that the general should not keep this booty, even though it was his property. What was he to do with it, if not use it for the benefit of the people and the gods? So the *triumphatores* gave a banquet and consecrated a religious building.

I shall not enumerate the monuments built by the *triumphatores*, but merely recall that all of them – trophies,[153] temples, temple porticoes[154] or theatre-temples – were religious buildings or buildings with a religious pretext. This explains the enigma of Pompey's theatre. Above this monument, dedicated after the triumph of 61, rose a temple of Venus Victrix, and in theory the theatre was merely an annexe to the temple, 'the steps of which formed his theatre'.[155] The whole complex was dedicated as a sanctuary.[156] Why? Religious explanations have been offered and we have been reminded that, for the Greeks, a theatrical performance was a sacred rite, and the linking of a temple with a theatre not unknown to them.[157] The true explanation is that *triumphatores* were obliged to build monuments of a religious character and that Pompey, wishing to give the people a theatre, therefore made this a mere prolongation of a sanctuary consecrated to the goddess whose protection had given him victory. This was an example of a process of secularization which was completed at the beginning of Augustus's reign, when, as we shall see, *triumphatores* were required to repair the roads.

In the same way, every *triumphator* could provide a feast for the people on the pretext of inviting a god to attend (*invitare deum*)[158] and of consecrating to the god, so as to ward off side-effects and the spirit of envy, one-tenth of his gains. An old Roman custom required that merchants should consecrate to Hercules, the god of Rome's market, a tenth of the profits they owed to the god's protection.[159] This money was most frequently employed to mount a banquet for all comers (*cena popularis*) which, as described earlier, had no other purpose in principle than to consume the flesh of the victims sacrificed to the god.[160] A fruit merchant was able in this way to pay the tithe three times over during his life, so effective was the god's protection.[161] The *triumphatores* used this very grocerly custom as a pretext, just as candidates used the pretext of funeral games and Pompey the pretext of thanking Venus Victrix, and provided a banquet for the whole people after their triumph.[162] Sulla, after his own triumph, 'consecrated the tenth of all his substance to Hercules' and 'feasted the people sumptuously'.[163] After his minor triumph (*ovatio*), Crassus 'feasted the people at ten thousand tables and made them an allowance of grain for three months'.[164]

For, as we see, the plebs had become accustomed to the *triumphator*'s adding some *largesses* to his banquet, usually in the form of a distribution of measures (*congii*) of oil, whence the name of *congiarium* given first to a distribution of oil and then to distributions in general, including distributions of money. Lucullus distributed wine to the citizens. Caesar was the first to give them money, to celebrate his triumph in 46.[165] The pioneer of this practice was perhaps Acilius Glabrio, who, as has been mentioned, was elected to the censorship for having distributed *congiaria* of oil to the people:[166] this happened, I presume, on the occasion of the triumph over Antiochus which he celebrated in 189.

6. The corn dole and the moral order

The corn dole was, by definition, the antithesis of euergetism. The *largesses* of the senators had political motives, as we have seen. The distributions (or alleged distributions) of free or cheap corn to the plebs of Rome, however, were unquestionably a social institution – but a *state* institution, established by law. For private euergetism was in no position to replace the state in this domain. The aediles had no desire to ruin themselves for the sake of the plebs. The cost of such quantities of corn was beyond the scope of private fortunes, huge as these would seem to our eyes. The organization of the distributions was too complex a task to be entrusted to private initiatives, which are by nature no less amateurish than generous. It is characteristic that in Rome this social institution, which was genuinely political, was not the responsibility of *euergetai* and had been wrested from the state by class struggle. But let us begin by analysing the institution itself, which bore no resemblance to what is sometimes imagined.

Everybody knows that all of Rome's citizens, or a section of them, received every month, at a low price or free of charge, a certain quantity of corn, that these distributions were established in 123 by a law of the tribune Gaius Gracchus, and that they continued until the end of the Empire. They can be regarded as a 'welfare-state' measure or else stigmatized as an encouragement to idleness, as by Cicero: 'Gaius Gracchus brought forward a corn law. It was agreeable to the masses, for it provided food in abundance without work. Loyal citizens were against it, because they thought that it was a call to the masses to desert industry for idleness, and saw that it was a drain upon the Treasury.'[167] That is the cliché. The truth seems to me both more complex and more interesting. In the time of Gaius Gracchus there was no question of distributions: the state confined itself to guaranteeing the sale of a certain quantity of corn to every consumer who had the money to buy it. Then, under the opposing pressures of the *optimates* and the *populares*, the institution evolved, and eventually became fossilized and insulated. Starting with Caesar, and thereafter till the end of the Empire, the state distributed 150,000 'purses' of free grain to certain privileged persons, and these purses were almost honorific. The centre of gravity of the problem had shifted. To ensure his supply of food the average Roman henceforth relied on the Imperial service of the Annona, which supervised the corn market and regulated free enterprise. The corn dole was no more than a picturesque survival. Class struggle, failure of euergetism, recourse to the state: this is what constitutes for us the interest of this story.[168]

THE PROBLEM OF CORN

The Gracchan law did not aim to enable the plebs to live in idleness and to purchase its abstention from politics at the price of its inertia. It was not a measure of public assistance or charity. Its principle was not the division of the benefits of conquest among all the citizens of the conquering people. It sought merely to apply in a serious way the principle which affirmed that corn was not a commodity like others and that it was the state's task to act so that the market was supplied with corn. This was a principle that went back much further than the Gracchi and was not special to Rome. The Greek cities acknowledged it, too. But in Rome the aediles were applying this principle in an amateurish way:[169] that, in brief, was the history of corn in Rome before the law of Gaius Gracchus.

In Rome, providing bread was, along with circuses, one of the two major tasks of the aediles. The *cura annonae* was of equal importance with the *cura ludorum*; the aediles had to ensure that there was always enough grain on the market and that its price was right. This was a pressing and arduous task. The powers and the skill of the aediles were no longer sufficient, any more than were the funds at their disposal, for a city which had grown too large. At the end of the Republic Rome had at least half a million inhabitants, in a peninsular Italy with a population of less than five million (slaves not included). Such a large amount of corn was needed to feed this gigantic agglomeration that the neighbouring regions were not up to the task. Thünen's circle was extended widely, so that transport costs increased the price of corn to a considerable extent – or would have done if Rome had not, fortunately, been near the sea. Even then one needed to know where corn could be found. The 'invisible hand' did not suffice, and the state had to use its own resources for getting information and its own means of exerting pressure, because the merchants were neither as well informed nor as powerful as the situation required. As soon as famine threatened, speculation started. In 57 Rome experienced famine and riots. The hungry plebs thought that the dearth was a punishment from heaven because the rich had recalled Cicero from exile. The actual reasons for it were 'partly that the corn-growing provinces had no corn; partly that it had been exported to other countries, the demands of the dealers being, as we are asked to believe, extortionate; partly that it was being stored in custody', not to be released until the famine reached its height.[170]

The magistrates in office in the provinces saw it as their duty to combat speculation and help their colleagues in Rome. Cicero, when quaestor in Sicily, 'had dispatched an enormous quantity of corn [to Rome] at a time of very high prices'.[171] As governor of Cilicia he succeeded, without using coercion or humiliating anyone, but simply by force of authority and persuasion, in getting the Greeks and the Roman businessmen to hand over corn which they had doubtless intended to hoard until prices rose still further.[172]

Nevertheless all this did not go very far, or rather, in accordance with the tendency of the age, the service of the Annona was a series of improvisations rather than a continuous enterprise. Each year the responsible authorities invented, or failed to invent, a different solution to their problem. The Republic did not organize the supply of food (the Empire was to do this), nor does it seem ever to have fixed a maximum market price.[173] In good years and bad the aediles or the Senate had recourse to three solutions: forcing the merchants' hand; putting on the market some of the grain acquired by the state as booty or taxation, fixing the price and also the quantity that each citizen could purchase;[174] and arranging for corn to be bought by brokers using credits provided by *senatus consultum*.[175] The first solution was unreliable, and the other two came up against disapproval from the Senate, who claimed to fear the exhaustion of their Treasury, for the state's money ought not to be wasted. The people had to comfort themselves with the thought that some years were better than others, and the aediles had to tell themselves that nobody is expected to do the impossible.[176] In short, whether by windfall, law or *senatus consultum*, the problem of corn found only irregular solutions.

The aediles did what any amateur could do. Did they try a fourth solution, patronage?[177] I think I can answer 'yes' for the last century B C. Their distributions of cheap corn were called *largesses*, but the word *largitio* is not decisive by itself: it describes the democratic or demagogic intention, but not the source of the funds drawn upon, and it was used of the demagogic laws of the tribunes which exhausted the Treasury for the benefit of the plebs. A glance at the written record shows Cicero writing:

Unless the whole question of corn values had to be regarded in relation to the seasons and the current market prices, and not simply as a matter of numbers and quantities, those three half-pecks a head of yours, Hortensius, would never have been so welcome, which you measured out in so sparing proportions and distributed to the people of Rome to the great satisfaction of everyone; for the high market price made your gift, which seems a small thing in itself, seem large because of the circumstances. Had you chosen to bestow the same quantity on the people of Rome when corn was cheap, your benefaction would have excited laughter and contempt.[178]

Did the aedile Hortensius use his own money for this *largesse*? I believe he did, for it would have required a law or a *senatus consultum* for the Treasury to be unlocked for him, and that would have been a major business. Besides, his *largesse* seems to have been an isolated gesture: we are not told that he renewed it at regular intervals through the year.[179] Such a gesture was better calculated to make the charitable aedile popular than to solve the problem of food supply over a period of many months. To distribute twelve litres of corn per head to a few hundred thousand citizens, losing a few sesterces per measure, was not a ruinous undertaking: the public games that this same Hortensius had given probably cost him a lot more. Even so, not every aedile was so generous, and the name of one who was would not be forgotten.[180]

Patronage by the aediles was confined to symbolic gestures which helped to secure their election as praetors or consuls – gestures regarded in the same light as the splendour of their games. The aedileship had become a special sort of magistracy. The real function of the man who held it was to make *largesse*: he distributed a little corn or oil in the same way as he provided games.[181] 'The generosity of the aediles consisted in celebrating the Roman Games splendidly, for the resources of that time, and in repeating them for one day; also in giving ... measures of oil for each precinct.'[182] At the end of the Republican period the problem of corn, which was still being dealt with by extraordinary and unsystematic measures, was to serve the magnates as a pretext for having the Senate confer on them those commands (themselves extraordinary) which, more than the magistracies, had become the real instruments of political power. In 57 Pompey was appointed commissioner for corn, with full powers in this sphere throughout the Empire, for a period of five years.[183]

FROM FAIR PRICE TO FREE CORN

Gaius Gracchus's corn law was intended to put an end to this lack of system, but without exhausting the Treasury. It required the Roman state to have corn permanently on sale at a price equal to[184] or even lower than[185] the normal. Every citizen of Rome, rich or poor, who wanted to buy this state corn and could pay for it had the right to do so.[186] However, in order to prevent speculation and to save the state from ruin, it seems certain that no citizen was allowed to buy more than a certain number of bushels per month – we do not know how many.[187] This was neither free distribution nor public assistance. The Gracchan law organized the sale of grain by the state at a fixed price in order to prevent famine and speculation. Did the state obtain the corn from its provinces, in payment of taxes? Did it buy the corn? We do not know. At any rate, the law prescribed that the necessary organization should be undertaken, in particular the establishment of a network of public granaries.[188] There was no question of supporting the plebs in idleness, since the corn was not free, since man does not live by corn alone, and since the citizens had to feed not only themselves but also their families and their slaves. It seems unlikely that they were not obliged to buy extra grain on the private market. As for the Treasury, which was very rich, the burden was easily borne: that calculation has been made.[189] We shall see below how it was that such a sensible law could arouse the wrath of the *optimates*.

When the market price of corn was higher than the price fixed by

the state, the loss, or profit forgone, was borne by the Treasury. As
the Treasury's resources came mostly from the tribute paid by the
provinces, it was at the expense of the Empire's subjects that the
Gracchan law promised to the citizens living in Rome that they would
always be able to buy a certain quantity of bread cheaply. The reform
of Gaius Gracchus was made possible by the reduction of ultra-rich
Asia Minor to the status of a Roman province a dozen years earlier;
moreover, the Roman plebs was patriotic and imperialistic.[190] Does
this entitle us to suppose that the principle behind the Gracchan law
was to share more equitably the fruits of conquest among all members
of the conquering people? I cannot believe so. What Gracchus did was
inspired by the spectacle of poverty in Rome and Italy, not by the
abstract idea that the dividends had not been shared out fairly. If the
Roman plebs had been enjoying a standard of living which was decent
according to the norms of the time, Gaius would not have bothered
to raise this standard further by making a point of principle of sharing
out the common inheritance; he would have seen no disadvantage in
leaving the revenue of Asia in the coffers of the Republic, the true
titleholder. His aim was a guaranteed subsistence, not an equal division
of gains amongst all payees or a reduction of relative inequality. Now
that the Treasury was full, thanks to Asia and other conquests, there
was no further excuse for a refusal to lift the plebs out of its poverty –
that was all. The people should be guaranteed a minimum, because it
was now possible to do so. For the ideal of an equal division of
national revenue to be more than a rhetorical justification, one needs an
intellectual bird's-eye view enabling one to take in the whole of society
and to calculate whether its benefits are equally distributed. But this is
not the way of things; no one can adopt this view instinctively, without
documentary evidence and technical skills – and such bookishness is
hardly likely to rouse social feelings. Gaius and his plebeians, like
everyone else, saw their society only from ground-level. In the social
panorama that met their eyes, they could see that there were rich and
poor, that the coffers of the state were not empty, and that the
wretchedness of the poor exceeded the absolute acceptable limit. This
was why they began to talk of unequal distribution of dividends, and
to protest that those who shed their blood to enlarge the Empire were
not receiving their fair share of the conquest. In doing this they were
not appealing to a principle (one which would never have occurred to
them if there had not been absolute destitution), but were developing
an ideology, an allegory of justice in which the body politic was

likened to a share-issuing company, in order to make more concrete the idea that everyone had a right to a livelihood.

This was enough to arouse the indignation of the conservative oligarchy. Soon after the lynching of Gaius Gracchus his law was repealed, or rather mitigated to the point where Cicero could write that in its new form it was acceptable to all decent people.[191] The fatal mechanism was thereby set in motion. The *optimates* had repealed the law, so the *populares* tried to restore it, and not without the inevitable overbidding. The *optimates* themselves, through opportunism, took the same path. I have mentioned that in 62, when Catiline's army was still a threat, Cato hastily initiated a corn law. There is no point in going into the details of these successive laws, which are little known anyway. The fact that needs to be brought out, as I see it, is that under successive or combined blows by conservatives and *populares* the principle behind the Gracchan law was distorted. In the end the corn laws no longer organized the sale at a fixed price of a maximum quantity of grain to any purchaser who was a citizen and inhabitant of Rome, but free distribution of a certain amount to every citizen in Rome. Distribution free of charge was an innovation by the tribune of the plebs Clodius in 58.[192] Thus for a dozen years, from Clodius to Caesar, the cliché did correspond to the reality, with the Roman plebs being fed for nothing by the state.

Twelve years after Clodius, Caesar, while unable to solve the problem, dealt with it in a way which, albeit opportunist, nevertheless lasted for four centuries. He fossilized the institution. The beneficiaries of free grain numbered 320,000. Caesar decided that the state would continue to distribute corn free of charge, but to a number of citizens limited permanently to 150,000. This served to block the leakage of public funds and the demographic flood. Not being able to abolish a popular institution, Caesar pruned it a little and, above, all, fossilized it.

THE FOSSILIZED INSTITUTION

Under the Empire this fossilized institution continued as a survival. We shall see later that the Emperors retained it in order to enhance the splendours of their capital.[193] For the average plebeian his daily bread was not this free bread, reserved for a few privileged persons, but the bread he could buy on the market, or that the Emperor sold to him when there was famine. When ancient historians write of the Roman plebs under the Empire, they do not see it as a population maintained in idleness but as 'the common people at Rome, being accustomed to buy their food day by day and having no public interests save the grain supply'.[194] In this sphere as in others the Empire had put an end to amateur efforts. The *cura annonae* passed from the four aediles to the very powerful Imperial service of the Annona. Famines and hunger riots did not disappear (as Tacitus and Ammianus Marcellinus assure us), but the improvement was palpable. The price of corn varied from year to year. At least the service of the Annona worked with a seriousness and a continuity in its efforts such as the aedileship had not shown. To be sure, it had at its disposal much greater resources.[195] The victualling of Rome was ensured in several ways apart from the supply of free corn. First there was private initiative: merchants sold corn in Rome and rich landowners had to bring in the grain produced on their estates. Sometimes the Emperor intervened to prevent a price increase. One year when the people complained of the high price, Tiberius 'fixed a definite price to be paid by the buyer, and himself guaranteed the seller a subsidy of two sesterces the peck'.[196] But above all the service of the Annona controlled huge quantities of grain which certain provinces supplied as tax-payments; when there was famine, the Emperor sold his corn to the plebs.[197] For the state alone was capable of organizing the regular supply of food to this enormous accumulation of people. The state alone possessed corn obtained by non-economic methods. The state alone could have it transported to Rome without regard to cost, by using shipowners who were given subsidies and exemptions in exchange, by guaranteeing the carriers' profits and meeting any losses due to shipwreck.[198] The state alone had the necessary network of informers in the provinces,[199] and with it also many means of persuasion.[200] The chief reason why the state had the advantage over private enterprise was that, for the sake of law and order in its capital, it did not shrink from selling its corn at a loss. What did the state actually do with its corn? It used it in two ways, according to the rather meagre information we possess. First a certain number of privileged persons, including the soldiers of the praetorian guard, enjoyed the permanent right of grain at a reasonable price. Second, when there was famine, the Emperor sold corn cheap to the plebeians. Thus apart from the 150,000 'purses' of free corn, the service of the Annona had re-created something like the law of Gaius Gracchus – on a permanent basis for the privileged persons, and for all the citizens in time of famine.[201]

We can now understand why the victualling of Rome could not

be left to the care of *euergetai* like the aediles. So vast and ruinous a task called for state action. We can understand, too, why the state distributed its corn free or at a low price to the population of Rome: it was because this agglomeration, too big for the private enterprise of the period, could not be supplied with food by the laws of the market, whereas the state could allow itself to sell at a loss. If the Republic, and later the Empire, guaranteed cheap bread to the Roman people, this was not in order to depoliticize it or to maintain it in idleness but because, before the Industrial Revolution, the cost of transport was too high and, more broadly, because private enterprise was not up to the task. The state gave its grain away, partly or entirely, so as not to sell it at too high a price to an impoverished population. That was all.

Let us now return to the 150,000 persons who had the right to receive free corn, and devote a few pages to technical details which may interest the reader if he fancies himself as a detective. These persons can be regarded as privileged, I think, if we judge by the way they were recruited and by the pride they show in mentioning in their epitaphs that they had received bread from the state.[202] One would be quite wrong to see them as needy people, ashamed of relying on public charity. But neither is their pride some 'ideological' oddity showing what prestige was accorded in those days to idleness, or to the title of descendant of conquerors of the Empire, inheriting from one's glorious ancestors the right to be fed by the provinces. Besides, 'fed' would be the wrong word. A few bushels of free corn every month did not suffice to keep anyone alive, so that in time of dearth the Emperor had to double or quadruple the ration in order to save the beneficiaries from having to buy extra corn on the private market.[203] The free corn was thus a supplement to income, a privilege comparable to that possessed in Russia by Party members who can buy goods cheap in shops reserved for them. It was a privilege that gave rise to much envy; and after the great fire of 64 Nero temporarily stopped these distributions of free corn and devoted all the grain held by the state to feeding the plebs.[204]

But how were the 150,000 fortunate ones chosen? We do not know what criteria Caesar used for the initial selection. We do know that subsequently, as beneficiaries died, their right passed to new ones who were chosen by lot (*subsortitio*) among the citizens.[205] That is the truth but not, I think, the whole truth. The Empire, author and master of the privilege and guarantor of their daily bread to the rest of the plebs, did not resist the temptation to reserve a few 'purses' of free corn not to the most needy but to persons who had served it well. Such were the soldiers of the Imperial guard, from Nero's reign onward,[206] and also some corporations in state service, like those of the flautists and the horn-players.[207] Above all, though, the Empire was unable to resist a further temptation, namely of selling a certain number of 'purses' of corn. Three passages in the *Digest* which have seemed rather obscure[208] speak of the purchase of *tesserae frumentariae*, coupons for free corn.[209] There were thus two or even three ways of acquiring the privilege: by luck of the draw, by engaging in certain public employments, and by purchase. One of the passages in question says, in fact: 'A woman had, in her will, instructed her trustee to buy for X a *tessera frumentaria*, thirty days after her death. However, as X began to enjoy possession of this *tessera* as a gift [*ex causa lucrativa*] during the woman's lifetime and cannot claim what he already has, I ask whether he can take proceedings. Paul answers that he must be given the value of the *tessera*, because this type of trust consists in value [*quantitas*] rather than in kind.'[210] We must deduce that nobody had the right to hold two 'purses' of corn. Having received one as a gift, the person mentioned cannot inherit a second. The state thus sold a certain number of free-corn privileges, or, as people still said, a certain number of 'tribes' – for these old electoral constituencies were no longer anything but frameworks for grain distributions, now that elections had been abolished.[211] The *Digest* considers elsewhere the case of a person who in his will bequeaths a 'tribe' to one of his freedmen, whose heir is a senator.[212] Now members of the senatorial order did not have the right to receive the corn dole.[213] So would the senator inherit the 'purse' of corn? No indeed, the jurist replies, but he could inherit the value thereof.[214] No doubt the Empire needed money and sold everything it had to sell: privileges, and also jobs in government service. For just as it had introduced the practice of selling the right to free corn, it had also introduced the selling of minor civil service posts (*militia*) and beadle-ships (*decuria*), and these jobs were sold and bequeathed, provided that the new owner was qualified to hold them.[215] 'If a *tessera frumentaria* is left to X and X dies, some consider that the bequest is cancelled, but this is wrong, because when one bequeaths a *tessera* or a *militia* it is the value of the thing that is bequeathed rather than the thing itself.'[216]

7. Patronage of the state

To conclude, I shall discuss a completely fresh set of facts. At the end of the Republic, when the age of the magnates arrived, with Pompey and especially Caesar and his successor Octavius, and when personal power triumphed, patronage of the state developed. The master of the day, merging in his person the public and the private man, paid certain public expenses out of his personal resources, which were enormous.

POLITICS BECOMES PRIVATE ENTERPRISE

In appearance this is merely an extension of everything described above; and if one were to reduce the study of human realities to the study of values and the study of values to the study of words, the *liberalitas* of Caesar or of Octavius Augustus would be the continuation of the *liberalitas* of Scipio. In reality, however, there had been a double break in continuity. In the first place there was a quantitative break. The magnates were no longer satisfied with giving the plebs a festival: they maintained their armies and they embellished Rome so as to make it a royal capital without the name. Consequently, while the *euergesiai* were the same as before – spectacles and buildings – their significance had changed along with their scale. The motivations behind them were new because the political structure inducing these motivations was itself new: oligarchy had been replaced by monocracy. The political power of the magnates was itself a new thing in Rome; it was not the power of a magistrate or of the senators writ larger – it had changed its character, it was supreme. The state belonged to the magnates. Hence the two reasons for their *largesses*: they made the machine work, even at their own expense, because they were its masters, and they gave expression to their supreme majesty in the form of *largesses*. These were already the two prime motivations of the expenditure that would be undertaken by the Emperors. The line between a magnate and an Emperor is unclear. Octavius Augustus was both, and until Nero's death the Roman state was to live half on tax revenue and half on the private fortune of the Julio-Claudian dynasty.

The Roman oligarchs were not Hellenic notables. Unlike the latter they did not pay the expenses of their functions. On the contrary, they enriched themselves in their government positions, and when they found they had to contribute something they complained loudly. However, they considered themselves the owners rather than the managers of their *imperium* and exploited it unscrupulously for their personal benefit. Furthermore, every great personage, even if he possessed no official mission, was regarded as a public man and was allowed an extensive right of political initiative. Ambitious or enterprising, the great man dipped into his purse in order to be the patron of his own political career. Crassus said that nobody could aspire to become a magnate (*princeps*) unless he had income enough to maintain an army.[217] Pompey, defending in Spain the cause of the Republic against the rebellion of Sertorius, complained bitterly that he had not received any money: 'Weary with writing and sending messengers to you,' he writes to the Senate, 'I have exhausted the whole of my private fortune and expectations ... What, in the name of the immortal gods, do you think of me? Do you suppose that my own resources are equal to an exchequer ... ?'[218] But this same Pompey had begun his career during the civil war by raising a private army in Picenum, which was completely in his family's clientage.[219] This kind of initiative showed that the age of personal power was at hand. A few years later, the young Caesar was on his way to Rhodes to take lessons from a teacher of rhetoric when he learned that King Mithridates had burst into the province of Asia. Like the Cid gathering 300 friends to fight the disembarking Moors, Caesar raised a little private army, took command of native troops and checked the enemy. It was as though the province of Asia had no governor.[220] Twenty years later, Caesar was to pursue in Gaul a policy of conquest that was absolutely personal, breaking with the Roman political tradition;[221] and he did this partly at his own expense (that is, using the immense booty he collected from the temples of the Gauls).[222] It was with his own resources that he raised four of the eight legions with which he conquered Gaul. Moreover the Senate decided to take upon itself the payment of the four legions.[223] Similarly, in 44 Octavius persuaded the Senate to reimburse him for the money he had spent on the private army he had raised to protect the Republic.[224] The time had already come when the magnates contending for supreme power took over the Treasury while accusing each other of doing so,[225] and when the Emperor Octavius Augustus could write, in his own funeral eulogy: 'At the age of nineteen I acquired an army by my own initiative and with my own resources, an army with which I freed the state from oppression by the tyranny of a faction.'

A GRAND THEORY: 'LUXURY' AND 'DECADENCE'

How had matters reached this point – personal power, and with it patronage of the state? Contemporaries had their own explanation, which is so curious that it deserves some attention. According to them, luxury was responsible for the fall of the Republic and the establishment of the monocracy, for luxury means decadence and ambition. Poor states are virtuous, but rich ones succumb to softness, or to internal rivalries. Here we recognize a theory which enjoyed fame for over 2,000 years, a theory which seemed self-evident to Plato,[226] Polybius,[227] St Augustine,[228] Dante,[229] Swift,[230] Montesquieu and Rousseau, before falling into oblivion. The most concise exposition of the theory is given by Polybius.

When a state has weathered many great perils and subsequently attains to supremacy and uncontested sovereignty, it is evident that under the influence of long-established prosperity, life will become more extravagant and the citizens more fierce in their rivalry regarding office and other objects than they ought to be. As these defects go on increasing, the beginning of the change for the worse will be due to love of office and the disgrace entailed by obscurity, as well as to extravagance and purse-proud display.

Polybius is thinking of the economic development and the political and social crises of the Hellenistic cities. He is thinking of the 'demagogues' who, making *largesses* for the people out of their own fortunes, or even out of public funds, established a moderate oligarchy under which the people lost the habit of docile obedience (as we have seen earlier) and competition for power became livelier because, as we say today of our democracies, the regime was pluralistic.[231] Power was the object of competition among several men and several groups and had nothing totalitarian about it. In this Polybius sees decadence, and he ascribes this tiresome evolution to an order of causes which he considers more important than any other, namely the development of wealth, of 'luxury', of 'prosperity'. The concepts are rather vague (at what point does prosperity begin, and what does it consist of?) and so also is the causal link (what sort of evolution is without economic causes, among others?) – so vague, indeed, that this theoretical schema can serve to explain more or less any process at all in history.

If luxury softens peoples, wealth corrupts oligarchies. It gives the poor a desire to raise themselves above their condition, which is fatal to the social order, or else it raises up parvenus who lack the virtues of the old nobility. Plutarch thinks that social mobility contributed to the fall of the Roman Republic. Before the era of the civil wars, he writes, 'it was equally opprobrious to dissipate one's fortune and not to remain in the poverty of one's fathers'. For Dante, the 'decadence' of Florence was due to the new nobles:

> *La gente nova e' subiti guadagni*
> *orgoglio e dismisura han generata,*
> *Fiorenza, in te, sí che tu già ten piagni.*

But above all, wealth corrupts the old nobility itself, by filling its members with a spirit of ambition and rivalry which is fatal to the peaceful functioning of society. The causal link is psychological, as we see. Under the name of oligarch (a name that was always pejorative in Greece, where everyone was somebody else's 'oligarch') Theophrastus conceptualized what we should call 'the oligarchic personality' – a psycho-political type, a sort of characterology of political opinions. His oligarch is a man who wants power and wealth. For Sallust wealth gives rise to the 'oligarchic personality' that ruins nations; luxury engenders greed, ambition, impiety, venality and disloyalty. Oligarchy is nothing but a hardened, greedy caste which refuses to open its ranks to the new men who still retain the ideal of governing the city. And since wealth is the primary cause of this decadence, Sallust (and Cicero with him) attach excessive importance to a detail which seems to them the principal link in the chain, namely the indebtedness of the oligarchy. The taste for luxury means that too many young senators who want to live at their ease borrow, because they prefer not to sell their property and eat into their capital. Having done this, they no longer see in politics anything but the source of the money which will enable them to repay their creditors, and they rule Rome's subjects as though the latter were milch-cows. If only lending at interest were to be banned, the young nobles would again find an ideal in politics: this is the miracle-cure.[232]

RESOURCES OF THE MAGNATES

We return now to our purpose, which was to show how, at the end of the Republic, personal power was associated with a new phenomenon, patronage of the state. The economic theory of decadence throws light, though doubtless one-sidedly, on one of the factors that brought about the triumph of personal power. The magnates of the first century BC had financial means which the senators of the second century had not yet acquired – the Senate held the purse-strings and they could do nothing without its consent. Polybius could write: 'The Senate ... has the control of the Treasury ... The consul, when he leaves with his army ... appears indeed to have absolute authority in all matters necessary for carrying out his purpose; but in fact he requires the support of the people and the Senate ... For it is obvious that the legions require constant supplies, and without the consent of the Senate neither corn, clothing nor pay can be provided.'[233] Consequently the oligarchy always managed to pull back into line those of its members who had thrust themselves forward. In the first century, however, the city, having become an empire, offered such abundant means for action to anyone who was able to grasp them that personal power became established for the simple reason that it was now possible. The provinces were a reservoir of money and resources, an arena for the conquest of glory. The plebs could be seduced or manipulated in the *comitia tributa*. The immense possibilities for 'making money' that were now open to a politician enabled him to acquire extensive clientages. The army was devoted to its chiefs and relied on them for grants of land. These four means for action vanished under the Empire, when Augustus, not caring to leave the way open for rivals, established an administrative system worthy of a great empire. In other words, the triumph of personal power was due to the institutional defects of the Republic. The city which had become a state had grown without transforming itself and adapting to its new greatness. The 'Roman revolution' of Octavius Augustus was needed in order to effect that adaptation. As for the class struggles, one cannot fail to recognize their intensity, nor can one deny that they furnished soldiers and supporters to the magnates. Nevertheless, I do not think they were the principal cause of the Roman revolution, whatever others have said.[234]

METAMORPHOSIS OF EUERGETISM: THE EXPRESSION OF SOVEREIGNTY

With tremendous resources at its disposal, the euergetism of Caesar, Octavius and Agrippa had nothing in common with that of the senatorial oligarchy, because the power they wielded had itself nothing in common with the power of a magistrate or a senator. It was sovereign power – already equivalent to the power of the Emperors. Now when a man is all-powerful, he no longer commands in person. He looks down from on high, and is not responsible for the mistakes of his ministers, his angels. When one rules alone one rules indirectly, being above all other authorities and not taking their place. On the other hand one embodies the majesty of the state. Octavius, and even Caesar, were sovereigns, and theirs was the euergetism of sovereigns. Their *largesses* were not to be compared with those of a magistrate, or a *triumphator* or a candidate. They engaged in no private liberalities but behaved as though already Emperors.

Their liberalities served to express their sovereign majesty. This was a characteristic feature. In Greco-Roman antiquity, in the world of the *polis*, a sovereign did not express his majesty by having a palace built for himself: that would have been the conduct of an oriental despot. Instead, he made *largesse* to his fellow citizens, or erected public buildings. The Florence of Dante and the Medici, which was a *polis* in almost every respect, nevertheless did not possess quite the same outlook – as witness the Pitti palace. During the last years of Cosimo the Elder, says Machiavelli, Pitti became the real master of Florence, 'to the point where it was no longer Cosimo but Pitti who ruled the city'. Pitti 'grew so confident in his power that he began to build an edifice that was truly royal in its magnificence; never before had a mere citizen erected such a palace'.[235] If Pitti had been a Roman senator, he would, instead of expressing his grandeur by the size of his palace, have called to mind a maxim that the Roman oligarchy had drawn from its long experience, and which, for Cicero, condensed the wisdom of euergetism: 'The Roman people hate private luxury, they love public magnificence.'[236]

Pompey had well understood that wisdom: 'Pompey himself, up to the time of his third triumph, had a simple and modest house. After that, it is true, when he was erecting the famous and beautiful theatre which bears his name, he built close by it, like a small boat towed behind a ship, a more splendid house than the one he had before. But even this was not large enough to excite envy . . .'[237] Octavius Augustus too, who never had a palace, spent all his life in the house of Hortensius on the Palatine Hill (it was an Élysée rather than a Louvre), and had a villa belonging to his granddaughter razed to the ground because it was too big.[238] To enhance his Imperial residence Octavius availed himself of a religious pretext. He caused a public temple of Apollo to be built in a section of the grounds of his house on the Palatine where lightning had struck, an occurrence which, according to the *haruspices*, meant that the god wished to have a home in that place. To this temple Octavius added a portico housing two libraries, Latin and Greek. These were all public buildings, not to be confused with the Emperor's residence, although modern archaeologists often treat them together as a single group. Suetonius, however, praises the modesty of the house of Hortensius, where the Emperor lived, and carefully distinguishes from it the temple and the portico, which he discusses in a different chapter devoted exclusively to public buildings.[239]

Like Caesar before him, Octavius was no despot, but a good Emperor. Both Caesar and he celebrated the festivals of their regime – but using the cover of the public games. Instead of building themselves palaces, they built temples. They embellished the capital under colour of raising monuments as *triumphatores* or *euergetai*. In their capacity as *euergetai* they dipped into their own coffers just as though these were the public Treasury. 'By shows, buildings, *largesses*, banquets, [Caesar] had conciliated the ignorant crowd; his own followers he had bound to him by rewards, his adversaries by a show of clemency,' wrote Cicero.[240] But clemency is the virtue of a despot, not of a citizen. Sallust knew of no clemency but that of the Roman people.[240] Just so, according to Cicero, it was by his generosities that Caesar gained the position of king.

ROME AS CAPITAL: CAESAR AND AUGUSTUS

In 54, during the Gallic War, the future dictator was able to show, by the buildings he erected, that his was a national destiny and the stature of a monarch. We are so used to seeing the senators make *largesse* that Caesar's buildings in the Forum do not appear to have surprised his historians.[241] However, there was *largesse* and *largesse*. As we have seen, nobody had hitherto taken it into his head to offer the Roman people a public monument unless he was a *triumphator*. Caesar took the first step in this direction. It is easy to see what his intention was. In 54 he held half the power, the other half being held by Pompey. These two glorious proconsuls had come to an agreement to control Rome and the Empire. However, Caesar was far from Rome – he had just crossed the Rhine and then raided into Britain – whereas, in Rome, Pompey had in 55 inaugurated his temple and theatre with exceptional pomp, and these buildings were grander than anything previous *triumphatores* had ever put up. Without waiting for his own triumph, Caesar sought to have his own monuments in Rome. These were the forum and basilica which were to bear his name, and also the Basilica Aemilia – the reconstruction of which he tactfully entrusted to a descendant of the man who originally built it, Aemilius Paullus, giving him the money needed for the task. The booty of Gaul was the source of the hundreds of millions which were invested in this monumental complex, a worthy match for Pompey's.[242]

I shall not dwell on the great works and constructions accomplished or planned by Caesar as dictator, between 48 and 44.[243] It was left to Octavius Augustus and his party, once in power, to do what the Republican administration had failed to do, and win for the new regime the merit of giving Rome the look of a capital city. The budgetary allowance that the Republic gave to its censors, praetors or aediles had been insufficient for great works, and private euergetism was restricted to *triumphatores*. Augustus used his personal resources to finance building work, encouraged the members of his party and the *triumphatores* to restore monuments and highways, and urged private persons to beautify the city with buildings both public and private. We shall see later how Rome was thus transformed from a city-state to an Imperial capital, and what this capital meant for the Emperors.

The metamorphosis of Rome's buildings, of which contemporaries were well aware, was due to Octavius together with the principal members of his party.[244] Nevertheless a distinction was established between the latter and the Emperor which itself became traditional. The Emperor alone could have public buildings erected or repaired, when he was pleased to do so, in Rome at least, and he made the most of his right. (In the eulogy of himself that he had carved on his tomb and which is known as the *Res Gestae*, Augustus draws up an impressive list of the Roman buildings which he erected, and of which only a few were triumphal.) The members of his party put up buildings in Rome only in their capacity as *triumphatores*, as immemorial custom allowed. The rule became absolute in the early period of the Empire, with the Emperors reserving for themselves alone the monopoly of euergetism in Rome, their capital. Any private person who wished to become a voluntary *euergetēs* had to display his generosity in some town other than Rome. The rule was already tacitly established under Octavius Augustus, I believe, since buildings for which members of his family or his party were responsible were erected exclusively as the result of triumphs. One debatable case, however, is that of the Emperor's closest confidant, his high admiral Agrippa. He was the strategic genius who had destroyed the fleet of Sextus Pompeius and was the real victor of the battle of Actium over Antony and Cleopatra; but, initiating another tradition by which triumphs also became a monopoly of the Emperors, Agrippa always refused to celebrate a triumph. Nevertheless, the admirable group of monuments which he erected on the Campus Martius five years after Actium was triumphal in spirit, if not formally. 'In honour of the naval victories he completed the building called the Basilica of Neptune and lent it added brilliance by the painting representing the Argonauts.'[245] The Pantheon, 'temple of all the gods', was also a sanctuary both military and dynastic, consecrated to Mars, to Venus Victrix, to Caesar, 'and to all the other gods'. That *et cetera* was intended, I imagine, to embrace implicitly Apollo, the god of Actium, whom Octavius had reserved for himself, just as he had attributed to himself the glory of the actual victory. Agrippa's non-triumphal buildings were set up far from Rome, at Nîmes or Merida, distant colonies which the regime wanted to make citadels of the Octavian party and strongpoints of Roman rule in the provinces.

In Rome itself, Octavius Augustus built only in order to edify the public mind. By turning Rome from a city of brick into a city of marble, the Augustan regime sought to suggest to everyone that, far from pursuing partisan ends, it had taken in hand the higher interest of the state, whose buildings were in those days its visible embodiment. Out of respect for that great object which transcended them all, private persons should also show respect for the regime which cared for it.

NATIONAL FESTIVALS

An identical evolution took place as regards triumphs and the aedileship. These two old-established occasions for *euergesiai* now gave place to politically symbolic gestures. When Caesar or Agrippa triumphed or were aediles, they did not follow the precedent of *triumphatores* and aediles of the past, even if outwardly they acted in the same way but on a larger scale. Once they were in control, the festivals they gave were no longer mere gifts by *euergetai* – they were festivals of the established regime and had acquired a political implication. They did not merely add to the history of the word *liberalitas*. The four triumphs in one that Caesar celebrated in 46, after returning home as a conqueror with no more enemies to beat and being appointed dictator for ten years, were the high festival of the new regime. Their splendour and the *largesses* of all kinds that were distributed in connection with them remained long in the people's memory.[246] Public opinion declared in favour of the conqueror by not shunning the festival. Similarly, the sumptuous aedileship of Agrippa in 33[247] was an exceptional function (Agrippa was made aedile when he had already become consul)[248] exercised in exceptional circumstances. The year 33 was to be the last in which Octavius would hold triumviral powers. In principle, on 1 January 32 there should no longer be any power higher than that of the consuls, and Octavius would henceforth be merely a private person.[249] He did not need to be more than that in order to remain in control, for he spent the year 33 in provoking a war between Rome and the Egypt of Antony and Cleopatra, confident that he would be carried forward by a wave of Italian nationalism that would keep him in power even when his official authorization had lapsed. And that was indeed what happened. But first he had to make sure of public opinion. That, I believe, was why he profited by the year 33, when he was still master, to confer upon his close associate Agrippa the aedileship which thus possessed decisive political importance and was to leave an indelible memory. With good reason, since Agrippa 'agreed[250] to be made aedile, and without taking anything from the public Treasury repaired all the public buildings and all the streets ... Furthermore he distributed olive oil and salt to all, and furnished the baths free of charge throughout the year for the use of both men and women; and in connection with the many festivals of all kinds which he gave ... he hired the barbers, so that no one should be at any expense for their services.'[251] What this unusual aedileship foreshadowed was the institution of the prefecture of the City.

PATRONAGE, NOT PATRIMONIALISM: AUGUSTUS

As legitimate, and soon legal, head of the Empire, Octavius Augustus was always to play a dual role. On the one hand he was a sort of supreme magistrate, armed with legal or quasi-legal powers. On the other, he continued to present himself as a mere private individual who, out of love for the public weal, had one day assembled a private army and liberated the state, like the Cid or the young Caesar – outstanding merits which entitled him to exceptional personal authority (*auctoritas*). In short, he was half prince and half national hero, or, as they said in those days, a saviour. As a saviour who was now a mere private person he would continue his work by becoming a *euergetēs*. His private fortune was to become, in practice, one of the two or three public coffers of the Treasury; Augustus would be a patron of the state. This we know thanks to the excellent interpretation of the *Res Gestae* by Nilsson and Wilcken.[252]

What do we find in the *Res Gestae*? Two sorts of things, as is indicated by the full title of this funeral eulogy: the 'political acts [*res gestae*] by which Augustus brought the inhabited world under the rule of the Roman people, and the expenses [*impensae*] he incurred on behalf of the Roman state and people'. These expenses are listed with a book-keeper's precision and are not like the ordinary expenses of a state. For example there is no mention of the pay of the legions, but only of distributions of money to the population of Rome, *congiaria*, corn bought privately and distributed to the plebs, *euergesiai* performed with the proceeds of booty. The whole, pompously recapitulated at the end of the text, amounts to 600 million sesterces. For such a tally of liberalities, many of which were made in coin, he must certainly have needed to increase the amount of specie in circulation, which could not have been considerable at that time. (This must have resulted not in inflation, but in a decline in the number of exchanges by barter.)[253] Sometimes the relation between these *largesses* and public expenditure, items which are visibly distinct from one another, is clearly seen: 'On four occasions I rescued the Treasury with my money. When a special coffer, the military Treasury, was created on my initiative, I contributed to it 42 millions from my personal fortune ...' There can be no doubt that Augustus is not speaking as a head of state proud of the public expenditure he has ordered, but as a patron of the state proud of the *largesse* he has made to the people or the state from his private fortune – the huge fortune bequeathed to him by Caesar and half of which he passed on to his successor Tiberius – and also from the booty of his triumphs which, like all *triumphatores*, he regarded as his own property. This evidence would have been acknowledged from the start if Mommsen had not, for once, introduced a false notion. Mommsen was one of those geniuses that a branch of learning enjoys only twice or thrice in a thousand years, and his *Public Law* is among the greatest monuments of moral and political science, besides being one of the most lucid books ever written. But on one occasion he grasped the wrong end of the stick, and would never thereafter let go. He was absolutely convinced that the principal coffer of the Roman Empire, called the Fiscus, was the Emperors' private possession. For Mommsen, Augustus had not been the patron of the state: on the contrary, the state had belonged to him. Consequently, when the *Res Gestae* said that Augustus had made *largesses* from his fortune, this was to be understood as meaning that he had done it at the expense of the Fiscus. We shall see later the nineteenth-century preconceptions that lay behind this theory. It was abandoned fifty years ago, and its passing enabled Nilsson and Wilcken to show that the expenses listed in the *Res Gestae* were really *euergesiai*.

A no less significant discovery has been added more recently by Jean Béranger, showing that patronage by the Emperors did not end with the death of Augustus, but continued until the tragic fall of Nero – so long as the dynasty founded by Augustus endured and the private fortune of Caesar and Augustus, steadily increased by legacies and the booty of Imperial triumphs, was passed on by inheritance from Emperor to Emperor together with the crown. This transforms the picture we formerly had of the Imperial finances in the first century, and especially our picture of the dynastic succession. The Senate and the army well knew that nobody had the means to rule unless he possessed so huge a fortune, with the inevitable result that the crown remained the property of Augustus's descendants. This is clearly shown by a phrase in Tacitus that Béranger was the first to translate exactly. In Augustus there died 'an aged prince, a veteran potentate, who had seen to it that not even his heirs should lack for means to perform their public function [*provisis heredum in rem publicam opibus*]'.[254] From Augustus to the death of Nero, the Roman Empire thus had two sources of revenue. Most expenditure was met from the state's coffer (or rather, from the two coffers it now possessed: the old Treasury and the newly organized Fiscus); other expenditure, however, and particularly such as might make its author popular, was undertaken by the Emperors using their private fortune. When Nero promised to contribute 60 millions a year to the state at a time when the public finances were running low, he meant, I think, that this sum would be taken by him from his private income.[255] Imperial patronage came to an end with Nero's death. After him, the dynasty of parvenus which succeeded the one founded by Augustus confiscated the private fortune of its fallen predecessor. The lands which had belonged to Augustus and his heirs and successors belonged thenceforth to the state or to this new dynasty, and the income from them went, it is said, to fill a third public coffer, called the Patrimonium.[256]

AUGUSTUS AS MAGISTRATE AND *EUERGETĒS*

To conclude this chapter, let us see the *Res Gestae* in its true light. It was the eulogy of a magistrate and the epitaph of a *euergetēs*, not that of a sovereign; nor was it a political testament, as Mommsen claimed, nor anything comparable to the triumphal inscriptions of the oriental potentates and of some Hellenistic kings. Augustus, continuing the Republican tradition of munificence, boasts in his funeral eulogy only of his private *largesses*, saying nothing of the public expenditure he decreed as the state's first magistrate. The founder of the Empire does not see himself as a sovereign. He defines himself in relation to the state and sees his personal patronage as separate. Less than a century later, his successor Trajan would have a more Imperial way of looking at the matter and would be congratulated, by his official panegyrist, for having distributed a *congiarium* 'out of his revenue', meaning from the public coffer of the Fiscus. This meant thinking like a real sovereign, for whom all his public decisions are meritorious. Augustus, however, does not claim to give an account of his public acts, and the *Res Gestae* is not his political testament: the document sets forth everything in the Emperor's political activity which redounds to his personal honour. This is easy to understand when we compare it with the humble epitaphs of municipal magistrates, hundreds of which have been found by archaeologists throughout the Empire, and which I shall seek to examine in another book. What, in fact, do these epitaphs reveal to us? Two things, as in the *Res Gestae* – the things about which, according to the ideals of the time, a man had the best right to boast: his political activity (and in particular the 'honours' or public functions that the city had awarded to him) and his *euergesiai*. All these epitaphs run roughly as follows: 'X was duumvir of his city and was the first to exhibit to the plebs a combat of ten gladiators.' The deceased boasts of these gladiators because, by definition, he was not obliged to undertake that *euergesia* and open his private purse; accordingly it can be inscribed among his personal merits. Again, it may be that fifteen gladiators fought; but he speaks only of the ten for which he paid himself, the five others having been 'exhibited' thanks to a public *lucar*. If he was the first to engage in such *largesse*, that fact also entitled him to high praise. Similarly, in the *Res Gestae* the words 'I was the first to . . .', *primus feci*, recur like a refrain.

The very form of this self-glorification is Republican. The *Res Gestae* is unusual in epigraphy in being a first-person composition, a 'eulogy' (which did not necessarily have to be funerary or sepulchral).[257] Such self-glorification, rarely indulged in by Hellenistic notables, did not offend the modesty of Roman oligarchs.[258] A century and a half before Augustus a consul of the Republic had his eulogy carved, in his lifetime, in the hills of Lucania, the scene of his exploits: 'I had 917 runaway slaves hunted down in Sicily and I returned them to their masters. I was the first to cause shepherds to give place to ploughmen on the public lands. I had the forum and the temples built here.'[259] At whom was a eulogy like this directed? At mankind, at posterity, at eternity. The same is true of the *Res Gestae*.[260] We have wondered too much about whom Augustus was addressing in his self-glorification. Was it for the plebs of Rome that he listed his *euergesiai*? But the *Res Gestae* was reproduced throughout the Empire, its text was carved even in the sanctuaries of faraway Asia. Why then, it has been asked, does Augustus not address a single word to this provincial public? Is the text perhaps a patchwork, whose various pieces are not all of the same period, and are destined for different readerships? These are idle questions arising from the fundamental mistake of interpreting the glorification of sovereign majesty as 'Imperial propaganda' and the expression of that majesty as ideology. If Augustus speaks of the *largesses* he has provided for the city of Rome (and, in accordance with custom, for that city alone), this is not propaganda aimed at a particular public, the Romans; these *largesses* are to be counted to his personal merit, which he wishes to proclaim to heaven, and there is no more to it than that. An epigraphic text – the *Res Gestae* is an inscription – is not a document like a propaganda poster that one sticks on walls to be read by one's contemporaries: it is a monument carved for the information of all time.

CONCLUSIONS

Let us draw up the balance sheet. The euergetism of the Roman oligarchy, quite unlike that of the Hellenic notables, was not an expression of its superiority (the official honours, the pomp of power, lictors or the embroidered toga sufficed for that). Nor was it the gratuity given in return for an honorific sinecure: the empire of the world was no sinecure. Rather was it:

1. The desire to reign also over men's minds, and not merely to be obeyed; for this is the other aspect of politics. A magistrate gave games not just to please his future electors (who were only a handful of people) but to acquire prestige in the minds of all the plebeians of Rome, even though these were without political power. Agrippa performed his famous aedileship sumptuously in order to win the hearts of the Romans for the new regime, even though their bodies were of no use to him, since these plebeians had no place in the political arena. Those hearts were, in consequence, lost for the enemy, who immediately felt paralysed. Even for a politician other people are not mere objects, but also minds.

2. Rome was a democracy only in name. But the oligarchy, in order to 'depoliticize' the bodies, and still more to avoid alienating the

hearts, of the ordinary citizens, showed concern for them. They ought not to be left unaware that, whatever the harsh imperatives of politics, the inner feelings of the oligarchy were basically democratic. Hence the soldiers received *donativa* which proved to them that, even if they were no longer an army of citizens, neither were they the slaves of their generals; the *donativum* was a symbolic gift. Other symbolic gifts were those given by candidates to their electors. This was not electoral corruption; such gifts testified to the electors that although the candidates did not consider themselves mere mandatories, yet they were no haughtier on that account. In short, symbolic gifts proved that, while belonging to an oligarchy, one could still be Republican at heart.

3. The triumph was a special case. The self-glorification of the *triumphator* was expressed in *euergesiai*. He sought to display his superiority in gifts, in monuments. This almost unique state of affairs is explained by the popular character of the triumph. Military glory was the popular aspect of imperialism. (Savouring the delights of dominion itself could be a pleasure available only to a happy few.) Even so, until Pompey's time the monumental *euergesiai* of the *triumphatores* remained relatively modest. With the building of Pompey's theatre the custom changed its significance: by raising national monuments and giving national festivals the magnates showed that theirs was a national destiny which was based on their personal prestige (Pompey) or which consisted in their personal power (Caesar).

4. We thus arrive at something almost unique in history. The first dynasty of Emperors fuelled the engine of state to some extent by means of a huge personal fortune, which they took care not to confuse with the public Treasury. This was not 'patrimonialism': it did not consist in treating the state as private property. On the contrary, it was patronage in relation to the state. In the same way, between the Meiji Restoration and 1945 the emperor of Japan was able to finance his personal policy (or that of a clique hiding in his shadow) by means of his enormous private fortune.

5. Roman euergetism was even less a pretext for redistribution than was the Greek variety. A consul was not 'induced' to be charitable by the exercise of face-to-face moral pressure upon him. He was not compelled by gentle violence to open his granary in time of famine. A charivari directed against him would have amounted to sedition. That was why, in Rome, redistribution became a state problem and hardly ever operated through private patronage. Cheap bread was the state's bread.

The power of the oligarchy was not founded upon bread and circuses. Elections were accomplished through networks of influence and clientage. As for the bread, this was distributed, reluctantly, by the state. The oligarchy cannot be accused of having lulled the people by means of materialistic satisfactions: in their social attitudes these latifundists were, on the contrary, ferocious. They did not engage in *euergesiai* in order to obtain power or to keep it, but because they possessed power. Political power consists in reigning over men's hearts, in being loved. The colonel who 'knows how to make himself loved' by his regiment is kind because his role as colonel involves this: he is not kind in order that he may be promoted general by his men. The idea of depoliticization is thoroughly anachronistic. It would make sense in a modern Western state whose rulers hold power by delegation and have to convince their electors, but it is meaningless in periods when the rulers were masters, chiefs, who commanded because they had the right to command.

These chiefs performed *euergesiai* because they were chiefs. Every authority, even when exercised by absolute right, involves two special features. It has to justify itself by making clear that its aim is the good of the governed. And its relation with the governed is not a relation with robots but with minds. These two features explain the *euergesiai* and lie behind the anachronism mentioned above, in which a relation with humble subjects, among whom the master would like to be popular, is mistaken for a relation with constituents whom a candidate needs to convince.

The truth is that rationalism makes us deny the obvious. The oligarchs had no rational need to make themselves popular. They did not have to be loved by the plebs in order to hold on to their power. But they could not help themselves – they wanted to be loved. Could it be that politics is not what people think it is, or not only what people think it is? Is it perhaps an inner relationship between minds? The Imperial period, which I shall now analyse, will show us, with the clarity of a blueprint of political philosophy, that this is indeed the case.

Notes

1. In practice, the senators were drawn exclusively from among the *equites*, because only the latter could be elected to a magistracy. Senators' sons were *equites* before they became (if they became) senators

themselves. The *equites* aspired to enter the Senate. Families which had once been senatorial but no longer had a member in the Senate fell to equestrian rank, but could rise to the Senate once more if one of their members was elected to a magistracy: this happened with Sulla's family. The *equites* were an order, while the senators were former magistrates, equestrian in origin, who formed the Council of government. But something caused the Senate itself to become an order, counterposed to the equestrian order, namely 'the closing of the Council', i.e. the fact that membership of the Senate became, in practice, hereditary. Thereafter people spoke of senatorial families, in which one member at least, through having been a magistrate, belonged to the Senate, while the rest were *equites*. See Mommsen, *Staatsrecht*, vol. III, pp. 501 and 508; C. Nicolet, *L'Ordre équestre à l'époque républicaine*, vol. I, p. 253; P. A. Brunt in *Annales, Économies, Sociétés*, 1967, pp. 1095–6.

2. M. Gelzer, *Kleine Schriften*, vol. I (Franz Steiner, 1962), p. 134.

3. It is F. Hampl's merit to have rid the history of the Republic of its cant: 'Römische Politik in republikanischer Zeit und das Problem des Sittenverfalls', in *Historische Zeitschrift*, CLXXXVIII (1959), especially pp. 510–11.

4. M. Gelzer, *Kleine Schriften*, vol. I, p. 202. The absence of any salary for the performance of public functions confined politics to an oligarchy of notables: see M. Gelzer, 'Die Nobilität der römischen Republik', a work of fundamental importance, in his *Kleine Schriften*, vol. I, pp. 17–135, especially p. 38 (read 'das Claudische Gesetz' instead of 'das Flaminische Gesetz'); Eng. tr. *The Roman Nobility*, 1969.

5. See the articles 'Optimates' (H. Strasburger) and 'Populares' (C. Meier) in Pauly-Wissowa, vol. XVIII, 783, and Supplement X, 555; R. Syme, *Sallust* (University of California Press, 1964), pp. 17–18; M. Gelzer, *Kleine Schriften*, vol. I, pp. 170 and 199; L. Ross Taylor, *Party Politics in the Age of Caesar* (University of California Press, 1971), p. 13; and the distinctions introduced by P. A. Brunt, *Social Conflicts in the Roman Republic* (Chatto and Windus, 1971), p. 95.

6. On *dignitas*, see P. Boyancé, 'Cum dignitate otium', in his *Études sur l'humanisme cicéronien* (Latomus Collection, 1970), especially pp. 114–23: 'pre-eminence in the city', 'prestige'; H. Drexler, 'Dignitas', in *Das Staatsdenken der Römer*, R. Klein (ed.) (Wiss. Buchgesell., 1966), pp. 231–54; C. Wirszubski, 'Cicero's "cum dignitate otium": a reconsideration', in *Journal of Roman Studies*, XLIV (1954), especially p. 12.

7. H. Drexler, 'Die moralische Geschichtsauffassung der Römer', in *Gymnasium*, LXVI (1954), p. 174. On Cicero's political career, which had been a triumphal progress until his exile, see H. Strasburger, *Concordia Ordinum* (Hakkert, reprinted 1956), p. 38.

8. Caesar, *Civil War*, I, 9, 3: 'Sibi semper primam fuisse dignitatem vitaque potiorem' (contrast the words *dignitas patriae* in Cicero's *Ad Atticum*, X, 4). Catiline, too, justified his conspiracy by concern for his *dignitas*: Sallust, *Catiline*, 35, 3; cf. D. C. Earl, *The Political Thought of Sallust* (Hakkert, reprinted 1966), p. 95. For the strictly private and personal character of Caesar's civil war, the problem is vigorously tackled by C. Meier, *Entstehung des Begriffs Demokratie* (Suhrkamp, 1970), pp. 70–75 and 121.

9. M. Gelzer, *Kleine Schriften*, vol. III, p. 23: *Caesar, Politician and Statesman* (Harvard, 1968), p. 5. Hence the astonishingly chaotic air of Roman political life, which surprises us today, used as we are to a slower pace and a more coherent succession of periods (succession of constitutions, presidents, ministries, etc.). With its magistrates and tribunes who are all so many petty sovereigns, Roman politics resembles a country where rival or allied bands wage guerrilla warfare. One band achieves a local success in the *comitia tributa*, another band is equally lucky in the *comitia centuriata* or the Senate. Within less than eighteen months Cicero is first exiled, then recalled from exile – two *coups de main* struck in opposite directions, not the consequence of a political reversal. One might even say that Rome had no 'policy', in the sense of a consistent political line; cf. Gelzer, *Kleine Schriften*, vol. II, p. 15. The Senate alone represented continuity.

10. Mommsen, *Staatsrecht*, vol. II, p. 424, and vol. III, p. 228. The land tax was levied only in cases of necessity and it would have seemed scandalous if it had been an ordinary source of revenue. There is a passage as clear as one could wish in Cicero, *De Officiis*, II, 21, 74.

11. On this tax, see P. Guiraud, *Études économiques sur l'Antiquité* (Hakkert, reprinted 1967), pp. 160–203.

12. Mommsen, *Staatsrecht*, vol. II, p. 998.

13. The liberality 'must be left to the free decision of the ward' (who will perform it, if he so wishes, when he grows up): the guardian cannot decide for him (*Digest*, XXVI, 7, 12, 3).

14. Mommsen, *Staatsrecht*, vol. I, p. 240. For the Senate's control of the Treasury, see vol. III, p. 1143.

15. For the institutions, see Mommsen, *Staatsrecht*, vol. II, pp. 517–22; Friedländer in Marquardt, *Staatsverwaltung*, vol. III, pp. 482–9; G. Wissowa, *Religion und Kultus der Römer* (C. H. Beck, reprinted 1971), pp. 449–67; Habel's article on 'Ludi Publici' in Pauly-Wissowa, Supplementband V, cols. 608–30.

16. Mommsen did not develop his theory in vol. I of his *Staatsrecht*, pp. 241 or 295, or in vol. II, p. 517, but later, in vol. II, pp. 999 and 1000, note 2, and p. 1129 (these references are not given in the index to *Staatsrecht*). It was in the course of a polemic with Hirschfeld about

the legal status of the Imperial *fiscus*, identified with the *mutuum* of private law, that he included the Republican games in this identification, a matter to which we shall return in chapter IV, section 5, notes 94 and 100: cf. Hirschfeld, *Die Kaiserlichen Verwaltungsbeamten* (Weidmann, reprinted 1963), p. 12, note 2, who questions Mommsen's theory.

17. References in Mommsen, *Staatsrecht*, vol. III, p. 509, note 2: 're- demptos ab aerario vectigales quadrigas' (Asconius); it is not known which magistrate was entrusted with the farming of them for the Treasury (*Staatsrecht*, vol. II, pp. 426, 447, 555). Most recently, E. Badian, *Publicans and Sinners: private enterprise in the service of the Roman Republic* (Blackwell, 1972), p. 16; C. Nicolet, *L'Ordre équestre*, p. 330.

18. Gamalian inscription at Ostia (*Corpus Inscriptionum Latinarum*, XIV, 375; Dessau, no. 6147): 'in ludos cum accepisset public[e] lucar, remisit et de suo erogationem fecit.'

19. Dio Cassius, LVI, 47, says that an actor who 'would not enter the theatre for the stipulated pay' was supported by the spectators, and the tribunes of the plebs were obliged to ask the Senate to authorize them to spend more on their games than was allowed by law. (We know that Augustus had laid down a maximum amount for magistrates' personal contributions to the cost of their games.) Suetonius, *Tiberius*, 34, says that the Senate was required to 'recidere mercedes scaen- icorum'. And Tacitus, *Annals*, I, 77, says that the Senate took measures 'de modo lucaris et adversus lasciviam fautorum'. Was the *lucar* the maximum amount the magistrates could spend? Was it synonymous with *mercedes scaenicorum*?

20. For the classical interpretation of *lucar*, see Mommsen, *Staatsrecht*, vol. II, pp. 61 and 66, note 1; Wissowa, *Religion und Kultus*, p. 451, note 6. The word appears in the *senatus consultum* concerning the secular games of Claudius or Domitian (*Corpus*, VI, 32324: 'de lucari ludo- rum'). The meaning 'actors' salary' emerges from the glosses (G. Goetz, *Thesaurus Glossarum Emendatarum*, vol. VI, p. 656) which explain *lucar* by μισθὸς θεατρικός or μισθὸς ἀπὸ φίσκου (many of the games, under the Empire, were the responsibility of the Emperor and his Fiscus) and from Tertullian, *De Scorpiace*, 8, 3: St John the Baptist's head was cut off as *lucar* for the dancer Salome. What has complicated matters is that there is another word *lucar*, related to *lucus*, which means 'wood', or 'sacred grove' (*Corpus*, I, second edn, 1730 and 401, cf. p. 720; Degrassi, *Inscriptiones Liberae Rei Publicae*, nos. 504 and 556). It has therefore been supposed that the *lucar* of the games was a tax or a farm paid for the exploitation of the sacred groves, the income from which was assigned to meet expenditure on the public games. In antiquity etymologists already associated *lucar* with *lucus*: 'Why do

they call the money expended upon public spectacles *lucar*? Is it because, round about the city, there are, consecrated to the gods, many groves which they call *luci*, and they used to spend the revenue from these on the public spectacles?' (Plutarch, *Moralia; Quaestiones Romanae*, 88); other passages in I. B. Pighi, *De Ludis Saecularibus Populi Romani* (reprinted 1965), p. 63. For all aspects of the games, the Treasury had to deal with an impresario, the *locator scaenicorum* (Dessau, no. 5207). Finally, I will quote the inscription *Corpus*, V, 5128 = Dessau, no. 6726: a *euergetēs* of Bergamo provided free funerals for his fellow citizens by paying on their behalf the *lucar Libitinae*, which the municipal Treasury had farmed; this *lucar* cannot have been anything but the payment due to the undertakers and mourners. Compare a *euergesia* by the Emperor Nerva, who provided free funerals for the Roman plebs; this explanation we owe to Liebenam, *Römisches Vereinswesen*, p. 251, and B. Laum, *Stiftungen*, vol. I, p. 114.

21. For the figures, see Marquardt, *Staatsverwaltung*, vol. II, p. 85, and vol. III, p. 488; also Wissowa, *Religion und Kultus*, p. 451, note 7.

22. Livy, XXII, 10 (cf. Plutarch, *Lives*, Flacelière edn, vol. III, p. 237, note) and the comparisons made by Wilhelm, 'Neue Beiträge', VI' CLXXXIII in *Akad. der Wiss. in Wien, Sitzungsberichte* (1921), p. 48; see also *Corpus*, III, 14195, 5 and 7.

23. G. Dumézil, *La Religion romaine archaïque* (Payot, 1966), p. 545. On the generally non-magical character of the games, even in very ancient times, see H. Le Bonniec, *Le Culte de Cérès à Rome*, p. 330.

24. Livy, XXXVIII, 35; on 'renewal', see Wissowa, *Religion und Kultus*, pp. 393, 423, 454; Friedländer in Marquardt, *Staatsverwaltung*, vol. III, p. 485; cf. Mommsen, *Staatsrecht*, vol. III, p. 1061 and p. 1062, note 3.

25. See especially Livy, XXV, 12, and Macrobius, *Saturnalia*, I, 17, 25. I shall not supply the copious bibliography of these games, of the Greek rite, or of Marcius's prophecy.

26. *Inscriptiones Graecae*, XII, 7, 241 (cf. XII, 7, 22). In Rome there was the same recourse to a *stips* for a *lectisternium* (Macrobius, I, 16, 13: Wissowa, *Religion und Kultus*, p. 428, notes 4 and 5). See also note 99.

27. G. De Sanctis, *Storia dei Romani*, vol. IV, 1, p. 493; W. Kroll, *Die Kultur der ciceronischen Zeit*, vol. I (Wiss. Buchgesellschaft, reprinted 1963), p. 98. We know that Sulla was defeated for the praetorship because he had tried to skip the aedileship.

28. Cicero, *De Domo Sua*, 43, 110: 'muneris splendore'.

29. This has to be pointed out, because sometimes the texts refer to *ludi* as *munera*, despite the very clear difference between the games, *ludi*, and the *munera* – the latter word being used in the very special sense of

'gladiatorial spectacles'. When the texts use the word *munus* to describe the *ludi* they mean it to be understood in a different way, as meaning 'a gift': the word *largitio* was also used (Livy, XXV, 2, 8). For the use of *munus*, 'gift', to mean the public games, see Cicero, *De Domo Sua*, 43, 110; Livy, VI, 42, 12; Cicero, *Pro Murena*, 18, *passim* and 26, 53: 'praetura probata in jure, grata in munere [i.e. in ludis]'; *De Officiis*, II, 16–17 '(munere ... sumptus aedilitatis)'; Cicero imitates this style, *In Verrem*, I, 12, 36: 'hoc munus aedilitatis meae populo Romano amplissimum polliceor' (for this use of *polliceri* see Asconius, *in toga candida*, p. 88 (Clark)).

30. Mommsen, *Staatsrecht*, vol. II, p. 519, note 1; Suetonius, *Caesar*, 10: *ludos et cum collega et separatim edidit*; Plutarch, *Life of Cato the Younger*, 46. Men were afraid of becoming aedile at the same time as a richer colleague whose games would eclipse everything else (Caelius, in Cicero, *Ad Familiares*, VIII, 3). To stop colleagues outbidding each other, Augustus decided that no praetor could spend more than the other for his games (Dio Cassius, LIII, 2).

31. Scaurus and Hypsaeus had been *triumviri monetales* together. The coinage mentioned by Mommsen (reference in the previous note) relates to their joint triumvirate, not to their aedileship: E. Sydenham, *The Coinage of the Roman Republic* (Spink and Son, 1952), p. 151, no. 912.

32. Summary list of the sumptuous aedileships in Marquardt, *Staatsverwaltung*, vol. II, p. 86, and vol. III, p. 488; Cicero, *De Officiis*, II, 16, 57. Cf., to the contrary, Plutarch, *Life of Cato the Younger*, 46.

33. E. Sydenham, *The Coinage of the Roman Republic*, p. 146, no. 885; p. 147, no. 890; p. 153, no. 921.

34. P. Veyne in *Bulletin de correspondance hellénique*, XC (1966), pp. 146–7; many examples could be quoted, but I will add only Aristotle, *Rhetoric*, I, IX, VI, 38: εἰς πρῶτον ἐγκώμιον ἐποιήθη.

35. *Tria patrimonia*, see Cicero, *Pro Milone*, 35, 95; Asconius, *In Milonianam*, p. 31 (Clark).

36. Seneca, *De Beneficiis*, II, 21.

37. Friedländer in Marquardt, *Staatsverwaltung*, vol. III, p. 488, note 6.

38. Cicero, *Ad Quintum Fratrem*, I, 1; IX, 26. Cf. also Livy, XL, 44.

39. Dio Cassius, XLVIII, 53: 'All were anxious, not so much to hold office for any considerable time at home, as to be counted among the ex-officials, and so secure the offices and military forces outside of Italy.' See also Cicero, *In Verrem*, II, 2.

40. Cicero, *Ad Atticum*, II, 19, 3: At the games in honour of Apollo, 'at Caesar's entry the applause dwindled away; but young Curio, who followed, was applauded ... Caesar was much annoyed ... [Pompey and Caesar] are annoyed with the knights who stood up and clapped Curio.' The knights (*equites*) sat in the seats of honour in the theatre.

41. L. Robert, 'Épigrammes satiriques de Lucilius', in *L'Épigramme grecque: entretiens sur l'Antiquité classique* (Fondation Hardt, vol. XIV, 1969), p. 201: 'These spectacles were more popular in antiquity than are, in our day, boxing or even football and cycling'; see Cicero, *Pro Murena*, 19, 38–40.

42. Cicero, *Pro Cluentio*, 150; *Pro Plancio*, 12; *De Lege Agraria*, 2, 2; Sallust, *Jugurtha*, 85, 3.

43. J. Lambert, *Amérique latine: structures sociales et institutions politiques* (PUF, 1963), pp. 211–13.

44. Plutarch, *Life of Cato the Elder*, 3.

45. Id., *Life of Brutus*, 46.

46. Id., *Life of Lucullus*, 35; *Life of Pompey*, 3. The military discipline of that time bore no resemblance to ours, and had none of the spirit of our army regulations. The soldiers argued with their generals and appealed to them loudly (*Life of Pompey*, 41). The commanders pleaded with their men, distributed presents among them – and also did not shrink from decimating them (Suetonius, *Caesar*, 65–70: *Augustus*, 24); because he who loveth well also chasteneth well. For an authority which in character was more paternal than governed by regulations, winning respect meant winning love. The same was true, under the Empire, of the relations between Corbulo and his troops (Tacitus, *Annals*). It was characteristic of the system that a Roman military commander could plead with his troops, or let them plead with him (Corbulo), without losing his authority. If this occurred in a modern army it would signify that the army was falling apart; but that was not the case in Rome, where obedience was always somewhat like a family relationship.

47. Plutarch, *Life of Lucullus*, 33; on the evolution of the *donativa*, from military reward to *largesse* made to soldier-clients, see J. Harmand, *L'Armée et le Soldat à Rome de 107 à 50* (Picard, Paris, 1967), p. 468; cf. H. Delbrück, *Geschichte der Kriegskunst*, third edn, vol. I (De Gruyter, reprinted 1964), p. 389.

48. When technique is primitive and production inadequate, the worst-placed producer is still needed for the community to be able to subsist, even if his output is meagre. Equilibrium is not fixed at the lower margin and the under-productive producer is supported by resources other than his own: see K. Wicksell, *Lectures on Political Economy*, Robbins (ed.), vol. I, p. 143; N. Georgescu-Roegen, *La Science économique* (Dunod, 1970), pp. 262 and 268; J. Ullme, 'Recherches sur l'équilibre économique', in *Annales de l'Institut Henri-Poincaré*, vol. VIII, fasc. 1, pp. 6–7 and 39–40.

49. Plutarch, *Life of Crassus*, 15.

50. Id., *Life of Cato the Younger*, 50.

51. Cicero, *Pro Murena*, 35, 74ff.
52. Plutarch, *Life of Cato the Younger*, 49–50 and 8.
53. Ibid., 15 and 11.
54. See, for example, Plutarch, *Life of Lucullus*, 3. These gifts to ambassadors are called *xenia* (Mommsen, *Staatsrecht*, vol. II, p. 553, note 3; vol. III, p. 1153, note 2).
55. Plutarch, *Life of Cato the Younger*, 12 and 16; he did not neglect physical exercise: 5.
56. Ibid., 18.
57. Ibid., 18 and 19; cf. J. Stroux, 'Die Versäumnisbüsse der Senatores', in *Philologus*, 1938, pp. 85–101.
58. Plutarch, *Life of Cato the Younger*, 40.
59. Ibid., 18 and 38. Scipio Africanus, on the contrary, refused to let the Senate check his accounts, and tore them up (Polybius, XXIII, 14).
60. Plutarch, *Life of Cato the Younger*, 18, 36 and 38.
61. Aristotle, *Politics*, II, 10 (1270a15) (Tricot), quoted by Latte. Cretan inscriptions show that the custom of holding these banquets survived well into the Imperial epoch, thanks to euergetism.
62. Mommsen, *Staatsrecht*, vol. III, pp. 894–5.
63. Ibid., p. 894, note 2; Wissowa, *Religion und Kultus*, p. 500, note 2; J. Marquardt, *Das Privatleben der Römer* (2nd edn, Leipzig 1886), pp. 208–9, and *Staatsverweltung*, vol. III, pp. 349–50.
64. Wissowa, *Religion und Kultus*, pp. 419–20. The flesh of the victims at the public sacrifices was sold off by the quaestors for the benefit of the Treasury (Mommsen, *Staatsrecht*, vol. II, p. xii, note 1). The banquets in which the entire population shared were those provided by private persons in connection with funerals or as their tithe to Hercules; those provided by the 'producer', like *missilia*, during some public games (Friedländer, *Sittengeschichte*, vol. II, p. 16; Friedländer in Marquardt, *Staatsverwaltung*, vol. III, p. 495); and the old-established popular jollifications like the *Septimontium* (Wissowa, p. 439, note 4; Marquardt, *Privatleben*, p. 208, note 4; *Staatsverwaltung*, vol. III, p. 190). I shall examine elsewhere, in a study of the ode *Nunc est bibendum*, the feasts held by private individuals on the occasion of a public ceremony or a national holiday, and also the banquets at which, in the same circumstances, the senators invited the plebs to their table.
65. Dio Cassius, XLVIII, 34.
66. Varro, *De Re Rustica*, III, 2, 16. These birds appeared on the menu of every banquet worthy of the name: Seneca, *To Lucilius*, 122, 4. For funerals and their public character, see a well-known passage in Polybius, VI, 53.
67. Cicero, *In Vatinium*, 12, 30; Horace, *Satires*, II, 3, 86: 'epulum arbitrio Arri'.

68. Cicero, *In Vatinium*, 13, 31. The explanation of this rule of protocol is probably that the funeral banquets were more dynastic than funereal: they were celebrations in honour of the *heres factus* who was succeeding as head of the family.

69. Livy, XXXIX, 46: 'funeris causa ... toto foro strata triclinia'. For the senators, see references in Mommsen, *Staatsrecht*, vol. III, p. 894, note 3.

70. Livy, VIII, 22.

71. Id., XXXVIII, 55. The *mulsum* and *crustum* distributed are the same as the γλυκισμός mentioned in the preceding chapter.

72. Id., XLI, 28: 'mortis causa patris tui'.

73. Seneca, *De Brevitate Vitae*, 20, 6: 'operum publicorum dedicationes et ad rogum munera'; cf. *Digest*, 31, 49, 4.

74. Dio Cassius, XXXVII, 51 (in 60 BC).

75. Cicero, *Pro Sulla*, 19, 54: 'gladiatores quos testamento patris videmus deberi' (in 62): cf. *In Vatinium*, 15, 37: 'cum mea lex vetet gladiatores dare nisi ex testamento'. Agrippa bequeathed to the people, besides his gardens (P. Grimal, *Les Jardins romains*, p. 193), free baths (Dio Cassius, LIV, 29). Cf., in the municipal towns, *Corpus*, I, second edn, 1903a (Dessau, no. 5671; Degrassi, no. 617): 'lavationem in perpetuom'; *Digest*, XXXII, 35, 3; see also Dio Cassius, XLIX, 43.

76. Dio Cassius, XLVIII, 32.

77. Bequests to a community (*universitas*) or to a number of people, named man by man (*viritim*), had, I believe, two origins. One of these was due to Hellenistic influence; I shall examine elsewhere an Oscan inscription which commemorates the bequest of a public building at Pompeii. The other origin was the one described here, derived from funeral customs. In Rome itself, bequests to the people soon ceased, for the Emperor reserved for himself the monopoly of euergetism in his capital. In other cities, however, they occurred very often, and in this matter fact preceded and outstripped legal provisions. We must remember that the *jus civile* reasons about actual practices and fits them as well as it can into its concepts, more often than it tries to lay down the rules of the game. On bequests to cities the best account is certainly the one given by L. Mitteis, *Römisches Privatrecht*, vol. I (Leipzig, 1908), pp. 377–80: he says that the right of cities to receive bequests had doubtless always been recognized *de facto*.

78. G. Ville, 'Les jeux des gladiateurs dans l'Empire chrétien', in *Mélanges d'archéologie et d'histoire de l'École française de Rome*, 1960, p. 307; E. F. Bruck, *Ueber römisches Recht in Rahmen der Kulturgeschichte*, pp. 64–7.

79. Max Weber contrasts the Greek games, in which the aristocracy took part, with the games and shows of Rome, in the last two pages of his

study *The City*: the pride of the Roman oligarchs forbade them to compete under the gaze of the crowd.

80. See note 73 (*ludi scaenici* given as *ludi funebres*). For other mentions of gladiators at funerals, see Livy, *periocha* 16 (cf. Valerius Maximus, II, 4, 7); XXIII, 30; XXVIII, 21; XXXI, 50; XXXIX, 46; XLI, 28; Terence's *Adelphi* was performed at the funeral games of Aemilius Paullus (Marquardt, *Staatsverwaltung*, vol. III, p. 529, note 8).

81. F. Münzer, *Römische Adelsparteien und Adelsfamilien* (reprinted 1963), p. 168, note 1.

82. Cicero, *Ad Familiares*, II, 3, 1: 'declarandorum munerum'; *De Legibus*, II, 24, 61: 'funus indicatur'; cf., in Varro, *De Lingua Latina*, the expressions *indictivum funus* and *indicere funus*.

83. Cicero, *De Legibus*, II, 24, 61: 'dominus funeris utatur accenso ac lictoribus'; Mommsen, *Staatsrecht*, vol. I, p. 391, note 6; on funerary bas-reliefs of the Imperial period which commemorate the gladiatorial shows given by some municipal *euergetēs*, even if this man were a *sevir* and a mere freedman, the *euergetēs* is always accompanied by lictors: I. Scott Ryberg, *Rites of the State Religion in Roman Art* (American Academy in Rome, 1955), pp. 99–101.

84. The term first used was *munus gladiatorium*, a 'gift consisting of gladiators', an expression which must have appeared in some public announcement of a funeral composed in the style of an advertisement; compare the emphatic style of the parody given by Cicero, *In Verrem*, I, 12, 36, mentioned above, note 29. The vocabulary of Roman euergetism is very composite: *munus* is Indo-European in origin, but *liberalitas* is a literal rendering of the Greek *eleutheriōtēs* and *largitio* is of Etruscan origin (J. Heurgon, 'Lars, largus et Lare Aineia', in *Mélanges André Piganiol*, 1966, p. 656); as for *sportula*, this is the Greek σφυρίς (L. Robert, *Hellenica*, XI–XII, p. 479).

85. It has been shown by G. Ville (*Mélanges ... de l'École française de Rome*, 1960, p. 306) that it is wrong to suppose that in 105 the *munus gladiatorium* had become a regular show, as was claimed by Buecheler in his *Kleine Schriften*, vol. III (reprinted 1965), p. 497.

86. Cf. P. Veyne in *Latomus*, 1967, p. 735.

87. References in M. Gelzer, *Caesar, Politician and Statesman*, pp. 37–8.

88. Plutarch, *Life of Pompey*, 55: when Cicero was consul he had a law passed against canvassing, and yet he defended Murena, who was accused of this offence. Ought we to blame Cicero for political back-scratching? Or praise him for taking account of the higher imperatives of politics, since, if Murena were found guilty, the door would be open for Catiline's men? The dilemma is unreal, and both explanations are true (Cicero, *Ad Familiares*, I, 9, and XI, 28).

89. Mommsen, *Strafrecht*, pp. 865–72.

90. 'Sub titulo "patri se id dare"'", writes Asconius, p. 88 (Clark); Cicero's law against canvassing forbade candidates to give gladiatorial shows, except when executing a trust (*In Vatinium*, 15, 37; *Pro Sestio*, 133). So as to provide another *munus*, Caesar used the pretext of commemorating his daughter, something for which there was no precedent (Suetonius, *Caesar*, 26), the custom being to honour the memory of one's parents only.

91. Mommsen, *Gesammelte Schriften*, *Jurist. Schriften*, vol. I, p. 229; *Strafrecht*, p. 868, note 1, and p. 875; *Lex Genetivae*, art. 132; Cicero, *Pro Murena*, 32, 34 and 35, 73; for invitations extended to a whole tribe (*tributim*), 32, 67. For electoral corruption under the Empire, see Mommsen, *Strafrecht*, p. 867, note 8, and p. 869, note 3: and in the municipal towns, *Digest*, 48, 14.

92. In the second century a good *munus* cost more than 700,000 sesterces (Polybius, XXXI, 28), or the pay of 1,500 soldiers for one year (P. A. Brunt, *Italian Manpower*, p. 411). On the importance of wealth in political life, see Gelzer, *Kleine Schriften*, vol. I, pp. 110–21.

93. For references and discussion of the figures, see Gelzer, p. 118, note 463. 'Promising' money to the electors on condition that one was elected was called *ronuntiare*: Cicero, *Pro Plancio*, 18, 45; Seneca, *Ad Lucilium*, 118, 3.

94. The two brothers Lucullus, who were very fond of one another, presented themselves for the aedileship at the same time. The people, knowing that the elder had waited for his brother to reach the qualifying age before himself becoming a candidate, were touched and elected both of them: Plutarch, *Life of Lucullus*, 1.

95. See the story about Mamercus in Cicero, *De Officiis*, II, 17, 58.

96. Plutarch, *Life of Sulla*, 5, following Sulla's own memoirs. Plutarch goes on: 'But subsequent events would seem to show that Sulla does not confess the real reason for his failure. For in the following year he obtained the praetorship, partly because he was subservient to the people, and partly because he used money to win their support.'

97. Livy, VIII, 22 and XXXVII, 57, 11: 'congiaria habuerat'.

98. Cicero, *Pro Murena*, 18, 37.

99. There are three examples of this: L. Scipio (Pliny, *Natural History*, XXXIII, 48); M. Oppius, who became famous because, during the proscriptions of the triumvirs, he had saved his father by carrying him on his shoulders, like a second Aeneas (Dio Cassius, XLVIII, 53; Appian, *Civil Wars*, IV, 41); and Egnatius Rufus, who, by euergetism, had organized a force of private firemen in Rome (Dio Cassius, LIII, 24). These collections taken up in the theatre itself (Dio Cassius, XLVIII, 53) were evidently a continuation of the ancient precept of the soothsayer Marcius (see above, note 25). The yield of these

collections must have constituted a trivial amount which, needless to say, reimbursed the magistrate only symbolically.

100. Plutarch, *Life of Brutus*, 10; cf. *Auctor de Viris Illustribus*, 82, 4: a poor aedile 'juri reddendo magis quam muneri edendo studuit'.

101. Cicero, *Ad Familiares*, II, 2 and 3; on the splendour of Curio's *munus* (for Curio did give a *munus*, despite Cicero's advice), see Pliny, *Natural History*, XXXVI, 116–20; two years later, Curio was elected tribune of the plebs. When advising Curio to make a career by means of his higher merits, Cicero was thinking of his own experience: he had distinguished himself by the courage he showed against Sulla's protégés and was elected consul despite the relative lack of brilliance of his aedileship (*De Officiis*, II, 17, 59).

102. Cicero, *Ad Atticum*, IV, 18, 2 (IV, 16, 6); on the aedileship of Scaurus, see above, notes 31 and 32. Cicero's *Ad Familiares*, XI, 16 and 17, should be mentioned, and especially II, 6, 3, in which the various factors in an election are cited: political positions (which mattered more than would be supposed from modern analyses which give excessive emphasis to clientage alone); shows (*munera*); and the recommendations of the consuls.

103. Cicero, *In Pisonem*, 1, 2: on the *existimatio*, see C. Meier, *Res Publica Amissa, eine Studie zu Verfassung und Geschichte der späten römischen Republik* (Franz Steiner, 1966), p. 8.

104. For clientage and recommendation, see Gelzer, *Kleine Schriften*, vol. I, pp. 62–132. For the processions, to which the electors were not indifferent, see Gelzer, pp. 63, 66, 67, 99, and note 313. This claque included numerous plebeians who came along only to be present, since 'if poor men have nothing but their vote, then, even if they vote, their support is valueless' (*Pro Murena*, 34, 71); the processions of supernumeraries which, in the street or in the Forum, enabled a lord to be distinguished from a mere mortal were to be continued in a very particular type of clientage which flourished under the Empire (see below, chapter IV, note 362). In addition, these processions served to ensure the physical safety of the candidates, violence having always been a feature of Rome's political style: A. W. Lintott, *Violence in Republican Rome*, p. 74.

105. Cicero, *Pro Sestio*, 53, 114, speaking of a tribune who was not too demagogic: 'tulerat nihil' (i.e. 'nullam legem').

106. See C. Meier's article on 'Populares' in Pauly-Wissowa, Supplementband X, col. 561 (this notable article should be the starting-point for any sociological study of political parties in Rome). The re-elections of Marius to the consulate and the elections of 71, 55, 52 (Asconius, *In Milonianam*, p. 314 (Clark)) and 50 were political in character, but in 60 political divisions failed to overcome the bonds of

clientage (Meier, *Res Publica Amissa*, pp. 197–9). Was Cicero's election in 64 a political affair? It all depends on when the menace from Catiline became clear, and legend seems to have placed that moment earlier (Meier, p. 18, note 67; R. Syme, *Sallust* (1964), pp. 66, 75, 89; R. Seager, 'The first Catilinarian conspiracy', in *Historia*, 1964, pp. 338–47).

107. On factors in elections, see M. Gelzer, *Kleine Schriften*, vol. I, p. 62ff., C. Meier, *Res Publica Amissa*, p. 8, and index under 'Wahlen', p. 330.

108. References in Meier, p. 194, note 199; Gelzer, vol. I, p. 113; on the *divisores*, see Mommsen, *Staatsrecht*, vol. III, p. 196, note 2: *Strafrecht*, p. 869, note 4; T. P. Wiseman, *New Men in the Roman Senate, 139 BC–14 AD* (Oxford, 1971), p. 83 and p. 134, note 1.

109. Plutarch, *Life of Cato the Younger*, 42.

110. Cicero, *In Verrem*, I, 8, 22–3; on the Romilia, Verres' tribe, see L. R. Taylor, *The Voting Districts of the Roman Republic* (American Academy in Rome, 1960), p. 264, cf. p. 294. It was shaming not to receive the votes of one's own tribe (Cicero, *Pro Sestio*, 53, 114; cf. *De Domo Sua*, 19, 49: 'tribum suam non tulit'; Suetonius, *Caesar*, 13). Murena distributed money to his fellow tribesmen (*Pro Murena*, 34, 72). Plancius, who, as will be seen in the third paragraph, had his town of Atina and his tribe well under control, distributed money to that tribe not in order to purchase its support but because the bond of clientage obliged him to make *largesse* to his fellow tribesmen (Cicero, *Pro Plancio*, 19, 46–7). On the electoral role of the tribes, see Mommsen, *Staatsrecht*, vol. III, pp. 197–8; on the weight of the municipal votes in the *comitia*, see L. R. Taylor, *Roman Voting Assemblies* (Ann Arbor, 1966), p. 67; T. P. Wiseman, *New Men in the Roman Senate*, pp. 137–42.

111. Every member of the equestrian order (and every senator, too: there was no difference between the two orders in this sphere) found his own method of self-enrichment. The father of Aemilius Scaurus, a patrician, engaged in the coal trade (*Auctor de Viris Illustribus*, 82, 1) and Atticus, as is well known, traded in books. For the mule-back transport business, which occupied for a time the future Emperor Vespasian, see Wiseman, *New Men in the Roman Senate*, pp. 84, 88, 104. Besides the enduring enterprises, which differed from one family to another and were like long-term speculations, we must also doubtless assume that there were numerous 'one-off' speculations: this is indeed how Petronius depicts the affairs of Trimalchio, and those of Atticus were not very different (G. Boissier, *Cicéron et ses amis*, pp. 134–5). Two modern anecdotes will illustrate this climate of improvisation, ingenuity and speculation which one needs to understand before talking about 'enterprise', attitude to 'work', and 'capitalism'. First, Samuel

Pepys, *Diary*, 26 September 1666, after the Great Fire of London, when the writer was a high official in the Admiralty. He records that he and Sir William Penn, commissioner of the Navy, 'walked in the garden by moonlight, and he proposes his and my looking into Scotland about timber, and to use Pett there; for timber will be a good commodity this time of building the City. And I like the notion, and doubt not that we may do good at it.' Second, Tallemant des Réaux, *Historiettes*, vol. II, p. 733 (Adam). The humanist Peirarède 'is a Huguenot teacher, a native of Bergerac and of fairly good family. He has a farm near Bergerac. He hears that salt beef is being sold at a high price in Bordeaux, where ships are being stocked up for a voyage. He slaughters his cattle, salts them and puts them on a boat, in which he himself embarks. On another occasion he had noticed that trees for wine-presses were selling very well in Bordeaux. He has a small wood of well-grown trees cut down. He sees that by making the wine-press trees half a foot shorter than usual he can make a substantial profit, and so he reduces their length and conveys them to Bordeaux.' The economic activities of the Roman nobility deserve systematic study.

112. Mommsen, *Strafrecht*, p. 868: Cicero, *Pro Murena*, 32, 6, 7.

113. Suetonius, *Augustus*, 40, 2.

114. Augustus considered introducing the postal vote: Suetonius, *Augustus*, 46, 3.

115. Plutarch, *Life of Pompey*, 66.

116. E. S. Stavely, *Greek and Roman Voting* (Thames and Hudson, 1972), p. 22.

117. Cornelius Nepos, *Life of Atticus*, 4, 3; cf. Taylor, *Party Politics*, p. 57; Meier, *Res Publica Amissa*, p. 193.

118. Cicero, *Pro Sestio*, 109; Mommsen, *Staatsrecht*, vol. III, p. 408; Taylor, *Party Politics*, p. 60.

119. Cicero, *Pro Murena*, 18, 37–9 and 33, 69. Lucullus should have celebrated his triumph three years earlier, and the coincidence of the triumph with the candidature of his lieutenant Murena was obviously intentional. After a war the soldiers went back home and then came to Rome for the triumph: Plutarch, *Life of Pompey*, 43.

120. Plutarch, *Life of Crassus*, 14; *Life of Pompey*, 51 and 58.

121. Cicero, *In Verrem*, I, 54; Meier, *Res Publica Amissa*, p. 193, notes 191 and 192.

122. Taylor, *Party Politics*, pp. 59–61. The *comitia tributa* who exiled Cicero are a pack of bandits, that is, of Roman plebeians, whereas the *comitia centuriata* who recalled him from exile are the flower of all Italy, *cuncta Italia*. The Italian notables travelled to Rome to vote, being summoned thither by Pompey (an unusual procedure: Marquardt, *Staats-*

verwaltung, vol. I, p. 65); cf. also P. Grenade, *Essai sur les origines du principat* (De Boccard, 1960), p. 231.

123. Taylor, *Party Politics*, p. 60 and p. 206, note 59.

124. Cicero, *Pro Murena*, 23, 47: the 'homines honesti atque in suis civitatibus et municipiis gratiosi' are opposed to 'confusio suffragiorum'. Cicero himself wanted a *lex tabellaria* which would put an end to the secret ballot: 'when elective, judicial and legislative acts of the people are performed by vote, the voting shall not be concealed from citizens of high rank, and shall be free to the common people' (*De Legibus*, III, 10; cf. 33–9); on the *leges tabellariae*, cf. J. A. O. Larsen, 'The origin of the counting of votes', in *Classical Philology*, XLIV (1949), especially p. 180.

125. Cicero, *Ad Familiares*, XIII, 11. For his part, Cicero cultivated the friendship of Reate (*Ad Atticum*, IV, 15, 5; *Pro Scauro*, 27, p. 481, (Schoell): 'Reatini qui essent in fide mea'; cf. Nissen, *Italische Landeskunde*, vol. I (reprinted 1967), p. 313; on Axius, a local notable and senator, see Syme, *Sallust*, p. 9).

126. *Pro Murena*, 40, 86.

127. L. R. Taylor, *The Voting Districts*, p. 273.

128. Ibid., p. 257.

129. *Pro Murena*, 20, 42; cf. W. V. Harris, *Rome in Etruria and Umbria* (Oxford, 1971), pp. 241–5; T. P. Wiseman, *New Men in the Roman Senate*, p. 139. The 'generosity' (*liberalitas*: this word has several meanings) referred to here is the quality shown by a magistrate who, while keeping within the framework of the laws, applies regulations with humanity: the same meaning is found in *In Verrem*, II, 3: 'ex liberalitate atque accommodatione magistratum'; Berve, article 'Liberalitas' in Pauly-Wissowa, XIII, col. 82. Regarding levies of troops, it must not be forgotten that, even after Marius's time, not all legionaries were professional soldiers and that many of them were mobilized against their will or that of their patron; Murena may have won the goodwill of the Umbrian notables and latifundists by *not* taking their peasants for the army; the myth of Marius putting an end to conscription was demolished by P. A. Brunt, *Italian Manpower* (Oxford, 1971), p. 408ff., and R. E. Smith, *Service in the Post-Marian Roman Army* (University of Manchester, 1958), pp. 46–50.

130. Because, although the tribe was the electoral framework, the real electoral basis was the town: Stavely, *Greek and Roman Voting*, p. 198 and note 372.

131. *The Voting Districts*, pp. 184–294, with R. Syme's critical notes, 'Senators, tribes and towns', in *Historia*, 1964, pp. 105–24. Seven senators, descendants of ancient *gentes majores*, were registered in the Palatina, side by side with the freedmen of Rome and Italy.

132. Quintus Cicero, *Handbook of Electioneering*, 8. On the constant relations maintained by the senators with the Italian towns and their notables, see T. P. Wiseman, *New Men in the Roman Senate*, pp. 47ff. and 136ff.; E. Fraenkel, *Horace*, p. 305.

133. Asconius, *In Milonianam*, p. 31 (Clark), cf. p. 53; on senators who assumed municipal responsibilities, see Wiseman, pp. 45 and 87; on the *equites*, see Nicolet, *Ordre équestre*, p. 420.

134. *Pro Plancio*, 22, 54; Taylor, *The Voting Districts*, p. 243; Wiseman, pp. 141 and 252, note 324. There is dispute about the origin of the *gens* Plautia: K. Beloch, *Römische Geschichte bis zum Beginn der punischen Kriege* (De Gruyter, 1926), p. 338.

135. On relations in general between the *homines novi* and their home towns and tribes, see Wiseman, p. 137ff.

136. On Juventius Lateranensis, see F. Münzer, *Römische Adelsparteien und Adelsfamilien*, p. 48, note 1; on his Papiria tribe and Tusculum, his home town, see Taylor, *The Voting Districts*, pp. 222 and 273 (cf. Syme in *Historia*, 1964, p. 125).

137. *Pro Plancio*, 8, 19–20; on Atima, see Taylor, pp. 243 and 275, cf. 290.

138. Except for the small amphitheatre of Statilius Taurus.

139. Polybius, 32, 12; Sallust, *Catiline*, 7, 6.

140. Cf. Syme, *The Roman Revolution*, p. 57, note 4.

141. Plutarch, *Life of Pompey*, 45, as interpreted by E. Badian, *Roman Imperialism in the Late Republic* (Oxford, 1968), p. 78.

142. P. A. Brunt, *Social Conflicts in the Roman Republic* (Chatto and Windus, 1971), p. 39, from which I have derived these views.

143. Mommsen, *Staatsrecht*, vol. I, p. 240, and vol. III, pp. 1126–40.

144. Ibid., vol. II, p. 452.

145. I shall return to this in the following chapter.

146. For example, it was not until the coming of the Empire that an *aerarium militare* regularly supplied the means for the retirement of veterans. The Republic left it to each *imperator* to obtain a special law for the settlement of his veterans on the land, and thereby acquire a clientage; cf. J. Harmand, *L'Armée et le Soldat à Rome de 107 à 50*, p. 474. In the case of Cicero, a politician rather than a statesman, a man who knew little of public business (his vision being limited by the walls of the Senate and a narrowly 'parliamentary' outlook), and one more inclined to cherish lofty convictions than to perceive real problems, propose concrete solutions and foresee the outcome of events, a very lively Roman patriotism turns into a conservative, romantic love of an idealized past.

147. Mommsen, *Staatsrecht*, vol. II, p. 453.

148. Besides the *cura annonae* of Pompey in 55, we have here a praetor who is absent from his court: he was *avocatus propter publici frumenti curam*

(Asconius, *In Cornelianam*, p. 59 (Clark)) – certainly as an extraordinary arrangement (*Staatsrecht*, vol. II, pp. 238 and 671).

149. I presume that Q. Marcius Rex, the praetor entrusted by the Senate (Pliny, *Natural History*, XXXVI, 15, 121) with the task of repairing the old *aqua Marcia*, was given this task as an extraordinary appointment – possibly because this building had been erected by his ancestors (this was a consideration that counted for much: see, e.g., Cicero, *On Statues*, 36–7); a coin shows the statue raised to him: Sydenham, *The Coinage of the Roman Republic*, p. 153, no. 919. On the curators of public buildings, see Mommsen, *Staatsrecht*, vol. II, p. 670. Marcius received 180 million sesterces (Frontinus, *De Aquae Ductu*, VII, 4).

150. T. Didius, who triumphed over the Celtiberians in 93 (*Fasti Capitolini*, Degrassi (ed.) (Paravia, 1954), p. 107), according to the coin in Sydenham, p. 149, no. 901: T DIDI IMP VIL PVB; no other evidence.

151. Plutarch, *Life of Caesar*, 5; cf. H. Strasburger, *Caesars Eintritt in die Geschichte* (1938), pp. 13 and 86.

152. Restored in 78 by *senatus consultum* (Sydenham, p. 147, no. 833: AIMILIA REF S C M LEPIDVS), it was rebuilt by Aemilius Paullus, to whom Caesar gave 36 million sesterces (Plutarch, *Life of Caesar*, 29; *Life of Pompey*, 58, etc.) in an act of political calculation (M. Gelzer, *Caesar, Politician and Statesman*, p. 178). A doubtful case is that of inscriptions such as *Corpus*, VI, 31602: 'P. Barronius Barba aed. cur. grados refecit', or the inscription of the praetor Naevius Surdinus on the paving of the Forum (P. Romanelli, 'L'iscrizione di Nevio Surdino nel lastricato del Foro Romano', in *Gli archeologi italiani, in onore di A. Maiuri* (1965), pp. 381–9); did this aedile and this praetor pay for the work themselves, or did they receive a sum from the Treasury? I presume that, if they had paid for it, they would have said so; the role of an aedile as a builder is easily explained (Mommsen, *Staatsrecht*, vol. II, p. 507); as for the praetor, he may have acted as curator or as the official responsible for that quarter of the city (vol. II, pp. 238 and 516); compare the different wording of the inscriptions quoted in vol. III, p. 1136, note 3. We know that between 74 and 22 there were no censors and that consuls, praetors and aediles replaced them in some of their functions. I do not know of any other example of buildings erected or repaired by private persons. The Basilica Porcia was built with public money (Plutarch, *Life of Cato the Elder*, 19); likewise the Basilica Sempronia (Livy, XLIV, 16); the temple of Hercules and the Muses was built *ex pecunia censoria* (*Latin Panegyrics*, VII, 3); the Tabularium was built *de senatu sententia* (Dessau, nos. 35 and 35a; Degrassi, *Inscriptiones Liberae Rei Publicae*, nos. 367 and 368); the Capitol was restored with public money, since Caesar pressed Catulus to present his accounts (Dio Cassius, XLIII, 14; Appian, *Civil Wars*, II,

26, 101, etc.). For a list of other monuments, see T. Frank, *An Economic Survey of Ancient Rome*, vol. I, pp. 183–7, 286–7, 331–3, 369–71.

153. On trophies and *fornices* (arches of the Fabii, of Scipio, of Dolabella and Silanus, of Stertinius, etc.), see M. Nilsson, 'Les bases votives à double colonne', in his *Opuscula Selecta*, vol. II, p. 992, and *The Origin of the Triumphal Arch*, vol. II, p. 1012.

154. Metellus's portico enhanced the temples of Jupiter Stator and Juno Regina (Wissowa, *Religion and Kultus*, p. 123); the Porticus Minucia was connected with the temple of the Lares Permarini (22 December was the *natalis* of the 'Lares Permarini in porticu Minucia').

155. Tiro, quoted by Aulus Gellius, X, 17: 'cujus gradus vicem theatri essent'.

156. Tertullian, *On Spectacles*, 10, 5: 'non theatrum, sed Veneris templum nuncupavit'.

157. The facts will be found (if not a correct interpretation of them) in J. A. Hansen, *Roman Theater-Temples* (Princeton, 1959), pp. 43–55. The explanation often given is that Pompey wished 'to avoid censure for building a permanent theatre' (S. B. Platner and T. Ashby, *A Topographical Dictionary of Ancient Rome* (Oxford, 1929), p. 516; J. van Ooteghem, *Pompée le Grand, bâtisseur d'empire* (1954), p. 407).

158. I shall discuss these Roman *theoxenia* elsewhere, and here merely refer to Dessau, no. 154, line 10ff., and to the *Thesaurus Linguae Latinae*, under 'Invitare', which devotes a section to *invitare deos*.

159. Wissowa, *Religion und Kultus*, p. 277; J. Bayet, *Les Origines de l'Hercule romain*, p. 326. The technical term is *pollucere* (Dessau, no. 3411, Degrassi, no. 136: *decuma facta, poloucta*; cf. the commendable correction by Godefroy to the text of the *Agobardinus* in Tertullian, *Ad Nationes*, II, 7, 17).

160. Plautus, *Trinummus*, line 468; E. Fraenkel, *Elementi plautini in Plauto*, p. 22. An ordinary merchant invited only his family and friends (Dessau, no. 3428, as late as 184 A D); after Augustus, when the Emperors reserved for themselves the monopoly of euergetism in Rome, as will be seen in chapter IV, section 8, the 'tithes to Hercules' to which everyone was invited ceased to be part of the Roman scene.

161. Dessau, no. 3413.

162. D. van Berchem, *Les Distributions de blé et d'argent à la plèbe romaine sous l'Empire* (1939), p. 120.

163. Plutarch, *Life of Sulla*, 35. Any flesh not eaten was thrown into the Tiber. This was certainly a ritual practice; in Greece it was impious to allow the guests to take any of the food away with them.

164. Plutarch, *Life of Crassus*, 2 and 12; Athenaeus, V, 65.

165. Plutarch, *Life of Lucullus*, 37; Suetonius, *Caesar*, 38; Dio Cassius, XLIII, 21; Appian, *Civil Wars*, II, 102.

166. See note 97. Livy, XXXVII, 46. *Triumphatores* were not the only ones to pay the tithe to Hercules: see in Cicero, *De Officiis*, II, 17, 58, the description of the banquet given by Aufidius Orestes.

167. Cicero, *Pro Sestio*, 48, 103. See the penetrating essay by J. Béranger, 'Les jugements de Cicéron sur les Gracques', in *Aufstieg und Niedergang der römischen Welt*, H. Temporini (ed.), vol. I (De Gruyter, 1972), p. 732.

168. The bibliography is considerable, but the corpus of sources very limited. They can be reviewed by consulting preferably: Marquardt, *Staatsverwaltung*, vol. II, pp. 114–35; G. Cardinali's article on 'Frumentatio' in De Ruggiero's *Dizionario epigrafico* (Bretschneider, reprinted 1961); D. van Berchem, *Les Distributions de blé et d'argent à la plèbe de Rome sous l'Empire* (thesis, University of Geneva, 1939); P. A. Brunt, *Italian Manpower, 225 BC–AD 14* (Oxford, 1971), pp. 376–82.

169. Van Berchem, *Les Distributions de blé et d'argent*, p. 18; C. Meier, *Res Publica Amissa*, p. 110, note 277.

170. Cicero, *De Domo Sua*, 5, 11.

171. Id., *Pro Plancio*, 26, 64.

172. Id., *Ad Atticum*, V, 21, 8.

173. The story recounted by Livy, II, 34, 7, may in fact be explicable by a mistake on the part of the author or of his source, transposing to the fifth century an arbitrary fixing of the price of the corn which the Republic, much later, was to receive from its province of Sicily as tax or requisition. When a censor fixed the maximum price of a wine (Pliny, *Natural History*, XIV, 14, 95) he did this in his capacity of censor of morals (Mommsen, *Staatsrecht*, vol. II, p. 382).

174. Cicero, *In Verrem*, II, 3; Livy, XXXI, 4: 'a huge quantity of grain, sent from Africa by Publius Scipio, [the aediles] sold to the populace at four *asses* a measure'; XXX, 26; XXXI, 50; XXXIII, 42: 'The curule aediles ... distributed to the people one million measures of grain at two *asses* per measure. The Sicilians had brought this to Rome as a mark of respect to Gaius Flaminius himself and to his father' (cf. E. Badian, *Foreign Clientelae, 264–70 BC* (Oxford, 1988), pp. 158 and 161). We may presume that the oil Caesar had distributed as a *congiarium* in 46 (Suetonius, *Caesar*, 38; Dio Cassius, XLIII, 21) was provided by Africa, as a tax-payment (Plutarch, *Life of Caesar*, 55).

175. For his *cura annonae* of 57 Pompey received 40 million sesterces (Cicero, *Ad Quintum Fratrem*, II, 5, 1). The Lex Terentia Cassia of 73 and the *senatus consultum* (Mommsen, *Staatsrecht*, vol. III, p. 1130) opened an annual credit of nearly three million sesterces for purchases of corn in Sicily: Cicero, *In Verrem*, II, 3 and 5; cf. J. Carcopino, *La Loi de Hiéron et les Romains* (1914), pp. 178–80 and 273; the year 75 was troubled by famine (Sallust, *Histories*, II, 45 (Maurenbrecher)) and, as aedile, Hortensius had had to distribute corn (*In Verrem*, II, 3).

176. Coins commemorate the aediles of former times who distributed corn at a low price: Sydenham, *The Coinage of the Roman Republic*, p. 54, no. 463, and p. 60, no. 494 (cf. Pliny, *Natural History*, XVIII, 4, and XXXIV, 11); p. 61, no. 500 (cf. Pliny, XVIII, 3).

177. There is a list of the *largesses* of aediles in Marquardt, *Staatsverwaltung*, vol. II, pp. 114 and 136; see also Mommsen, *Staatsrecht*, vol. II, p. 503, note 1, who concludes: 'In most cases it is impossible to say whether the aediles were the organs of public generosity or financed their *largesses* out of their own resources.'

178. Cicero, *In Verrem*, II, 3.

179. The *largesses* of aediles were always isolated gestures (note 175), and when Seius distributed oil *per totum annum* Pliny makes express mention of this.

180. The most famous was the aedile Seius, who sold a bushel of corn to the people at a low price and also oil for a whole year: Cicero, *De Officiis*, II, 17, 58; Pliny, *Natural History*, XV, 2, and XVIII, 16: Seius paid for everything himself; Cicero adds that it did not ruin him ('nec turpi jactura, nec maxima').

181. Cicero, *De Officiis*, II, 16, 57: 'And yet I realize that in our country, even in the good old times, it had become a settled custom to expect magnificent entertainments from the very best men in their year of aedileship.'

182. Livy, XXV, 2, with commentary by F. Münzer, *Adelsparteien und Adelsfamilien*, p. 188.

183. Cf. Mommsen, *Staatsrecht*, vol. II, p. 672; E. Meyer, *Caesars Monarchie*, p. 118. In June 44 Brutus and Cassius were appointed commissioners for corn and ordered to go to Asia and Sicily to buy it (Cicero, *Ad Atticum*, XV, 9 and 12): they were indeed in real need of an excuse to leave Rome. On the extraordinary commissioners for corn, see note 148 and Mommsen, *Staatsrecht*, vol. II, pp. 671, 238, 571–2.

184. F. Heichelheim, *Wirtschaftliche Schwankungen der Zeit von Alexander bis Augustus* (1930), p. 74.

185. P. A. Brunt, *Italian Manpower*, p. 376. (Under Gaius's law grain was sold at a little over one and a half sesterces the bushel, which was, apparently, less than half the normal price.) Throughout the early period of the Empire the 'fair price' of a bushel of grain (eight litres) was, in everyone's opinion, four sesterces (or one *denarius*). For example, in the second century some plebeians thank a *euergetēs* for selling them grain at one denarius the bushel in time of famine (*Corpus*, XI, 6117). At Antioch in Pisidia, during a famine, the governor of the province fixed the price of a bushel at one *denarius* (D. M. Robinson, 'A new Latin economic edict from Pisidian Antioch', in *Transactions of the American Philological Association*, LV (1924), p. 7). In Sicily, even

in Verres' time, the *frumentum aestimatum* stood at one *denarius* the bushel (Cicero, *In Verrem*, II, 3 *passim*). In the *Res Gestae* (15, 2 and 4) Augustus stops counting in sesterces and counts in *denarii* when speaking of distributions of corn, for he is thinking of the equivalence of one bushel and one *denarius* (U. Wilcken, *Berliner Akademieschriften*, vol. II, p. 6, note 1). Actually, one ought first of all to consider whether the problem of the price of corn has one meaning only. In my opinion, we have to see the matter as follows. The larger part of the corn consumed was not the object of monetary transactions at all: many peasants used their corn for their own subsistence, and most wage-earners were paid in corn, which they ate and did not resell. Furthermore, since the currency served as measure of value in Rome, it was the time-honoured custom to measure the value of corn at one *denarius* the bushel, this being the *justum pretium*. That was nominal and irrefutable, since this corn was not acquired in the market and was not exchanged. One was simply able to hire a workman for a nominal wage of so many *denarii*, which one paid in corn: this corn never confronted other commodities which were the object of truly monetary transactions. This nominal price of corn could remain fixed and proverbial for decades, just like wage rates. But when a famine occurred, self-sufficiency and payment in corn for services rendered no longer fed the people adequately. They had to buy their corn in the market, where, of course, its value was greater than one *denarius* the bushel. Corn thus circulated at two levels. On one of them corn had no price, except nominally, while on the other it had its market price. In case of famine, the authorities undertook to sell corn at its *justum pretium*, its nominal price, the effects of this being either nil or catastrophic. A natural consequence was that the social groups that were paid in corn were better off than those paid in coin.

186. We know a case of a former consul going to buy his state corn (Cicero, *Tusculan Disputations*, III, 20, 48).

187. Subsequent corn laws fixed a maximum of five bushels per month (Brunt, p. 378). Cato gave his slaves four bushels per month (*De Agri Cultura*, 56).

188. G. E. Rickman, *Roman Granaries and Store Buildings* (Cambridge, 1971), p. 173.

189. P. A. Brunt, *Italian Manpower*, p. 240. To the same effect, see E. Badian, *Roman Imperialism in the Late Republic* (Blackwell, 1968), p. 49. On Gaius's action as a whole, see P. A. Brunt, 'The army and the land in the Roman Revolution', in *Journal of Roman Studies*, 1962, p. 70; 'The Roman mob', in *Past and Present*, 1966, p. 18.

190. E. Badian, *Roman Imperialism in the Late Republic*, pp. 47–8. On the other hand, the organization of the taxes in Asia by Gaius Gracchus

was intended by him to be as favourable to the provincials themselves as to the Treasury; cf. E. Badian, *Foreign Clientelae, 264–70 BC*, pp. 184 and 287.

191. *De Officiis*, II, 21, 72 (M. Octavius's corn law, which was in fact the abrogation of Gaius's: Cicero, *Brutus*, 222).

192. Dio Cassius, XXXVIII, 13: προῖκα. Cicero, *Pro Sestio*, 25, 55, implies that Clodius was indeed the initiator of free grain, and so does Asconius, p. 8 (Clark). On the state of Rome's finances after the law of 58, see P. A. Brunt, 'Porcius Cato and the annexation of Cyprus', in *Journal of Roman Studies*, LV (1965), especially p. 117.

193. See below, chapter IV, section 8.

194. Tacitus, *Histories*, IV, 38.

195. On the Imperial service of the Annona, see O. Hirschfeld, *Verwaltungsbeamten*; on the companies of shipowners and merchants, J. P. Waltzing, *Étude historique sur les corporations professionnelles chez les Romains*, vol. II, pp. 19–115 *passim*; generally, Marquardt, *Staatsverwaltung*, vol. II, pp. 125–35; cf. also P. Baldacci, ' "Negotiatores" e "mercatores frumentarii" nel periodo imperiale', in *Istituto Lombardo, Rendiconti* (*Classe de Lettere*), vol. CI (1967), pp. 273–91, which I have been able to read through the kindness of André Tchernia.

196. Tacitus, *Annals*, II, 87; the price of grain in Rome was, depending on estimates and years, either two, three or four sesterces the bushel (Baldacci, pp. 279–82).

197. Marquardt, vol. II, pp. 125–7.

198. Suetonius, *Claudius*, 18.

199. The prefect of the Annona had agents in the various provinces: Mommsen, *Staatsrecht*, vol. II, p. 1043, note 4.

200. Pliny praises Trajan for never having extorted corn under colour of buying it (*Panegyricus*, 29, 5).

201. Suetonius, *Augustus*, 41: 'In times of food shortage he often sold grain to every man on the citizens' list at a very cheap rate; occasionally he supplied it free; and doubled the number of free money-coupons [*tesserae nummariae*].' Thus, privileged persons had the right to buy from the Emperor at any time a certain quantity of corn, evidently at a favourable price, and the *tessera nummaria* was the token of this right. In time of famine the Emperor doubled the number of coupons held by each privileged person (so that this person could get all the food he needed from the Annona, without needing to buy extra corn on the private market). Furthermore, the Emperor had corn sold to the plebeians at a very low price in time of famine. It would seem that the praetorians, before obtaining the right to a ration of free grain, originally formed one group of the privileged persons who had a permanent right to buy grain from the Emperor (Tacitus, *Annals*, XV,

72; Suetonius, *Nero*, 10; cf. Rostovtzeff in Pauly-Wissowa, VII, under 'Frumentum', especially col. 181; M. Durry, *Les Cohortes prétoriennes* (De Boccard, reprinted 1968), p. 269).

202. For these epitaphs, see Dessau, nos. 6063–70; *L'Année épigraphique*, 1928, no. 70; D. van Berchem, *Les Distributions de blé et d'argent*, pp. 36–43.

203. Dio Cassius, LIII, 2, and LV, 26.

204. Id., LXII, 18; cf. van Berchem, p. 75. A vigorous measure in which – as often under Nero – we can perceive the action of the Imperial council (*consilium principis*), which seems to have been particularly talented, at least at the beginning of this reign.

205. Suetonius, *Caesar*, 41.

206. See the end of note 201.

207. J. P. Waltzing, *Étude historique sur les corporations*, vol. I, Addenda, p. 519.

208. Van Berchem, *Les Distributions de blé et d'argent*, p. 49.

209. *Digest*, XXXI, 49, 1; V, 1, 52, 1: 'If a testator instructs his trustee to buy *tesserae frumentariae* for his freedmen ...'; XXXI, 87 pr.

210. *Digest*, XXXI, 87 pr., which is very close to Justinian's *Institutes*, 2, 20, 6; on *causa lucrativa* in this passage, see Jacques Michel, *Gratuité en droit romain* (Free University of Brussels, Institut Solvay, 1962), p. 419. See also B. Biondi, *Successione testamentaria e donazioni*, second edn (Giuffrè, Milan, 1955), p. 394.

211. *Fragmenta Vaticana*, 272, and *Digest*, XXXII, 35 pr.; Mommsen, *Staatsrecht*, vol. II, p. 447, note 4.

212. *Digest*, XXXII, 35 pr.

213. Mommsen, *Staatsrecht*, vol. II, p. 447, note 4; p. 461; cf. p. 472.

214. Same solution in *Digest*, XXXI, 87 pr. (mentioned in note 210), in XXXII, 11, 16 (a *militia* is left, by mistake, to a slave, who, as such, cannot take up this employment: the slave's owner will receive the value of the *militia*), and in XXXI, 49, 1 (mentioned in note 216).

215. Since a slave could not hold this post. On the sale and bequest of *militiae*, see *Codex Justiniani*, VIII, 13, 27; *Digest*, IV, 4, 3, 7; XXXI, 22 ('a *militia*, or the sum that can be obtained by selling it'); XXXII, 11, 16; XXXII, 102, 3 (if you bequeath a *militia* your heir will also have to pay to the legatee the gratuity or *introitus* which the new official has to give to his superior or colleagues when taking up office); XXXIV, 1, 18, 2 (a freedman cannot take up a *militia* which has been bequeathed to him). For the sale of *decuriae*, see *Fragmenta Vaticana*, 272, and the fact that certain ushers were *immunes* (see chapter IV, note 341). I have not been able to read G. Kolias, *Aemter- und Würdenkauf im frühbyzantinischen Reich* (1939).

216. *Digest*, XXXI, 49, 1. All these passages in which appointments as officials are put on the same footing as military appointments (*militiae*) evidently relate to the Roman administration as it was in the fourth century (or towards the end of the third) and may be later interpolations in the *Digest*.

217. Plutarch, *Life of Crassus*, 2; we must take this as 'an army', not as 'a legion' (as is suggested by J. Harmand, *L'Armée et le Soldat à Rome*, p. 171, note 170), for Cicero also reports this saying (*De Officiis*, I, 8, 25) and writes *exercitum alere*; cf. also Pliny, *Natural History*, XXXIII, 134. For the interpretation of *princeps* in this phrase, see M. Gelzer, *Caesar*, p. 40, note 2; but it will be observed that *princeps* can mean 'leader of a party' (Caesar, *Gallic War*, VI, 11: each faction among the Celts has its *princeps*) and I think that this is what the word means here.

218. Sallust, *Histories, Letter of Pompey*, 2 and 9 (II, 98 (Maurenbrecher)); cf. Plutarch, *Life of Sertorius*, 21, and *Life of Pompey*, 20.

219. Velleius Paterculus, II, 29: 'ex agro Piceno, qui totus paternis ejus clientelis refertus erat'; Plutarch, *Life of Pompey*, 6. Cf. C. Cichorius, *Römische Studien* (Wissensch. Buchgesell., reprinted 1961), p. 158; M. Gelzer, *Kleine Schriften*, vol. I, p. 95; Syme, *The Roman Revolution*, pp. 28 and 92; Wiseman, *New Men in the Senate*, p. 41; E. Badian, *Foreign Clientelae*, p. 228; J. Harmand, *L'Armée et le Soldat à Rome*, p. 446; M. Gelzer, *Pompeius* (Bruchmann, 1949), p. 36.

220. The story 'shows the provincial administration of that period in a strange light', writes M. Gelzer, *Caesar*, p. 24; on the facts, see H. Strasburger, *Caesars Eintritt in die Geschichte* (1938), p. 84.

221. D. Timpe, 'Caesars gallischer Krieg und das Problem des römischen Imperialismus', in *Historia*, 1965, p. 189.

222. M. Gelzer, *Caesar*, pp. 167–8.

223. *Gallic War*, I, 10, 3 and II, 1, 1; Suetonius, *Caesar*, 24; M. Gelzer, *Caesar*, p. 124, note 1; P. A. Brunt, *Italian Manpower*, p. 467; J. Harmand, *L'Armée et le Soldat à Rome*, p. 171.

224. Dio Cassius, XLVI, 29.

225. R. Syme, *The Roman Revolution*, pp. 130–31; E. Gabba, *Appiano e la storia delle guerre civili* (La Nuova Italia, 1956), p. 194, note 1; Dio Cassius, XLVI, 46 and LIII, 22; Appian, *Civil Wars*, III, 94, 387.

226. *The Republic*, 372e ff.; 422a ff.; *Laws*, 677b–679d.

227. Polybius, VI, 57.

228. *Civitas Dei*, I, 30–33; II, 18–21.

229. *Inferno*, 16, 73; cf. *Paradiso*, 15, 97; 16, 49.

230. *Gulliver's Travels*, 3, 9, end. See also N. Nassar, *La Pensée réaliste d'Ibn Khaldun* (PUF, 1967), pp. 169, 178, 205.

231. Polybius, VI, 9. The theme of the demagogues' *largesses* at the Treasury's expense is familiar in Cicero and comes from Polybius, XX, 6 and XXIV, 7. Polybius suspects these demagogues of seeking to establish their tyranny (as Chaeron had done in Sparta (Polybius, XXIV, 7); Molpagoras, at Cius (Polybius, XV, 21), made his rule popular by the same means).

232. Dante, *Inferno*, 16, 73:

> A glut of self-made men and quick-got gain
> Have bred excess in thee and pride, forsooth,
> O Florence! till e'en now thou criest for pain.

Cf. *Paradiso*, 16, 67. Theophrastus, *Characters*, 26, 1. Sallust, *Catiline*, 10ff.; *Jugurtha*, 41ff.; Sallust or Pseudo-Sallust, *Letters to Caesar*, 1, 5; 1, 7–8; 2, 5; 2, 7; 2, 10. Cicero, *De Officiis*, II, 21, 75 to 22, 78; 23, 84 to 24, 85.

233. Polybius, VI, 13–15.

234. The explanation in terms of class struggle is fully developed in Fustel de Coulanges, *Histoire des institutions politiques de l'ancienne France*, vol. IV: *Les Origines du système féodal*, p. 94. Octavius's supporters were his father's veterans; and the men active in the civil war were not all sons or grandsons of ruined peasants. The history of the civil wars would be comprehensible without the agrarian crisis.

235. *Istorie fiorentine*, 7, 4.

236. Cicero, *Pro Murena*, 36, 76: 'Odit populus Romanus privatam luxuriam, publicam magnificentiam diligit.'

237. Plutarch, *Life of Pompey*, 40.

238. Suetonius, *Augustus*, 72, cf. 57; G. Lugli, *Roma antica: il centro monumentale* (Bardi, Rome, 1946), p. 409ff.

239. Suetonius, *Augustus*, 29. On the other hand there was not, in the grounds of Augustus's house, a temple of Vesta, rivalling the one in the Forum, but merely an altar, as has been shown by A. Degrassi, *Scritti vari di antichità*, vol. I, pp. 451–65. For another sign of Augustus's modesty, his refusal to have a monumental entrance with a pediment (the *fastigium* being reserved for temples), see A. Alföldi, *Die zwei Lorbeerbäume des Augustus* (Habelt, 1973), p. 14.

240. *Second Philippic*, 45, 116; Syme, *Sallust*, p. 119; Sallust, *Jugurtha*, 33, 4. A quite different point of view is that of M. Treu, 'Zur clementia Caesaris', in *Museum Helveticum*, V (1948), p. 187.

241. There is a break between Caesar and the various *principes* who preceded him (see the list of them in Wickert's article on 'Princeps' in Pauly-Wissowa, vol. XXII, cols. 2014–29); Scipio invented a new style of political relations; as general and as candidate he made *largesse*; neither Marius nor Sulla was particularly munificent.

242. Cicero, *Ad Atticum*, IV, 16, 14 (IV, 17, 7); Suetonius, *Caesar*, 26; Pliny, *Natural History*, XXXVI, 103 (for Caesar's Forum the purchase of the site alone cost 100 million sesterces); Meyer, *Caesars Monarchie*, p. 200; Gelzer, *Caesar*, pp. 140, 168, 177. Caesar was evidently authorized by a law to build on this site. Regarding the Basilica Aemilia it will be observed that the custom was to entrust the responsibility for reconstructing a public building to a descendant of the magistrate who (using public money, of course) had originally built it (notes 149 and 152); the Curia Hostilia, rebuilt by Sulla, was reconstructed by his son Faustus Sulla. In fact it was considered that the descendants of great families had a right and a moral duty with regard to the monuments which perpetuated the names of their forefathers (note 149). Caesar tactfully respected this sentiment. In practice, the fact that he entrusted the reconstruction of the building to Aemilius Paullus meant that he left the name of Aemilius associated with it and that the rebuilt basilica did not take the name 'Basilica Julia' (like the Greeks, the Romans attached the greatest importance to the builder's right to give his own name to his monument: see Mommsen, *Staatsrecht*, index, under 'Bauwesen'). Caesar also had good political reasons for conciliating Paullus: see Suetonius, *Caesar*, 29, where he writes bluntly: 'Caesar again won over the other consul – Aemilius Paullus – with a heavy bribe' – so that his proconsulate in Gaul might not be terminated.

243. Gelzer, p. 314; Meyer, pp. 388, 427, 497. These buildings were the subject of laws which Caesar caused to be passed (Cicero, *Ad Atticum*, XIII, 33a, 2).

244. Strabo, V, 3, 8: 'The early Romans made but little account of the beauty of Rome, because they were occupied with other, greater and more necessary matters; whereas the later Romans, and particularly those of today and in my time, have not fallen short in this respect either – indeed, they have filled the city with many beautiful structures.' I shall discuss in chapter IV the triumphal edifices erected by the *viri triumphales* under Augustus. The Emperor encouraged his party and all the rich men of Rome to embellish the city: Suetonius, *Augustus*, 29: 'principes viros saepe hortatus est'; Agrippa invited the rich to present to the public the works of art in their possession (Pliny, *Natural History*, XXXV, 26). Cf. chapter IV, note 314. When Tigranes founded Tigranocerta, his capital, 'every private person and every prince vied with the king in contributing to its increase and adornment' (Plutarch, *Life of Lucullus*, 26).

245. Dio Cassius, LIII, 27. Agrippa completed and dedicated the Saepta Julia, 'instead of undertaking to repair a road' (id., LIII, 23). We know that Augustus had the roads repaired by *triumphatores* as their triumphal monument (chapter IV, notes 337 and 339). For the Pantheon, see J.

Beaujeu, *La Religion romaine à l'apogée de l'Empire: la politique religieuse des Antonins* (Les Belles Lettres, 1955), pp. 118–23. I am aware that the addition 'and to all the other gods' is frequently met in prayers or hymns (G. Boissier, *La Religion romaine d'Auguste aux Antonins*, vol. I, p. 101, note 5) and is intended to appease the jealousy of those other gods; but the point is that this addition is rare in inscriptions (Veyne in *Latomus*, 1965, p. 936, note 1) and not every temple was a Pantheon. For wordings such as 'to Zeus, to Heracles, to Poseidon and to all the other gods', see Dittenberger, *Sylloge*, no. 1122; Servius, *Ad Georgica*, 1, 21; a note in the Kiesling-Heinze edition of Horace, *Carmen Saeculare*, 73; G. Appel, *De Romanorum Precationibus* (Religionsgesch. Vers. und Vorarb., VII, 1909), p. 83, note 3; and, especially, E. Fraenkel, *Aeschylus: Agamemnon, a commentary*, vol. II, p. 262. For the *monumenta Agrippae* in the Campus Martius, see M. Reinhold, *Marcus Agrippa, a Biography* (Bretschneider, reprinted 1965), pp. 74–5 and 96; for Agrippa's buildings at Nîmes (the Maison Carrée especially; the Enceinte de Nîmes was a gift from Octavius himself) and at Emerita (the theatre), see Reinhold, pp. 90 and 94; for the significance of the ramparts of Nîmes, see P. A. Février, 'Enceinte et colonie de Nîmes à Vérone, Toulouse et Tipasa', in *Revue d'études ligures*, XXXV (1969), p. 277.

246. E. Meyer, *Caesars Monarchie*, pp. 385–7; M. Gelzer, *Caesar*, pp. 284–6; D. van Berchem, *Les Distributions de blé et d'argent*, p. 120. Velleius Paterculus, II, 56, shows how the people remembered this.

247. For the facts, see M. Reinhold, *Marcus Agrippa, a Biography* (Bretschneider, reprinted 1965), pp. 46–52; see especially Dio Cassius, XLIX, 43.

248. On this *aedilitas post consulatum*, see Mommsen, *Staatsrecht*, vol. I, p. 537, note 1. No other example of a consular aedile is known.

249. R. Syme, *The Roman Revolution*, pp. 276–80; cf. Mommsen, *Staatsrecht*, vol. II, p. 719. For a different interpretation, see U. Wilcken, *Berliner Akademieschriften zur alten Geschichte und Papyruskunde*, vol. I (Zentralantiquariat der Deutschen Demokratischen Republik, Leipzig, 1970), pp. 208–27: *Das angebliche Staatsreich Octavians in Jahre 32* (Octavius's powers lasted until 31 December 32, not until 31 December 33). See now P. Herrmann, *Der römische Kaisereid* (Vandenhoeck and Ruprecht, 1968), p. 87.

250. 'Voluntarily', ἑκών: Dio Cassius uses the language of Greek municipal euergetism. It is true that, in the period of which he speaks, it was increasingly difficult to find aediles, because this honour was a ruinous one (Dio Cassius, XLIX, 16 and LIII, 2). Dio has in mind a generous *euergetēs* who 'does not have to be pressed' to assume a function and who makes *largesse*. As Agrippa had made *largesse*, Dio presumes that he had not needed to be pressed to accept the aedileship.

251. Dio Cassius, XLIX, 43; cf. Pliny, *Natural History*, XXXVI, 121.

252. M. Nilsson, in an article which appeared in Swedish in 1912 and was republished in translation in his *Opuscula Selecta*, vol. II (Gleerup, Lund, 1952), pp. 930–37: 'The economic basis of the principate of Augustus'. The discovery was made, independently, by U. Wilcken, in 1931: see now his *Berliner Akademieschriften zur alten Geschichte und Papyruskunde*, vol. I, pp. 342–55: *Zu den impensae der Res gestae divi Augusti*, with a correction of detail in vol. II, p. 8, note 1: *Zur Genesis der Res gestae*. See also T. Frank, 'On Augustus and the aerarium', in *Journal of Roman Studies*, XXIII (1933), p. 143; W. Ensslin in *Rheinisches Museum*, LXXXI (1932), p. 335; Garzetti in *Athenaeum*, XLI (1953), p. 321.

253. Here are my own suppositions on this subject. We know that it is very difficult, at any time, to calculate the quantity of specie in circulation (for attempts at estimates for the twentieth century, see J. Rueff, *Théorie des phénomènes monétaires: statique* (Payot, 1922), p. 104). Estimates range between one-fifth and one-thirteenth of the annual national product, with each writer trying to conceive the amount of specie needed for transactions: see Alfred Marshall, *Money, Credit and Commerce* (Macmillan, 1924), p. 45, note 7. For example, Galiani estimated that the 18 million ducats existing in the kingdom of Naples sufficed for 144 million transactions every year (C. Rist, *Histoire des doctrines relatives au crédit et à la monnaie*, p. 98). 'Now we know very imperfectly what is the quantity of currency in most countries, and we know nothing at all as to the average rapidity of circulation' (W. S. Jevons, *Money and the Mechanism of Exchange*, 1875, p. 336). Attempted estimates of the number of coins struck, themselves highly hypothetical (R. Turcan, 'Pour une étude quantitative de la frappe du bronze sous le Haut-Empire', in *Congresso internazionale di numismatica*, 1965, pp. 353–61; P. R. Franke and M. Hirmer, *La Monnaie grecque* (Flammarion, 1966), p. 29 and bibliography, p. 146), do not tell us what total number of coins was circulating at a given moment. Nevertheless, it is possible to establish the order of magnitude of this number; we know, for instance, that Tiberius left in the Treasury 2,700,000,000 sesterces (Suetonius, *Caligula*, 37) and that a public loan of 100 millions was sufficient to re-establish the circulation of money (Tacitus, *Annals*, VI, 17; Suetonius, *Tiberius*, 48). We may therefore assume that, in the early Empire, the quantity of specie might amount to a number of billions of sesterces which, at most, could be counted on the fingers of two hands. What was the effect of Augustus's 600 millions, under these conditions? Quite apart from the non-quantitative effects, an injection of fresh currency may cause prices to rise, but it may also be absorbed by an increase in the population, or by a multiplication of the stages of production and sale (the volume of intermediate transactions increas-

ing in relation to the unchanged final product), or by a reduction of the velocity of circulation (in particular, if expensive goods like real estate become more often the object of transactions, money will need to be hoarded so as to obtain the liquidities needed for the acquisition of these goods). But the most likely effect is that more exchanges will be effected by money payments, instead of by barter. We must not forget that, in Rome, some rents and most wages were paid in kind. A workman received his food in the form of a certain quantity of corn; a story about Augustus, in Macrobius, *Saturnalia*, II, 4, 28 is illuminating. Cf. Cantillon, *Essai sur la nature du commerce* (Institut National d'Études Démographiques, reprinted 1952), pp. 70 and 98; J. Marchal and J. Lecaillon, *Théorie des flux monétaires* (Cujas, 1967), pp. 27 and 31; J. M. Kelly has discerned the problem clearly, in a book on a quite different subject, *Roman Litigation* (Oxford, 1966), pp. 76–9.

254. J. Béranger, 'Fortune privée impériale et État', in *Mélanges offerts à Georges Bonnard* (Droz, Geneva, 1966), pp. 151–60, commenting on Tacitus, *Annals*, I, 8. Béranger writes: 'It was by means of the private law of inheritance that Augustus ensured his political succession, the principate being a conquest won in advance thanks to the resources which the *princeps* left to his heirs. Owing to the absence of a constitutional regulation (unthinkable because incompatible with the fiction of the *res publica*, an untouchable dogma) it was the *opes* that conferred, transmitted and perpetuated the principate.'

255. Tacitus, *Annals*, XV, 18: 'se annuum sescenties sestertium rei publicae largiri'. The difficulty is this. When the Emperors speak of their *largesses*, the word means sometimes (and no doubt especially at the beginning of the Empire) a *largesse* which the Emperor makes as an act of patronage *out of his private fortune*, and so the word '*largesse*' is here to be taken literally. Much more often, however, and almost regularly from Vespasian onward, the Emperors' '*largesses*' represent expenditure drawn from public funds (the Fiscus, the Patrimonium, or even the Treasury), but which are verbally attributed to the Emperors' *largesse*, in a sort of monarchical style of expression, just as the most ordinary administrative act was attributed to 'the King's bounty'. Was Nero using this monarchical style? If so, we must understand either that he paid into the coffers of the Treasury (managed by the Senate) 60 millions taken from the coffers of the Fiscus (managed by the Imperial administration), or more simply still that he decided to increase by 60 millions the ordinary total of public expenditure, from whichever of the public coffers it was drawn. But what if, on the contrary, Nero's words are to be taken literally? In that case, as a good patron, he gave to the state 60 millions taken from his private income and paid into the Fiscus (or into the Treasury, it matters little which).

What inclines me to favour the second interpretation is that Nero intended, by his *largesse*, to fill the vacuum then existing in the Fiscus, which had been exhausted by the previous Emperors: so that this was neither a payment from the Fiscus into the Treasury nor additional expenditure, but a payment out of Nero's private purse into the Fiscus.

256. O. Hirschfeld, *Die kaiserliche Verwaltungsbeamten*, pp. 9 and 19. See chapter IV, note 92.

257. On the *Res Gestae* as *elogium* rather than political testament, see Dessau, in *Klio*, XXII (1929), p. 266; E. Hohl, in *Klio*, XXX (1937), p. 323; on the use of the first person, J. Gagé, *Res gestae divi Augusti*, second edn (Les Belles Lettres, 1950), p. 28; H. H. Armstrong, 'Autobiographic elements in Latin inscriptions', in *University of Michigan Studies, Humanistic Series*, vol. III: *Latin Philology*, C. L. Meader (ed.) (Macmillan, 1910; Johnson Reprint, 1967), p. 261: 'autobiographic record' (the (the funerary and sepulchral character of which is not essential); G. Misch, *Geschichte der Autobiographie*, vol. I (Francke, Bern, 1949), p. 230 (Eng. tr. *History of Autobiography in Antiquity*, vol. I (London, 1950), pp. 223–4), on the use of the first person in Greek and Roman epigraphy.

258. Self-glorification, whether in the first or the third person, sepulchral or non-sepulchral, was alien to the Hellenistic notables: they glorified themselves by having engraved the decrees in which their city had awarded public honours to them. 'Under the Empire Roman epitaphs came to give a degree of personal detail which has little parallel in Greek epitaphs; even the Republic has, as far as its great families were concerned, its pleasure in *elogia*, real or fictitious,' writes A. D. Nock, in *Essays on Religion and the Ancient World*, vol. II (Oxford, 1972), p. 778. We can contrast with the *Res Gestae* an epitaph of the genuinely Hellenic sort, that of Virgil: 'Mantua bore me, Calabria [i.e. Apulia] took my life, now Naples has me: I sang of pastures, of crops and of heroes.' This epitaph says nothing, or almost nothing, of what the man was or did (it seems to assume that all human lives are much the same, in our common human condition); the only individual variations are the place where one is born and the place where one dies. One is a man, and does not perform individual exploits. Cf. *Aeneid*, XII, 546: 'Here was thy bourne of death; beneath Ida was thy stately home, thy stately home at Lyrnesus, in Laurentine soil thy sepulchre.' This epitaph may be called etiological, following the practice of those historiographies which, instead of recounting the history of a city, restricted themselves to telling of its foundation. All cities are alike and their life is made up of more or less the same sort of events; the only thing one needs to know is that they existed and how they began. For this kind of epitaph, cf. N. I. Herescu in *Ovidiana*, 1958, p. 422.

259. *Corpus*, I, 638 (and p. 725) and 833; Degrassi, no. 454.
260. G. Misch, *Geschichte der Autobiographie*, vol. I, especially p. 288 (Eng. tr. p. 276); W. Seidle, *Sueton und die antike Biographie* (C. H. Beck, 1951), p. 179.

CHAPTER IV

The Emperor and His Capital

It was the Emperor who provided Rome with the bread and shows spoken of by Juvenal; sometimes he provided free baths.[1] The municipal notables did as much in their respective cities. 'The kings of the Gentiles,' says the Gospel according to St Luke, 'exercise lordship over them; and they that exercise authority upon them are called benefactors [*euergetai*].'[2] The *Res Gestae* of Augustus is the epitaph of a patron of the state. Were not the successors of Augustus merely *euergetai* of Rome and of their Empire as a whole? Their propaganda, or what we term their propaganda, celebrates their liberality, and their *euergesiai* are identical with those of the oligarchs of the Republic and of the municipal notables. If we had to take the ancients at their word, we should say that liberality, the aristocratic virtue, was a royal virtue as well. Is not the monarch the supreme model, the perfection of humanity, according to Dio of Prusa? We should surely wonder whether the basis of the Imperial power was liberality, a human virtue, or charisma, a divine one, and we should conclude that the Emperor reigned as a *euergetēs* and was deified for his benefactions.

Was the Emperor a *euergetēs* in the same way as a notable or as a member of his Senate? No, except by name. As Louis Robert once wrote to me, the Imperial mantle is not discarded like that, it cannot be left in the cloakroom. The municipal notables gave games by virtue of their social superiority and because their relation to politics (the petty politics of the autonomous communes) was a delicate matter. The senators of the Republic, who were engaged in very high politics, gave games in order to show the people that, even if they did little *through* the people, they did a lot *for* them, and also to remind the electors that they were beholden to the senators, and not their mandators. But what about the Emperor? He was not satisfied with merely taking a share in high politics. He was the sole sovereign, and could say, '*L'État, c'est moi.*'

The Republican state was a moral person different from its passing representatives. It was also an entity created by the patriotism or the sense of political duty of the senatorial 'collective'. As person and entity it expressed its majesty by a display of official ceremony, and it justified its authority by presenting its commandments as obligations to which everyone had to submit, out of obedience and patriotism. Now, however, the state was the Emperor. The kingly style replaced the appeal to each man's civic sense by an exaltation of the personal virtues of the Emperor. Instead of obeying out of devotion to the state, people were to trust in the sovereign's providence. As for the ceremonies of the Republic, these would now surround the very person of the monarch.

To present the impersonal law as the individual will of a virtuous sovereign, who gave the people bread and circuses out of euergetism, and conversely to present the individuality of the monarch, who showed himself to the people at the Circus, as an incarnation of the majesty of the state: herein lay the whole secret of Imperial euergetism.

1. *Autonomy and heteronomy*

HETERONOMY, ABSOLUTE RIGHT, PUBLIC OPINION

There are two poles to political obedience: I may claim to be obeying only for my own good and as though I were my own legislator, and in this attitude I am autonomous; and I obey someone else. The formal reasons for this dualism are many. The 'someone else' may not always wish to do me good (politics involves conflicts of opinion or interest), or wishes to do me good against my will (he forbids me to lean out of the window of a railway carriage in motion): or else he wills something on my behalf (I only dream of having a crack at the hereditary enemy, but it is necessary for the head of state to take the steps signifying a declaration of war, because I do not have the necessary knowledge). Thus I end up giving my obedience once for all on a basis of perpetual credit, as it were, instead of considering on each separate occasion whether or not to obey. This is all the more important because politics is carried on 'in real time' and cannot wait. There is not time to convince everyone and the principle of *compelle intrare* has to be applied, for time presses.

To this day, these formal truths remain 'eternal', and apply to the United States no less than to the Roman Empire, though politics and social reality diversify them. As we know, political authority can come from three sources: from the ruled, from the gods (absolute right) or from the nature of things. If the monarch's power is not delegated to him by the persons under his rule and he reigns by absolute right, he will not be reabsorbed into his function: he will be himself, he will reign because he is master, and this will call for some ceremony on his part. Since he is the master it is only from virtue, from euergetism, that he does good to his subjects: he is not their servant. Finally he will be a god, or a ruler by the grace of God, for whence else could come his right to command men by virtue of being their superior, if it does not come from men? Imperial euergetism and deification of the Emperors are two effects of the same cause.

The monarch would not be able to separate himself from his function unless he were capable of abandoning it, but this he cannot do, since it is a right that belongs to him: a property-owner does not abandon his property. As against this, the monarch possesses such virtues that, to ensure my well-being, all that is needed is for him to be himself. Imperial euergetism was a sort of cult of the universal expressed in the royal individual. It contained two contrasting elements, the kingly style on the one hand, and pomp and circumstance on the other. The former reduced universality to the monarch's individual virtues, while the second conferred a universal value upon that individuality. The monarch was the state, and was invested with the majesty of the state.

The kingly style ascribed to the Emperor's bounty the public institutions themselves and even the most commonplace administrative decisions. If we were to take this phraseology literally (and it has happened), we should suppose that the Emperor was the owner of his Empire and knew no law other than his own will, as has also been alleged of the Hellenistic kings.[3] Through his bounty the Emperor ensured Rome's supply of bread, and through his clemency officials and soldiers who had served him were allowed to retire in comfort.[4]

On the other hand the monarch's person had a public aspect. He enjoyed the private relationship of a father or of a patron with the plebs of his capital. The events of his family life were occasions for rejoicing or mourning for all his subjects and he accorded, or allowed to be accorded, divine honours to his favourites.[5] He displayed in Rome and at the Circus a degree of pomp which turned the Eternal City into something like a king's court.

The private became public and the public became private. The monarchical function was a private possession, but this possession rendered public services. This would not have been the case if the Emperor had not been seen as having an absolute right to reign. For that to be so, however, the social, economic and mental state of the Roman world would have to have been such as to make the mass of the ruled so passive that they could not do other than submit to their rulers without passing judgement on them. In other words, there did not then exist the phenomenon called public opinion, which cannot coexist for long with absolute right, or consequently with the euergetism of a sovereign who is a god or who reigns by divine right. For public opinion does not consist in rebelling, suffering silently or being discontented, but in claiming that one has the *right* to be discontented and that the monarch, even when his ministers may have misled him, can nevertheless be at fault – whereas a property-owner cannot be at fault in relation to what is his own property. Of course the monarch is not a property-owner like other property-owners: he has duties to his subjects. But we know that he cannot fail in these duties, because he is infallibly good and euergetic. Therefore one cannot sit in judgement upon him.

2. Submission or public opinion

THE EPOCH WHEN NOBODY TALKED POLITICS

Manifestations of public opinion occur under all regimes, even if only in popular songs celebrating the king's latest victory, and conversely we find submission everywhere (the government being spoken of as 'them'): in all places and at all times there is autonomy and heteronomy. Everywhere, too, there is apoliticism, in the sense that public opinion, if it exists at all, does not itself make policy, but merely comments *post facto* on decisions taken by those to whom it has surrendered the care of politics. Even so, a gulf separates the political life of the Roman Empire or of an *ancien régime* monarchy from that of a modern democracy. Today public opinion passes judgement on the government; then, the people loved their sovereign and right-thinking persons praised submission as the duty of every loyal subject. Only the senatorial caste, the narrow ruling class who had knowledge of public business and public events, represented a sort of public opinion; decency compelled them to act responsibly and not to contradict the people's notion of the Emperor.

One would strangely misunderstand the realities of the past if one failed to appreciate that the people's love for the sovereign is a sentiment that has always existed, or nearly always, and that when the Emperor's name was spoken, this had to be done in the respectful and affectionate tone in which Catholics used to speak the name of the Pope. Evidence of this love was to be found everywhere: festivals and ceremonies, the Emperor's portrait displayed in all the shops, popular imagery.[6] This was not a sentiment that men chose to cultivate but one that was induced, like children's love for their father, and so it was automatically transferred to the next Emperor, or to a successful usurper.

The people loved their sovereign, they considered that taxes were too heavy, and they set a bulkhead between these two ideas. They despised the *publicani*[7] (who absorbed popular resentment in the same way as do the police in our day) so as not to express a view about Caesar. The Emperor's name was spoken with respect, but people did not have political opinions and political discussion was unknown. Things must have been somewhat more complicated among the senators. When they talked among themselves they can hardly have failed to let it show that they thought public affairs were going from bad to worse. But whoever spoke in that vein stopped, or was stopped, before he could criticize the reigning prince. If he defied that taboo, it would mean that a plot was being hatched against the Emperor, and that the critic was its recruiting sergeant.

So what did the people talk about when they discussed public affairs? The thousands of graffiti and painted inscriptions to be read on the walls of Pompeii surprise us, for there is not a single one that we should call political – only repetitions of 'Long live the Emperor' (*Augusto feliciter*). The Emperor is not politics. The latter, with its disputes and discussions, was purely local and concerned elections (if elections they were and not, as I believe, acclamations) and the necessities of life. Hundreds of 'electoral' acclamations painted on the walls of Pompeii have preserved for us the names of the local notables and *euergetai* who 'gave gladiators' or ensured the supply of bread. Likewise in the *Satyricon*, Trimalchio's guests talk about the meetings of the municipal Council, about notables who grow fat at the expense of the poor, about the high price of bread about the latest gladiatorial combat provided by a local *euergetēs* who is only a pretentious fellow, about a notable of the good old days who was respected and loved by all the plebs for his authority and honesty. At the same time, these guests rise to drink a toast to the Emperor, as protocol required.

SUBMISSION IN REVOLT

People talk about the prince, what he looks like. If the scene is Rome itself, people talk about the shows he provides. They talk of the 'good news' (*euangelia*), i.e. of the official announcement of a victory or of a happy event in the reigning family. Or else they revenge themselves on the Emperor by mocking him; in spite of what I wrote earlier, there is indeed one political graffito at Pompeii, directed against Nero, but it is an obscene graffito.[8]

In Rome, at Vespasian's funeral, a mime was given the task, 'according to custom', of following the procession in order to imitate the voice and mannerisms of the late prince and mock his meanness.[9]

Real opposition was either raised in the Emperor's own name or directed against his evil ministers, in order that he might be better served. Peasant revolts in Russia took place on the pretext of a non-existent decree by the Tsar, and in Rome the plebs believed more than once that Nero was not dead, but would return: there were several 'false Neros'.[10]

On other occasions discontent took the form of unhappy love. If only the monarch knew what was going on! But his ministers are deceiving him. The *vox populi* blamed Antiochus VII for trusting too much in wicked courtiers.[11] The just man who is suffering prefers to think that the monarch does not know the truth, because, if he did, that would mean all hope was gone. Since the monarch only acts virtuously he cannot be knowingly bad. All one can do is to sigh, 'God is too high above us and the Tsar too far away.'[12]

Accordingly political life was fairly simple. The monarch's only duty to the people was to make himself 'popular', and we shall see what that meant. In his non-symbolic political activity, however, he needed to take into consideration only the opinion of the senators and the attitude of the praetorian prefect, the provincial governors and the army commanders. He had no need to observe the reactions of the people, whose docility was taken for granted. If a popular revolt broke out, it would be like an earthquake. Politics consisted in stopping up holes as they appeared: an invasion here, a peasant or nationalist rebellion there, sometimes a financial crisis. Political action was often as peremptory as a police operation, the recipe being to strike down everything that moved, without thinking. In that way one could be more certain of success. Some of the religious persecutions require no explanation more subtle than that.

LEGAL RELATIONS

Heteronomy and autonomy being indissociable, the monarch both frightens and reassures, but as his power does not come to him from men,[13] any offence against the law is at the same time a revolt against the personal authority of the sovereign or his representatives, and is punished accordingly. In so far as it dealt with non-citizens, Roman penal practice knew no law. It exercised coercion, the penalties being left to the discretion of governors, who were 'sent by [the Emperor] for the punishment of evildoers and for the praise of them that do well', as the First Epistle of Peter has it.[14] In the governor's eyes there might be delinquency, even if no crime had been committed, when a provincial persisted in an attitude which, though perhaps innocent in terms of the law, was yet refractory to an order given him by the governor. I do not know whether Christianity is a crime in itself, Governor Pliny writes to his Emperor, but, while awaiting your instructions on that point, I have taken provisional measures: 'I interrogated them whether they were Christians; if they confessed it I repeated the question twice again, adding the threat of capital punishment; if they still persevered I ordered them to be executed. For whatever the nature of their creed might be, I could at least feel no doubt that contumacy and inflexible obstinacy deserved chastisement.'[15]

Intractability was punished even more severely than a breach of the law. On the other hand, a worthy citizen was not honoured: at most, one expressed satisfaction with his conduct. The Emperor and the governors did not award honours and statues, like the cities and the provincial leagues of cities, but confined themselves to public acknowledgement of the merits of a certain person in an official letter; instead of the civic 'honours' we have the 'testimonials' (*testimonia*, *martyriai*) of the Imperial authorities. In Rome itself, when statues of deserving magistrates were set up officially they were erected by the Senate, not by the Emperor, who was honoured but did not honour others.[16] The subjects of the Empire were in the Emperor's service; they were not autonomous citizens who acted more or less well. The Emperor was an individual and could not do homage to another individual without lowering himself; only a city, which was an entity, could do that.

The Emperor was not an entity, and his legal relations with his subjects lacked the anonymous coldness of the law. He did not act merely as legislator or judge. Besides his laws and constitutions, he could address the people in edicts which were in the nature of episcopal letters. In them the Emperor issued orders, but also, and more frequently, he gave advice, imparted information or handed out reprimands; for a father addressing his children can say whatever he likes to them.[17] By means of edicts the Emperor replied to insults, explained the good intentions that inspired his decisions,[18] deplored a brawl between supporters of rival gladiators, and invited the *equites* to come and listen to his speeches.[19] He reassured the people when an eclipse occurred. He educated them: Augustus 'even read whole volumes aloud to the Senate, and issued proclamations commending them to the people – such as ... Rutilius's *On the Need for Smaller Buildings*'.[20] Questions of elementary good behaviour were not beneath his attention, nor was spelling. Claudius went far enough in those two domains, but he was not the only one. Tiberius 'issued an edict against promiscuous kissing and the giving of good-luck gifts at New Year',[21] and there is reason to suspect that Hadrian decided that henceforth Romans should write *servos* and *vivos* instead of *servus* and *vivus*.[22]

The legislation of modern nations includes protective regulations, such as the banning of drugs, whereby the state seeks to defend individuals against themselves. Nevertheless this protective role is exercised in an impersonal style. When a Roman Emperor exercised it, and generally when he acted as legislator, he expressed himself as though addressing children: he blamed, threatened, rebuked. Augustus reprimanded by edict the spectators in the theatre who had hailed him as 'Master'. On one occasion, when the people called on him to fulfil his promise of a distribution, he told them that he would keep his word (for Emperors make promises just like ordinary men who are free to give or withhold their word); but on another occasion, when he was asked to give a *congiarium* for which he had not made any pollicitation (for Emperors make pollicitations, just like ordinary *euergetai*) he reproached the people for their impudence and declared by edict that 'though he had intended to make them a money present, he would now tighten his purse-strings'.[23] In a message to the people of Alexandria, the text of which is available to us on a papyrus, Claudius informed those pogrom-loving people that this time he would not investigate, but that he was ready to take severe measures 'against any who do it again'.[24]

Imperial legislation was itself a continuous creation. The Emperor had no hope that his laws would remain effective of their own accord, and ceaselessly reminded his children of the rules they were forgetting to obey. Often his constitutions were simply proclamations intended to remind people to obey a certain law (the French Constitution of 1791 authorized the king to issue similar proclamations). When we see the Theodosian Code periodically repeating the same prohibitions, and coming out a hundred times, in the same terms, against patronage of the weak by the strong, or against recommendation[25] and clientage, our first impulse is to say that the law was powerless to transform the social order, or that these constitutions emanated from a weak power whose authority became bogged down in the passive resistance of the countryside and of local autonomy. The astonishing thing, however, is not that these orders were not carried out, but that they were given. It was as if the Emperor was concerned not so much to be obeyed as to prove to his people that he shared the principles and the sufferings of his subjects; as if the law was not essentially imperative but aimed also at bearing witness (the same could be said of the edicts of the Chinese emperors or of the papal bulls of the Middle Ages).

When the laws are decisions by a sovereign people, the latter does not need to justify them to itself; at most it explains its actual intentions, for the benefit of the executive. But when the laws emanate from a master, he has to justify them in order to justify himself in his subjects' eyes. The constitutions of the Emperors have an ethical foundation. It is a pity that, all too often, the Codes in which they are collected have not retained the preambles. When the complete text has come down to us we are able to see that the sovereign displays an acute social sense, affirming his desire to improve those parts of the Imperial structure which are in decay and to 'advance it by his philanthropy and his *euergesiai*'.[26] The Emperor boasts of the lofty principles which inspire him, and of the prosperity of his reign. He takes up the defence of the humble against petty local tyrants, municipal notables and his own agents.[27] If he fixes by edict the maximum price of all commodities, the preamble to this edict states that the merchants are responsible for high prices and denounces the unrestrained appetite for gain.[28] In general, the manner in which legislation is expressed is not shy of incidentally passing moral judgement on forbidden actions: 'Be the landowners not so impudent as to offer their patronage to the peasants.' This style was to be that of the ordinances of the kings of France.

Historians are sometimes tempted to suppose that this sermonizing legislation is peculiar to the later Empire. Is not the impression of baroque ponderousness that we form of late antiquity largely due to this rhetoric? This is only an illusion caused by the accidental conservation of certain documents; the rare early Imperial edicts whose preambles have been preserved are no less moralizing and over-subtle.[29] We need to think not of two successive stages in an evolution but of the dual image which the Imperial regime presented at all times.

Why this moralizing style? Because there was autonomy at the heart of heteronomy. The sovereign could not expose himself to the suspicion of acting arbitrarily or for selfish motives. Outwardly, his liberality as a legislator was as absolute as that of any ordinary private person who creates whatever obligations he chooses when he signs a contract; but the arbitrariness of a private person's will is unbecoming in a public man who is supposed to aim at the good of all.

Moreover, the public man in question was a master; in him the functionary and the public man were inseparable. He therefore had to justify to his subjects every one of his actions, including those in his private and family life. We, today, are in the habit of distinguishing, among the deeds of a head of state, between his formal acts, which have legal consequences, his material acts, which are usually ceremonial ('opening flower-shows'), and his private acts. The Romans, on the contrary, made no such distinction. Augustus explained to the Senate and people of Rome why he behaved so severely towards his daughter Julia; Caligula listed in an edict the reasons for his marriage; after the death of Britannicus, Nero declared in an edict that 'as he had now lost a brother's help, his remaining hopes centred in the state, and all the more tenderness ought to be shown by the Senate and people towards a prince who was the only survivor of a family born to the highest greatness'.[30]

Under the Republic the people were theoretically sovereign, but in practice (and also according to Cicero) the sovereign was the Senate. The same ambiguity existed under the Empire, as is proved by that ideology-in-gestures known as 'ceremonial'. In the palace ritual the Emperor was sometimes the successor to the magistrates of the Republic, the senators' peer, and sometimes a Hellenistic or oriental monarch.[31] The lawyers saw the Emperor as an appointed official, but the people and the ideologues saw him as a 'Good King', in other words, a father. The *Digest*, the most important item of debris to survive from that old Empire, is the work of lawyers with a sharp style and clear (even if not systematic) minds: it is the only work of Roman thought that can stand comparison with Hellenic reason. For the jurists, the Emperor is only a law-giver, and when they discuss the basis of his authority, they place this expressly in the mandate he receives from his people: 'What the Emperor has decided possesses the same authority as a law of the people, because the people have conferred their own sovereignty upon the Emperor.'[32] Contrast with this the Codes. In them the Emperor himself speaks, addressing his benevolent and imperious messages to his subjects, and doing so in an inflated style that corresponds to his subjects' lofty conception of him.[33]

3. The sovereign by absolute right

The idea that a government does not of itself possess the right to govern, but is a mere mandatory, probably defines the most important moment in the whole of political history.[34]

MASTER, GOOD MASTER, SOLE MASTER

When the general condition of society is such that public opinion is only embryonic, the sovereign reigns because he has the right to reign; the heteronomic pole is given prominence by institutions, ceremonial and popular feeling. Sociologically, the absence of public opinion entails, politically, sovereignty by absolute right, which in turn entails ideologically the sovereign's euergetism.

Under every regime political reality is the same: in order to obey what is good, that is, to obey myself, I must nevertheless obey other people. This sad truth is not to be ascribed to economic reasons, because it is due not to scarcity of goods but to plurality of wills. However, this essential fact matters less than the contingent factors which modify it. When the people are sovereign, the business of ideology is to explain that, although obeying myself alone, I nevertheless submit myself to a will which is not often my own. Heteronomy is the problem. I shall be told that I bow myself democratically to the will of the majority, or that the Party is my own 'vanguard'. When the monarch is the real sovereign, on the contrary, the business of ideology is to explain that, although I obey a will that is not my own, I am none the less obeying myself, in the sense that I obey for my own good. Here it is autonomy that is not obvious. Ideology will then tell me that the monarch is good, euergetic. At the heteronomic pole the monarch reigns by himself, but at the autonomic pole he reigns for me. He is a euergetic master, majestic and good, and Imperial euergetism is the proof of this goodness and this majesty.

Whoever possesses, by absolute right, authority over a community is greater than that community. He has rights over it which it does not have over him. No matter if he exercises only a small part of these rights and if the monarch is, in practice, nothing more than a great judge or warlord. He is the master, and if he confines himself to a limited role, this is because he so chooses. Nobody limits his power; he is not restricted to a defined function. The origin of his authority matters more than its extent. Since he levies taxes or dispenses justice, he is the sovereign *in general*, for only society itself, or its ruler, can legitimately levy taxes, dispense justice or make war. Otherwise, taxation would be a racket, justice would be personal vengeance and war would be a private vendetta. Whoever holds the monopoly of even one of these legitimacies will be seen to be the sovereign in general.

If the Emperor is my master, and a good master, he must be infallible. I cannot mistrust him. Therefore, he must assuredly make his decisions by a sort of instinct, without deliberation, and consequently alone. I believe this all the more easily because I do not know what goes on behind the scenes. In my eyes, all sovereignty is personal. If the Emperor appoints a grand vizier, a praetorian prefect, that man can only be a delegate of the Emperor, even if it is he who wields power in reality, for the Emperor can dismiss him with a word.

The monarchical regime, which has truly existed only in exceptional reigns, has succeeded for thousands of years in making people believe in its existence. Its chief merit, which has enabled it to last so long, is that it is not monarchical, but serves as cover for informal team-governments. Throughout history most monarchs have been what Weber calls *Dilettanten*, amateurs, who spent their time drinking and hunting. At least the Roman Emperors certainly worked harder than the kings who created France. But did they take decisions – and what does 'taking decisions' mean? As they possessed only the information that the Emperor's council conveyed to them, they did not so much take decisions as were made to take them.

It follows that the individual peculiarities and private life of the sovereign assume immense importance in the eyes of his subjects. This has nothing in common with the 'star system'. 'Stars' embody publicly something private, the human condition and its dreams, whereas the obsessive curiosity shown in relation to royalty as individuals remains *political*.

When Commodus appeared in the amphitheatre in the role of gladiator, he was not trying to enhance the brilliance of his crown by assuming the laurels of a champion, and the public did not admire him as a star gladiator, forgetting that he was the Emperor. What the spectators admired was the fact that their sovereign possessed all gifts and realized all human potentialities (the rich and powerful owe it to themselves to actualize every aspect of man's estate, since they have the means to do so). The spectators were also pleased that the master was showing the plebs that he shared their sporting interests and did not despise the people's culture. Commodus was making himself popular *as sovereign*.

The star system, on the contrary, solves a problem of the sociology of cognition. On what objects is the universal curiosity about the human condition, both everyday and fairy-tale, to be given satisfaction? The broadcasting of information is limited by society's rules and pruderies. It is not for just any individual to interest the public in his very ordinary private life, and only public men have the right to publish their memoirs. The only solution is to interest ourselves in the private lives of singers – or if one is educated, in the private lives of great writers.

The Roman plebs judged the Emperor by his pleasing manner and his attitude, distant or popular, at the games in the Circus, because only somebody informed and rational can judge a specialist directly on the basis of his professional competence. We judge him usually by the impression of sincerity or self-confidence that he is able to convey. And besides, the plebs were more desirous of having a benevolent master than of having as Emperor a virtuoso of high politics. 'The common man,' wrote Tacitus, 'usually judges Emperors by their looks and by the charm of their manners.' But Tacitus himself was no different, in that he judged Emperors by such indirect indications as were available to him, and with reference to his own political interests. He judged them by the sobriety of their private lives and their egalitarian ways with the senators. With an Emperor, the worthiness of his private life allows us to presume that he will not be a tyrant, a slaughterer of senators (Tacitus, of course, was a senator). Furthermore, this worthiness is a matter of concern in its own right, for a depraved Emperor insults the ideal of senatorial gravity and challenges the Senate's authority in the regulation of morals.

THE CAUSE OF GOOD, BUT NOT RESPONSIBLE FOR EVIL

A person's whole existence seemed to depend upon the Emperor, whether he were good or bad, for the Emperor was identified with the state and with society. 'The terror of his name will make our cities strong, the harvest of our fields will wear out our sickles and the fruits of our trees will surpass the promise of their flowers.' It was to him that were due good harvests, the daughters of good weather, and likewise bad weather was a punishment from the gods for the sins of Israel or of its king.[35] Thanks to Augustus, sheep might safely graze, the countryside was fertile, sailors voyaged across peaceful seas, and the chastity of the home was untroubled by adultery.[36]

All the world's happiness and all the world's woe ultimately depend on the monarch, good weather included, for misfortunes are due to our sins,[37] and luck is a matter of merit.[38] After all, famine is a social fact no less than a natural one, and so the government has something to do with it. Already under the Republic the magistrates of that regime, including Cato the Elder,[39] took credit for the fact that, when they were in office, the weather had been good and there had been no problem in making one year's crop last till the next year's harvest was ready for reaping. Naturally, people did not believe these things implicitly: they were ideas, not perceptions. But when one was in the right mood, or propriety demanded it, one surrendered to these ideas.

People 'only half-believed' in these things, and at some moments more than others, because, the social world not being transparent, they hesitated between two notions of the Emperor's actions. Either the sovereign was the government, which governed well or not so well, or the sovereign ensured, not that society was better or worse, but that it existed at all. Sometimes people muttered against the Emperor, through his unworthy ministers, and at other times he was held responsible for good harvests. Under the second hypothesis the monarch is good by virtue of the mere fact that he reigns: a good half of Imperial euergetism comes down to this, as will be shown in some detail.

The monarch does not so much govern as cause society to exist. This is true of all sovereigns, by virtue of their very function. Yet I shall attribute this functional role to the sovereign's individual virtue (putting aside the logical idea that the sovereign could be a bad man) and I shall love him for his goodness, because we all spontaneously confuse the sentiments we choose to have and those that are induced: everyone 'loves his father'.

From this it follows that in my eyes the sovereign will, at least now and then, be responsible for everything good and *not* responsible for anything bad, a privilege he shares with Divine Providence, charismatic leaders and the Muse of inspiration. Providence causes things to go well; and when they go badly, it serves as a refuge that enables the virtuous man who suffers to justify himself against the world and to think that in heaven there is a being who is on his side.

To believe this more easily, I refrain from imagining the Emperor actually taking a particular political decision (in time of crisis, it is through his continued unruffled existence that he inspires the saving actions of his servants). Therefore the Emperor cannot be spoken of as skilful or intelligent, any more than one could say this of the gods. His individuality will be exclusively ethical. His virtues will be sung, but it would be disrespectful to discuss his political qualities. These he may or may not possess, since he is merged with his function, and this function is unchanging and providential. He is a virtuous sovereign, not a charismatic leader, a conception that is too modern, appropriate to societies with a public opinion, in which the leader rises to power not through a right he possesses but through the force of circumstances, the objective fact that he is the best man – a fact which is as good as popular delegation and may take its place.

Since every regime is both heteronomous and autonomous, a sovereign will reign by his right to do so, but he will reign for my good. His absolute right will then be elevated into divine right, or into the deification of the Emperor, and the fact that he reigns for my good will be elevated into Imperial euergetism. And since he is the state, he will display the pomp of a great property-owner and the Empire will be regarded as his patrimony. All this is logical and to explain it there is no need to call on ideas of charisma, primitive mentality or depth psychology.

4. *The deification of the Emperors and the notion of charisma*

The cult of the monarch is a subject on which it is easier to write 200 pages than twenty, for the documentation is enormous and has been well studied.[40] The difficulty lies in explaining the facts without taking the simplistic path of saying that people are so odd that they can believe anything and for any reason. The reader must be given the means to appreciate that in their shoes he would have shared their beliefs.

Belief in the divinity of the sovereign strikes us as astonishing on two counts. We are astonished at ourselves and at others. How is it possible to get into such states of mind and exalt a man to the point of making him into a sort of god? Whence come the delirium of Nuremberg and the 'cult of personality'? The other astonishment is ethnographical. How can peoples be so outlandish as to say that a mortal is a god? The idea surprises us in them, and the feeling surprises us in ourselves.

DID THEY REALLY BELIEVE THAT THE MONARCH WAS A GOD?

The first of these points is the easier to deal with. Nobody, even the most primitive of primitives or the least of Pharaoh's subjects, ever believed that his sovereign was a god, if only because he knew that the sovereign would die, and also because he could see him as a creature of our world, visible to our eyes, whereas the gods do not, as a rule, let human beings see them, but belong to a different ontological sphere from real objects. Primitive man feels very strongly about his sovereign, but his feelings are not exactly the same as those, no less strong, that are stirred in him by the idea of a real god, Osiris or Apollo. He may hold his sovereign to be superhuman, to be a man with the supernatural gift of curing scrofula. To believe that a mortal is sacred is commonplace and easy, but to believe that he is a god is quite another matter.

The Egyptians, we may recall, took Pharaoh both for a 'god' and for a man whom the gods would judge after death. The Greeks and Romans were no more ingenuous. Like the Egyptians, they 'believed', as a form of words, that kings and Emperors, whether alive or dead, were gods; but as to putting this belief into practical effect . . . Reacting against the tendency to take the religious texts literally, Nock made a revealing observation: there does not exist a single votive offering to the divinity of an Emperor, alive or dead. Thousands of Greek and Latin inscriptions state that the Emperor is a god; thousands of other inscriptions are ex-votos to some god, thanks for a favour of one sort or another – a cure, a lying-in, a successful journey, recovery of lost property. But not one of these ex-votos takes a king or an Emperor for a god. When a Greek or a Roman, while sincerely hailing the Emperor as a god, felt the need of a genuine god, he never addressed himself to the Emperors of whom it is sometimes alleged that they channelled to their own advantage the religious sensibility of their subjects.[41]

It is therefore not a matter for surprise that the change that came after the Emperors had been converted to Christianity was barely noticeable. The same sentiment continued, with an alteration in words or concepts which were quite ready to become their own contraries, provided that the sentiment survived. On 1 January 1946, when Emperor Hirohito declared on the radio, 'I am not a god,'[42] nothing changed in the sentiments of the Japanese people. In one sense they had always known it, and in another sense they went on not wanting to know it.

The ancients did not deceive themselves. They knew and repeated that the deifying of an Emperor was not so much a religious belief as a decision taken, namely to award him 'honours equal to those of the gods' (*isotheoi timai*), meaning sacrifices and altars,[43] the external signs of the respect due to the gods. The deifying of sovereigns proves that political feelings about them were intense. It proves also that between our feelings and our public acts there lies a wide zone of expressions which are imposed or at least organized, made official, or quite simply ritualized and conventional. The difference is like that between passion and the more or less burdensome bonds of marriage.

It has long been said that the cult of monarchy was established by sovereigns in order to base their power upon religious feeling.[44] If so, we must marvel that their people took them at their word and believed on demand. For human nature to have changed so much in thirty centuries is quite as surprising as for the foundations of politics in those distant days to have been so different from what they are now. In reality, we all realize that Pharaoh or the Emperor were gods because they were sovereigns and not sovereigns because they were gods. And what does 'religious' mean? Is a patriotic and monarchical festival, even one that opens with a sacrifice offered to the divinity of the monarch, religious in the same sense as a prayer addressed to a god in a moment of strong emotion, or a votive offering promised to a god in a moment of despair? I do not mean to hint that the cult of monarchy was insincere: there is nothing more sincere, likewise, than a patriot's cult of the national flag,[45] but even though love of the flag may be an intense feeling, it is not a religious one. Far from explaining patriotism, it derives its sincerity from love of country. Love of the flag is not the basis of patriotism, and nobody will turn political philosophy upside down on the grounds that, in some armies, the national emblems are accorded homage that might be described as religious in character.

A more recent interpretation, which has not solved these difficulties, has the merit of stressing the sincerity of the cult of monarchy and making it 'understandable'. But it has not analysed that confused feeling which the ancients did not themselves explain; it tries instead to get us to experience it as they did, in all its confusion, to this end multiplying suggestions of an impressionistic kind.

Its great merit is to have perceived that the cult of monarchy was no less spontaneous than sincere. In the Greco-Roman world adoration of the sovereign began most commonly on the initiative of his subjects, or, rather, of the autonomous cities, and not with a decree by the sovereign himself. The Emperor did not *cause* himself to be worshipped, as is sometimes thoughtlessly said; he *let* himself be worshipped. If he organized his own cult he was a tyrant. The cult of Augustus, organized in the Italian cities around the *seviri augustales*, was invented by certain cities, which were imitated in this matter by their neighbours, and those in turn by *their* neighbours (which process gave rise to local variations in this institution).[46] It was not created by the central authority. On other occasions it happened that a Greek city, or an association of the cities in a given province, formed the project of offering an annual sacrifice to the reigning Emperor, doing this on the altar of the town's principal divinity, and placing the Emperor's sacred image in the temple of that divinity, seating it beside the latter on the same throne,[47] or else celebrating a provincial festival in honour of the reigning god. The city or the province then made known to the Emperor their intention to honour him in this way and asked for his permission.[48] They did not receive from him an order to do this; it was of their own volition that numberless Greek cities deified the living Emperor (or rather recognized that he had a divine nature, as the sacramental formula put it).[49] True, it did also happen that deification was instituted by the central authority itself: Antiochus the Great introduced the cult of himself and became his own supreme pontiff. Even in these cases where spontaneity was absent, however, the sincerity of the people is not open to doubt, for there is plenty of evidence of the fervour with which the ceremonies of the Imperial cult were celebrated.

LOVE OF THE MONARCH, AN INDUCED FEELING

We still need to make this fervour understood. A whole school has gone to great lengths to suggest to the reader's imagination the affective component of the cult of monarchy (at the risk of overestimating it and crediting the most conventional exaggerations with complete emotional content). It has studied the official or didactic expositions by priests and poets of the theology of the Imperial power. It has charted the associations of ideas which enhanced the cult of monarchy (for example, the link between Imperial ritual and the Circus). It has revealed the richness of the theme rather than located the heart of the problem. In fact, in conformity with Lucien Febvre's principle that a religious fact has religious causes, it has sought to explain in religious terms this apparently religious phenomenon, the true explanation of which is to be found in the political structure. An affect, whether religious or not, explains nothing; on the contrary, it is explained by the structure that induces it. Affectivity has few variations, and similar feelings can be induced by widely differing organizations – by a divine-right monarchy or by a simple subgroup like the patriarchal family. Nor can monarchical sentiment be explained by the associations of ideas it arouses. It is not even certain that, in this depiction of the sentiments involved, the central place has always been held by the sentiment which must not be forgotten, which must indeed be kept in view more than any other, namely love of the monarch, a sentiment so natural that only its absence would surprise us.

IT IS BETTER TO BE CALLED A GOD THAN TO BE TAKEN FOR A DEMI-GOD

A certain man is, by virtue of his function, more than a man. That is the attitude, sincere and spontaneous, in which representation and affect are inseparable from one another. A gulf lies between this and saying that the man is a god. It would seem less absurd and more appropriate to see in this mortal a divine man (or, in our own mythology, a 'man of genius'). How did it come about that he was called a god, and why was he not, instead, called a demi-god? Here we move from spontaneity to institution. 'He is a god!' is a consciously paradoxical expression, which seeks to intensify humility and justify a further intensification, realized in actions, namely the rendering of a cult. The word 'god' is a metonym which is used for the sake of the very violence it does to what is obvious. This violence presupposes a certain credibility (which would be possible under paganism but unthinkable with the Christian God); it also requires that a public authority should impose it, or at least that the community should impose it on itself, or permit it, and turn it into an institution or at least a custom that people can observe with a straight face.

Nobody ever thought of proclaiming that Jupiter was a god, because nobody doubted this. The statement: 'Yes, he is a god!' is never used of a god. But it is meritorious to say this of the Emperor. For genuine gods other hyperboles are resorted to – for instance, henotheism: 'Thou art for me the only god, or, rather, thou art all the gods at once!' Where the sovereign is concerned, one remains at a lower pitch: thou art truly a god *for me*! 'It is a god who wrought for us this peace,' a poet makes a simple shepherd say about Octavius; 'for a god he shall ever be to me; often shall a tender lamb from our folds stain his altar.'[50] The procedure is attributed to a fictitious shepherd, but it was employed by real worshippers. It begins as the expression of a moment of emotion: Octavius is here one of the 'gods of the instant' spoken of by Usener.[51] All that is needed is to ritualize the procedure and Octavius will be a god for ever. And why not ritualize it? Saying is doing in this case. It is enough for me to acknowledge someone as a god for him to *be* a god for me, especially as I should not have acknowledged him as a god if he had not been one already. The sacred is not created, only discovered.

The monarch is a god. Which means that he reigns by his own right and also, paradoxically, that he is less than a demi-god, a mere hero. A demi-god has deserved his power through his personal merits and has been judged by his works, whereas the title of god is attached to the crown and passes automatically to the monarch's successor.[52] The sovereign will thus be able to remain a god, even in times when *pronunciamentos* or palace revolutions are toppling thrones.

The ancients applied the titles of god,[53] hero[54] or demi-god[55] almost indiscriminately to eminent writers, conquerors or those great men of inspiration whom we should call geniuses. In the case of monarchs, however, they were not indiscriminate in their choice of title, but soberly decided to call them gods, never heroes or divine men. Where sovereigns were concerned, the vocabulary was reclassified so as to create a contrasting pair. There was good reason for this. In order to be a god the monarch needs only to reign, just as the gods are what they are without having to deserve to be it. A god performs exploits because he is a god. A hero, on the contrary, becomes a hero because he performs exploits. In the Middle Ages, when monarchs were, if not gods, at least sacred beings and kings by the grace of God, it was unusual for them to be saints after the Merovingian period. Louis IX was canonized for his personal merits, which were different from the divine grace attached to the monarchy as such.[56] The Emperor was a god, and not half a god, because one is not more or less an Emperor. He was the only living man in his Empire whom his subjects had the right to proclaim god, if they wished: it was his monopoly.

We should, therefore, stop saying that the Greek kings and the Emperors were deified because, in the Hellenistic period, the line between gods and men became uncertain (and also, through henotheism, between the gods themselves). The truth is precisely the opposite. For the benefit of the sovereign the notion of a god was restored in all its classical clarity. What was obliterated here was not that clarity but the rule of modesty which ordained that men should know themselves and be aware that they were not gods; and also that old-fashioned respect which required men to give their due to *all* the gods, forbade sentimental whims, and did not allow a worshipper to choose one among the gods and proclaim that, for him, this god was all the gods in one. The Emperor was not deified because the gods were no longer easily distinguished from heroes and men (the Emperor was very clearly distinguished from both), but because men no longer found it scandalous to deify other men in a sentimental way. They deified many dead people. That is why the Greco-Roman cult of the sovereigns has something about it that is anodyne, moderate and even sometimes Voltairean, with nothing of the 'oriental' ponderousness of the cult of the Pharaohs. For the Egyptians continued to consider that a man is not a god, so that deifying Pharaoh was an almost tyrannical act of violence, an assault by a potentate upon human modesty. A Hellenistic king, however, did little violence to people's consciences when he had himself, or let himself be, worshipped: it was just sentimental weakness.

THE NUANCES OF DEIFICATION

We see then that different societies proceed, each in its own way, from the feeling of royal sublimity to institutionalized deification. Societies often do not make this transition. The sovereign by absolute right confines himself to being a high priest or having himself anointed. Pharaoh was a god and so was the emperor of Japan, but their neighbours, the kings of the ancient Middle East and the emperor of China, were merely mortals protected by the gods or exercising a divine authority. Moreover, the word 'god' does not carry the same meaning everywhere, and for the Romans the only thing that a god had in common with what we call a god was the name.

The transition from sentiment to deification happens all the more unevenly because it is a historical event and even a voluntary act, indeed a political decision. The Hellenistic cities spontaneously deified kings, by analogy with the cult they rendered to their founders and *euergetai*.[57] We read in Plato that, for the philosophers, the guardians of the city, after their deaths, 'the state will set up monuments and sacrifices, honouring them as divinities, if the Pythian Oracle approves, or at least as men blest with a godlike spirit'.[58] In Roman Italy the Emperors refused to accept the worship of their Italian subjects, just as Gandhi and Nehru refused to allow temples to be dedicated to them.[59] The cult of the sovereign was permitted only to the provincials. Developed by priests and magistrates, this cult always had something conventional and contrived about it. The intellectuals and notables who devised it affected to improve upon the humility felt by the masses towards the sovereign. The cult of the monarchy never corresponded to a popular *belief*, but it did correspond to a popular *feeling*.

Did the institutionalized cult add anything to this feeling induced by submission, and did it reinforce that submission, as is commonly said of ideologies? The effect varied. The feeling itself, which was not inter-individual like filial love, did not even establish a bond of personal fidelity between the Emperor and his subjects: after the next *pronunciamento* the new Father of the People would find the love of an entire people automatically transferred to him. But what if the feeling served as pretext for a cult, for regulated forms of behaviour, for socially obligatory expressions (like politeness, or mourning)?

Let us begin by making the distinction, to which the ancients were very sensitive, between the princes who were worshipped and those who had themselves worshipped. The latter were tyrants who wanted to be loved on command. In one of Seneca's tragedies an attendant of the tyrant asks his master: 'Does public disapproval deter thee not?' The tyrant replies, 'The greatest advantage this of royal power, that their master's deeds the people are compelled as well to bear as praise.' The truly powerful man, he goes on, is known by his ability to wrest praise from others. 'Where only right to a monarch is allowed, sovereignty is insecure' (*precario regnatur*, a legal expression).[60] These verses, written by someone with practical experience of what he was talking about, show what this symbolic addition to his oppressive power meant to a prince. It was fairly Platonic, affecting the form of obedience. The king was not trying to make his subjects more docile than they already were or to subdue an opposition, nor was he preparing them to obey despotic or revolutionary commands; he wanted them to realize that they owed him obedience because he was a great man, or a superhuman being. When Antiochus the Great, returning from the long expedition in which he had almost repeated the exploits of Alexander, established a state cult of monarchy, he expected to receive from his subjects the homage due to a hero. Did he not rival Hannibal for the title of most famous man of his time? When Caligula had himself worshipped he claimed that his subjects admitted to themselves that the basis of the Imperial authority was beyond human grasp.[61] This was an attempt as vain as it was tyrannical, for it is futile to try and impart to large numbers of people strong feelings which they do not have of their own accord. When one tries to politicize people, one either wins the strong support of a handful of militants, or else one wins large numbers only superficially, and bewilders them. Antiochus succeeded, apparently, because he was generally admired, and he did not leave behind the memory of a tyrant; whereas Caligula, who attracted admiration less spontaneously, left an evil memory to posterity.

The existence of a cult of the sovereign is always a political symptom. It is not accidental that in Macedonia, a national and patriarchal kingdom where the grandees talked with their king as equals,[62] the royal portrait does not even appear on coins, at least until the reign of the authoritarian Philip V.[63] A symptom, therefore, but one whose significance depends on the context. For example, under the Empire, the Greek cities spontaneously multiplied cults of the living ruler or of members of the Imperial family. Were these the 'flatteries' of 'degenerate' Greeks? Almost the contrary. These cities looked on themselves not so much as communes of the Empire as little autonomous states, albeit 'satellites' of a foreign city. In fact their relation to the Empire was closer to being an informal dependence, a power relation and, in that sense, an international relation, than to being a well-regulated system of administrative units.[64] They did not render a cult to the foreign Emperor in the manner of humble subjects worshipping a master who is above their heads; in the case of the Greeks the cult bore a diplomatic and international significance (it was thus the successor to the cult of the Roman people). It was comparable to the exaltation of friendship with the USSR in the people's democracies. The city that worshipped the Roman Emperor acknowledged that it was and wished to be a *de facto* satellite of Rome; consequently its relations with Rome had to be *de jure* those of two distinct states. In the second century BC, when Greece, though already 'satellized' by Rome, was not a Roman province, and no Roman soldier was stationed on its soil, exaltation of the friendship of the Romans, '*euergetai* of the universe', was the way in which the pro-Roman parties in the cities proclaimed their attachment to their too-powerful protectors.[65]

The institutionalized cult certainly did add something to natural feelings and did not confine itself to expressing them, for when a declaration of love is more than an emotional outburst and assumes a canonical form, it becomes a promise, obedience to oneself against oneself, and ultimately obedience to another person. The mere fact that the expression of feelings has become obligatory creates awareness of the presence of an authority and of a possible penalty for non-conformity. Nevertheless, let us not over-simplify. Political life does not gravitate exclusively to the poles of spontaneity and constraint. It is more varied; it does not consist merely in keeping people under control, but also takes subordinate needs into account. Often the cult of monarchy is only a ceremonial, and the purpose of a ceremonial is not so much symbolic violence as a way of escaping one of those inconveniences that lend picturesque confusion to everyday life, with its conflicts of interest. From time to time a monarch has to make his existence publicly known, for reasons that do not matter here, and this is called a public holiday. Now the monarch cannot do this without surrounding himself with solemn ceremony, so as to bridge the gap between the significance of his august presence and the ordinariness of the particular moment. Unfortunately every ceremonial demands a script, like a ballet, and that script has to be composed; the Imperial cult was introduced in order to supply the need. It was only ceremonial, and one cannot blame ceremonial for being what it is.

THE OUTWARD MARKS OF RESPECT

A ceremonial is innocent so long as one is in agreement on the principles involved and so long as it adds nothing to these principles. It begins to seem burdensome when its principles, implicit or unconscious, are contested. For the Christians the Imperial cult was not arbitrary, since it implied a notion of divinity which could not be theirs. However, the pagans did not even understand the Christian idea of divinity, so that instead of seeing the martyrs as adversaries they saw them as stiff-necked persons who were merely stupid or perverse.[66] This is why symbols have a substance of their own, are hard to separate from what they symbolize, and are not empty. It is always precarious to show contempt for a flag while insisting that one respects the country of which it is an empty symbol. Perhaps one does indeed respect that country, but by rejecting the symbol one fails in respect for something else which, even if not the country, does nevertheless exist.

The Christians learnt this to their cost. On the one hand the Imperial cult was only the symbol of a political loyalty to the sovereign which very few Christians rejected. On the other, it existed in itself and implied a whole religious system which for the pagans was so self-evident that they could not imagine any other. The conflict between the Christians and the Imperial cult was a conflict between a religion of dogmas and a religion of rites. Obedient to St Paul's teaching, the martyrs were ready to respect the Emperor's majesty, but they refused to express their loyalty in a rite of worship. The public authorities and the people were furious at this subtle distinction which they did not trouble to understand, and no less furious at the very disobedience shown by these incomprehensibly stubborn persons. Combined with this authoritarianism, the lack of understanding resulted in a hatred of the Christians which failed to disentangle its different causes. In their confusion of thought the public authorities ended by punishing the Christians, justifying their severity by the fact that the Christians repudiated the Emperor's majesty itself. This oft-encountered process of false conceptualization brings about the mistaken belief that symbols 'adhere' to the thing symbolized, so that an attack on the former means an attack on the latter. This gives rise to the dualistic illusion which forgets that the symbol has an existence of its own and treats it as a mere reflection, and then is astonished to find that this reflection possesses sufficient solidity to provoke hatreds.

With the persecution of the Christians it was as with the Imperial cult itself: political in its ultimate cause, it was religious in its material cause, in the symbols to which it was attached. The Christians were detested as rebels and as atheists, and these two 'causes' were complementary: the one was not merely the symbolic reflection of the other. St Polycarp was ordered by the governor to treat the Emperor as a god: 'Swear by the Fortune of the Emperor and I will let you go.' The crowd, meanwhile, shouted: 'Death to the atheists!' Polycarp answered that he was ready to honour the sovereign, because he had 'been taught to honour in the proper way the rulers and authorities, who have been ordained by God', but not to worship him.[67]

We note that the Roman authorities and the crowd did not call upon the martyr to believe in the Emperor's divinity, to confess this, but required from him what in our armies are called the outward marks of respect. The Imperial cult adhered to the ritualism of classical paganism: it was made up of festivals and rites, with piety consisting in performance of these rites with the utmost precision.[68] This does not mean that it was entirely outward show. Nothing helps better to understand ritualistic religions than our military parades, in which the way to show the most authentic zeal is to march past 'in impeccable order', without so much as a wrong crease in the regimental colours. Let us imagine, too, that the march-past is followed by a popular and traditional festival. Ritualism has the great advantage of putting one on automatic pilot where affects are concerned; one is not consciously zealous, but this does not mean that one fails to show zeal.

The persons present at these ceremonies followed, with attention either pious or casual, the progress of a ritual elaborated by specialists in the art. They were not interested in the details; all they wanted was that it should be a real ceremony. At most, one of them might, out of curiosity, ask for explanation of some feature of the ritual, and marvel at its pious ingenuity. For rites essentially symbolize nothing, any more than music does. They do not necessarily refer one back to a different reality, to beliefs. They form a species of behaviour *sui generis* in which what matters is to do things ceremoniously, the details remaining arbitrary. These details may concern music, or dancing, or some gratuitous complication of technical gestures, as in table manners. Why this gesture, or that ritual vestment? Why not another? For no reason at all: the only thing that matters is that it should be this and no other. Why is the sacrificial altar lozenge-shaped and not square? So that it should not be shaped any old how, that is the point. Subsequently, of course, explanations for everything are invented. A part of brahminical literature is made up of symbolic interpretations of ritual, each more ingenious than the last. It is even the case sometimes that these interpretations are not *post eventum* but constitute the true explanation, for when one has to invent a ritual, the task can be eased by resorting to symbolism. This is like going over from pure music to programme music, the resource of limited imaginations. The fact remains that rites are essentially expressions, ways of showing politeness to the gods, and not symbols. Were we to analyse in detail the Imperial theology and liturgy, we should certainly learn a lot about the cultural and religious context of the time, but nothing more about the Emperor and the idea people had of him – apart from this assertion, repeated with a thousand variations: he reigns by himself, and so he is more than a man. Except perhaps also a secret doubt: even if he is more than a man, is he really a god? It is indeed symptomatic that, in the Roman Empire, the cult of the sovereigns rarely took an extreme form, that of the blood sacrifice. Most often it was merely a matter of offering a few grains of incense. Only at some public ceremonies were victims offered to the deified Emperor, as to genuine gods.[69]

THE MULTIFUNCTIONAL NATURE OF THE IMPERIAL CULT

Going beyond this basic explanation, the cult of the sovereigns also served other functions. It was no exception to the general probability that one and the same social fact may serve several functions and bring several satisfactions; why, indeed, should it serve only one function? Among these functions were euergetism and ceremonial.

The spirit of paganism consists of rites and festivals. The Imperial cult also served to provide public rejoicings, which were of course financed by *euergetai*. So praiseworthy a pretext as worshipping the Emperor could not decently be rejected. In the first century AD the pretext for gladiatorial shows was usually a celebration of the reigning dynasty.[70] The 'provincial assemblies' of the Roman Empire were also a response to the desire for festivals (gladiatorial combats, at ruinous cost, formed the centrepiece of their sumptuous revels).[71] They were a response also to the cities' need to come together in order to deal with the Roman governor of a province, and this was an additional reason for making the Imperial cult the pretext for their meeting, so as to emphasize their loyalty to the central authority.

Then there was the ceremonial aspect. In that era when leisure activities were not paid for by the people as individuals, but were collective, free and public, they always had something solemn about them. In antiquity almost everything that was solemn and much that was ideological was borrowed from religion, which consequently seems to permeate the whole of social life (this is the element of truth in the thesis of Fustel de Coulanges). A city, a *collegium*, a *euergetēs* plans to organize festivals or banquets, even games. The festival will have a religious tone, the banquet will follow a sacrifice, and the games will be dedicated to a god – but to which god? The only one on whom everyone can agree is the reigning Emperor (or his deified predecessors). In fact another deity could serve as all-purpose god, namely the god who protects the city. Both the Emperor and the tutelary deity were often used for the purpose mentioned. If some public edifice was about to be erected – a bridge, a gate for the town, perhaps even a sundial – it needed a fine inscription, if only so that people might read the name of the *euergetēs* responsible: and so it was inscribed that the building had been dedicated by this patron to the local god, to the Emperor and to the city itself.[72]

Sovereign by absolute right and sometimes all-purpose god – that was the Emperor, and the experiment of analysis *in vivo* represented by the triumph of Christianity confirms my own analysis, for after becoming Christian, the Emperor remains what he was before.

Long before the triumph of Christianity the Imperial cult had gradually become pompous and despotic. The procedure to be followed grew increasingly solemn. The Emperor's titles, official or invented by 'flattery', which had to be recited, became longer and longer, and his subjects competed in humbling themselves before the master, the *dominus*. The official portraits became more and more hieratic: whereas the first-century Emperors were given the faces of intellectuals or of young gods, like the Hellenistic kings, those of the fourth century resemble, in their portraits, Byzantine Christs or Mussolinian hierarchs. The baroque ponderousness of the later Empire is due to two things, namely this ritualizing of political symbolism and the affected and 'de-realizing' rhetoric which dominates the prose of that period.[73]

What was the reason for this ponderous pomposity? Was it a defensive reaction by an Empire which, threatened by barbarians and by *pronunciamentos*, closed ranks anxiously around its leader? I do not believe so at all. The truth is simpler. Exaltation of the Emperor had been hindered by two obstacles: the senatorial aristocracy did not like to see the Emperor assuming the air of a master, and the hegemonic, 'colonial' structure of the Empire meant that deification of the living sovereign, admissible and even praiseworthy where provincials were concerned, was intolerable for Italians, citizens of the metropolis. But the institutional transformation of the third century meant that Rome was municipalized and Italy provincialized, while the senatorial aristocracy lost all their power. Henceforth there were no obstacles to protestations of humility before the sovereign majesty.

And that applied even when this majesty was embodied in a Christian Emperor. The Christian (or Arian) sovereigns still expected the *adoratio* from their courtiers. 'A sacred oracle or a divine privilege signed by our divine will': those are the terms in which a Christian Emperor, in 424, spoke of his edicts and privileges.[74] Being essentially political, the deification of the Emperors was maintained, almost intact, for the benefit of the Christian Emperors who reigned by the grace of God.[75] The Emperors and their laws were never more consistently described as divine and sacred than in the Empire's Christian century: it was then, for the first time, that the sovereigns were called *divi* in their own lifetime.

The priests of the Imperial cult also continued to exist, because the divinity of the Emperor provided a pretext for *euergesiai* and festivals. There would be Christian Imperial priests in Roman Africa.[76] In Gaul a Christian epitaph found near Saint-Gaudens celebrates the piety and splendour of a notable who was, I imagine, the Imperial *flamen* of his province and provided a hunt in the amphitheatre, applauded by the people.[77] But then charity took over. Ammianus Marcellinus tells us of a prefect of Rome named Lampadius: 'When this man, in his praetorship, gave magnificent games and made very rich *largesses*, being unable to endure the blustering of the commons, who often urged that many things should be given to those who were unworthy of them, in order to show his generosity and his contempt of the mob, he summoned some beggars from the Vatican and presented them with valuable gifts.'[78] These are the words of a pagan.

CHARISMA

Let us now pass from sociological history to historical sociology. We perceive some vague similarities but also numerous differences between the deification of monarchs in olden times and present-day examples of the exaltation of heads of state. All that need be said is that Max Weber's concept of charisma is too vague and that distinctions have to be made. Charisma, according to Weber, means 'the extraordinary quality of a man (it does not matter whether this is real, alleged or supposed), a quality which rises above the commonplace',[79] and this charisma is found not only in the realm of politics.

Outside politics, charismatic persons include the leaders of religious, poetical, philosophical, psychoanalytical and other sects whom their followers see as having knowledge of truths which have been imparted to them alone, truths that minds other than theirs could not discover. Moreover, a certain authority radiates from such a person, so that, as well as admiration, his followers feel dependent on him. We know of the incredible fervour which surrounded Père Enfantin or Stefan George: and the Fourth Gospel enables us, even better than the Synoptics, to see the charisma that Christ exercised over his disciples.

Charisma is often accompanied by the power to perform miracles, though this power is not its exclusive privilege. In every society it is normal for any exceptional or even important person to enjoy the reputation of possessing a 'gift' and to be asked to cure a sick child. A monarch, too, may be endowed with such powers: Pyrrhus had the gift of healing and a blind man had his sight restored by the Emperor Hadrian.[80] The kings of France and England cured scrofula, and this gift was attached to their crown more than to their person, or even to their dynasty. Needless to say, a king is a miracle-worker because he is a king, and not a king because he is a miracle-worker; the sublime and even sacred concept of kingly power suffices to explain why a miraculous gift was attributed to those who wielded it. That is merely a detail of anecdotal interest; what is more important is the superhuman concept of sovereign power.

The Roman Emperors were regarded by the people as the owners of their Empire. They were themselves and lived for themselves, took their ease in the manner of rich men, and it was plain to see, from their *largesses* and from the luxurious display of their dwellings, that they were 'kings of the castle'. Good kings, too: a component of their characters was a natural liberality which made them *euergetai*.

Such was the popular political philosophy. But did it correspond to the administrative realities? Did the immense machinery of the Empire function according to the same principles as the management of a private patrimony? That remains to be seen.

5. *The Emperor: owner and 'boss'?*

The Bibliothèque Nationale in Paris was for a long time called the Bibliothèque du Roi. British warships are called Her Majesty's ships. In the Roman Empire people spoke of the public Treasury or the public domains as 'Caesar's money' and 'Caesar's domains'. Must we deduce from this that the sovereign owned his Empire? Because some of his subjects sometimes swore an oath of fidelity to him, because the plebs of the capital were sometimes called the Emperor's clients, because the soldiers received from each Emperor, on his accession, a present called the *donativum*, should we conclude that the Roman Empire was an extremely archaic type of society in which ties of personal fidelity took the place of political obedience and that the Emperor was the 'boss', the *capomafioso* of his Empire? This is a difficult problem, and also an unprofitable one to examine. If I were the reader I should skip this chapter.

WAS THE EMPIRE A PRIVATE ENTERPRISE?

In the nineteenth century, under the influence of the Code Napoléon, jurists constructed the juridical system around the notion of absolute right: every juridical subject was supposed to possess a certain number of rights. Some jurists then tried to construct public law on the basis of the same notion: the sovereign commands because he has the right to command. From that concept it is easy to move to the idea that the sovereign himself is owner of the realm, which is seen as a kind of private property.

Historians and sociologists have been influenced by this idea. Mommsen thought that the Fiscus, the state Treasury, belonged to the Emperor, who would have been able to bequeath to anyone he liked the domains of the crown and the yield of taxation. Anton von Premerstein reduced Imperial politics to sociology and considered the Principate to be the continuation, on the gigantic scale of a monopoly, of the networks of personal devotion established between the magnates of the Republic's last phase and their followers. Max Weber thought that the Imperial regime was 'patrimonialist': the sovereign governed by means of his slaves, freedmen and procurators, and thus recruited the Empire's officials from among persons who were personally dependent on him.[81]

In order to administer the Empire, the Emperor certainly had some high officials called procurators, on the model of the 'procurators' to whom rich private persons entrusted the administration of their patrimonies.[82] The mass of government clerks were slaves or freedmen of the Emperor.[83] Yet these Imperial slaves were not his private household. They were, so to speak, 'slaves of the crown', remaining in their posts when there was a change of Emperor. By private law, the Emperor's heirs had no claim on them; instead, they became the slaves of the next man to ascend the throne.[84] The Emperor was not like some sheikh who dispatches one of his servants whom he knows well in order to settle some matter of importance to his authority. He did not choose his officials from among his slaves, he bought slaves so as to make officials of them. These men were slaves rather than wage-earners because the market was not as all-inclusive then as it is today (one did not purchase men's labour, but attached men to one's person), and because engagement for life was the regular solution in ancient societies for the problem of recruitment; the monastic orders follow this principle even today.[85] The officials were slaves of the Emperor rather than of the state (*servi publici*) for historical reasons: Augustus was a successful soldier who was gradually transformed into a monarch, and who on his own initiative complemented the old institutions which had become inadequate by adding to them his bureaucrats and procurators.

That is public which fulfils public purposes: other criteria have no weight. Let us look at those high officials, the Imperial procurators. They were undoubtedly officials, because in cases of embezzlement they were charged before the Senate, like magistrates.[86] But basically they would no less have been officials if they had been regarded as their master's servants and if it had been necessary to bring them before an ordinary court, as when somebody sued the procurator of a private individual. What does it matter, after all, whether remedy lies through the ordinary courts, as in England, or through the French Conseil d'État? It is no more than a point of administrative law.

Let us therefore distinguish between four orders of facts. First, the kingly style. The domains of the Fiscus were called the Emperor's estates and the blocks of stone taken from the public quarries were marked *C(aesaris) n(ostri)*, 'property of our Emperor', just as the hulls of British warships bear the letters *H(er) M(ajesty's) S(hip)*. That does not take us very far. What is more important, the Fiscus and the administration were directly dependent upon the monarch, just as in any monarchy worthy of the name. Augustus had constructed a new state apparatus which was outside the Senate's control. His alleged patrimonialism was simply his monarchy, as against the senatorial oligarchy to which he was obliged to leave the rest of state power. But things were not altogether as schematic as that. In those days, dependence was not always as straightforward as is obedience based purely on regulations. A bureaucrat was not a mere wage-earner and the soldiers of the Imperial guard were not content merely to collect their pay in return for their service. They wanted, in addition, to have a personal and symbolic relationship with the Emperor, as we shall see later. Moreover, we remember that Augustus was a patron of the state and that, far from dipping into the public coffers as though they were his own, he drew on his own resources to meet the state's needs. Did not his successors follow his example? The emperors of Japan and of Ethiopia acted in the same way, down to 1945 and 1974 respectively. The successors of Augustus did likewise, as will be seen. This enables us to clarify the much discussed question of the public coffers of the Roman Empire, which has been distorted by preconceptions arising from modern law.

THE EMPIRE'S FOUR TREASURIES

I shall try to be both brief and clear. The Roman Empire had no less than four treasuries, which is a lot. This plurality was due partly to historical reasons, but it could also correspond to a plurality of owners. Perhaps, despite appearances, one of these coffers belonged to someone other than the state? Therein lies the whole problem.

The first coffer was the Treasury strictly so called, the *aerarium*. This was the old coffer of the Republic, which had no other. It continued to be dependent on the Senate and, for old times' sake, it was called 'public' *par excellence*, and even 'the people's Treasury'. Nevertheless, this Treasury had become very unimportant. What mattered was the Fiscus, created by Augustus; its revenue was of the order of half a billion sesterces, and it depended exclusively upon the Emperor.[87] Of the other two coffers, we know little else but their names. One was very ancient and went back, perhaps, to Augustus: it was called the Patrimonium of the Emperor or of the Caesars, which may mean much or nothing.[88] Similarly with the other, which was called the Private Fortune or the Private Account (*Res Privatae*, *Ratio Privata*) and of which we have evidence from the time of Antoninus Pius.[89] It would be too simple to assume that the difference between Treasury, Fiscus, Patrimonium and Private Fortune amounted merely to an accountant's distinction, a division between different sections of a balance-sheet. That is doubtless true of two or three of these coffers,[90] but not of all, for there are texts which imply that the Emperor disposed of certain revenues in his private capacity.

Everyone agrees that the distinction between the old Treasury and the others, introduced in the Imperial period, is historical in origin. A triad dear to the modern mind seems made to measure for the later three: property of the state, property of the crown, private fortune of the Emperor. The property of the state belongs to the nation and is managed by the sovereign. The property of the crown belongs to the successive wearers of the crown; with each new reign or dynasty it passes automatically to the new Emperor or the new ruling house. The private patrimony belongs to the sovereign in his capacity as a private person: he can bequeath it in his will just as he likes, to whomsoever he chooses.[91] This patrimony can be the fortune which the Emperor possessed when he was a mere senator and nothing yet seemed to destine him for the Imperial throne. All this is quite straightforward. Now let us see how the three Roman coffers fit these three modern concepts. After some hesitation, out of respect for Mommsen, it was agreed, contrary to his view, that the chief treasury, the Fiscus, was the property of the state, just like the Treasury of the Republic, and in fact no one since then has ever doubted or could doubt that this was the case. But what about the Emperor's private patrimony? Does that correspond to the coffer called the Patrimonium? Or to the Private Fortune? Mitteis favoured the former answer, Hirschfeld the latter.

Hirschfeld's doctrine has become almost beyond dispute.[92] The Treasury, which dates from the Republic, and the Fiscus, established by Augustus, were, according to him, the property of the state. At the time of Nero's violent death, when the Julio-Claudian dynasty came to its end, the huge private fortune which the Julio-Claudian family inherited from Augustus was confiscated and became crown property, passed on to the succeeding dynasties: this was the Patrimonium. As for the Private Fortune, that was what its name suggests – the wealth that an Emperor possessed when he came to the throne or which he acquired privately in the course of his reign.

I shall try to show that this division is anachronistic. The concept of 'property of the crown' was alien to the Romans, for it is not natural in a regime in which the throne is a non-hereditary magistracy. The Treasury and the Fiscus were indeed public coffers, as nobody doubts. But alongside them there was only the private fortune of the different Emperors. We find that, through channels which we shall describe, this private patrimony of the reigning Emperor frequently passed, wholly or in part, to his successor as a legacy or inheritance. This means that the Augustan system of patronage of the state was unfailingly perpetuated. This private patrimony probably corresponds to the coffer called the Patrimonium, as Mitteis thinks.[93] As for the Private Fortune, which was no more private than the Bibliothèque du Roi, this was a third public coffer, distinguished from the Fiscus only by an accountant's separation of items.

However, we must first go back over a long-dead problem, because it revives from time to time. Was the Fiscus really a public treasury?

Should we not take seriously a juridical text which states that the domains of the Fiscus are the Emperor's private property? Was not the Fiscus, then, the private patrimony of Caesar, as Mommsen claimed it to be?[94] Let us be clear about this. Mommsen did not claim that the word 'Fiscus' meant the private fortune which the Emperor possessed when he ascended the throne. He could not be unaware, indeed, that the Fiscus was kept filled by means of taxes, and served the needs of the state. But he wondered whether, by a peculiarity of Roman law, this coffer was perhaps formally treated as the Emperor's private property while materially remaining public in character, owing to the source of the money it contained and the use made of this money.[95] The interest of this little problem will lie in reminding us that, far from being the majestic construction that one might have hoped, Roman law, even where it is clearly set forth (as in the *Digest*, but certainly not in the actual laws, edicts and codes), is bad at conceptualizing and is even less systematic than English law.[96]

MOMMSEN'S THEORY

Mommsen's theory is complicated. It seeks to reconcile certain common-sense notions with the language of our sources, which say that the Fiscus was not a public institution (though it remains to be seen whether 'public' meant here what Mommsen thought it meant). The sources say, again and again, that the Fiscus belongs to the Emperor[97] and contrast it with the old Treasury, which alone is said to be public and belonging to the people, so that *populus* and Treasury are synonymous. The quaestors of the Treasury are excluded from the administration of the Fiscus, which is the preserve of the Emperor's procurators. Accordingly, it appears that the Fiscus belongs to the Emperor, since, if it does not belong to the people, it must belong to somebody.

Needless to say, the Fiscus bore no resemblance to a piece of private property. It was a state institution and was just like any other fiscal organ of yesterday or today. It was filled in part by taxes, and a mere private person does not levy taxes; and what it contained was used to operate the state machine. Finally, Mommsen holds that the reigning Emperor could not bequeath the Fiscus to whomsoever he liked. In the same way as any other public institution, it remained at the service of his successor on the throne. So perhaps (Mommsen is not very precise on this) the reigning Emperor disposed of the Fiscus in his will, just like any piece of private property, but took care to leave it to the person who was to be his successor, or otherwise his will was not honoured.[98]

If I have understood Mommsen aright, the private character of the Fiscus was a legal fiction. It is in the nature of a fiction that we must not deduce from it any more consequences than those for which it was invented. The Fiscus was not the Emperor's property in order to allow him to leave the Treasury to some favourite in the same way as he left his rings. The Emperor possessed the Fiscus because it was necessary for this Treasury to belong to some legal person; otherwise, the Fiscus could have been plundered without anyone being robbed.

The Fiscus did not come under private law, nor could the Emperor make use of it as though it were private property. Why, then, could it be considered private, as our sources seem to allege? What practical consequences followed from this fiction? When we read Mommsen we find only one such consequence. If we are to believe a number of items of evidence, one of which has some weight,[99] the first concern of certain Emperors, on the day they ascended the throne, was to bequeath to their children everything they possessed. That could have been due to kindly thoughtfulness: what need had the Emperors, thenceforth, for their fortune? It could also have been a precaution, to ensure that the family's patrimony was not confiscated and lost to their children in the event of their being victims of a revolution. Mommsen prefers to think that the Emperors wanted to circumvent the rule of law which identified the Emperor's property with the Fiscus, and which could have resulted in the Emperor's patrimony no longer passing to his heirs but rather to whatever person might succeed him on the throne. In short, under the pretext that the property of the Fiscus was formally the Emperor's own property, Mommsen concludes from this that, materially, the Emperor's property belonged to the Fiscus.[100]

THE FOREIGNNESS OF ROMAN LAW: A LAW WITHOUT CONCEPTS

The various sources, legal and other, declare in two ways that the contents of the Fiscus belong to the Emperor. Most commonly this is merely a matter of kingly style. Reacting against that style, a 'good' Emperor, Pertinax, decided one day that Caesar's domains should no longer be so called, because they really belonged to the state.[101] In the same way, the Queen of England could, if she chose, do away with the expression H(er) M(ajesty's) S(hip).

On another occasion, however, we have something more than a matter of style, for the adjective 'private' is here used by a lawyer, Ulpian, who draws consequences from it.[102] In Rome, when a private person misused public land, obstructed traffic on the public highway, or allowed to dangle from his balcony a piece of material which took the light from the floors below, the magistrate had the power to stop him doing these things. He pronounced an 'interdict' and called upon the offender to remove the offending object. This was an order: there was no need for any court action. Ulpian wonders whether the interdict could be pronounced on the territory of the domains of the Fiscus in the same way as on public land, and is inclined to think not: 'I consider that this interdict does not apply to land belonging to the Fiscus, because, on this land, a mere private person can neither do anything nor prevent anything.' Ulpian has earlier explained that public land is definable by the fact that it belongs to nobody in particular, so that one can no more suffer obstruction on it than take possession of it for oneself.[103] By this criterion the land of the domains of the Fiscus was not public in that sense. It consisted in fact of planted and cultivated fields, not of public gardens open to everyone. Ulpian goes on as follows: 'The domains of the Fiscus are, in fact, so to speak [*quasi*], the private property of the Emperor.' This passage has been much discussed. But surely it is obvious that the domains of the Fiscus are here described as private only in relation to the criterion adopted, and in order to contrast them with a public garden or the public highway.[104]

This is confirmed by the next passage. 'If, therefore, someone commits an offence there, this interdict will not apply, but in the event of a dispute, those who are in charge of these domains will be the judges to settle it.' Ulpian alludes to one of the 'privileges of the Fiscus' which withdrew the administration of the Imperial domains from common law and made it sole judge of any conflicts that private persons might have with the Fiscus.[105] Strange logic. Ulpian begins by saying that, since the domains of the Fiscus are not public, they are private, and since they are private, no interdict can apply to them. He ought to conclude from this that, on the domains of the Fiscus, the ordinary judges have jurisdiction, and that, just as a private person would do if he saw some stranger installing himself on his property, the Fiscus can only appeal to the courts – for example, by applying for a prohibitory injunction. But on the contrary he concludes that the representative of the Fiscus will himself settle the dispute, being both judge and party. There could be no better way of proving that, if the domains of the Fiscus are not public in a very special sense of that word, neither are they private: they are simply public in a different sense of that word.

In this passage in Ulpian, the domains of the Fiscus are private in the sense that they are not 'open to the public'. In most of the texts, and in the kingly style, however, they are private in the sense that they are not included among the old-established public institutions of the Republican period. 'Public' here has a historical meaning. As everyone always knew, the old Treasury was public. The Fiscus was a newcomer which made its entrance as timidly as the Imperial monarchy itself, and won its 'third' position only gradually. It remains the case that, from the beginning, nobody doubted that it was an institution such as we should call public, and *not* the Emperor's property. When translating this principle into formal statements, however, those concerned proceeded empirically and with prudence. The principle, indeed, was 'self-evident', and was not given formal expression. Hence the difficulty encountered in studying the problem: we must avoid asking of Roman law questions which arise from the standpoint of the rational norm, but which Roman law did not ask itself, although it could not avoid dealing with them *de facto*. This is the same difficulty that exists with all disciplines wherein the matter is subject to a norm. Must we ask a philosophy to answer questions which we want answered for the sake of establishing its internal coherence, but which this philosophy has not asked itself? Historically, the answer seems clear at first glance: we must restrict ourselves to what the philosopher or the jurist said. Yes; but what if despisèd logic, seeing the door shut, has come in through the window?

The sums held in the Republic's Treasury were regarded as public money (*pecunia publica*). This meant that any dispute concerning this money between the state and an individual was dealt with in accordance with the principle of authority; private law and procedure did not apply. Against the Treasury private persons could not go to the courts. They could only appeal to the censor to reconsider their case, and the censor, being both judge and party, decided as he wished. The state was not subject to common law.[106]

When Augustus set up the Fiscus and the other monarchical institutions, outside the apparatus of the Republican state and against it, there was at first a period of uncertainty. The Fiscus was a public coffer, but different from what had till then been regarded as *pecunia publica*. The procurators of the Fiscus were certainly public agents, but they were not on the same footing as the old-established magistrates. Certain 'interdicts' could be pronounced only on public land. That was the hallowed formula; should it be interpreted according to the letter or according to the spirit? The literal interpretation was adopted first. Despite an underlying awareness that the Fiscus was public, it was at first made subject to common law. Then, from Claudius's time onwards, the Fiscus, like the Treasury, became both judge and party in its own cases. Subsequent evolution was complicated but eventually, and very quickly, the Fiscus, thanks to its privileges, escaped altogether from the sphere of the ordinary judges, and became subject to *cognitio* alone.[107] The end was thus a triple division: there were public cases, fiscal cases and private cases.[108]

We needed to discuss Mommsen's theory at some length because, in my opinion, certain details remained to be clarified and because the idea is still current that, in the beginning at least, the Fiscus belonged to the Emperors.[109] This is a mistake. The simple truth is that the Fiscus was a monarchical institution and that, furthermore, the Roman state drew a great part of its resources not from taxation but from the immense Fiscal domains which it exploited just as a rich landowner would. Through the organ of the Fiscus the state was the largest latifundist of the whole Empire. Here we observe a familiar duality. With us, too, the state is at once a public authority (it orders us to pay taxes) and a private landowner (indeed a privileged private landowner, according to the French system of the 'public domain' and the Roman system of the privileges of the Fiscal domains).

THE EMPEROR'S PRIVATE WEALTH AS INSTRUMENT OF GOVERNMENT

Even if the Emperor was not a patrimonialist, however, he was the patron of his Empire. A brief study of the two other public coffers, the Patrimonium and the Private Fortune, will enable us to establish this. More precisely, a text of Pliny the Younger, if correctly understood, implies that, a century after Augustus, the Emperors continued to possess an enormous private fortune which they bequeathed to the senator whom they wished to succeed them, just as Augustus had done. But Pliny, while revealing the existence of this private patrimony, does not utter its official name. Was that name 'the Patrimonium', as

I believe, or 'the Private Fortune', as the most widely held view has it? It matters little which of these two coffers corresponded to the private wealth of the Emperors. All that we need do is to establish that, besides these public coffers and this private wealth, there was no third category, the 'property of the Crown' so dear to modern writers.

In the panegyric of Trajan which Pliny delivered soon after that Emperor came to the throne, the orator praises the Emperor for his disinterestedness: instead of keeping his huge fortune to himself, he has sold 'many of his inherited estates',[110] and a lengthy catalogue of lots for sale is being circulated. Besides which, the Emperor is distributing some of his finest properties as free gifts.

What was the source of this enormous fortune? Certainly not Trajan's natural father, an old senator who was not one of the richest, but rather his predecessor and adoptive father, the Emperor Nerva, who had chosen him as successor; 'You have bestowed on us as a gift,' exclaims the panegyrist, 'some of the loveliest properties, making over to us the very inheritance for which you were chosen and adopted, which was made yours by a reasoned decision.' Was Nerva then so rich? The immense inheritance he left to his adopted son and of which the latter disposed so freely included, among other things, a villa which had never belonged to anyone but the Emperors,[111] and a park which had formerly belonged to 'a famous general', most probably Pompey the Great. In reality this inheritance consisted of the spoils of noble families, the homes of senators – which are glad, says the orator, to see returning within their walls new owners who are also senators. Yet Pliny does not speak of the confiscations, does not recall any bloodstained memories. One might imagine that this immemorial patrimony of the Caesars was made up of inherited wealth and of those legacies which, obedient to convention, senators never failed to leave to the reigning Emperor.

I therefore believe that Trajan had in his possession the enormous patrimony of Augustus, considerably increased in the course of a century. Through legacies, inheritance or confiscation, this patrimony passed down from Emperor to Emperor. At Nero's death the new dynasty of the Flavians must have seized the inheritance of the Augustan family. Then came Nerva, who appointed as heir, in accordance with private law, his adopted son Trajan. This was how Trajan became the owner of the domain of Pausilypum which Vedius Pollio had once left to Augustus.[112]

The hinge of this argument is that the private patrimony of the Augustan house must have been confiscated by the Flavians, an illuminating hypothesis which we owe to Hirschfeld.[113] But Hirschfeld did not believe that the Flavians held on to it. In his view, they turned it into 'property of the crown'. The rest of the system which is generally accepted today follows from this idea. After the confiscation, it is held, there was the coffer called the Patrimonium, which consisted of the property of the crown, and also the coffer called the Private Fortune – the latter corresponding to the last category of Imperial property which it seems logical to distinguish, namely the private fortunes of the different Emperors.

But why should the Flavians have turned the inheritance of the Caesars into a possession of the crown? Here is Hirschfeld's reasoning: 'The new dynasty of the Flavians, together with the Emperors who succeeded them, entered into possession of the patrimony of the Caesars at the same time as they acquired the name of Caesar.' In fact from the Flavians onward, the *cognomen* 'Caesar', which was peculiar to the Augustan family, became the name of every reigning Emperor and also of his heir presumptive; 'but this patrimony necessarily lost, thereafter, its character as family property and acquired that of property of the crown, attached to possession of the throne'.[114] This 'necessity' exists only for modern eyes; in Rome, where the throne was never regarded as hereditary,[115] there could be no dynastic property. The Emperor was a magistrate who could not decide beforehand who should be his successor, even if he could smooth the way for him. I think that, by taking the *cognomen* of 'Caesar', the Flavians wanted to link themselves artificially with the fallen dynasty whose heritage they had seized in the bloody circumstances of the years 68 to 70. Trajan was to inherit it; he did not come into possession of it as 'property of the crown'. More than a century later the Emperor Macrinus was to sell off the property of another fallen dynasty, the Severi.[116]

In practice, inheritance of the private patrimony decided succession to the throne, unless revolution or confiscation supervened. Of course, when Augustus left two-thirds of his fortune to Tiberius and a third to Livia, that was not a sharing-out of the throne.[117] He did not have the right to divide it or to bequeath it. But, as Jean Béranger has shown so convincingly, this fortune gave such power to the heir that he was forthwith marked down as the next Emperor. 'It was not an inconsequential matter of chance that the Emperor was the richest man in his Empire.'[118] That was the case with the Augustan family and it was the same, I think, with the subsequent dynasties.

This private fortune, which was also the strongest of the Emperor's instruments of government, was both the weapon and the prize of each *pronunciamento*. But now the fallen Emperor or his heirs found themselves despoiled not only of the colossal inheritance but also of the private patrimony which had belonged to the unfortunate ruler before he came to the throne. This explains a feature which fascinated Mommsen.[119] Let us imagine a senator and his patrimony. He becomes Emperor. By inheritance or by confiscation he gets possession of his predecessor's enormous wealth, as private property, not as property of the crown. This wealth becomes part of his patrimony, just as if he had inherited it from one of his uncles. In the event of revolution, all of that property will be confiscated, for the fortunate victor will certainly not carry courtesy so far as to leave to the heirs of the fallen dynasty the property which would have come to them if their father had not climbed so high. Confiscating inheritances on one pretext or another was one of the chief resources of Rome's rulers. We appreciate therefore the wise precaution taken by Pertinax (who was to reign for only three months): the very day he came to the throne, he divided his patrimony among his children.[120] The daughter of his successor Didius Julianus (who reigned for a few weeks) had less luck. When her father was condemned to death by the Senate, she was stripped not only of her title of princess of the blood (*Augusta*) but also of the patrimony which her father had taken the vain precaution of transferring at once to her.[121]

This, then, was the private heritage which enabled the Emperors to go on being patrons of the state. We still need to discover whether to call it Patrimonium or Private Fortune.

Patrimonium, surely. For this coffer existed from the time of Claudius, from the dynasty inaugurated by Augustus, and we have just seen that there was no break in the history of the Imperial patrimony — it was not born in 69 as 'property of the crown'. What was called the Patrimonium in the second century was the same patrimony that had belonged to Augustus. The Private Fortune, on the other hand, is not mentioned before the middle of the second century. For another argument, when one of the Emperor's subjects made his sovereign his heir or legatee, the heritage apparently went to the Patrimonium and not to the Fiscus or the Private Fortune; thus the Patrimonium included the property which the Emperor possessed or acquired in his personal capacity.[122] We still have to examine a certain much-disputed passage in Ulpian. I will spare the reader this – he has already seen the traps that Roman law lays for the jurists of today – and put what I have to say about it in a note.[123]

As for the last of the three coffers, the Private Fortune, everything points to its *public* character.[124] It was outside the scope of common law and enjoyed the same privileges as the Fiscus.[125] Its paper-work was sometimes the same as that of the Fiscus.[126] I think that the domains of the so-called Private Fortune are what is meant by the 'possessions of Caesar' mentioned in some writings. In Rome, when some treasure was discovered on private land, the finder kept half the value while the other half went to the landowner. If it was found on public land, this half went to the city; if on land belonging to the Fiscus, to the Fiscus; and if the discovery was made on one of Caesar's possessions, this half went not to Caesar or to his Patrimonium, but again to the Fiscus.[127] It was these possessions of Caesar, I imagine, that Pertinax wanted to deprive of the name 'possessions of Caesar', because they were public.

What, then, was this Private Fortune? We do not know. Was it a coffer different from the Fiscus? A mere subdivision of the Fiscus, entrusted with the management of the domains, as Mitteis supposes? A sort of civil list, since in it the Emperor's account is separate from the Empress's? At all events, let us not assume anything too simple. The finances of the Empire were as complicated and confused as those of the French *ancien régime*; they lacked that elegant orderliness which permits the construction of attractive hypotheses and, in the absence of documents, the fabrication of probable history.

THE EMPEROR AND THE ARMY: SOLDIERS FOR SALE?

The Emperor had a huge private fortune which enabled him to be the leading *euergetēs* of his Empire. The Empire's public Treasury was under his exclusive control. The bureaucracy was under his hand, and only the great military commands, together with almost all the governorships of the provinces, continued to be reserved to the senatorial caste. Nor was that all: the Emperor was the supreme head of the armies.

But was he this *ex officio* or in his personal capacity? Here the question of patrimonialism resurfaces. Some think, indeed, that the soldiers were not so much the agents of authority as the liegemen of the Emperor, to whom they were bound by the military oath. Moreover, money seems to have been so important in the relations between the Emperor and the armies that it often looks as though he was buying the obedience of his troops. He distributed money among them, *donativa*, which are regarded as one of the exotic and scandalous peculiarities of Caesarism. The army or the Imperial guard, say historians both ancient and modern, were for sale to the highest bidder, and set on the throne the pretender who made them the best offer. Liegemen or mercenaries? The truth is more commonplace but less simple.

The direct relation between the Imperial authority and the army was twofold: the Emperors commanded the armies and the armies appointed the Emperors, or allowed them to be appointed. The Emperor was the exclusive master of foreign policy: the foreign nations that had trembled before the Senate of the Republic now trembled before him alone.[128] He was the master of the army, made all promotions,[129] recruited and raised as many soldiers as he wanted.[130] Soldiers swore their oath to his name and to his images, which decorated their standards.[131] When he inspected an army, the Emperor put on military garb and himself took over command.

Apart from military ceremonial and inspections, the Emperor's relationship with his soldiers was as impersonal as with the mass of his officials. Only the fighting Emperors – Trajan, Severus, and later Constantine or Julian the Apostate, with their *comitatenses* around them – appear as leaders of men. Other military leaders, who were not sovereigns, were no less worshipped by the troops they had led to victory, and their popularity with the troops threatened the throne.[132] The fact remains that, although not a citizen army, neither was the Imperial army a band of liegemen devoted to their leader, the sovereign. It was an army of professionals who pursued a trade that was profitable to them. They knew that their pay and their careers depended on the Emperor's office, and they took no heed of the Senate.

Nevertheless, Premerstein is right in a way. These professionals were not a species of official. The impersonal relationship between them and their trade, their sovereign (whoever he might be) and their standards, was that of a privileged body which elevates its interests into an *esprit de corps*. It had all the zeal of a subgroup's own particular patriotism. Men entered the army as one enters holy orders; until Severus's time, soldiers were not allowed to marry. They belonged to a world apart, and a privileged one. In the face of the peasant masses, those men who were so lucky as to be soldiers represented authority, and they had swords and money. In this Empire in which the state had been thrown upon society like great blocks of stone, the state machine felt superior to society and did not merge with it. Being a soldier was not a trade like any other.

The statutory relations between this body and the Emperors were paralleled by a relationship of a different kind. The Emperors were required by custom, in various circumstances and especially on their accession, to give their troops a *donativum*, a money present. We must dwell awhile on this institution, which is well known, mainly on the anecdotal level, and whose history I do not think has yet been written.

The *donativum* was a gift of some thousands or tens of thousands of sesterces per man.[133] Mere delay in paying it cost more than one Emperor his throne, it is said.[134] This inaugural gift was paid by the Emperor to the soldiers of the legions stationed on the Empire's distant frontiers just as to the praetorians who guarded the Emperor in Rome.[135] However, our sources speak chiefly of the *donativum* paid to the praetorians, who are accused of having sold the throne on more than one occasion. Thus in 193, after an Emperor (Pertinax) who favoured the Senate had been murdered by the guard, there were scandalous scenes, if we are to believe a senatorial historian: 'Just as if it had been in some market or auction-room, both the City and its entire empire were auctioned off. The sellers were the ones who had slain their emperor, and the would-be buyers were Sulpicianus and Julianus, who vied to outbid each other ... They gradually raised their bids up to 20,000 sesterces per soldier. Some of the soldiers would carry word to Julianus, "Sulpicianus offers so much; how much more do you make it?" And to Sulpicianus in turn, "Julianus promises so much; how much to you raise him?"'[136]

Is this a partisan caricature? In part only. The praetorians and the senators were the only political forces capable of making an Emperor in Rome itself, and a pretender who was too much liked by the one group was in danger of incurring the dislike of the other. The sovereigns who are supposed to have lost or gained their throne on account of a *donativum* (Claudius in 41, Galba in 68, Didius in 193) were also sovereigns whose nomination had been disputed between the Senate and the praetorian guard. The guard murdered Emperors who were too 'senatorial', whether they had hastened to pay the *donativum*, like Pertinax,[137] or whether they had delayed payment for too long, like Galba. The fact remains that, in these political conflicts, the *donativum* always played a role. Refusal to make the accession gift seems to have angered the guard not so much because of the money they were not getting as because of implied repudiation of a principle. Galba, wrote the senator Tacitus, made a great mistake in saying too loudly 'that he was sent to select, not buy, his soldiers ... There is no question that their loyalty could have been won by the slightest generosity on the part of this stingy old man. He was ruined by his old-fashioned strictness and excessive severity – qualities which we can no longer bear.'[138] The praetorians became angry about the *donativum* with Emperors whom they disliked for other reasons. The accession gift had symbolic value and was, so to speak, the raw nerve. The hostility of the guard towards a 'senatorial' Emperor focused on the question of the *donativum* and we shall see that after they had chosen an Emperor to their liking, their choice was also sealed by the *donativum*.

Other sources, indeed, present the accession gift in a less caricaturing light. The following scene takes place in Paris in 360, and Ammianus Marcellinus, a reliable writer, is the author.[139] Julian, the future Apostate, is as yet only a Caesar or sort of vice-Emperor, and has just fought a triumphant campaign on the Rhine which has saved Gaul from barbarian invasion. This young hero is adored by his troops, who have a grievance against the reigning sovereign, Constantius Augustus: the latter wants to separate them from their leader and send them to fight, far from their families, at the other end of the world. In vain has the court done everything possible to prevent Julian from winning his soldiers' hearts. It has cut off his supply of funds and the young prince has only enough to feed and clothe his men.[140] He cannot distribute to them, in addition, the *largesses* in gold and silver which had become customary in the later Empire, supplementing payment in kind.[141] Nevertheless the soldiers want Julian and him alone.

And so, one fine day in 360, the army and the population of Paris go and tear the young Caesar from the palace where he is hiding – for he fears the perilous honour they wish to confer on him, even while in his heart he longs for it – and they proclaim him sovereign in full title, Augustus. A usurper in spite of himself, or almost, Julian now has only the choice between death, which will be his fate if he fails, and the Empire. Meanwhile he promises his troops, as an accession gift, five gold *solidi* and a pound of silver per man, which was the customary rate.[142] We can be sure that when they heard the news, old Constantius and his court exclaimed that Julian had bought the Imperial title for five *solidi* and that the soldiers in Gaul were venal. This is all the more likely because Julian himself accused Constantius's agents in Paris of trying to bribe his men.[143]

THE *LARGESSES* TO THE SOLDIERS

Abandoning the idea that the *donativum* was the actual purchase price of a throne put up for auction, are we then to see in it a mere inconsequential formality? No, we are not; for symbols are not merely reflections of reality, they are a part of it, which our eyes take as indices to the whole, just as smoke is a feature of certain phenomena of combustion. But not all combustion gives rise to smoke. For the accession gift to have sealed the accord between a popular Emperor and his army and for this gift to have become on other occasions the 'raw nerve' in a political antagonism, the relation between the Emperors and their army must have included something special, without which no symbol would have emerged from it.

I should add straight away that this special feature was historical. We ought not to be too ready to explain it by the natural tendency to introduce symbols into any relationship which is not strictly a matter of regulations. We know that the choice of the gift, among all other possible symbols, is always largely historical, and that other symbols could have been preferred. Gifts to the army upon accession, or on any other occasion, were by no means a universal phenomenon in ancient monarchies. Roman soldiers received a *donativum*, and so did the Roman plebs, but the Imperial officials did not. On the other hand the last shah of Iran gave a coronation *donativum* to his officials not so long ago. More recently still, in Britain, the gift went in the opposite direction, when the soldiers were vigorously canvassed to subscribe to a wedding gift for Princess Anne. To symbolize a personal relationship between the sovereign and the army, the gift can function equally well in either direction; if the sovereign is a father of his people, the army ought to show filial affection. To be sure, it could show this in words and gestures rather than with money.

The existence of the *donativum* in Rome was due to historical reasons, but these were not the ones commonly supposed. The accession gift was not a continuation of the *largesses* made to the armies in the epoch of the civil wars. Its origins are more unexpected, being located in the realm of last wills and testaments.

During the civil wars at the end of the Republic,[144] the magnates Sulla, Caesar, Octavius, Antony and Brutus distributed money to their troops whenever they needed to revive enthusiasm,[145] and their subordinates did the same.[146] It would be interesting to know the psychology of the troops who received these '*largesses*' (that was the approved term), and there are two passages which reveal this to us. A few months after the murder of Caesar, Octavius tried to rally fighters to his banner for the struggle against Antony. He succeeded in winning over all the veterans living in Casilinum and Calatia; 'and no wonder,' writes Cicero, 'when he is giving them 500 *denarii* apiece'. This sum seems to me substantial, not merely symbolic, but all the same it was not enough to hire a man. Those veterans needed to wait till after victory to have their future assured. The 500 *denarii* are an advance on profits to come. Cicero adds that the legions in Macedonia 'refused to take Antony's bounty, or so he says, heaped insults on him and left him still haranguing'.[147] We see that these troops were interested, but not venal; they were honest 'workers with the sword' rather than mercenaries in the pejorative sense of the word.

On another occasion Octavius tried to corrupt Antony's supporters. He made some initial symbolic *largesses* to them, followed by more and more substantial promises, assuring them that he would look upon them as long-standing supporters of his, rather than as soldiers. Out of 10,000, only 1,000 gave way (others allege that 3,000 was the figure). 'The rest then took their departure, but presently they remembered the toils of agriculture and the gains of military service ... And so ... they repented and, seizing upon their former pretext for the sake of appearances, they armed themselves and went back to him,' leaving Antony's party for that of Octavius, which seemed the more promising prospect.[148] These professional soldiers appear to have had divided souls. They fought for money, but they seem also to have had a personal loyalty to, even a political preference for, a particular leader, Caesar or Antony, and found it hard to change this. Perhaps their souls were simpler than that, and personal loyalty was, in those ancient times, equivalent to what we call professional inertia. They disliked abandoning Octavius or Antony just as, today, a middle-class person dislikes changing his profession or a skilled worker refuses to go and live on the other side of the country in response to changes in the labour market. Antony's soldiers did not like sacrificing the habits, the comrades and the investments, material and moral, that they already had in a particular party.

The '*largesses*' of the civil wars were informal wage supplements paid before the expected victory. The soldiers certainly counted on not having to rest content with their pay. These *largesses* nevertheless pleased them when they came, because, although tacitly understood to be due, they were not looked for on fixed dates, and their arrival gave men more heart for the fight. The *donativa* of the Empire were not like that. Before they became primarily the accession gift of a new Emperor, they were the legacy left by the late Emperor to two groups of people – the army and the plebs of Rome. In fact the *donativum* to the soldiers and the *congiarium* to the Roman plebs always went together,[149] which means that the Emperors considered the soldiers and the citizens of Rome to be under their special protection.

This was indeed the case. In his panegyric of Constantius, Julian compares the Emperor to a shepherd. The mass of his subjects are his flocks and the soldiers are his good sheep-dogs. These are the two categories of the population.[150] Such ideas had a very long history. When Augustus constructed his system of personal power in opposition to the senatorial oligarchy, he reserved to himself two control levers – the army and the City of Rome, which epitomized the entire Roman people. Augustus wanted to have the soldiers on his side and to close Rome against any possible rivals who might use the City as the theatre in which they would court popularity. In constitutional terms, this was called *imperium proconsulare* in the provinces[151] and *cura Urbis* over the City of Rome, which ceased to be an autonomous commune.[152] Now in those days it was the custom to be very liberal when drawing up one's will: something should be left to all one's friends, neighbours and dependants, without exception. So on the death of Augustus it was learnt, when his will was read, that he had left 43 millions to the citizens of Rome and about 50 millions to the soldiers.[153] In his lifetime Augustus had always taken care to treat his subjects like one big family. When his grandson Gaius Caesar joined the army, he gave a money present to the troops 'because then for the first time they had Gaius taking part with them in their exercises'.[154]

Augustus's legacies to the soldiers and the plebs were executed by his heir Tiberius, who succeeded him on the throne. Tiberius in his turn left millions to the soldiers and the plebs, which were distributed by his heir and successor Caligula.[155] The latter went mad and was murdered. It was then, say our sources, that the *donativum* was born.[156] Placed on the throne by the praetorians, in dramatic circumstances, the new Emperor, Claudius, had no legacy to distribute. He needed to thank the soldiers for their support and to seal his accord with them, and this was all the more necessary because the Senate was slow to confirm the choice made by the praetorians. 'Claudius assembled and addressed the army, binding them by oath that they would remain loyal to him. He presented the praetorian guard with 5,000 drachmas apiece and their officers with a proportionate sum and promised similar amounts to the armies wherever they were.'[157] The legacy had become an accession gift, and the tradition became fixed. At the death of Claudius, Nero 'promised a donative after the example of his father's bounty'.[158]

For about two centuries the *donativum* remained what it had originally been – the sign of a family relationship between the Emperor and the army. It was distributed at every accession[159] and other payments were made when the heir presumptive came of age[160] or received the title of Caesar.[161] Finally, a *donativum* might be paid to reward cohorts that had stayed loyal to the Emperor during an attempted *coup d'état*.[162]

THE NATURE OF THE IMPERIAL AUTHORITY

The *donativum* had enabled Augustus to demonstrate to everyone that the army depended on him alone. What, after his time, could have been the political implications of these *largesses*, which were at once symbolic and substantial (at each change of Emperor a praetorian received a sum equivalent to several quarters' pay)? The implications depended on the political weight of the body of troops in question. So long as the legions were too far from the centre of power to be able to make Emperors, except in revolutionary circumstances, the *donativum* was seen by them as a right they had acquired, but which lacked any special significance. Only a denial of this right would have meant something and caused trouble. For when purely historical causes have resulted in the selection of a symbol, whatever this may be, two effects follow: the symbol ceases to be thought about, and it becomes impossible to go back on it; whoever rejects this symbol which is both banal and hallowed is seen as violating the social pact.

From the viewpoint of the praetorian guard, however, the *donativum* was always a raw nerve and never taken for granted, because the guard always had a say in the election of a new Emperor. This fact is bound up with a curious aspect of the Imperial system.

In Weber's terms, the Empire was a traditional regime which assumed false appearances of formality and constitutionality.[163] By 'traditional' is meant that it was based on power relations which, however informal, were accepted by public opinion and held to be both legitimate and lasting. At Augustus's death the regime 'reproduced itself'.[164] These power relations were dressed up in constitutional robes which had been arbitrarily retailored. Scholarly discussions of the legal foundations of Imperial authority have been as voluminous as they have been meagre in convincing conclusions. The more recent discussions on its ideological foundations have been still more Byzantine: what have people not looked for behind the 'authority' which Augustus claimed to possess? That word was merely the laudatory way he had of talking about his position of strength.[165] He could allow himself to talk about it in noble terms because public opinion accepted his rule. Public law played no part in this. Should we write, for example, that after Vespasian at the latest, the creation of the Emperor by the army was regarded as being legal (*rechtsgültig*)?[166] What had legality to do with it? An Emperor has died, and so the political forces in position look for a new Emperor. The choice is improvised on the basis of the realities of the moment. Nobody dreams of consulting the constitution or remembering what custom dictates. If the Senate, terrified, stays silent, nobody will ask for its views, and the Emperor will be chosen by the army. Then the Senate, so as not to be reduced to nullity, will hasten to confirm the army's choice. If the Senate feels strong enough on another occasion to put forward a name, it will sound out the feelings of the guard so as to see whether it is prepared to acclaim the Senate's candidate.

What then were the forces usually present in the political arena? There was the authority of the late Emperor, if he had been able to win the approval of public opinion for his chosen successor; the Senate, by virtue of its prestige; and the guard, through its weapons. In time of revolution there were also the legions on the frontiers, with *their* weapons. Very exceptionally, the population of Rome took to the streets.[167] As for those revolts of the lower orders which try to overthrow the dynasty and, if they succeed, end by founding a new one, Rome, like China or Russia, knew many of them, but none succeeded even in attaining the dimensions of the revolt of Spartacus in earlier times. And as for the notables, they ruled or tyrannized over their cities, but the machinery of state remained beyond their grasp.

The power of the Senate and that of the guard were left confronting one another. The praetorians did not always or especially claim to impose on Rome an Emperor conformable to certain political interests. What they wanted, above all, was that the Emperor should not be made without them, for mere possession of political power is a satisfaction, no less than the use that can be made of it. From this followed jealousy between the praetorians and the Senate. Would the Emperor emerge as the Senate's man or the guard's? In this conflict over political self-respect, the way in which the Emperor gave his *donativum* was a sure indication; an Emperor who gave it grudgingly would be someone who wanted to reduce the guard to a role of mere obedience and deny it the dignity of a political force on which he relied. Would he take action to deny the guard that dignity? He would hardly have had the opportunity to take the risk; but he had already gone too far if he entertained contemptuous thoughts about the praetorians.

Such was the *donativum* in the early Empire: in the eyes of all citizens, an assertion of the Emperors' control of the army; in the eyes of the legions a simple entitlement; and in the eyes of the guard an indication of its political prestige, about which it was very touchy. Now we shall see the transformation undergone by the *donativum* in the third and fourth centuries, when it became on the one hand something like the wages of old-time servants, and on the other a gratuity by means of which the Emperors showed their men that they looked on them as 'family friends' of the ruling power.

IN THE LATER EMPIRE: 'WAGES' AND GRATUITIES

In Molière and Balzac we see servants being paid by their master in three ways: they are fed and clothed; they have the right to money wages which are paid to them more or less regularly (a master who is poor or miserly may neglect to pay them for years on end); and they may also receive gratuities if their master is pleased with them. This was more or less the situation of soldiers under the later Empire, because the '*annonae*' in kind had become the guaranteed part of their pay, whereas devaluation had affected the element received in coin, and because the *donativum* (the word had changed its meaning) had become a regular supplement to pay since the Emperors had taken to granting it every five years, to celebrate the fifth and tenth anniversaries of their accession, which had turned into major festivals.[168] In short, the soldiers were guaranteed maintenance in kind, but the supplements in gold and silver that should have been added to this were not always paid regularly – Julian, it will be remembered, had never been able to pay them. So that when these supplements, called pay (*stipendium*) and *donativum* were paid at last, the Emperor who distributed them seemed to be making a gift; he exhorted his soldiers to be brave and loyal in exchange for what they were receiving,[169] he won their goodwill[170] and he refreshed their enthusiasm.[171] The *donativum* had in principle become as regular as the *stipendium*, and both were paid when the sovereign was able to pay them.

This wrongly gives the soldiers of that time the air of having no longer any professional ideal and of thinking only of money.[172] The same could be said, no more or no less, of the armies of the early Empire: but they had received their pay automatically. The soldiers of the fourth century profited by their close relationship with a fighting Emperor to try and wrest their wages from him when they thought they had him at their mercy. After taking a town in Assyria, Julian's soldiers raised the question of money with him, but he rebuked them and they did not insist.[173] They had not grown greedy. It was the system of remuneration that had, in respect of one half of it, become informal, and that was what led to scenes worthy of Molière. Being a bad payer, the state, when it did deign to pay, seemed to be giving presents. One had to be rough in demanding one's due from the state.

In addition, the state gave genuine presents, on the occasion of victories[174] and of the accession of an Emperor, for since the *donativum* had become part of the soldier's pay, an authentic accession gift had come into existence in all but name.[175] The fourth-century army was something quite unprecedented. It was no longer strung out along distant frontiers like the legions of old (protection of the frontiers would soon be abandoned to undistinguished soldier-farmers). The spearhead of the army now consisted of a group of several tens of thousands of men, the *comitatenses*, who accompanied the Emperor and went to war with him – men who beheld their sovereign with their own eyes, whom he consulted and appealed to, and with whom he discussed matters of grand strategy.[176] At each change of Emperor the men in office had these soldiers ratify by acclamation the nomination of the new Emperor and also that of his heir.[177]

This huge army did not have the same political pretensions as the few thousand praetorians of former times, but it did have a corporate pride, and wanted to be a privileged body, distinguished from the crowd by Imperial favours.[178] The accession gift proved to it that the new Augustus was, in this respect, what it expected every sovereign to be. These soldiers were non-political. They did not claim to make the Emperor themselves, but they desired that, through the favours he showed them, the ruler whom they did not fail to acclaim should testify that he considered them his faithful sheep-dogs and did not

344

confuse them with the mass of sheep. In many ancient societies, being one of the ruler's servants meant enjoying a prestige among the people that it is hard for us to imagine; nothing else marked off one man from another.

In short, if we trace it back to its origins, we see that the *donativum* is a historical accident. Augustus, whose position as monarch was precarious, had been obliged to give symbolic expression to his control of the army, and in accordance with a Roman testamentary custom the symbol *par excellence* was a gift or a legacy in kind.

Let me expand this little tale of the *donativum* into a sociological conclusion. Modern historians have concerned themselves mainly with the social origins of the Roman army or of its officers and their class position: were the *pronunciamentos* at heart a revolt of the rural masses, among whom the soldiers were recruited, against the 'bourgeoisie' of the cities? This is seeing only half of the problem, and probably the less important half at that. An army is also an institution which has an *esprit de corps* and which reacts as such. The praetorians did not wish to govern because they were of Italian bourgeois origin but because the guard possessed strength and prestige. The armies of the various provinces did not make *pronunciamentos* against the Senate as the organ of the 'bourgeoisie' but in order to sweep away those chatterers, drive out an incapable ruler and save the Empire; or quite simply so that it should not be said that it was a rival army, in another province, that made all the Emperors. The armies represented only themselves and their ideals, the myths and interests of their corporation. As for social class, class positions and other civilian ideas, soldiers and officers had left them behind when they joined the army.

THE ROMAN MODIFICATION OF THE IDEAL TYPE

This protracted discussion of the Imperial army, finances and administration leads us to negative conclusions. There is no trace of patrimonialism in Rome's institutions, except in the vocabulary used (the minor officials being called slaves or freedmen of the Emperor, not of the state). In practice the separation between the state apparatus and the persons of the successive rulers was rigorous. There was just one exception: alongside the different public coffers (which were the Emperor's private property only nominally), certain Emperors inherited a huge personal patrimony which they employed for political ends, thereby acting as *euergetai* of the state. Apart from that, they were magistrates.

As for the alleged relations of clientage between the Emperor and his subjects or soldiers, these were non-existent: the *donativum* was not a pledge of such bonds. To suppose that an immense state, in which the relations between sovereign and subject are relations of anonymous obedience, can be compared to a band of followers is frankly to lose one's sense of historical realities. We must not allow a few trees to hide the forest from us. Premerstein curiously exaggerated the importance of the oath to the Emperors. Texts, inscriptions, papyruses all show clearly that the Emperor's tens of millions of subjects obeyed him, as taxpayers, legal subjects, patriots and soldiers, in the same way as all subjects obey in all states in the world – they obeyed him as the head of state. Almost all the details in Premerstein's book are correct, but the total effect is very misleading. The great historian has been the victim of a philological convention, that of seeking to interpret the realities of an epoch solely through the concepts and symbols of that epoch. Consequently one is not allowed to assert that the sky over Rome was blue and that Romans had two arms and two legs, if chance has it that these facts are not mentioned in any of the ancient writings which have survived.

To see the difference, as regards patrimonialism, between Rome and the Hellenistic states, it is enough to recall a fact of some weight. The Greek kings could leave to whomsoever they chose, not their crowns of course, or the royal lands or the contents of their coffers, but their kingdom as a whole. They bequeathed it as though it were a plot of land, and their wills had the force of law.[179] We know that Rome inherited in this way, absolutely legally, both Asia and Cyrene. This oddity was, as I see it, in conformity with the way things were done in the semi-barbarian East.[180] It also followed from the fact that a Greek king was regarded as a conqueror, a crowned adventurer, a gatherer of lands. We see the contrast with Rome, where the Emperor did not even have the right to appoint his successor in his will. The foundation of Greek monarchy was the right of conquest (a kingdom was 'land won by the spear'), but the Imperial regime was a magistracy.

This was how the ideal type of the sovereign by absolute right was modified in Rome. The Emperor's role was profoundly affected by the fact that, before being an empire, Rome had been a city. Hellenistic thought and reality observed a very sharp contrast between cities and kingdoms: it was the great divide of those days. The Emperor was a civic personage. He was a magistrate and a *euergetēs*. He was not the owner of his Empire, but he could be its patron, as we have seen. We shall see also that, when he made *largesse*, he did not do it on the scale or with the carelessness of an oriental potentate or a Hellenistic king.

Nevertheless, even when he was not making *largesse* and even when he was executing acts of law, he called them *euergesiai*, 'benefactions' performed by the Good King that he was by definition.

6. *The Emperor's benefactions*

If the Emperor had been the owner of the Empire, everything would be very simple: there would be no public law at all, and all political life would be improvised at the potentate's whim. The Empire was not run like that, of course, and its machinery of state was more complex and formal than family life; it needed laws, regulations, bureaucrats. The problem is, as we shall see, that the language of the kingly style attributed the public acts of the sovereign, as well as his private acts, to his virtues and in particular to his liberality; these acts were presented as so many benefactions. People thus affected to believe that the sovereign could have nothing to do with an abstraction like the state and that, consequently, any relation between his subjects and the state apparatus was a relation with the sovereign's person, the person of a benefactor.

When he became Emperor, Antoninus 'gave largess to the people, and, in addition, a donation to the soldiers, and founded an order of destitute girls, called Faustinianae in honour of Faustina [the Empress]. Of the public works that were constructed by him the following remain today ...'[181] This catalogue of acts, taken from a late historian, was canonical. Liberalities, or what were called such, were an important part of the Emperors' activity in the eyes of the average Roman. *Liberalitas* is the Latin word for the quality that makes a *euergetēs*: the Greek word *euergesia*, or good deed, was translated as *beneficium*, benefaction.[182] Ancient historians talk endlessly about the liberalities and benefactions of the Emperor, and either approve or disapprove of them according to their political and religious opinions.[183]

Yet the Emperor could not be a run-of-the-mill *euergetēs*. How could one distinguish, in him, between the private person who performed public services, like a notable, and the sovereign who merely fulfilled his proper tasks? The texts speak of his bounty, and we need to 'understand' them and speak their language, but at the same time we have to refrain from always taking them at their word, and must distinguish between what the Romans did and what they thought they were doing. When Vespasian, 'out of his liberality', established chairs of rhetoric with the money of the Fiscus, i.e. the product of taxes, there was no difference between him and a minister of education who establishes chairs in the Sorbonne, and only a turn of kingly style caused him to be called a *euergetēs*; while this style recalls not so much the rhetoric of the inscriptions that celebrated the *euergesiai* of the notables as the monarchical phraseology of the French *ancien régime*. In the study of Imperial euergetism, the question is no longer one of knowing the private motives that impelled a private person to sacrifice his wealth for the public good, but of knowing why a public personage attributed his public actions to his private virtues.

The question is not an easy one, for the sovereign's activity was not unitary. The different measures he took were to some extent matters of applying regulations but also to some extent matters of discretion. Automatic application of the law to an individual case; mercy for a condemned man who would have been murdered rather than punished by the letter of a law too generally conceived; a decision in the field of foreign policy – these were three types of public action related to very different principles. Did Imperial euergetism belong to one of these types, and were the words 'liberality' and 'benefaction' technical terms? Or did all this mean simply that ideology and the kingly style described as benefactions very different types of action, public or private, so long as the beneficiaries had reason to be glad of them?

THE BENEFIT OF THE LAW

It is the second hypothesis which is correct. Take for example the word 'benefaction'. Whatever may sometimes be said, this is never a technical term, and it cuts across very different types of action by the Emperor. *A priori*, a benefaction by the Emperor might be one of three things: the mechanical application of a rule to an individual case, as when a veteran is allowed to retire on pension;[184] departure from the letter of the law in an individual case for the sake of equity or simple charity; or an unjustifiable favour, a royal caprice embellished with the name of 'pardon'. A *beneficium* could be any of these, but in practice the term was applied mainly to the most ordinary administrative decisions, because these were the most frequent: grant of the right to citizenship,[185] admission into the equestrian order,[186] authorization given to a private person to take water from an aqueduct.[187] Benefactions were any and every public act which gave unalloyed pleasure.

It was rare, however, for the benefaction to be a royal pardon. The sovereign's prerogative of pardon did exist, but in pagan antiquity it was less talked about than in the Middle Ages.[188] On the contrary, when people thought about the virtues of the Emperor, or his benefactions, they hardly considered the condemned men he might have pardoned, for the image of the executioner's sword checked as it descends evokes associations of ideas that are not likely to foster love for a ruler. The word 'benefaction' was more usually applied to privileges: immunities from taxation, revenues of public domains allotted to an autonomous city,[189] citizenship accorded to veterans who had the right to it or to an entire city which had deserved it. Should we say with Mommsen that a *beneficium* was a 'useful right'? Or with Alvaro d'Ors that it was not a privilege but rather a discretionary measure which, far from contradicting the other rules, as a privilege would, was in conformity with them?[190] The two definitions complement one another, and the problem does not lie there; an immunity is a privilege, citizenship is not a 'useful right'. In reality, *beneficium* had no definite meaning and was often a redundant expression, which has passed into our own legal vocabulary. 'To receive citizenship by the benefaction of the Prince [*beneficio imperatoris*]' meant simply receiving it 'by virtue of a decision by the Emperor', and 'to enjoy the rights which the Lex Julia grants to mothers' could be put as 'to enjoy them by benefit of that law [*beneficio legis Juliae*]', i.e. to benefit from the provisions of the law.

What we need to know is in which cases there was a personal decision by the Emperor rather than the automatic application of a rule, a benefaction by the Emperor rather than benefit of the law. *A priori*, this would happen in two cases: when the Emperor broke the law and when it fell to him to decide whether the law was applicable in a particular instance. In the first case he granted a pardon, an immunity or a privilege; in the second, he exercised discretion by virtue of the executive power vested in him – as when he ruled that a veteran did indeed fulfil the conditions that enabled him to claim citizenship. And if there was no rule for the Emperor to apply, or of which he could suspend the effect, we are surprised to find that the ancient writers do not use the word 'benefaction' – that they do not, for example, say that an officer has been decorated for bravery as a result of the Emperor's benefaction. For no legislator would have tried to define formally in advance what brave actions should attract decorations: the Emperor judged the facts in their materiality and in his own soul and conscience. If a military decoration had been called a benefaction this would have seemed to imply that favour rather than merit had dictated the award.[191]

When Frontinus writes that 'Augustus also determined by an edict what rights those should possess who were enjoying the use of water according to Agrippa's records, thus making the entire supply dependent upon his own grants',[192] he means that the Emperor reserved to himself the decision to award these concessions to the beneficiaries – concessions that were given, and even required, within the framework of a rule. For one could not ask the Emperor for just any favour; there was a limiting rule, and the Emperor could decide that henceforth no one would have the right to solicit a particular favour.[193] Other advantages were granted on request; but as the beneficiary had first been obliged to make the request, the kingly style did not fail to ascribe the granting of the concession to the Emperor's beneficence.

In short, the idea of benefaction was derived from an essentialist mode of thinking. Benefactions were not identifiable by their nature as royal pardon or privilege but by the person who granted them. Being good in essence, the Emperor did nothing but good. The reader will perhaps remember that when we discussed the ancient conception of work, we observed that it was based not so much on a classification of activities as on a classification of men. Depending on whether or not a man was a notable, trade would be regarded either as an inessential activity or as the occupation that defined him socially. The Emperor was good, even when he did no more than apply the law. Not that he could feel the slightest temptation to be bad; but he was not restricted by the law, like an ordinary official – he was free, and therefore virtuous. Whereas that modest pen-pusher, the Emperor's procurator, who actually took the decision whose merit was credited entirely to the Emperor, was not a benefactor because he was not free: he was not the Law incarnate and he worked for someone else.

The same ideology of benefaction and gratuitousness underlay private law and shows there its real nature in the same way. For lawyers, when one hired the services of a craftsman, this was a contract which obliged one to pay the poor man his wage; and if one failed to pay it, he could sue. A poor man worked: he was not his employer's benefactor. But if one sought the advice of a notable who 'pursued the profession' of rhetorician, advocate or doctor, that was not hiring labour. These professional men were regarded as conferring a benefit upon those who employed them and, over many centuries, they were not paid 'salaries'. True, one did not fail to thank them for their benefaction by giving them a present. But, also for many centuries, they were not able to sue if they received nothing from the person they had benefited.[194] Here we see the Romans deceived by themselves and their own ideology.

The image of the monarch as author of benefactions conforms, if not to constitutional law and administrative realities, at least to popular thinking and the declarations of panegyrists. For Dio of Prusa the monarch's craft falls into two parts, of which one is obligatory and the other free; the latter is the euergetic part, which a good ruler prefers. 'Blessings he dispenses with the most lavish hand, as though the supply were inexhaustible.' This liberality proves that he has a pleasing character: for the good ruler 'it is a pleasure to show favours to good men and true'.[195] Dio does not ask himself whether it is from his own pocket or at the taxpayer's expense that the Emperor does all this, and whether these good men and true are the Emperor's favourites or his agents, who receive these presents as their wages. For him it is enough to think that the monarch is generous, because it is agreeable to think oneself ruled by a pleasant prince, even if one does not personally benefit from his favours.

THE MONARCHY, MERCY AND CHARITY

The 'mirror of the true prince' which Seneca addressed to Nero under the title *De Clementia* is an invitation to equity. Through failure to perceive that its problematic is of Platonic origin, it has been wrongly thought that there is a contradiction in this treatise and that, in it, Seneca gives two successive definitions of mercy: mitigating equity or justice, and re-establishing equity.[196] Latin thinkers were not immune to self-contradiction, but Seneca had a philosopher's mind, as much as or even more than Lucretius, and in his *De Clementia*, as in the rest of his work, only the necessities and psychological *longueurs* of an exhortation to virtue (one needs time in order to convince) appear to drown the clarity of the concept.[197]

Seemingly, Seneca agrees with the popular notion of mercy, namely that which we find in the Gospels or in Confucius. 'Mercy is the moderation which remits something from the punishment that is deserved and due ... Mercy consists in stopping short of what might have been deservedly imposed.' 'Deserved' by what criterion – equity, or the letter of the law? Seneca is careful not to clarify this point immediately. He is aware that from a philosopher's standpoint it is not advisable to remit an equitable punishment, and will explain that point later, at length. But he also knows that, in the eyes of his Imperial pupil, more aesthete than reasoner, the distinction between the two mercies may seem to be an argument about words, *de verbo controversia*; common sense confuses the two conceptions, which look so similar.

For the benefit of the young prince we shall confine ourselves to the confused symbols of common sense. It is even desirable that he should mistake Platonic mercy for the other sort, excessive though it be. It is indeed more attractive, and it is better to pardon a criminal with the thought that one is doing good, than to punish an innocent person with the thought that one is observing the demands of equity. If Nero can believe he is good, he will be flattered, and even more disposed to behave accordingly. In the eyes of a pedant we shall only be half-right, but on the other hand we shall have won our point.

In modern systems of law, this equitable mercy has assumed legal form: mitigating circumstances, reprieve, individualization of penalties – all things that had little place in Roman law, so that individual decisions by the monarch had to fill the gaps in the law. I will not inflict upon the reader a lecture from a course in Roman law on the judicial role of the Emperor. It may be more useful to recall that, throughout history, there is an ideal type of the monarch's judicial power which we find more or less completely realized and modified in a great number of societies, from the Egypt of the Ptolemies to the empire of the Negus. The sovereign intervenes in four ways in the exercise of justice: he personally adjudicates cases which he considers particularly serious; the parties may, instead of appealing to the ordinary courts, address themselves directly to the justice of Solomon ('the cadi's justice', as German lawyers put it) which the monarch himself exercises by virtue of his prerogative, either sitting under an oak-tree like Louis IX or replying by rescript to petitions or *enteuxeis*; appeals may be passed up from the courts for final decision by the monarch; and the monarch may exercise a right to pardon, the details of which need not concern us.

CLASSIFICATION OF THE STATE'S TASKS

The flattering mirror that Seneca held out to his Imperial pupil reflects only one of the Emperor's activities, his role as judge. In order to review the principal actions by the Emperors which were seen as benefactions, we must first distinguish between different types, so as not to lose our bearings.

1. The Emperor individualizes a rule, according to Plato, or mitigates it, according to the Gospels.

2. There are acts wherein the Emperor behaves as a private person, displaying the ostentation of a millionaire and the bounty of a good shepherd.

3. 'Royal caprice' – the sovereign heaps favours, public or private, more or less arbitrarily, upon his favourites or supporters.

4. The monarch – if necessary contradicting his ministers – reacts against the tendency of the state machine to abuse its power, to do (out of excessive zeal) more than is necessary or to overlook non-political considerations.

5. The office of the sovereign is not merely to lay down the law or give orders: he also performs services. Authority has social tasks and promotes economic or spiritual interests.[198] Besides exercising constraint, it also shows initiative.

6. The list of a state's tasks varies historically and is therefore capable of extension. It would be a benefaction if an Emperor were to take in hand public assistance or education.

It will be noticed that, in listing all these nooks and crannies in which the ideology of royal euergetism might nest, I have left out the activity that is most characteristic in a sovereign, namely politics itself, acts of government. Bounty relates to the *non-political* aspect of the monarch's occupation, and Dio of Prusa seems to have vaguely perceived this. A victory of the Imperial armies is not, strictly speaking, a benefaction. A saviour is not a *euergetēs*. The victory is an event, and nothing is less like an event than the regular exercise of a virtue. Public life consists of two parts. One is made up of 'events', which never augurs well, since it is always best if nothing happens. The other, which presents no problems, is what I am about to describe. The ruling power busies itself with two things: it has an activity which consists in distributing benefits, and it carries out works – both physical, in stone or marble, and abstract, in the form of institutions. The list is doubtless canonical, for we find this great balloon of hot air in Napoleon's *Mémorial de Saint-Hélène*: 'My last days would have been devoted to visiting all parts of the Empire, erecting monuments and scattering benefits wherever I went.' During this time, adds the Corsican dictator, political affairs would have been looked after by my son.

Monuments and benefactions. A third term could have been added, namely gifts. But Napoleon, as a true Roman, considered, like the Emperors of Rome, that it was not for a magistrate to make gifts.

Yet the monarch who heaps *largesses* upon everyone who approaches him, for one reason or another, is a timeless figure. Eumenes of Pergamum, we are told, 'was most eager to win reputation, and not only conferred more benefits than any king of his time on Greek cities, but established the fortunes of more individual men'.[199] For the Hellenistic kings competed for prestige on the international scene with the cities and with other monarchs. But it was not the same with the Roman Emperors, who held the stage alone. For the Romans there was, in a sense, only one state in the world – their own. (Tacitus talks of the Parthians as barbarians whose rulers possess all the proverbial features of oriental potentates, including luxury.) What was to be expected of barbarians was not appropriate to the first magistrate of the Empire. Latin writings only celebrate the Emperor's gifts discreetly, the sole exception being his acts of patronage in the Italian sense: Vespasian left behind the reputation of a patron generous to men of culture. The gift in its crude form was seen as characteristic of a barbarian kinglet. This was because, among the barbarians, the political arena was occupied only by a few dozen lords, so that the ruler would be safe on his throne if he could win a group of grandees to his side by making *largesses* to them which would be either the price or the symbol of their support. The Empire, however, was a machine in which the political personnel were numerous and specialized, a civilized and constitutional *res publica* whose sovereign needed to be earnest.

The Emperor did, of course, distribute money or land to his friends, his supporters and the senatorial caste, and the texts ascribe all these *largesses* to his liberality.[200] In reality, these acts of his were more variegated. Some gifts were purely private, while others were public but considered as having been given as rewards. Let us go into the details, which seem less well known than they should be.

1. Like every other citizen, the Emperor had the right to indulge in liberalities from his private fortune. When Britannicus died, Nero distributed the estates of that unfortunate prince among his favourites. We must understand that, in accordance with the custom of the senatorial oligarchy, he gave these friends a part of Britannicus's heritage, which had come to him by civil law; since Nero, I presume, inherited the property of Britannicus, who was his relative by adoption, had no *heredes sui*, and must have died intestate.[201]

2. But the Emperor could also distribute public domains belonging to one of the Empire's treasuries. These *largesses*, however, were made on an official pretext which dated from the Republican epoch, namely

the rewards of persons who had deserved well of the state (*bene meriti*). Such rewards were so many benefactions by the Emperor, and the medieval period was to keep the word in a technical sense when it spoke of 'benefices'.[202]

The practice is known to us especially for the epoch of the Christian Emperors, thanks to the *Codex Theodosii*. A score of constitutions speak of lands which had belonged to the Fiscus or the Private Fortune before being given away by Emperors to individuals.[203] We glimpse a huge shifting of landownership; but to whose detriment and to whose advantage? The laws do not tell us, and Godefroy presumed that the domains mentioned in these constitutions were the property of the pagan temples which, vacant and obsolete, had been given to the Church.[204] Modern writers, however, think that they were lands distributed to the supporters of the reigning Emperor.[205] What strikes us, when reading these long-winded laws, is that none of them says anything about the Church or about the merits of veterans. They remain very discreet on the beneficiaries' claims on Imperial liberality. One of the laws does give us a glimpse of the mass of leeches that swarmed upon the confiscated domains of Constantine II, who had been declared a public enemy. They competed in soliciting the *largesses* of the Emperor, and petitions abounded.[206]

Nevertheless, on three occasions, these laws do offer motives for the donations, at least in vague terms. The lands were being given, they say, as reward for exertions and merits, to persons who had deserved well of the state.[207] Here we recognize a traditional formula that dates back several centuries. At the end of the Republic, when *imperatores* founded colonies or undertook, on the strength of a law, to distribute lands, they were allowed the privilege of excepting from the distribution certain pieces of land which they could grant, in full possession, to anyone they chose. However much their political opponents might be scandalized by these *loca excepta, concessa, possessa*, the practice was none the less hallowed by custom.[208] It was justified by the consideration that the *imperator* had given these lands as reward to persons who had well deserved such reward (*locum bene merenti dedit*).[209] No doubt the Emperors merely inherited this right of the *imperatores* of the Republic, and despite the silence of our sources, these *largesses* may have played an important part in certain political circumstances.[210] It remains characteristic that these royal favours were covered by a principle of universal application. That is what is called being statesmanlike.

THE SENATE: ORDER OR ORGAN?

There was another sort of Imperial *largesse* whose political importance contributed to the regular functioning of the institutions (if by this regularity we mean customary, tacit, even preconceptual rules), namely the *largesses* made by the Emperors to senators who were not well-off. These made it possible, over and above the official rules for recruitment, to ensure co-option to the ruling caste. If a senatorial family was burdened with debts and no longer had the capital which the law required every member of the Senate to possess; if an *eques* who was worthy to enter the Senate lacked this capital; if a senator could not assume a magistracy because he was unable to finance the games entailed by this dignity – in all such cases the Emperor could, by his liberality,[211] give the persons concerned the sum they needed if he thought fit to do so.

At first sight there could be nothing simpler than this favouritism, but if we look closer we see that the Emperor's bounty to senators shows that there were two systems of recruitment to the Senate, real and bogus. Officially, the conditions for admission to the supreme assembly were governed by rules: a man needed to possess land to the value of one million sesterces (which was the case with several thousand citizens); it was necessary also, as A. Chastagnol has divined, to enjoy expressly the right to seek public honours in Rome (which was not the case with many citizens who were of provincial origin);[212] finally, it was necessary either to be made a magistrate by the Senate and the Emperor or to be oneself the son of a senator.[213] In reality, all that mattered was to be considered desirable as a senator by the existing senators and by the first among them, the Emperor. The senatorial order intended to choose freely the persons worthy to enter it or to remain in it, and to do this it would, if need be, smooth down the formal rules. The Emperor's liberality made it possible, when necessary, to transform the property-qualification regime into a system of co-option – for the benefit, say, of some impecunious but warmly re-commended country gentleman. The same applied to entry into the equestrian order, except that in this case the liberalities which made it possible to circumvent the property qualification were private, being in the nature of clientage, *patrocinium* or *suffragium*.[214] Behind the formal appearances, co-option was everywhere the great maxim of the Roman oligarchy, together with political clientage.

But why? Because the relationship between the Senate and society as a whole was not what sometimes seemed to be supposed. The senatorial 'order' was not a social class, needless to say; and the very word tells us that. But neither was it an order in the sense of the orders of the French *ancien régime*, or even in the sense in which one spoke of the order of *equites* in Rome. The Senate was an organ, not a group. It consisted of several hundred persons, as was appropriate to an assembly, and not of some tens of thousands, as would be appropriate to a nobility. It was an order in the same sense in which people spoke of the order of the *seviri augustales*, that organ of the municipal cult of the Emperors which included, at most, a few dozen freedmen. Like the *Parlement* of the *ancien régime*, the Senate was heterogeneous in relation to society as a whole, as was proper for a specialized organ. It was not there to epitomize society, to represent it or even to crown it by forming its upper class. Therefore it claimed the right to be sole judge of its own recruitment, and not to be hindered by any mechanical rules. The Senate alone knew what it had to be, what it must perpetuate, and it had no accounts to render to a society in which it was not the summit. It was an edifice, the highest to be seen in the city. Its psychology was not that of a delegation from a class or caste, but that of a *conservatoire*, an academy or an order of knighthood (in the sense of the French *ancien régime*). It was not a club of latifundists but the *conservatoire* of political wisdom and service to the state.

It would thus be wrong to see entry into this political academy as the normal culmination of upward social mobility. The Senate was no more the summit of society than the *Parlement* of the *ancien régime* was the summit of the 'bourgeoisie'. In some great family, one son might become a senator while the other remained an *eques* – indeed, by numerical proportion this was frequently the case. The richest Greek families never sought to enter the Senate.[215] They did not choose the mission of service to the Emperor, and doubtless considered that the triumph of a great house consisted in tyrannizing over their own city or province and making everyone there tremble, even the Roman governor. Entering the Senate meant a specialization rather than a consecration. The state machine was not similar in structure to the aggregate of cities which composed the Empire. The composition of the senatorial order was not a representative sample of society as a whole, and the entry of Africans into the Senate indicates only very indirectly and partially the enrichment of Roman Africa; the choice of Richelieu as Louis XIII's first minister is no more reliable as an index of the upward social mobility of the south-west of France. Much study has been devoted to the geographical origin of senators. The information is very interesting in that it enables us to know the Senate better, but it does not help us to a better understanding of Imperial society or even of the tendencies of its politics. The dynamic of the Catholic Church, after all, is not determined merely by the fact that, from the sixteenth century until recently, all its popes have been Italian.

The agent through whom co-option to this political *conservatoire* was effected was the Emperor himself: his liberality resolved the conflicts between the letter and the spirit of the rule. This spared the Senate the disagreeable task of purging itself. When a great family lost its money and was threatened with exclusion, the Emperor became the master of its fate. He could either pay the family's debts or allow the rule to take effect against it. In the latter case the senators were secretly relieved at being rid of a colleague who detracted from the honour of their corporation as a whole and of each of its members, but were still more relieved at not having to get rid of him themselves. Furthermore, they had the satisfaction of being able to blame the sovereign for the feeling of uneasiness which the removal of one of their kind always left with them. Accordingly, they criticized not the deed itself but the way it was done, and accused the Emperor of showing lack of delicacy. 'It is not quite proper for a prince to bestow a gift in order to humiliate,' wrote Seneca;[216] 'a goodly number were found to make the same request, and he [Tiberius] ordered them all to explain to the Senate why they were in debt, and under this condition he granted them specific sums. But liberality that is not, it is censorship . . .' The wretched Tiberius was never in luck. This senator-Emperor, an enthusiast to the point of snobbery for the senatorial order to which he belonged with every fibre of his being, had obviously wanted to show his respect to the supreme assembly, to allow it to judge for itself the fate of its members and to avoid any appearance of monarchical arbitrariness. He could not have chosen a worse moment; at bottom, the Senate never wished to decide, and in this matter less than in any other. What it secretly wanted was to have no responsibility in any sphere and to be able, at the same time, to feel resentment against the Emperors who deprived it of all responsibility. If actually given some responsibility, it quickly found a pretext for making difficulties, becoming fastidious and evading the responsibility – for what reason, we shall see at the end of this book.

AN ARCHAIC FISCAL SYSTEM

Largesses to the senators were an undeclared political necessity and fulfilled a function that it was advisable to overlook, so that it was convenient to treat them as an example of the Emperor's liberality. Let us now review the other Imperial liberalities. Some were public tasks of state which the language of the kingly style associated with the Emperor's euergetism. Others were genuine *euergesiai* performed by the Emperor, which nevertheless became public tasks simply because the Emperor could not cease to be a public personage. In this way the historic list of the state's traditional tasks was lengthened. This happened in the case of patronage to intellectuals and aid to victims of natural disasters. False *euergesiai* comprised public buildings and remissions of taxes.

A ruler could win the gratitude of his subjects in no better way than by abolishing a tax, reducing temporarily the fiscal burden of a province, or remitting taxpayers' arrears of payments due to the Fiscus.[217] A famous piece of sculpture in the Forum shows the Emperor Hadrian ordering that the bonds of debt held in the public Treasury be burnt.[218] Reliefs of this kind were attributed to the Emperor's liberality by a turn of kingly style, but also because the state machine was seen as a brigand – plundering the taxpayers for its personal advantage – which was half true.

The fact remains that remissions of taxes were not private whims, but public decisions concerning the public fiscal system. They served two public purposes: to avoid shearing the sheep too closely, lest they be flayed alive, and to avoid public squandering of prestige. The economic importance of these abatements could be considerable in those days. It affected the structure more than the conjuncture. The very fact that substantial variations could be made in the fiscal burden is another archaic feature of the system.

In pre-industrial societies the sheep's wool was very short and taxation had consequences that affected geography. If we read the reports of travellers of past centuries we note that when they came upon a region that was well cultivated and prosperous, they at once assumed that the prince who ruled there did not overburden his subjects with taxes, whereas a too heavy burden of taxes was enough to impoverish a neighbouring principality.[219] We see how the tax burden varied according to the master's caprice or to regional custom. Of certain regions of the Roman Empire which, though arid and even desert, were nevertheless inhabited and cultivated, it was said that 'the only reason men have for settling there is that they are free from all taxes'.[220] Taxation policy had effects on habitat that were as strong as physical geography. Roman taxation is a subject about which little is known. One has a feeling, however, that for purely historical reasons the burden of taxes was very unequal between one province and another. Some considerable economic fluctuations, such as the growth of the province of Asia from the time of the Flavians onwards, may have had a fiscal cause. Some taxes were fixed dues, while others were changed only after long periods and based on assessments that were revised too rarely. A wise ruler ought, therefore, to intervene to reduce the rate of taxation if the harvest happened one year to fail in a given province; the Emperor's action would correct the imperfect rule and constitute a *euergesia*. He would also correct it in order to draw a province out of long-term poverty. When the philhellene Nero,[221] out of his 'greatness of soul', 'did good' to all Greece when that country was ruined,[222] and granted it 'independence and immunity from taxation', this apparent quixotry may in fact have been an example of true high politics. When Julian the Apostate was the ruler of Gaul, that country's taxes were reduced from 25 gold *solidi* to 7[223] – though, to be sure, this merely meant shifting the burden on to the other provinces.[224] The good shepherd had to take care both of the state's needs and of the economic interests, permanent or seasonal, of the different provinces.[225]

Reality and pastorals are two different worlds. The burden of taxes varied notably and notoriously, depending on whether the ruling Emperor exercised self-control or was greedy for luxury and buildings: 'huge edifices which are quite unnecessary, and hordes of high officials [*aulici*, which does not mean "courtiers"] can easily cost more than legions.'[226] From Caligula to Constantine, some Emperors have richly deserved their reputation for prodigality. Besides their monarchical ostentation, we can accuse them, without much risk of error, of plundering the public funds on a gigantic scale, for this has been the rule rather than the exception throughout history.[227]

There was no great difference between the financial methods of the Roman state and those of a rich private individual. The state's tasks were few and were often occasional or performed only at discretion. An Emperor might increase the pay of his guards, build himself a palace of gold, go to war, or do none of these things. If in fact he did build or fight, he would exhaust the Treasury, which might contain reserves equivalent to one or two years' taxes;[228] for like private persons, the state had its income and also a resolve to put some money aside for a rainy day. A spendthrift Emperor devoured the savings made by his predecessor, like a son consuming his patrimony. Once the Treasury was empty, the Emperor would have to resort to increasing the burden on his subjects. He would not, like present-day states, be able to pay for a war without extra taxation by ceasing to renew the national capital. On the other hand, he might decide to do without his war or his palace.

Conscious of their margin of freedom, Emperors did not shrink from speaking ill of their greedy predecessors, since the tax burden was a political choice more than a necessity of state. They admitted that taxation might serve the most selfish interests of the ruler. Julian declared to his peoples that he was not 'an Emperor who had an eye solely to gain' and claimed: 'I have not made it my aim to collect the greatest possible sums from my subjects.'[229] Imperial coins blatantly celebrate the suppression of abuses and fraud (*calumnia*) on the part of the Fiscus.[230] It was accepted that subjects could with impunity excoriate the preceding dynasty and the peculation committed by its high officials,[231] the golden age having begun only with the present reign.[232] The political options of antiquity did not lie where we should look for them, in rival programmes of constitutional or social policy, but where we should *not* look for them – in administrative options or even in the mode of obedience, the style of command. An Emperor either obliged one to acclaim him or he did not, he was either too fond of building or he was not. Since taxation was a matter of political choice rather than administrative continuity, Emperors did not feel solidarity with their predecessors where fiscal matters were concerned and were not afraid to sow in the minds of their peoples those doubts which are fatal to all governments. Taxation belonged to the realm of political choice, not of state continuity, and an Emperor had the right to choose a different policy from that of his predecessor.

BUILDING AS A POLITICAL ACT

Tax reliefs were thus due partly to budgetary rationality and partly to a political, and consequently personal, choice made by the Emperor. It was the same with another task of the states of those days, namely the creation of public buildings. The Emperor had useful buildings erected, which it was his duty to do, and this could be presented as a *euergesia* only through the kingly style. He also erected other buildings to satisfy his taste for building, his desire to give expression to his majesty or quite simply his royal fancy for a favourite city. It must be added that, before becoming one of the tasks of the state or of princely caprice, building activity had been a personal *euergesia* which went back to the role played by Augustus as patron of the City. In this way the list of the tasks to be performed by the central power grew longer.

Let me quickly sketch an outline.[233] During the early period of the Empire, the public buildings erected in Rome were exclusively the work of the Emperor or the Senate. Magistrates and *euergetai* had no right to build within the *Urbs*. Outside Rome, in Italy and the provinces, public buildings were put up by the cities, by local magistrates who erected them *ob honorem*, or by patrons, by provincial governors, in exceptional cases by the Senate,[234] or by the Emperor. The central authority thus manifested itself through buildings in Rome itself and throughout the Empire.

This was an innovation in comparison with the Republic, and the author of it was Augustus in his role as patron. The Republican state concerned itself only with Rome and neglected to build in the other Roman towns, not to mention the distant cities. From the Social War onwards, at least, the Roman censors had ceased to build in the municipal towns[235] which, in this respect too, became so many cities independent of the *Urbs*. On the other hand the Roman aristocrats, as *euergetai* or local magnates, were keen to build in the towns of Italy; for instance we have seen Calpurnius Piso, consul in 58, and Cassius's brother assuming the five-year duumvirate at Pola and providing ramparts for this colony.[236] Augustus imitated the aristocrats, thereby filling an administrative gap, because his example was followed by the Emperors who succeeded him. The ramparts of Trieste, Fanum, Nîmes and Iader were built by Augustus, as was the aqueduct at Venafrum.[237] I hardly need to list the Imperial buildings erected in Italy and the provinces. It is enough to have shown that Augustus's patronage was the origin of a public service and that it caused the Imperial government to abandon the narrow outlook of the City, which was that of the Republican censors, in favour of that of a great state.

Even so, it was not because Augustus acted as a patron that the Imperial buildings of his successors came to be attributed to their liberality or their *indulgentia*. It was because the buildings would not have existed had there not been a decision by the Emperor: either the Fiscus supplied the necessary sum or the central authority simply authorized the town to build it at its expense.[238]

The liberality of the sovereign was all the more palpable in that, when he financed the construction of a building in Italy or in a province, the money did not come from Rome. The Emperor authorized the governor to dip into the coffers of the Fiscus of his province, into which tax revenue was paid before being sent to Rome, to the Imperial palace on the Palatine, at the centre of the Eternal City, where the Empire's Treasury was located; for the principle of a single coffer for all revenues did not exist. When Domitian writes to a governor of Bithynia, 'Place the sum expended to the article of my benefactions', he does not merely mean that this sum is to be put down to his gracious expenditure (for that order would not be given to a provincial governor but to the central services of the palace).[239] He is authorizing the governor to have the sum in question paid to him by the Fiscus of the province and to justify the absence of that amount when the revenue is sent to Rome by recording it as a liberality on the part of the Emperor. This is why many inscriptions attribute buildings to the liberality or the complaisance (*indulgentia*) of the sovereign. He has relinquished a sum of money which had been paid to him in taxation and given it to the city, which has thus been enabled to put up its building.

Actually, nothing good might be done by anyone in the Empire without the Emperor being the *euergetēs* really responsible. Here let me comment on a passage which, though well known, has been poorly understood. In 298 a rich notable of Autun decided to restore the schools in this large town, out of his own pocket. This *euergetēs* had been a teacher of rhetoric, and after a long career in the schools his qualities as a humanist had brought him the position of secretary to one of the Emperors. When his employment came to an end, the Emperors allowed him to continue receiving his salary as secretary, which was high enough to make the managing director of a large firm envious today. Once he had come to his generous decision, our *euergetēs* hastened to inform his fellow citizens. His speech, which we can still read,[240] was similar to many other municipal speeches which are all so many public announcements of pollicitations whereby *euergetai* assume a commitment to their fellow citizens and enjoy the gratitude of the latter in advance.[241] The inhabitants of Autun were not the only ones to hear this typical address. The provincial governor was also there, and for good reason, because only he could ratify the municipal decree accepting the solemn promise and, if he thought fit, authorize the proposed building work. The relations between the cities of a province and its governors were always ill-defined, like so many things in Roman public law, and in practice the governor intervened in municipal affairs whenever he thought fit, unless the city was strong enough to resist him. When expenditure was at issue, the governor would intervene more often than ever, because the cities were too much inclined to go in for prestige spending. He intervened also if an 'ambitious decree' was passed, i.e. a decree voted under the pressure of some local petty tyrant who was having himself flattered by his fellow citizens.[242] The position of the *euergetēs* of Autun was more delicate than might be supposed, especially because another Cerberus was present. The assembly at which he spoke was attended by a noble old man named Glaucus, whose role in this affair seems mysterious at first sight. He was probably the curator of the city, an attentive watchdog where municipal finances were concerned. In Africa the dedicatory inscriptions on public monuments of the later Empire almost always associate the name of the provincial governor and that of the city's curator with the name of the *euergetēs*. The speech delivered at Autun does this in advance.[243] Here, then, we have a *euergesia* of the ordinary sort; except that the Emperor has to figure in it and everything grand that is done must be due to 'the happy times we live in'. Our Autun rhetorician does not fail to ascribe his own *euergesia* 'to a sacred *largesse*', i.e. to the Emperor's liberality: he says and repeats that the Emperor, by continuing to pay him his splendid salary, is really the founder of the building he is financing.[244]

For the state or the city manifest themselves through their buildings – all 'monuments' of their providential majesty, which endures while individuals pass. 'The majesty of the Empire,' wrote an architect, 'was expressed through the eminent dignity of its public buildings.'[245] Flavius Josephus blames Caligula for putting his egoistic narcissism before the welfare of his subjects and not undertaking any of the great and truly royal works which benefit generations both present and to come.[246]

With our excessively rational minds we readily wonder whether these buildings were really useful, whether three aqueducts were indispensable to Aix-en-Provence, and if the Roman taste for building was not 'ludic' in the multiform sense that Huizinga gives to that word. Let us say that the public buildings were expressive and that their rationalism was adapted to the possibilities of action which existed in their time. In these constructions the state, which often seemed so remote, became tangible, and ceased to be either prosaic or greedy like its own tax-gatherers. The buildings, being public, showed that the state was not selfish, and their solidity showed that the state was durable and saw further into the future than individuals were able to see. The immensity of the constructions demonstrated that the sovereign could accomplish what private individuals never could. And besides, it was important that the government should be doing something and not appear to doze in self-satisfaction and negligence. This, at least, was what was said by the notables who built and by the public authorities who congratulated themselves on having done something wonderful when they erected yet another ruinously costly aqueduct. As for the people, did they really feel the shiver of awe that was expected of them? Rather less than expected, and it was in this sense that the buildings were expressive: they spoke in order to speak rather than in order to be heard. But this was itself 'symbolic violence'. The people could see with their own eyes that, above their heads, there existed an authority which did things that were impressive and somewhat mysterious, while being concerned only with itself and its own purposes. How could one argue with a state like that? How could one compare with its power and intelligence?[247]

But the master must also be just, and all the large towns of the Empire had to be able to show some proof of the Emperors' benevolence. Hadrian beautified Italica, in Spain, where his family possessed the freedom of the city, but while visiting Nîmes, he also initiated there a basilica with bas-reliefs (now in the archaeological museum) so fine that we must assume that he sent sculptors from the Imperial workshop to carve them on the spot. (We may speculate, too, as to whether the high reliefs found at Italica, which are of great merit, were not produced by the same artists. They should be compared with the statues found on the banks of the Canopus and re-erected in Hadrian's palace at Tibur.) Roman Nîmes was an important town.[248]

From this issued a curious custom, which has precedents in Hellenistic[249] and Republican times and shows that the Empire and the old city system were juxtaposed rather than integrated.[250] The Emperors often accepted the supreme magistracy of a city of their Empire, which could be either a large town or a tiny one, and delegated a prefect to perform its duties in their name.[251] This gave them the opportunity to present some fine gift to the place during their year of office: they behaved as *euergetēs ob honorem*.[252] The Emperor Hadrian was thus a municipal magistrate in Naples, Athens and several small towns in Latium, as well as in his birthplace Italica. 'In almost every city he built some building and gave public games.'[253] The Emperor Constantine was a magistrate in Athens and the city awarded him a statue, like the local notables. 'To repay Athens for this compliment he bestowed on her annually a gift of many tens of thousands of bushels of wheat . . .'[254]

The list of state responsibilities was further extended in two main ways. The state allowed private persons to utilize an activity which it had originally developed for its own use (the postal service, or public transport). The sovereign's private patronage, his euergetism, his charity, and so on, which employed public means, became public services. In a society which holds euergetism or charity in high esteem, how could the monarch fail in these duties without disappointing his subjects? In a society where the state itself possesses resources it would offend natural feeling if it were to leave people to die of hunger, without doing anything, as Burke, mocking the tub-thumpers, advises it to do.[255]

In the event of a natural catastrophe, fire or earthquake, the Emperor came to the aid of the victims just as the private *euergetai* and the Hellenistic kings had done.[256] This was the case with Tiberius and Nero after the fires in Rome; the action taken by Nero, or rather by the informal group which ruled in his name and was perhaps headed by Seneca, was particularly remarkable.[257] Besides 'acts of God', the Emperor also helped his subjects in cases of 'acts of the king's enemies', but with much less zeal than where natural catastrophes were concerned. The state would seem to acknowledge a certain guilt on its part if it relieved ills in which it was itself involved. Besides, the state is an organ of command and does not want to be mistaken for a friendly society which repairs the damage its activity may have done to some of its voluntary adherents. Nevertheless, Vespasian urged the notables of Cremona to rebuild their city, which had been sacked during the civil war that brought him to the throne.[258] Occasionally the Emperor even intervened in a financial crisis, to maintain credit in a year when nothing was available for borrowing because money was being hoarded.[259] Money and credit, which are 'conventions', depend on the state's initiative, like weights and measures, or the alphabet in the ancient East. All these gracious interventions that smelt of money were taken *ipso facto* to be *euergesiai*.[260]

PUBLIC ASSISTANCE, DEMOGRAPHY AND RATIONAL CONDUCT

Finally, we need to pay close attention to a highly original institution, namely the family allowances, or *Alimenta*, which the Emperor caused to be paid to Italian citizens so that they could bring up more children. Was this a work of beneficence, or was it an act of policy to promote a higher birth-rate? The *Alimenta*, the regulations governing which are known in some detail, present a familiar type of historical problem: is the rational explanation of certain behaviour likely to be the true one? And if not, how can we discover its true motivation? The difficulty of such a problem always lies in the details.

This was how the institution operated. Its benefits applied to Italy alone. In the various cities of the peninsula Trajan or his successors had established, once for all, a fixed loan-fund, from which landowners could borrow money for an indefinite period, paying a low rate of interest and offering cultivated lands as security. The Emperor never reclaimed his capital and did not seize the property pledged as security as long as the borrower kept up his interest-payments. These payments, however, did not go into the Emperor's coffers but were used, in each city, to pay a certain number of pensions to the children of poor citizens. For example, in the small town of Veleia, 245 legitimate sons received a monthly pension of 16 sesterces, 34 legitimate daughters one of 12, an illegitimate son also one of 12, and an illegitimate daughter one of 10.[261] These figures had been fixed immutably, since the Emperor had established, once for all, a fund of a specific amount and the rate of interest was also fixed. Unfortunately we do not know the answer to a crucial question. Was it possible for the landowners who had committed themselves, and to whom the Emperor had lent capital he would never reclaim, to return this capital and stop paying interest, on condition that they found other landowners to take their place as contributors to the fund? Or were they personally committed for ever?[262]

The institution was much celebrated. Its humble beneficiaries thanked the Emperor for his liberality,[263] while the political world praised him for ensuring the survival of the Italian race.[264] Everyone agreed in hailing the *Alimenta* as an *indulgentia*, an expression of the ruler's kindness;[265] whether it was beneficence or birth-rate policy, he had spent his money on a new and gracious task. Subsequently, the Empresses established a fund to provide pensions for daughters of the poor.[266]

Was the aim of this institution solely to assist children? Did not Trajan also intend to assist Italian agriculture and were not the landowners who pledged their land the real beneficiaries of the *Alimenta* scheme rather than its milch-cows? Was the institution not a land bank as well as a work of public assistance? This is the first problem. The second is to know whether this public assistance was humanitarian, like the private foundations which the *euergetai* of that time established for poor children, or if 'reasons of state' had moved the sovereign to 'multiply the numbers of the king's subjects and of cattle', to use Turmeau de la Morandière's vigorous phrase.

Helping poor children was certainly among Trajan's purposes. If he had merely wanted to establish a land bank he would have pocketed the interest on his loans. But did he want to create such a bank and develop Italian agriculture? These are the intentions which interest us. We wonder if Imperial euergetism may have been the vehicle of an economic policy and if a state of antiquity was undertaking the task of intervening in the economy.

Let us put ourselves in the Emperor's position. If he had had in mind only the birth-rate or public assistance, and had been indifferent to the fate of agriculture, the institution would have been no different from what it was. Trajan would have invested the state's funds just the same in agricultural enterprises, for there was no better investment for a 'father of his country'. These enterprises were durable, they did not proceed by successive separate operations like the ventures of maritime trade, and they were economically stable. Legally, or rather administratively (the *Alimenta* were a public institution not subject to civil law), these enterprises were easy to control. Whatever his real aim may have been, it was in Trajan's interest to lend to landowners.

From their own point of view it was in these landowners' interest to accept the Emperor's advances, since they did so without compulsion. It seems certain that the lands pledged to the Emperor were pledged voluntarily and that these were not forced loans in any sense. Since the landowners had an interest in subscribing to the scheme, the children were not its sole beneficiaries. Objectively, Trajan helped both groups.

And subjectively? Trajan did not use coercion. That may have been because he was interested in the landowners for their own sake and did not regard them merely as milch-cows for the children. It may also have been that he was a liberal ruler in economic matters (as indeed he was)[267] and desired that the cows should give their milk freely.

Do the details of the regulations, the conditions imposed on the subscribers, enable us to judge the ruler's intentions?

We do not know if the landowners who had pledged their land could disengage, if they wished, and produce a substitute. If that was the case, the *Alimenta* would deserve the noble name of land bank. If they do not deserve it, this does not matter, since the perpetual subscribers joined the scheme voluntarily. But their free will may have been lured into agreement rather than convinced by sound economic arguments. They may have forgotten the perpetual interest-payments (which were admittedly low — one-twelfth of the rent of the most heavily burdened land)[268] and looked only at the large lump sum they were to get immediately; and so, since the dining-room needed redecorating ... If that was what happened, Trajan would have given money to farmers but would not have aided Italian agriculture.

However, this would prove nothing about the Emperor's intentions, for the methods of economic policy in those days were very crude. No condition seems to have been imposed on the borrowers regarding the use they were to make of the Emperor's money. Of course, the methods of extending credit selectively to enterprises, much talked about nowadays, had not yet been invented. On the other hand, we observe that Trajan was strict in the way he selected candidates for loans. He refused pledges that were too small, accepting as security only land of a value higher than 20,000 sesterces. Perhaps he wanted to favour large-scale enterprises, as being more dynamic. Perhaps, even certainly, his agents refused to 'water' pocket-handkerchief-sized tracts of land, which would have uselessly complicated the task of the administrators who had to collect the interest-payments. As we see, the Emperor, or his agents, never sacrificed the children to the landowners. Trajan did what he could, what his times understood as being rational, and what was compatible with his other purpose, public assistance; he did not want to sacrifice either purpose to the other. The agricultural side of his institution was crudely conceived. Was this because he was not interested in it? No; but because he did not think very deeply about it. Every landowner could receive a payment if he provided adequate sureties; for Italian agriculture to develop it was enough to provide it with finance. The *Alimenta* were constructed in Roman concrete: a solid structure, but the design is so crude that we cannot make out whether Trajan had any aim besides promoting a higher birth-rate and whether he also wished to favour cultivation and animal husbandry.

But what do the details of the design matter, since the monument itself is there to see? The *Alimenta* effected a huge allocation of credit to Italian agriculture, and so Trajan indeed helped that activity, by supplying it with money. He killed two birds with one stone, could not have failed to see this, and could not have done otherwise than consider himself a ruler who had undertaken the noble task of helping the peasantry. A mere private person who becomes a *euergetēs* by establishing a fund for public assistance has only a limited outlook; he is not concerned with the economic effects of his investments, only with the children for whose benefit the fund is intended. A sovereign, however, takes a wider view: public assistance matters to him, but agriculture matters as well. The *Alimenta* have been the subject of long discussions among modern historians. In my opinion, there are two errors of method to be avoided. One ought not to judge of Trajan's intentions on the strength of our own view of the rationality of his measures. And one ought not to reduce a sovereign who is a *euergetēs* to the dimensions of a private *euergetēs*, on the pretext of respecting the uniqueness of every historical period and explaining the Romans exclusively on the basis of their own values, or what we consider those values to be.

Having thus done something for agriculture at the same time as for deprived children, the Emperor stopped there. The *Alimenta* did not open the way to a policy of economic intervention in general. This was often the case with policy in antiquity – an isolated measure would be taken which did not lead to a consistent activity. A sovereign thought he had done wonders if he erected an institutional monument, often a picturesque one, whose usefulness was more doubtful and which soon fell into ruin, but which enabled the problem to be forgotten while nevertheless continuing to prove by its existence that the government cared. A 'work' is less rational than an activity, but it is more conspicuous and it entitles one to sit back once one has seen that it is good.

As regards the children rather than the farmers, the *Alimenta* were also a work, but was it a work of beneficence? Was the Emperor more concerned with the birth-rate than with philanthropy? Let us not make our minds up too quickly, for we need to distinguish between what Trajan did, what he was able to do, what he wanted to do, what he believed he was doing, and the degree of consciousness he may have had of his own belief.

THE DEMOGRAPHY OF THE PAST

The *Alimenta* would seem designed to bring relief to a certain number of unfortunate people rather than to encourage parents to have children. At Veleia the allowances paid numbered 281. If we assume that the beneficiaries received these allowances until they reached the age of sixteen,[269] that would mean that, each year, fewer than twenty new children appeared on the list of those entitled to allowances. Given that the territory of Veleia had no more than 10,000 inhabitants and that the birth-rate would not have exceeded 20 per 1,000, one child out of ten, at the most, would have been entitled to an allowance, and future parents could not be sure in advance of benefiting from the Emperor's aid. Such uncertainty was unlikely to make them decide to have another child. For lack of money, the Emperor could do no better than provide this lottery. Veleia was only one out of a thousand towns in Italy, and its *Alimenta* cost the Fiscus a million sesterces.

The institution was not well conceived, but nevertheless its purpose was certainly more 'natalist' than charitable. The Romans were quite well aware of demographic problems, even if their means of intervention in that sphere were very limited. Periodical censuses informed them very precisely of the number of inhabitants of the Empire,[270] but more sophisticated data, such as the birth-rate, were obviously unknown to them.[271] However, far from underestimating the importance of demography, the ancients seem rather to have exaggerated it, just as we do when we attribute the cause of wars to overpopulation or when we mechanically explain the 'decline' of the Roman Empire by a fall in population, seen as the most obvious apparent cause. In no less mechanical fashion Polybius explains by depopulation (and here we scent his myth of 'the good old days') the relative decline of old Greece compared with the rapidly growing Hellenistic world. We wonder on what numerical data he might have based his theory.[272]

All the same, Polybius had a head for aggregates and large numbers. Not everyone was like him. Where the size of armies or of populations was concerned, the ancients rarely had any notion of orders of magnitude; thousands and millions were sometimes the same for them. For example, they had no hesitation in ascribing the decadence of a state to the losses in human lives suffered in a politically fatal battle like Pharsalus or Mursa.[273] Trajan wanted to do something to increase the birth-rate, but he had no leverage on the problem. He did what he could, distributing money at random.

The official statements prove nothing as to the Emperor's true intentions. They do indeed ascribe a 'natalist' purpose to the *Alimenta*, but rather too solemnly, and this justifies systematic doubt on our part. The children who have been helped in this way, writes Pliny, will people the barracks and the tribes – in other words, will be future soldiers and future electors.[274] If we are to believe the orator, the allowances were intended to raise up a crop of useful citizens. But this was only a rhetorical cliché; for a full hundred years the tribes had not voted, and the armies were recruited mainly in the provinces. Yet the cliché was neither vacuous nor unrooted in reality. Trajan was not facing the fact that the Empire's real strength lay outside Italy and wanted to maintain the hegemonic, 'colonial' structure of Roman dominance. He was consequently inclined to believe in an eternal essence of 'the Roman people' (that is, of Italy), a nation of citizen-soldiers. Italy had long ceased to be that. But Trajan or Pliny saw it not as it was but as it was thought to be, because their idea of it was aetiological, essentialist. For them Italy possessed a national spirit, or more precisely a way of being, a character and an activity which had nothing to do with the 'events' that made up the biography of the 'person' called Italy.

Furthermore, we note that throughout history, whenever a publicist wishes to praise some sovereign for having encouraged an increase in population, he tends to talk about the army, saying that the prince provided himself with future soldiers. We find this all the way from the *Panegyrici Latini* to Daniel Defoe.[275] The army was the most tangible indicator of an abundant population and the argument most likely to appeal to a ruler, since demographic problems presented themselves on the military and political planes rather than in economic terms.

If that was so, 'they will people the barracks' might be merely a rationalization intended to give an impression of political earnestness. We can imagine that the *Alimenta* were less rational in their intentions than was claimed in the official statements. It is not enough to declare one's concern – it has to be proved. There is the same suspicious exaggeration in the earnestness shown by the Christian Constantine. He also established *Alimenta*, but his aim was not demographic. Nor, if we believe the preamble to his law, was it exclusively charitable.[276] The Christian ruler claims to be concerned with his subjects' morality: aid to necessitous families will save the children dying of hunger and their parents from being drawn into crime – infanticide or the selling of new-born babies. We suspect that Constantine wants to assume the severe expression of a censor, because a ruler ought not to seem to soften; he must perform acts of charity with an air of hardness.

'NATALISM' AND COLONIALISM

Unlike Trajan, Contantine gave no priority to boys over girls, but aided any child who was in need. Trajan directed a larger number of allowances to boys and to legitimate children. Does that prove that his institution was more civic and 'natalist' than beneficent? No, Trajan may also have wished to reconcile arithmetically a charitable aim with additional considerations such as the privileges of the 'first sex' and concern for propriety, just as he balanced the interests of the children and the farmers. Such mutual impediments between interests (as Leibniz would say) always muddle the rationality of an action and make it harder to decipher.

Public assistance or promotion of birth-rate? We find ourselves reduced to deciding on the basis of the historical context or of our idea of human nature. The answer will be complicated.

Two facts show that Trajan's real purpose was the birth-rate, namely the cost of the institution and its extension to the whole of Italy. The *Alimenta* must have cost the Fiscus several billions. It was not natural for the state to ruin itself for the benefit of the poor when there was no class struggle, in a civilization which looked on beneficence as the moral ornament of beautiful souls, not as something made obligatory by ethics and theology. From the Hellenistic period, and still more in Trajan's century, private *euergetai*[277] and queens[278] set up funds to help citizens' children in particular towns – though these beneficent foundations were much rarer than *euergesiai* that involved ostentation and festivals. If a state extended this beneficent practice to an entire nation, it must have had an important political aim. Not that a state is indifferent to non-political values, if it can reconcile these with its aims, or can sacrifice to them only a charitable margin. Agriculture is politically important, but so also are children, when one sees in them the future of the race rather than poor creatures to be relieved.

A natalistic enterprise above all, the *Alimenta* did not have as their chief purpose ostentation any more than beneficence. True, outward show played a big part in the Emperor's behaviour. But a detail which is decisive in the context of the times reveals that Trajan's motive was not to make a display of euergetism. The *Alimenta* were an Imperial liberality which benefited all Italy, and not Rome alone. Now it was understood that Rome was the stage on which Emperors showed themselves off and made *largesses*. Rome alone received bread and circuses. The other cities of the Empire were left to private euergetism, which was strictly excluded from the capital. Since Trajan established his *Alimenta* in Italy, he was pursuing a political aim and not a 'symbolic' one: he wanted to strengthen that pillar of the state, the Italian race.

Before making his subjects happy by taking the trouble to be king, a monarch's duty is to sustain the state and its apparatus. He must ensure the availability of certain provisions, prevent an efflux of gold and have a plentiful population. From this standpoint, two policies were conceivable in those days. Either the Roman Empire was a hegemony of Italy over the provinces or else the Imperial monarchy unified and equalized everything beneath it, so as to transform the hegemony into a multinational state.

The second of these policies was followed, beginning, I believe, under Trajan's own successor, the philhellene Hadrian, who was a successful Nero, an aesthete with political sense. Philhellenism was the first stage in the 'decolonization' of the Empire, for the Greek nation was the most civilized nation (it was considered to be civilization itself) and it lived in cities. The historic role played by Hadrian becomes apparent only if we appreciate that the manifestations of decolonization are to be sought not among those who wielded hegemony over the provinces, or in the content of this hegemony, but in the relationship itself, in the form of obedience. Nothing changed politically or economically. Hadrian made no modifications in the system of provincial government (on the contrary, it was Italy that was destined to be reduced, one day, to an ordinary administrative province), nor did he abolish taxes. But he treated the provincials as his subjects, made them feel he was their Emperor and not the ruler of an alien master race. He spent a large part of his reign far from Rome and Italy, staying in the different provinces, turn and turn about, an innovation which broke with the haughtily stay-at-home tradition of the Emperors, who used to remain among their own Roman people. The 'symbolic' significance which these journeys acquired in people's minds must have been considerable. Being no longer despised is something that counts politically. Historians are just as much inclined as politicians to forget this fact, which is why the historical importance of Hadrian is still underestimated.

During the second century, in Hadrian's coinage and the historical bas-reliefs of his reign, as also in the romances of Apuleius, the provinces cease to appear as an exotic and inferior 'otherness', and the theme of the Roman people as master race disappears. The *Alimenta* of Trajan are the last expression of the hegemonic policy which preserved, on an Imperial scale, the obsolete outlook of the City. But by virtue of that very fact, this measure of natalist policy was, objectively, the same thing as a work of public assistance, a *euergesia* in favour of deprived children, with only the scale of the institution distinguishing it outwardly from the private foundations I have mentioned. The motives of Trajan and those of the *euergetai* were certainly very different, but the narrowness of the old ideal of civic solidarity caused the results to be very similar in these two cases.

THE AMBIGUITIES OF PHILANTHROPY

In the city system an ideal of solidarity among privileged persons united the members of the civic body and required them to help one another, for the sake of friendship among equals and so as to ensure the firmness of the political structure. Political motivation and natural generosity came together to realize this ideal. 'Reasons of state' needed to find support in feelings of benevolence; yet these feelings 'selected their own poor' and, with the best intentions in the world, were unable to see beyond the political circle of fellow citizens, like a Lady Bountiful who takes the view that before concerning ourselves with immigrant workers we should look after indigenous people. Consequently every institution for civic assistance was open to two partial interpretations, one exclusively political while the other highlighted the philanthropic motives – the latter not being the 'ideological cover' of the other! The same private foundation might have been as much civic as charitable, depending only on the psychology of its author, assuming that he was clear about his own motives. In short, the word 'political' can be taken in a material sense or as referring to ultimate aims, just as 'economic' can signify 'material' or 'interested'. A political purpose is not realized through political motives alone. And so it was said that civic life demanded also a certain degree of friendship among all the citizens.[279]

The partial ambiguity between reasons of state and philanthropy reappears in another political and ideological current of the time. The jurists and the Emperor's council readily asserted the higher interests and rights of the state, over and above all feudal relations, against

absentee latifundists who left their land uncultivated while the neighbouring peasants were dying of hunger, and against the Emperor's
agents themselves, procurators and soldiers, who oppressed the weak
through excess of zeal or for the purpose of extortion. The Emperor
took the side of the humble, whether they were Roman citizens or
peasants in a remote province, for his interest was naturally to protect
them from local petty tyrants who would fleece them to his detriment.
This policy merged with a philanthropic trend in public opinion which
is represented for us by Dio of Prusa.[280]

We can conclude that the *Alimenta* were both aid to children and
aid to agriculture, since the state distributed money to both the former
and the latter. The financial rationality of the epoch looked no further
than that. This aid to children had behind it a political motive, natalism,
but objectively it was indistinguishable from a work of civic solidarity.
It would be amusing to know Trajan's own idea as to what he was
doing. He certainly did not censure his political motives, which his
period approved. But there was also a philanthropic trend running
through that period, and Trajan must have profited by the ambiguity
to congratulate himself on having deserved the fine title of *euergetēs*,
since that was what he was objectively. The point is not that he
deceived himself as to his real motives and falsely credited his work to
philanthropy rather than to political prudence. It was the distinction
between these virtues themselves that must have been confused in his
mind. Policy doubtless seemed to him the serious, grown-up form of
generous and naïve inclinations. The *euergetai* of his time set up private
foundations for the benefit of deprived children. With the *Alimenta*
Trajan thought he was doing the same thing, but in a truly Imperial
and responsible way. The fact remains that a politician of the Republican epoch would have blushed to think himself a philanthropist. He
would have considered that he ought to 'impose discipline' and not
soften his heart, and to that end he was ready to go too far rather than
not far enough. We see what an inextricable jumble is constituted by
our uneven awareness of our own motives, the arbitrary way in which
virtues are classified historically, the mutual impediment of interests,
the coalescence of 'causes', material and final, the tendency of heterogeneous attitudes to strike beyond their target. Trying to bring
order into all this by cutting it in two (putting reality on one side and
ideologies or 'mental constructs' on the other) amounts to sabotaging
historical analysis. Since policy and public assistance partially coincided
in their effects, and since it was possible by that time to talk in terms

of philanthropy, it happened, in the course of decades, that the public-assistance aspects of the *Alimenta* were gradually developed for their own sake. Trajan's successors were to establish in Italy, in the names of the Empresses, additional relief funds, and where these were concerned the 'second sex' would not be overlooked. The Empresses could refer to the old tradition of civic solidarity: dowering orphan girls was in the interest of the civic body and was the duty of every good citizen, in the eyes of the Athenians and of the Senate of the Roman Republic; it is useful to the state that women should have dowries and so be able to marry, a jurisconsult was to write.[281] No doubt, but this was more true of a senator's daughter than of a poor man's, yet the Empresses' *Alimenta* were obviously intended for poor people. It is in this way that good feelings, which 'select their own poor' and remain captives of the mental framework of their time (for wishing and knowing are two different things and goodwill does not automatically include knowledge), also tend to outgrow this very framework. And the thinking of an epoch is not shaped in isolation but depends on its whole character, good feelings included.

7. What ideology is for and how people believe it

The monarch is 'the *euergetēs* common to all'.[282] People did not talk in those days about the craft of kingship; instead they exalted the virtues of the reigning prince. From the second century A D, on official bas-reliefs and on the reverse sides of coins, official art developed a whole iconography in which these virtues were symbolized by feminine figures, to which a cult was sometimes devoted.[283] The bureaucratic style we have inherited from the later Empire, in which the Emperors called themselves Our Serenity or Our Liberality, has perpetuated into our own time veneration for the virtues of the Roman Emperors.[284] In his diary Marcus Aurelius imbues himself with his princely duties and observes (admittedly with extreme complacency) that he possesses innumerable good qualities, one of which is that he is a democrat (that is his own word);[285] by which we may understand that he allowed his counsellors and the senators complete freedom to voice their views. There we have Marcus Aurelius as he saw himself and as he wished to be. As against that, the ideology which publicly exalted his virtues must have been, in his eyes, a sort of costume for grand occasions, to which the philosopher-monarch resigned himself, no doubt, as to one of his duties as sovereign or as a ceremonial detail of no consequence.[286]

THE GOOD KING: PROPAGANDA OR IDEOLOGY?

Referring to this public parade of virtues, modern historians have fallen into the habit of talking about 'Imperial propaganda'. The word is not very appropriate ('expression' would be more exact than 'propaganda', as will be seen later), and politically it sounds a false note. If the exaltation of virtues was propaganda, that would be a grave matter, because it would be equivalent to '*il Duce a sempre raggione*', and this would indicate a dictatorial and mobilizing regime. Propaganda and dictatorship can exist only in societies with a public opinion. How could one become a dictator in an old monarchy where there was no public opinion to master and befuddle? And to what end? When Caligula or Commodus had themselves acclaimed by the plebs in the Circus, in the theatre or in the arena, this was not for any material political purpose but for the sole pleasure of being acclaimed and reigning absolutely in their hearts. Propaganda, however, conditions public opinion so as to make it carry out or agree to a certain political undertaking. Propaganda mobilizes public opinion so as to drag it out of political indifference, fill it with strong feelings and prepare it for 'events'. The ideology of the Good King, on the other hand, the noble kingly style, keeps the people in a state of heedlessness and exalts the least disturbing of routines under the most paternal of regimes.[287]

The Roman Emperors no more made 'propaganda' than did the kings of France. Even a tyrant (in the ancient sense of the word) like Louis XIV was not trying to rally fresh 'supporters' when his narcissism savoured the homage that the people renders to great kings. Monarchical display is not a political programme and teaches nothing to the masses that they do not think already. When subjects regard their king as a sort of saint, it is normal for them to treat him as such, because when one has faith in a saint, one venerates him. This veneration expresses a pre-existing humility and adds nothing thereto. Propaganda *informs* and acts upon minds, whereas display *expresses*.[288] The ideology of the Good King, or rather ideology in general, is not what one might suppose. Ideology is a specific phenomenon, an activity of the subject. If it were not so, we should wonder what mystery could enable a king, merely by trying to make people believe in his goodness, to ensure that his subjects did indeed believe this, passively, regardless of the truth and of their own interests. People do not succeed in making us believe just anything they choose, and we do not believe just anything. One ideology is not like another, and belief in a Good King is not belief in government by consent and in the sovereign people. For ideology is not a blind 'drive', but a judgement which takes account of the facts and of the condition which is ours historically. It is suggested by reality, from which it extrapolates tendentiously. In other words, the tendency to justify what exists constitutes one of the factors which combine to shape opinions, together with the other reasons, good or not so good, that cause us to believe whatever it is we believe. For example, we spontaneously confound society and its sovereign (only a trained specialist will have clear ideas on that matter). In particular, we take the king to be the author of our happiness or, contrariwise, of all our woes. Is he not responsible for the bad weather, or at least for the shortage of food? There is a certain amount of evidence pointing that way: after all, if the king did not let the monopolists do as they please, there would be bread for all. Some other evidence contradicts this: are the monopolists solely responsible for the shortage? But one of my reasons for extrapolating the *positive* evidence is my bitterness at being without bread. For an ideology to 'take', the facts must not contradict it too flagrantly, there must be no insuperable credibility gap. We shall see later why, in politics, there is a margin.

Despite the legends about 'mystification', the ideology of the Good King is secreted, in the first place, not by the king but by his subjects themselves. There is no need for the ruler to inculcate this belief: their own condition is enough for this. Ideology does not reproduce the established order; it is this order which reproduces ideology in the minds of successive generations.

This spontaneous ideology is taken over by the king for his own advantage. When he addresses his subjects he talks about his goodness, his bounty. Why? So as not to lose his credit by failing to correspond to the people's notion of him and also to justify himself in his own eyes. The second reason may be the chief one. It is enough to read the memoirs of public men to observe that it is with the craft of kingship as with other professions: the kingly function needs to believe in the activity which exalts it, just as teachers of Latin believe in Latin and French wine-merchants believe in the worth of the wines of France. Rather than being propaganda aimed at conditioning opinion, official discourses on the monarch's euergetism are corporate apologetics. On paper, it can be claimed that this mania for apologetics is identical with the defence of material interests, but experience refutes this monism. Self-justification is not universal. The prince may prefer to shut himself up in his own arrogance and treat his people as subhuman; that was how the ancients saw the tyrant. And apologetics is not a rational form of behaviour: very frequently it fails in its effect. It aims not so much at effectively defending its particular brand of goods as at proclaiming before heaven that the prince is just (the style, the tone of voice, do not deceive on that point). Nobody is deliberately wicked, for nobody is ready to admit that he is wicked and resolved to be in the wrong.[289]

8. The expression of majesty

After the king's goodness, his majesty. We have seen up to now why the Emperor was nominally a *euergetēs*. His public acts were so many benefactions because, reigning as he did by himself, he was not obliged to reign for other people. But Imperial euergetism also covered another sphere, in which the ruler was not content to call his public acts *euergesiai*. In this new sphere he performed *euergesiai* which, were it not for his need to express his majesty, he would not have performed. The recipient of these benefactions was the City of Rome alone. The Emperor provided it with bread and shows.

This tendency of the sovereign's to express his majesty is no more rational than his need to justify himself: the means are not proportionate to the ends. Justification and expression lend themselves secondarily to ideological uses or to 'machiavellian' rationalizations, but they are not primarily weapons, and that is why they can be dear to both sides. The people would be disappointed if the king did not call himself good and if he did not display his grandeur. On his part, the king wants to satisfy himself and has little notion of the effect his ostentation produces on the spectator. When he raises triumphal arches he wants, first and foremost, to leave to posterity monuments of himself, in the face of heaven. Far from engaging in 'Imperial propaganda', he is ready to proclaim his own glory even if nobody is listening. Let us give the name 'expression' to this irrational ostentation, this narcissism, or at any rate this need to speak on his own behalf.

ACTION, INFORMATION, EXPRESSION, EXPRESSIVENESS

Above Trajan's Forum Trajan's Column still raises its shaft, and around it winds, like a picture-puzzle round a stick, in twenty-three spirals, a frieze of 144 scenes that celebrate episodes in Trajan's conquest of Dacia and exalt the Emperor's own role in it. Archaeologists examine this frieze with binoculars. We may doubt whether Trajan's subjects paid much more attention to it than do the Romans of today – whether they rushed to see this spectacle and stupefy themselves by circling the Column twenty-three times with their heads thrown back.

The Column is no more propaganda than the Gothic cathedrals were visual catechisms. It is ornamented with reliefs showing figures because, being a monument, it could not exist without speaking or speak without saying something. It therefore contains a message; it tells in detail of Trajan's campaigns so as to express his glory, but this detail seems to have interested the sculptor himself more than it interests the passers-by. It is with Imperial majesty as with the star-strewn sky that expresses the glory of God. What is more expressive than the sky? But in order to perceive its expression we do not need to itemize the stars one by one – the overall effect is enough. It is even better not to itemize them, for the sky would seem to be repeating itself, like a ceremony that goes on for too long. A monument before heaven to Trajan's glory, the Column confirms that Rome, the Imperial capital, was, like most capitals in pre-industrial societies, a stage on which the splendour of the sovereigns, reigning or dead, was expressed by monuments, ceremonies and institutions. The ruling power obtained additional prestige from the very irrationality of its expressions, which spoke for themselves and were proudly indifferent to their audience. Grandiloquent nonsense has always been the privilege and sign of gods, oracles and 'bosses'. Monuments and ceremonies are like the wind, which gives utterance while gazing elsewhere, very high above our heads, in an unknown tongue whose general sense we grasp.

KINGLY DISPLAY AND SYMBOLIC VIOLENCE

The Emperor's majesty expressed the existing political relations and added little to them. Its absence alone would have worried people. One would need a very purified imagination to look upon the Great Sultan as just another man when one saw how thoroughly the minds of his subjects were submissive to him. And the seraglio where he lived was as splendid as was fitting for such a master. If his subjects had not been submissive to him, this excessively beautiful palace would have been merely a millionaire's folly.

In the confused whole which we call ideology or display let us distinguish between two types of fact: some are appropriate to the conditioning of minds, but others are merely the result of this conditioning. Thus, (1) the display whereby the sovereign perpetuates his name in history, or allows his subjects to behold his majesty, merely follows from the already established relations; the same is true (2) of ideology in the strict sense, or the need to believe that what exists is justified; and the same can be said (3) of the patriotic festival, the cult of the monarchy, in so far as the subjects express therein the love which they have been induced, in another connection, to feel for a saviour. It is difficult to conceive of a peaceful monarchy without display and without veneration of the royal person; a challenge to these outbuildings would constitute an indirect attack upon the main edifice.

The personal superiority expressed by display extends to everything, since the master commands by the right to command which belongs to a higher species. Those who belong to that species eat better and live more luxuriously. Luxury and pleasures form part of the display. It is with rulers as with rich men, when public opinion accepts the superiority of their wealth: they have to mark themselves off from ordinary mankind by realizing all the potentialities of that wealth. What are these potentialities? That is a question of good taste. One king will become a charioteer or a gladiator, another will drink heavily. The king ought to be the happiest man in his realm. Aristotle noted with amazement that 'some tyrants, we know, start the day and continue for days on end in a state of inebriation, and even do so for the express purpose of letting others see how supremely happy and fortunate they are'.[290] It was counted a merit in the Hellenistic kings that they led a rich life, *tryphē*.[291] The word is used in the passage in St Luke's Gospel where we read: 'Behold, they which are gorgeously apparelled, and live delicately, are in kings' courts.'[292] At the banquets of Demetrius Poliorcetes, drunkenness was part of the display; the Besieger of Cities got drunk for the same reason that he haughtily refused to accept the petition which a poor woman held out to him, despite the patriarchal tradition of the Macedonian monarchy.[293] He wished to set himself above all other men. Another excellence is idleness. The masses are not interested in the king working; the outward show of his happiness requires that he be free from that servile obligation. His providence does not reassure unless it exists yet does nothing, takes no concrete political decision that would call to mind the actual government which governs well or ill. In short, the king does nothing: he expresses the monarchy, in other words himself.

However, the Roman Emperor had fewer facilities than other rulers to distinguish himself in this way. He did not drink but instead was a *euergetēs*. He was a magistrate no less than a prince, and, as Cicero says, the Roman people abhorred private luxury but approved of luxury shared with the public. Imperial luxury was not just selfish consumption, it was also consumption by a *euergetēs* who provided his capital with shows. The selfishness of the ruler who drank alone was regarded (wrongly) as the behaviour of a tyrant. In an act of propaganda, in the true sense of that word, Vespasian demolished the Golden House which Nero had built for himself,[294] and erected on its site the amphitheatre of the Colosseum, destined to receive within it the Roman people.

THE ETERNAL CITY SERVES AS A COURT

In this case, the expression 'Roman people' has to be taken in its narrow sense – the population of the City of Rome. It alone received from the Emperor bread and circuses, which were not a means of rule over the vastness of the Empire.

If euergetism consists in calling the sovereign's public acts 'bounties', its sphere of action obviously extends to the Empire as a whole. But when it signifies the display that surrounds the sovereign's person, it moves with that person and its sphere of action is on the scale of an individual: a residence, a town, a court or a capital. Antiquity, however, was an era of cities, not of courts. The City of Rome, the city *par excellence*, took the place of a court for the Emperors, who gave it bread and circuses as they might have fed their courtiers and arranged ballets for their courtiers' entertainment. For the Emperors had no courtiers. They lived in the company of a few chosen friends, who were always present at their banquets and travelled along with them.[295] We should not be surprised at the fact that Suetonius talks at such length about the shows put on at Rome by the Emperors: under France's *ancien régime* people talked no less about what went on at court.

Down to the fall of the Western Empire Rome was to retain the prestige and some of the privileges of the old historic capital that it had been for many centuries. As a ceremonial survival from the era of city-states, the population of Rome was regarded as being the master race, the conquering nation, and bread and circuses were their right as lords. From Augustus's time onwards, however, these ragged lords were also courtiers of a sort, for Rome had ceased to be a city-state and had become the capital – more precisely, as we shall see, a capital of the pre-industrial type. Sometimes the two functions uncoupled: when the Emperor travelled, he took his euergetism with him and held shows wherever he went.[296] Three full centuries after Augustus, Constantine, by royal whim, moved his capital, making Constantinople the rival of Rome. The new Imperial city had, like Rome, its palace, its forum, its Senate, its Circus and its corn dole.[297]

In the apocryphal advice to Augustus that Dio Cassius puts in the mouth of Maecenas we read: 'Adorn this capital with utter disregard of expense and make it magnificent with festivals [*panēgyreis*] of every kind.'[298] Rome, pre-industrial-type capital of an absolute monarchy, was a 'shop-window' like Versailles or the Paris of Napoleon. In the Turkish Empire, wrote Volney, the only town 'over which the sultan took any trouble which was not taken elsewhere' was his capital.[299] The sovereign focused on the stage of his display all the efforts and resources of a society that did not have much to spare. The Emperor's relationship with Rome was quite special. Two expressions tell us this – expressions which are sometimes misinterpreted. Rome, *urbs sacra*, was the holy city, i.e. the Imperial city, and it was *urbs sua*, the city that was wholly devoted to the Emperor, wholly his.[300]

This explains the very special urban layout of Rome. It was no longer a city of classical and Hellenistic antiquity, built around its forum and its acropolis, but a royal residence, like many oriental cities. Augustan Rome was ruled by prefects in the monarch's name, to some extent like Alexandria or Pergamum.[301] We must forget the Seven Hills, and imagine an accumulation of human beings drawn thither by the mere presence of the monarchical apparatus and its colossal expenditure. This population was dominated by the raised mass of the Emperor's palace in the centre, and watched over from the outside by the huge barracks of the praetorian guard, established at a point on the edge of the city, like the Bastille, the Tower of London or the Turris Antonia in Jerusalem.

Rome was a royal capital and no longer a city-state. That is, at bottom, the significance of Juvenal's *panem et circenses*. The last link with the past was cut when Augustus ended the election of magistrates by the people of Rome. Reduced to its tribunes of the plebs and a few supernumeraries, this people would thereafter play only a ceremonial role in certain official pageants.[302]

And yet the Imperial regime also lost by this change. The cohabitation of this local population and the Emperor, the obsession with the capital as 'shop-window', had the effect of municipalizing the government's outlook. Rome, like the court of Versailles, assumed disproportionate importance in the concerns of the ruler. Reading Suetonius, one might suppose that bread and circuses constituted half of all Imperial policy, and the *Res Gestae* confirms that this impression is only too correct.

This disproportion did not result from machiavellian calculation, but from hypersensitivity to popularity and display. Rome was not a city where people were likely to mount the barricades, and after the creation of the praetorian guard, their swords were the only ones that counted politically.[303] Take the case of Agrippina, who, after the death of Britannicus, sees her position undermined. What can she still rely on? She thinks of the praetorians and she thinks of the senators. (The latter enjoyed such prestige that if the Emperor quarrelled with them, he thereby opted for a fundamental political line, which was not to be done lightly. The senators controlled provinces and armies. In addition, they cherished an old dream, more vengeful than realistic, of arming their clients and freedmen and holding the Imperial guard in check.)[304] She did not think for one moment of the people of Rome. If the Emperors had been able to confine their concerns to ruling and had not had to express themselves, they would have attached no importance to the capital city. Trajan proclaimed that his power was based on entertainments and shows no less than on serious things (*seria*), but he admitted that if he were to neglect the latter he would be heading for catastrophe, whereas by neglecting the futilities he would only be risking unpopularity (*invidia*). Let those who do not mind being unpopular cast the first stone. In the bestiary of politics, alongside Machiavelli's lion and fox, there is room for the peacock.[305]

Proximity to the City and the obsession with shows gave rise to a picturesque circumstance: the amateur acting of some 'bad' Emperors who appeared in person before the people as charioteers or gladiators. Since the powerful among men are supposed to actualize all human potentialities, why not those? Nero displayed his talent as a charioteer at least once in the presence of the Roman public, before competing victoriously as a performer in the Greek contests. Commodus fought as gladiator with wild beasts in the Colosseum.[306] Sporting activities were much cultivated and many Emperors tried their hands in private at the gladiator's art, fencing.[307] Between doing that and performing before the assembled people there was a wide gulf, which was crossed less often than has been supposed.[308] There were even two gulfs. Could an Emperor submit himself to the judgement of the vulgar? Could he engage in vulgar sports? For there are sports and sports. Hunting was polite, but fencing and charioteering were not. More precisely, the Emperor had to decide whether making a spectacle of himself was proper (as the Greeks thought) or degrading (as the Romans thought). He had to consider whether sporting or theatrical activity was a noble profession or an occupation for mountebanks. In Greco-Roman culture the two views confronted each other. Most senators regarded fencing as a vulgar amusement and a despicable occupation, yet a few members of the best society nevertheless descended into the arena to fight, and so did one or two Emperors.[309]

MONOPOLY OF IMPERIAL EUERGETISM IN ROME

After circuses, bread. All Emperors showed a practical concern for their capital which they could not show for the Empire as a whole. No city was to be compared to Rome in that respect; an important argument in those days when the least of little towns emulated each other like little nations.[310] Rome alone had free bread, *congiaria* and an *annona*. Juvenal's *panem* is not free bread, but that which the service of the Annona busied itself to bring to the market of Rome, either as tax revenue or through organizing the activity of traders.

Why was so much trouble taken? For the sake of good admin-istration: on this depended the prestige of the ruler, who had to be more liberal towards 'his City' than the private *euergetai* towards their respective cities. And for the sake of display: the sovereign had the same personal relations with the urban plebs as an *ancien régime* king with his courtiers. For Rome to be the jewel-case wherein the sover-eign's splendour shone, it was necessary that the sovereign should shine there alone, and that senators and *euergetai* should not compete with him in munificence. The Intendant Fouquet learnt to his cost that in monarchies propriety forbids that anyone should outshine the king, a circumstance which tends to restrict individual initiative.[311]

However, Rome possessed a Republican heritage which hindered this Imperial exclusiveness and which had to be suppressed or restricted. This was done by Augustus. He put an end to the Republican *euergesiai*, shared with the magistrates the right to present shows, reserved for himself a near-monopoly of public building, and beautified Rome so that it might be worthy of its status as capital of the monarchy. The story seems little known, and I shall tell it in some detail. The detail is complicated. Before reserving for his own patronage the monopoly of euergetism in Rome, Augustus began by encouraging patronage on the part of his own lieutenants, so that the disappearance of private euergetism in Rome followed immediately upon its highest development. The explanation is that Augustus was both the leader of a party and the head of state. The party leader encouraged his supporters to win the hearts of the plebs, while the sovereign tended to reserve this work to himself as a monopoly. The sovereign did not detach himself all at once from the party leader, hence the initial detour.

For Tacitus it was a matter of course for private munificence to be excluded from the City and for the ruler to treat it as his monopoly. The senatorial historian relates with sadness the last success of Republican euergetism at the beginning of Tiberius's reign:

About the same time Lepidus asked the Senate's leave to restore and embellish, at his own expense, the basilica of Paullus, that monument of the Aemilian family.[312] Public-spirited munificence was still in fashion, and Augustus had not hindered Taurus, Philippus or Balbus from applying the spoils of war or their superfluous wealth to adorn the capital and to win the admiration of posterity. Following these examples, Lepidus, though possessed of a moderate fortune, now revived the glory of his ancestors. Pompey's theatre, which had been destroyed by an accidental fire, the Emperor promised to rebuild, simply because no member of the family was equal to restoring it, but Pompey's name was to be retained.[313]

Philippus, Balbus and Taurus — the three *triumphatores* whom Augustus had allowed to adorn Rome — had, respectively, restored a temple of Hercules, restored a temple of Diana and erected the first stone amphitheatre in the City. It would be easy to prolong the list of buildings of the Augustan epoch that were the work of *triumphatores* and *viri triumphales*, and which had been financed by the spoils of war, the *manubiae*, in accordance with tradition.[314]

This apogee was followed by swift decline. How could *triumphatores* continue to build, when there were no more *triumphatores* and the Emperor reserved for himself the right to a triumph?[315] The same Imperial monopoly extended, in Rome, to euergetism, and in the Empire to many other things. In the City,[316] as elsewhere, *opera publica* were no longer dedicated to anyone but the sovereign or members of the reigning family.[317] The Greeks had to give up awarding temples, games or divine honours to the governors of their provinces.[318] The process was slow, and took place *de facto* more than *de jure*, but it was complete by the end of Tiberius's reign at the latest. As regards euergetism, Augustus himself had perceived its political dangers at the time of the affair of Egnatius Rufus.[319] This aedile had made himself popular by organizing, privately, a fire brigade. The people elected him praetor and subscribed to reimburse him for the costs of this honour. Rufus let popularity go to his head, and presented himself as candidate for consul. Arrested on a charge of conspiracy, he was executed and the Emperor formed a public fire brigade. The last conflict took place under Vespasian, as a result of the initiative of a man who was behind the times. 'Helvidius had proposed that the Capitol should be restored at public expense and that Vespasian should assist in the work. This proposal the more prudent senators passed over in silence, and then allowed to be forgotten.'[320] The Emperor could not tolerate any *euergetēs* in his capital other than himself.

A division then took place which was to last until the later Empire, when Rome, municipalized and once more an ordinary city, lived under its prefect's authority like other cities under that of their curators, and when it had *euergetai* just like those other cities, because the Imperial monopoly over Rome had ended.[321] Before that time and during the whole of the early period of the Empire, the division took the following form: in Rome the Emperor alone had the right to erect public monuments, and no *euergetēs* could do so. In principle the Senate also had the right to build, but in practice it merely set up honorific statues of Emperors and magistrates, or monuments to the Emperors' glory.[322] The Emperor also possessed the exclusive right to provide Rome with extraordinary games and *munera*, while the ordinary games and *munera* continued to be provided by the magistrates.[323] Logically, the Emperor should have reserved for himself a complete monopoly where shows were concerned, but the Republican institutions remained in being and the ruler had to compromise with them. Outside Rome, of course, in municipal towns and foreign cities, shows and buildings continued to be free from the Imperial restriction.[324] Finally, public *largesses* of all kinds, which continued to be permissible elsewhere than in Rome, were reserved for the Emperor in the capital. Henceforth, he alone would distribute money to the plebs, together with banquets or *epulae* and *congiaria*, and he alone would be honoured by the plebs. It goes without saying that Rome had no *patronus* other than the Emperor, '*pater patriae*'. The last person to distribute money to the Roman people in a private capacity was apparently Herod the Great, during a visit to Rome.[325] The Emperor was the sole *euergetēs* and the sole *patronus* of his City. And while legacies to other cities became common, the practice ceased of making bequests to the Roman plebs in the manner of Caesar, Balbus or Acca Larentia. Henceforth only the Emperors left money to the Roman people. As for private persons, they doubtless left to the Emperor himself what in former times they would have left to the people.[326] It must be added in fairness that all these restrictions had their logical compensation: Rome was the only city in the Empire where no collective charge fell on the inhabitants and in which *munera municipalia* were unknown.[327] Nor, of course, did Rome enjoy municipal autonomy.

A passage in Dio Cassius shows vividly how Augustus dimmed the splendour of shows and *largesses* offered by others than himself.[328]

Of the public banquets, [Augustus] abolished some altogether[329] and limited the extravagance of others.[330] He committed the charge of all the festivals to the praetors, commanding that an appropriation should be given them from the public Treasury, and also forbidding any one of them to spend more than another from his own means on these festivals, or to give a gladiatorial combat unless the Senate decreed it, or, in fact, oftener than twice in each year or with more than 120 men.[331]

While the Emperor alone was providing extraordinary shows, which were the finest, erecting all the public buildings (except the monuments which the Roman Senate and people raised in his honour), and distributing *largesses* to the people of Rome, the members of the senatorial aristocracy organized routine entertainments and maintained at their own cost the roads and aqueducts of Rome, which did not bear their names. In the later Empire, when Rome was municipalized, the major senatorial magistracies were also municipalized. The fortune of a senator was frozen as a pledge to the Senate, just as a municipal decurion had to pledge his fortune to his *curia*.[332] The games given by the consuls and praetors were to be higher in cost than a minimum fixed by law, as in the municipalities, unless these officials were obliged to repair the aqueducts instead of giving shows and distributions.[333] But this municipalization had already begun in the early Empire, although the facts are not well known and the process of evolution was hesitant.[334] The first tendency was to limit expenditure by the senators and the splendour of their shows. The praetors were not allowed to spend more than three times as much as the amount contributed by the Treasury.[335] Claudius limited to a single day the *instauratio* of the Circus games.[336] As in the municipal towns, the next step was from expenditure on games to expenditure *pro ludis*. Augustus had already asked the *viri triumphales* to devote their *manubiae* to road repairs.[337] Agrippa was entrusted with the dedication of the Saepta Julia, Dio Cassius tells us, 'instead of undertaking to repair a road'.[338] We may translate this 'instead of' into the language of municipal epigraphy: Agrippa dedicated the Saepta *pro pollicitatione straturae*, in the guise of a pollicitation concerning road repairs. Suetonius also tells us that Claudius imposed a gladiatorial show on the quaestors *pro stratura viarum* (those are his words).[339] We must conclude from this that, before Claudius's time, Rome's quaestors, like common municipal magistrates, had been required to pay for the upkeep of the roads. Finally, in his treatise on aqueducts, Frontinus says that the reservoirs into which the water flowed were called either *opera publica* or *munera*, and that the latter were the finer.[340] The reader will have no doubt that, as their name indicates, these *munera* had been built by the curators of the aqueducts, or perhaps by the quaestors, at their own expense instead of their gladiatorial shows. And the súpreme insult: already in Claudius's time Roman priests had to pay the Treasury a sum *pro introitu*.[341]

THE PLEBS AS 'CLIENT' OF THE EMPEROR

The *euergesiai* of the aristocrats were thus lost to sight in the anonymity of a repair job or in the coffers of the Treasury. Those of the Emperor were personalized: shows, buildings, distributions, all resulted from his personal decisions. For the Emperor had a special relationship with the plebs of his capital. He treated them as his family and left them legacies. When Octavius Augustus cut his beard for the first time, or celebrated his birthday, he invited everyone to the feast, and in his will he left a million to each of the tribes.[342] On their part, the citizens presented New Year gifts to the Emperor. In the third century, when Heliogabalus married, the entire population of Rome, invited to the wedding, made merry and drowned their joy in drink.[343] The Emperor was thanked for his *largesses* like a *euergetēs*: for example, the thirty-five tribes raised a statue to Trajan, who had given them extra seats in the Circus.[344] Between the Emperor on the one hand and the Senate and people of Rome on the other, exchanges of gifts and honours took place incessantly. Caligula's 'daughter's birth gave him an excuse for further complaints of poverty. "In addition to the burden of sovereignty," he said, "I must now shoulder that of fatherhood" – and promptly took up a collection for her education and dowry. He also announced that New Year gifts would be welcomed on 1 January; and then sat in the palace porch, grabbing the handfuls and capfuls of coin which a mixed crowd of all classes pressed on him.'[345] The grotesqueness of Caligula does not lie in his behaviour as such (Augustus had also received New Year gifts from the Roman plebs) but in his lack of tact and disinterestedness. Augustus had acted differently:

When the Senate and the people once more contributed money for statues of Augustus, he would set up no statue of himself, but instead set up statues of Salus Publica, Concordia and Pax. The citizens, it seems, were nearly always and on every pretext collecting money for this same object, and at last they ceased paying it privately, as one might call it, but would come to him on the very first day of the year and give, some more, some less, into his own hands; and he, after adding as much or more again, would return it, not only to the senators but to all the rest.[346]

The relationship between the Emperor and the people of Rome was not so much civic as like that between a father and his family.

Comparable to the *donativa* which set the Imperial guard apart from ordinary citizens, the *congiaria* indicated that there was a special relationship between the sovereign and his capital. These distributions of money to the plebs took place at irregular intervals, and especially when a new Emperor ascended the throne.[347] We do not know whether the entire free population shared in them, or only those citizens who also benefited from the distributions of free corn. The amount of these liberalities was of the order of several hundred sesterces, differing from case to case. This was enough for a person to live on, frugally, for some months. It cost the taxpayers tens of millions. As the Emperor reserved for himself the monopoly of this *largesse*, which was private in origin, the plebs became his client – or would have if they could have regarded him as a mere private person, and if they had not known that his successor, whoever he might be, would grant the same *largesses*. To these distributions of money were added the bread, the oil and the meat which the services of the Annona distributed more and more frequently and which became regular in the third century. A passage from this period shows that the privileges enjoyed by the capital made an impression on observers: the Greek Philostratus compares these *largesses* to the economy of the Cyclopes, 'who, they say, live idly while the land provides for them, neither planting nor sowing anything'; property and exchange could not exist, and 'everything would have no value and belong to everyone, like in the Forum Boarium',[348] which was where the headquarters of the Annona stood.

As for the free corn, this was a picturesque survival which, of course, the kingly style ascribed to the Emperor's liberality. By the transformation of Rome into an Imperial city the Gracchan institution became filled with new meaning: the plebs who received free corn were expressly seen as the Emperor's clients, and when the sources talk of the Emperor's clients, that is all they mean.[349]

THE URBAN SOCIOLOGY OF ROME

Imperial Rome had a population made up of persons who lived directly on expenditure by grandees and by the palace, and of persons who lived on it indirectly, either as parasites on the first group or by working for them. These plebeians reacted in ways unknown to the masses of industrial society, having a passion for shows and a highly original relation with politics, or rather with the palace.

There is a marked contrast here with the astonishingly self-disciplined masses of the industrial countries of our time, which no longer get themselves crushed to death on occasions when great crowds assemble – as happened at the coronations of tsars, and more recently at the funerals of Nasser and Stalin. The Roman plebs, who included many *lazzaroni*, were enthusiastic fans of the stars of the theatre and the arena or of the teams of charioteers, the 'factions' of the Circus.[350] Brawls, quite non-political in character, broke out between the groups of supporters, organized into clubs.[351] The policing of the shows was a great responsibility; ancient historians tell us the names of stars who were put to death or exiled because they had occasioned or provoked disturbances.[352] Was this the outlook of a police state which mistrusts anything that moves? Not merely that. The quarrels connected with sports or 'pantomimes' (a medley of opera and ballet) were genuinely hard to control, for they could start off more serious mob actions.[353] All antiquity lived in expectation or fear of the general riot which did eventually come, and which, beginning in the Circus, almost cost Justinian his throne.[354] No less dangerous, or suspect to the police, were the clubs or *collegia* of every kind, based on trades or on religious beliefs.

What made matters worse was that, in Rome, the Circus factions were apparently held to be unequal in distinction.[355] They had no political colouring, were not disguises for political tendencies (Rome was not Byzantium, and in the case of Byzantium we need to distinguish between periods). But it seems that persons of good taste, and also 'good' Emperors, tended to be for the Blue faction, whereas popular taste favoured the Greens. However, this was more a matter of personal temperament than of well-defined politico-social lines. None were at bottom more Green than the persons who thought they were Blue, and those who should have been Blue were Green at heart. The trouble was that the Emperor himself had his preferences and his stars, so that booing his favourite gladiators could be taken to be, or actually was, an expression of opposition. Caligula had honourable men executed 'merely for criticizing his shows',[356] and Vitellius 'executed some of the commons for disparaging the Blues, on the suspicion that such criticism was directed against him'.[357]

The ancients were the first to be surprised at all this, but they knew one thing, namely that the craze for shows was a disease of their very large towns – Rome, Alexandria, Antioch. It is hard to attempt urban psycho-sociology almost two thousand years after the events. The sociology of Rome is barely known to us, and despite a mass of writings and tens of thousands of inscriptions, unknowable. We are left with the probabilities which are also called 'laws of history', and a phrase in Tacitus which I think gives me my Ariadne's clue. When Nero died, writes the historian, 'the respectable part[358] of the common people and those attached [*annexa*] to the great houses, the clients and freedmen of those who had been condemned and driven into exile, were all roused to hope. The lowest classes, addicted to the Circus and theatre, and with them the basest slaves . . . were cast down . . .'

The difficulty about this passage is that it uses as its frame of reference the relations of clientage, whereas we should use a different one. We should inquire whether the Roman plebs included many unemployed, *disoccupati* or *lazzaroni*, whether they lived by their labour or by the alms of their protectors. But Tacitus does not despise 'the lowest classes' for their idleness. He lived in a world where work was not the best way of earning one's living and where personal service was honourable. He despises 'the lowest classes' because, belonging to nobody, they are nothing: no fealty gives them substance. They are the lowest stratum of the human race, crumbling into dust. As they have no social discipline, there is nothing serious about them and they devote their whole time to leisure occupations. How are we to pass from the 'clients/non-clients' frame of reference to that of 'workers/ idlers'?

The Roman plebs worked.[359] Some of them were dependent on the grandees in various ways (clientage in the narrow sense of a complete livelihood being the least important of these ways). And Rome had its idlers, its *lazzaroni*, its 'dangerous classes'. When we think about the economy of ancient cities, which consumed without producing much, we are tempted to imagine the cities of the Empire as being like those of present-day Latin America – vast agglomerations in which hundreds of thousands of former peasants live wretchedly in shanty towns. Despite the legends, there is no regular link to be established between this idle class and the distributions of free bread on which all the forms of demoralization are blamed. The free bread did not go far to support a man; man does not live by bread alone; this bread was an honourable privilege which was bought or which one obtained through the protection of a patron; and it was distributed only to 150,000 privileged persons in a city that may have had a million inhabitants. The free bread was not alms. As for the service of the Imperial Annona, which mattered much more than the old privilege of free bread, this ensured a supply of bread at the normal price, and one had to work in order to be able to buy it. The Roman plebs did not want alms, they wanted work. Vespasian refused to use a machine to transport a column, so as not to deprive the poor of their livelihood.[360] The Colosseum was doubtless built by the hands of the plebs. We can conceive of four categories among the poor inhabitants of Rome. There would be the huge households of the great families, made up of slaves and freedmen. There would be the shopkeepers and craftsmen who, free or freedmen, supplied the rich and the rest of the population, and whom we know fairly well from their epitaphs. There would be a mass of semi-unemployed, looking for work. And there would be the *lazzaroni*, who were numerous in Rome because, when in direst poverty, one can find more means for survival in a city, in contact with the rich and in the anonymity of an impersonal crowd, than can be found in the countryside. Let us now turn to the clients.

When Tacitus says that the respectable part of the people were 'attached' to the great houses, he probably does not mean that the plebs had affection for the old oligarchy in general and were favourable to it politically, but rather that the various plebeians depended in some way upon particular old families. They were made up, I imagine, of three types: the freedmen, the protégés and the clients in the strict sense of the word.

The great families surrounded themselves with a circle of dependants whom they needed to enhance their prestige: 'clients and faithful freedmen and workers rendered their services to them.'[361] These hard-working freedmen were former slaves of the household who had stayed under their ex-master's roof and went on serving him as before. There were also freedmen who had set up as craftsmen or shopkeepers and were legally required to pay dues to their master, in money or in kind, and to come and offer him homage.

As for the protégés, I am assuming that they existed, without being able to prove it. We may suppose that the lesser people counted on the protection of one or other of the great families, worked for it and loved it, and that neighbourhood relations decided the choice of a protector. Montesquieu wrote in his travel memoirs: 'The people of Venice are the best in the world. They will endure patiently if a great man does not pay them, and, if they go three times to see a creditor and he tells them that, if they come again, he will have them beaten, they submit in patience and do not come again. It is true that, if a great man has promised his protection, he will give it, whatever may happen.'

Finally the clients, in the special sense that the word acquired under the Empire. Clientage was an institution for display.[362] The great houses needed people to come and fill their reception rooms in the morning and to accompany them in the streets, for a Roman lord was never alone, even in the most intimate moments of his life.[363] In exchange for this quite well-defined service, the client received a wage that was no less formal, the *sportula*,[364] which he drew when he came to the house. This wage was six sesterces a day, or a good wage for a workman of Balzac's time. It was a lot for a man of the people, but too little for the upper class. The clients were privileged persons who were discontented with their lot, because, far from being men of the people, they were unfortunates who had been 'recommended', or else starveling poets.[365]

Let us leave aside those who, under the Empire, formed the true clientage. The salons of the great were also visited by 'friends' (who sometimes called themselves 'clients' in order to emphasize their deference).[366] These were persons, both young and not so young, *equites* and senators, who cultivated their relationships for the sake of political careers, because everything was done by co-option and recommendation.

These networks of dependence upon the senatorial families did not encompass all the plebs. Many freedmen set up on their own, abandoning their patron and no longer paying homage to him – an infidelity that was one of the proverbial calamities deplored in those days. The numerous Imperial freedmen were something different again: as officials or ex-officials they lorded it among the plebeians and had clients of their own, 'many clients' perhaps,[367] for everybody considered it a point of honour to protect someone else and every unfortunate found another worse off than himself. There remained the unemployed who looked for work from the Emperor or the grandees; the *lazzaroni* who did not look for work and who had sufficient strength of character to live without worrying about the morrow (not everyone can be a *lazzarone*); and finally 'the basest slaves', whom we can imagine as being like the 'insolent lackeys' of the eighteenth century, scroungers and rowdies who contributed to the disorders at public entertainments.[368]

AFFECTIVE RECEPTIVITY AND THE COURTIER ATTITUDE

All these people, respectable or not, went more or less regularly to public entertainments, and the senators were particularly assiduous, out of both duty[369] and inclination (in their salons they argued for and against the attractions of the Circus just as people have argued in our day about television).[370] However, Tacitus's complaint regarding these entertainments refers only to that section of the plebs who were not dependent on the great houses, and his complaint is political. Whereas the dependent plebeians were socially and politically under the thumb of the senatorial oligarchy, the unattached ones, being indifferent to politics, felt affection for the sovereign alone, that giver of games and visible prince who let himself be loved without expecting these plebeians to act as his dependants.

The complaint about excessive love for shows is doubly mytho-logical. The unattached plebs did, perhaps, attend the Circus more often than the other section, but this tendency of theirs was seen as characteristic. Their affective receptivity in relation to the shows and the stars of these shows was taken as symbolic of their social 'avail-ability'. These plebeians were a kind of human dust which floated in all the winds of opportunity or current events. Besides, there really was a category of persons for whom the Circus was the main thing in their lives – the *lazzaroni*, who were recruited more on the basis of character than of socio-economic situation. Like the notables of the cities, these beggars were men of leisure who were interested in culture – their own culture. For his polemical purpose Tacitus identifies the entire unattached plebs with them.

For Rome had changed a great deal since the end of the Republic. From a city it had become a capital in which work was not everyone's chief concern and which served as the sovereign's court – in short, a 'royal city'. Its inhabitants were incapable of civic life, just as, in earlier times, those of Alexandria had been.[371] They no longer felt that they were masters and citizens of their own city, but rather the monarch's household. According to the account given by Tacitus, their outlook was comparable to that of the courtiers of Versailles. The plebs watched the sovereign as he lived, and his outsize image became obsessive with them, the sole topic of conversation. They ran after the pleasures that the ruler provided for them and which made up the events of their lives, together with their daily bread.

In the end, consequently, the attitude of the capital towards the master of the Empire, which was very different from that of the inhabitants of the Empire towards their sovereign, was comparable, to a considerable degree, to the attitude of those inhabitants towards the local notables of their respective cities.

If we read Greek inscriptions we see that, in the eyes of the governed, the government was embodied in two very different sorts of person. Close to them were their familiar masters, the notables, who were fellow citizens. But above everyone, very high and very far away, were 'the authorities', i.e. the Roman authorities, the Emperor and the provincial governor. These, the 'authorities' *par excellence*, are called in inscriptions *hoi hēgoumenoi*, and Dio of Prusa (one should not trust some of his translators) does the same. These are the powers-that-be whom St Paul wished to be obeyed, and in Luther's translation of the Bible they were to become the sadly famous *Obrigkeit*.[372]

Under the Imperial authorities the masses in the cities bowed their heads and submitted to a political relationship that was impersonal and unilateral. With the notables, however, their relationship was familiar and bilateral. The masses took part in the internal quarrels of the city Council, acted as chorus in the rivalries between local notables, and in all circumstances constituted an audience which acclaimed, booed or 'induced' a *euergetēs* to open his purse.

This leads us to re-examine the question of the depoliticization of Rome by the Circus.

9. The Circus and politicization

Love cannot be reduced to an asymmetrical, even unequal, relationship and to personal satisfactions; it is also 'desire for the other's desire'. Nor is politics merely a matter of power and material interests. Between the Emperor, the plebs and a *terzo incomodo*, the Senate, a sentimental drama was played out for which the public entertainments were the setting and the symbol. Given by the Emperor or in his presence, the shows were a material satisfaction, but they also allowed the sovereign to prove to his capital that he shared popular feelings (*popularis esse*). They were also a ceremony at which the Emperor was acclaimed. One might therefore talk of depoliticization. The material and symbolic satisfactions of the Circus subjected the plebs to their master. One could also say that there was something democratic in this *largesse* and this homage that the Emperor paid to the most representative city of his Empire.

Words count for little here. Democracy? But though the Emperor reigns *for* the people, he does not reign *by* it. Depoliticization? Under this confused notion there is the vague idea of an exchange of satisfactions. But politics is not exchange, even unequal exchange, of homogeneous quantities; it is adjustment to heterogeneous situations.[373] Let me first set forth the fascinating picture of Rome's public entertainments and the Roman year, with its many holidays, and then I shall try to define these shades of meaning.[374]

THE SHOWS: FOUR MONTHS' HOLIDAY

Under the Empire the shows in Rome were given exclusively by the magistrates and the Emperor. Private persons had lost the right to give gladiatorial *munera*. The magistrates received a sum from the Treasury, but they greatly exceeded these credits, and the cost of the games ran into hundreds of thousands, or rather millions, of sesterces. They gave the regular *ludi*, that is, theatrical performances and chariot races in the Circus. The Emperor reserved for himself all the extraordinary shows, which were frequent, and usually took the form of spectacles in the arena, fights between gladiators in the amphitheatre (but also *venationes*, wild-beast hunts). There it was that condemned men were beheaded, burned or thrown to wild animals to provide an additional show. As we see, the old distinction remained between the *ludi*, solemn and public games in the Circus and the theatre, and the *munera* in which gladiators fought each other or wild beasts. These *munera* continued to be extraordinary, and ceased to be private only to become Imperial: the modern expression 'gladiatorial games' is an absurdity which Latin did not commit before the third century.[375] However, besides the Imperial gladiators, any magistrate could add an exhibition of gladiators to the normal programme of his games; and above all, under the Empire there was a *munus* which became, in Rome, public and obligatory. It was given by the quaestors, who no longer gave at Praeneste the games which Sulla dedicated to the Fortuna of that town, in the name of the Roman state, as I shall try to show elsewhere.

The ordinary *munus* of the quaestors and the ordinary games, which were given by the aediles, the praetors and the consuls, occupied each year a number of holidays totalling two months at the beginning of the Empire, three months under Tiberius, four months at the end of the second century, and six months in the later Empire.[376] The extraordinary games and the *munera* given by the Emperor were additional to these. In 112 Trajan became consul and 'on 30 January gave the signal for fifteen days of games in the three theatres, with three days of distributions of gifts and lottery tickets to the public; on 1 March he gave the signal for the Circus, with thirty races'. Four years earlier he had given a *munus* with more than 4,000 pairs of gladiators, which lasted for 117 days between 4 June 108, when the shows began, and 1 November 109, because it had been necessary to leave out the days when the courts were sitting and those that were occupied by the regular festivities.[377]

The Emperor attended some of these spectacles in person, namely those of which he was himself the author, those that were given for his good health and prosperity or for his birthday, and even some of those which had a magistrate as author and president (for the two functions went together). In the last-mentioned cases the Emperor honoured the magistrate concerned, and enhanced his games, by being present in the seat of honour (this is the real meaning of the verb *praesidere*).[378] Concerning Tiberius, who did many things in quite the opposite way to his successors (for the Imperial monarchy was still taking shape in his reign), Suetonius mentions an oddity: he gave no shows whatsoever and attended only very rarely those that were given by others.[379] Suetonius exaggerates. In reality, at the beginning of his reign, Tiberius demonstrated his pro-senatorial feeling by 'presiding' over the magistrates' games so as to honour their authors. In short, the sovereign was often present at the Circus, the theatre or the amphitheatre, in the front row, or in his box at the Circus (which in my view was not originally a sanctuary for the Imperial person).[380] Even when given by somebody else, a show at which he 'presided' became a ceremony in his honour.

All this means that Rome lived a life of festivals, with several months of them every year, spaced out in series of several days at a time, as the religious calendar dictated. The public spent these months of leisure in the Emperor's company, living with him almost to the same extent as courtiers with their king. Ruler and spectators spent a third or a quarter of their time together at the shows. Even if the Emperor was absent, the games began with an act of public homage to him. They were equivalent to court festivals, at which the ruler's person inevitably figured as the star. We read in Phaedrus's fables an authentic account of one of these shows.[381] A magistrate, a nobleman, is giving games in the theatre. The curtain rises (or, rather, 'falls') on a tragedy or a 'pantomime' and the choirs sing a cantata: 'Rejoice, Rome, in security, for your prince is well.' And the whole public stands up respectfully at these words. Wishing good health to the Emperor was the standard formula for these acts of homage performed at a show.[382] The Senate, the equestrian order and the plebs hailed the sovereign, and their rhythmic acclamations were gradually codified and accompanied by music, culminating in the Byzantine ceremonial of the Circus.[383] The victory of one of the chariot factions in the Circus was a good opportunity to hail, in a symbolic ritual, the perpetual victory of the sovereign and to transform the Circus ceremonies into a sort of triumph.[384] Nor were the shows the only public occasion when the inhabitants of Rome beheld their Emperor. They also saw him giving judgement in person in the Forum (the attitude of the Emperors on these occasions is an essential item in their characterization by Suetonius), distributing *congiaria* with his own hand (official sculpted reliefs and the reverse sides of coins show us the scene),[385] throwing gifts or lottery tickets to the people (Caligula enjoyed watching them fight over these)[386] and presiding over solemn sacrifices; not to mention the Emperor's solemn entries into his capital. Thus, 'the greater part of the year was being given up to ... days of thanksgiving and holidays'.[387]

It followed that the shows became, in several ways, a political arena, because there the plebs and their sovereign came face to face. There the Roman crowd honoured their Emperor, demanded that he should grant them pleasures, made known to him their political demands, and either hailed or attacked the Emperor under colour of applauding or booing the shows. Thus the Circus and the amphitheatre acquired disproportionate importance in Rome's political life. Even when the Emperor was not present in person at some show (even Commodus was sometimes absent),[388] the Imperial insignia were apparently always placed on his seat, where they could be seen by everyone.[389] The show was an official ceremony. The crowd knew that the show was laid on for them, that they themselves were the 'carnival queen' and that the authorities wanted to please them.[390] They felt at home at the Circus and in the theatres (and so, in times of political agitation, it was to those places that they hastened in order to assemble and demonstrate).[391] Because the shows were the people's festivals, the author of the games, when this was the Emperor, devoted those days to the people's service and humbled himself before them.[392] Claudius addressed the spectators as 'my masters' (*domini*) – he whom, as sovereign, the crowd normally addressed as 'our master' (*dominus noster*). When Augustus was absent from shows ('sometimes he did not appear until the show had been running for several hours, or even for a day or more'), he would first ask the public's pardon and recommend to them the acting president whom he had appointed to take his place.[393] The sovereigns readily accorded the public the extra pleasures they asked for. Domitian regularly attended the gladiatorial combats given by the quaestors, so as to enable the people to ask him to bring on some of his Imperial gladiators, who performed before the people in their court costume.[394] The ruler made himself especially popular by agreeing to reward the actors or champions whom the public liked best. When the spectators wanted the Emperor to reward one of their stars by sending a purse down to the track, they apparently expressed themselves in the following way: they would shout to the man himself, in the guise of good wishes, 'May the Emperor be good to you!' (*habeas propitium Caesarem*).[395] But the crowd also profited by the opportunity to demonstrate politically, and the shows were the scene of political disturbances.[396] It was at a show that the crowd successfully pressed Galba to execute Tigellinus,[397] complained about the high price of corn,[398] 'desperately entreated Gaius [Caligula] to cut down imposts and grant some relief from the burden of taxes',[399] and chanted their desire for peace.[400] The shows were a court ceremonial and a *tête-à-tête* between the Emperor and his court of citizens.

Those Emperors who liked to work were inconvenienced by the

tyranny of the shows. Caesar had displeased the people by reading dispatches or petitions during shows.[401] (In our day, on the contrary, a minister who takes the plane from Paris to Nice has to be seen at work during the flight.) Augustus was careful not to behave like Caesar; 'nor did he himself dislike such amusements, and he thought it citizenlike [*civile*] to mingle in the pleasures of the populace [*vulgus*].'[402] Marcus Aurelius did not like official pomp. At the beginning of his diary he mentions that his teacher, Rusticus, had advised him not to wear his robe of state when inside the palace, and he learnt from the gods and from his father and predecessor that within the palace there was no need for guards, official costumes, torches and statues. The shows bored him, for the shouts of the crowd prevented him from concentrating on his state papers[403] and, besides, there was nothing more monotonous than what went on in the amphitheatre, where, he says, one always sees the same thing.[404] All the same, he had to strike a happy medium, for the same reason as Cicero in his day. Antoninus had taught him to do neither too much nor too little in the matter of Imperial *euergesiai*.[405] He congratulated himself on 'his freedom ... from hunting for popularity with respect to men by pandering to their desires or by courting the mob: yea, his soberness in all things, and steadfastness; and the absence in him of all vulgar tastes and any craze for novelty'.[406] These were all allusions to the problem of the shows, at which the philosopher-Emperor made a point of not engaging in amateur acting, while respecting the tradition which required that an Emperor should not disdain whatever gave pleasure to the people. Julian the Apostate, however, took a high line, and thereby drew on himself the animosity of the people of Antioch because he did not go to the theatre often enough, and devoted only his spare time to the shows, so that the crowd greeted him with hostile shouts.[407] But most of the Emperors did not dislike the shows, at which they had their majesty acclaimed, showed their love for their fellow citizens and savoured their popularity. Marcus Aurelius, who did not like the games, disliked also 'public acclamations and every sort of adulation',[408] meaning the court liturgy and the organized acclamations.

In short, Juvenal tells us that the Roman plebs were resigned to the Imperial regime and appreciated the advantages it was able to offer them. For his part, the sovereign respected tradition and let himself be seen during the shows so as to testify to his popular tastes. When a ruler is not seen as the mandatory of those under his rule, he makes a point of multiplying proofs that at least he reigns *for* them. Democracy?

No; indeed, the shows were also a liturgy of power by absolute right. The old word 'popularity', under the French *ancien régime*, expressed the two sides of the coin. 'Let [the king] render himself popular,' says Montesquieu.[409] 'The common people require so little condescension that it is fit they should be humoured; the infinite distance between the sovereign and them will surely prevent them from giving him any uneasiness.'

By being present often at the shows, or else by giving shows frequently, an Emperor made it clear that he was not contemptuous of the plebs. In his presence the spectators did not behave like a public which was there for its own pleasure and ready merely to give a curious glance at the great man. They assumed an attitude of deferential familiarity. Even the stiff Constantius, from whom everything was to be feared, understood the precise line he had to tread: 'On several occasions, when holding equestrian games, he took delight in the sallies of the commons, who were neither presumptuous nor regardless of their old-time freedom, while he himself also respectfully observed the due mean', like Marcus Aurelius.[410] By their freedom of speech, or *libertas*, the public tried to prove to itself that the Emperor was a familiar, complaisant and loving master.

ANCIENT CONCEPTIONS OF FREEDOM

In ancient times there were three conceptions of freedom, for there were three issues in politics. One conception was that of the classical city: a citizen is free if, holding power by turns with the others, he is given orders only by himself. The other conception is much less well evidenced, as a result of the almost total loss of that ancient historiography which a Frenchman would call left-wing. Here, however, is a specimen. The demagogue Hippo proposed 'a distribution of land, urging that liberty was based on equality, and slavery on the poverty of those who had naught'.[411] Plutarch, who reports this proposal, contrasts this execrable freedom to the true freedom, which he calls *parrhēsia*. Being able to speak without fear to the sovereign, to address him as equal to equal (*isēgoria*), that was *libertas*, freedom of speech; and that was what freedom meant under the Empire. This was the freedom that Marcus Aurelius was glad to allow to his subjects. His was, he wrote, 'the conception of a state with one law for all, based upon individual equality and freedom of speech and of a sovereignty which prizes above all things the liberty of the subject'.[412] In practice, that meant that Marcus Aurelius would be a 'good' Emperor, respecting the Senate, whose advice he would seek (from the standpoint of the form to be taken by obedience, it is more important to do people the honour of asking their advice than it is to follow that advice: the ruler should 'engage in dialogue'). It meant also that Marcus Aurelius would really listen to the divergent views of his privy councillors. The Imperial *libertas* is for those political agents the Senate and the council, and for them only (it has nothing to do with the rights of man and the citizen). Whereas the plebeians have the right to the Emperor's love, the Senate has the right to be heard. In its extent, this liberty bears a misleading resemblance to that of the classical city, which also extended to the political agents alone. In the city, however, those agents were the sovereign body of citizens. Under the Empire they were the sovereign's councillors. The notion of 'counsel', somewhat forgotten by the moderns,[413] enjoyed for thousands of years an importance equal to that of representative democracy nowadays. If Marcus Aurelius listened to his councillors, he did not do so merely out of genuine generosity: he knew that it was in his political interest to listen to them.

PLURALISM, COUNSEL AND DESPOTISM

It was in his interest 'not to be Caesarified',[414] for pride prevents one from tolerating outspokenness, from listening to persons who have something to say that is useful to the state, and from allowing oneself to be contradicted.[415] This seems to have called for some effort from Emperors who were all-powerful and almost worshipped. In those far-off days the pluralistic regime, in which several groups divide and dispute the possession of power, did not exist. What took its place to some degree was the council. The sole sovereign had to wield power in a way that allowed him to escape from his solipsism. He had to see with eyes other than his own, by calling on councillors who would epitomize for him, if not his subjects and their interests, at least the outlook of reasonable people. The councillors did not represent the people, they enabled the sovereign to survey his problems as ruler.

A despot who tolerates around him only flatterers, and punishes the bringers of bad news (the classic example of this was Tigranes, king of Armenia, in Plutarch's *Lucullus*), harms himself in many ways. He will be given only good news and will be virtually blind. He will offend his subjects' pride by giving them orders without having asked their advice. He will no longer take account of the interests of the different groups among his subjects. Finally, he will deprive himself of the heuristic instrument called the topic. Every deliberation has to solve two problems: to find the right key among all those placed on the council's table, and to make sure that every possible key has been thought of. Only an excessively Cartesian mind would claim to possess a method capable of viewing problems from every possible angle. Less megalomaniac minds know that, when it is no longer a matter of unrolling from a *primum verum* those long chains of reasoning beloved of geometricians, method gives place to topic,[416] the aim of which is to try to think of everything, without being sure of success. The topic means a list, prepared in advance, of all the data and all the possible solutions in relation to a certain problem. If no topic is available, or if the problem is unique, one tries to replace topic by 'brainstorming', and councillors are useful for that. One lets the councillors talk quite freely, in the hope that, amid the flood of stupidities and displeasing views they will disgorge, the right solution will appear.

The council being a master-word in ancient politics, love having its price, and freedom bearing several meanings, antiquity's notion of tyranny is clarified. The relation between the Emperor and the Senate will also be clarified.

A tyrant can be, in the first place, a man whose policy runs contrary to the material interests of a section, large or small, of his subjects. Those who are disfavoured will feel oppressed, deprived of material freedom, and they will say that the tyrant is selfish in that he does not pursue *their* policy, even if he does not pursue a policy that is merely his own. In order to impose his policy, the tyrant will perhaps resort to violence, which will either be legalized or remain arbitrary.

Violence can also be used by a tyrant to keep himself in power. That means a state apparatus which imprisons the community of which, ideally, it is the organ. This case always combines with the one previously mentioned, since this political apparatus necessarily continues to pursue a certain policy. Nevertheless, it is marked off from it conceptually and by shades of meaning. Proselytes who impose a state religion because religion interests them materially do not have quite the same mentality as brutes whose only interest in life is power and who impose the state religion merely in order to debar rivals from power.

Finally, the tyrant can be a man whose delight in the exercise of power derives entirely from the servitude that he imposes on some of his subjects. He wants to be obeyed absolutely, or even worshipped. He will drink and make display of his *dolce vita*. Sometimes he will despise popularity and will not seek to be loved by the plebs; at other times he will require from the grandees a mendacious flattery that deprives them of dignity. He will no longer listen to any advice.

So many social groups, and in each group so many types of interest, mean so many different tyrants. It seems to me that what Montesquieu calls despotism combines the first and third definitions: arbitrariness and humiliation. To see how confused the notion of 'tyrant' is, it is enough to think of Nero, tyrant to the Senate but popular with the plebs of Rome alone, less interested in power than in being worshipped, but resorting to violence in order to remain in power against subjects who want to overthrow a man who humiliates them for no reason at all. By demolishing his Golden House Vespasian tried to convince the people that Nero had been 'selfish', like all tyrants. It is true that Nero wanted to be worshipped and consequently led a very 'godlike' private life, which angered the grandees and probably most of his subjects as well. But this way of life was admired by the Roman plebs, his courtiers. Far from being selfish, Nero was the first Emperor to build public baths for the Romans. But that was precisely, in the eyes of some, his worst misdeed: Nero's altruism benefited not the Senate but the plebs. And Senate and plebs were rivals, which was why, around the Circus, a triangular battle of political conceptions was joined.

THE SULTAN, THE MANDARINS AND THE PLEBS

For at the Circus or in the amphitheatre there was a third personage whose susceptibilities were no less easily aroused than those of the plebs, namely the Senate. The plebs wanted to be loved by the Emperor, the Senate meant to be respected by him. Each group defended only its own freedom, and the higher dignity claimed by the Senate was in no way the rampart of universal freedom.

Unfortunately, the Senate's conception of its dignity ruled out that of the plebs. For the Senate, an Emperor who conformed to their political ideal would be content with making himself popular; only a tyrant would court the plebs by heaping public festivities upon it like flowers. It was useful for rulers to cause the regime to be loved, in their persons, so that the people might more willingly obey all who were in authority, even though the people in question were the inhabitants of Rome alone, a mere one per cent of the Empire's population. It was no less reassuring that, by making himself popular and going no further, the Emperor implied that he thought of his power as that of a magistrate. The Senate did not like tyrants, who tended to prefer the plebs to them. Between a popular magistrate and a tyrant, the difference lay in intentions. A good Emperor like Trajan might give 100 days of entertainments because the Senate understood that his need for popularity required it, but that he was pro-senatorial at heart.

This was not all. At the games the Emperors had themselves acclaimed by the people, which was acceptable except when it went too far. When that happened, Emperors exposed a tyrannical conception of their authority, and this was less tolerable to the Senate than to the plebs. The worst stage was reached when certain Emperors demanded to be acclaimed by the Senate itself; these were usually the same ones who decimated the ruling group by driving senators to suicide by accusing them of high treason or, as it was put, lese-majesty.

In the reigns of such men the senators looked on the Emperor as an idol, red with their blood, that they were forced to worship. The remarkable passage I am about to quote is as concrete as a private conversation. Dio Cassius, a senator himself, describes for us a scene in which he was both spectator and actor.[417] The events take place in the amphitheatre, where the tyrannical Emperor Commodus is personally fighting wild beasts in the arena.[418] The senators have been shouting out 'whatever we were commanded', for acclamations were not left to their improvisation but were regulated like official slogans. 'Thou art lord and thou art first, of all men most fortunate. Victor thou art, and victor thou shalt be; from everlasting, Amazonian, thou art victor.' 'Having killed an ostrich and cut off its head,' the historian tells us, 'he came up to where we were sitting, holding the head in his left hand and in his right hand raising aloft his bloody sword; and though he spoke not a word, yet he wagged his head with a grin, indicating that he would treat us in the same way.' In the homage he thus obliged them to pay to his spoils, the senators recognized, or thought they recognized, a tacit threat to their own heads; but at the time their problem was to refrain from bursting out laughing. 'And many would indeed have perished by the sword on the spot, for laughing at him (for it was laughter rather than indignation that overcame us), if I had not chewed some laurel leaves, which I got from my garland, myself, and persuaded the others who were sitting near me to do the same, so that in the steady movement of our jaws we might conceal the fact that we were laughing.'

The Senate wanted to be respected because it wanted to obey the Emperors in a way that was appropriate to its own political power and material wealth. But a tyrant preferred a plebs whose love he could win, to senators between whom and himself there was mistrust. An Emperor who was jealous of his authority wanted all his subjects to be merely 'his people'. If he lacked political sense, or simply patience, if he did not realize that there was more than one way of making oneself obeyed, his clumsiness or his pride got the better of his calculation of the balance of strength, and then instead of handling the Senate's dignity with care, he felt more comfortable amid the plebs of his capital.

In pre-revolutionary China there were, as in Rome, emperors both good and bad, if we are to believe the mandarins who wrote their history. It was not that the policy of the one kind was materially very different from that of the other; but the good emperors showed much more respect for the mandarin caste, whereas the bad persecuted and humiliated the mandarins and governed only through their entourage of eunuchs. We may, following Weber, apply the term 'sultanism' to the conduct of the bad emperors:[419] they refused to show respect to the caste which raised its head higher than the general level of the emperor's subjects.[420]

Both types of emperor were to be found in Rome, where the Senate held the position of the mandarins, while that of the eunuchs was held by the Emperor's freedmen, his prefects and the council. The first-mentioned could be veritable grand viziers, and the council was the real organ of government, the real informal sovereign.[421] However, a third actor came in to complicate the tragedy. Republican tradition forbade the Emperor to live shut up in a Forbidden City, as in Peking, so that the people of the capital sometimes counted for more, with certain Emperors and for ancient historians, than the rest of the Empire's population.

Sultanism or not, the dilemma was not new; it resulted from the logic of politics and not from any tradition of oriental despotism. In 222 BC Ptolemy Philopator became king of Egypt and could think himself free of rivals (foreshadowing Nero, or rather several Roman Emperors, he had carried out some pruning in his own family, disposing of his brother and of the queen mother). Thereafter, 'he began to conduct himself as if his chief concern were the idle pomp of royalty, showing himself as regards the members of his court and the officials who administered Egypt inattentive to business and difficult to approach' and neglecting public affairs 'owing to his shameful amours and senseless and constant drunkenness'.[422]

Polybius depicts for us elsewhere the ideal type of such a ruler as this: 'But when [kings] received the office by hereditary succession and found their safety now provided for, and more than sufficient provision of food, they gave way to their appetites owing to this superabundance, and came to think that the rulers must be distinguished from their subjects by a peculiar dress, that there should be a peculiar luxury and variety in the dressing and serving of their viands ... The kingship changed into a tyranny: the first steps towards its overthrow were taken by the subjects, and conspiracies began to be formed.' Polybius emphasizes that these plots were due to the pride of the ruling strata. 'These conspiracies were not the work of the worst men but of the noblest, most high-spirited and most courageous, because such men are least able to brook the insolence of princes.'[423] The great Greek historian seems to be predicting the many senatorial conspiracies against Imperial sultanism. To the arrogance of the Greek kings of Egypt was contrasted the Macedonian monarchy, in which the nobles could speak freely with their king – a freedom of speech that foreshadowed the *libertas* dear to the Roman Senate.

'MAD CAESARS', PURGES AND MOSCOW TRIALS

When compared with the ideal type, the case of the Caesars is individualized by the shows, with the presence of the plebs, and by the very special nature of the Senate. The senators were creatures much more complex than the officials of a Hellenistic king or than the Macedonian nobles. They wanted to govern, or at least to control, and at the same time they did *not* want to do so. This inner conflict, and this alone, was the cause of the famous struggle between the Senate and the Imperial authority, which tolerated each other only at the cost of hypocrisy, except when one slaughtered the other. And the Senate bore a grudge against the Emperors for its own unwillingness to rule.

The regime of the Caesars, the dyarchy spoken of by Mommsen, juxtaposed monarchy and republic, the latter being epitomized by the Senate. The long struggle between the two centres of authority was not, despite appearances, fought over the sharing of power. The Senate was in a false position in relation to its governing role, which was either too big for it or not big enough. At bottom, the senators had given up governing and were relieved that the Emperor had taken this burden off their shoulders. But now the contest concerned a 'symbolic' issue that was considerable: the Emperor's respect for the Senate became the great matter. Would a ruler who needed the acclamations of the plebs also respect the Senate?

Let me briefly clarify the logic of the situation which accounts for this. Christian kings were hereditary, like the kings of ancient Macedonia, and likewise had a nobility to respect; when these two features are present, we find a patriarchal monarchy, without arbitrariness or arrogance. If, however, one or other of these features is absent, the temptation of sultanism draws near. Either the king will behave arrogantly to the high officials who are dependent on him or else fear of losing his throne will cause him to see in every nobleman a possible pretender; in the first case we shall have Ptolemy Philopator, in the second the 'mad Caesars' who massacre senators.

For Caesarism was based on an absurdity. The Emperor, though sovereign by absolute right, had been made Emperor by his subjects. Could they give unconditional respect to their own creature? Would they hesitate to take back the crown they had given? There were indeed more attempts at usurping the throne than there were successful Emperors. The Caesars ought to have been created by virtue of a mechanical rule, heredity, the earthly imitation of divine law. When nobody can be a kingmaker, nobody can envy kings, and persons inclined towards usurpation will hesitate if they need to replace not merely one transient prince but a whole dynasty. Hauriou said that there were only three legitimate sources of authority – divine investiture, heredity and popular mandate.[424] The Emperors sensed the absurdity of their status. When they received their power from the hands of the Senate they therefore pretended to hesitate a little and engaged in that comedy of refusing power which we find in many societies.[425] They affected to accept the crown only on the Senate's insistence. By pretending in this way that they had been given power by their peers and were no worthier of it than any other senator, they made those peers acknowledge that the Senate, by insisting that they accept the crown, had renounced the right to take it back.

The 'mad Caesar' type is to be found wherever a non-delegated sovereignty has no assured legitimacy.[426] Let us undertake a mental experiment. Instead of a monarchy by absolute right, let us assume an accidental, *de facto* sovereignty. The general secretary of the Party clings to power in the name of his own genius, yet in the name of Lenin's 'democratic centralism' he is only the appointed official of the Party, which could replace him with someone else. He will therefore need to strike at random, which has good exemplary effect. He will not try to hit at precise opponents but rather at the permanent challenge to his legitimacy represented by the very existence of the Party. Then madness soon takes over from logic. There is danger everywhere, and so it is elusive. The ruler loses his head and becomes the first to believe in the crimes he attributes to his victims. When we are afraid of others we believe that they hate us, and we are afraid of them when we doubt our own legitimacy. Against such doubts nothing can prevail with us, even total submission and worship, because these doubts have their sources within ourselves: Stalin was the first to consider himself a usurper.

The 'mad Caesar' type is the mirror-image of this. Rome had the equivalent of Soviet Russia's purges and show trials and its morbid suspiciousness. Every senator was subject to suspicion, a state of affairs which continued right down to the end of the Empire. Ammianus Marcellinus writes of the Emperor Constantius that in his reign, 'as if it were prescribed by some ancient custom, in place of civil wars the trumpets sounded for alleged cases of high treason ...' and 'free rein was given to general calumny'. 'While in administrative affairs he was comparable to other Emperors of medium quality, if he found any indication, however slight or groundless, of an aspiration to the supreme power, by endless investigations, in which he made no distinction between right and wrong, he easily surpassed the savagery of Caligula, Domitian and Commodus.'[427] The purges of the Senate were the inverse of Stalin's purges. Stalin was an appointed official who claimed that his irremovability was legitimate, as though it arose from the nature of the situation. The 'mad Caesars' were owners of the state whose irremovability was not much more legitimate, in their subjects' hearts, than if they had been mere appointed officials. Formally, though, the two terrors were similar, in that they were diseases of deficient legitimacy, not material conflicts or conflicts of authority.

THE EMPEROR AND THE SENATE BLAME EACH OTHER FOR THEIR OWN INNER CONFLICT

Nor was this all. The dyarchy of the Emperor and the Senate was founded on another absurdity. The Emperor had to govern in collaboration with an organ, the Senate, which was too powerful to behave like a mere council without responsibility and yet was not powerful enough to be able sometimes to impose its sovereign will. Therefore from the beginning of the Empire the senators chose not to govern but instead to become a rubber stamp and an honorific assembly, provided that the reigning Emperor honoured them. They were almost as powerless under good Emperors as under bad ones. At least the good Emperors showed them respect and asked their opinion, or pretended to. The absurdity lay in reducing to the role of a mere council an organ whose members had an independent existence, whereas genuine councillors should be nobodies.

The Senate was too great to function as a council without responsibility. Councillors can allow themselves freedom of speech only if they are men who are nothing in their own right. The senators, however, had not been created by the Emperor to perform that office but had entered the supreme assembly because they were men destined to govern provinces and command armies. In the mouths of such men the slightest objection sounded like revolt, and the slightest initiative seemed to challenge the Emperor's own initiative. They were unable to say anything, nor did they wish to, for their pride forbade them to offer advice which might not always be followed. There was nothing they could do. The army, the Fiscus, foreign policy, all were in the Emperor's domain. They had some fragments of sovereignty (the administration of Italy, for example) and the function of councillors. The fragments were too few for them, and they were too great for the function. They confined themselves to rubber-stamping the Emperor's decisions, while hoping that he would be tactful enough not to do them the dubious and dangerous honour of asking their advice, and that he would be kind enough to await their acclamations without demanding them: they would never be delivered late.[428]

From the beginning of the principate the Senate vigorously renounced a governing role. In vain did Tiberius seek to consult it on all manner of things, even the army and war, which were his prerogative.[429] The Senate did not believe in his sincerity, and they were right, for he was in no less a state of inner conflict than they were: 'an Emperor who feared freedom while he hated sycophancy'.[430] These contradictions reduced the ruler to neurasthenia, and his reign ended in a bloodbath. There was conflict between Senate and Emperor not because the Senate wanted a share of power but because it did *not* want it.

Their problem is understandable. High politics was not allowed them, and occupying themselves with petty politics was just as dangerous, and more humiliating. The following anecdote is significant.[431] Under Nero a senator named Thrasea, a man of principle, thought that it was necessary for the state that the Senate should make greater use of its freedom of speech (*rem publicam egere libertate senatoria*). Accordingly he transformed into a lively debate a discussion about a routine *senatus consultum* concerning a matter of no great importance – whether to authorize a certain city to have a greater number of gladiators fighting in a show than the law allowed. His colleagues waxed ironical at the expense of this senator who thought he could teach senators their duty. ' "Why," it was asked, "if he thought that the public welfare required freedom of speech in the Senate, did he pursue such trifling abuses? Why should he not speak for or against peace and war, or on the taxes and laws and other matters involving Roman interests?" ' And Thrasea had indeed been careful not to touch on such matters. He replied that he had merely wished to preserve the honour of the Senate and symbolically maintain the principle of *libertas*, while being aware that it was impossible to exercise it. Was the game worth the candle? The overwhelming majority of the senators probably considered that it was better not to descend to arguing about trifles, but instead to insist on receiving honorific treatment. Let the Emperor command alone, and command whatever he wished, always provided that he commanded in a way that respected the dignity of the supreme assembly.

What with the dubious legitimacy of the Emperors and the awkward distribution of roles between Emperor and Senate, the Imperial system was dysfunctional, as the saying goes, and accordingly bred personality disorders and mental instability. The mental health of the Caesars was severely tested by this rickety organization. They had to appear in too many different roles: incarnate god, modest Senator among his peers, responsible (*gravis*) magistrate, popular magistrate, Good King, majestic sovereign, administrator in his council ... They were strange figures, those rulers of the early Empire, tormented by their contradictions to the threshold of madness (which some crossed), inclined to persecution mania, changeable, exhibitionistic, cultivated, moving from simple humanity to aestheticism or to a brutality which was in fact traditional in the ruling caste.[432]

The attitude of the senators was no less divided. As high officials they supported the Emperor, as senators they saw the Emperor as their successful rival. By his existence the sovereign drove the Senate to abandon its share in sovereignty, and so he was a tyrant. But he honoured the Senate, and so he was a good ruler. The solution found was to proclaim that Caesarism was bad but the reigning Emperor was good. The young senator Lucan, bound to Nero by literary comradeship, wrote an epic poem to the glory of the last defenders of the Republican regime, but which included an exalted eulogy of his Emperor. We are needlessly astonished by this dithyramb. Pliny the Younger and Tacitus also repeat that Caesarism is a necessary evil, that all previous Emperors have been bad and that the paradise of free speech for senators has returned only with the ascension to the throne of the good prince who reigns today. Marcus Aurelius himself admired Brutus and Thrasea;[433] the Emperors were themselves senators and politically the Senate was their real family (like the Party for a Bolshevik leader); their disputes with the senators distressed them like a family quarrel.

LOVE OF THE PLEBS

This was why the Emperor, if he was arrogant, could not tolerate the Senate. These men could not be, for him, a mere administrative nobility, a cog in the state machine, since they existed independently of him, were not his creatures. During the third century the Senate was to be gradually replaced by a new office-holding nobility. In the early period of the Empire, Emperors on bad terms with the Senate preferred to it the plebs of the capital, with whom their relations were easy and among whom they felt that they were really reigning. They gave the plebs plenty of shows. Claudius gave numerous shows only because he was good-natured; Trajan did the same as a matter of policy and display, and Lucius Verus because his intelligence was at no higher level. But all the other Emperors who, in Suetonius or Dio Cassius, bear the reputation of great givers of shows, did what they did *systematically*; for Caligula, Nero, Domitian, Commodus or Caracalla, persecuting the Senate, winning adoration and pleasing the plebs all went together. Nero left to history the memory of an evil man, but among the plebs of Rome his memory was no less popular three centuries after his tragic death than in his lifetime.[434] For the Emperor as for the Senate and the people, what was at stake in the conflict was Platonic (it was a drama of jealousy) and the splendour of the shows was the sign which confirmed that the Emperor preferred the plebs to his true family.

The plebs was happy to be no longer cast as Cinderella. Besides, it mistrusted the senatorial caste, and with good reason. We see this clearly in the year 41. Caligula had just been murdered. The senators 'were eager to regain their former prestige and earnestly aspired, since after long years they now had the chance, to escape a slavery brought

414

upon them by the insolence of the tyrants. The people, on the other hand, were jealous of the Senate, recognizing in the Emperors a curb upon the Senate's encroachments and a refuge for themselves.' They were glad that the soldiers were going to make Claudius Emperor, for they 'supposed that his securing the throne would avert from them any civil strife such as had occurred in Pompey's day' – the vendettas of the Republican oligarchy obsessed with *dignitas*.[435]

The plebs liked to see the bad Emperors humiliate the nobles.[436] In the trials for lese-majesty by means of which the Emperors drove senators to suicide, there was a detail which aroused the horror of respectable people, namely that denunciations and testimonies by slaves against their masters were accepted.[437] This was felt by some not as a social scandal but rather as an act of 'impiety', a violation of family relationships, like parricide.[438] Others must have seen in it an act of revenge wherein the last became the first.[439] Caligula was aware of these shades of feeling, and in the improvised theatre which he had had had set up under his balcony, 'no seats had been set apart either for the Senate or for the *equites*, so that the seating was a jumble, women mixed with men and free men with slaves'.[440] Now in Rome the disposition of seats at shows was, in most cases, very strictly arranged, so as to represent the social order (just as in Germany, until 1848, the stalls of a theatre were reserved for the nobility). We can imagine what a shock was produced by this innovation introduced by Caligula, who wanted everyone under him to be merely 'people' at the shows which he attended, as though at home, looking down from his balcony, as 'the master of the house' and not just the state's first magistrate.

Thus the shows, in Rome at least, had been politicized by the people, the Emperor and the Senate with, as the issue at stake, or the significance sought, the form to be taken by relations between them. They had been politicized because they were public throughout the Empire. They were official ceremonies which theoretically formed an element in the state religion (except for the gladiatorial *munera*, which were, so to speak, a matter of custom and folklore). This was a politicization which calls into question what we think of as private life and leisure, and which leads us to wonder what politics really is. Is it a specific entity, just as religion, or games and entertainments, are also entities? Or is it the *way* things are? Or is there a third possibility? That a city should, through its state apparatus, make foreign policy, or take on a new master, is something that seems to conform to the natural order –

the city is engaging in politics. But when the city decides to concern itself with popular diversions, to organize them and make them public affairs, is that also politics? And if furthermore it 'politicizes' them, is it not stepping out of its proper role and abusing what we call politics?

Conclusion: festival and folklore

When euergetism, Imperial or private, is not raising public monuments, it is giving festivals and shows to a city. This was so much in line with the spirit of the age that private associations, which freely imitated the institutions of the cities, did the same, and had their own *euergetai*. An example is provided by those private religious associations which were what we call the various schools of philosophers. In Aristotle's 'school', at the Peripatos, they kept alive the spendthrift and corrupt habits of their master, whose hair-style and private life, unworthy of a philosopher, were recalled in antiquity only with repugnance.[441] The school had its banquets, two per month, and its rector was responsible for organizing them. The participants paid a modest contribution and the rector himself found the balance of the cost from his own resources. To be sure, there was a different rector each month, so that every member of the school held the office in turn, and thus it was not really euergetism, more a tontine. All the same it was expensive, so that only rich men could become Aristotelians and take part in the scientific researches of the Peripatos; 'many there were who refused to join it, just as one keeps away from a corrupt city where there are too many choregies and liturgies'.[442] Each one paying in turn, or making the rich pay – the Peripatos combined the disadvantages of both systems; where the rich pay too much, the city is definitely corrupt. There lies a prime political problem of euergetism – material interests, the question of money.

This painful question was certainly as important in those days as it is in ours; to doubt that would be to doubt the very nature of everyday human life. The fact remains, however, that politically the major problem of euergetism, in the eyes of the ancients, was that of the form of obedience rather than that of material interests. Polybius, Cicero or the anti-Nero senators refused to give their approval to *euergesiai* and shows not so much from dislike of any redistribution of the cake as from resentment at the sight of tatterdemalions thinking they had rights instead of obeying like devoted servants. This is understandable. They were rich, they were notables or senators, even

Emperors. Political relations mattered more to them than economic interests. Why then were they nevertheless *euergetai*? Because shows, in those days, were official, just as the monuments raised by the *euergetai* were public. Notables and oligarchs were public men. The shows might well be, in the eyes of some of them, a corrupt sort of politics, but they were politics none the less, and so, as public personages, they had to take a hand in them.

This is why the ancients distinguished between three things where we see only two. We contrast public life with private or everyday life. They distinguished between the city's business, private life and festivals. Polybius evokes somewhere the return to normal conditions in the Peloponnese after the Social War: 'As soon as the Achaeans had the war off their shoulders, electing Timoxenus as their *stratēgos* and resuming their customs and their normal mode of life, they set themselves ... to re-establishing their private fortunes, to repairing the damage done to their lands, and to reviving their traditional sacrifices and festivals and various local religious rites.'[443] There is the same triple division in Juvenal's *panem et circenses*. The Roman people, the poet exclaims, no longer wants to vote, it has renounced public life, and is interested only in its bread and its festivals. For us, 'bread and circuses' would be taken together and mean private life, with its necessities and its luxuries, its leisure activities, in contrast to political activity, public life.

Summary

Bread and circuses, euergetism, thus meant politics for three reasons that were different and unequal, corresponding to the three proverbial issues of sociology: money, power and prestige.

The first reason, about which our contemporaries think too exclusively (because they reason as persons living in indirect democracies) is redistribution, meaning an approximation between justice and the *status quo*, between the two aims of politics. This explanation is not absurd, and it is certainly true for other periods of history. In those far-off times, however, when running the economy was not yet a profession, the political class regarded its economic advantages merely as means of sustaining its political and social superiority. Euergetism as redistribution did exist, but subordinately. An illuminating passage which we are surprised to come upon in Fronto tells us why:

The Roman people are held fast by two things above all, the corn-dole [*annona*] and the shows ... [and] the success of government [*imperium*] depends on amusements as much as more serious things; neglect of serious matters entails the greater loss, neglect of amusements the greater discontent; food-largess is a weaker incentive than shows; by largesses of food only the proletariat on the corn-register are conciliated singly and individually [*singillatim et nominatim*], whereas by the shows the whole population [*universum*] is kept in good humour.[444]

The second reason was that the state machine felt or believed that it was threatened by certain interests of its subjects, who wanted entertainments and bread. We know that when authority decides to impose discipline, this is a heterogeneous option which, for psychological reasons, goes beyond what is needed: 'if we allow the people to have festivals, innocent enough affairs in themselves, they will suppose that they are free to do whatever they like, and they will no longer be willing to obey or to fight.' Several solutions to this problem were conceivable. First, festivals: public enjoyments were confined to certain limited moments. This was convenient the rulers, who could decide whether the festival was to be patriotic or religious. Confinement to one day obtained for the ruled some effects of externality, by concentrating satisfactions and material resources; besides which there was the pleasure of variety – it is pleasant if one day is not like another. If the festival was dedicated to the gods, there would be no moral problem to worry about. (Aristippus, the philosopher of pleasure, was criticized for his corrupting doctrines. 'Being reproached for his extravagance, he said, "If it were wrong to be extravagant, it would not be in vogue at the festivals of the gods."')[445] In short, it is good to provide recreation from time to time for the childlike people, in the interests of authority itself.

Finally, in that period when there was nothing between direct democracy and authority by absolute right, the possession of power had some unreal effects. The rulers wanted to offer symbolic proof that they were in the service of the ruled, for power could not be either a job, a profession or a piece of property like any other. The right to be obeyed is a superiority, and every superiority needs to be expressed, since otherwise it will cause itself to be doubted; for there is not much difference between actualization and expression (when people talk of 'conspicuous consumption', this is a prosaic rationalization of the phenomenon of expression). And politics, like love, is an inner relation of consciousnesses. A master is not a thing, an *aliud*, he is a man like me, an *alter ego*, and what he thinks of me affects me in the idea I have of myself. Hence the requirements which it is merely playing with words to call 'symbolic' (they symbolize nothing, they exist for their own sake) and which it would be naïve to despise as being too Platonic.[446] Once more we face the three issues of politics: Who commands? What does he command? In what tone does he command?

Notes

1. Dio Cassius, LIV, 25, 1; cf. Dessau, nos. 5671–3 and 6256.
2. Luke 22: 25.
3. W. Schmitthenner, 'Ueber eine Formänderung der Monarchie seit Alexander', in *Saeculum*, XIX (1968), p. 31. Generally, W. Schubart, 'Das hellenistische Königsideal', in *Archiv für Papyrusforschung*, XII (1936), p. 1; A. J. Festugière, 'Les inscriptions d'Asoka et l'idéal du roi hellénistique', in *Mélanges J. Lebreton*, vol. I (1951), p. 31. On the Emperor as author and guarantor of the law and protector of the weak, see W. Schubart, 'Das Gesetz und der Kaiser in griechischen Urkunden', in *Klio*, XXX (1937), p. 54. Cf. A. von Premerstein, *Vom Werden und Wesen des Prinzipats*, p. 174.
4. See below. The soldiers of Lambaesis put their pay and the Emperor's liberalities on the same footing: Dessau, nos. 2445, 9099, 9100.
5. Hadrian's Antinous had a predecessor, Themiso, favourite of Antiochus Theos, who was deified (Athenaeus, 289f).
6. Fronto, *Epistolae ad Caesarem*, IV, 12; Tertullian, *Apologeticus*, 35; *De Idololatria*, 15 (Friedländer, *Sittengeschichte*, vol. I, p. 166, and vol. III, p. 62). A study of the popular imagery of the Emperors, on which there are innumerable monographs but no synthetic work, would require a whole book. I will mention only (and with reverence) A. Alföldi's work on the cake-moulds of the Danubian provinces, published in the *Laureae Aquincenses V. Kuzsinsky dicatae*, vol. I (Budapest, 1938), pp. 312–41. When Imperial 'good news' (cf. *Inscriptiones Graecae in Bulgaria*, vol. II, no. 659) was brought by messengers (see the *cenotaphia Pisana* in *Corpus Inscriptionum Latinarum* (hereafter *CIL*), XI, 1421), private persons hung wreaths on their doors: 'quod januam ejus, subito adnuntiatis gaudiis publicis, servi coronassent', wrote Tertullian, *De Idololatria*, 15, 7–8 (cf. *Codex Justiniani*, XII, 63, and *Codex Theodosii*, VIII, 11, 1: 'publicae laetitiae nuntii'). The sovereign's portraits were regarded as lucky charms: H. Stern, *Le Calendrier de 354* (Geuthner, 1953), p. 89; which probably explains why they are so frequent among cheap carved stones and glassware; cf. also G. Picard, *Les Trophées romains* (De Boccard, 1957), p. 336. On Imperial art

serving as model for religious iconography, see E. Will, *Le Relief cultuel gréco-romain* (De Boccard, 1955), p. 350. Note, at Chiusi, the epitaph of a 'pinctor Augustorum sive omnium bonorum virorum' (*CIL*, XI, 7126).

The everyday rituals exalting the Emperor provide a vast field for study. There were toasts for hailing the sovereign's name (Petronius, *Satyricon*, 60, 7); the practice of consecrating every public edifice, even a sundial, to a great god, to the Emperor and to the city (I shall return to this later); the practice of associating the Emperor with the god whom one thanked in ex-votos (inscriptions of the type *Augusto sacrum, Apollini v.s.l.m.*); and the practice of saluting the Emperor at the beginning of public and private documents (thus, in the regulations of a *collegium* at Lanuvium, *CIL*, XIV, 2112, col. 1, 14: 'quod faustum felix salutareque sit imp. Caesari Trajano Hadriano Aug ..., nobis, nostris collegioque nostro'). In France we had the practice of saluting the king's name at the beginning of wills: Villon does this in his *Grand Testament*, 56. In funerary foundations an Imperial anniversary was often chosen for distributions of *sportulae* (E. F. Bruck, *Ueber römisches Recht in Rahmen der Kulturgeschichte* (1954), p. 98); thus, *CIL*, VI, 10234 and 33885; a banquet founded in honour of the Emperor would be held on his birthday: *CIL*, X, 444; at every opportunity people cry 'Long live the Emperor!' (*Augusto feliciter, felix Augustus:* or *propitium habeas Augustum*). A perpetual foundation would be placed under the protection of the Emperor's name – to fail in respect to the foundation would thus be an act of impiety towards the Augusti (Dunant and Pouilloux, *Thasos*, vol. II, p. 78).

7. Besides the Gospels, see Dio of Prusa, *Orationes*, IV, 98 and XIV, 14.

8. *CIL*, vol. IV, no. 2338; cf. J. Carcopino in *Bulletin de la Société nationale des antiquaires*, 1960, p. 155.

9. Suetonius, *Vespasian*, 19: cf. M. Nilsson, 'Der Ursprung der Tragödie', in *Opuscula Minora Selecta*, vol. I, p. 104. On the insult which averts bad luck and the vengeance of fate, see J. G. Frazer, *The Golden Bough*, abridged edition (Macmillan, 1971), p. 750; E. Welsford, *The Fool* (Faber and Faber, 1935), p. 66.

10. Much could be said about revolutionary Messianism in Rome. Revolt was not launched against the Tsar, but in his name: only in the nineteenth century does the proletariat try to take over the state in order to carry out a social revolution (L. von Stein, *Geschichte der sozialen Bewegung in Frankreich*, preface, sees in this the originality of the nineteenth century). Before that time risings were the work of cranks or of rebels who had formed the notion – apparently mad, but sometimes successful – of becoming Emperor. This delirium of ambition was a feature of the old societies; see Tacitus, *Annals*, II, 39,

and IV, 27, and compare a curious passage from Sun Yat-sen quoted by Simon Leys, *The Chairman's New Clothes* (1977), p. 56 – at the beginning of the twentieth century the founder of China's revolutionary party, which was to put an end to that ancient empire, came upon a number of crazy people of this sort who joined his party with this purpose in mind.

11. Plutarch, *Sayings of Kings and Commanders*: 'Antiochus' (*Moralia*, 184e); cf. E. Bikerman, *Institutions des Séleucides*, p. 50, note 2.

12. J.-L. van Regemorter, *Le Déclin du servage* (Hatier, 1971), pp. 39–40. The pair consisting of the good king and the wicked vizier (the good ship's captain and his wicked mate) is familiar in group dynamics.

13. Romans 13: 1.

14. I Peter 2: 13–14.

15. Pliny the Younger, *Letters*, X, 96, 3; Mommsen, *Strafrecht*, p. 80. The question has been much discussed: cf. Sherwin-White, *The Letters of Pliny, Commentary*, p. 699. The passage seems clear: coercion is one thing, the penal law (in the strict sense of the word 'law') is another.

16. Mommsen, *Staatsrecht*, vol. III, p. 1186.

17. This is briefly indicated by Mommsen, *Staatsrecht*, vol. II, p. 905, note 1: 'Unlike a law, an edict does not necessarily contain an order; it may merely convey information, advice or warnings'; cf. vol. I, pp. 202 and 208.

18. Suetonius, *Augustus*, 28, 31 (end), 56.

19. Id., *Caligula*, 30, 54.

20. Id., *Augustus*, 89; Dio Cassius, LX, 26.

21. Suetonius, *Tiberius*, 34.

22. The spelling with -*vos* instead of -*vus*, current in the Republican period, reappears in the second century of the Empire, and it seems that this fashion began under Hadrian.

23. Suetonius, *Augustus*, 53 and 42; cf. Velleius Paterculus, II, 81, 3. Here are some examples of Imperial pollicitations: Tiberius promises the Senate to repair Pompey's theatre (Tacitus, *Annals*, III, 72); Augustus had promised to pay for repairing the aqueducts of Rome (Frontinus, *De Aquae Ductu*, 125); Nero promises to contribute to the rebuilding of private houses, after the fire of Rome (Tacitus, *Annals*, XV, 43); Titus promised more than he could give (Suetonius, *Titus*, 8). We know of the pollicitations of Antoninus at Ostia (*CIL*, XIV, 98; Dessau, no. 334) and Puteoli (*CIL*, X, 1640: Dessau, no. 336). It will be remembered that King Antiochus Epiphanes, as a good *euergetēs*, also made pollicitations to the *poleis* (Livy, XLI, 20). See also *Panegyrici Latini*, XII, 19, 1.

24. Claudius's letter is in Hunt and Edgar, *Select Papyri*, vol. II, no. 212.

25. Favouritism and corruption: *suffragium*; see G. E. M. de Sainte-Croix,

'Suffragium', in *British Journal of Sociology*, V (1954), p. 33; A. H. M. Jones, *The Late Roman Empire*, vol. I, p. 391. Sometimes, in fact, the men in power refuse to submit to the law and sometimes all agree in preferring favouritism to fair play; for everyone, individually, hopes to gain by this. See Ammianus Marcellinus, XX, 5: Julian's soldiers obtain a promise from the new Augustus that promotions will take place exclusively on grounds of merit – but then, soon afterwards, one of the army units asks for a favour to be granted to it which violates this rule. We know that in Rome it was as today in Corsica or Calabria: relations governed by rules coexist with relations of clientage and the two are connected in complex ways.

26. Papyrus of Alexander Severus on the gold for the crown; Grenfell and Hunt, *Fayum Papyri*, no. 20; Hunt and Edgar, *Select Papyri*, vol. II, no. 216; cf. W. Schubart in *Archiv für Papyrusforschung*, XIV (1941), p. 58; S. L. Wallace, *Taxation in Egypt* (Princeton, 1938), pp. 282 and 351; J. Moreau, *Scripta Minora* (Carl Winter, 1964), p. 34. On the theme of the prosperity of the current reign, see note 213 of my chapter II and add: Pliny, *Letters*, X, 23 and 37: Pseudo-Seneca, *Octavia*, 834 ('saeculi nostri bonis corrupta turba'); *Panegyrici Latini*, V, 18, 1. See A. Alföldi, *Studien zur Geschichte der Weltkrise des dritten Jahrhunderts* (Darmstadt, 1967), p. 41. On a Danubian cake-mould, a product of popular art and a testimony to monarchical feeling, we read: 'As the Emperor is well, we live in a golden age' (Alföldi in *Laureae Aquincenses*, vol. I, p. 319). However, each reign had its detractors, its *obtrectatores temporum*: a law of 393 orders that they be shamed and punished (*Codex Theodosii*, IX, 4: 'si quis imperatori male dixerit', 1). See below, note 232.

27. *Codex Theodosii*, I, 29, 3: 'We have done all we could to establish institutions in the interest of the common people'; ibid., 5: the harmless and peaceful peasantry must not suffer harassment; ibid., I, 16, 7: 'Cessent rapaces officialium manus, cessent, inquam'; ibid., X, 4, 1: the Emperor defends the lower orders against his own stewards.

28. Dessau, no. 642.

29. See the edict of Nerva quoted by Pliny, *Letters*, X, 58, 7. It opens as follows, in a style no clearer than that of the *Codex Theodosii*: 'There are some points, no doubt, Quirites, concerning which the happy tenor of my government itself issues an edict; and a good prince need not be narrowly scrutinized in matters wherein his intention cannot but be clearly understood. Every citizen may rest assured, even without a reminder, that I gave up my private repose [*quieti*: on this word's meaning see Wissowa, *Religion und Kultus*, p. 333] to the security of the public in order to dispense new benefits and confirm those of my predecessor.' It is wrong to draw a contrast between the bureaucratic style of the later Empire and that of the early Empire. The real contrast

is between the precision of thought (but not of vocabulary, see below) of private law and the confusing imprecision of the language of public law, in every epoch. The *Digest* is a chaos of clear ideas, the *Codex* is a realm of confused rhetoric. The imprecision of the vocabulary and the turgidity of the style are such that some of these constitutions cannot possibly have been understood, even in fields such as taxation where the Emperor certainly intended his laws to be applied. Questions like the way the land tax was assessed, or the difference between the various public coffers, are almost insoluble. The reason is twofold. The *Digest* is made up of extracts from the writings of jurisconsults who speak for themselves and form a sect proud of its traditions of rigour and clarity, whereas the rhetorical training of the bureaucracy, a veritable humanist mandarinate, made them incapable of precision but very much concerned to express themselves with majestic pomposity.

30. Suetonius, *Augustus*, 65; *Caligula*, 25; Tacitus, *Annals*, XIII, 17. Compare the numerous edicts of the Chinese emperors translated by E. Backhouse and J. O. P. Bland, in *Annals and Memoirs of the Court of Peking* (1914).

31. A. Alföldi, *Die monarchische Repräsentation in römischen Kaiserreiche* (Darmstadt, 1970). The second image completely eclipses the first during the third century, and this is what is meant by the transition from the Principate to the Dominate (Alföldi, *Studien zur Geschichte der Weltkrise des dritten Jahrhunderts* (Darmstadt, 1967), p. 374). It was the result of the eclipsing of the senatorial nobility by the new administrative nobility.

32. Ulpian, *Digest*, I, 4, 1 pr.: cf. Léon Duguit, *Traité de droit constitutionnel*, vol. II, p. 640 and vol. I, p. 595.

33. There was the same division in the minds of the Emperors. Marcus Aurelius rejected official acclamations (*Meditations*, I, 16, 13) but nevertheless allowed an apotheosis to be awarded to his wife (Julian, *Banquet*, 9 and 35). Julian, who criticizes him for this, made a display of his own contempt for the external forms of prestige; but his subjects gave him no credit for it (E. Stein, *Histoire du Bas-Empire*, J.-R. Palanque (ed.), vol. I, 2, p. 504, note 44).

34. R. Aron, *Études politiques* (Gallimard, 1972), p. 79.

35. Ammianus Marcellinus, XXVIII, 5, 14: 'In [the Burgundians'] country a king ... lays down his power and is deposed if, under him, the fortune of war has wavered, or the earth has denied sufficient crops; just as the Egyptians commonly blame their rulers for such occurrences.'

36. Horace, *Odes*, IV, 5, 13: cf. P. Margouliès, *Anthologie de la littérature chinoise*, p. 147.

37. John 9: 1–2, may be cited as the *locus classicus* on this point. Plague and famine are sent to punish the world's crimes (Jeremiah 14) or those of the Emperor. It was the same in China (M. Weber, *Religionssoziologie*, vol. I, pp. 298, 311 and note 2, 397). We should not suppose, however, that the 'primitive mentality' held this belief absolutely: a remarkable passage translated by Margouliès, *Anthologie de la littérature chinoise*, p. 177, cf. pp. 145 and 208, has profound implications for the complexity of 'belief'.

38. It is not an absurd idea to judge a leader by his luck rather than by his merit, since, the links in the chain of causal connection being largely hidden from us, there is some probability that this 'luck' is actually due to the leader's merit – so says a theoretician of probability, Georgescu-Roegen, *La Science économique, ses problèmes, ses difficultés* (Dunod, 1970), p. 200. See also F. Bailey, *Stratagems and Spoils, a social anthropology of politics* (Blackwell, 1969), pp. 131 and 148; M. Nilsson, 'Natural catastrophes', in his *Opuscula Minora Selecta*, vol. III, p. 427; on the theme of the *annus felix*, see the *Thesaurus Linguae Latinae*, II, 118, under *annus*; cf. Alföldi in *Jahrbuch für Antike und Christentum*, VIII–IX (1965–6), p. 68. The following references may be cited: Nero, delivering the funeral oration of the Emperor Claudius, praises the late ruler for the good luck of his reign (Tacitus, *Annals*, XIII, 3); Rome saddles Commodus with responsibility for plague, famine and fire (Herodian, I, 14, 7; pp. 28–9 (Stav.)). Famine is always seen as a wonder, a sign (Tacitus, *Annals*, XII, 43). Later, when the harvest failed, the Christians were blamed (Tertullian, *Apologeticus*, 40). In its last effort against Christianity, paganism ascribed famine to the anger of the gods who were being abandoned (Symmachus, *Relatio*, 16). As will be seen, the theme comes close to several others: that a leader's good luck is a sign of merit (Cicero, *Pro Lege Manilia*); that bad weather is a proof of the gods' anger (*Iliad*, XVI, 385–8: a storm proves that Zeus is angry with unjust judges); that the good king procures good harvests for his subjects (*Odyssey*, XIX, 111). Polybius disdainfully allows to the vulgar this belief that bad weather is a sign of divine wrath (XXXVI, 17). We are not surprised to see that at Tibur the aediles put up a dedication (on their leaving office, no doubt) to the goddess of good crops, *Felicitati* (*CIL*, I, 1481, XIV, 358; Dessau, no. 3700; Degrassi, no. 89). See also a strange but corrupt passage in Seneca, *Naturales Quaestiones*, IV, 7; cf. Mommsen, *Strafrecht*, p. 122, note 2. See also Petronius, *Satyricon*, 44, 10.

39. In his oration *De Felicitate Lustri Sui*. It was said against Scipio that his censorship had been *infelix* (Lucilius, 394 (Marx)), by which we understand that the harvests had been bad (contrast *lustrum felix* in *Panegyrici Latini*, VIII, 'Thanks to Constantine', 13, 3). It was a

common notion that the fortunate events of a given year were due to the eponymous magistrate of that year (L. Robert, *Hellenica*, I, p. 11, and XI–XII, p. 547). Velleius Paterculus (II, 36) congratulates Cicero on having been consul in the year when Augustus was born. Virgil congratulates Pollio on being consul in the year when the Messianic Child is born (there is no reason to assume that Pollio, because he receives these congratulations, must be the child's father). Bad weather proves that the gods are angry with Catiline (*In Catilinam*, III, 8); since Cicero returned from exile the harvests have been good (*Post Reditum in Senatu*, 14, *Ad Quirites*, 8; *De Domo Sua*, 5–8; cf., for the contrary view, *Ad Atticum*, IV, 1). On the king's responsibility for bad weather the essentials of the subject are fully covered by B. de Jouvenel, *De la souveraineté* (Librairie de Médicis, 1955), pp. 52, 55, 63. When public calamities are not attributed to the king, the blame for them is laid on 'marginal' elements – Jews, lepers, etc. – or on beggars (Philostratus, *Life of Apollonius*, 4, 10).

40. F. Taeger, *Charisma, Studien zur Geschichte des antiken Herrscherkultes*, 2 vols. (Kohlhammer, 1957 and 1960); cf. L. Cerfaux and J. Tondriau, *Un concurrent du christianisme: le culte des souverains dans la civilisation gréco-romaine* (Desclée, 1957). The most penetrating account is that given by Nilsson, *Geschichte der griech. Religion*, vol. II, pp. 132–85 and 385–93. The common view is to be found in G. Gurvitch, *La Vocation actuelle de la sociologie*, vol. I, p. 446 (he admits elsewhere that it is not certain that the kings of Dahomey and the Sudan, whom he originally gave as the last cases of kings really taken to be gods, were actually taken for gods). I have not read *Le Culte des souverains dans l'Empire romain* (Fondation Hardt, Entretiens sur l'Antiquité classique, vol. XIX, 1974). Finally, the *Essays on Religion and the Ancient World* by A. D. Nock (Oxford, 1972) contain passages of incomparable value.

41. This illuminating remark is made by A. D. Nock, *Essays on Religion*, p. 833, cf. p. 780; and in *Gnomon*, VIII (1932), p. 518 and XXVII (1955), p. 245.

42. J. Stoetzel, *Jeunesse sans chrysanthème ni sabre*, p. 91. R. Guillain, *Le Peuple japonais et la guerre, choses vues* (1948), p. 40: 'To see the emperor as a living god is wrong. For the Japanese he is only a higher being, exceptional but not a god; and for him to be a god, moreover, it would be necessary that the Japanese mind be metaphysical enough to grasp the very meaning that *we* attach to the word "god". The truth is, probably, that the emperor is the man who has not the right to be a man: he is Authority.' An outstanding work by L. Bréhier and P. Batiffol, *Les Survivances du culte impérial romain, à propos des cultes shintoistes* (1920), studies the Imperial cult in the time of the Christian

Emperors, with a view to deciding whether it was possible to allow Japanese converts to Christianity to perform the rites of worship of the Mikado which were incumbent upon officials.

43. Dittenberger, *Sylloge*, no. 390, line 25, and no. 624, lemma; Wendland, in *Zeitschrift für neutestam. Wissenschaft*, vol. V, p. 339; A. D. Nock, *Essays*, p. 724, note 23; C. Habicht, *Gottmenschentum*, p. 196, note 23, and p. 212. In an edict (Hunt and Edgar, *Select Papyri*, vol. II, no. 211), Germanicus rejects the 'acclamations hailing him as equal to the gods' with which he is welcomed by the Alexandrians.

44. E. Bikerman, *Institutions des Séleucides*, p. 257, disagrees.

45. The analogy between the Imperial cult and the Roman cult of the military standards is specifically stressed by A. D. Nock, *Essays*, pp. 657 and 780.

46. Cf. Veyne, in *Bulletin de correspondance hellénique*, XC (1966), p. 146, in which I omitted the most important reference: Mommsen, *Hermes*, XVII, p. 640: cf. *Staatsrecht*, vol. III, p. 803.

47. A. D. Nock, *Essays*, pp. 202–51: L. Robert, *Études anatoliennes*, p. 64.

48. See, e.g., Caligula's letter to the *koinon* of the Boeotians (*Inscriptiones Graecae*, vol. VII, no. 2711, col. 3, line 29), the letters from Tiberius to Gytheion (L. Wenger in *Zeitschrift der Savigny-Stiftung*, Roman. Abt., XLIX (1929), p. 300) or Claudius's letter to the Alexandrians (*Select Papyri*, vol. II, no. 212).

49. C. Habicht, *Gottmenschentum und griechische Städte* (C. H. Beck, 1970), p. 173: 'The divinity of the person honoured is the condition for the establishment of this cult, and not its result.' This may be understood in two ways. First, the Greek cities did not deify the kings or, later, the Roman governors, automatically, just because they were Authority; they deified them so as to acknowledge in them a personal merit, as 'saviour' or '*euergetēs*', that is, as having performed a heroic deed, or as 'founder' (they maintained a cult of founders). On this non-automatic deification cf. C. Werhli, *Antigone et Démétrios*, p. 94. Heroes, founders and benefactors are acknowledged to be gods because of their personal deeds. In a more general sense, however, nobody decides that a man or a place is divine: one *discovers* that he or it was already divine, and adapts one's conduct to the discovery. The result is that the decrees founding a cult usually say, 'The god X will receive a cult from the city' rather than 'X will be a god and receive a cult.' In this sphere, saying is doing, and X is *hailed in passing* with the title of god, without it being said that the title is being expressly *awarded*; cf. Veyne in *Latomus*, XXI (1961), p. 61, note 1.

50. Virgil, *Eclogues*, I, 6; on the statement 'He is a god!' or 'He will be a god for me', see Usener, *Götternamen*, p. 291 and note 17, and A. D. Nock, *Essays*, vol. I, p. 145, note 51. I cannot agree with O. Weinreich,

Ausgewählte Schriften, vol. II (B. R. Grüner, 1973), pp. 171–97, 'Antikes Gottmenschentum', who compares the deification of the Emperors to the notion of divine men like Epicurus (see my note 53). I prefer to follow L. Bieler, mentioned in note 55.

51. H. Usener, *Götternamen: Versuch einer Lehre von der religiösen Begriffs-bildung* (Schulte-Bulmke, Frankfurt, reprinted 1948). This very great work, which has had no successors, is still today one of the most promising contributions toward a science of religions. On how it can be used and on the gift it has for dispersing the commonplaces about the *mana* and other Durkheimianisms (subsequently covered by Wagenwoort with a phenomenological veil in which there is nothing phenomenological but only a certain skill in writing that creates a night in which all cats are grey), see P. Boyancé, *Études sur la religion romaine*, pp. 4–7.

52. I am not talking about the spontaneous cult of the Greek cities for kings, governors and even, with some variations, for Emperors.

53. See Polybius, XII, 23, 3: 'Epicurus is a god, yes, a god,' cries Lucretius on two occasions, with passion.

54. For 'hero' in the sense of 'writer of genius', see Longinus, *On the Sublime*, 4, 4; 14, 2; 36, 2.

55. On demi-gods, or rather 'divine men' such as Socrates, Homer, Apollonius of Tyana and Jesus, see L. Bieler, *Theios Aner, das Bild des göttlichen Menschen in Spätantike und Frühchristentum* (Wissenschaftl. Buchgesellschaft, 1967), especially p. 12, on the Emperors.

56. A. D. Nock in *Gnomon*, VIII (1932), p. 518.

57. Besides Habicht, *Gottmenschentum*, see Nock, *Essays*, p. 249, and L. Robert in *Bulletin de correspondance hellénique*, 1926, p. 499, and in *Comptes rendus de l'Académie des inscriptions*, 1969, p. 60, note 1.

58. *The Republic*, 540bc. Which, alas, raises the very big question of gods *in* Plato and *the* God *of* Plato. The trouble is that Plato never speaks of his God, unless we assume that for him the Good is God. It is true that, if God existed for Plato, he could only have been the Good. But Plato does not speak of him.

59. W. Mühlmann, *Messianismes révolutionnaires du Tiers Monde* (Galli-mard, 1968), p. 291.

60. Seneca, *Thyestes*, 204–15; see also an explicit passage in Plutarch, *Life of Demetrius*, 30.

61. Philo of Alexandria, *Embassy to Gaius*, 11, 76 (Smallwood): 'In the first stage of this infatuation [Caligula] is said to have taken this line of argument. "Those who have charge of the herds of other animals, ox herds, goat herds, shepherds, are not themselves oxen nor goats nor lambs, but men to whom is given a higher destiny and constitution, and in the same way I who am in charge of the best of herds, mankind,

must be considered to be different from them and not of human nature but to have a greater and diviner destiny." '

62. Polybius, V, 27, 6.

63. F. Taeger, *Charisma*, vol. I, p. 353; W. W. Tarn, *Antigonos Gonatas*, p. 250. I am not speaking of the cult decided on by the cities, but of a cult demanded by the king himself.

64. D. Nörr, *Imperium und Polis in der hohen Prinzipatszeit*, especially pp. 115–23.

65. On the Romans as *euergetai* of the entire universe, or *euergetai* of all the Greeks, see L. Robert, in *Comptes rendus de l'Académie des inscriptions*, 1969, p. 57; H. Volkmann, 'Griechische Rhetorik oder römische Politik?' in *Hermes*, LXXXII (1954), p. 467. Later the theme was to be extended to all the Emperor's subjects, and he was styled 'pacifier of the universe' or 'founder of peace' (Alföldi, *Monarchische Repräsentation*, p. 217; F. Schulz, *Principles of Roman Law*, p. 112). On this theme see also C. Habicht in *Athenische Mitteilungen*, LXXII (1957), p. 248.

66. On the Christians' obstinacy, see Marcus Aurelius, *Meditations*, XI, 3, 2. He denies that the martyrs show in any way the courage of the wise, seeing in them only dissidents by nature.

67. *Martyrium Polycarpi*, 10. On the persecution by Decius and the requirement to sacrifice to the gods as pledge of loyalty, see A. Alföldi in *Klio*, XXXI (1938), p. 323.

68. P. Boyancé, *La Religion de Virgile*, p. 73. On the point that what the authorities demanded of the Christians was not faith (*religio*) but rites (*cerimoniae*), see L. Koep in *Jahrbuch für Antike und Christentum*, 1961, pp. 58–76.

69. Wissowa, *Religion und Kultus*, p. 425. It is, in general, not possible to say where human honours ended and worship began. The Emperor might have his statue in the temple of a god either as a cult statue or as a statue offered to the deity as a sort of ex-voto; he might decide that any insult to these 'sacred images' would count as sacrilege; he might be identified, by apposition, with a deity ('Nero Dionysus') or be taken to be the second edition, so to speak, of a deity ('Nero the new Dionysus'). The Emperor or Empress were even sometimes identified with an abstraction which was itself personified or deified ('Sabina Concordia'). What complicates things still further is that the real gods themselves lost their personalities by transformation into concepts or forces (Nock, *Essays*, p. 34). The Emperor might even be identified with a goddess: Demetrius with Demeter (Nilsson, *Geschichte*, vol. II, p. 151); Caligula dressed up as Venus (Suetonius, *Caligula*, 52); for other examples see Alföldi, *Studien zur Geschichte des 3. Jahrhunderts*, p. 46; cf. Veyne in *Latomus*, XXI (1962),

pp. 52 and 83. See below for my views on the cult of the Imperial virtues.

70. As at Pompeii; to my knowledge, the only example of a funerary *munus* in the Imperial period is to be found in Pliny, *Letters*, VI, 34; cf. Suetonius, *Tiberius*, 37.

71. See L. Robert, *Les Gladiateurs dans l'Orient grec*.

72. Veyne in *Latomus*, XXI (1962), pp. 65 and 82; XXVI (1967), pp. 746–8; also *CIL*, XIII, 1449: temple of a Celtic Pluto, dedicated to the divinity of the Emperors.

73. Rhetoric admirably analysed by E. Auerbach, *Mimesis*, on the basis of examples from Ammianus Marcellinus and St Jerome.

74. *Codex Theodosii*, XI, 21, 3; on *adnotatio* (which I have translated as 'privilege'), cf. I, 2, 1, and VIII, 5, 14 – a decree signed by the Emperor's own hand. It was not until 425 that this same Emperor finally banned the cult of the Imperial images (XV, 4).

75. The *locus classicus* is the soldiers' oath, given by Vegetius, 2, 5: 'The military mark, which is indelible, is first imprinted on the hands of the new levies, and as their names are inserted in the roll of the legions they take their usual oath, called the military oath. They swear by God, by Christ, and by the Holy Ghost; and by the Majesty of the Emperor who, after God, should be the chief object of the love and veneration of mankind. For when he has once received the title of August, his subjects are bound to pay him the most sincere devotion and homage, as the representative of God on earth.' I have not been able to read W. Ensslin, 'Gottkaiser und Kaiser von Gottes Gnaden', in *Sitzungsberichte der bayer. Akad.*, 1943, 6.

76. *CIL*, VIII, 450, 10516 (in the year 525), 23045a, to be complemented by Diehl, *Inscriptiones Latinae Christianae*, nos. 126 and 387–9. See also Mgr Duchesne, 'Le concile d'Elvire et les flamines chrétiens', in *Mélanges Louis Renier*, p. 159.

77. Inscription of Valentinus published by Le Blant, *Inscriptions chrétiennes de Gaule*, vol. I, p. xcv and no. 595a; A. Diehl, no. 391. This must be an Imperial priest of Novempopulania who gave a *venatio* in the amphitheatre (unless *cuneos* is merely a memory from *Georgics*, II, 509) and who, as representative of his city, passed on a municipal decree to the assembly of Novempopulania. Cf. also A. Bigelmair, *Die Beteilung der Christen am öffentlichen Leben in vorkonstantinischer Zeit*, pp. 114–19; on the duties of the Christian *euergetēs* and magistrate, see in Hefele canons 2, 3, 55 and 56 of the Synod of Elvira and canon 7 of the Council of Arles.

78. Ammianus Marcellinus, XXVII, 3, 6.

79. M. Weber, *Religionssoziologie*, vol. I, p. 268.

80. The facts from antiquity have been collated by M. Bloch, *The Royal*

Touch (London, 1973), pp. 28–43. I do not know how we ought to interpret the fact that the Hellenistic kings were invoked in the mysteries (Nilsson, *Opuscula Minora Selecta*, vol. III, p. 326) and that there were Imperial mysteries in Roman Asia (H. W. Pleket, 'An aspect of the Emperor's cult: imperial mysteries', in *Harvard Theological Review*, LVIII (1965), p. 331). Among the superstitions surrounding the sovereign's person, the following has not been commented on: the Roman plebs believed that Domitian had special 'good luck' which ensured that the Circus faction he preferred – the Greens – always won their races. This is the explanation of Martial's epigram, XI, 33. Under Byzantine protocol, however, the Emperor was held to have won in the persons of whichever faction came first in the chariot-races: A. Grabar, *L'Empereur dans l'art byzantin*, p. 65.

81. A. von Premerstein, *Vom Wesen und Werden des Prinzipats* (Johnson Reprint, 1964); M. Weber, *Economy and Society*, vol. I, p. 228; *Religionssoziologie*, vol. II, pp. 69 and 253; *Rechtssoziologie*, pp. 262 and 306 (Winckelmann). See also Wickert's article on 'Princeps' in Pauly-Wissowa, XXII, 2, cols. 2500–508.

82. On the Imperial procurators, see O. Hirschfeld, *Die kaiserlichen Verwaltungsbeamten bis auf Diokletian* (1905, reprinted by Weidmann, 1963); H. G. Pflaum, *Les Procurateurs équestres sous le Haut-Empire romain* (Maisonneuve, 1950), and *Les Carrières procuratoriennes équestres*, 3 vols., 1960–61. See also his article on 'Procurator' in Pauly-Wissowa, XXIII, 1, cols. 1240–79.

83. There are three mutually complementary studies: H. Chantraine, *Freigelassene und Sklaven in Dienst der römischen Kaiser, Studien zu ihren Nomenklatur* (Franz Steiner, 1967); G. Boulvert, *Esclaves et Affranchis impériaux sous le Haut-Empire: rôle politique et administratif* (Jovene, Naples, 1970); R. P. C. Weaver, *Familia Caesaris, a social study of the Emperor's freedmen and slaves* (Cambridge, 1972).

84. Boulvert, *Esclaves et Affranchis impériaux*, p. 447. Weaver, *Familia Caesaris*, p. 6. It was the same with the Emperor's 'friends'. Their role was more official than their title would suggest: 'they did not lose their position at the death of the Emperor whose friends they had been' (Friedländer, *Sittengeschichte*, vol. I, p. 84); 'it was they who provided the essential continuity in imperial policy' (J. Crook: *Consilium Principis: imperial councils and counsellors*, p. 29, cf. p. 115).

85. M. Crozier, *Le Phénomène bureaucratique* (Seuil, 1963), p. 243.

86. Pflaum, *Les Procurateurs équestres*, p. 8.

87. The Fiscus presents difficult and tangled problems which are now much debated. I will list them, while first emphasizing that the question of the public character of the Fiscus is one thing and that of its legal personality is another:

1. Before the word *fiscus* was used to mean *the* Fiscus it meant 'a coffer' − one belonging to a private person, or a provincial coffer of the *aerarium* in a senatorial province, or else a coffer of what would later be the Fiscus. This point is now cleared up.

2. From the time of Vespasian, perhaps, the different coffers (*fisci*) for the taxes levied by the Emperor were actually brought together under a central palace service, the Fiscus.

3. Or, at least, it was towards the middle of the first century that the singular '*Fiscus*' gradually came to be used to mean the totality of these coffers, that is, *the* Fiscus; this usage seems to me to be proved from Seneca, *De Beneficiis*, IV, 39, 3.

4. It is one question to know whether the Fiscus, or *a* fiscus, was a legal person and whether, when a procurator obliged an unwilling taxpayer to pay up, he was acting in his own name or in the name of the Fiscus as a person: this is a mere question of legal technique.

5. It is quite another question to know whether the Fiscus was an entity in the service of the state or whether it was literally the property of the Emperor, who, as Mommsen thought, could bequeath to a private person the contents of the coffers of the Fiscus.

6. It is another question again to know whether there was fiscal law that differed from private law and public law.

7. Finally, the literary sources say that the contents of the coffers of the Fiscus belong to the Emperor − they are his; but this is a mere manner of speaking and, in my view, we cannot draw any conclusion from the passage in Seneca, *De Beneficiis*, VII, 6, 3. For a different interpretation of the two passages in Seneca, see the article by my colleague G. Boulvert, 'Le fiscus chez Sénèque', in *Labeo*, XVIII (1972), p. 201.

On the Fiscus the essential information is to be found in Hirschfeld, *Verwaltungsbeamten*, pp. 1–29; C. H. V. Sutherland, 'Aerarium and fiscus during the early Empire', in *American Journal of Philology*, LXVI (1945), p. 151; A. H. M. Jones, 'The Aerarium and the Fiscus', in *Journal of Roman Studies*, XL (1950), p. 22. The discussion, revived by F. Millar (*Journal of Roman Studies*, LIII (1963), p. 29), gave rise to a study by P. A. Brunt which seems conclusive, 'The Fiscus and its development', in the same journal, LVI (1966), p. 75. See the article by Rostovtzeff on 'Fiscus' in Ruggiero's *Dizionario epigrafico*, vol. III, p. 96, and the articles on 'Fiscus' in Pauly-Wissowa, VI, col. 385 (Rostovtzeff) and Supplementband X, col. 222 (Uerödgi). The word *fiscus* has recently appeared in an inscription in Asia: Hermann and Polatkan, 'Das Testament des Epikrates', in *Akad. der Wiss. in Wien, phil.-hist. Klasse, Sitzungsberichte*, CCLXV, 1, 1969. On the 'privileges of the Fiscus' there is a detailed exposition by Mitteis, *Römisches Privatrecht*, vol. I, pp. 366–75, and a striking summary by Sohm, Mitteis and Wenger, *Institutionen, Geschichte und System des römischen Privatrechts* (1926 edition), p. 199, note 5. For example, the Fiscus could inherit (whereas, in Rome, non-physical persons could receive legacies only).

88. From Claudius's time the expression used was 'the Patrimony of the Caesars', in the plural, which thus implied, if not Claudius's predecessors, at least all the members (*Caesares*) of the ruling family: Dessau, no. 1447; Pflaum, *Carrières procuratoriennes équestres*, vol. I, p. 88; *CIL*, XI, 3885 and 5028. See A. Kärnzlein's article on 'Patrimonium' in Pauly-Wissowa, Supplementband X.

89. On the date, see now Pflaum, *Carrières procuratoriennes*, vol. II, pp. 598 and 811, and, especially vol. III, p. 1005; cf. H. Nesselhauf, 'Patrimonium und res privata', in *Historia Augusta, Colloquium* (Bonn, 1963), p. 73.

90. R. Orestano, *Problema delle persone giuridiche in diritto romano* (Giappichelli, Turin, 1968), p. 252: 'The contrast amounts to a mere distinction in accounts, a distribution between different headings in the balance-sheet.'

91. F. Preisigke, *Girowesen im griechischen Aegypten* (Olms, reprinted 1971), p. 188.

92. *Verwaltungsbeamten*, p. 18: followed, without any new arguments, by A. Masi, *Ricerche sulla res privata del princeps* (Giuffrè, Milan, 1971).

93. L. Mitteis, *Römisches Privatrecht bis auf die Zeit Diokletians* (1908), p. 361; followed by E. Stein, *Histoire du Bas-Empire*, J.-R. Palanque (ed.), vol. I, 1, p. 45 and note 131; and by M. Kaser in his admirable *Römisches Privatrecht*, vol. II (Beck, 1959), p. 103, note 2. This was already the thesis maintained by Karlowa, but with very unsound arguments, which Hirschfeld had rebutted.

94. *Staatsrecht*, vol. II, p. 998, 1003, 1007 and 1135.

95. Ibid., vol. II, p. 999, note 1: 'Der formell dem Kaiser, reell dem Staate gehörige Fiskus.'

96. This was at first a non-systematic law. It proceeded by topic, and the systematic aspect was, most of the time, only 'vaguely sensed' (P. Koschaker, *L'Europa e il diritto romano* (Sansoni, 1962), pp. 160, note 2, 289, 328). Also, its use of concepts was traditional rather than rigorous (P. Wieacker, *Vom römischen Recht* (Leipzig, 1944), p. 28). This 'topical' law contrasts with the civil code, which was 'axiomatic' law (T. Viehweg, *Topik und Jurisprudenz*, 1953); on the analogy, cf. U. Wesel, *Rhetorische Statuslehre der römischen Juristen* (Heymanns, 1967), p. 89. The fundamental study is probably that by M. Kaser, 'Zur Methode der römischen Rechtsfindung', in *Nachrichten der Akademie in Göttingen* (1962), fasc. 2.

97. For example, Pliny, *Panegyricus*, 27, 3 and 41–2; cf. Mommsen, *Staatsrecht*, vol. II, p. 998, note 2. To be sure, in the *Digest* the Emperors

constantly refer to *Fiscus meus* or *Fiscus noster*; but this means 'the Fiscus which is under my authority', not 'the Fiscus which belongs to me'. They likewise say 'my procurator' (*Codex Justiniani*, I, 54, 2 and 10, 8, 1), 'our procurator' (3, 3, 1; 3, 13, 1; 3, 26, 1 and 2), 'my friend and count' (Dessau, no. 206), 'my friend and procurator' (*CIL*, X, 8038), 'our legate and friend' (Dessau, no. 423), 'our soldiers' (Brigetio tablet). But they would not, I think, have said 'my proconsul', because a proconsul depended on the Senate, not on the Emperor.

98. *Staatsrecht*, vol. II, p. 1135, cf. p. 1007.

99. That of Dio Cassius, LXXIV, 7, 3. The other testimonies are in the *Historia Augusta*, 'Antoninus', 7, 9 and 12, 8 (cf. 4, 7 and perhaps 4, 8), and 'Didius Julianus', 8, 9. I shall suggest below (see text at note reference 119) a different interpretation of these passages.

100. By the same reasoning Mommsen ought to have concluded that every *triumphator* who kept his *manubiae* and every magistrate who became the owner of the *lucar* of his games lost thereby the patrimony they possessed and had to sink it entirely in their games or their triumphal monument, unless they had taken the precaution of transferring it to their children on the eve of their triumph or of their games! Mommsen does, in fact, identify the case of the Fiscus with that of *lucar* and booty – see *Staatsrecht*, vol. III, p. 1129, and vol. I, p. 241; vol. II, p. 1000, note 2.

101. Herodian, II, 4, 7.

102. *Digest*, XLIII, 8, 2, 4. Very little attention is given to this prohibition *ne quid in loco publico vel itinere fiat* in our manuals of Roman civil law, because, to our modern eyes, this is not civil law. But it was for the Romans, for whom civil law meant everything that concerned the interests of private persons (*Digest*, I, 1, 1, 2). This detail shows how far from historical, and how much dominated by modern ideas, the study of Roman law still is.

103. *Digest*, XLIII, 8, 2, 2.

104. In the *tabula alimentaria* of the Ligures Baebiani, the landowners whose estates adjoin a public highway are said to have the people as their neighbour (*adfinis populus*) whereas those whose land borders an Imperial domain have as their neighbour the Emperor (*adfinis Caesar noster*).

105. P. A. Brunt, 'Procuratorial jurisdiction', in *Latomus*, XXV (1966), p. 461.

106. F. Schulz, *Principles of Roman Law*, p. 177.

107. Mitteis, *Privatrecht*, p. 364; Mommsen, *Staatsrecht*, vol. II, pp. 203, 226, 964, 1007, 1021–5. For the situation before and during Claudius's reign, see Tacitus, *Annals*, IV, 6, and IV, 15; XII, 60; Suetonius, *Claudius*, 12; Dio Cassius, LVII, 23, 5.

108. On this threefold division, see *Codex Justiniani*, VII, 49, 1: 'Causa *sive* privata *sive* publica *sive* fiscalis'; Mommsen deals strangely with this passage and manages to find in it a twofold division: *publica* on the one hand and *privata* and *fiscalis* on the other (*Staatsrecht*, vol. II, p. 999, note 1) – yet the texts sometimes contrast *privatus* with *fiscalis* (e.g. *Codex Justiniani*, VIII, 40, 11 and VII, 75, 3).

109. Even F. Schulz believes this: *Principles*, p. 177, note 6. It is curious that he does not seem to be struck by the historical impossibility of the hypothesis. A sly, precarious monarch, a dictator looking like a magistrate, Augustus was in the weakest possible position to treat the money from taxes as his own property.

110. Pliny, *Panegyricus*, 50: 'multa ex patrimonio', 50, 2.

111. Ibid., 50, 6: 'nunquam nisi Caesaris suburbanum'.

112. Hirschfeld, *Verwaltungsbeamten*, p. 19, note 4 and p. 18, note 2.

113. Ibid., p. 19.

114. Mommsen, *Staatsrecht*, vol. II, p. 770.

115. Ibid., vol. II, p. 1135.

116. Dio Cassius, LXXVIII, 11, 3.

117. *Staatsrecht*, vol. II, pp. 1007 and 1135. The Emperor's heir was usually his successor. It should be recalled that, in Roman private law, every will is essentially the nomination of one or more heirs (the will consists less in a transmission of property than in the designation of the moral continuator of the testator: as a consequence of this, the moral continuator or continuators receive the goods of the deceased, or part of them). One could nominate anyone at all as one's heir: there was nothing simpler than to disinherit one's children or eldest son. The father of a family does not merely pass on his belongings, he thereby decides the future of his house. Together with the dowry system, nothing did more to shape Roman society, with its paternalism and its apparent respect for women. (Roman marriage was a *de facto* condition, like concubinage or the material possession of an object, but this fact had legal consequences. What distinguished concubinage from marriage was the dowry: a man could not dismiss his wife without returning her dowry.)

118. H. Nesselhauf in *Historia Augusta Colloquium, Bonn, 1963* (Habelt, 1964), p. 79: 'Without this sound financial foundation the principate would have stood much more insecurely on its basis, which was the regulation of the succession. His inheriting of this gigantic patrimony predisposed the heir to succeed to the throne.' Suetonius, *Caligula*, 14, is very clear on this point: 'On [Caligula's] arrival in the City the Senate (and a mob of commoners who had forced their way into the House) immediately and unanimously conferred absolute power upon him. They set aside Tiberius's will [*voluntas*] – which made his other

grandson, then still a child, joint-heir with Caligula . . .'

119. See note 99.

120. Dio Cassius, LXXIV, 7, 3.

121. *Historia Augusta*, 'Didius Julianus', 8, 9.

122. Into which coffer fell legacies left to the Emperor? Our only source is the *Digest*, XXXI, 56 and 57 (cf. Dio Cassius, LXIX, 15, 1). Under Claudius there was a procurator of the Patrimonium and the inheritances (Dessau, no. 1447) and under Severus a procurator of the inheritances of the private Patrimonium (H. G. Pflaum, *Carrières procuratoriennes*, vol. II, p. 599, no. 225), but as our teacher Pflaum points out, his *cursus* needs reinterpreting (vol. III, p. 1006) since we have learnt that the *Ratio Privata* was already in existence under Antoninus.

123. *Digest*, XXX, 39, 7–10, and XXX, 40. Karlowa explained this passage badly, but Hirschfeld, in rebutting him, fell into the opposite error (*Verwaltungsbeamten*, pp. 21–5). Yet Karlowa was right: the Patrimonium was indeed the Emperor's private wealth. There is another commentary on this passage in Ulpian, in F. De Martino, *Storia della costituzione romana*, vol. IV, 1965 edn (Jovene, Naples), p. 819. This is how I am tempted to understand the passage in question. In Roman law the heir who is the moral continuator of the deceased and executes his legacies can be charged by the deceased to buy a certain piece of property which he wishes to leave to one of his legatees. It may happen that this property is not for sale, so that this article of the will cannot be executed literally. The jurists then ask themselves in what cases the heir must give to the legatee, instead of the property, its value (*aestimatio*) in money. On this question Ulpian makes an observation. If a testator bequeaths goods which are very unlikely to be purchasable, it must be concluded that he was not in his right mind. The heir will not have to pay the equivalent in money, not because the principle that one may bequeath goods one does not own is invalid, but quite simply because the testator was obviously not *compos mentis*. And Ulpian gives examples. Theoretically, we might say, Louis XIV could have sold Versailles, but it was not likely that he would have done this or that one of his subjects would have instructed his heir to buy it for a third party. Ulpian says that one could not buy the Imperial villa at Albano (which was Domitian's Versailles), because it was the Emperors' residence (*usibus Caesaris deservit*: we see here an expression which must have been a technical term, for we meet it again in Dessau, nos. 9024 and 9025). Going further, Ulpian conceives of the case of a private estate which is absolutely private, but whose private owner happens to be the Emperor, who includes it in his Patrimonium (he is obviously not talking about the estates of the Fiscus, which are the public

domain of the Roman state). Ulpian then mentions a common-sense truth: an heir would find it hard to go and see the Emperor (or, rather, a procurator of the Patrimonium) to offer to buy his land. We know, of course, that Emperors did sometimes auction off their private wealth, and we saw Trajan do this (I say that Trajan must have sold his patrimony by auction because that was the usual way of selling things: see Mommsen, *Juristische Schriften*, vol. III, p. 225). But that was a great 'historic' decision which marked an epoch; in normal times a procurator of the Patrimonium sold nothing without an express order from the Emperor, and there could be no question of an heir going to ask the Emperor, as a favour, to sell him a piece of land so that he might execute a legacy. These are common-sense considerations and we should not see in them juridical theory and concepts. Nevertheless, what Ulpian writes does prove that the Patrimonium was the Emperors' private wealth, for otherwise he would not have taken as his example this particular case of a private property which no testator with common sense would have thought to be easily purchasable. I will translate the example into a modern French setting: 'If a testator charges me to buy the Place de la Concorde' (Ulpian says the Forum and the Campus Martius), 'the Élysée or La Boisserie at Colombey-les-Deux-Églises ...' Everyone will agree that La Boisserie is here regarded as the private property of a head of state; if not, why take it as an example?

124. In contrast to the most widely held view, this is the conviction of E. Beaudouin, *Les Grands Domaines dans l'Empire romain* (1899), p. 31; of L. Mitteis, *Privatrecht*, p. 361; of M. Kaser, *Privatrecht*, vol. II, 1959 edn, p. 103, note 2; and of Tenney Frank, *An Economic Survey*, vol. V, p. 78.

125. *Digest*, XLIX, 14, 6, 4: 'Everything that applies to the privileged status of the Fiscus applies also to the Private Fortune of Caesar and of the Augusta' – which seems to point to a distinction between the Emperor's fortune and that of the Empress.

126. *Codex Justiniani*, II, 7, 1 (this passage would imply that the Private Fortune was a subdivision of the Fiscus rather than a fourth coffer: in fact, L. Mitteis and E. Stein, *Histoire du Bas-Empire*, vol. I, p. 115, suppose that confiscated and escheated properties were taken over by the Fiscus, which transferred the management of them to the Private Fortune). Two other arguments from the later Empire tend to confirm that the *Ratio Privata* was public. First, we know that the lands of the *Ratio Privata* (or *Res Privata* as was also said) were subject to emphyteusis, whereas the *fundi patrimoniales* were 'sold' in perpetuity, *salvo canone*; this regime was the one which also applied to the estates of

private persons. See Mitteis, *Privatrecht*, p. 361. Secondly, the law in the *Codex Theodosii*, XI, 1, 6, 2, shows that as late as 323 the *fundi patrimoniales* of the Emperor paid tax, whereas, at the beginning, those of the *Res Privata* did not. See Beaudouin, *Les Grands Domaines*, pp. 151–5.

127. *Digest*, XLIX, 14, 3, 10 (apparently a rescript of Marcus Aurelius and Lucius Verus). The summary in Justinian's *Institutes*, II, 1, 39 is so laconic that it is hard to make out whether Hadrian had already dealt with the case of treasure trove on Caesar's possessions: it would be important to know this in order to determine the date of origin of the *Ratio Privata* (all we do know is that it was already in being under Antoninus). I do not believe that Hadrian had dealt with this case: in the *Institutes* the word *convenienter* ('conformably' or 'consistently') seems to indicate that what is meant is a logical consequence of Marcus's rescript rather than a measure taken by Hadrian.

128. Mommsen, *Staatsrecht*, vol. II, pp. 953–7; cf. vol. III, pp. 1158 and 1173.

129. It was an exceptional honour for a victorious military unit to be allowed to choose its officers (Tacitus, *Histories*, III, 49) or to award decorations themselves (Dessau, no. 2313). From the fact that the Emperor made appointments at all levels Caligula had drawn the conclusion that the will of any officer (down to the rank of *primus pilus* inclusive) in which the deceased did not thank the Emperor for his promotion by bequeathing him a legacy should be annulled as 'an ungrateful will' (Suetonius, *Caligula*, 38). The custom was for the Emperor to be thanked with a legacy for any career, civil or military, and also, if the testator was a senator, to bequeath a legacy to him (for the Emperor was himself a senator, and the senators redistributed, through legacies, part of their patrimony among their best-liked colleagues). Caligula was right in principle: in the Romans' eyes the only ridiculous feature of his action was that he applied the principle right down to the rank of *primus pilus*. See Hirschfeld, *Kleine Schriften*, p. 516; *Verwaltungsbeamten*, p. 110; Marquardt, *Staatsverwaltung*, vol. II, p. 294; J. Gaudemet, 'Testamenta ingrata et pietas Augusti, contribution à l'étude du sentiment impérial', in *Studi in onore di Arangio-Ruiz*, vol. III, pp. 115–37. I have not read R. S. Rogers in *Transactions of the American Philological Association*, 1947, p. 140. Cinna (the conspirator) left all his property to Augustus (Seneca, *De Clementia*, 16). Legacies to the Emperor provide the key to Petronius, *Satyricon*, 76, 2: 'My master made me co-heir with the Emperor.' For officers, see a revealing anecdote of Valerius Maximus, VII, 8, 6 (VII, 9, 2), and note that the person mentioned, T. Marius Urbinas, really existed and his epitaph has been found (Groag in *Klio*, XIV, p. 51, on *CIL*, XI, no. 6058;

Premerstein, *Vom Wesen und Werden des Prinzipats*, p. 105).

130. Mommsen, *Staatsrecht*, vol. II, pp. 847–54.

131. On the military oath and the cult of the Imperial images in the army, see Premerstein, pp. 73–99. Note that, until the Severi, there was nevertheless no real cult of the living Emperor or even of his *genius* in the armies.

132. For example, Germanicus (Suetonius, *Tiberius*, 25), Corbulo or Lusius Quietus.

133. In general, on the *donativum*, the fundamental study is still Fiebiger's in Pauly-Wissowa, vol. V, cols. 1543–4, which has the merit of bringing together all the references, at least for the early Empire. The institution has been little studied. See, however, E. Sander, 'Das Recht der römischen Soldaten', in *Rheinisches Museum*, CI (1958), p. 187, and H. Kloft, *Liberalitas Principis* (Böhlau, 1970), pp. 104–10. The *donativum* is strangely absent from the reverse sides of coins. (There are no grounds for seeing, as do Mattingly and Sydenham, an allusion to the *donativum* in the legends MONETA AVG.)

134. According to Tacitus, *Histories*, I, 5, 25, 37 and 41.

135. Had the legionaries a right to the *donativum*, like the praetorians? The sources testify to this as regards Augustus's legacies to the army and also those of Tiberius, distributed by Caligula. Regarding the first *donativum* properly so called, distributed by Claudius at his accession, Josephus says that the legions had their share (*Jewish Antiquities*, XIX, 247). The *donativum* mentioned by Tacitus, *Histories*, IV, 36 and 58, must on the other hand be a military reward, and should not be identified with what is mentioned by Dio Cassius, LXV, 22. Did the *alae* and the auxiliary cohorts have a right to the *donativum*? The sources are silent on this, for Tacitus, *Histories*, IV, 19, speaks rather of a military reward. Domaszewski thinks that the auxiliaries did not have a right to the *donativum* (*Neue Heidelberger Jahrbücher*, IX (1899), p. 218), and Sander that they did, from the time of the Severi. For the third century, see J.-P. Callu, *Politique monétaire des empereurs*, p. 311.

136. Dio Cassius, LXXIII, 11. To the *donativa* of 193 are ascribed partial responsibility for the devaluation of the *denarius*: J. Guey, in *Bulletin de la Société nationale des antiquaires*, 1952–3, p. 89; T. Pekary, 'Studien zur röm. Wahrungspolitik', in *Historia*, VIII (1959), p. 456.

137. Dio Cassius, LXXIV, 1, 5 and 8.

138. Tacitus, *Histories*, I, 5 and 18.

139. Ammianus Marcellinus, XX, 4; C. Jullian, *Histoire de la Gaule*, vol. VII, p. 222.

140. Ammianus, XVII, 9, 6 and XXII, 3, 7 (see, however, on a *donativum* which Julian distributed in Gaul, Sulpicius Severus, *Life of St Martin*,

4, Fontaine (ed.), vol. II, p. 597. Note that *donativum* and booty are two different things: see below, note 174). Julian complains about this in his *Letters*, 17 (Bidez).

141. At first the soldiers had the right to '*annona*' in corn and to clothing (or its value in money, the *canon vestium*). Later, they received each year wages paid in money, called *stipendium* (this is the *annuum stipendium* of which Julian speaks: *Letters*, 17, 8 (Bidez); it was paid in regular fashion, *more solita*, says Ammianus, XVII, 9, 6). Finally they had the right to a *donativum* paid every five years, for the Imperial *vicennalia* and *decennalia* (E. Seeck, *Untergang der antiken Welt*, vol. II, Anhang, p. 545, note 27, and, with new documents, A. H. M. Jones, *The Later Roman Empire*, vol. II, p. 623, and vol. III, p. 187, note 31). But both *stipendium* and *donativum* were felt to be gifts rather than payments due, and the two words, after a long period when they were used together (*Codex Justiniani*, XII, 35, 1; *Historia Augusta*, 'Tacitus', 9, 1; Diocletian, Maximum Price Edict, preamble; Ammianus Marcellinus, XVII, 9, 6; Paul in *Digest*, XLIX, 16, 10, 1, opposite XLIX, 16, 15), are treated by Ammianus Marcellinus as more or less synonymous (see the long chapter 28, 6). *Stipendium* and *donativum* were both seen as that part of the soldier's pay which he received in money, in contrast to what was paid to him in kind, i.e. food and clothing: for those two words also went together; the soldier 'veste et annona publica pascebatur' (Vegetius, 2, 19), except when there was *adaeratio* for the clothing (on the *canon vestium*, see *Codex Theodosii*, VII, 6, 5 = *Codex Justiniani*, XII, 39, 4). In the 'ideological' texts the soldier is fed and clothed (Julian, *Panegyric of Constantius*, 32, and *Letters*, 109 (Bidez); the pupils of the Imperial school of sacred music also received food and clothing as their only wages). Whatever took the form of a payment in gold or silver seemed, by contrast, to be a gift. 'Money is barely mentioned in the *Codex Theodosii* when pay is being discussed,' writes Godefroy in his paratitle to book VII of the *Codex*. And yet, when we read Vegetius, 2, 20, who gives us the atmosphere of the third century, we sense that the *donativum* had become a sort of regular gratification. However, this evolution had been 'overtaken' by the other evolution which caused any payment in gold or silver to be regarded as a gift (R. MacMullen, 'The emperor's largesses', in *Latomus*, XXI (1962), p. 159). The *stipendium* was looked on more as a moral debt of the ruler towards the army than as a payment needed if the soldier was to live. Was he not, indeed, both fed and clothed? And the soldier was grateful when he received it, the *stipendium* seeming like a reward, especially when it was distributed, for example, at an Emperor's accession (Ammianus, XXII, 9, 2). This was why *stipendium* and *donativum* became synonymous. Study of these words as they are used

in the *Historia Augusta* leads to the expected conclusion, which can be summed up thus: this work employs the words in their fourth-century sense and cannot be used for the second and third centuries. For *stipendium* in the sense of *donativum*, see *Historia Augusta*, 'Caracalla', 2, 8; 'Maximini duo', 18, 4; 'Max. and Balb.', 12, 8; 'Albinus', 2. On the evolution of soldiers' pay in the third century, see J.-P. Callu, *La Politique monétaire des empereurs romains de 238 à 311* (De Boccard, 1969), pp. 295–300. On the *adaeratio*, see the remarkable review of Santo Mazzarino by Marrou in *Gnomon*, XXV (1953), p. 187; Callu, pp. 290–94; a new document: W. L. Westermann and A. A. Schiller, *Apokrimata: Decisions of Septimius Severus on legal matters* (1954), discussed by Pekary in *Historia*, 1959, p. 468. Study of the *adaeratio* has recently been renewed, however, by A. Cérati, *Caractère annonaire et Assiette de l'impôt foncier* (1975), pp. 153–80, which is now essential reading. On the phenomenon in the Hellenistic armies, cf. Launey's *Recherches sur les armées hellénistiques*, vol. II, p. 779.

142. E. Stein, *Histoire du Bas-Empire*, vol. I, p. 429, note 209.

143. Julian, *To the Council and People of Athens*, 11. Ammianus Marcellinus himself accuses the usurper Procopius, whom he disliked and whose attempt miscarried, of buying his soldiers, who were mere mercenaries (*vendibiles milites*, XXVI, 6, 14). We perceive, however, as we read him, that the supporters of this usurper – the only one, perhaps, who appeared in the East in that century – respected in him the blood of Constantine that ran in his veins. On the other hand Ammianus has not one word of reproach when Valentinian promises money to the soldiers for his election after a stormy meeting (XXVI, 2, 1): Ammianus was a supporter of legality.

144. References in the article on 'Donativum' by Fiebiger in Pauly-Wissowa, vol. V, col. 1543.

145. There is a characteristic passage in Caesar, *Civil War*, I, 39, 3: 'largitione militum voluntates redemit.' I stress the point that the word *donativum* is not used before the Empire.

146. *Alexandrian War*, 48 and 52. All these *largesses* must be distinguished from those referred to in the previous chapter. Custom required that generals should leave a share of the booty to the soldiers (Livy, XXX, 45, 3; hence Suetonius, *Caesar*, 38: 'praedae nomine', and *Res Gestae*, 3, 18: 'ex manubiis'). In the Hellenistic world the soldiers were promised a bonus in the event of victory.

147. *Ad Atticum*, XVI, 6, 2.

148. Appian, *Civil Wars*, III, 42. This passage is extremely valuable by virtue of its subtlety and precision: Appian must here be following his source very closely.

149. E.g. Tacitus, *Annals*, XII, 41, and XIV, 11; Suetonius, *Nero*, 7; Pliny,

Panegyricus, 25, 2; Herodian, VII, 6, 4, and III, 8, 4; Dio Cassius, LXXIII, 1, 5, and VIII, 76, 1.

150. Julian, *Panegyric of Constantius*, 28.

151. On the provinces with armies, see Mommsen, *Staatsrecht*, vol. II, p. 840: cf. pp. 847 and 869.

152. Ibid., vol. II, p. 1032.

153. Tacitus, *Annals*, I, 8; Dio Cassius, LVI, 32, cf. LVII, 5 and 6; Suetonius, *Augustus*, 101.

154. Dio Cassius, LV, 6.

155. Id., LIX, 2 and 3; Suetonius, *Tiberius*, 76.

156. Suetonius, *Claudius*, 10: Claudius was 'the first of the Caesars to purchase the loyalty of his troops'. Claudius renewed his *donativum* one year later: Dio Cassius, LX, 12.

157. Josephus, *Jewish Antiquities*, XIX, 247.

158. Tacitus, *Annals*, XII, 69; cf. Dio Cassius, LXI, 3.

159. References in Fiebiger's article in Pauly-Wissowa.

160. Tacitus, *Annals*, XII, 41; Suetonius, *Nero*, 7.

161. *Historia Augusta*, 'Hadrian', 23, 12 and 14; Dio Cassius, LXXVIII, 19 and 34. When Galba adopted Piso he caused a scandal by not promising a *donativum* (Tacitus, *Histories*, I, 18; Suetonius, *Galba*, 17).

162. Tiberius after the fall of Sejanus (Suetonius, *Tiberius*, 48) or Nero after Piso's conspiracy (Tacitus, *Annals*, XV, 72; Dio Cassius, LXII, 27).

163. We have seen that it was also a charismatic regime, though in a sense different from Weber's. Belief in the Emperor's divinity and love of the Emperor were not the basis of legitimacy and of the fact that people obeyed without coercion or needing to be convinced step by step. They were a feeling induced by the recognized (legitimized) existence of the ruling power, its traditional character (see next note). A father is adored because he is a father; he is not a father because he is adored. There is nothing here in common with the individual genius-leader or with the dictator whom people in exceptional circumstances want to believe is a genius.

164. See the shrewd criticism of Weber's confused notion of traditional action given by Alfred Schulz, *Phenomenology of the Social World* (Heinemann, 1972), p. 91 (note) and pp. 197–8. Reacting against the brisk and deliberately somewhat cursory nominalism of Weber, Schulz shows that inertia and habit cannot serve as a final explanation and that consequently Weber's famous theory of the three bases of power in untenable.

165. On the Imperial regime, see the excellent passage in R. Orestano, *Problema delle persone giuridiche*, pp. 217–32, on the non-institutional character of the Imperial authority: 'The Emperor was neither a magistrate nor a *privatus*,' just as the Fiscus, which depended on him, was

neither public nor private. He had indeed been awarded the tribunician power and the proconsular *imperium*, but this was only a language of analogy, for 'these powers were henceforth distinct from the actual exercise of the corresponding magistracies'. There was good reason for this, since they were awarded for life and were subject to no geographical limits. The principate has nothing in common with the old Republican magistracies and the 'constitution'. All the same, it is observable that neither is the principate a mere brute fact, a power relation, or, in noble terms, an expression of the personal *auctoritas* of an individual, since, when this individual dies, a new Emperor is created with the same power as before and beneath the same constitutional trappings. Thus, Weber would say, a regime with a traditional foundation has been established. Let us admit that nothing was more frequent in Rome than these informal and legitimate 'brute facts': examples are the relations between the Emperor and the Senate, those between Greece and Rome between about 190 and 60, and those between a governor and the Roman or Greek cities of his province. Was this judicious empiricism which everywhere identified hidden reasons? I cannot believe so. An unwritten constitution and respect for traditional rules? Definitely not. Neither the Emperor, nor Rome in its dealings with the Greeks, nor the governors had any time for 'fair play'. They took all the power they could. The truth of the matter is that Rome completely lacked the bureaucratic and organizing spirit (it is wrong to confuse 'hegemony' with 'organization' or 'superstitious regard for norms and precedents' with 'juridical spirit'), nor did she have the idea of 'rules of the game' to be respected in relations between equals. She had the sense of hegemony and, under the name of *fides*, further insisted that loyalty was her moral due. On the notion of *auctoritas*, which has received little useful study, and which formed part of the trappings with which Rome clothed power relations and elevated them into loyal and loftily moral submission, see Alföldi, *Monarchistische Repräsentation*, pp. 192–5, and the definitive passage in J. Béranger, *Recherches sur l'aspect idéologique du principat* (Reinhardt, Basel, 1953), pp. 114–31. An alternative conceptualization, from a different standpoint, is seen in K. Loewenstein, *Beiträge zur Staatssoziologie* (Mohr, 1961), pp. 3–33: 'The constitutional monocracy of Augustus, for a morphology of types of regime'. For the so-called charismatic (in the vaguest sense of the word) aspects of the Imperial authority, see F. Schulz, *Principles of Roman Law*, pp. 180–83.

166. Mommsen, *Staatsrecht*, vol. II, p. 843, note 3.

167. Tacitus, *Histories*, III, 79–80.

168. There is already mention of a *donativum* for the *quinquennalia* in Dio Cassius, LXXVI, 1. For the quinquennial *donativum*, see A. H. M.

Jones, *The Late Roman Empire*, vol. III, p. 187, note 31; E. Stein, *Histoire du Bas-Empire*, J.-R. Palanque (ed.), vol. I, p. 116; Mattingly and Sydenham, *The Roman Imperial Coinage*, vol. VII, by Bruun, p. 57. On the importance of money gifts in addition to pay, see Alföldi, *Studien zur ... Weltkrise des 3. Jahrhunderts*, p. 415. On the relations between the land tax and the military *annona*, the question has been treated afresh by A. Cérati, *Caractère annonaire et Assiette de l'impôt foncier*, pp. 103–51.

169. Ammianus Marcellinus, XV, 6, 3.
170. Id., XXII, 9, 2.
171. Id., XXIX, 5, 37; XXXI, 11, 1.
172. Jullian, *Histoire de la Gaule*, vol. VIII, p. 120: 'The soldier's real cult is the cult of money; between the soldiers and their leaders a continual bargaining goes on.' In Molière's plays the servants, fed and clothed by their master, stay loyal to him even when they are not being paid, but, nevertheless, they loudly demand their wages – not because they are greedy but because their master does not pay them regularly.
173. Ammianus Marcellinus, XXIV, 3, 3. 'The soldiers, who in the past have often been fooled, demand their *stipendium* in cash down,' writes the author of *Panegyrici Latini*, XI, 1, 4. Beneath the vague phrasing there is also a very precise reference in Claudian, *Eulogy of Stilicho*, 2, 148: 'Thou neglectest not thy soldiers in peace, and dost not only enrich them when war is toward. Thou knowest that belated gifts, offered in fear to those hitherto scorned, earn no gratitude.'
174. Ammianus, XXIV, 3, 3. On the other hand, in XVII, 13, 31, Constantius tells his soldiers that the booty will be their sufficient reward. Thus the *donativum* paid in gold and silver is contrasted with the booty in kind.
175. By the time of the Severi, troops who made a *pronunciamento* were already demanding a distribution of money as their reward: Dio Cassius, XLVI, 46 (cf. Herodian, III, 6, 8) and LXXIX, 1. Julian persuaded his soldiers by means of a gift to submit to his newly acquired authority: Ammianus, XXII, 9, 2.
176. Ammianus, XIV, 10, or XXIV, 7.
177. After the influential men of the court or of the army had met and chosen an Emperor, there remained the delicate task of getting him acclaimed by the army (Ammianus, XXVI, 1). Sometimes the army gave its approval 'with the consent of all (for no one ventured to oppose)' (XXVI, 4, 3); but on other occasions cries were heard. If the orator was able to assume a tone of authority, there might be no further incident (XXVI, 2, 11). It was the same when the Emperor's heir was proclaimed (XXVII, 6).
178. Dio of Prusa, *Orationes.*, I, 22: the Good King calls his soldiers his

comrades in arms, those who live with him his friends, and the mass of his subjects his children. Julian, *Panegyric of Constantius*, 6: the mass of subjects look on the monarch as their sovereign, but the soldiers expect something more – presents and favours.

179. The classic example is the will of Ptolemy VIII Euergetes II, *Supplementum Epigraphicum Graecum*, vol. IX, no. 7. See U. Wilcken, *Akademische Schriften*, vol. II, p. 23; E. Will, *Histoire politique du monde hellénistique*, vol. II, p. 305. For the will of Attalus of Pergamum, see ibid., p. 351. Despite recent comments, the will of Ptolemy VIII is certainly a will, and not political advice. Against the widespread view that Egypt was the Emperors' private domain, see A. Stein, *Aegypten unter römischer Herrschaft*, p. 98, and M. Gelzer, *Kleine Schriften*, vol. II, pp. 368–70.

180. Justin, XXXVII, 4, 5 (cf. Will, *Histoire politique du monde hellénistique*, vol. II, p. 392); XXXVIII, 7, 10: Mithridates inherited foreign kingdoms which were left to him on account of his magnificence. Polybius, XXV, 2, 7; Eumenes of Pergamum, out of pure bounty, gave the city of Tios to Prusias.

181. *Historia Augusta*, 'Antoninus', 8; Suetonius, *Domitian*, 12: 'Unfortunately, the new building programme, added to his expensive entertainments and the rise in army pay, were more than Domitian could afford ...' This passage is discussed by R. Syme, 'The imperial finances under Domitian, Nerva and Trajan', in *Journal of Roman Studies*, XX (1930), p. 55, and C. H. V. Sutherland, 'The state of the imperial treasury', ibid.,, XXV (1935), p. 150.

182. On *beneficium* as the equivalent of *euergesiai*, see e.g. a bilingual inscription at Delos, Degrassi, *Inscriptiones Liberae Rei Publicae*, no. 363; or the *Grammatici Latini*, Keil (ed.), vol. IV, p. 567, top.

183. The pagan Zosimus (II, 38) condemns the *largesses* of Constantine (A. Chastagnol, in *Historia Augusta, Colloquium 1964–5* (Habelt, 1966), p. 34) but the *Life of Constantine* (I, 43, 1) by the Christian Eusebius thoroughly approves of them.

184. E.g. Hyginus in the *Gromatici Veteres*, p. 121, 9, (Lachmann-Rudorff): 'agros veteranis ex voluntate et liberalitate imperatoris ... assignavit.'

185. Mommsen, *Staatsrecht*, vol. II, p. 890, cf. vol. III, p. 134. Citizenship is due to the Emperor's 'benefaction', *CIL*, II, 1610 and 2096; Ulpian, *Rules*, 3, 2; Pliny, *Panegyricus*, 37, 3; Dessau, no. 9059, 2 (end). It is due also to the Emperor's 'complaisance' (*indulgentia*): Seston and Euzénnat in *Comptes rendus de l'Académie des inscriptions*, 1971, pp. 470 and 480.

186. Dio Cassius, LV, 13: Seneca, *De Beneficiis*, III, 9, 2: 'beneficium vocas dedisse civitatem, in quattuordecim deduxisse'; cf. A. Stein, *Der römisch Ritterstand*, pp. 23 and 73.

187. Frontinus, *De Aquae Ductu*, 99, 3. As I understand it, this passage indeed shows that *beneficium* is equivalent to 'decision'. Augustus in fact reserves to himself the right to decide who should receive the privilege of taking water from an aqueduct (as we should put it). In Latin and in the kingly style it is put thus, that he 'numbered the totality of things of this kind among his benefactions' (*tota re in sua beneficia translata*). This implies, furthermore, that the right to take water was a favour that one was allowed to request from the Emperor: for one was not allowed to ask him for just anything at all (see note 193). The same idea appears in Suetonius, *Claudius*, 23: the Emperor decides that permissions to take leave, which formerly had to be requested from the Senate, will henceforth be included among his benefactions. I should explain in the same way *Digest*, I, 2, 2, 49, on the *jus publice respondendi*.

188. On the prerogative of mercy, see Mommsen, *Strafrecht*, p. 262, note 1 (the references should be checked, as Mommsen's notes are muddled; cf. Suetonius, *Tiberius*, 35; *Claudius*, 14; Tacitus, *Annals*, III, 24), p. 483 and p. 1042. See also *Codex Theodosii*, headings IX, 37 ('De abolitionibus') and IX, 38 ('De indulgentiis criminum'); Mommsen, *Staatsrecht*, vol. II, p. 884; vol. III, pp. 358 and 1069. On the individualization of penalties and what we should call mitigating circumstances, see *Strafrecht*, p. 1039; on amnesty, intercession and provocation, *Strafrecht*, p. 452. W. Grewe, *Gnade und Recht* (1936), is a theoretical study of the prerogative of mercy. This prerogative 'assumes that the state is regarded as a transcendent being' (p. 51), and it belongs to a divine-right monarchy or to a deified king. It coincides chronologically with divine right and the theme of royal bounty (p. 59). However, this is not, in my view, the only possible justification or rationalization of the prerogative of mercy.

189. Mommsen, *Staatsrecht*, vol. II, p. 1126. In general, on royal 'benefaction', see *Thesaurus Linguae Latinae*, vol. II, s.v., col. 1886, line 66; *Dizionario epigrafico*, vol. II, s.v., p. 996. On the Hellenistic origins, see M.-T. Lenger, 'La notion de bienfait (philanthropon) royal et les ordonnances des rois lagides', in *Studi in onore di V. Arangio-Ruiz* (1952), vol. I, p. 483. The *philanthropa* are not a particular sort of legal act, and this word is not a technical term; it is the name of certain ordinances, certain *prostagmata*.

190. A. d'Ors, *Epigrafía jurídica de la España romana* (Madrid, 1953), p. 20. I heard this great Spanish jurist explain that the benefaction was so called because it was not a spontaneous action on the Emperor's part: one had to ask him for it. It could be granted automatically and was often the most commonplace of rights, but one was obliged to 'present the request'. Some benefactions had to be asked for (*petere*), while for

others one had to wait until they might be granted (*praestari*), without presenting any request: *Digest*, I, 2, 2, 49.

191. Another word which, like *beneficium*, is not a technical term, is *judicium*, of which I have prepared a detailed study. *Judicium* is not a 'judgement' but the good opinion one has of someone, the fact that one 'judges him to be good', and it is also a 'decision', by transfer from the Greek *krima* or *krisis* which acquired this meaning in the Hellenistic phase of the language. In practice, *beneficium* and *judicium* complement each other: the former signifies a favour given from bounty, the latter a decision based on one's personal esteem for someone, so that *judicium* is used, in Imperial Latin, to mean 'appointment to a post' (and we find this meaning of the word in the *Song of Roland*, verse 262).

192. See note 187.

193. In the address by 'Maecenas' to 'Augustus' in Dio Cassius (L II, 37; cf. LIV, 24), Maecenas advises Augustus not to allow cities to give themselves pompous titles which arouse the jealousy of rival cities, and adds: 'And all will readily yield obedience to you ... in this and in every other matter, provided that you make no exceptions whatever to this rule as a concession to anybody ... Consequently, you ought not to allow your subjects even to ask you ... for what you are not going to give them.' A constitution of 338 (*Codex Theodosii*, XV, 1, 5) forbids provincial governors to grant a certain immunity: 'Henceforth such requests shall not be accepted' (*in posterum aditus similia cupientibus obstruatur*); this *aditus* is what Majorian's *Novella* 4 calls the *licentia competendi*, the right to ask for a certain benefaction. *Aditus* here translates the Hellenistic Greek *enteuxis* (as in the Vulgate, from the Septuagint: P. Collomb, *Recherches sur la chancellerie et la diplomatique des Lagides* (1926), p. 52). It is a request addressed nominally to the king, or directly to an official, and either having or not having the aim of introducing a solicitation (cf. Latin *adire praetorem*, *adire judicem*). For the *enteuxis* introducing a solicitation, see E. S. Seidl, *Ptolemäische Rechtsgeschichte* (J. J. Augustin, 1962), pp. 65 and 89. In Latin one would say that by means of a request, written or spoken (*aditus*, *aditio*), one obtains a *beneficium*, and in Hellenistic Greek that by an *enteuxis* one obtains a *philanthropon*.

194. On this vast question, see, for a sample, *Digest*, X I, 6, 1 pr. and L, 13, 1; M. Kaser, *Römisches Privatrecht*, vol. I, 1971 edn, p. 569.

195. Dio of Prusa, *Orationes*, I, 23–4 and III, 110; cf. above, note 178. For Dio, whose rhetoric takes to extremes the theme of the Good King by absolute right, the king is really conceived as a rich private person who possesses the kingship. This rich property-owner has his private life, like everyone else, and his friends, as is his right. He makes *largesses* to his friends, which is to his credit. Those who know him well can tell

others of these generous characteristics of his, which inspire a favourable notion of his character. Moreover, as I shall explain at the end of this section, this king is *essentially good*. This is Dio's way of saying that this rich private property-owner nevertheless fulfils, through his property, a *public function*, that he is 'at the service of the public', which public 'benefits' from the office he performs. He reigns by himself and he reigns for us, and in so doing he is good. We readily believe that when Dio exalts the Emperor's goodness he wishes to remind the Emperor of his duties, and that this heralds the 'golden age' of the Antonines. But it would also be possible to argue that by reducing the sovereign function to private goodness, albeit essential, Dio is a theoretician of absolute monarchy, the theme of the goodness of the king who reigns for us merely serving as an 'ideological cloak' for the fact that he reigns by himself and not in the name of the ruled. Objectively, Dio's discourse has both of these meanings. All that remains is to know which were, in their own time, Dio's subjective intentions. Was he emphasizing absolute right only so as to remind the king of his duty to be good? Or on the contrary was he emphasizing the king's goodness only so as to assert absolute right and monarchical absolutism? I shall examine this problem elsewhere.

196. Thus T. Adam, *Clementia principis, der Einfluss hellenistischer Fürsten-spiegel auf den Versuch einer rechtlichen Fundierung des Prinzipats durch Seneca* (Klett, Stuttgart, 1970).

197. I agree on the essence of the matter with M. Fuhrmann, 'Die Allein-herrschaft und das Problem der Gerechtigkeit: Seneca, De Clementia', in *Gymnasium*, LXX (1963), pp. 481–514. But perhaps we interpret the facts somewhat differently.

198. G. Jellinek, *Allgemeine Staatslehre*, 1922 edn, pp. 180 and 622.

199. Polybius, XXXII, 8.

200. For detailed references hereafter, see H. Kloft, *Liberalitas principis: Herkunft und Bedeutung; Studien zur Prinzipatsideologie* (Böhlau, 1970).

201. The existence of private liberalities by the Emperor seems to me to be expressly proved in an edict of Nerva quoted by Pliny, *Letters*, X, 58, 9: 'quod alio principe vel privatim vel publice consecutus sit'.

202. The origin of the word and the difference of meaning were pointed out by F. de Coulanges, *Origines du système féodal*, p. 179, note 1.

203. *Codex Theodosii*, V, 12, 3, and 16, 31; X, 1, 1 and 2 and 8; X, 8, *passim*; X, 9, 2 and 3; X, 10, *passim*; XI, 20, *passim*; XI, 28, 13 and 15; XII, 11, 1.

204. Godefroy, paratitle to *Codex*, X, 8, and notes to X, 1, 2; X, 10, 6; XI, 20, 5 and 6. These are forfeit properties (X, 8, *passim*) which belong to the Fiscus (law of Constantine, X, 1, 2) or to the Private Fortune (X, 10, 6). Depending on the period, empty and forfeit properties fell

to one or other of these coffers. I have not been able to read R. His, *Die Domänen der römischen Kaiserzeit* (1896), p. 33.

205. C. Pharr, *The Theodosian Code and Novels* (Princeton, 1952), note to X, 1, 2.

206. *Codex*, X, 8, 4.

207. *Codex*, X, 1, 1: 'pro meritis obsequiisque'; X, 8, 3: 'pro laboribus suis et meritis': XI, 20, 4: 'in bene meritos de re publica'.

208. Cicero, *De Lege Agraria*, II, 2, 11, 12. Why was it consecrated? For the same reason that a victorious general was allowed to claim as his own property part, at least, of the booty, or that provincial governors were allowed to keep for themselves or to distribute among their friends any windfalls, together with the savings they might make on their credits – which were, as we saw in the previous chapter, considerable. For these were great lords and not mere state servants. This has nothing to do with law, and Mommsen gave himself trouble to no purpose (in this being historically typical of nineteenth-century legalism) when he based the general's right of ownership upon a distinction between loan and deposit. The plundering of public funds is the most universal fact in world history, and the plunderers were rarely troubled by legal fictions. The state apparatus exists by itself, as a confraternity, and it exists for the public good, as an organ. The confraternity treats public property as its own and awards itself little favours, with the same simplicity as the employees of a big store buy goods there at a reduced price which the management does not allow to ordinary customers. However, the state apparatus must also, to some extent, perform its role as an organ – must at least 'go through the motions'. Consequently, the general who keeps the booty for himself feels that this money burns his fingers, and so he spends part of it on the construction of a public monument. This he certainly does not do because the booty had been allotted to him only as a deposit! Besides, the general has the booty in his clutches, and who would care to dispute it with him by force of arms? Similarly, the *imperator* who distributes land is on the spot and can do whatever he likes, which makes it only too easy to understand why he yields to temptation. His weakness is natural, and it would be best to legitimize it, since nobody either can or wants to prevent him from yielding to it. The sole reservation is that, the state being an organ of the public good, he will feel obliged to 'go through the motions' by proclaiming that the land he has distributed by favour-itism is a reward for merit.

209. References in *Gromatici Veteres: Schriften der römischen Feldmesser*, Lach-mann-Rudorff edn, vol. II, pp. 387–9: vol. I, p. 197, 10: 'Excepti sunt fundi bene meritorum.' It remains to discover whether the allotments of land to deserving individuals were recorded in a certain *Liber*

Beneficiorum wherein were entered at least the Emperor's grants of public land to cities (*Gromatici*, vol. I, p. 203, 1; p. 295, 12; p. 400, 12). This is hard to decide. The only source is *Gromatici*, p. 295, 13, where the word *alicui* is very vague; it could just as easily mean a veteran who has obtained land in the normal way, for his regular retirement! What did this mysterious Book of Benefactions contain? All that we know is that at least from Trajan's time one official was responsible for Benefactions (Dessau, nos. 1792 and 9030; *CIL*, VI, 8626 and 8627). In the later Empire there was to be the *scrinium beneficiorum* (*Notitia Dignitatum*, West (ed.), XII, 32).

210. We need to recall at some length the twofold policy of Constantine. First, to win the support of the new ruling caste, the new administrative nobility, the 'clarissimate' in the sense given to that word in the later Empire (a *clarissimus* of the fourth century was as different from one of the second century as one of Napoleon's barons was different from a baron *tout court*; in the later Empire the equestrian order practically disappeared and every high official was at least a *clarissimus*). This new ruling caste emerged not from a political or social revolution but from the transformation of institutions and the army between 260 and 310. The political personnel of Constantine's time was as different, from every standpoint (including its literary culture), from that of the early Empire as the political personnel of nineteenth-century France was from that of pre-Revolutionary times. So ended the Hellenistic and Roman period of ancient history. Constantine meant to heap favours upon this new caste, like Napoleon creating barons and counts and making them wealthy. But secondly, Constantine wished also to be reconciled with the Senate in the strict sense, with the clarissimate in the old meaning of the word (like Napoleon trying to reconcile the nobility of the *ancien régime* and to take them into his service). And Constantine was able to make his friends wealthy (Eutropius, X, 7; Eusebius, *Life of Constantine*, I, 43, 1). On Constantine's approaches to the old Roman clarissimate, see A. Alföldi, *The Conversion of Constantine and Pagan Rome*, pp. 118–22.

211. The Emperor pays debts: Kloft, *Liberalitas*, pp. 77–8 and 101–4. The Emperor pays for games: Suetonius, *Augustus*, 43; *Historia Augusta*, 'Hadrian', 3, 8, and 7, 10. Many rich men fled from membership of the ruinous senatorial order (Dio Cassius, LIV, 26; cf. XLVIII, 53 and LX, 27) or preferred the service of the Emperor and the procuratorships (Tacitus, *Histories*, II, 86); cf. A. Stein, *Der römische Ritterstand*, pp. 189–200.

212. A. Chastagnol in *Mélanges Pierre Boyancé*, p. 165.

213. Mommsen, *Staatsrecht*, vol. I, p. 498 and vol. III, p. 466. On the relation between the senatorial order, meaning the persons who sat in the

Senate, and senatorial rank in the wider sense (including the senators' wives and their relatives as far as cousins thrice removed), see Mommsen, *Staatsrecht*, vol. III, p. 468, and also *Codex Justiniani*, XII, 1, 1.

214. Pliny, *Letters*, I, 19; Martial, IV, 67.

215. F. Millar, 'Herennius Dixippus: the Greek world and the third-century invasions', in *Journal of Roman Studies*, 1969, p. 21.

216. *De Beneficiis*, II, 7–8.

217. On fiscal reliefs, see Mommsen, *Staatsrecht*, vol. II, p. 1015; Marquardt, *Staatsverwaltung*, vol. II, p. 217; Kloft, *Liberalitas*, pp. 120–24; index to Godefroy's edition of the *Codex Theodosii*, under *indulgentia* and *reliqua*. Tax-abatements were a *liberalitas*: this word is used by Ammianus Marcellinus, XXV, 4, 15, and by the *Panegyrici Latini*, VIII, 14, 1. There are numerous papyrological documents, e.g. an edict of Hadrian in 135, in Preisigke-Bilabel, *Sammelbuch griech. Urkunden aus Aegypten*, vol. III, 1, no. 6944.

218. Dio Cassius, LXIX, 8. On these reliefs, see W. Seston in *Mélanges d'archéologie ... de l'École française de Rome*, XLIV (1927), p. 154, who shows that they relate to Hadrian and not to Trajan. Cf. M. Hammond in *Memoirs of the American Academy in Rome*, XXI (1953), p. 127; R. Brilliant, *Gesture and Rank in Roman Art* (Memoirs of the Connecticut Academy, XIV, 1963), pp. 108 and 128.

219. See C. Wilson, *Economic History and the Historian, Collected Essays* (Weidenfeld and Nicolson, 1969), p. 114: 'Taxation and the decline of Empires, an unfashionable theme'.

220. Sulpicius Severus, *Dialogues*, I, 3. The reference is to the desert area along the coast of Cyrenaica or Tripolitania.

221. Dittenberger, *Sylloge*, no. 814. On another occasion Nero intended to abolish customs duties (Tacitus, *Annals*, XIII, 50–51), which was not at all an absurd idea; cf. B. H. Warmington, *Nero: Reality and Legend* (Chatto and Windus, 1969), pp. 65 and 118.

222. U. Kahrstedt, *Das wirtschaftliche Gesicht Griechenlands in der Kaiserzeit: Kleinstadt, Villa und Domäne* (Dissertationes Bernenses, 1954).

223. Ammianus Marcellinus, XVI, 5, 14.

224. When he became Augustus, Julian hesitated to 'injure the public prosperity by granting a particular indulgence to any' (*Letters*, 73 (Bidez)). He refused to remit *all* arrears of taxation (*reliqua*), as that would particularly benefit the rich, who alone had been able to get permission to delay payment: the poor were required to pay up at once (Ammianus, XVI, 5, 15).

225. Proportioning the tax burden to the economic situation of each region: two striking examples are the edict of Hadrian mentioned in note 217 and the *Panegyrici Latini*, VIII, commented on by A. Cérati, *Caractère annonaire et Assiette de l'impôt foncier*, p. 315.

226. *Panegyrici Latini*, XI, 11, 2.
227. Sombart, *Der moderne Kapitalismus*, vol. I, 2, p. 664.
228. Dio Cassius, LXXIII, 8, 3. At the death of Antoninus the public coffers contained 2.7 billion sesterces. According to Suetonius, Nero and Domitian, spendthrift rulers, exhausted the contents of the Treasury.
229. Julian, *Letters*, 73 (Bidez). In an edict to which I have already referred (note 26), Alexander Severus writes: 'I am not interested in money, but wish rather to advance the well-being of the Empire by my philanthropy and my *euergesiai*; so that the governors and procurators sent out by me, whom I have selected with the greatest care, ought to be inspired by my example and show the greatest possible moderation; for the provincial governors will learn a little more each day that they should put all their efforts into sparing the nations to which they have been appointed, if they can see the sovereign himself ruling the Empire with so much self-respect, moderation and restraint.'
230. Mattingly, *Coins of the Roman Empire in the British Museum*, vol. III, p. xlvii: FISCI IVDAICI CALVMNIA SVBLATA; cf. Suetonius, *Domitian*, 12.
231. *Panegyrici Latini*, XI, 4, 2.
232. To the references given above, chapter IV, note 26, add Tertullian, *De Pallio*, 1, 1 and 2, 7; Symmachus, *Relatio*, 1.
233. There is no overall study of the subject. E. De Ruggiero's *Lo Stato e le opere pubbliche in Roma antica* (Turin, 1925), pp. 78–111, deals only with the city of Rome itself. The main lines can be discerned from Marquardt, *Staatsverwaltung*, vol. II, pp. 90–92; Hirschfeld, *Verwaltungsbeamten*, p. 266; Mommsen, *Staatsrecht*, vol. II, 2, p. 1100, note 2 (by 'the Emperor's private coffer' Mommsen, in conformity with his theory, means the Fiscus), and vol. III, p. 1145; Friedländer, *Sittengeschichte*, vol. III, pp. 28–32. Some monographs: F. C. Bourne, *Public Works of the Julio-Claudians and the Flavians* (Princeton, 1946); R. MacMullen, 'Roman imperial building in the provinces', in *Harvard Studies in Classical Philology*, LXIV (1959), pp. 207–35 (he studies especially the buildings constructed by the armies); D. Tudor, 'Les constructions publiques de la Dacie romaine d'après les inscriptions', in *Latomus*, 1964, p. 271; C. E. van Sickle, 'Public works in Africa in the reign of Diocletian', in *Classical Philology*, 1930, p. 173. Sometimes an Emperor and a *euergetēs* collaborate: Herodes Atticus wrote to Hadrian that Alexandria Troas lacked water and asked him for 12 million sesterces in order to bring water into the town; as the cost proved to be greater than that sum, Herodes paid the excess, or, rather, had it paid nominally by his son, to whom he gave the necessary

amount (Philostratus, *Lives of the Sophists*, I, 26, p. 537, beginning, and II, 1, p. 548, end).

234. The buildings erected elsewhere than in Rome by the Roman Senate and people (on the significance of the S P Q R formula, see Mommsen, *Staatsrecht*, vol. III, p. 1258) were usually put up in honour of the Emperor. Thus, Suetonius, *Tiberius*, 5 (Fundi); Dio Cassius, LI, 19 (Actium). The arches at Rimini and Benevento are cases in point. The temple of Venus Erycina was restored by the Treasury on the initiative of Claudius (Suetonius, *Claudius*, 25; Mommsen, *Staatsrecht*, vol. III, p. 1145, note 1); on *opera publica* in Asia and Bithynia, see *CIL*, V, 977 and Hirschfeld, *Verwaltungsbeamten*, p. 266, note 1. More generally, see F. J. Hassel, *Der Trajansbogen in Benevent: ein Bauwerk des römischen Senates* (Verlag Philipp von Zabern, 1966), pp. 2–9.

235. Mommsen, *Staatsrecht*, vol. II, p. 249; Marquardt, *Staatsverwaltung*, vol. II, p. 88; D. Kienast, *Cato der Zensor, seine Persönlichkeit und seine Zeit* (Heidelberg, 1954), studies the constructions by the censors of 174 at Pisaurum, Fundi and Potentia.

236. *CIL*, V, 54; Degrassi, *Inscriptiones Liberae Rei Publicae*, no. 639; *Inscriptiones Italiae*, X, 1, no. 81, cf. A. Degrassi, *Scritti varî*, vol. II, p. 913; R. Syme, *The Roman Revolution*, p. 465, note 1: 'From his father Cassius inherited a connexion with the Transpadani'; Tacitus, *Histories*, II, 72: 'in Istria ... for there the ancient Crassi still possessed clients, lands and popularity'.

237. *CIL*, XI, 6219 (Dessau, no. 104: *murum dedit*); V, 525 and addenda, p. 1022 (Dessau, no. 77: 'murum turresque fecit'); XII, 3151 ('portas murosque coloniae dat'); III, 13264 ('parens coloniae, murum et turris dedit'); X, 4842 (Dessau, no. 5743), with the new readings in *L'Année épigraphique*, 1962, no. 92.

238. When a governor had a bridge repaired by imposing a charge and an obligation to furnish labour upon the nearby town, it was the Emperor who *pontem restituit* (*CIL*, III, 3202; Dessau, no. 393): the Emperor had given authorization for this to be done. True, the Emperor in question was Commodus, whose egocentric tendencies were doubtless known to his political staff. The Emperors in general were inclined to subordinate all public building work to their authorization: Pliny, *Letters*, X, 37–42, and Macer, *Digest*, L, 10, 3, 1.

239. Pliny, *Letters*, X, 58, 5, explained by O. Hiltbrunner, 'Miszellen', in *Hermes*, LXXVII (1942), p. 381. When a construction is said to be due to the Emperor's *indulgentia* we may understand, on the whole, that the Emperor has authorized it; or that he has authorized the governor to impose extraordinary charges in order to have it done; or that he has sent money for the purpose; or that he has permitted a share of the province's taxes to be used to pay for the task (see, e.g.,

CIL, III, 7409; P.-A. Février, in *Mélanges André Piganiol*, p. 223). A
special case is when the Emperor assigns the revenues of a temple to
pay for building work: from this we must deduce that these revenues
had been assigned to the Fiscus (*CIL*, III, 7118, Dessau, no. 97; *CIL*,
III, 14120; cf. *Inscriptiones Creticae*, vol. II, p. 139, no. 6, and vol. IV,
p. 356, no. 333: the Emperor restores buildings *ex reditu Dianae* or *ex
sacris pecuniis Dictynnae*).

240. *Panegyrici Latini*, V, speech by Eumenes at Autun.

241. On the public announcements which the pollicitating *euergetēs* made,
by letter or speech, of his future *euergesia*, as yet only a promise, see
Pliny, *Letters*, I, 8: Pliny's address to his fellow citizens of Como is the
obvious parallel to our *Panegyrici Latini*, V. A very good imaginary
example of such a speech is given in a Latin novel translated from
Greek (J. P. Enk in *Mnemosyne*, 1948, p. 231), the *History of Apollonius,
King of Tyre*, 47 (Riese) (the entire novel, which deserves detailed
analysis, is valuable for Imperial-period Greek euergetism: see also
chapters 9 and 10). A real example is Apuleius, *Florida*, XVI, 35-9, or
Lucian, *Death of Peregrinus*, 15. Examples are not rare in Latin and,
especially, Greek epigraphy: see in particular *CIL*, X, 4643, at Cales.
In general see Waltzing, *Corporations professionelles chez les Romains*,
vol. II, p. 454, and L. Robert, *Études anatoliennes*, p. 379. The speech
or letter which the *euergetēs* addressed to his city is of great importance
because it constitutes a public commitment to carry out the promise.
Thus at Narbonne a *euergetēs* says at the end of his letter: 'You will
regard this letter as equivalent to a legal act in proper form' (*epistulam
pro perfecto instrumento retinebitis*) (*CIL*, XII, 4393). Did the *euergetēs*
deliver his speech before the assembled people or before the Council
only? Eumenes of Autun chose the first-mentioned procedure, while
Pliny the Younger is quite proud of having chosen the other (*Letters*,
I, 8, 16). In any case, it was necessary to inform the city of the intention
of *euergesia* that one had formed, because the city had either to accept
or to reject the promise (Gaius, *Institutes*, II, 195, concerning a legacy;
but we must generalize – as the *euergesia* is to be a monument erected
on public land, the city has to decide whether or not to authorize the
euergetēs to take over a piece of this land for his building). To thank
the *euergetēs* for his letter or his speech, the city sends him a decree of
honours or of 'testimony', which has the advantage of committing
him a little more firmly to performance of his promise; for examples
of such decrees see Degrassi, *Inscriptiones Liberae Rei Publicae*, no. 558;
Dessau, no. 154 ('ut gratiae agerentur munificentiae ejus'). The crucial
question remains: did the promise, by letter or public speech, commit
the *euergetēs* in law? Did his speech enable the city to go before the
governor's tribunal and demand that the promise be carried out? This

is the great question of pollicitations in Roman 'private' law: one need only read *Digest*, L, 12. In short, the speech of Eumenes at Autun conforms to the general pattern in every respect.

242. On the 'ambitious decrees', see *Digest*, L, 9, 4 pr. The governor looked after the public buildings in the cities and reported on them to the Emperor (Pliny, *Letters*, X, 37–42; *Digest*, L, 10, 3; I, 16, 7, 1; I, 18, 7). On relations between the governor and the autonomous city, see D. Nörr, *Imperium und Polis in der hohen Prinzipatszeit*, p. 36; J. H. Oliver, 'The Roman governor's permission for a decree', in *Hesperia*, XXIII (1954), p. 163. A very good example appears in *Tituli Asiae Minoris*, vol. II, no. 175: the city of Sidyma asks the governor of Lycia, by decree, for permission to build a *gerousia*.

243. For the central role of the *curator rei publicae* in the later Empire, when he was the real ruler of the city (the magistrates being no longer anything more than liturgists), and made dedications and so on, see, e.g., *CIL*, XIV, 2071, 2124, 2806, 3593, 3900, 3902, 3933, to name but a few. Before a *euergetēs* was granted a public place to build his edifice, the curator's permission was sought: *CIL*, XI, 3614, or X, 1814. On the role of the curator in the matter of public buildings, see *Année épigraphique*, 1960, no. 202. In the inscriptions we read that a building, or even a statue, has been erected 'with the confirmation of the city's curator and under the governor's authority' (thus *CIL*, VIII, 5357, cf. 1296). In general, see L. Robert, *Hellenica*, I, p. 43; H. Seyrig, *Antiquités syriennes*, vol. III, p. 188 (reprinted from *Syria*, 1941, p. 188); Jouguet, *Vie municipale de l'Égypte romaine*, p. 463; H. Seyrig in *Bulletin de correspondance hellénique*, LI (1927), p. 139; S. Cassario, 'Il curator rei publicae nella storia dell'impero romano', in *Annali del seminario giuridico, Università di Catania*, II (1947–8), pp. 338–59. Let me briefly remind the reader of the difference between the *curator rei publicae* of the early Empire, a stranger to the city, appointed by the Emperor and confining himself to guardianship of the city, and the *curator rei publicae* as he became during the third century, when he was chosen from among the local notables, appointed for an indefinite period, elected by the council itself, and entrusted with actual management of the city and its budget; moreover, he undertook no *euergesiai* (whereas the magistrates had lost control of the actual government of the city and were now no more than its milch-cows).

244. *Panegyrici Latini*, V, 3, 4; 11, 1; 16, 5. I have examined above (note 72) the custom of dedicating buildings to the reigning Emperor. It could also happen that a building bore the Emperor's name although he did not erect it: at Thugga the Aqueduct of Commodus was built by the town (Poinssot in *Mélanges Carcopino*, p. 775) and at Apamea the Bath of Hadrian was built *ex pecunia publica* (*CIL*, III, 6992).

245. Vitruvius, I, 1, 2.
246. *Jewish Antiquities*, XIX, 2, 5.
247. Nor is that all. Needs and desires vary in kind according to resources. In that period the people may have ascribed to the public buildings, that is, to the setting in which they lived, much greater importance than people do today, when the setting of their lives is the private home and the transport system. In those days the people lived in *tabernae*, each family in a single room which served as both dwelling and workshop or shop. There was hardly any furniture (owning furniture rather than not owning it meant one had made a start towards luxury). The only movable goods that were owned by the many were clothes, which were expensive (people left their clothes as security when borrowing from usurers, just as the nineteenth-century workman pawned his mattress). In other words, the main part of the setting of private life was public. Living amid fine but useless public buildings was like living in a fine apartment, among fine furniture; it was a real source of individual satisfaction. See how Pausanias writes of 'Panopeus, a city of the Phocians, if one can give the name of city to those who possess no government offices, no gymnasium, no theatre, no market-place, no water descending to a fountain, but live in bare shelters just like mountain cabins [*kalybai*], right on a ravine' (X, 4, 1). I deliberately translate *kalybai* here by *gourbis* [Arabic for 'shacks' or 'huts' – Trans.] because, in the bilingual texts, *kalybē* is how Latin *mappalia* is rendered. This is the case in the fragments of the Greek translation of the *Aeneid* in *Rylands Papyrus*, 478b (Cavenaile, p. 11) and in the *Grammatici Latini*, vol. IV, p. 583 (Keil): '*magalia, kalybē*'. Nobody would have enjoyed living in the place Pausanias describes, and the poor people of that neighbourhood must have longed for an 'exodus from the countryside' and migration to a real town.
248. Hadrian heaped benefactions upon his native town, Italica: R. Syme, 'Hadrian and Italica', in *Journal of Roman Studies*, LIV (1964), p. 144. In this he was following the example of his father, a notable of Italica whose horoscope has, by the merest chance, come down to us. The Moon, Saturn and Jupiter had made him 'fortunate and very wealthy and a donor of many gifts and donations for his native city' (F. H. Cramer, *Astrology in Roman Law and Politics* (American Philosophical Society, 1954), p. 163). There is no space to discuss the benefactions of the Severi to their native town, Leptis Magna. Julian adorned Constantinople because, he wrote, he was born there (W. Ensslin in *Klio*, XVIII (1923), p. 164). In other cases it was a matter not of royal caprice but of party politics. An example of this is Nîmes, which was loaded with favours by Augustus and Agrippa, who built there an enormous enclosing wall, a water-supply and the temple now called

the Maison Carrée. To be sure, southern Gaul needed a large fortified place of refuge into which a whole army could retreat, and since this was needed, it might as well be built at Nîmes as anywhere else. But there was also a positive reason for the choice of Nîmes. My friend Christian Goudineau has brought to my attention a passage in Caesar's *Civil War*, I, 35, 4, where it is said that Pompey, as patron of Marseilles, assigned to that city the territory of the Volcae-Arecomici, i.e. the territory belonging to the Celtic town of Nîmes. Now all becomes clear. The civil wars at the end of the Republic saw, in Gaul and elsewhere, the same phenomenon which is well known to us in Greece and Asia through the evidence of Strabo, Plutarch, et al. The different native cities took sides with one or other of the Roman magnates who were fighting each other, with a view to the benefactions they expected from them, and also on the basis of the antagonisms between neighbouring cities. Nîmes had been deprived of part of its territory by Pompey for the benefit of Marseilles; so when Caesar besieged Marseilles, Nîmes declared for Caesar, and remained loyal to his adopted son Octavius Augustus. Nîmes was a Caesarean city; it was Caesar's base in Gaul. After his victory, Caesar restored the Volcae-Arecomici to Nîmes (thus reconstituting the vast territory possessed by Nîmes under the Empire), while at the same time he considerably reduced the territory of Marseilles for the benefit of Arles and Aix-en-Provence (see the writings of M. Clerc). I will mention one parallel case. On account of its loyalty to Octavius Caesar in his conflict with Cassius, the city of Tarsus was given autonomy, a vast territory, control of the sea and the river, and so on. Similarly, the territory of Nîmes under the Empire extended to the Rhône, which was of major importance in a period when rivers were the only good means of transport. See Dio of Prusa, *Orationes*, XXXIV, 8; Dio Cassius, LVII, 31, and Appian, *Civil Wars*, V, 7. On the basilica of Plotina and its sculptures, see the references assembled by E. Linckenheld in his excellent article 'Nemausus' in Pauly-Wissowa, XVI, cols. 2297–8. For the Hermes and Aphrodite of Italica, in Seville Museum, see Garcia y Bellido, in *Les Empereurs romains d'Espagne, colloque du CNRS*, 1965, pp. 20–21. For the sculptures at Hadrian's villa at Tibur, see *Fasti Archaeologici*, vol. IX, no. 5028, and vol. X, nos. 3682ff., 4441ff.

249. L. Robert, *Études épigraphiques et philologiques*, pp. 139 ('Did not the honorary sum paid by a king have to be especially splendid?': when a king became the eponym of a city he gave it a fine gift) and 143–50.

250. On the Emperors as magistrates of cities, see Mommsen, *Staatsrecht*, vol. II, pp. 813 and 828; id., *Juristische Schriften*, vol. I, pp. 304, 308 and 324; Marquardt, *Staatsverwaltung*, vol. I, p. 169; W. Liebenam,

Städteverwaltung im römischen Kaiserreiche (Bretschneider, reprinted 1967), p. 261; L. Robert, *Hellenica*, VIII, p. 75.

251. On the other hand, there are no examples, after Augustus's reign, of an Emperor becoming patron of a city. (Or let us say more precisely 'receiving the honorific title of patron of a city', for the patronate was not a thing, a function either formal or informal, but an honorific *title*, a word. One was not a *euergetēs* because one had been chosen to be patron of the city; one received the title of patron for the *euergesiai* one had performed or would perform. The alleged 'institution' of the city patronate is to be compared to the honorific *titles* which the Greek cities awarded to their benefactors, such as *euergetēs*, foster-father of the city, son or father of the city. The city patronate needs to be completely restudied.) The Emperor no longer wished to have the title of patron of a city, which was suitable for mere private persons, and after Augustus no reigning Emperor was a *patronus* (L. Harmand, *Le Patronat sur les collectivités publiques*, pp. 155–6; the only alleged exception, p 164, is non-existent: the Nerva in question is not the Emperor of that name but one of his ancestors, who was governor of Asia in the time of the triumvirs. In *Latomus*, 1962, p. 68, note 4, I was guilty of the same confusion, though it had been pointed out several times: in the second edition of the *Prosopographia Imperii Romani*, letter C, no. 1224, under 'Cocceius'; by Syme, *The Roman Revolution*, p. 266, note 3; by J. and L. Robert, *La Carie*, vol. II, p. 103, note 7). The title of patron was proscribed as far as the Emperor was concerned. In the same way, among the titles which the Greek cities awarded to their *euergetai*, that of 'father of the homeland' disappears under the Empire, because it resembled too closely the Imperial title of *pater patriae*, and was replaced by a modest 'father of the city' (L. Robert in *Antiquité classique*, 1966, p. 421, note 5). It could happen that senators were magistrates of a city, like the Emperor. It could also happen that a local magistrate was absent and had himself replaced by a prefect. But then a difference of protocol was established between them and an Emperor who had been replaced by his prefect. The senator was not replaced by a prefect (there were thus two duumvirs in office, one of them a senator of Rome) and the absent magistrate had a colleague (there were thus two magistrates at the head of the city – one a duumvir and the other the prefect of the absent duumvir). However, when an Emperor was a city magistrate, one person alone was at the head of the city, namely the prefect who represented him and who had no colleague. This regime was introduced after Augustus. During his reign there were still numerous cases where a senator who was a duumvir had himself replaced by a prefect; this was done by Statilius Taurus at Dyrrhachium (*CIL*, III, 605). On this see G. L. Cheesman,

'The family of the Caristanii at Antioch in Pisidia', in *Journal of Roman Studies*, III (1913), p. 256. Like the facts mentioned in the preceding note, and like those I shall describe in connection with the Emperor's monopoly of *euergesiai* in Rome itself, these were details of protocol which gave the Emperor a position as unique sovereign and not merely as one magistrate among his peers. See notes 317–19.

252. This is my hypothesis, at any rate. However, apart from the two examples mentioned above, the sources tell us either of Imperial *euergesiai* to cities or of Emperors as magistrates of cities, but never of both together. This is an unfortunate mischance resulting from the nature of our documentation. It should be noted, moreover, that the institution evolved both before and after Augustus and Tiberius. Under Augustus the institution still retained its Republican and Hellenistic character; the city elected the Emperor to the office of duumvir just as it would have elected a senator and as the autonomous Greek cities used to elect a king – as a sort of noble and powerful stranger, so that it was almost a relationship in international politics. The city also elected princes of the blood (like Germanicus), whose place was taken by prefects. These prefects who stood in for the Emperor or a prince of the blood were nominated by the city itself (Dessau, no. 2689). We see here a case of sentimental relations between powers which, though unequal, were independent or at least autonomous. This was the period when the Imperial authority consisted of magistracy plus personal charisma. After Tiberius, there is thus no example of a prince of the blood, when he was a city magistrate (as he could continue to be, like any other senator), daring to have his place filled by a prefect or prefects. Furthermore, the single prefect who stood in for the Emperor, and this one alone, was no longer appointed by the city, but by the Emperor himself (see the Salpensa tablet, Dessau, no. 6088, article 24: 'If Domitian Augustus accepts the duumvirate and appoints a prefect . . .').

253. *Historia Augusta*, 'Hadrian', 19, 1–3.

254. Julian, *Panegyric in Honour of Constantius*, 6.

255. *Third Letter on a Regicide Peace*, 1797.

256. E.g. the gifts of the kings to Rhodes after the earthquake, or the gifts of Opramoas to the towns of Lycia after another earthquake (*Tituli Asiae Minoris*, III, no. 905, XVIIb, cap. 59). Another form of liberality can be mentioned: when corn was short in a province or a provincial city and there was famine, the Emperors sent corn there (see Rostovtzeff's article on 'Frumentum' in Pauly-Wissowa, VII, 1, cols. 184–5). This liberality is sometimes recorded on Greek coins of the Imperial period.

257. For the facts, see Kloft, *Liberalitas*, p. 118; Liebenam, *Städteverwaltung*,

p. 172; Friedländer, *Sittengeschichte*, vol. III, p. 28. On the *munificentia* of Tiberius after the fire on the Caelian Hill, see Suetonius, *Tiberius*, 48. But Laodicea, destroyed by an earthquake, 'recovered itself by its own resources' (Tacitus, *Annals*, XIV, 27).

258. Tacitus, *Histories*, III, 34. This was a public appeal for euergetism. It is not a unique case: Pliny, *Letters*, X, 8 (24), 1 (Nerva).

259. This was the well-known crisis of 33, resulting from ill-considered measures (Tacitus, *Annals*, VI, 16–17; Suetonius, *Tiberius*, 48; cf. Dio Cassius, LVIII, 21). It has been frequently commented on, from Cantillon (*Essai sur la nature du commerce en général* (Institut national d'études démographiques, reprinted 1952, p. 168) to H. Crawford ('Le problème des liquidités dans l'Antiquité classique', in *Annales, Économies, Sociétés*, 1971, p. 1229) and especially J. M. Kelly, *Roman Litigation* (Oxford, 1966), pp. 76–9.

260. The word *munificentia* is found in Suetonius, *Tiberius*, 48. For the modern idea of the nation as a mutual-aid society, see L. Duguit, *Traité de droit constitutionnel*, vol. II, p. 73, and vol. III, p. 469.

261. Dessau, no. 6675, beginning.

262. On the *Alimenta*, see bibliography in Veyne, 'Les alimenta', in *Les Empereurs romains d'Espagne, colloques du CNRS*, 1965, pp. 163–79 and appendix. Now see also P. Garnsey, 'Trajan's alimenta: some problems', in *Historia*, XVII (1968), p. 381; M. Pfeffer, *Einrichtungen der sozialen Sicherung in der griechischen und römischen Antike* (Duncker and Humblot, 1969), pp. 122–7 and 175. I am not reproducing here the conclusions of studies I have previously published on the *Alimenta*.

263. References in H. Kloft, *Liberalitas Principis*, p. 97. A Terracina bas-relief relates to this theme; it has been examined by P. Strack, *Reichsprägung, Traian*, p. 47, and reproduced by G. Lugli in the work which he published on 'Anxur-Tarracina' in *Forma Italiae* in 1927.

264. Dessau, no. 6106: 'Trajan has in view the eternity of Italy'; Pliny, *Panegyricus*, 28, says of the children whom the Emperor helps that 'the army and citizen body will be completed by their numbers'. It is necessary, nevertheless, to avoid making the mistake I made twenty years ago by endowing this 'eternity of Italy' with too exact a meaning. It does not mean the eternity of the Italian race as condition for the continued existence of the state. What we have here is kingly style, not ideology. *Every* decision by the Emperor, on whatever subject, ensures the eternity of the state, in that it is good and contributes to salvation. For example, if the Emperor concerns himself with checking speculation in land and preventing the cities from filling themselves with ruined houses, he is thereby also caring for the eternity of Italy (Dessau, no. 6043, beginning).

265. On *indulgentia*, see J. Gaudemet, *Indulgentia Principis* (Università di

Trieste, Conferenze romanistiche, 1962). Other references in Veyne, *Les Empereurs romains d'Espagne*, *colloques du CNRS*, 1965, p. 166, note 20; W. Waldstein, *Untersuchungen zum römischen Begnadigungsrecht: abolitio, indulgentia, venia* (Dissertationes Aenipontanae, XVIII, Innsbruck, 1964); *Dizionario epigrafico*, vol. IV, p. 50, under 'Indulgentia'. A very early example of the word would be a coin of Patras mentioned by M. Grant, *From Imperium to Auctoritas*, p. 295, if it really dates from Tiberius's reign. On *indulgentia* in connection with gladiatorial combats, see Mommsen, *Epigraphische Schriften*, vol. I, p. 513; L. Robert, *Gladiateurs en Orient grec*, p. 274. The inscription *CIL*, XI, 5375, at Assisi, provides an example of *indulgentia* used of persons other than the Emperor: 'ex indulgentia dominorum' – but a slave is speaking.

266. *Historia Augusta*, 'Antoninus Pius', 8, 1; 'Alexander Severus', 57, 7; 'Antoninus the Philosopher', 25, 6. A relief in the Albani collection relates to these charities (S. Reinach, *Répertoire des reliefs*, vol. III, p. 147).

267. Pliny, *Letters*, X, 54–5.

268. *Les Empereurs romains d'Espagne*, p. 173.

269. Cf. *Digest*, XXXIV, 1, 14, 1.

270. See, e.g., the censuses of Augustus in P. A. Brunt, *Italian Manpower* (Oxford, 1971), pp. 121–30. We know that the apparent sharp increase in the number of Roman citizens between the last Republican census and the censuses of Augustus was not due to a large-scale and rapid increase in the citizen population, as Tenney Frank curiously supposed, but quite simply to a change of method. The Republican censuses took account only of the male citizens of military age, but the Imperial ones included *all* citizens, regardless of age or sex. Beloch, who possessed a sense for large numbers, had guessed that this was so, and it is to Brunt's credit that he has followed Beloch. I wonder whether we have not got extracts from the census registers in a list of centenarians compiled, town by town throughout Italy, by Phlegon of Tralles, which includes women as well as men (*Fragmenta Historicorum Graecorum* (Müller), vol. III, pp. 608–10; Jacoby, *Fragmente der griechischen Historiker*, 2b, 1185, no. 37; cf. Pliny, *Natural History*, VII, 163).

271. A passage in Caesar seems to me to give us an idea of the methods of demography in ancient times. In his *Gallic War*, I, 29, Caesar writes, 'Of the Helvetii ... there were about 92,000 able to bear arms. The grand total was about 368,000.' Now the first figure is exactly one-quarter of the second. Moreover, we know the tendency the ancients had to overestimate the numbers of enemy armies (note what Delbrück, in his *Geschichte der Kriegskunst*, showed regarding the Persians' numbers in the Median wars and at the time of Alexander's

conquests). We also know the legend according to which, among the barbarians, there were as many warriors as free adult men. Caesar would not have been displeased to have it believed that with six legions he conquered an enemy three times their number. So this is what he did. He knew that, broadly, the number of citizens, women and children included, was four times the number of male citizens of military age. (We saw in the previous note that, under the Republic, only the last-mentioned were recorded in the census, and that must have led curious-minded people to wonder what fraction they constituted of the total citizen population. Doubtless the conventional proportion agreed on was, in round figures, one-quarter.) Caesar found in the Helvetians' own records, as he tells us, that this nation numbered 368,000; he divided this figure by four and boldly asserted that all the men of military age were combatants.

272. Polybius, XXXVI, 17. See, as against this, in II, 62, Polybius's very remarkable account of the lack of resources of the Peloponnese.

273. For Pharsalus, see Lucan, *De Bello Civili*, VII, 387ff.; for Mursa, Eutropius, X, 12. The subject is timeless: in the Middle Ages the inability of the Franks to resist the Norse invasions was explained by the losses of population in 850–53.

274. Pliny, *Panegyricus*, 26.

275. *Panegyrici Latini*, VI, 2, 4; Defoe quoted by Sombart, *Der moderne Kapitalismus*, vol. I, 2, p. 810.

276. *Codex Theodosii*, XI, 27, 1–2. For echoes of the *Alimenta* in the iconography and epigraphy of the fourth century, see Veyne in *Les Empereurs romains d'Espagne*, p. 169, note 35, and L. Robert in *Revue de philologie*, XLI (1967), p. 82. It is necessary to *prove* one's concern; it is not enough to declare it. Jules Ferry or Lyautey claimed to be conquering Indo-China or Morocco in order to open up markets 'for our traders and our bankers' (who only half-believed it). They were obliged, indeed, to seem to have serious reasons for what they were doing. Their real motive was to avenge the defeat of 1871 by 'making French influence felt' throughout the world. I have always wondered why persons who desire to hate imperialism and colonialism need to insist that these phenomena are always economic: it is not clear why they would be less hateful if they were non-economic.

277. *Les Empereurs romains d'Espagne*, pp. 165 and 168.

278. L. Robert in *Annuaire du Collège de France*, 1971, p. 516.

279. This is the 'patrimonialist' theme, according to which loans between citizens, mutual aid or liturgies maintain or even establish the bond of citizenship. Within the framework of the citizen body and in the egalitarian ideology of the Greek city, euergetism and beneficence between citizens were inspired by the same motives and differed only

in scale, not in nature. A good citizen would do good to all his peers and to each one individually, being both *euergetēs* and philanthropist. His euergetism would be neither a way of showing off his superiority nor a gratuity to compensate for the monopoly of political rights: it would be performed as between equals. The Roman municipal inscriptions of the Imperial period say in the same way that a certain *euergetēs* was liberal 'towards the citizens as a whole and towards each one of them', *universis et singulis*. In his *Oration on the Chersonese*, 107 (70), Demosthenes lists *euergesiai* and acts of beneficence together. 'If anyone were to ask me to say what good I had really done to the city ... I could tell how often I had been trierarch and *chorēgos*, how I had contributed funds [*eisphorai*], ransomed prisoners, and done other like acts of generosity.' The same could be said of American euergetism.

280. *Les Empereurs romains d'Espagne*, p. 167.

281. *Digest*, XXIII, 3, 2.

282. Petition to Ptolemy Philopator in 220 BC (*Enteuxeis* papyrus no. 82) in Edgar and Hunt, *Select Papyri*, vol. II, no. 211. On the title of '*euergetēs*-king', the theme of the sovereign benefactor, philanthropist and also saviour, see A. D. Nock, 'Soter and Euergetes', in his *Essays on Religion and the Ancient World* (Oxford, 1972), pp. 720–35; B. Kötting in the *Reallexicon für Antike und Christentum*, vol. VI (1966), pp. 849–56; other references in W. Spoerri, *Späthellenische Berichte über Welt, Kultur und Götter* (Basle University dissertation, 1959), p. 194, note 30; on royal philanthropy, references in J. H. Oliver, *The Ruling Power, a study of the Roman Empire through the Roman Oration of Aelius Aristides* (Transactions of the American Philosophical Society, XLIII, 4, 1953), p. 930. On the non-philosophical origin of this idea, see A.-J. Festugière, *La Révélation d'Hermès Trismégiste*, vol. II, pp. 303–9. With Julian the Apostate, the ideal of philanthropy shows Christian influence: J. Kabiersch, *Untersuchungen zum Begriff der Philanthropia bei Julian* (Harassowitz, 1960).

283. On the virtues, see G.-C. Picard, *Les Trophées romains* (De Boccard, 1957), pp. 371–464; Syme, *Tacitus*, vol. II, p. 754. The frontiers are vague between allegorical talk (when one speaks of Imperial Liberality in the same way that Zola invoked Truth and Justice during the Dreyfus affair), deification (for altars were set up to Liberality and sacrifices offered to it), and the concrete noun (for *a* liberality was a *congiarium*); see L. Robert, *Hellenica*, IX, p. 55, note 2. For personifications on coins, the three books by Strack replace the old studies by W. Koehler, *Personifikationen abstrakter Begriffe auf römischen Münzen* (Königsberg University dissertation, 1910), and Gnecchi, 'Personificazioni allegoriche sulle monete imperiali', in *Rivista italiana di numismatica*, XVIII (1905). Many references are given in a valuable

study by G. Manganaro, 'La dea della casa e la Euphrosyne nel Basso Impero', in *Archaeologia Classica*, XII (1960), p. 189. On the vague frontier between personifications and geniuses, see P. Veyne, 'Ordo et Populus, génies et chefs de file', in *Mélanges de l'École française de Rome*, 1961, pp. 264–74. For deified personifications in Hellenic and Hellenistic religion, see the second edition of Nilsson's *Geschichte der griech. Religion*, vol. I, p. 812; vol. II, pp. 198, 206, 282, 296 and 378. On priestesses of the divinized Imperial Virtues in the Greek world, cf. Veyne in *Latomus*, XXI (1962), p. 55, note 1. For the cult of *Pistis*, i.e. *Fides*, see L. Robert, *Laodicée du Lycos*, p. 321, note 7. On a statue of Imperial *Educatio*, L. Robert in *Revue de philologie*, XLI (1967), p. 82. On historical bas-reliefs the personifications are often hard to identify. The key to this iconography has in many cases been lost. It must not be forgotten that these reliefs frequently bore inscriptions – painted or, rarely, engraved – which gave the names of the personifications represented; cf. *Mélanges de l'École française de Rome*, 1960, p. 198, note 1.

284. *Codex Theodosii*, X, 10, 12: 'ex consensu Nostrae Liberalitatis': cf. R. M. Honig, *Humanitas und Rhetorik in spätrömischen Kaisergesetzen* (O. Schwartz, Göttingen, 1960), pp. 71–3; this work deals with the moralizing sentiment and 'rhetoricalization' of late Imperial legislation and thereby contributes to study of the ideology of the Imperial virtues. Cf. also, for the early Empire, R. Frei-Stolba, 'Inoffizielle Kaisertitulaturen', in *Museum Helveticum*, 1969, pp. 18–39.

285. Marcus Aurelius, *Meditations*, I, 14.

286. On the wearing of costumes of state by Marcus Aurelius (who refused to put them on inside the palace, except at ceremonies), see *Meditations*, I, 7, 4, which is well explained by A. S. L. Farquharson, *The Meditations of Marcus Antoninus*, vol. II (Oxford, 1968), p. 445.

287. Not that antiquity was ignorant of propaganda, far from it! Propaganda exists only if one is trying to convince (whether by good or bad arguments is immaterial), and this is something one does only with persons who have retained some degree of autonomy. Propaganda must be distinguished from expression (or ritual, if that term be preferred) and also from 'symbolic violence', that is, from the threat of possible actual violence. In real life these different aspects are intermingled. A good propagandist surrounds himself with the official insignia of power, so as to inspire, in those whom he wishes also to convince, a virtuous respect for legitimate authority. Also the intensity of an effort of propaganda, or the fervour that the authorities put into it, constitutes a veiled, symbolic threat. If the ruling power is strong enough to set up loudspeakers in every street, or if it brings religious passion into the official ideology, that warns all citizens that this power

will not tolerate the slightest blasphemy against the official dogma, and that it possesses as many tanks as loudspeakers. This being understood, propaganda, official display and symbolic threat are to be distinguished as concepts, and they are distinct in reality as well. A party which is not in power will engage solely in propaganda (or in self-expression). These criteria having been laid down, there *was* propaganda in antiquity. During the civil wars at the end of the Republic the magnates sought to win followers through a pamphlet war. During the wars of the Diadochi the successors of Alexander tried to win over the independent or autonomous Greek cities. On the other hand, when Virgil or Horace sang the praises of Octavius Augustus in power they were not making propaganda. They were expressing a love for the saviour of the nation with which their hearts were filled to overflowing (it is expression when one speaks for oneself and not for the benefit of other people). Secondly, they were in this way transmitting, whether consciously or not, the 'symbolic violence' constituted by the moralizing monarchist conformism established by the Augustan party in power. The reader of Horace is made to feel that one could not oppose this conformism without incurring ridicule and the real risks entailed in playing at dissidence. But Horace and Virgil do not undertake to *convince* their reader. At most they try to impress him, to overwhelm him, by presenting the monarchist dogma as something which is 'self-evident' and that nobody could question. They 'bear witness', as the phrase goes, and when a witness has an entire state machine behind him, his testimony overwhelms.

288. On the value of the so-called Imperial 'propaganda' some significant observations have been made by L. Wickert ('Der Prinzipat und die Freiheit', in *Symbola Coloniensia: Festschrift für Joseph Kroll*, especially p. 123). Antoninus Pius celebrated LIBERTAS on his medallions, but his successor, Marcus Aurelius, whose ideal it was to reign so as to ensure liberty to all the subjects of the Empire (*Meditations*, I, 14), never celebrated LIBERTAS. The tyrant Commodus, however, did celebrate it, on coins of gold, silver and bronze. Wickert consequently writes: 'This is not primarily propaganda aimed at influencing public opinion, but rather the solemn statement of an ideal ... It is not exactly propaganda which, in order to deceive public opinion, emphasizes those maxims of government which are the very ones least applied, but a fairly Platonic homage paid to the ideal of the principate ...' What, however, should be taken much more seriously is the monopoly of information held by the Emperor: W. Riepl, *Das Nachrichtenwesen der Altertums*, pp. 408, 435.

289. St Augustine, *Confessions*, X, 23: 'I have had experience of divers that would deceive, but not a man that would willingly be deceived ...

All which love any other thing would gladly have that to be the truth, which they so love.'

290.   *Politics*, 1314b30.

291.   J. Tondriau, 'La tryphé, philosophie royale ptolémaïque', in *Revue des études anciennes*, L (1948), p. 49; D. Levi, *Antioch Mosaic Pavements*, vol. I (Princeton, 1947), p. 206, note 41; L. Roberts, *Hellenica*, XI–XII, p. 344.

292.   Luke 7: 25.

293.   See Plutarch's *Life of Demetrius*.

294.   A. Boethius, *The Golden House of Nero* (Ann Arbor, 1960), especially pp. 108 and 127.

295.   J. Gagé, *Les Classes sociales dans l'Empire romain*, p. 197: 'There was no Imperial court in the true sense.' F. de Coulanges, *Origines du système féodal*, p. 229: the Emperor had no courtiers, only dining and travelling companions. This was indeed the custom of the great lords: they had their regular retinue of *convictores* (see K. Meister in *Gymnasium*, LVII (1960), p. 6). On the duties of these companions, see Marcus Aurelius, *Meditations*, I, 16, 8; cf. Friedländer, *Sittengeschichte*, vol. I, p. 85.

296.   Dio Cassius, LXXVII, 9 and 19; Tacitus, *Histories*, II, 61; Suetonius, *Caligula*, 20; *Historia Augusta*, 'Hadrian', 18. When Trier became a capital a Circus Maximus was built there which could rival Rome's: *Panegyrici Latini*, VII, 22, 5.

297.   See, e.g., Alföldi, *The Conversion of Constantine and Pagan Rome*, pp. 112–14; E. Stein, *Histoire du Bas-Empire*, J.-R. Palanque (ed.), vol. I, p. 127. On state-provided bread in Constantinople, see the article 'Frumentatio' in De Ruggiero's *Dizionario epigrafico*, vol. III, cols. 282–7.

298.   Dio Cassius, LII, 30.

299.   *Voyage en Syrie*, 12.

300.   I have given about thirty examples of this use of *meus*, *tuus* and *suus* in *Latomus*, 1967, pp. 742–4. To these one may add Dessau, nos. 396, 487, 5592 ('urbis suae'); *Codex Theodosii*, VIII, 5, 32 ('populi Romani nostri'); Symmachus, *Relatio*, I ('senatus amplissimus semperque vester'); Dittenberger, *Sylloge*, no. 835a ('his Greece'); L. Robert in *Comptes rendus de l'Académie des inscriptions*, 1970, p. 14 ('his universe', when speaking of the Emperor's power over the universal Empire); Dessau, no. 6090 ('per universum orbem nostrum').

301.   Alexandria: Mommsen, *Staatsrecht*, vol. II, p. 1032, note 2. Pergamum: Dittenberger, *Orientis Graeci Inscriptiones*, no. 217, note 12.

302.   On this ceremonial role played by the plebs, see Syme, 'Seianus on the Aventine', in *Hermes*, LXXXIV (1956), p. 260; cf., for the iconography, P. Veyne in *Mélanges de l'École française de Rome*, 1961, p. 256. In 356, on her solemn entry into Rome, the Empress Eusebia had

money distributed 'to the presidents of the tribes and the centurions of the people' (Julian, *Panegyric of the Empress Eusebia*, 19).

303. The plebs could not withstand professional soldiers: Tacitus, *Annals*, XIV, 61. What Rome experienced were hunger riots in which the plebs attacked the prefects of the City or of the Annona (e.g. Tacitus, *Annals*, VI, 13; Ammianus Marcellinus, XIX, 10; Symmachus, *Letters*, Seeck (ed.), in the 'Auctores Antiquissimi' of the *Monumenta Germaniae* (reprinted 1961), preface, p. lxx.

304. Tacitus, *Annals*, XIII, 18.

305. Fronto, p. 199 (van den Hout); cf. Syme, *Tacitus*, p. 41. In *Plebs and Princeps*, p. 136, Yavetz considers that the Emperors cultivated their popularity with the plebs for the sake of the support the latter could give them. However, what happened seems to me to have been less rational than this would imply.

306. The exhibitionism of the 'mad Caesars' themselves has been exaggerated. Most of the time the Emperors performed as charioteers, gladiators, hunters or actors only within their palace, in their private theatre or in the court amphitheatre (*amphitheatrum castrense*; see Hirschfeld, *Verwaltungsbeamten*, p. 314, correcting a traditional misunderstanding of Suetonius's *ludi castrenses* (*Tiberius*, 72). These shows were not open to the public. The audience consisted of the Emperor's guards and senators invited by him ('privato spectaculo', says the *Historia Augusta*, 'Heliogabalus', 22). Nero began by playing the charioteer and the actor in private. Of Commodus, Dio Cassius, LXXII, 17, says expressly that he never drove a chariot in public, that he performed as gladiator only in his palace, but that he was seen in the role of hunter both in private and in public. (On this point, see below, note 418.) Caracalla and Heliogabalus drove chariots only in private (LXXVII, 10, and LXXIX, 14). Nero was the only Emperor to drive a chariot in the Circus Maximus in Rome (Suetonius, *Nero*, 22).

307. E.g. *Historia Augusta*, 'Didius Julianus', 9 ('armis gladiatoriis exerceri'). We must distinguish between public performances and the reproach of being privately interested in popular sports: precise distinctions are vital here. In Greece it was noble to race chariots at Olympia and the *Inschriften von Olympia* (Dittenberger) show that more than one prince of the blood did this – e.g. Tiberius, before he came to the throne. But to perform in public as an actor was a different matter, even in Greece: it was something more than racing a chariot which one did not drive oneself.

308. Friedländer, in Marquardt, *Staatsverwaltung*, vol. III, pp. 490 and 491.

309. Gladiatorial combats might have become just as noble as were tournaments in a later period. Already *equites* took part in them, but public opinion remained uncertain whether this was a degrading spectacle

(which was, of course, the view taken by the satirical poets) or a noble sport; see Dio Cassius, LVI, 25, and LVII, 14. The problem was that this sport was a paid occupation followed by persons of the lowest origin (this constituted, indeed, the problem of the status of jesters and actors throughout history). There is a sharp contrast between Greece, where citizens took part in the games, and Rome, where only professionals performed (the status of actors in the theatre being problematical). This contrast is clearly noted by Tacitus, *Annals*, XIV, 20, and by Cornelius Nepos, preface to *Atticus*. Then there were the sports properly so called, which do not presuppose an audience, such as hunting, the noble sport *par excellence*. But it was convenient to engage in this in an arena, a place where shows were put on, and, for the benefit of the populace, the Emperors also organized public hunts in the arena. This was how Commodus came to descend to a public exhibition of his talents as a hunter in the arena. (Under Domitian, the Emperor and the senators whom he invited confined themselves to hunting in the private amphitheatre of Domitian's palace at Albano: Juvenal, IV, 99.)

310. During the civil war of 69 Piacenza was sacked because its magnificent amphitheatre had aroused the jealousy of the other cities: a number of facts of this kind are brought together by R. MacMullen, *Enemies of the Roman Order*, pp. 168 and 185. It was forbidden to erect public buildings without the Emperor's permission, especially if a city wanted to do this merely to keep up with a neighbouring city (*ad aemulationem alterius civitatis*), says the *Digest*, L, 10, 3. A governor writes to a Greek city that it was 'a noble and ancient city, and at the same time, through its recent constructions, in no way inferior to those which demonstrate their prosperity' (L. Robert, *Études anatoliennes*, p. 302; cf. *Digest*, I, 16, 7 pr.: 'If a governor visits a city which is neither important nor a provincial capital, he has to put up with hearing it praised, and he will not decline to listen to a public eulogy of the place, for this is a point of honour with provincials.' In his letter to the city our governor merely reproduces the terms of the eulogy of their city which the inhabitants pronounced before him). A *euergetēs* of Oxyrhynchus presents a gift to the city 'so that this city may be in no way inferior to the rest' (*Oxyrhynchus Papyri*, vol. IV, no. 705). Cf. also T. Frank, *An Economic Survey of Ancient Rome*, vol. IV, p. 809. It was therefore necessary that no other city should be able to compete with Rome: the age of the 'functional' capitals established in secondary cities had not yet arrived.

311. Tacitus, *Annals*, XIII, 53: 'quo plerumque cohibentur conatus honesti'.

312. He had to ask permission because the basilica, though erected by a

euergetēs, had none the less become a public monument. Nobody could touch it without permission from the Senate, which still bore responsibility for public buildings (Mommsen, *Staatsrecht*, vol. III, p. 1136, note 3; vol. II, pp. 1044, 1046, note 1, and 1051).

313. Tacitus, *Annals*, III, 72.

314. Augustus encouraged *viri triumphales* to embellish Rome (cf. above, note 258), as we are told by Velleius Paterculus, II, 89, reproduced almost literally by Suetonius, *Augustus*, 29. Sosius repaired or erected the temple of Apollo, Ahenobarbus that of Neptune, Munatius Plancus that of Saturn, Domitius Calvinus the Regia, Cornificius the temple of Diana. See Platner-Ashby, or L. Homo, *Rome et l'Urbanisme dans l'Antiquité*, p. 339; R. Syme, *The Roman Revolution*, pp. 141 and 402. Under the Empire building work by victorious generals came to an end, for a very good reason: the booty did not belong to the generals any more, but to the Emperor alone (E. Sander, in *Rheinisches Museum*, CI (1985), p. 184).

315. Mommsen, *Staatsrecht*, vol. I, p. 135; vol. II, pp. 854, 885; vol. III, p. 1234.

316. There is only one possible exception. Trajan seems to have allowed the 'kingmaker' Licinius Sura to build the Thermae Suranae on the Aventine, bearing his own name: Aurelius Victor, *Epitome*, XIII, 6; Dio Cassius, LXVIII, 15; cf. R. Syme, *Tacitus*, p. 35, note 5, and p. 231.

317. A monument could be dedicated to an individual, just as we dedicate a book. The Greeks dedicated buildings to the Roman *imperatores* and governors, instead of dedicating them to the gods, as had been the custom. We observe that, under the Empire, *opera publica* were dedicated exclusively to the reigning dynasty or to the Emperors in general (Dessau, no. 3976: 'Numinibus Augustis, fanum Plutonis posuerunt') and I have interpreted a passage in the *Digest* in this sense (*Latomus*, 1967, p. 746, note 1); see Mommsen, *Staatsrecht*, vol. II, p. 950. When we see, in Rome under the Empire, a chapel consecrated to the *clarissimus* who built it (Dessau, no. 1203), we can confidently conclude that this was a private place of worship. We should mention the almost exceptional case of the library at Ephesus, dedicated to the consul Ti. Julius Celsus Polemianus: his name appears in the accusative form in the inscription on the building, which housed his statue and those of his Virtues and was 'like a vast monument in his honour': J. Keil in *Forschungen in Ephesos*, second edn, vol. V, (Oesterr. Archäol. Institut, 1953), I, p. 62.

318. Syracuse had celebrated 'Marcellia' and 'Verria', but could do so no longer under the Empire: see Nilsson, *Gesch. griech. Religion*, second edn, vol. II, p. 38; L. Robert, *Hellenica*, II, p. 38; Syme, *The Roman Revolution*, pp. 405, 473; id., *Tacitus*, p. 513. See also note 251.

319. Dio Cassius, LIII, 24; Velleius Paterculus, II, 92; R. Syme, *The Roman Revolution*, pp. 371, 402.

320. Tacitus, *Histories*, IV, 9 (Mommsen, *Staatsrecht*, vol. II, p. 950, note 1, and vol. III, p. 1145, note 2).

321. In the later Empire Rome was municipalized. The Senate was thenceforth merely equivalent to a council of decurions, and relations between the prefect of the City and the Senate were those of a *curator civitatis* with the local *curia*. See E. Stein, *Histoire du Bas-Empire*, vol. I, p. 121; A. H. M. Jones, *The Later Roman Empire*, vol. II, p. 687, and, for the shows, p. 537. In the fourth century the public buildings in Rome bore the name of the city's prefect, the names of the Emperor and the Senate being added only if they had contributed to their cost (A. Chastagnol, *La Préfecture urbaine à Rome au Bas-Empire*, p. 353). Similarly, in the municipal towns, the *opera publica* bore the name of the *curator civitatis*. Moreover, the prefect of the City often took to assuming the honorific title of *patronus*: for the first time, Rome had *patroni* like the other cities. Finally, in the fourth century ordinary private persons obtained the right to build in Rome. Chastagnol (*Fastes des préfets de la Ville*, p. 16) quotes a list of senators who subscribed to erect a building. The *Codex Theodosii*, XVI, 1, 11, allows anyone the right to repair Rome's buildings. As for the baths of Neratius Cerialis (Dessau, nos. 1245–6), I do not know whether they were public or private.

322. The last building erected in Rome, before the fourth century, by someone other than the Emperor or the Senate, was doubtless the theatre of Balbus, or else the Porticus Vipsaniae, built by Agrippa's sister. By virtue of the dyarchy, the Senate, in its own name and that of the people (hence the formula SPQR, which first appears under the Empire: Mommsen, *Staatsrecht*, vol. III, p. 1257), raised monuments in Rome to the glory of the Emperors: temples of Vespasian and Titus (*CIL*, VI, 938), arch of Titus (VI, 945), Trajan's column (VI, 960), arch of Septimius Severus (VI, 31230), arch of Constantine (VI, 1139) – as if some rule of modesty prevented the Emperors from honouring themselves. Apart from monuments of this kind, the Senate's authority was reduced to erecting statues on public land (*Staatsrecht*, vol. III, p. 1185), even on that of the Imperial forums (*Staatsrecht*, vol. I, p. 450; also Tacitus, *Annals*, XV, 72; cf. Dessau, no. 273; Suetonius, *Vitellius*, 3, 1), and to having them removed (*Staatsrecht*, vol. III, p. 1190). On the duality of the *curator operum publicorum* and the *procurator operum publicorum*, see Hirschfeld, *Verwaltungsbeamten*, pp. 265–72, and Pflaum, *Carrières procuratoriennes équestres*, vol. II, p. 600.

323. Friedländer, in Marquardt, *Staatsverwaltung*, vol. III, p. 490.

324. While respecting the law which forbade a freedman to give *munera*

without special permission and the rules which fixed a maximum for expenditure on gladiators. Furthermore, provincial governors, whether senators or *equites*, had no right to give *munera* (Tacitus, *Annals*, XIII, 31: cf. Mommsen, *Epigraphische Schriften*, vol. I, p. 523). They would have ruined the people under their administration by providing shows at the expense of the latter and excusing themselves, as a result of these shows, for plundering them.

325. Josephus, *Jewish Antiquities*, XVI, 128. Unless we are to understand that Herod gave the money to Augustus to distribute himself.

326. Hence the *Digest* mentions legacies left to cities, but never refers to a case of a legacy to the Roman people.

327. Apart from the dues paid by the *corporati*, Rome knew no *munera civilia* except the *tutelae*. Consequently, when the *Historia Augusta* presents as a *munus* the Senate's legations to the Emperor (who alone could receive them: *Staatsrecht*, vol. II, p. 680), we must conclude that, once more, the *Historia Augusta* is transposing to the third century the institutions of the fourth ('The Three Gordians', 32). On senatorial *immunitas*, see E. Kuhn, *Die städtische und bürgerliche Verfassung des römischen Reichs*, vol. I (1864; Scientia Verlag, Aalen, reprinted 1968), pp. 223–4.

328. Dio Cassius, LIV, 2; cf. Hirschfeld, *Verwaltungsbeamten*, p. 286.

329. On the banquets which, during certain festivals, the senators gave to the plebs or to their clients, see, e.g., Marquardt, *Privatleben*, p. 208.

330. No doubt the feast (*recta cena*) was replaced by a distribution of *sportulae* (cf. Suetonius, *Nero*, 16: 'publicae cenae ad sportulas redactae').

331. Claudius renewed this ban (Dio Cassius, LX, 5).

332. In the later Empire the patrimony of the *curiales*, like that of the decurions, could not leave the *curia*. Recorded in the public registers, it was frozen (*Codex Theodosii*, VI, 2, 8) and was in pledge to the *curia* (C. Lécrivain, *Le Sénat romain depuis Dioclétien*, p. 86).

333. On the expenditure and honorary sums of the praetors and consuls of the later Empire for their games (unless, *pro ludis*, they repaired aqueducts), see the *Codex Theodosii*, VI, 4, *passim*; *Codex Justiniani*, XII, 3, 2 (cf. R. Delbrück, *Consulardiptychen*, Textband, p. 68). In general, see E. Kuhn, *Die städtische und bürgerliche Verfassung*, vol. I, pp. 206–7. For the sumptuosities of Symmachus's son when he provided shows (Symmachus, *Letters*, IV, 8, 3; Olympiodorus, fragment 44), see A. Chastagnol in *Historia-Augusta Colloquium 1964–5*, p. 62; Friedländer, *Sittengeschichte*, vol. II, p. 41; Alföldi, *Kontorniaten*, p. 40.

334. Mommsen, *Staatsrecht*, vol. III, p. 900, denies in general the existence of an honorary sum for the magistracies in Rome even under the early Empire. The auctioning of priesthoods by Caligula (Suetonius,

Caligula, 22; cf. Dio Cassius, LIX, 28) recalls the selling of priesthoods in the Hellenistic epoch, mentioned in chapter II.

335. Dio Cassius, LIV, 17; but cf. LV, 31.

336. Id., LX, 6.

337. See especially Suetonius, *Augustus*, 30, and Tibullus, I, 7, 57–62; R. Syme, *The Roman Revolution*, p. 402. The Emperor also had roads repaired himself: Mommsen, *Staatsrecht*, vol. III, p. 1146, note 1.

338. Dio Cassius, LIII, 23.

339. Suetonius, *Claudius*, 24; Mommsen, *Staatsrecht*, vol. II, p. 534; cf. Tacitus, *Annals*, XI, 22, and XIII, 5; Suetonius, *Domitian*, 4, and *Vita Lucani*, 2, 10; Friedländer in Marquardt, *Staatsverwaltung*, vol. III, p. 487. Cf. Veyne in *Revue de philologie*, 1975, p. 92, note 1.

340. *De Aquae Ductu*, 3, 2.

341. Suetonius, *Claudius*, 9. Turning to ordinary officials of very low rank, the inscription *CIL*, XIV, 4012 (Dessau, no. 5387) presents a difficulty. An *accensus velatus* is here said to be *immunis*. Should we believe, with Mommsen (*Staatsrecht*, vol. III, p. 289, note 3), that he was exempted from paying the honorary sum for entry upon his *decuria*? Or does it refer to an immunity from the *munera* of Ostia or of the *corporati* of Rome (*Fragmenta Vaticana*, 138, quoted by Dessau)?

342. Suetonius, *Augustus*, 57; *Caligula*, 42; Dessau, nos. 92, 93, 99; Dio Cassius, XLVIII, 34; LIV, 30; LV, 26. For Augustus's will see especially Suetonius, *Augustus*, 101. Compare the other Imperial wills known to us (I do not speak here of the ones to be found in the *Historia Augusta*): those of Tiberius (Suetonius, *Tiberius*, 76), Caligula (*Caligula*, 24) and Claudius (*Claudius*, 44). On the New Year gifts from the people to their Emperor, see the ethnographical comparisons of M. Nilsson, *Opuscula Minora Selecta*, vol. I, p. 274.

343. Dio Cassius, LXXIX, 9.

344. Dessau, no. 286: See 'liberalitate optimi principis'.

345. Suetonius, *Caligula*, 42. See Friedländer, *Sittengeschichte*, vol. I, p. 90. Cf. Dio Cassius, LXXII, 16 (Mommsen, *Staatsrecht*, vol. III, p. 900).

346. Dio Cassius, LIV, 30 and 35. A *euergetēs* honoured by the award of a statue shows tact if he uses the public funds destined for this purpose to set up a statue of a god, or of the Emperor, rather than his own effigy. This explains the epigram in the *Greek Anthology*, XVI, 267, which the editors compare with Pliny, *Letters*, I, 17. More generally, one had always to make reciprocal gifts and take care not to be left behind in this ritual. There is an example in the *History of Apollonius of Tyre*, chapter 10, which I mentioned in note 241. Fleeing from the king of Antioch, whose daughter he has seduced, Apollonius lands at Tarsus, which is suffering from famine. Apollonius makes a public speech of pollicitation to the city: if the city will protect him, he will

supply it with 100,000 bushels of corn at 8 *asses* (*octo aeris*) the bushel. The city agrees and buys the corn at this low price (in Greek it would be said that Apollonius has made a *paraprasis*): 'but Apollonius, not wishing to lose his royal dignity and be considered a merchant rather than a donor, gave the money back to the city, for its own use' (*utilitati*; cf. Dessau, no. 6252: 'voluptatibus et utilitatibus populi plurima contulit'). However, the city does not wish to be found wanting in this matter of gifts, and so it uses the money returned by the *euergetēs* to erect in the forum a statue of Apollonius in a chariot.

347. D. van Berchem's work, *Les Distributions de blé et d'argent à la plèbe romaine sous l'Empire* (Geneva University thesis, 1939), pp. 119–76, renders it unnecessary to say much about the *congiaria*.

348. Philostratus, *Heroicus*, I, 5 (661; p. 129 (Kayser)).

349. On free corn and the *annona* see above, section 6 of chapter III. On corn as liberality, see Kloft, *Liberalitas Principis*, pp. 88–95. On the much discussed problem of the clients of the Roman plebs, see D. van Berchem in *Rendiconti della Pontificia Accademia*, XVIII (1941–2), pp. 183–90, on the inscription *CIL*, VI, 32098f – or quite simply Mommsen, *Staatsrecht*, vol. III, p. 444, note 4; cf. p. 173, note 4, and p. 461.

350. The word *factio* meant the colours or teams of charioteers, the 'stables' and also the theatrical companies – not the popular clubs of supporters and fans of these factions, for which the word was *populus* or *pars*. This was established by A. Maricq, 'Factions du cirque et partis populaires', in *Académie royale de Belgique, Bulletin de la classe des Lettres*, XXXVI (1950), especially pp. 400–402.

351. This same proselytism on the part of the *lazzaroni* made them enthusiasts for palace revolutions (Tacitus, *Histories*, I, 35 and 36). It would be wrong to identify this fervour of anarchic mobs, for and against high-ranking personages, with the revolutionary fervour of modern mobs: Tacitus, *Annals*, XIV, 61, talks rather of clientage.

352. E.g. a pantomime actor, the first Pylades of that name, exiled by Augustus (Dio Cassius, LIV, 17; Suetonius, *Tiberius*, 37). The biographer of Hadrian mentions as a curious fact that this Emperor never exiled an actor or a charioteer. For the fourth century, see Ammianus Marcellinus, XV, 7, 2.

353. Tacitus, *Annals*, XIII, 25: 'gravioris motus terrore'.

354. Besides the Nika riot, the civil war of 609–10 is said to have been a war between the Blues and the Greens. But that was due to the very special organization of the Hippodrome in Byzantium, and no conclusion can be drawn from it regarding the *factiones* and clubs of the early Empire.

355. This seems to me to be the real point of the question, and in such a

matter subtle distinctions are all-important. The factions were not political parties in disguise, nor were they associations political in part (by virtue of the fact that associations generally fulfil more than a single function): they merely had different status values. Liking polo more than football or buying a record-player rather than a TV set is not a disguised expression of political opinion, either. One might even be tempted to assert that, in the early Empire, the factions bore no permanent *political* colouring. It was simply that when an Emperor was said to favour the Greens, the opposition would shout, 'Down with the Greens!' and vice versa, just as they would boo a particular actor if the Emperor showed a liking for him. Supporting this scepticism is the fact that Vitellius and Caracalla, whom one would have presumed to be for the Greens, the popular faction, supported the Blues. Nevertheless, I do think that the Blues and the Greens bore a permanent status association. The Blues were the favourite stable of the elite, and the Emperor's personal sympathies did not automatically make them the official team or the opposition team. My justification is that in the *Satyricon*, 70, 10, Trimalchio, master of all forms of elegance, is for the Blues and reproaches his guests, who are men of less social pretension, for being supporters of the Greens (this cannot be a matter of chance but, in Petronius's writing, an *ethos*, a characteristic feature). So we can sum up as follows: there were two choices and these were taken up unevenly, but without there being any politico-social implication in this circumstance. Moreover, the upper class and the Emperors were divided between these two choices. The choice one made was more a matter of individual temperament than of class standing. (There was a time when football and tennis, bourbon and scotch, television and record-players were unevenly favoured; but, within the upper class itself, choices made between them remained largely individual.) From the way that Marcus Aurelius, *Meditations*, I, 5, speaks of the Greens and the Blues we might well suppose that he was as much a supporter of the one faction as of the other. See, on all this, the very different positions taken up by R. MacMullen, *Enemies of the Roman Order*, p. 170, and R. Goossens in *Byzantion*, 1939 (the latter seems to me to exaggerate seriously). On the Circus factions in Byzantium itself, regarding the well-known thesis of Manijlovic on their politico-social significance, one should now consult A. Cameron, *Porphyrius the Charioteer* (Oxford, 1973), pp. 232–9. He suggests that the problem is almost as complicated and subtle as that of the causes of the revolution of May 1968 in France, arouses almost as much personal passion among historians, and inspires the writing of almost as much nonsense. But what is important for us is that Rome, even in the fourth century, was not Byzantium. Brawls did not arise solely from the rivalry between the Blues and Greens but also from differing attitudes to a particular gladiator or actor. Apart from the sporting or artistic proselytism which remains their chief explanation, they assumed political colouring only occasionally and in a secondary way (see the next two notes). We could say the same of the *claque* at the theatre and the opera in the eighteenth century or under the Napoleonic Empire: zeal for art was sufficient to make men come to blows, but sometimes political passion also played a part in it.

356. Suetonius, *Caligula*, 27.

357. Id., *Vitellius*, 14. Suetonius mentions this behaviour and that of Caligula as the bizarre conduct of tyrants. This means that partisan feeling did sometimes lead people to criticize an actor or an entire show for purely political reasons, but that such cases remained sufficiently incidental for the ruling power to close its eyes to these fringe expressions of partisanry. The politicization of the shows did not go so far as to oblige the Emperor to sacrifice to the maintenance of order two sacrosanct principles. One was that the Emperor placed himself at the service of the citizens when he arranged games for their entertainment (he addressed them as 'My masters', as we shall see): he was their supplier, and everyone has the right to be dissatisfied with a supplier (cf. Petronius, *Satyricon*, 45, 13). The other principle was that the Roman people, at the Circus or at shows, had the right to free speech (*libertas*, Ammianus Marcellinus, XVI, 10, 13) and it was they who judged each performer or each champion: the president had only to bow to their decision. In general, the shows constituted a festival, a leisure activity: the 'Circus' is the opposite of politics. Caligula and Vitellius were doubly odious, because they 'politicized' the Circus and because they refused to the public the right possessed by every audience not to be satisfied with what is offered to it.

358. Tacitus, *Histories*, I, 4. On this phrase, see Friedländer, *Sittengeschichte*, vol. I, p. 223 (Eng. trans., vol. I, p. 195); R. Syme, *The Roman Revolution*, p. 404, note 5; Z. Yavetz, *Plebs and Princeps* (Oxford, 1969), p. 152; and the notable article by R. Marache, 'La revendication sociale chez Martial et Juvénal', in *Rivista di cultura classica e medioevale*, III (1961), especially p. 41. The same splitting of the plebs into two sides happened when the Flavians attacked Vitellius. While one section of the plebs took up arms to defend Vitellius (Tacitus, *Histories*, III, 58, 69, 79–80; cf. Suetonius, *Nero*, 44), the grandees armed their men against him (*Histories*, III, 64). Again, when the mob sided with Octavia against Poppaea, the latter's supporters declared that this mob was not the plebs but merely the private clientage of the Empress (Tacitus, *Annals*, XIV, 61).

359. An original view of the matter will be found in I. Hahn, 'Zur poli-
tischen Rolle der Plebs unter dem Prinzipat', in *Die Rolle der Plebs im
spätrömischen Reich* (Akademie Verlag, Berlin, 1969), p. 49. In the
synthesis I am attempting I rely not so much on the documents (they
are few, and not such as to be of great assistance with regard to
economics or geography) as on resemblances and comparisons. Indeed,
that would also apply to any other synthesis one might attempt where
this question is concerned.

360. Suetonius, *Vespasian*, 18.

361. Fronto, p. 127 (van den Hout).

362. Marquardt, *Privatleben*, vol. I, pp. 204–12; Friedländer, *Sittengeschichte*,
vol. I, pp. 223–32. In some cases the patron housed his clients rent-free
(*Digest*, IX, 3, 5, 1 and XXXIII, 9, 3, 6).

363. Tacitus, *Annals*, XIII, 44, quoted by P. Lacombe, *La Famille dans la
société romaine* (Bibliothèque anthropologique, vol. VII, Paris, 1889),
p. 308 – an opportunity here to recommend warmly this admirable
work, which was considerably before its time, was underrated, and
then forgotten when its hour came round.

364. On its rates of payment, see Marquardt, *Privatleben*, vol. I, p. 211,
note 7.

365. On the poets, see the article by Marache mentioned in note 358.

366. See, e.g., Tacitus, *Histories*, III, 66 (Vespasian as former client of
Vitellius).

367. Trimalchio's treasurer-paymaster speaks of a garment which one of
his own clients has given him for his birthday (*Satyricon*, 30, 11). A
freedman says in his epitaph: 'I had many *clientes*' (*CIL*, VI, 21975).

368. *Digest*, XI, 3, 1, 5: a slave 'in spectaculis nimius vel seditiosus'.

369. When Commodus fought wild animals in the arena it was best for the
senators not to show lack of appreciation of the show. Dio Cassius,
LXXII, 20–21.

370. Pliny, *Letters*, IX, 6.

371. On Alexandria, see Polybius, XXXIV, 14.

372. On 'the Roman authorities' in Greek inscriptions, see L. Robert, *Études
anatoliennes*, p. 51 and note 2.

373. R. Aron, *Études politiques* (Gallimard, 1972), p. 156.

374. Along these main lines the following works complement each other:
Friedländer in Marquardt, *Staatsverwaltung*, vol. III, pp. 482–7 and
503; Hirschfeld, *Verwaltungsbeamten*, pp. 285–7; Mommsen, *Staatsrecht*,
index, under 'Spiele', and *Epigraphische Schriften*, vol. I, p. 509. The
public games and *munera* must not be confused with the court shows
which the Emperor organized in his palace. When Caligula and Nero
acted as charioteers this doubtless happened within their court (Marquardt, vol. III, p. 490).

375. The earliest example is in Minucius Felix, *Octavius*, 37, 11. In the life of Hadrian in the *Historia Augusta* we find both *gladiatorium munus* (7, 12) and *ludi gladiatorii* (9, 9). This is an indication of a late rewriting; in the life of Trebonianus Gallus, 3, 7, we find *ludos gladiatorios*. However, in 357 the *Codex Theodosii* still has *gladiatorium munus* (15, 12, 2). See Wissowa, *Religion und Kultus*, p. 465, note 9.

376. On the duration of the games, see Friedländer, *Sittengeschichte*, vol. II, p. 13 (Eng. trans. vol. II, p. 11); H. Stern, *Le Calendrier de 354* (Geuthner, 1953), p. 70.

377. L. Vidman, 'Fasti Ostienses', in *Rozpravy Československé Akademie Ved.*, LXVII (1957), fasc. 6, years 108 and 112.

378. On *praesidere*, see Mommsen, *Staatsrecht*, vol. I, pp. 402 and 407; vol. II, p. 824. It is clear that the organizer of the games, who 'produces' them (*edere*), is the one who presides at them (*praesidere*) when the Emperor is not there (cf. Suetonius, *Augustus*, 45: 'suam vicem ... praesidendo'). *Edere* and *praesidere* are used synonymously in Tacitus, *Annals*, III, 64.

379. Suetonius, *Tiberius*, 47: but cf. Dio Cassius, LVII, 11, and cf. *Historia Augusta*, 'Hadrian', 8, 2.

380. This is a hotly disputed question. See Alföldi, *Monarchische Repräsentation*, p. 160, and J. Gagé, *Les Classes sociales dans l'Empire romain*, second edn (Payot, 1971), p. 203. Many facts are assembled by T. Bollinger, *Theatralis Licentia, die Publikumsdemonstrationen an den öffentlichen Spielen* (Schellenberg, Winterthur, 1969), pp. 74–7. I will mention three problems only. (1) We need to know whether the *pulvinar* of Augustus at the Circus (*Res Gestae*, 19, 1, and appendix 2) was the sanctuary where the images carried in the *pompa circensis* were deposited, or was the Imperial box. It is certain that, in the early Empire, this box was merely a box. The Emperor showed himself to his subjects by coming to the front of it, or else withdrew to the back, behind curtains. Could we not make a distinction between, on the one hand, the *pulvinar ad Circum*, a sanctuary so called on account of the divan on which the images of the *pompa* were deposited, and on the other a *pulvinar* or divan of honour on which the Emperor and his family took their seats (Suetonius, *Claudius*, 4) and which was installed in the Imperial box (which was not a sanctuary) at the Circus? (2) Was the box at the Circus in Constantinople a reproduction of the Imperial box in Rome? See A. Piganiol in *Byzantion*, 1936, p. 383. (3) Where was the box of the author of the games? The place of honour was in front of where the author sat, *contra munerarium*, in the terms of an honorific decree of Cumae studied by A. Degrassi, *Scritti varî*, vol. I, p. 480. We can relate to this an instance of the pride of the tribune Amphilochus, who, in the Circus of Antioch, took up a position

opposite the Imperial box, *ex adverso imperatoris* (Ammianus Marcellinus, XXI, 6, 3).

381. Phaedrus, *Fables*, V, 5 (fable 100): 'Erat facturus ludos quidam nobilis.' ⸮

382. 'Laetare, incolumis Roma salvo principe', in Phaedrus. The hero of this tale is known to us, his epitaph having been found (Dessau, no. 5239). Bücheler was mistaken in thinking that these must have been extraordinary *ludi* held for Augustus's health: at all shows the audience invariably wished good health to the Emperor (Dio Cassius, LXXII, 2). Cf. in the Acts of the Arval Brothers, acclamations such as 'imperator Augustus, ex cujus incolumitate omnium salus constat'; Dessau, no. 451: 'te salvo, salvi et securi sumus'; *CIL*, IV, 1074 (Pompeii graffito): 'vobis salvis, felices sumus perpetuo'.

383. Alföldi, *Monarchische Repräsentation*, pp. 79–84.

384. A. Graber, *L'Empereur dans l'art byzantin* (Paris, 1936), pp. 144–7.

385. Kloft, *Liberalitas Principis*, pp. 99–101; R. Brilliant, *Gesture and Rank in Roman Art*, pp. 170–73. Hence the occasional discussions, when a *congiarium* was being distributed, between one of the beneficiaries and the Emperor himself: 'Hermeneumata pseudodositheana', in Goetz, *Corpus Glossariorum Latinorum*, vol. III, p. 36.

386. Josephus, *Jewish Antiquities*, XIX, 1, 13. On *missilia* and *sparsiones*, see Friedländer, *Sittengeschichte*, vol. II, p. 17; Regling in Pauly-Wissowa, vol. V, 1, col. 852, under 'Missilia'; H. Stern, *Le Calendrier de 354*, p. 152.

387. Dio Cassius, LX, 17.

388. Id., LXXII, 13.

389. Id., LXXIII, 17: 'As for the lion-skin and club . . . in the amphitheatres they were placed on a gilded chair, whether [Commodus] was present or not.' The novelty here seems to me to be not that the Imperial insignia were placed on the empty throne (which was perfectly normal), but that these insignia were a club and a lion-skin, which made the living Emperor a new Hercules. Ceremonial and iconographic use of an empty throne on which were placed the insignia of the ruler was quite commonplace: J. W. Salomonson, *Chair, Scepter and Wreath: historical aspects of their representation* (Groningen University thesis, 1956). There was no 'funerary symbolism' in this, except in a secondary way; it was a real feature of the ceremonial.

390. It was considered shrewd and praiseworthy for a great personage to affect to share the popular enthusiasm for shows; such conduct was *popularis* (Tacitus, *Histories*, II, 91).

391. Tacitus, *Histories*, I, 72; in the towns of Asia Minor in the Imperial epoch the theatre played the same role.

392. Alföldi, *Monarchische Repräsentation*, pp. 64–5. Other references in Z. Yavetz, *Plebs and Princeps*, p. 98; cf. Suetonius, *Claudius*, 21.

393. Suetonius, *Augustus*, 45.
394. Id., *Domitian*, 4; cf. *Historia Augusta*, 'Hadrian', 19, 6: 'histriones aulicos publicavit'.
395. This emerges from Pliny, *Letters*, VI, 5, 5: 'propitium Caesarem, ut in ludicro, precabuntur'; the formula is familiar in inscriptions: Dessau, no. 5084a ('habeas propitium Caesarem') and no. 2610; *CIL*, VI, 632 and 9223; XI, 8; XIV, 2163.
396. On political demonstrations at shows, see Friedländer, *Sittengeschichte*, vol. II, p. 7; R. MacMullen, *Enemies of the Roman Order*, with many references and a very subtle account; Yavetz, *Plebs and Princeps*, pp. 18–24; T. Bollinger, *Theatralis Licentia* (see note 380); also *Digest*, XI, 3, 1, 5: a slave 'in spectaculis nimius vel seditiosus'.
397. Plutarch, *Life of Galba*, 17.
398. Tacitus, *Annals*, VI, 13.
399. Josephus, *Jewish Antiquities*, XIX, 1, 4.
400. Dio Cassius, LXXV, 4. The historian is astonished at the (always rather surprising) fact that a crowd of demonstrators come to agree on shouting the same thing at the same time. It is often hard to make out, in the ancient texts which report what acclamations saluted a certain great personage and how many times they were repeated, whether the acclamations were spontaneous (so that the number might be significant, just as we note how many times a singer is 'recalled' to receive applause) or were slogans dictated by the authorities. In Dio Cassius the acclamations are dictated (LXXII, 20). See Alföldi, *Monarchische Repräsentation*, pp. 79–87; E. Peterson, *Heis Theos: epigraphische, formgeschichtliche und religionsgeschichtliche Untersuchungen* (Göttingen, 1926), pp. 141–5. Even student audiences applauded their teachers of rhetoric with stereotyped acclamations: Philostratus, *Lives of the Sophists*, II, 24, pp. 270, 282 and 286 of the Wright edition (Loeb). Tacitus, *Annals*, XVI, 4: 'certis modis plausuque composito'.
401. Suetonius, *Augustus*, 45.
402. Tacitus, *Annals*, I, 54.
403. If we are to believe the *Historia Augusta*, 'Marcus Aurelius', 4, 1; cf. Friedländer, *Sittengeschichte*, vol. II, pp. 4–5.
404. Marcus Aurelius, *Meditations*, VI, 46.
405. Ibid., I, 16, 25: on the threefold possibility of shows, buildings or *congiaria*, cf. Syme, *Tacitus*, p. 226.
406. *Meditations*, I, 16, 15; the allusion to shows seems clear to me and the passage ought to be commented on in that sense.
407. Zosimus, III, 11, 4–5. Julian took his revenge by writing the *Misopogon* (see especially chapters 4, 5 and 9 of that work). This Emperor had been obliged to give up his plan of reforming the shows (*Letters*, 89 (Bidez, 304bc)).

408. *Meditations*, I, 16, 13; cf. I, 17, 5, and I, 7, 4.

409. *Esprit des Lois*, 12, 27 (Eng. trans., *The Spirit of Laws*, vol. I (1897), p. 220).

410. Ammianus Marcellinus, XVI, 20, 13. Ammianus, who 'spoke Greek in Latin', because for him Latin was a foreign language (Norden, *Kunstprosa*, p. 647), writes of 'ludi equestres' because he thinks in Greek (*agōn hippikos*). He means the *Circenses*.

411. Plutarch, *Life of Dio*, 37; cf. chapters 4, 6, 28 (end), 29, 34. Marcus Aurelius had learnt to admire Dio (*Meditations*, I, 14, 2).

412. *Meditations*, I, 14, 2. Liberty, in the primary sense of the word, thus means direct democracy, as against an absence of reciprocity between rulers and ruled. Under the Empire, however, people took a 'sour grapes' view of this liberty. Men were too corrupt, the territory of the Empire was too vast, and a sovereign was needed, for men had become incapable of self-discipline. This is Tacitus's main idea, but we come upon it everywhere, e.g. in Longinus, *On the Sublime*, 44, 10 (and one cannot quote against this 44, 5, where the writer is really talking about the 'equitable' hegemony of Rome over Greece). On liberty as freedom of speech, see Polybius, IV, 31, 4; cf. II, 38, 6; V, 9, 4; VII, 10, 1; Syme, *Tacitus*, p. 558; C. Wirszubski, *Libertas as a Political Idea at Rome* (Cambridge, 1960); MacMullen, *Enemies of the Roman Order*, p. 63. Suetonius, *Tiberius*, 28: 'He ... would often say that liberty to speak and think [*mentem*] as one pleases is the test of a free country'; and in the Senate he once said (29): 'You will, I hope, forgive me if I trespass on my rights as a senator by speaking rather more plainly than I should [*libertas*].'

413. W. Hennis, *Politik als praktische Wissenschaft* (Piper, 1968), p. 65: 'Rat und Beratung im modernen Staat'.

414. Marcus Aurelius, *Meditations*, V, 30, 1.

415. Ibid., I, 6, 4; I, 16, 4; VI, 30, 13.

416. W. Hennis, *Politik und praktische Philosophie* (Luchterhand, 1963), p. 89: 'Topik und Politik'. In general, on topic, see W. Krauss, *Operations Research, ein Instrument der Unternehmensführung* (Verlag Moderne Industrie, 1970), p. 160: 'The two great methods of natural science, topic and Cartesianism'.

417. Dio Cassius, LXXIII, 20–21. On Commodus as hunter, cf. J. Aymard, *Essai sur les chasses romaines* (De Boccard, 1951), pp. 537–56. On acclamations, see L. Robert, *Études épigraphiques et philologiques*, p. 111, note 2. Caracalla, too, killed wild beasts in the arena: Dio Cassius, LXXVII, 6.

418. Where did this scene take place? I think that it was indeed in Rome, at a public show (the people were sitting on the steps). Dio speaks of an amphitheatre, without further definition. This might be the

amphitheatrum castrense, the Emperor's private arena (see above, note 306), or the arena at Lanuvium (for Commodus did fight in that arena, according to the *Historia Augusta*, 'Commodus', 8, 5; Commodus had a house at Lanuvium, where he was born; have we here another private arena?), But if the 'amphitheatre' the historian mentions was not the one in Rome, he would undoubtedly have said so. Besides, the people were there.

419. M. Weber, *Economy and Society*, vol. I, pp. 231–2.

420. On the conflict between eunuchs and mandarins, see Weber, *Religionssoziologie*, vol. I, p. 427.

421. J. Crook, *Consilium Principis* (Cambridge, 1955). Two recent documents: Seston and Euzénnat in *Comptes rendus de l'Académie des inscriptions*, 1971, p. 468; J. H. Oliver, 'The sacred gerusia and the emperor's Consilium', in *Hesperia*, XXXVI (1967), p. 331.

422. Polybius, V, 34.

423. Id., VI, 7; on Macedonian freedom of speech, V, 27, 6.

424. Hauriou, *Traité de droit administratif*, 1919 edn, p. 25.

425. J. Béranger, *Recherches sur l'aspect idéologique du principat*, pp. 137–69. We find this also in Russia (A. Besançon, *Le Tsarévitch immolé*, p. 103), among the tyrants of Sicily (Polybius, VII, 8, 5) and elsewhere (Veyne in *Latomus*, XXI (1962), p. 62).

426. On the lack of a rule of hereditary succession in Rome, owing to the meritocratic ideology, see L. Wickert, 'Princeps und Basileus', in *Klio*, XVIII (1943), p. 10.

427. Ammianus Marcellinus, XIX, 12, 1, and 21, 16, 8. On the use of torture, in connection with this passage, see Mommsen, *Strafrecht*, p. 407, note 4.

428. For the good Emperors, even the best of them, were no less ritually acclaimed than the bad: see Pliny, *Panegyricus*, 2, 7–8.

429. Suetonius, *Tiberius*, 30: never, even under the Republic, had the Senate been, in theory, so powerful as it was under Tiberius.

430. Tacitus, *Annals*, II, 87; cf. I, 72; Syme, *Tacitus*, p. 427.

431. Tacitus, *Annals*, XIII, 49.

432. Some stories told by Seneca, *De Ira*, I, 18 or II, 6, are thought-provoking, as is the account of a violent outburst by Hadrian given in Galen, *De Animi Affectuum Curatione*, vol. V, p. 17 (Kühn).

433. *Meditations*, I, 14, 2.

434. We are surprised to find Nero's portrait on one of the contorniate medallions on which the senatorial aristocracy displayed those ideals that it wished to popularize, whether this aristocracy was pagan or Christian (following the well-conceived finishing touch given by Santo Mazzarino to the thesis set forth in Alföldi's *magnum opus*; see Mazzarino, 'La propaganda senatoriale nel tardo impero', in *Doxa*,

IV (1951), p. 140). An Emperor is not loved because he gives games, but to the extent that these games are a sign of his favourable attitude to the plebs; 'as though by some sixth sense, the urban plebs preferred one bestower of largess to another. The significance of this "sixth" sense – which Tacitus calls *inanis favor* – is very obscure,' but of its existence there can be no doubt, writes Z. Yavetz, *Plebs and Princeps*, p. 43. In fact, Trajan, a 'good' (pro-senatorial) Emperor, left behind no fond memory among the plebs, despite his splendid games.

435. Josephus, *Jewish Antiquities*, XIX, 3 (2), 3.

436. Yavetz, *Plebs and Princeps*, pp. 114–16, has guessed that they liked this, even though the sources to which he refers do not say so. Pliny, *Letters*, IX, 13, 21, mentions 'that reproach which was thrown upon the Senate by the other orders of citizens, that while severe towards the rest of the community, it let its own members escape its justice by a sort of mutual connivance'.

437. Mommsen, *Strafrecht*, p. 350, note 2, and p. 414, notes 6 and 8. Josephus, *Jewish Antiquities*, XIX, 1, 2 (cf. XIX, 1, 16) speaks of 'doulocracy', rule by slaves. Accusation by a slave was no less acceptable, in trials concerning lese-majesty, than evidence given by one.

438. Virgil, *Aeneid*, VI, 613 ('dominorum fallere dextras', with Norden's note); a slave revolt is an attack upon a personal relationship, not upon the social order. Four verses earlier Virgil has spoken of persons who killed their father, cheated their client, hated their brother or were adulterers.

439. In hell, says Lucian, the rich will bear the burdens of the poor for 25,000 years. On the theme of the social world turned upside down, see Bolkestein, *Wohltätigkeit und Armenpflege*, p. 475; S. Luria, 'Die Ersten werden die Letzten sein: zur "sozialen Revolution" im Altertum', in *Klio*, XXII (1929), p. 405.

440. Josephus, *Jewish Antiquities*, XIX, 1, 13; Suetonius, *Caligula*, 26; on the freedom of shows established by Caligula, see Bollinger, *Theatralis Licentia*, p. 18. D. van Berchem, *Distributions de blé et d'argent*, p. 62: 'The audience at the games ought to represent a systematically arranged picture of Roman society.' The second Africanus made himself unpopular by assigning reserved seats to the Senate (Valerius Maximus, IV, 5, 1, and II, 4, 3). For reservation of seats, see Mommsen, *Staatsrecht*, vol. I, p. 406; vol. III, pp. 519 and 893.

441. This anti-Aristotelian tradition is familiar from many stories told by Aelianus, and from Polybius, I, 28, 4; XII, 24, 2.

442. Athenaeus, XII, 547e; Wilamowitz, *Antigonos von Karystos* (Wiss. Buchgesellschaft, reprinted 1967), p. 263, cf. 83; Boyancé, *Culte des muses*, p. 319.

443. Polybius, V, 106, 2.

444. Three passages provide the best commentary on Juvenal's *panem et Circenses*.

(1) Cicero, *Ad Atticum*, XVI, 2: 'For my part the better the news is, the more it annoys and pains me that the Roman people use their hands not for defending the constitution but for clapping.'

(2) Plutarch, *Precepts of Statecraft*, 29. 'Those who give such bribes should bear in mind that they are destroying themselves when they purchase great reputation by great expenditures, thus making the multitude strong and bold in the thought that they have power to give and take away something important.'

(3) Fronto, p. 210 (Naber), 200 (van den Hout) (*Principia Historiae*, 17), which I have just quoted. The *congiaria* do not seem to have been reserved to the *plebs frumentaria* in the technical sense of the expression – those who possessed the right to the corn dole – and I have therefore interpreted freely the words *frumentariam plebem* as meaning the people for whom getting their daily bread is a problem.

445. Diogenes Laertius, II, 68. For an example to illustrate the idea that, for psychological reasons, solutions which are incoherent or have confused motives tend to go beyond what is rationally necessary, let me recall that Christian ascetic theology teaches that it is not enough to renounce evil pleasures, nor even to give up dangerous ones: one must also deprive oneself of some permissible pleasures, because whoever enjoys without restriction all the delights he is allowed is very close to slipping into enjoyment of those which are forbidden. What really lies behind the idea of depoliticization is probably the ascetic concept, too. Someone who enjoys non-political pleasures will be a poor militant; though theoretically possible, it is psychologically difficult to take an interest both in political activity and in romantic novels. This reminds one a little of the Christian idea that sensuality is an implacable foe of divine love. A historian must acknowledge that these mutual exclusivities are not without foundation in human psychology and character. Let the psychoanalysts explain this. (The author has personal reasons – which are not reasons of scientific disdain, but quite the contrary – for not getting too close to psychoanalysis.) The myth of depoliticization *projects* upon the plane of political concepts a truth of characterology: those who are enthusiastic about politics are less so about bread and circuses, because nobody is enthusiastic about two things at once. To the same effect: 'Two contrary qualities cannot coexist in the same subject; the love of God and the love of the creature are contrary the one to the other, and so cannot dwell together in the same heart' (St John of the Cross, *The Ascent of Mount Carmel*, I, 6).

446. I am thinking here of the distinction drawn by some psychoanalysts (if I understand them aright) between the real, the symbolic and the imaginary.

INDEX

FOR THE BEST IN PAPERBACKS, LOOK FOR THE

In every corner of the world, on every subject under the sun, Penguin represents quality and variety – the very best in publishing today.

For complete information about books available from Penguin – including Puffins, Penguin Classics and Arkana – and how to order them, write to us at the appropriate address below. Please note that for copyright reasons the selection of books varies from country to country.

In the United Kingdom: Please write to *Dept E.P., Penguin Books Ltd, Harmondsworth, Middlesex, UB7 0DA.*

If you have any difficulty in obtaining a title, please send your order with the correct money, plus ten per cent for postage and packaging, to *PO Box No 11, West Drayton, Middlesex*

In the United States: Please write to *Dept BA, Penguin, 299 Murray Hill Parkway, East Rutherford, New Jersey 07073*

In Canada: Please write to *Penguin Books Canada Ltd, 2801 John Street, Markham, Ontario L3R 1B4*

In Australia: Please write to the *Marketing Department, Penguin Books Australia Ltd, P.O. Box 257, Ringwood, Victoria 3134*

In New Zealand: Please write to the *Marketing Department, Penguin Books (NZ) Ltd, Private Bag, Takapuna, Auckland 9*

In India: Please write to *Penguin Overseas Ltd, 706 Eros Apartments, 56 Nehru Place, New Delhi, 110019*

In the Netherlands: Please write to *Penguin Books Netherlands B.V., Postbus 195, NL–1380AD Weesp*

In West Germany: Please write to *Penguin Books Ltd, Friedrichstrasse 10–12, D–6000 Frankfurt/Main 1*

In Spain: Please write to *Alhambra Longman S.A., Fernandez de la Hoz 9, E–28010 Madrid*

In Italy: Please write to *Penguin Italia s.r.l., Via Como 4, I-20096 Pioltello (Milano)*

In France: Please write to *Penguin Books Ltd, 39 Rue de Montmorency, F-75003 Paris*

In Japan: Please write to *Longman Penguin Japan Co Ltd, Yamaguchi Building, 2–12–9 Kanda Jimbocho, Chiyoda-Ku, Tokyo 101*

Modern Ireland 1600–1972   R. F. Foster

'Takes its place with the finest historical writing of the twentieth century, whether about Ireland or anywhere else' – Conor Cruise O'Brien in the *Sunday Times*

Death in Hamburg   Society and Politics in the Cholera Years 1830–1910
Richard J. Evans

Why did the cholera epidemic of 1892 kill nearly 10,000 people in six weeks in Hamburg, while most of Europe was left almost unscathed? The answers put forward in this 'tremendous book' (Roy Porter in the *London Review of Books*) offer a wealth of insights into the inner life of a great – and uniquely anomalous – European city at the height of an industrial age.

British Society 1914–1945   John Stevenson

A major contribution to the *Penguin Social History of Britain*, which 'will undoubtedly be the standard work for students of modern Britain for many years to come' – *The Times Educational Supplement*

A History of Christianity   Paul Johnson

'Masterly ... a cosmic soap opera involving kings and beggars, philosophers and crackpots, scholars and illiterate *exaltés*, popes and pilgrims and wild anchorites in the wilderness' – Malcolm Muggeridge

The Penguin History of Greece   A. R. Burn

Readable, erudite, enthusiastic and balanced, this one-volume history of Hellas sweeps the reader along from the days of Mycenae and the splendours of Athens to the conquests of Alexander and the final dark decades.

Battle Cry of Freedom   The American Civil War
James M. McPherson

'Compellingly readable ... It is the best one-volume treatment of its subject I have come across. It may be the best ever published ... This is magic' – Hugh Brogan in *The New York Times Book Review*

PENGUIN POLITICS AND SOCIAL SCIENCES

Comparative Government S. E. Finer

'A considerable *tour de force* … few teachers of politics in Britain would fail to learn a great deal from it … Above all, it is the work of a great teacher who breathes into every page his own enthusiasm for the discipline' – Anthony King in *New Society*

Karl Marx: Selected Writings in Sociology and Social Philosophy
T. B. Bottomore and Maximilien Rubel (eds.)

'It makes available, in coherent form and lucid English, some of Marx's most important ideas. As an introduction to Marx's thought, it has very few rivals indeed' – *British Journal of Sociology*

Post-War Britain A Political History Alan Sked and Chris Cook

Major political figures from Attlee to Thatcher, the aims and achievements of governments and the changing fortunes of Britain in the period since 1945 are thoroughly scrutinized in this readable history.

Inside the Third World Paul Harrison

From climate and colonialism to land hunger, exploding cities and illiteracy, this comprehensive book brings home a wealth of facts and analysis on the often tragic realities of life for the poor people and communities of Asia, Africa and Latin America.

Housewife Ann Oakley

'A fresh and challenging account' – *Economist*. 'Informative and rational enough to deserve a serious place in any discussion on the position of women in modern society' – *The Times Educational Supplement*

The Raw and the Cooked Claude Lévi-Strauss

Deliberately, brilliantly and inimitably challenging, Lévi-Strauss's seminal work of structural anthropology cuts wide and deep into the mind of mankind, as he finds in the myths of the South American Indians a comprehensible psychological pattern.

The Victorian Underworld Kellow Chesney

A superbly evocative survey of the vast substratum of vice that lay below the respectable surface of Victorian England – the showmen, religious fakes, pickpockets and prostitutes – and of the penal methods of that 'most enlightened age'. 'Charged with nightmare detail' – *Sunday Times*

Citizens Simon Schama

The award-winning chronicle of the French Revolution. 'The most marvellous book I have read about the French Revolution in the last fifty years' – Richard Cobb in *The Times*. 'He has chronicled the vicissitudes of that world with matchless understanding, wisdom, pity and truth, in the pages of this huge and marvellous book' – *Sunday Times*

Stalin Isaac Deutscher

'The Greatest Genius in History' and the 'Life-Giving Force of Socialism'? Or a tyrant more ruthless than Ivan the Terrible whose policies facilitated the rise of Nazism? An outstanding biographical study of a revolutionary despot by a great historian.

Jasmin's Witch Emmanuel Le Roy Ladurie

An investigation into witchcraft and magic in south-west France during the seventeenth century – a masterpiece of historical detective work by the bestselling author of *Montaillou*.

The Second World War A J P Taylor

A brilliant and detailed illustrated history, enlivened by all Professor Taylor's customary iconoclasm and wit.

Industry and Empire E. J. Hobsbawm

Volume 3 of the *Penguin Economic History of Britain* covers the period of the Industrial Revolution: 'the most fundamental transformation in the history of the world recorded in written documents.' 'A book that attracts and deserves attention ... by far the most gifted historian now writing' – John Vaizey in the *Listener*

PENGUIN ARCHAEOLOGY

Archaeology and Language   The Puzzle of Indo-European Origins
Colin Renfrew

'His most important and far-reaching book: the pace is exhilarating, the issues are momentous … *Archaeology and Language* breaks new ground by bringing the findings of the two sciences back into relationship more successfully than any other scholar in this century … We have come a long step closer towards understanding human origins' – Peter Levi in the *Independent*

The Dead Sea Scrolls in English   G. Vermes

This established and authoritative English translation of the non-biblical Qumran scrolls – offering a revolutionary insight into Palestinian Jewish life and ideology at a crucial period in the development of Jewish and Christian religious thought – now includes the Temple Scroll, the most voluminous scroll of them all.

Hadrian's Wall   David J. Breeze and Brian Dobson

A penetrating history of the best-known, best-preserved and most spectacular monument to the Roman Empire in Britain. 'A masterpiece of the controlled use of archaeological and epigraphical evidence in a fluent narrative that will satisfy any level of interest' – *The Times Educational Supplement*

Before Civilization   The Radiocarbon Revolution and Prehistoric Europe
Colin Renfrew

'I have little doubt that this is one of the most important archaeological books for a very long time' – Barry Cunliffe in the *New Scientist*. 'Pure stimulation from beginning to end … a book which provokes thought, aids understanding, and above all is immensely enjoyable' – *Scotsman*

The Ancient Civilizations of Peru   J. Alden Mason

The archaeological, historical, artistic, geographical and ethnographical discoveries that have resurrected the rich variety of Inca and pre-Inca culture and civilization – wiped out by the Spanish Conquest – are surveyed in this now classic work.

FOR THE BEST IN PAPERBACKS, LOOK FOR THE

PENGUIN RELIGION

Adam, Eve and the Serpent Elaine Pagels

How is it that the early Church, advocate of individual free will, came to preach the doctrine of original sin and to regard sexual desire as the inherent and shameful enslavement of humanity? This paradox is explored by the author of *The Gnostic Gospels*.

Islam in the World Malise Ruthven

This informed and informative book places the contemporary Islamic revival in context, providing a fascinating introduction – the first of its kind – to Islamic origins, beliefs, history, geography, politics and society.

The Orthodox Church Timothy Ware

In response to increasing interest among western Christians, and believing that a thorough understanding of Orthodoxy is necessary if the Roman Catholic and Protestant Churches are to be reunited, Timothy Ware explains Orthodox views on a vast range of matters from Free Will to the Papacy.

Judaism Isidore Epstein

The comprehensive account of Judaism as a religion and as a distinctive way of life, presented against a background of 4,000 years of Jewish history.

Mysticism F. C. Happold

What is mysticism? This simple and illuminating book combines a study of mysticism with an illustrative anthology of mystical writings, ranging from Plato and Plotinus to Dante.

The Penguin History of the Church: 4 Gerald R. Cragg
The Church and the Age of Reason

Gerald Cragg's elegant and stimulating assessment of the era from the Peace of Westphalia to the French Revolution – a formative period in the Church's history – ranges from the Church life of France under Louis XIV to the high noon of rationalism and beyond.

Political Ideas   David Thomson (ed.)

From Machiavelli to Marx – a stimulating and informative introduction to the last 500 years of European political thinkers and political thought.

On Revolution   Hannah Arendt

Arendt's classic analysis of a relatively recent political phenomenon examines the underlying principles common to all revolutions, and the evolution of revolutionary theory and practice. 'Never dull, enormously erudite, always imaginative' – *Sunday Times*

Ill Fares the Land   Susan George

These twelve essays expand on one of the major themes of Susan George's work: the role of power in perpetuating world hunger. With characteristic commitment and conviction, the author of *A Fate Worse than Debt* and *How the Other Half Dies* demonstrates that just as poverty lies behind hunger, so injustice and inequality lie behind poverty.

The Social Construction of Reality   Peter Berger and Thomas Luckmann

Concerned with the sociology of 'everything that passes for knowledge in society' and particularly with that which passes for common sense, this is 'a serious, open-minded book, upon a serious subject' – *Listener*

The Care of the Self   Michel Foucault
The History of Sexuality Vol 3

Foucault examines the transformation of sexual discourse from the Hellenistic to the Roman world in an inquiry which 'bristles with provocative insights into the tangled liaison of sex and self' – *The Times Higher Education Supplement*

Silent Spring   Rachel Carson

'What we have to face is not an occasional dose of poison which has accidentally got into some article of food, but a persistent and continuous poisoning of the whole human environment.' First published in 1962, *Silent Spring* remains the classic environmental statement which founded an entire movement.

FOR THE BEST IN PAPERBACKS, LOOK FOR THE

PENGUIN POLITICS AND SOCIAL SCIENCES

Comparative Government   S. E. Finer

'A considerable *tour de force* ... few teachers of politics in Britain would fail to learn a great deal from it ... Above all, it is the work of a great teacher who breathes into every page his own enthusiasm for the discipline' – Anthony King in *New Society*

Karl Marx: Selected Writings in Sociology and Social Philosophy
T. B. Bottomore and Maximilien Rubel (eds.)

'It makes available, in coherent form and lucid English, some of Marx's most important ideas. As an introduction to Marx's thought, it has very few rivals indeed' – *British Journal of Sociology*

Post-War Britain   A Political History   Alan Sked and Chris Cook

Major political figures from Attlee to Thatcher, the aims and achievements of governments and the changing fortunes of Britain in the period since 1945 are thoroughly scrutinized in this readable history.

Inside the Third World   Paul Harrison

From climate and colonialism to land hunger, exploding cities and illiteracy, this comprehensive book brings home a wealth of facts and analysis on the often tragic realities of life for the poor people and communities of Asia, Africa and Latin America.

Housewife   Ann Oakley

'A fresh and challenging account' – *Economist*. 'Informative and rational enough to deserve a serious place in any discussion on the position of women in modern society' – *The Times Educational Supplement*

The Raw and the Cooked   Claude Lévi-Strauss

Deliberately, brilliantly and inimitably challenging, Lévi-Strauss's seminal work of structural anthropology cuts wide and deep into the mind of mankind, as he finds in the myths of the South American Indians a comprehensible psychological pattern.

PENGUIN PHILOSOPHY

I: The Philosophy and Psychology of Personal Identity   Jonathan Glover

From cases of split brains and multiple personalities to the importance of memory and recognition by others, the author of *Causing Death and Saving Lives* tackles the vexed questions of personal identity. 'Fascinating ... the ideas which Glover pours forth in profusion deserve more detailed consideration' – Anthony Storr

Minds, Brains and Science   John Searle

Based on Professor Searle's acclaimed series of Reith Lectures, *Minds, Brains and Science* is 'punchy and engaging ... a timely exposé of those woolly-minded computer-lovers who believe that computers can think, and indeed that the human mind is just a biological computer' – *The Times Literary Supplement*

Ethics   Inventing Right and Wrong   J. L. Mackie

Widely used as a text, Mackie's complete and clear treatise on moral theory deals with the status and content of ethics, sketches a practical moral system and examines the frontiers at which ethics touches psychology, theology, law and politics.

The Penguin History of Western Philosophy   D. W. Hamlyn

'Well-crafted and readable ... neither laden with footnotes nor weighed down with technical language ... a general guide to three millennia of philosophizing in the West' – *The Times Literary Supplement*

Science and Philosophy: Past and Present   Derek Gjertsen

Philosophy and science, once intimately connected, are today often seen as widely different disciplines. Ranging from Aristotle to Einstein, from quantum theory to renaissance magic, Confucius and parapsychology, this penetrating and original study shows such a view to be both naive and ill-informed.

The Problem of Knowledge   A. J. Ayer

How do you *know* that this is a book? How do you *know* that you know? In *The Problem of Knowledge* A. J. Ayer presented the sceptic's arguments as forcefully as possible, investigating the extent to which they can be met. 'Thorough ... penetrating, vigorous ... readable and manageable' – *Spectator*